D0459758

Ireland: A Cultural Encyclopædia

Ireland: A Cultural Encyclopædia

General Editor
BRIAN DE BREFFNY

FACTS ON FILE – NEW YORK

First published in the United Kingdom in 1983
by Thames and Hudson Ltd., London

Published in the United States of America in 1983
by Facts On File Inc.
460 Park Avenue South, New York, New York 10016

Library of Congress Cataloging in Publication Data

Main entry under title:

Ireland: a cultural encyclopaedia.
    1. Arts—Ireland—Dictionaries.   2. Ireland—
Dictionaries and encyclopedias.   I. De Breffny, Brian.
NX546.A1I73   1983   700′.9415   83-1533
ISBN 0-87196-260-8

Printed and bound in Japan

Contents

Map of Ireland showing principal towns and sites mentioned in the encyclopaedia.

Introduction and reader's guide

The purpose of an encyclopaedia is to present a succinct body of classified information on all branches, or one specified branch of knowledge. The specification for this volume in Thames and Hudson's series of illustrated encyclopaedias being *Irish culture*, it would have been only too easy when planning this encyclopaedia to have floundered in a sea of nearly indefinable complexities of the word culture. While it appeared reasonable to limit the specification *Irish* to include that which originated in, occurred in, or emanated from, or was closely associated with, Ireland as a geographical entity, the question of what should be included as expressions of the term *culture* remains a vexatious one which cannot be easily resolved.

As general editor, in planning this work I opted, therefore, to err on the side of including what might be considered a cultural expression rather than limiting the subjects to a conservative interpretation of the term. By broadly interpreting culture to mean the aesthetic endeavour of a people and the manifestation of their intellectual, artistic and even social development, I have planned this work to embrace a very wide range of subjects including, for example, neolithic sites, the Ogham alphabet, Celtic monasticism, illuminated manuscripts, the reform movement of the Célí Dé (Culdees) and mythology, as well as the equestrian sports which are an important factor in Irish life and have inspired writers and painters, the history of costume and of furniture in Ireland, crafts such as weaving, lace-making, bookbinding, glass and ceramic manufacture and recent cultural developments such as photography, cinema, television, the Gaelic League, the Gaelic Athletic Association and the societies and institutions devoted to stimulate cultural activity or conserve its past manifestations. Such entries find their place in this work along with the more obvious subjects such as architecture, language, literature, music, painting, poetry, sculpture, stained glass and the theatre.

In addition to the references under subjects the reader will find individual biographical references for many persons selected as exponents of Irish culture over the centuries. The matter of this selection was not always easy. As general editor I have largely left the decision to the experts who have contributed the subject articles to select the exponents of their particular subject who might merit individual mention. In subjects such as poetry, literature and painting which all have vigorous contemporary expression, it has been much easier to select the luminaries of the past, those men and women who have secured an established place in the hall of fame, than to make a selection among contemporary poets, writers and artists. We have tried, therefore, to include as many of the latter as possible, conscious that some may not attain the stature of earlier great exponents of these arts but also of the usefulness to the reader of biographical data on these persons, not easily available in print elsewhere, if at all. And if some contemporaries have not found individual mention, let it not be taken as a reflection on their merit; I trust that they will not take offence but understand the difficulties in selection for the editor and his collaborators in attempting to cover an enormous body of knowledge within the physical limits of a volume of 150,000 words.

The arrangement of the encyclopaedia is simple. It is strictly alphabetical. A list of abbreviations used is provided. Cross-references are indicated by the use of SMALL

CAPITALS. Thus the name JAMES BARRY appearing in the article **painting**, or the house RUSSBOROUGH in the article **architecture**, alerts the reader to the fact that individual entries will be found alphabetically under **Barry** and under **Russborough**.

Wherever possible, some useful bibliographical references for further reading are appended to individual entries. The initials at the end of each entry are those of its author who can be identified by reference to the list of contributors. The map of Ireland and the lists (arranged by counties) of principal museums, art galleries and libraries, together with the names of the most important houses, castles and gardens open to the public, will, I hope, serve as useful appendices, especially for the visitor to Ireland.

I have no doubt that this encyclopaedia will prove to be immensely useful over the years to students, scholars, teachers and all those interested in Irish civilization, and that it will find its place on bookshelves along with the standard works on the individual subjects as an invaluable compendium of easily accessible information. The publication of this encyclopaedia is due, in the first place, to the initiative and enthusiasm of its publishers, Thames and Hudson, who have been foremost over the last decade in producing remarkable illustrated books on various expressions of the arts in Ireland, not least the handsome presentation of the Book of Kells; but its appearance has, of course, only been made possible by the co-operation of the specialists and experts who contributed the articles, and I most sincerely thank them for their collaboration not only in submitting their articles but also in making many helpful comments and suggestions generally.

Breffny
Castletown Cox, 1982

List of contributors

AA   Anders Ahlqvist, Statutory Lecturer in Old and Middle Irish, National University of Ireland at University College, Galway

JHA   J. H. Andrews, Associate Professor of Geography, Trinity College, Dublin

DB   Douglas Bennett, Warden of the Company of Goldsmiths of Dublin, and the author of *Irish Georgian Silver*

NGB   Nicola Gordon Bowe, Lecturer in Art History, National College of Art and Design, Dublin

PB   Patrick Bowe, Member of the Heritage Gardens Committee of An Taisce, and co-author of *Irish Gardens and Demesnes from 1830*

BB   Brendan Bradshaw, Fellow of St John's College, Cambridge

B de B   Brian de Breffny, General Editor

CEBB   Charles E. B. Brett, President of the Ulster Architectural Heritage Society

ECC   Edward C. Chandler, Photographic historian and author of *Photography in Dublin*

MC   Maurice Craig, Fellow of Trinity College, Dublin, and author of *Dublin 1660–1960*, etc.

AOC   Anne Crookshank, Professor of the History of Art, Trinity College, Dublin

BF   Brian Ferran, Art Director, Arts Council of Northern Ireland

R ff   Rosemary ffolliott, Editor of *The Irish Ancestor*, and co-author of *The Houses of Ireland*

KtG   Desmond Fitzgerald, The Knight of Glin, Formerly Deputy Keeper, Department of Furniture, Victoria and Albert Museum, London

CF-S   Christopher Fitz-Simon, Artistic Director of the Irish Theatre Company, and author of *The Irish Theatre*

WG   William Garner, Lecturer at the National College of Art and Design, Dublin

EG   Elgy Gillespie, Staff-writer, *Irish Times*

PH   Peter Harbison, Archaeologist, Bord Failte Eireann (Irish Tourist Board)

BH   Barbara Hayley, Lecturer, St Patrick's College, Maynooth

MH   Michael Herity, Professor of Celtic Archaeology, University College, Dublin

AGH   Anthony G. Hughes, Professor of Music, University College, Dublin

PJ   Patricia Jorgensen, Textile and fashion designer

PL   Paul Larmour, Lecturer, Queen's University, Belfast

CL   Colin Lewis, Lecturer, University College, Dublin

T McC   Thomas McCarthy, Poetry Critic, *Irish Times*

C MacG   Ciarán MacGonigal, Chairman, Hugh Lane Municipal Gallery of Modern Art, Dublin

PLM   Phillip L. Marcus, Professor of English Literature, Cornell University

KM   Kenneth Milne, Principal, Church of Ireland College of Education, Dublin

HLM   Lillias Mitchell, formerly Head of the Woven Textiles Department, National College of Art and Design, Dublin

GM   George Morrison, Film director

KBN   Kevin B. Nowlan, Professor of History, University College, Dublin

TÓB   Tomás Ó Beirne, Architect, An Foras Forbartha (National Institute of Physical Planning)

COʼC   Consuelo O'Connor, Chairman of An Taisce (The National Trust)

DÓC   Donnchadh Ó Corrain, Associate Professor, Department of Irish History, University College, Cork

DECP   David E. C. Price, Council Member, Wexford Festival

MR   Mairead Reynolds, National Museum of Ireland

ICR	Ian Campbell Ross, Professor of English Literature, Trinity College, Dublin
R	The Earl of Rosse
MFR	Michael Ryan, National Museum of Ireland
NS	Nicholas Sheaff, Director of the Irish Architectural Archive
GOS	George Simms, Formerly Archbishop of Armagh and Primate of All-Ireland
JT	John Turpin, Professor of the History of Art, National College of Art and Design, Dublin
GT	Gerald Tyler, Manager of Information and Exhibitions, Kilkenny Design Workshops
PFW	Patrick F. Wallace, National Museum of Ireland
JW	James White, Chairman of An Chomhairle Ealaíon (The Arts Council)

List of abbreviations

ARHA	Associate of the Royal Hibernian Academy
BBC	British Broadcasting Corporation
CEMA	Council for the Encouragement of Music and the Arts
EBA	Early Bronze Age
EEC	European Economic Community
EIA	Early Iron Age
GAA	Gaelic Athletic Association
HRHA	Honorary Royal Hibernian Academician
IELA	Irish Exhibition of Living Art
IGS	Irish Georgian Society
IRA	Irish Republican Army
JCHAS	*Journal of the Cork Historical and Archaeological Society*
JRSAI	*Journal of the Royal Society of Antiquaries of Ireland*
LBA	Late Bronze Age
NGI	National Gallery of Ireland
NLI	National Library of Ireland
NMI	National Museum of Ireland
NUI	National University of Ireland
PRHA	President of the Royal Hibernian Academy
PRIA	*Proceedings of the Royal Irish Academy*
RA	Royal Academician
RHA	Royal Hibernian Academy (Academician)
RIA	Royal Irish Academy
RIAI	Royal Institute of the Architects of Ireland
RTE	Radio Telefis Eireann
TCD	Trinity College, Dublin
UJA	*Ulster Journal of Archaeology*

The Encyclopaedia

The colour plates listed below illustrate the following entries in the encyclopaedia:

Abbey Theatre.

The Irish Literary Theatre, founded in Dublin in 1898 by Lady AUGUSTA GREGORY, EDWARD MARTYN and W. B. YEATS, evolved as the National Theatre Society Ltd in 1903; since 1904 the company has been housed in the Abbey Theatre (formerly the Mechanics' Theatre) and the adjoining Peacock Theatre. Its first financial benefactor was Miss A. E. Horniman of Manchester. The original aim was to present plays by Irish writers, on Irish themes, preferably with Irish actors. Lady Gregory favoured rural or folk subjects; Yeats was interested in something more 'remote, spiritual and ideal', concerning himself first with 'Celtic' mythology, in the manner of the French *Symbolistes*, later adding techniques from the Noh theatre of Japan.

The first writer associated with the Theatre to gain international recognition was J. M. SYNGE, followed by SEÁN O'CASEY. Synge's *Riders to the Sea* is possibly the greatest short tragedy ever written; his *The Playboy of the Western World*, a 'comedy laced with tragic feeling', is the archetypal Abbey play. WILLIE FAY was the earliest and most influential director; LENNOX ROBINSON, a popular playwright, directed the majority of productions 1910–35, with Arthur Shields and M. J. Dolan directing occasionally. Hugh Hunt was resident director 1935–8, followed for the next ten years by Frank Dermody, who was succeeded by Ria Mooney.

In 1951 the theatre was accidentally burned down and the company was accommodated in the Rupert Guinness Hall and the Queen's Theatre until its new building, designed by MICHAEL SCOTT, was opened in 1966; it contains an excellent smaller auditorium, the Peacock. Since the re-opening, Tomás MacAnna, Hugh Hunt, Alan Simpson, Lelia Doolan and Joe Dowling have held the post now known as Artistic Director.

The production of international classics, of contemporary foreign plays, and of plays by Irish writers dating from a period prior to the Abbey's foundation, has been resumed, but the Abbey continues to be the one theatrical institution which provides active encouragement for Irish playwrights, and where the works of many young Irish playwrights receive their first productions.   CF-S

Abbey Theatre. A scene from J. M. Synge's *The Playboy of the Western World*.

A.E.

(pseudonym of George William Russell; 1867–1935). Poet, theosophist, agricultural economist, editor and essayist; born at Lurgan, Co. Armagh, his creative life centred around Dublin, where he became the ironic, benign core of the Irish Literary Revival. A presence equal in stature to YEATS, he used vision rather than intellect. His poetry never lived up to the promise of *Homeward: Songs by the Way* (1894). He edited *The Irish Homestead*, 1904–23, and *The Irish Statesman*,

A.E. Portrait in oils by John Butler Yeats, painted in 1903. NGI.

1923–30. His essays still have great relevance in Ireland, particularly *Imaginations and Reveries* (1915). His letters, edited by Alan Denson, 1961, are full of advice, gossip and incisive political perception. *See* POETRY.   T McC

aisling. A distinctive genre of Gaelic POETRY which was particularly powerful during the early 18th century. It was a form of political verse, ornate in construction, in which the political message was covertly conveyed by the use of metaphor. A vision-woman (interpreted by Irish readers as Ireland) appeared to the drowsy poet and foretold the coming of a Stuart redeemer to Ireland. The greatest writer of aisling was AOGAIN Ó RATHAILLE who composed 'Gile na Gile' ('Brightness of Brightness') and 'An Aisling' ('The Vision').   T McC

Allan, Henry (1865–1912). Landscape and portrait painter; born in Dublin, he studied in Belfast, Dublin and Antwerp. His painting *The Little Matchseller* won the Royal Hibernian Academy prize in 1893. Elected ARHA 1895; RHA 1901; subsequently Treasurer of the RHA.   C MacG

Allen, Alfred (1925–). Poet and farmer; born in Co. Cork. His two collections of traditional poetry, *Clashenure Skyline* (1970) and *Interrogations* (1975), are full of wry common sense and prosodic skill.   T McC

An Chomhairle Ealaíon. *See* ARTS COUNCIL.

An Taisce (The National Trust for Ireland). *See* TAISCE, AN.

An Túr Gloine (The Tower of Glass). *See* TÚR GLOINE, AN.

Aosdána. An affiliation, established in 1981, of artists engaged in literature, music and the visual arts; its membership is restricted to a maximum of 150. The initial membership was nominated by the ARTS COUNCIL of Ireland, but from 1983 onwards new members are elected by the existing membership, election being a recognition of achievement and distinction in a creative discipline; the financial circumstances of an individual artist are not a consideration. A *cnuas* (burse) valued at £4,000 per annum for a period of five years can be awarded to those artists who are already members of Aosdána, and whose earnings are not sufficient to enable them to devote their energies to the full-time pursuit of their creative discipline; members of Aosdána who apply for the *cnuas* must reside within the jurisdiction of the government of Ireland at the time of applying for the *cnuas* and must continue to do so for the five-year period, but this does not prohibit a temporary absence.   C MacG

architecture. Apart from forts and small corbelled oratories and BEEHIVE HUTS, the earliest surviving built structures in Ireland are stone churches, possibly dating from the 7th or 8th century. The known history

Reconstruction of an early wooden church, built of oak logs and planks and roughly thatched with rushes.

of these (and of early wooden structure now lost) and an outline of building activity and architectural styles since then are described below in seven chronologically arranged sections: the early period (7th–12th centuries); Romanesque churches; Transitional and Gothic; the 17th century; the 18th century; the 19th century; and the 20th century.

The early period (7th–12th centuries)
The first churches built in Ireland were presumably constructed of mud or wood. Although, unlike the wooden stave churches of Norway, no example of an early Irish wooden church has survived, literary sources do give us some information about them. The old Irish name for a wooden church was *duirteach* (a house of oak), indicating the type of timber used in construction. Cogitosus, the late 7th-century biographer of St Brigid, describes in some detail the church of the double monastery at Kildare as it was in his day. Without actually saying that it was of wood, he tells us that it was large and tall, and had many windows; it was divided into three oratories by two timber partitions; one of these – decorated with paintings and linen hangings, and with a door at either end – ran across the body of the church, while the second was placed at right-angles to it. The abbess, nuns and widows entered by one door on the left-hand side of the church, while the priests and lay persons entered by a decorated door on the right.

A second important, yet little-known, description of a 7th-century wooden church, probably in Ireland, is found in the A-text of the *Hisperica Famina*, written in very obscure Latin. Michael Herren's recent translation suggests that it had square foundations (of stone?), and walls made of candle-shaped logs – perhaps similar to those surviving in the Saxon church at Greensted in Essex. Furthermore, the church may have had a vaulted roof, with square beams across it, as well as four steeples – probably one at each corner. The altar was in the centre of the church, and a portico stood in front of the only entrance, which was in the west wall. The church was furnished with innumerable objects which are, unfortunately, not described. These two descriptions suggest that there may have been a considerable variety in the size of wooden churches, which continued to be built in Ireland up to the 12th century. None of the traces of wooden structures uncovered during archaeological excavations on monastic sites in Ireland during the last 30 years is sufficient to provide an adequate reconstruction of a wooden church. Professor M. J. O'Kelly found six post-holes beneath the stone oratory on Church Island, Valencia, Co. Kerry; these O'Kelly tentatively reconstructed to give an oratory some 2 m. (6 ft.) wide and 3 m. (10 ft.) or more long. Only two post-holes were recovered at Reask in the same county, and no details have been published of the possible wooden churches excavated at Ardagh, Co. Longford, and Inishcealtra, Co. Clare. The post-holes found within St Vogue's church at Carnsore Point in Co. Wexford, which provided a radiocarbon date of AD 660 ± 80, were reconstructed by the excavators to suggest an original wooden structure 2·25 × 1·50 m. (7 ft 6 in. × 5 ft) – scarcely large enough to have been an oratory. At Derry in Co. Down, the late D. M. Waterman found the stone foundation, 68·5 cm. (27 in.) wide, of what may have been a church with an overall width of 4·10 m. (14 ft), and on this foundation a vertical timber 45·7 cm. (18 in.) in diameter had rested. The sleeper-trenches, 45·7 cm. (18 in.) and 22·8–30·4 cm. (9–12 in.) wide, which Waterman found at White Island in Co. Fermanagh, may also have contained material for a wooden church. With the exception of the radiocarbon date for the structure within St Vogue's church, none of these wooden remains have been dated. Those found in Co. Kerry are likely to have pre-dated the stone-roofed oratories on their respective sites.

With the exception of much later literary accounts of the building of stone churches associated with the 5th-century saints, PATRICK and Cianán of Duleek, the earliest historical reference to a stone church in Ireland is at Armagh in 788. Stone churches are recorded for Armagh and Kells in the 9th century, and it is only in the 10th century that stone churches are mentioned on smaller sites such as Tuamgraney, Co. Clare.

The surviving stone churches (*daimhliag* in Old Irish) which are likely to have been built before 1200 may be divided into four types, according to the difference in their ground-plan and the nature of the roofing materials used:

(1) Rectangular oratories built in the corbelling technique, so that the inward-sloping side-walls merge imperceptibly in a gradual convex curve into the roof. These oratories are found exclusively in the west of Ireland, where the only complete examples are on SKELLIG MICHAEL and at GALLARUS, both in Co. Kerry. The date of such oratories is often considered to be 7th or 8th century, but they could be as late as the 12th century.

St Mochta's House (or Oratory), Louth, a stone-footed building, probably 12th/13th century.

(2) Simple rectangular structures with upright walls. Some were roofed presumably with thatch or wooden shingles; they range in size from 3·35 × 2·13 m. (11 × 7 ft), as at Temple Benen on the Aran Island of Inishmor, to a length of more than 11·27 m. (37 ft) for Kilmacduagh Cathedral, also in Co. Galway (if it did not originally have a chancel). Most of the examples roofed in this manner are found in Co. Galway, Clare and Limerick. Other examples were covered by a stone roof, supported by a stone vault with a small croft above it. The largest example is St Kevin's church at GLENDALOUGH, Co. Wicklow; others include 'St Columb's House' at KELLS, Co. Meath, St Mochta's House in Louth and (in its original form) St Doulagh's at Balgriffin, near Malahide in Co. Dublin. It is likely that all of the stone-roofed examples date from the 12th century.

(3) Simple rectangular structures with the addition of *antae*, that is, projections of the north and south walls beyond the corners of the east and west gable-walls – a feature probably derived from wooden churches, as at ST MACDARA'S ISLAND. Many of the churches of this type have been altered subsequently by the addition of a chancel, possibly under the influence of type 4 (see below). As with type 2, churches of this type have differing roof materials. Those which had roofs of thatch or shingles vary in internal dimensions from 2·43 × 2·13 m. (8 × 7 ft) as at Teampull Dhiarmide on Inchcleraun, Co. Longford, to 14·63 × 9·14 m. (48 × 30 ft), as at Glendalough Cathedral. Those which were roofed with stone include the (now roofless) St Molaise's 'House' on Devenish in Co. Fermanagh, measuring internally 5·86 × 3·40 m. (20 ft × 11 ft 2 in.), which may have had a stone vault supporting the roof, and St Macdara's Island which did not.

The earliest historical evidence which could be used to date churches of this type is from the 10th century, though some of the surviving churches may possibly be earlier. The present cathedral at CLONMACNOIS in Co. Offaly may be identical with that mentioned in the old Irish annals as having been erected in the first decade of the 10th century, and the western part of the church at Tuamgraney, Co. Clare, may be the same as the church erected in 964 (according to the *Chronicon Scotorum*). Judged by its decoration, the church of St Molaise on Devenish is scarcely earlier than the 12th century, and the use of *antae* may have continued in the west of Ireland into the 13th century.

(4) Churches with a rectangular nave and a contemporary but smaller rectangular chancel. Most of the examples were presumably roofed with thatch or shingles, but CORMAC'S CHAPEL at Cashel in Co. Tipperary and St Flannan's Oratory, KILLALOE, Co. Clare, both have a stone roof, as the church at Kilmalkedar may also have had. The ground-plan for this type of church was probably introduced into Ireland from outside (perhaps England), in contrast to the other types which appear to represent a local development and which (with the probable exception of oratories of type 2) were apparently modelled in scale and plan on earlier wooden churches. The majority of churches with a contemporary nave and chancel can be dated by their Romanesque decoration to the 12th century.

Romanesque churches

Historical evidence suggests that Irish Romanesque churches date largely from the 12th century, but the style continued in use into the following century in what is known as 'The School of the West', which flourished almost exclusively west of the Shannon. It is, however, not impossible that some simple churches using rounded arches may be of the 11th century, though proof is totally lacking.

Whereas in England, and on the Continent, Romanesque churches were generally large structures, often with side-aisles which permitted the imaginative carving of capitals, Irish Romanesque churches – with the exception of those built by the Cistercians – were small in comparison. With a few minor exceptions, they consisted of a nave and a smaller chancel. But while the Irish Romanesque churches were comparatively small in scale, the various orders of the rounded arches gave masons considerable scope for the decoration of doors and chancel arches and occasionally windows too (e.g. the rare round example at Rahan, Co. Offaly). The decoration varies considerably. The zig-zag chevron, doubtless introduced from Norman churches in England, is predominant, but there is also an abundance of human heads, sometimes on door arches (as at Dysert O'Dea, Co. Clare, and Inchagoill, Co. Galway), or with interlaced hair on capitals (as at Rahan, or St Saviour's Church at Glendalough), and Cormac's Chapel at Cashel has many individual heads on the interior and exterior. Plant ornament is also popular, particularly in the triangles of chevron ornament, and surface geometrical ornament is found on the Nuns' Church at Clonmacnois. Animals are also encountered, some in high relief (as on the doorway in Killaloe Cathedral),

Romanesque decorated doorway at Dysert O'Dea, Co. Clare, featuring chevrons and, in the outer register, human heads; 12th century.

and where they are found interlaced with one another, they are usually the result of influence from the VIKINGS. It is the strong presence of such Scandinavian-derived interlaced animal ornament which makes the ornament of Irish, or Hiberno-Romanesque so different from that elsewhere.

The range of symbolical and human figure carving found in England and on the Continent is largely absent in Ireland, but it is quite probable that the decoration on Irish Romanesque churches had a symbolic significance now lost to us. Nevertheless, representational carving does survive in rare instances; one notable example is the sculpture under arches on the exterior west gable at Ardmore, Co. Waterford. The *Crucifixion* was carved on one lintel at Maghera, Co. Derry, and on another at Dunshaughlin, Co. Meath, but the subjects carved on Co. Donegal lintels – at Raphoe, Carndonagh and Clonca – have not yet been satisfactorily explained. The tympanum of the north doorway of Cormac's Chapel at Cashel, showing a helmeted centaur firing an arrow at a lion which crushes an animal beneath its paws, may symbolize the battle between good and evil. Kilteel, Co. Kildare, is unique in having figure sculpture on the jambs of the chancel arch.

The unique features of Cormac's Chapel were copied individually, though not collectively, in other

Romanesque north doorway of Cormac's Chapel, Cashel, Co. Tipperary, with carved decoration on the tympanum; 12th century.

Presumably it was this French builder-monk who suggested the apsidial chapels, a Continental feature not used elsewhere in Ireland. Cistercian abbeys were built to conform to the exigencies of the Order's rule: the architect was to strive towards utility and simplicity, reducing the elements to the minimum necessary and avoiding unnecessary decoration. The recommended layout was with the church, which was the highest building, to the north of a cloister, forming the centre of the abbatial complex and linked to the other buildings. To the east of the cloister was the chapter-house, the parlour, and the refectory with the monk's dormitory above it; to the west were garderobes and the buildings of the lay brothers with their dormitory. The most complete remains of this arrangement in Ireland are at JERPOINT ABBEY, Co. Kilkenny; the monks reached the east end of the church by a night stair from their dormitory and the lay brothers reached the west end of the church from their dormitory. As the lay brothers' buildings were erected more hastily and less expensively, they were the least sturdy and have been the first to become ruinous. The Cistercian abbeys and churches were built on a cruciform plan with the square-ended chancel of earlier Burgundian churches and chapels off the transept. A transverse screen divided the church, separating the worshipping monks at the east end from the lay brothers at the west end. Peculiar to most of the Cistercian abbey churches in Ireland was the positioning of the clerestory windows above the pillars of the nave rather than above the arches.

Within twelve years of its foundation Mellifont had eight daughter-houses: Bective Abbey, Co. Meath

churches such as St Cronan's, ROSCREA, Co. Tipperary (pointed gable over the west doorway), and Kilmalkedar and Ardfert, both in Co. Kerry (blind arcading). The church at Aghadoe, Co. Kerry, may have been built in 1158, but reliable dating evidence is lacking for most Irish Romanesque churches. In addition to those already mentioned, there are other fine examples of doorways decorated in the Irish Romanesque style at Monaincha and Donaghmore, Co. Tipperary, Killeshin, Co. Laois, Ullard and Freshford, Co. Kilkenny, White Island, Co. Fermanagh, Wicklow, part of St Mary's Cathedral, Limerick, Christ Church Cathedral, Dublin, and one now in the Church of Ireland Cathedral at Kilmore, Co. Cavan.   P H

Harold Leask, *Irish Churches and Monastic Buildings*, vol. 1, 2nd ed. 1977; Brian de Breffny and George Mott, *The Churches and Abbeys of Ireland*, 1976; Peter Harbison, Homan Potterton and Jeanne Sheehy, *Irish Art and Architecture*, 1978.

Transitional and Gothic

Work on the first Irish abbey of the Cistercian Order, at Mellifont, Co. Louth, began in 1142; the nucleus of the community was a group of Irish monks professed at Clairvaux, and in 1143 St Bernard sent a monk, Robert, from Clairvaux to assist in the building.

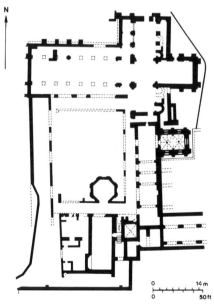

Plan of the Cistercian Mellifont Abbey, Co. Louth, begun in 1142; the church is located on the north side, with the adjacent cloister (with lavabo) at the centre of the complex (cf. p. 154).

The nave of the church at Boyle Abbey, Co. Roscommon, looking east; late 12th–early 13th century.

The ruins of Inch Abbey, Co. Down (founded 1187), showing the tall lancet windows of the choir.

(1147); Boyle Abbey, Co. Roscommon (1148); Monasternenagh, Co. Limerick (1148/51); Baltinglass Abbey, Co. Wicklow (1148); Kilbeggan Abbey, Co. Westmeath (1150); Inishlounaght Abbey, Co. Tipperary (1151); Newry Abbey, Co. Down (1153); and Abbeydorney, Co. Kerry (1154). Meanwhile St Mary's Abbey, Dublin (1147), was founded by Cistercians from Savigny in France. Other foundations followed: by 1200, nineteen more abbeys and a cell were founded in Ireland as descendants of Mellifont. St Mary's, Dublin, engendered Dunbrody Abbey, Co. Wexford (1180/82); and Grey Abbey, Co. Down (1193), Inch Abbey, Co. Down (1187), and the great Abbey of Duiske at Graiguenamanagh, Co. Kilkenny (1204/7), were all founded by Cistercians from England, and Tintern Abbey, Co. Wexford (1200), by Cistercians from Wales. The 13th century was to see further Cistercian expansion with five more foundations, the last being Hore Abbey, near Cashel, Co. Tipperary, in 1272.

Cistercian builders between 1150 and 1250 were subject to Transitional and later to Gothic stylistic influences; the fine lavabo (1200) at Mellifont has Romanesque arches but the delicate foliar decoration of the capitals and the effortless handling of the moulding bespeak the Transitional style. At JERPOINT ABBEY the arches of the nave are pointed in the Gothic style, while the capitals are Romanesque and the pillars differ as work progressed in the closing decades of the 12th century, from the earliest examples at the eastern end to the later ones at the western end of the nave. At Boyle Abbey, Co. Roscommon, the impressive ruins reveal English influence; unusually for Ireland, the clerestory windows are above the arches of the nave, and the church has marked similarities with Buildwas Abbey on the English–Welsh border. The tall lancet west window, in the latest part of the building, has affinities with Anglo-Norman churches in eastern Ireland. It has been suggested that the Christ Church Cathedral (Dublin) master (see below), who had worked in the West of England, also worked at Boyle.

Duiske Abbey at Graiguenamanagh, Co. Kilkenny, had the largest Cistercian church in Ireland, measuring just over 60 m. (200 ft) in length; the transept is 34 m. (112 ft) across, with three chapels in each arm – a plan identical in size and shape to the abbey church of Stratas Florida in Wales. Masons who worked on Christ Church Cathedral in Dublin may also have worked at Graiguenamanagh; here, the abbatial church was splendidly restored under the direction of the architect Percy Le Clerc in the 1970s. While Duiske had the longest church, the church of Dunbrody Abbey, where impressive ruins remain, is only about 1·50 m. (5 ft) shorter and it has a broader transept: 40 m. (130 ft) across with three chapels in each arm. The pointed arches of the nave rest on plain square piers.

Apart from the architectural ideas imported by the Cistercians, the determining factor in architectural development in Ireland, affecting as it did both ecclesiastical and secular building, was the settlement

The restored 13th-century church of Ballintubber Abbey, Co. Mayo, seen from the south-east.

there of the Anglo-Normans. The churches of the Anglo-Norman invaders reflect the vigour and wealth of their culture. The cruciform parish church built at New Ross, Co. Wexford, c. 1210 was more magnificent than most of the then existing Irish cathedrals. The building of Christ Church Cathedral, Dublin, which was finished c. 1240, was accomplished in two stages. The choir was built in the earlier stage in the late Romanesque style of English cathedrals; details of its design were subsequently adopted by the Augustinians in churches in the West of Ireland. The second phase of building seems to have been directed by an English master-mason who had worked at Droitwich and Overbury in Worcestershire; he is now referred to for convenience as the 'Christ Church Master'. The masons who worked under him probably also came from the West of England and the stone for the building was imported from near Bristol. The style of the nave, begun c. 1212 and finished c. 1235, is the Gothic of the West of England churches in the region of Evesham. Its use at Christ Church revealed to the Irish the soaring grandeur of such a nave and the beauty of a skilfully integrated clerestory and triforium.

The provincial Irish cathedrals of the Anglo-Normans were not built on such a grand scale as Christ Church or of Dublin's second cathedral, St Patrick's, with its three-tier elevation. Kilkenny Cathedral, however, is a distinguished building in the Gothic style, completed in the 1260s with a handsome broad nave; the aisles continue beyond the transept for a little more than half the length of the choir. The design of the east windows is so similar to that of windows in the Cistercian Abbey church at Graiguenamanagh that it is reasonable to suppose them to be the work of the same master or corps of masons. The later quatrefoil windows which light the clerestory are believed, like the quatrefoil in the west doorway, to be the work of a master mason who may be conveniently referred to as the Gowran Master because he appears to have worked also on the fine Collegiate church at Gowran, Co. Kilkenny. He has been described as 'the most gifted craftsman to work in Ireland during the 13th century'.

The plan of the 13th-century cruciform church of the Augustinian priory at ATHASSEL, Co. Tipperary, with chapels in the arms of the transept, owes a debt to the Cistercians although its style reveals the Anglo-Norman cultural influence of its founder, William de Burgh. Cistercian influence is apparent in other churches of the Augustinians in Ireland such as at Ballintubber, Co. Mayo, which has been restored. An awareness of changes in architectural fashion is evident in the 13th-century church of the Augustinian nunnery at Killone, Co. Clare, which has windows in three successive styles – Romanesque, Transitional and Gothic.

While the earliest churches of the mendicant Dominican and Franciscan orders who came to Ireland in the first half of the 13th century were simple buildings, by the end of the century the Dominicans at Kilmallock, Co. Limerick, were engaged on an impressive priory where building continued in the 14th century. The church has a splendid enfilade of six lancet windows lighting each side of the chancel and an elegant east window with five slender graduated lancets.

Almost every stage in the development of tracery from the mid-13th to the mid-15th century is illustrated in the windows of the Dominican priory church at Athenry, Co. Galway, the earliest being the tall lancets in the choir. The Dominican 'Black Abbey' at Kilkenny has a magnificent window in the south wall of the transept. It has five lights with mullions

The elaborate 14th-century window in the south transept of the 'Black Abbey' at Kilkenny, the largest of its type in Ireland.

ending in pointed cusps; above, within the intersecting lines, trefoils and quatrefoils are arranged with consummate skill.

The earliest Franciscan architectural achievements of any distinction are the 14th-century friary church at Castledermot, Co. Kildare, untypical of Franciscan building in its size and magnificence, thanks to a generous endowment, and the friary church at Ennis, Co. Clare, which has an impressive five-light lancet window.

A slackening in building activity is evident in the first half of the 14th century due largely to the distress and devastation caused by Edward Bruce's incursions. What building there was, was mostly in the form of repairs, improvements and additions to existing buildings. The stepped parapet seems to have been introduced at this time, probably from France or Catalonia; examples may be seen on Kildare Cathedral, on the 14th-century additions to Ardfert Cathedral, Co. Kerry, Cashel Cathedral, Co. Tipperary, and the Collegiate Church at Gowran, Co. Kilkenny.

The Black Death, which reached Ireland at mid-century, claimed many victims, indeed a large portion of the population died of the plague, including masons and builders. Consequently building activity came near to a halt and the tradition of high-quality workmanship declined. Not until the return of prosperity in the 15th century was there any architectural enterprise of consequence. There are examples of very fine work and design at Kilconnell, Co. Galway, where one tomb-niche has a canopy with bold geometrical tracery and another has Flamboyant tracery and, below, figures in ogee-headed niches; and at Strade, Co. Mayo, where the tomb-niche with Flamboyant Gothic tracery must be the most beautiful in Ireland. The work of a school of highly proficient masons at Callan, Co. Kilkenny, in the 15th century may be seen at Jerpoint Abbey, Co. Kilkenny, and Kilcooly Abbey, Co. Tipperary.

Small churches with a narrow nave and short chancel were built in the 15th century, some fortified by an adjacent tower at the east end which provided accommodation for the priest. Examples may be seen at Newcastle, Co. Dublin, and Taghmon, Co. Westmeath.

The high point of architectural endeavour in Ireland in the 15th century was the splendid and highly accomplished rebuilding of HOLY CROSS ABBEY, Co. Tipperary, under the patronage of the cosmopolitan 4th Earl of Ormond.

In the 15th century the Franciscan friars (who had become immensely popular in Ireland) embarked on an extensive phase of building, particularly in the Gaelic West and South-West. One of the earliest of the resulting friaries is Kilconnell, Co. Galway, built early in the century: its fine tomb-niches, one of which shows French influence, have already been mentioned. The size of the churches and the substantial claustral buildings are a remarkable witness to the industry of the friars and the generosity of their benefactors. One example is at Adare, Co. Limerick, where the friary

St Patrick's, Taghmon, Co. Westmeath, a 15th-century church building which incorporated a fortified four-storey tower.

was founded in 1464. The church is large, with chapels at the east end and a spacious aisled south transept. At Askeaton, Co. Limerick, there are impressive remains of the church built between 1420 and 1440 and also the cloister and refectory. Other impressive remains may be seen at Quin, Co. Clare (c. 1453), Muckross, Co. Kerry (c. 1448–1490), Moyne, Co. Mayo (built shortly before 1460), Rosserk, Co. Mayo (founded by the Third Order Regular before 1441), Ardfert, Co. Kerry, where the cloister and the south transept of the church are 15th-century additions, and Claregalway, Co. Galway, where the tower and a fine east window in the chancel were added to an earlier church. The largest and best preserved of the Franciscan friaries of the period is one of the last to be built, Ross Errily, Co. Galway (pl. 1), founded not earlier than 1498. The popularity of the friars is evident there for although it was in an isolated position in a sparsely populated region the church is large and has an unusual double transept to the north of the nave, larger than either the nave or chancel; the extensive claustral buildings range over a wide area. The extraordinary building phenomenon of the Franciscans terminated shortly before the Reformation with Creevelea Friary at Dromahaire, Co. Leitrim, founded in 1508; its nave and chancel church with south transept was built after 1512. To a lesser extent the Dominicans also built and improved their priories in the 15th century. One at Burrishoole, Co. Mayo, was built c. 1469. The last Dominican building venture was at Ballindoon, Co. Sligo, founded in 1507. The Augustinians, still less active in new building, nevertheless built a church and monastic buildings for their new foundation at Murrisk, Co. Mayo (1457); this church has unusual battlemented walls.

Secular building following the Anglo-Norman conquest of Ireland began with the urgent construction of forts to hold their positions as the invaders advanced through the country. The Norman castles were of two main types. One type had a massive rectangular keep or donjon such as that at Carrickfergus, Co. Antrim, begun in the 1180s and having a great unbuttressed

The 15th-century friary at Rosserk, Co. Mayo; the church within the complex consisted of nave and choir, with the tower above the screen.

defended by eight towers, five round and three rectangular, and within the walls are an outer middle and inner ward; the innermost ward is protected by a gate with a portcullis, contained in the massive keep. Early in the next century a great hall for audiences and banquets was added. Askeaton Castle, Co. Limerick, built about the middle of the century, also has an elegant detached great hall, there built over a vaulted kitchen and cellars with Decorated Gothic carving on the windows similar to that in the nearby Franciscan friary. The stepped battlement to be seen, for example, at Coolhull Castle, Co. Wexford, or Blarney Castle, Co. Cork (*c.* 1446) was a 15th-century innovation of uncertain origin.

The massive ruins of Trim Castle, Co. Meath, one of the principal Norman castles in Ireland, overlooking the River Boyne.

four-storey keep, 27 m. (90 ft) high and 16·75 × 18·25 m. (55 × 60 ft) in plan; and at Trim, Co. Meath, where building began in the 1180s but seems to have been completed thirty or forty years later. The massive square keep at Trim has walls 3·35 m. (11 ft) thick and stands in a large bailey surrounded by a fortified curtain wall. A peculiarly Irish development of this type of castle was the addition of cylindrical turrets at the corners of the keep, as at Carlow Castle and Ferns Castle, Co. Wexford, both built in the first quarter of the 13th century.

Many of the Anglo-Norman knights came to Ireland from Wales and the second type of castle which they introduced, a walled enclosure with a strong gatehouse, corner towers, and sometimes also intermediate towers, was inspired by the Welsh castles of Beaumaris and Harlech. Examples in Ireland are Liscarrol Castle, Co. Cork (13th century). Ballymote Castle, Co. Sligo (early 13th), and Roscommon Castle (1269). This too was the plan of the now much altered Dublin Castle and of Limerick Castle (early 13th century). One early castle belonging to neither type is Dundrum Castle, Co. Down, built at the end of the 12th century; the two-storey keep, 16 m. (52 ft) in height and 14 m. (46 ft) in diameter internally, is cylindrical and is similar to one built about the same time by the Earls Marshal at Pembroke in Wales. The cylindrical donjon at Nenagh was part of the outer defence, while the cylindrical Reginald's Tower at Waterford was a part of the town's walls.

A defensive development of the 14th century, when the country was in turmoil, was machicolation projecting from the upper wall-face of the castle with a row of openings through which missiles could be directed at intruders. However, as with ecclesiastical building, there was a lull in secular building in this century followed by renewed building activity with the return of more favourable conditions in the 15th.

Cahir Castle, Co. Tipperary, built early in the 15th century, is the most impressive of the medieval strongholds, providing as it does an excellent idea of the feudal castle complex. The high enclosing walls are

The battlemented ruins of Blarney Castle, Co. Cork; mid-15th century.

The restored Bunratty Castle, built *c.* 1450, with its four corner towers.

The concept of accommodation on several levels was a novel one which found lodgment in Ireland early in the 15th century in the form of the ubiquitous TOWER HOUSE, the multi-storey fortification-cum-residence. So many were built in Co. Meath alone (following the offer by the Government in 1429 of a bounty to those who built a small defensible castle) that by 1449 a limit had to be placed on the number constructed; in Co. Limerick alone four hundred tower houses were built. Town tower houses were built at Carlingford, Co. Louth and other towns, including Kilmallock, Co. Limerick, where the elegant four- and five-storey one-bay castles were decorated not only with stone carving but also with gilding.

Bunratty Castle, Co. Clare (*c.* 1450), is a fine example of the castle of an important magnate for whom the limited accommodation of a simple tower house was insufficient and to whom the medieval arrangement at Cahir Castle or Askeaton Castle may have seemed both uncomfortable and antiquated. The plan of Bunratty is a great rectangle flanked at the angles by four communicating towers, the southern and northern towers at the front of the castle are joined by a high broad arch rising to above the third storey and with a chamber above it on the fourth. The central block of Bunratty contains the main guard, a chapel, commodious private apartments and other chambers as well as an impressive paved great hall or audience chamber 14·60 m. (48 ft) in both height and length and 9·15 m. (30 ft) wide. The plan of Bunratty was to

become popular in the 16th and 17th centuries with the builders of 'strong-houses'.

The 16th and 17th centuries

The unsettled political, religious and administrative situation in Ireland in the 16th and 17th centuries was far from conducive to civic, ecclesiastical or domestic building activity.

With the dissolution of the monasteries following the Reformation the monastic establishments with their churches passed into the hands of lay proprietors who not infrequently adapted the conventual buildings for residential use for themselves and sometimes, as at Tintern Abbey, Co. Wexford, even the church. The parish churches and the cathedrals passed to the ministers of the Reformed faith. Thus the Protestant minority had more than enough church buildings at their disposal and only a few new churches were erected in areas of new settlement such as Kilbrogan Church at Bandon, Co. Cork (1610), in the late Gothic style or the new cathedral at Derry (1628), erected for settlers by the Corporation of the City of London and built by William Parrott in the Late Gothic style of older London City churches. Building activity increased after the Restoration but the need for new Protestant churches generally was still minimal. From that period, however, the simple rectangular Ballinderry Middle Church, Co. Antrim (1664), has survived. Occasionally additions were made to existing buildings such as the gallery added by Nicholas Langredg in 1616 for the Earl of Cork to the church at Tallow, Co. Waterford, probably the first galleried church in Ireland.

The Late Gothic style survived for a while in Ireland into the 17th century but eventually succumbed to the change of taste. Architects now appeared who made a deliberate study of design and actually supervised building operations.

As Dublin expanded and prospered some of its churches were rebuilt or repaired. St Werburgh's was rebuilt in 1662 but the work of the builder Thomas Browne was so shoddy that it had to be rebuilt again fifty years later; other dilapidated medieval parish churches in the city were restored and some were rebuilt. St Andrew's, Dublin (1670), on an elliptical plan, the design of William Dodson, demonstrates this architect's awareness of Renaissance architecture. It appears to have been the first church in Ireland to include Classical elements, but was so badly built that it soon collapsed. When the unpretentious new church of St Michan's parish (1685) was designed, albeit unimaginatively, by Sir WILLIAM ROBINSON, on a Renaissance plan, it was apparently the first instance of its adoption in ecclesiastical architecture in Ireland. Following the Restoration repairs and additions were carried out elsewhere in the country, such as the tower added by Thomas Smith and William Armstead to the cathedral at Cork shortly before 1677.

In the safety of the cities there was some domestic building. Timber cagework houses of the type still surviving at Chester in England were erected at Dublin and Drogheda in the latter decades of the 16th century.

A 16th-century urban merchant's dwelling: the façade of Rothe House, Kilkenny.

These have all vanished, but fortunately drawings made of some early in the 19th century exist to provide a record of their appearance. Limerick, Cork and probably other cities also had examples of cagework houses.

In Galway city 16th-century building was mainly in stone; it appears that the builders there were more subject to Continental than to English influence. The multi-family houses had ornately decorated doorways, some flanked by massive pillars; the principal apartments were on the piano nobile with shops below and less expensive accommodation above. The Rothe House at Kilkenny (1594) has survived as a rare example of a prosperous urban merchant's dwelling: it is built of stone, two storeys with mullioned windows over an arcaded ground floor fronting the street. As further accommodation was required the owner built two more houses on courtyards to the rear of the first one. Within the walled town of Youghal, Co. Cork, a gabled three-storey house now known as Myrtle Grove and dating from the end of the 16th century is very English in appearance and has been compared to an Elizabethan house in Devonshire. Outside the cities the defensible castle long remained the most practical residence of the landowner. The ORMOND MANOR HOUSE at Carrick-on-Suir, Co. Tipperary, must be seen as unique and outside the mainstream of architectural development in England, being in the Elizabethan Tudor style which its owner had come to appreciate while living in England in the

latter half of the 16th century and which he imitated on his return to Ireland.

Mallow Castle, Co. Cork, where building on a four-storey single pile began in the last decade of the 16th century on the ruins of an older castle, demonstrates concessions to domesticity in its many mullioned windows with chamfered hood-mouldings, but it had stout polygonal turrets for defence at the front corners and an angular turret to protect the front door. Not infrequently a defensible mansion was added to an existing tower such as at Donegal Castle (*c.* 1620) where mullioned windows were inserted in the tower to match the adjacent new gabled house and a fine Jacobean chimneypiece was placed in a chamber of the tower, or Leamaneh Castle, Co. Clare (*c.* 1640).

Mallow Castle, Co. Cork, built at the end of the 16th century on the ruins of an earlier castle.

Leamaneh Castle, Co. Clare, showing the four-storey mansion added to the existing tower, *c.* 1640.

Castle Balfour, Co. Fermanagh (1618), built at the time of the plantation schemes, reveals distinctive Scottish features.

Monea Castle, Co. Fermanagh, a typical 'plantation castle' built before 1620; the castle incorporates two round towers.

Rathfarnham Castle, Co. Dublin (1585), appears to be the first of a series of the type of defensible mansion known as a strong-house, its plan being a rectangular central block flanked with four rectangular turrets at the corners. Kanturk Castle, Co. Cork, built in the first decade of the 17th century, is four storeys in height flanked by five-storey communicating towers at the corners; it, too, follows this plan which found favour – the rectangular mansion with flanking angle towers. Kanturk exhibits an innovation in its fine Renaissance door and appears to be the first house to combine traditional Irish tower house architecture with both Tudor and Renaissance features; PORTUMNA CASTLE, Co. Galway, built early in the 17th century for Irish landowners who had lived in England, is more elegant, admitting further Renaissance elements. Other great houses of the period, such as Joymount at Carrickfergus, Co. Antrim, and the grandiose Charlemont, Co. Tyrone (c. 1622), have been demolished, but with the exception of the Lord-Deputy's palatial JIGGINSTOWN the 17th-century Irish country mansion rarely exhibited any features of current architectural style in England or continental Europe, as evidenced by Coppingers Court, Co. Cork (early 17th century), Monkstown Castle, Co. Cork (1636), or Ightermurragh, Co. Cork (1641). Burncourt Castle, Co. Tipperary (1641), is still in the Tudor architectural tradition with its mullioned windows, tall hexagonal chimney stacks, stringcourse, front door case with hood-moulding and a corbelled timber guard-walk linking the angle towers, archaic in comparison with contemporary country mansions in England and lagging behind English architectural fashion by as much as one hundred years. Even houses in the English tradition, such as Oldbawn, Co. Dublin (1635), were built in the Late Tudor style already old-fashioned in England.

The settlers of the Ulster Plantation schemes in the first half of the 17th century – the majority of whom came from Scotland – brought masons from Scotland who built castles and strong-houses in Ulster with such distinctive Scottish features as the round turret projecting from the upper angles of the building on rows of corbels and capped with a conical roof. Such construction may be seen at the ruined Castle Balfour, Co. Fermanagh (1618), or at Ballygalley Castle, Co. Antrim (1625). Monea Castle, Co. Fermanagh, built shortly before 1620, has two round towers corbelled out at their summit to carry rectangular chambers set directly above them with at least two courses of corbelling to support the projecting corners, a feature found in Scotland at Claypotts near Dundee.

Following the Restoration and in a period of relative calm and prosperity the administration encouraged new building in Dublin which expanded rapidly. Lessees of plots around what was to become St Stephen's Green were obliged by the terms of their lease from the Corporation to build in brick, stone and timber, with at least two storeys and a tiled or slated roof. Several streets of four-storey houses were built in the last quarter of the 17th century with their roof-ridge at right-angles to the street, its gable masked by quadrants sweeping up to curved or triangular pediments in the style fashionable in the Netherlands.

Outside the capital, Rathbeale Hall at Swords has an elegant 17th-century panelled interior and staircase. In Co. Louth, BEAULIEU, built in the 1660s, seems to have been the first wholly unfortified country house; it survives intact with its fine late 17th-century panelled drawing room and dining room, while a rather similar country house of the same period, Eyrecourt, Co. Galway, is now in ruins. Another distinguished country house of the same period, Ballintober, Co. Cork, of eleven bays, three storeys high with dormers in the top storey and wings *en échelon*, has also been demolished, as has the Duchess of Ormonde's palatial red-brick Dunmore House built in the 1670s near Kilkenny and which had a majestic carved staircase. Indeed knowledge of late 17th-century building is limited due to the disappearance of most of the important houses, including: the largest private house of that period, the Earl of Orrery's huge Charleville Castle, Co. Cork (1661), which had no less than fifty-six chimneys – it was burnt to the ground in 1690; and Sir John Perceval's Burton House, Co. Cork, in the late Caroline style for which the architect's design was presented by William Kenn in 1669 and subsequently executed with additions by Thomas Smith. The latter was also engaged in the building of the Southwell Gift Almshouses at Kinsale, Co. Cork (*c.* 1680). The almshouses in the main street of Youghal, Co. Cork (1614), which have unfortunately been allowed to fall into a perilous state of decay, were built for the 1st Earl of Cork by Nicholas Langredg, who also involved in improvements to the Earl's Lismore Castle.

The civic buildings of the 17th century have fared little better than the country houses. The Dublin Custom House (1638–40) was burned in 1711; Samuel Molyneux's old cruciform Dublin Four Courts (1608) rebuilt in 1695 by Sir William Robinson, has vanished. Fortunately, however, one distinguished building, Robinson's Royal Hospital, KILMAINHAM, Co. Dublin (1680–7), in the Classical style with skilfully handled Baroque features, has survived and has been restored.   B de B

For bibliography see p. 30.

18th-century buildings

The influence of Dutch building practice, which had been strong in Ireland in the late 17th century, persisted until the 1720s. It is identified by high-pitched roofs with bracketed eaves, near-triangular pediments, curvilinear 'Dutch' gables, and swan-necked pediments to doorcases. In the towns the gable-fronted houses were called 'Dutch billies'. The Red House, Youghal, Co. Cork (1706–15). Shannongrove, Co. Limerick (1709), and the Court House, Kinsale, Co. Cork (1706), are typical of the period.

The office of the Surveyor-General was the main architect's office in the early 18th century and in great demand for the supply of designs for all kinds of works, as well as Government and military buildings, and therefore highly influential in the development of Irish architecture. Col. THOMAS BURGH, who was appointed Surveyor-General in 1700, was capable of strong Classical work, e.g. in the Library of TRINITY COLLEGE (1712) and the façade of St Werburgh's, Dublin (1715), yet his Dr Steeven's Hospital (1721–3) is relatively archaic. Stylistically contemporary with the Hospital are Stackallen, Co. Meath (1719), and Damer House, Roscrea, Co. Tipperary (*c.* 1722).

Burgh was succeeded as Surveyor-General in 1730 by Sir EDWARD LOVETT PEARCE, who was then aged about thirty. The work of Pearce was the cornerstone of Irish Palladianism. His influence was widespread but his

The façade of St Werburgh's, Dublin, by Thomas Burgh, 1715.

identified works are few. They include BELLAMONT FOREST, Co. Cavan, CASTLETOWN, Co. Kildare, and the PARLIAMENT HOUSE, Dublin. After the death of Pearce in 1733 his pupil RICHARD CASTLE emerged as the leading Irish architect. Castle was fortunate to secure a series of large and important commissions which he executed in a thoroughly Palladian manner. At CARTON, Co. Kildare (1739–45), and RUSSBOROUGH, Co. Wicklow (1741–*c.* 1755), he used the hallmark of the Palladian style – the 'economic' layout – joining the main house to service wings by curved colonnades. In Dublin he designed Clanwilliam House (1738), which was quickly followed by other commissions. Though his buildings incline towards the severe, the incorporation of plasterwork by the FRANCINI brothers in many of his houses gives the interiors a Baroque magnificence. Castle died in 1751 and his assistant FRANCIS BINDON is thought to have completed several of his buildings.

Though there were few professional architects in practice before the late 18th century, there were a number of gentlemen-amateurs, architect-craftsmen and builders. Aspiring architects were assisted by the increasing number of pattern books in circulation. These included Andrea Palladio's *Quattro Libri . . .*, which were published in English in 1715 as *Four Books of Architecture*, James Gibb's *Book of Architecture* (1729). Colen Campbell's *Vitruvius Britannicus* (1715), Isaac Ware's *A Complete Body of Architecture* (1756) and William Pain's *The Builder's Pocket Treasure* (1763) which went through many editions. Irish architectural books included John Aheron's *General Treatise on Architecture* (1754) and *Twelve Designs for Country Houses* by Rev. John Payne (1757). Such books assisted builders to gain a knowledge of Classical detail, though in fact they became so imbued with the use of Classical proportions that the use of Classicism became second nature. The importance of pattern books is seen at Mount Ievers, Co. Clare (1737), which appears to have been inspired by the illustration of Chevening in Kent printed in *Vitruvius Britannicus*. Yet the 'strength, simplicity and sophistication' of the house derives solely from the skill of the architect John Rothery. The

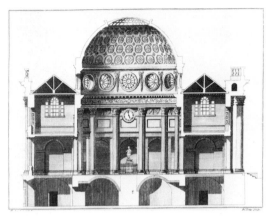

The Royal Exchange (now City Hall), Dublin, by Thomas Cooley, 1769: E–W section, from R. Pool and J. Cash, *Views of the most remarkable Public Buildings . . . in the City of Dublin (1780).*

Rothery family appear to have worked in the Clare, Limerick and north Cork area and retained the same style of early 18th-century Classicism from Doneraile Court, Co. Cork (1725), to Bowen's Court, Co. Cork (1776). Bindon continued the Palladian tradition in country-house architecture, as did the Italian-born DAVIS DUCART who introduced a Rococo flavour to Irish Palladianism. Among the gentlemen-amateurs was Nathaniel Clements (1705–77), who was closely associated with Richard Castle and built the Phoenix Lodge (1751–4). He is credited with a series of villas, including Colganstown, Co. Dublin, notable for its sophisticated economic layout. THOMAS IVORY, a professional architect, designed his finest building – a Mannerist essay – in the form of a farm at Kilcarty, Co. Meath (c. 1775). Perhaps the most polished example of the late Palladian period is Castleward, Co. Down (c.

The Custom House, Dublin, by James Gandon, begun 1781; watercolour by James Malton, 1793.

1762–73), attributed to James Bridges of Bristol. Robert Mack designed the imposing Powerscourt House, Dublin (1771), with its crusty granite façade and immense attic. Other architects active in the mid-18th century were JOHN SMYTH, JOHN ENSOR, GEORGE SEMPLE, HUGH DARLEY and JOHN ROBERTS.

The Gothick Revival was inspired by Romantic literature, as opposed to the later Gothic Revival which was archaeologically inspired. Early examples include the east lodge at Castletown, Co. Kildare (c. 1750), taken from a design published by Batty Langley in 1741, and the garden façade of Castleward, Co. Down. Moore Abbey, Co. Kildare (1767), was the first country house to be built completely in the Gothick taste. However, it was not till the 19th century that Gothick houses lost their Classical planning and their Classical interior decoration. In 1759 the architecturally conscious Bishop Pococke employed Sanderson Miller to work on St Canice's Cathedral, Kilkenny, but it was not till late in the 18th century that Gothick was used for new churches, e.g. by Thomas Cooley at Kells, Co. Meath, in 1778 and Ballymakenny, Co. Louth, in 1781; the style, however, went only skin deep.

The building of the Royal Exchange (1769), as the result of an architectural competition, marked the advent of Neo-Classicism in Dublin. This was the first architectural competition in Ireland, and was won by Thomas Cooley (1740–84). He also designed the Archbishop's palace, Armagh (1770), and Caledon, Co. Tyrone (1779). Though he died young, he trained FRANCIS JOHNSTON and it is thought that they collaborated on Rokeby, Co. Louth (c. 1784). Johnston then proceeded to design Townley Hall, Co. Louth (1794), in the unconventional neo-Greek style. Thomas Ivory designed Newcomen's Bank, Dublin (1781) in a flat, Adamesque style, and the same, chaste Neo-Classicism is to be seen at Downhill and the Mussenden Temple, Co. Derry, which has been attributed to Michael Shanahan of Cork (fl. 1770–95). SIR WILLIAM CHAMBERS, who is sometimes seen as the last of the Palladians and the first of the Neo-Classicists, commenced work on the Marino Casino, Clontarf, Co. Dublin, in 1758 and later supplied designs for the Public Theatre and Chapel of Trinity College, Dublin. However, it was his pupil JAMES GANDON who took the architectural plums of 18th-century Dublin with the Custom House (1781), the Four Courts (1786) and King's Inns (c. 1800). Though Gandon designed a number of small country houses and one great house, Emo, Co. Laois, in 1790, it was JAMES WYATT who was in greatest demand for country-house designs in the last three decades of the century.

19th-century buildings

The great famine of the 1840s divided the century demographically and economically. In the first half of the century economic power, and architectural initiative, was held by the Protestant Ascendancy; the population grew dramatically and the building industry expanded. In the second half of the century land agitation and a drop in agricultural prices undermined the landed society and architectural initiative passed to the Catholic Church, and to the new entrepreneurs.

Architecturally, the persistence of the Classical (Georgian) period as late as the 1850s, and the mid-century revolution in building materials emphasized the division of the century into two distinct halves. Changing methods in the production of brick and glass altered the face of domestic architecture, while iron and steel production facilitated great advances in engineering and the development of efficient transport services – both steamship links and internal railway networks – which brought the new materials to the farthest corners of the country.

The Act of Union had less effect on the architectural development of the country house than it did on Dublin where the great, politically motivated, families closed up their large houses and departed for London. However, much of the Georgian city had yet to be built; Fitzwilliam Square, Fitzwilliam Street, much of Leeson Street, Baggot Street and Mountjoy Square. Large though the houses in these streets were, the element of luxury had disappeared. The coming of the railways resulted in the building of imposing railway termini and, at the same time, the opening up of the coastline of Dublin Bay to suburban development. A distinctive design of suburban house, found only in Ireland, evolved in the environs of Dublin. This is called the 'top-entry' house, having a single storey over a high basement.

The first half of the century saw the rise of the home-grown architectural profession, culminating first in the establishment of the ROYAL HIBERNIAN ACADEMY in 1823 and secondly of the ROYAL INSTITUTE OF THE ARCHITECTS OF IRELAND in 1839. It would be appropriate therefore to consider first the work of FRANCIS JOHNSTON, who designed the Academy building in 1824. His work shows a fluidity of plan and a free interpretation of historical styles which could be seen as proto-Victorian. His pioneering work on the design of prisons and lunatic asylums suggested the path future public works architects should follow. James Gandon's pupil SIR RICHARD MORRISON commenced his career in the 18th century, though his particular blend of Neo-Classical and academic historicism came to fruition only in the second and third decades of the century. He was assisted by his son, WILLIAM VITRUVIUS MORRISON, who took a great interest in the finishing of interiors and is credited with the introduction of the Tudor-Gothic Revival style to Ireland. Johnston's nephew and pupil, William Murray, continued the Classical tradition and went into practice with George Papworth, who in turn continued building country houses in the Classical manner well into the 1850s. JOHN NASH was the one major English architect of the early 19th century to have an extensive practice in Ireland. His best Classical work is at Caledon, Co. Tyrone, and his best Gothic work, Lough Cutra, Co. Galway. The brothers JAMES and RICHARD PAIN came to Ireland to supervise the work at Lough Cutra and stayed on, James in Limerick and George Richard in Cork. The brothers are best known for their continuation of

The 'Black Church' (St Mary's Chapel-of-Ease), Dublin, designed in Gothick style by John Semple, 1830.

Nash's castle style and their series of churches and courthouses.

The ecclesiastical Board of First Fruits employed John Bowden (d. 1829) and others in a huge operation to rebuild half the existing Church of Ireland churches and build the same number of new churches. These churches, in a spiky, desiccated Gothick style, were run up in the first three decades of the 19th century. John Semple (fl. 1820–31) designed churches· which are unmistakable; they include the Black Church, Dublin (1828), which has a parabolic vault, and the 'Portuguese' Monkstown church, Co. Dublin, influenced by James Cavanah Murphy's *Batalha* (1795) and his *Arabian Antiquities of Spain* (1815).

During the Greek War of Independence (1821–33) several Catholic churches were built in the neo-Greek style which was seen as symbolic of liberty. The finest example is St Mary's Pro-Cathedral, Dublin, which was commenced in 1815, based on Chalgrin's S. Philippe du Roule, Paris (1764) and is attributed to John Sweetman; the portico was added in the 1840s by J. B. Keane.

St Mary's Pro-Cathedral, Dublin, begun in 1815, has a later portico (added in the 1840s) by J. B. Keane.

Rathdaire Church, Co. Laois, designed in the Hiberno-Romanesque style by J. F. Fuller; late 19th century.

An archaeologically inspired Gothic style developed in the 1840s and coincided with the emergence of the Catholic Church as a powerful cultural force in the country. A. W. N. PUGIN was in the vanguard of the effort to design ecclesiologically correct churches, though Irish architects such as William Deane Butler, who designed St Mary's Cathedral, Kilkenny (1843), Thomas Cobden in Carlow, Thomas Duff in Dundalk and Patrick Byrne in Dublin, were working in the same direction. The closest Irish follower of A. W. N. Pugin was J. J. MCCARTHY, who dominated Catholic church building in the 1850s and '60s. McCarthy's main rival was A. W. N. Pugin's son, E. W. Pugin, who was partnered by GEORGE ASHLIN. On E. W. Pugin's death in 1875 Ashlin became the dominant figure in church architecture, rivalled only by the successor to McCarthy's practice, WILLIAM HAGUE (fl. 1860–1900). The first church to break with both the Classical and French-English Gothic traditions was the University Church, St Stephen's Green, Dublin (1856), by J. Hungerford Pollen, in an Early Christian style. However, the Lombardo-Romanesque style achieved greater success because it emphasized the link with Italy. The rise of Irish nationalism prompted the revival of Hiberno-Romanesque. McCarthy used the style on the chapel at Glasnevin (1878), while Ashlin built a Hiberno-Romanesque monument to Cardinal McCabe, also at Glasnevin, in 1887 and Timothy Hevey (1845–78) built several churches with round towers in Co. Donegal. However, it is at Rathdaire, Co. Laois, by J. F. FULLER, that Hiberno-Romanesque reached its purest form. From there WILLIAM A. SCOTT led it off in revolutionary directions.

Up to the 1850s Joseph Welland (1798–1860) held a commanding position with the Ecclesiastical Commissioners of the Church of Ireland and designed over a hundred churches, while CHARLES LANYON from Belfast, William Atkins from Cork and Abraham Denny from Waterford were active in their own areas. By the 1850s attitudes towards historicism were

St Matthew's, Woodvale, Belfast, by Welland and Gillespie (1872), has a ground-plan based on the shape of a shamrock leaf.

changing and the Church of Ireland started to build highly eclectic and original churches. William Slater designed Kilmore Cathedral, Co. Cavan (1859), in an English 13th-century style, while Sir Thomas Deane designed TUAM Cathedral (1863) in a 13th-century Irish style (see DEANE AND WOODWARD). Sir Thomas Newenham Deane designed a remarkable, organic church at Westport, Co. Mayo (1872), and Welland and Gillespie built Derryaghy, Co. Antrim (1871), and St Matthew's, Woodvale, Belfast (1872), with its unique shamrock plan. The most important church built by the Church of Ireland in the late 19th century is undoubtedly the Cathedral of St Fin Barre, Cork (1865–76), in an early French Gothic idiom, by the great English medievalist William Burges (1827–81). Its magnificence derives from Burges's eye for composition, detail and furnishing. At the end of the century came the more conservative and supremely

Narrow Water, Co. Down, built *c.* 1832 in the Tudor-revival style by Thomas Duff.

St Fin Barre's Cathedral, Cork, designed by William Burges in French Gothic style, completed in 1876.

Tullira Castle, Co. Galway, rebuilt in Tudor style by George Ashlin (1880), was the home of Edward Martyn, a key figure in the Irish Revival.

confident St Anne's, Belfast (1899), begun by Sir Thomas Drew (1838–1910).

Historicism in country-house architecture led to the use of a wide selection of styles. The popular Tudor and Jacobean-revival style pioneered by the Morrisons was used by the Pains in Munster; by William Burn at Crom Castle, Co. Fermanagh (1834), and Muckross, Co. Kerry (1839); and by Thomas Duff (1792–1848) of Newry at Narrow Water Castle, Co. Down (*c.* 1832). More adventurous was Gosford, Co. Armagh (1820), by Thomas Hopper, which was the first Norman-revival castle in the British Isles, and the largest house in Ireland. An important landmark was Lough Fea, Co. Monaghan (*c.* 1827), by Thomas Rickman, the great historian of English medieval architecture. Adventures into the past continued with: the fairy-tale Killyleagh Castle, Co. Down (1849), by LANYON and LYNN; the High Victorian Adare Manor, Co. Limerick (1832–76), which was worked on by the brothers Pain, A. W. N. Pugin and P. C. Hardwick; and the Venetian Gothic Oak Park, Tralee, Co. Kerry (1857), by William Atkins. Of great importance is DROMORE CASTLE, Co. Limerick (1866–73), which E. W. GODWIN designed in a freely interpreted northern European Gothic style with strong medieval Irish influences. At the same time HUMEWOOD, Co. Wicklow, was built by William White; J. F. FULLER designed Ashford, Co. Galway (*c.* 1870), in a similarly muscular Gothic style and GEORGE ASHLIN tried his hand at castle building at Tullira, Co. Galway (1880). However, country-house design was taking on a more domestic character, as seen in Sir Thomas Drew's Lough Rynn, Co. Leitrim (1883), which is in an Elizabethan Renaissance style with a 'Queen Anne' interior.

The 19th century was notable also as a period of institutional building. The plan form and elevational treatment of courthouses were established by James Gandon in the 18th century and followed by Francis Johnston at Armagh (1809) and John Bowden at Derry (1817). Further handsome courthouses were built at: Cavan (1825) by William Farrell; Cork (1835) by the brothers Pain; Carlow and Tralee by W. V. Morrison, while those of Nenagh, Tullamore and

Broadstone Station, Dublin, by J. S. Mulvany, completed in 1850.

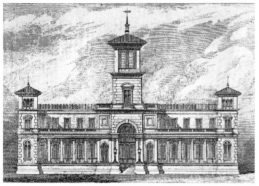

Amiens Street (now Connolly) Station, by William Deane Butler, 1844; engraving by J. Kirkwood from the *Handbook to the Dublin and Drogheda Railway*, 1844.

Ennis are by J. B. Keane. Most are Classical, being symbolic of the ancient origin of justice, while the gaols are Gothic fortresses guaranteed to fill their occupants with an appropriate sense of Gothic horror. Following the Poor Law legislation of 1838 union workhouses were built by George Wilkinson, who later published the invaluable *Practical Geology and Ancient Architecture of Ireland* (1845). In the wake of the famine a second wave of lunatic asylums was built (Johnston and Murray having built the first wave), followed by many convents and schools for the Catholic Church. Railway companies and banks erected buildings which inspired confidence and encouraged investment. John Skipton Mulvany (*c.* 1813–1870) designed the stations on the Dublin to Dun Laoghaire line and the 'Egyptian' Broadstone station (completed in 1850); Sancton Wood designed Kingsbridge (1845) and William Deane Butler built Amiens Street station in 1844. Meanwhile Sandham Symes built banks for the Bank of Ireland from the 1840s to the 1870s; William Caldbeck worked for the National Bank; William G. Murray for the Provincial and Sir Charles Lanyon for the Belfast Bank. The second half of the century saw an

increase in civic pride and the building of impressive town halls. These include: Sligo (1866) by William Hague; Dun Laoghaire (1879) by J. L. Robinson; Pembroke Town Hall, Ballsbridge, Dublin (1879), by E. H. Carson; Bray (1882) by Sir Thomas Newenham Deane; Rathmines (1896) by Sir Thomas Drew; and the grandiloquent Imperial-style Belfast City Hall (1899–1906) by Sir Alfred Brumwell Thomas.   WG T. Sadleir and P. Dickinson, *Georgian Mansions in Ireland*, 1915; Maurice Craig, *Classic Irish Houses of the Middle Size*, 1976; ——, *The Architecture of Ireland from the Earliest Times to 1880*, 1982; P. Harbison, H. Potterton and J. Sheehy, *Irish Art and Architecture*, 1978; B. de Breffny and G. Mott, *The Churches and Abbeys of Ireland*, 1976; B. de Breffny and R. ffolliott, *The Houses of Ireland*, 1975; ——, *Castles of Ireland*, 1977; D. Guinness and W. Ryan, *Irish Houses and Castles*, 1971; J. Sheehy, *The Rediscovery of Ireland's Past; The Celtic Revival 1830–1930*, 1980.

The 20th century

The Modern Movement came late to Ireland. Political events of the early part of the century, economic difficulties in the 1920s and 1930s and the scarcity of building materials during World War II severely restricted building activity. The majority of public buildings completed during that period were designed in a Neo-Classical manner. These included: University College, Dublin, by R. M. Butler (1918); the Royal Dublin Society buildings by O'Callaghan, Webb and Giron (1925); the Parliament House at Stormont, outside Belfast, by Sir Arnold Thornley (1932); the City Hall, Cork, by Jones and Kelly (1937); and Government Buildings in Kildare Street, Dublin, by J. R. Boyd Barrett (1942).

Although little attention was paid to the emerging philosophy of modern architecture, two significant buildings were completed in the first half of the century which did incorporate this new philosophy in their designs. The first was MICHAEL SCOTT's Irish Pavilion for the New York World's Fair of 1939. The extensive use of glass, walls which were curved in plan, and the handling of interior spaces proclaimed this to be a building in what was then the mainstream of the Modern Movement. The second was Desmond FitzGerald's Terminal Building at Dublin Airport (1941), which was for many Irish people their first direct contact with modern architecture. Like Scott's Pavilion, this building demonstrated the chief characteristics of modern architecture of the 1930s.

The first significant modern building of the second half of the century was the offices and bus terminal at Store Street, Dublin (1953), also by Michael Scott. Here was a large building on a prominent site close to Gandon's Custom House and the River Liffey and, being multi-functional, it was, in addition, a complex building. Its influence would have been far greater and the development of modern Irish architecture much accelerated had the significant body of young architects who were responsive to the spirit of the time been given an opportunity then to work out their ideas in practice. Economic factors prevented this happen-

Dublin Airport Terminal Building by Desmond FitzGerald, completed 1941, features a curvilinear plan and a convex façade (not shown) on the airfield side.

The New Library (1961–7) at Trinity College, Dublin, by Ahrends, Burton and Koralek, is flanked by the Museum (left) and Old Library.

ing and what might have been a new wave became only a ripple.

Nevertheless, some well-designed buildings were completed during the 1950s. These include: two technical schools in Co. Dublin, one at Inchicore (1956) by Robinson, Keefe and Devane, and one at Crumlin by Hooper and Mayne; several churches by Peppard and Duffy in Dublin and by Corr and McCormick in Limerick and Clare; and a College of Physical Education (1957) in Co. Dublin by Pearse MacKenna.

In Northern Ireland interest in modern architecture was inspired by the Festival of Britain (1951) but, as in the Republic, no major body of work emerged until the 1960s, with the exception of some school and hospital buildings designed by such architects as Houston and Beaumont, W. D. R. and R. T. Taggart, and Ferguson and McIlveen.

The early 1960s saw an upsurge in building activity which, although not maintained at a constant level subsequently, even so remains substantially higher than in the preceding decades. Many firms produced work of a consistently high standard during this period and many more produced good work sporadically, but the work of Michael Scott's firm has been dominant throughout the last two decades. Since 1953 the Royal Institute of the Architects of Ireland has awarded eight Triennial Gold Medals and four of these have been awarded to members of the Scott, Tallon, Walker firm. In addition, Ronald Tallon and Robin Walker have each been awarded the RIAI Medal for Housing. In 1975 Michael Scott received the Royal Gold Medal in London, thus sharing the honour of having received what may be considered the highest architectural award in the world with Walter Gropius, Frank Lloyd Wright, Le Corbusier and Mies van der Rohe.

The precision and clarity of the work of Scott, Tallon, Walker is reminiscent of Mies; theirs is, however, an interpretation rather than a reproduction, as can be seen from such buildings as the Television and Radio Broadcasting Centre, completed in three phases in 1962, 1967 and 1973, Wesley College in Co.

Dublin (1969) and Carroll's cigarette factory in Co. Louth (1970).

Another firm responsible for work of distinction was Stephenson, Gibney and Associates, formed at the beginning of the 1960s. Their competition-winning entry for offices for the Electricity Supply Board in Dublin was the first attempt to make a large modern building fit into an existing Georgian street; their other buildings include Dublin Airport Hotel (1972), Fitzwilliam Lawn Tennis Club (1973) and Arthur Gibney's Training Centre for the Irish Management Institute (1974) in Co. Dublin, which won an RIAI Gold Medal.

Several major competitions took place during the early 1960s. The first, for a new library building at TRINITY COLLEGE, DUBLIN, was won by Paul Koralek of Ahrends, Burton and Koralek; his design for a strongly sculptured concrete structure has merged well with the existing buildings on the campus.

Another competition arose from the decision of University College, Dublin, to move from the city centre to the suburbs, and called for the college development plan and the detailed design of the Arts and Commerce Building; it was won by Polish architect Andrzej Wejchert, who now runs a most successful practice in Dublin.

Two important competitions were held in Northern Ireland: one, for the Ulster Museum extension in Belfast, was won by Francis Pym; the other, for a County Hall in Ballymena, Co. Antrim, was won by English architects, Burman and Goodall. In both cases the resultant buildings were outstandingly successful.

Liam McCormick of Derry is the architect most closely associated with modern church building in Ireland. His innovative design ability and skilful use of mainly indigenous materials have produced many distinguished churches; St Aengus at Burt, Co. Donegal (1967), with its intriguing form and close relationship with the site, is the best known. Other well-designed churches include: Raymond McDonnell's Church of the Holy Spirit, Ballyroan, Co. Dublin (1968); Patrick Haughey's St Teresa's,

St Aengus, Burt, Co. Donegal (1967), by Liam McCormick.

The Church of the Holy Spirit, Ballyroan, Co. Dublin (1968), by Raymond McDonnell.

A recent housing development by Raymond McDonnell: The Paddocks, Dalkey, Co. Dublin.

Sion Mills, Co. Tyrone (1962); John Thompson and Partners' St Dominic's at Athy, Co. Kildare (1967); and Simon Kelly and Partners' Church of Mary Immaculate Queen at Barna, Co. Galway (1976).

Until recent years, with few exceptions, the standard of design of school buildings in Ireland has not been particularly distinguished. However, largely due to a policy of enlightened patronage pursued by the Department of Education, a number of interesting community schools have been completed. Among the most successful are those at: Ballincollig, Co. Cork, by A. & D. Wejchert (1976); Castletownbere, Co. Cork, by Murray, Murray, Pettit and Partners (1977); Don Henihan's brick-and-timber school in the Tallaght suburb of Dublin, completed in 1979; and Peter and Mary Doyle's school at Birr, Co. Offaly, which was finished in the same year.

The expansion of third-level education both in the Republic and Northern Ireland has led to the completion of a number of interesting buildings. The largest developments have been at Belfield for University College, Dublin, and St Patrick's College, Maynooth, Co. Kildare. Others include: the Ulster College, Jordanstown, Co. Antrim (1970), by Building Design Partnership; the Institute for Advanced Studies, Dublin (1971), by Stephenson, Gibney and Associates; Scott, Tallon, Walker's Science Building and Library at University College, Galway (1973); and Portadown Technical College in Co. Armagh (1973) by Shanks, Leighton, Kennedy and Fitzgerald.

Residential developments in Ireland usually take the form of low-rise, low-density single-family houses built in suburban estates. Indifferent design has characterized most of these in the past but standards are improving, particularly in the public sector; the development at Ringsend, Dublin (1979), by Burke-Kennedy, Doyle and Partners, and several other schemes in Dublin and some in Cork are noteworthy. Private housing-estate design is generally unremarkable, although several schemes by Raymond McDonnell are of a high standard, and Castlepark Village, Kinsale, Co. Cork (1972), by Denis Anderson of the Diamond, Redfern, Anderson partnership received international recognition.

Modern architecture in Ireland is frequently judged on the evidence of the speculative office buildings constructed in the 1960s, '70s and '80s on prominent city-centre sites; most of these projects are small by international standards, but usually far larger than the buildings which they replaced. Most are single-purpose buildings designed without regard for the detailed requirements of the ultimate – and at the design stage, usually unknown – occupier. It is, perhaps, significant that the more successful examples of this type have tended to be either larger or smaller than the average, to have accommodation for a variety of functions and to have been designed with a specific occupant in mind. These include: Desmond Rae O'Kelly's Dublin headquarters for the Irish Transport and General Workers Union (1964); P. L. McSweeney's Cork County Offices (1968); Robinson, Keefe and Devane's Irish Life Centre in Abbey Street,

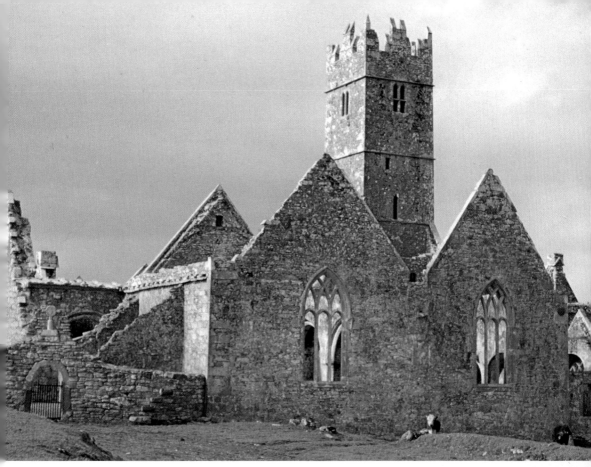

I, II **architecture.** Ross Erilly Friary, Co. Galway (*top*), the largest and best-preserved of the 15th-century Franciscan foundations; and the garden front, Kilruddery, Co. Wicklow, rebuilt in the 1820s by Sir Richard Morrison and William Vitruvius Morrison in the Tudor-revival style.

III **Arts and Crafts Movement.**
(*Left*) Door of the tabernacle in St Michael's, Ballinasloe, Co. Galway, by Mia Cranwill, 1926. The design, executed in gold and silver with enamelled bosses and inlays, shows Christ at Emmaus.

IV **Celtic Revival.**
(*Below*) Detail of a tapestry dossal showing the eagle – the symbol of St John – designed by Evelyn Gleeson and Katherine MacCormack and based on an illumination in the Book of Kells; the dossal was made for the Honan Chapel, Cork, by the Dun Emer Guild, *c.* 1917.

Dublin (1977); and Sam Stephenson's controversial but courageous Central Bank Headquarters, Dublin (1979). TÓB

David Evans, *An Introduction to Modern Ulster Architecture*, Ulster Architectural Heritage Society, 1977; Mathew J. McDermott, *Ireland's Architectural Heritage, An Outline History*, 1975; Tomás Ó Beirne, *A Guide to Modern Architecture in Dublin*, 1978.

Ardagh Hoard. Found in 1867 in Reerasta Ráth, near Ardagh, Co. Limerick, during potato digging, this hoard (now in the National Museum of Ireland) consists of a great silver chalice, a smaller bronze chalice (damaged at the time of discovery), three silver-gilt BROOCHES of the pseudo-penannular type and a silver-gilt penannular brooch of the type known as 'thistle' brooches. The silver chalice, 17·8 cm. (7 in.) high and 23·1 cm. (9 in.) in maximum diameter, is without doubt the finest work of metal in Ireland. Its large bowl of beaten silver is balanced by a large foot with a broad flange, and the two are united by a cylindrical stem through which runs a stout copper bolt. The rounded, gilt-bronze rim is applied, and two handles are provided for lifting. A decorated band of filigree panels and glass settings girdles the bowl below the rim, and two circular medallions decorate the sides. Ornament of great delicacy and technical sophistication occurs on the bowl girdle, the handles and their escutcheons, the medallions, the stem, the flange of the foot on both upper and lower surfaces, while, on the underside, there is an elaborate roundel surrounding the polished crystal which disguises the end of the bolt. Filigree wires of amazing delicacy and variety, glass, enamel, amber, malachite, gold granules, stamped silver, cast copper, and crystal are the materials used in the ornamentation. On the surface of the silver a Latin inscription, seen as a reserve against a dotted background, records the names of the eleven original apostles and St Paul. Delicately incised lines border the inscription, escutcheons and medallions, expanding below the latter two to form entwined animal heads. Comparisons with ms. illumination and with other examples of metalwork suggest an 8th-century date for the piece.

Of the pseudo-penannular brooches one, the largest, is less certainly dated to the 8th century, while the others may with confidence be ascribed to the 9th. The thistle brooch is of a sort which was in vogue in the 9th and 10th centuries, thus leading to the suggestion that the hoard was deposited in the Viking period about 200 years after the date of manufacture of the silver chalice. The bronze chalice is much simpler than the silver one – it appears to have had a funnel-shaped stem and proportions closer to those of chalices current in the Eastern Church. Like the silver chalice, the cup is an adaptation of a local form of bowl. MFR

Armagh, Book of (Trinity College, Dublin, library, no. 52; ms. consisting of 215 vellum leaves, measuring 19·5 × 14·5 cm.; 7¾ × 5¾ in.). This, the only surviving complete New Testament from the 9th century, was written by Ferdomnach, 'a sage and the very best

(*Above*) **Ardagh Hoard.** The 8th-century silver chalice, showing intricate and delicate applied decoration on sides and stem. NMI.

(*Right*) **Book of Armagh.** Page decorated with the symbols of the four Evangelists; 9th century. TCD.

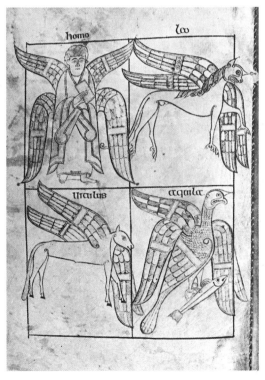

scribe in Armagh', who died in 845 (*Annals of Ulster*). The ms. is of special importance since it contains ST PATRICK's dossier, his Confession, Muirchú's life and Tirechán's memoirs; it was called Canoin Phádraigh. Delicate pen drawings of the symbols of the four evangelists and sensitively curved capital initials introducing each book of the New Testament add grace and dignity to the pages. Coloured initials in red, blue and yellow are found in St Paul's Epistles and at the beginning of Revelation. A quaint diagram of the heavenly city at the end is a remarkable example of fine writing and impressive layout. A later note records the fact that Brian Boroimhe viewed the book in the year 1002. Armagh's importance as a religious centre was firmly linked with St Patrick's apostolic activities there.   G O S

Armstrong, Arthur (1924–   ). Landscape painter; born at Carrickfergus, Co. Antrim, he studied at Queen's University, Belfast. Though largely self-taught as a painter, he also worked under the influence of GERARD DILLON and GEORGE CAMPBELL. Armstrong has painted and exhibited throughout Ireland and in Spain. His work is represented in many public collections in Ireland. Elected RHA 1972.   C MacG

Arts and Crafts Movement. As a result of the interest of Lady Aberdeen, Alice Hart, the Home Arts and Industries Association and others in the development of rural art industries, some minor arts, notably EMBROIDERY and woodcarving, flourished in the 1880s–90s. Interest was sustained by annual 'arts and industries' exhibitions such as those organized by the Royal Dublin Society (*see* DUBLIN SOCIETY).

Exhibitions were also held periodically by the Arts and Crafts Society of Ireland, which was founded in 1894 by Lord Mayo to foster the work of groups like the Fivemiletown Art Metal Workers and individuals like the bookbinder Sir Edward Sullivan. Gradually the peasant groups and the enthusiastic amateurs were joined by an increasing number of qualified art workers. The Society became more organized; in 1909 local committees were set up in the provinces and a Guild of Irish Art Workers was formed. By the 1920s a very high level of excellence was being achieved by certain craftsmen: the fine work of HARRY CLARKE in STAINED GLASS and graphic work, of WILHELMINA GEDDES in the same fields and also embroidery design, of OSWALD REEVES in enamelled metalwork, of Alice Brittain, Mia Cranwill and Nan Holland in jewellery. Various styles were apparent throughout the period, but whether in 'new art', 'Celtic', or other style, the best work was characterized by a mastery of technique and by the superb craftsmanship displayed. *See* CELTIC REVIVAL.   P L

Arts Council, The (Chomhairle Ealaíon, An). In the Republic the Arts Council is a statutory body, established by the Government in 1951. The Council's functions as defined by the Act by which it was set up are very broad: it is expected to stimulate public interest, promote the knowledge, appreciation and practice, and assist in improving the standards of the arts. The State, through the Department of the Taoiseach (Prime Minister), provides an annual grant-in-aid to artists and arts organizations who request financial assistance. In practice the Arts Council funds the Theatre, Dance, Visual Arts, Literature, Film, Music (including opera and traditional music) and all activities which can be classified under the heading 'Arts'.

Organizationally, the Council consists of seventeen members, appointed by the Prime Minister for a term of five years, who meet, usually, ten times in each year to consider questions of policy and applications for financial assistance. To assist it with its work the Council employs some twenty staff, including a Director and nine specialist Officers.

The Council would consider that the most essential element of its policy is that it must remain independent, both of Government and of the arts community. The Council is very aware of the difficult and necessarily subjective nature of many judgments in the arts. It believes that the most appropriate way of dealing with this problem is to ensure its own autonomy (while, of course, emphasizing its accountability to Government and the arts community).

The Council would consider improvements in the professional status and material well-being of artists as its major priority. An extensive system of bursaries, scholarships and awards has been in operation since the mid-1970s. This system is being steadily expanded and has recently been complemented by decisions to provide funding to artists' professional associations and by the introduction of AOSDÁNA, an affiliation of artists engaged in literature, music and the visual arts. Lower-ranking, but integral, aspects of the Council's policies are the emphasis being placed on the encouragment of the arts outside Dublin and the promotion of the arts in the education system. Finally, in a period of economic stringency, the Council has a vital role to play as an advocate, arguing that continued State support for the arts is essential.   J W

Armstrong, Arthur. *Rocks and Sea near Roundstone* (Co. Galway). Private Collection.

Arts Council of Northern Ireland. Now a State-sponsored organization, the Arts Council was first established in 1940 in Belfast as a Council for the Encouragement of Music and the Arts in Northern Ireland; initially funds were provided by the Pilgrim Trust and matched by the Ministry of Education for Northern Ireland, but since 1943 funding has been provided primarily by Government with some Local Authority contributions. The annual budget allocation has increased from an initial £3,000 to £2,500,000 in 1982/83. The Council is a limited company registered under the Companies Act (Northern Ireland) 1932. Its affairs are managed by a Board consisting of eighteen members. The Director is the principal executive officer. Administrative support is provided by professional staff responsible for subject and functional areas of the Council's programme. This programme is designed to increase the accessibility of the arts to the public throughout Northern Ireland and to improve standards of execution in all disciplines. In the visual arts, opportunities are provided for the public to be made aware of, and to experience at first hand, the work of Irish and foreign artists through exhibitions, loan collections, public commissions and related propaganda activities, including films on distinguished Irish artists and the publication of catalogues, monographs and surveys. Painters, sculptors, print-makers and craftsmen are assisted through awards, exhibitions and other patronage. The Council presents major exhibitions at the ULSTER MUSEUM; it also runs a gallery in central Belfast, as well as a studio print workshop situated on the outskirts of the city.

In drama the Council primarily ensures the survival of the Province's theatres. The Grand Opera House in Belfast was taken into public ownership by the Council, rehabilitated and reopened in 1980. Vital financial support is given to the Lyric Theatre and the Civic Arts Theatre in Belfast and the Riverside Theatre in Coleraine. The Council also funds touring companies performing in Belfast and at regional centres. In literature the Council helps, by supporting local publishing houses and magazines, to ensure that poets and creative writers have the opportunity to get their work published. Funding of the Ulster Orchestra represents the major contribution to the Province's musical life. This is supplemented by the deployment of funds in promoting tours by small musical ensembles or soloists. Financial support is also provided to assist in conserving traditional arts that might otherwise die out. Funds are also made available for a variety of innovative enterprises, both in performance and research in all disciplines. In the pursuit of its general aims and policies the Council organizes and promotes projects in community arts and the arts in education.   B F

Ashford, William (*c.* 1746–1824). Painter; born in Birmingham, he came to Ireland to work in the Ordnance Office of the Board of Works in 1764 and, apart from a few visits to England, remained in Dublin until his death. Starting as an amateur, he exhibited in

Ashford, William. *Classical Landscape* (detail), 1976. Private Collection.

the Society of Arts from 1767, beginning to submit landscapes in 1772. He was much influenced by Dutch art. When he left the Ordnance Office in 1778 he was a professional painter and the obvious successor to THOMAS ROBERTS who died in that year. His landscapes were so admired that he was invited to become the first President of the ROYAL HIBERNIAN ACADEMY, a great honour for a landscape painter. Most of his work was done for Irish landowners and is simply topographical, but it is inspired by his remarkable ability to capture the harmonious peace of cultivated land-scape.   A O C

Ashlin, George (1837–1921). Architect; trained with E. W. Pugin (1834–75) and married his sister. During his partnership with Pugin (until 1870) he designed the Augustinian Church, Thomas Street, Dublin (1862), and Cobh Cathedral, Co. Cork (1868–1918). His style is coloured by French Gothic and his churches could be mistaken for those of J. J. MCCARTHY. He designed churches for Templemore, Co. Tipperary, Midleton, Co. Cork, and Inchicore, Co. Dublin, in the French Gothic style, Carrick-on-Suir, Co. Tipperary, in the Lombardo-Romanesque style, and the O'Connell Memorial church, Cahirciveen, Co. Kerry (1884), with a dash of Hiberno-Romanesque, while the McCabe Memorial in Glasnevin Cemetery (1887), is a riot of Hiberno-Romanesque decoration. Ashlin

Ashlin, George. The McCabe Memorial (1887) in Glasnevin Cemetery; the carved decoration is by C. W. Harrison and Sons.

designed the parish church at Raheny, Co. Dublin, for Lord Ardilaun and built St George's, Killiney, Co. Dublin, for himself. WG

Athassel Priory, Co. Tipperary. Founded for Augustinian Canons at the end of the 12th century, the Priory became the largest medieval monastic complex in Ireland. The remains of the monastery, which cover 4 acres (1·8 hectares), are surrounded by a high wall with a gate-house and must altogether comprise the most impressive monastic site to be seen in Ireland. The 13th-century church, 64 m. (210 ft) in length, has two transepts, two aisles flanking the nave, a rebuilt tower over the crossing and a later smaller tower at the NW end. A screen-wall with a fine doorway divided the nave from the choir which was lit by four tall lancet windows on each side, similar to those in many other 13th-century Irish churches. There are extensive remains of the monastic quarters surrounding the cloister which lies to the south of the church. To the east are the sacristy, the dormitory, the chapter-house and other vaulted rooms. At the end of the west walk of the cloister the elaborate doorway led to the refectory on the first floor over vaulted basements of the building to the south of the cloister. B de B

Balfe, Michael William (1808–70). Violinist, singer and composer. Born in Dublin, he was commissioned by La Scala, Milan, to write the music for *La Perouse*, and was subsequently patronized by Rossini in Paris where he sang the role of Figaro in *The Barber of Seville*, 1827. Balfe wrote several operas, including *The Siege of Rochelle, Falstaff* (1838), *The Bohemian Girl* (1843), *The Sicilian Bride* (1852) and *The Knight of the Leopard* with a libretto based on Scott's *The Talisman*. B de B

Ballagh, Robert (1943–). Painter, graphic artist and designer; born in Dublin, he studied architecture at Bolton Street Technical School and became a full-time painter in 1966. He was awarded an Alice Berger Hammershlag Scholarship, the Douglas Hyde Gold Medal at the Óireachtas, and represented Ireland at many international exhibitions as well as at ROSC (1980); Ballagh has produced graphics and designed stamps for the National Postal Service. His work is represented in many public collections. C MacG

ballet. The Irish Ballet Company, established in 1973 and funded by the State, has its headquarters in Cork. It emerged from the amateur Cork Ballet Co. founded in 1947 by Joan Denise Moriarty, who was its inspiration as dancer, teacher, director and choreographer; she continues her work as Artistic Director of the Irish Ballet Company. Professor ALOYS FLEISCHMANN and the Cork Symphony Orchestra have been associated with the Ballet from its earliest years. The Company's Resident Choreographer is Domy Reiter-Soffer, its Designer Patrick Murray, and it has 14 solo dancers. A large repertoire embraces classical, romantic and modern works, while many of Miss Moriarty's own ballets incorporate movements adapted from traditional Irish dances. The Company travels throughout Ireland during the year, and now stages annual seasons in Dublin and Belfast, with regular visits to smaller centres. In 1980 it staged Miss Moriarty's *The Playboy of the Western World* in New York, with music by the Chieftains; the Company's repertoire includes her *The Táin*, Domy Reiter-Soffer's *Chariots of Fire, Shadow Reach, Paradise Regained* and *Medea*, as well as original work by Beck, Bournonville, Czarny, Darrell and Dolin.

The Dublin City Ballet, founded in 1979 by Louis O'Sullivan, who is also its Director, has already achieved high standards; Ann Courtney has proved herself a stimulating choreographer. The Company has the services of three solo dancers and corps de ballet of ten. In 1981 it presented 126 performances of three new productions.

Both companies have participated in productions of the Dublin Grand Opera Society. AGH

Balfe, M. W. The Dublin-born composer depicted in an engraving by Auguste Hüsfener.

Ballyglass, Co. Mayo. Townland near Bunatrahir Bay and the village of Ballycastle; two COURT TOMBS (of a group of 27 in the vicinity) were excavated by S. Ó Nualláin, 1968–72. A centre-court tomb with a two-chambered gallery at either end lay NW/SE, with the court entrance facing NE. Under the NW part of the cairn lay a near-contemporary rectangular post-built house measuring 13 × 6 m. (42 ft 6 in. × 19 ft 6 in.), with a separate room SE of the fireplace, and having its NW end porched. Finds associated with both house and tomb included plain Neolithic A pottery with rolled rims, and leaf-shaped arrowheads and concave scrapers of flint and chert. Wood from the house timbers yielded radiocarbon determinations indicating an average date of 2620 BC. Stake-holes and trenches provided evidence of a dwelling structure in the court of the second tomb in this townland; outside this tomb on the S side were found traces of a shelter open to the N.   MH
S. Ó Nualláin, 'A Neolithic House at Ballyglass, near Ballycastle, Co. Mayo', *JRSAI* 102 (1972), 49–57.

Ballykeel, Co. Armagh. Site of a PORTAL TOMB, 92 m. (300 ft) above sea-level, on the W side of Slieve Gullion, excavated by A. E. P. Collins in 1963. The main chamber, at the SE end of the rectangular cairn, 27·50 × 9 m. (90 ft × 29 ft 6 in.), had tall, matched portals with a doorstone between; these, with back-stone, supported a roofstone measuring 2·90 × 2·50 m. (9 ft 6 in. × 8 ft 3 in.). In the chamber were three necked bowls with channelled and corded decoration resembling basketry, one with stamped rosettes; a high concentration of phosphates in the floor of the chamber probably indicated ancient burials. The small cist at the NW end yielded sherds of a globular corded bowl, a small javelin-head and a discoidal bead.   MH
A. E. P. Collins, 'Ballykeel Dolmen and Cairn, Co. Armagh', *UJA* 28 (1965), 47–70.

Banville, John (1945–   ). Writer; Wexford-born, he is a journalist on the *Irish Press*. A complex modernist writer, he pushes against traditional forms and conventions. In elaborately structured novels, novellas and short stories he charts the 'philosophy of despair', creating an intricate connection between fiction and science, most notably in his major work, the tetralogy *The Newton Letter* (1982).   BH

bardic schools. The ancient bardic schools, pagan and pre-Christian in origin, survived the conversion of the people of Ireland to CHRISTIANITY in the 5th century and flourished as secular places of learning for poets, lawyers and historians for centuries after the defeat of the Druids. Usually these callings were hereditary and the same families would have provided both teachers and pupils. The training consisted of a rigorous period of disciplined preparation, which might last at least six or seven years. The IRISH LANGUAGE was used in the schools, and the history and law taught were Irish history and the ancient Brehon Code. Great importance was placed on committing learning to memory rather than having to rely on reference to the written word.

English observers in the 16th century have left some accounts of such schools and it would appear from Edmund Campion's account of a school which taught leech-craft that by that time there were medical schools organized in the tradition of the bardic schools. In the school described by Campion in 1571 ten adult male students lay on straw couches on the floor of a room with their books, chanting out their lessons. The pathologist Dermot O'Meara, a native of Co. Tipperary, who published a medical text in 1611, would have been trained in such a school before going to Oxford.

With the collapse of the Gaelic social system in Ireland in the 17th century the bardic schools lost their patrons and it seems that only a few managed to survive in remote places until the end of the century; one such was the school of the O'Davorens in the stone fort of Cahermacnaghten, Co. Clare; the COURTS OF POETRY in the 18th century were the heirs of the bardic school tradition. *See* EDUCATION.   B de B

Barre, William J. (1830–67). Architect; a pupil of Thomas Duff, he came from Newry and blazed a meteoric trail before his early death. He was a 'rogue' architect who loved innovation and ornament. In 1860 he won the competition for the Ulster Hall, Belfast. Barre designed several churches, the Crozier Monument, Banbridge, Co. Down, the Whitworth Hall, Drogheda, Co. Louth (1864), the opulent Danesfort, Belfast (1864), and the Albert Memorial, Belfast (1865).   WG
Durham Dunlop, *A Memoir of the Professional Life of William J. Barre*, 1868.

Barret, George (*c.* 1728–1784). Landscape painter; born in Dublin and educated at the DUBLIN SOCIETY Schools, he won a premium in 1747 for landscape painting. His views of the wild scenery of Co. Wicklow,

Barret, George. *Stormy Landscape*, after a painting by the 17th-century Italian artist, Salvator Rosa. NGI.

Barry, James. *The Trinity of Modern Commerce* (detail), painted for the Royal Society of Arts, London.

which were followed in the 1760s by paintings of scenes in North Wales and later of the Lake District and of southern Scotland, were among the earliest painted landscapes of such romantic scenery. He spent most of his career in London, where he became one of the founders of the Royal Academy (1768), but unfortunately his spendthrift habits forced him to paint many a potboiler, so that his reputation is not as high as his best pictures would justify. About 1780 in England he painted an illusionist landscape room for William Locke at Norbury Park, near Mickleham, Surrey – a splendid example of his ability to capture the atmosphere of mountainous scenery.   AOC

Barry, James (1741–1806). Painter; born in Cork, of modest parentage, and a pupil of ROBERT WEST, he is unique among Irish artists as a painter of subject pictures. His first known painting, *The Conversion by St Patrick of the King of Cashel* (1763), breaks new ground by illustrating a subject from ancient Irish history. After he went to London in 1764, he turned more to classical subject-matter under the influence of Reynolds and Athenian Stuart, and following a long visit to Rome, 1765–71, financed by EDMUND BURKE. Out of sheer desire to prove his ability to work on the grand scale, he painted (unpaid) a series of pictures between 1777 and 1784 for the Great Room of the Society of Arts in London; also, as one of the leading artists of his day, he was invited to paint scenes for John Boydell's 'Shakespeare Gallery'. His few portraits are of very high quality, ennobled by his personal sense of grandeur. His career at the Royal Academy, where he was Professor of Painting 1782–99, was wrecked by his own tragically difficult temperament. He died in poverty.   AOC
William L. Pressly, *The Life and Art of James Barry*, 1981.

Barry, Spranger. Engraving from *Bell's Edition of Shakespeare* (1776), showing Barry as Timon in Act V of *Timon of Athens*. NLI.

Barry, Spranger (1719–77). Romantic actor; born in Dublin, he first appeared at the Smock Alley Playhouse, Dublin, in 1744. He played with Garrick there and subsequently in London; he became Garrick's partner, then rival. 'Garrick commanded most applause, Barry most tears'. He opened and managed Crow Street Theatre, Dublin, 1758–66, and opened the theatre in Cork 1761. He is buried in Westminster Abbey.   C F-S

Barton, Mary Georgina (fl. 1895–1955). Landscape painter; born at Farnderg, Dundalk, Co. Louth, she studied at Westminster School of Art and in Rome, and exhibited at the Paris Salon, in Ireland and England. She was a member of the Water Colour Society of Ireland, the Society of Women Artists and of the Women's International Art Club. She is represented in the Hugh Lane Municipal Gallery of Modern Art, Dublin. Since the late 1970s her works have become much prized by collectors.   C MacG

Barton, Rose (1856–1929). Landscape painter; born in Dublin, she decided in the early 1880s to become a professional artist and first exhibited in London at the Royal Academy in 1884; she exhibited with the Old Water Colour Society, of which she was elected an Associate in 1893, and with the Royal Water Colour Society, to which she was admitted as a member in 1911, the first woman painter to receive this distinction. In 1898 she illustrated *Picturesque Dublin* by Frances A. Gerard and she herself published *Familiar London* (1904).   C MacG

Beaulieu, Co. Louth. Country house near Drogheda, built in the 1660s for Sir Henry Tichborne – the earliest such house in Ireland without fortifications; in the 'Artisan Mannerist' style, it is built of rubble-stone, plastered over, with brick dressing; unusually, the brickwork is finished proud of the wall face. The house has two main storeys with a dormered attic in the high, hipped, eaved roof which is carried on carved consoles. The entrance front has seven windows on each storey, the outer two on either side being set forward in symmetrical bays; the side elevation has six windows. Much of the 17th-century interior decoration has survived.   B de B

Beckett, Samuel (1906–). Writer and playwright; born at Foxrock, Co. Dublin, he is a commanding figure in European drama and fiction. He was awarded the Nobel Prize for Literature in 1969. Lived in France (1928–30), where he was greatly influenced by JAMES JOYCE; lectured in French at Trinity College, Dublin (1930–32), and during World War II joined the Resistance in France. His novels *Murphy* (1938) and *Watt* (1945) were the last written originally in English; living in France, Beckett writes in French, whose precision suits his clear, hard thought, seen in his trilogy of novels *Molloy, Malone Dies* and *The Unnamable* (1951–53). His grim tragi-comedy *Waiting for Godot*, produced in French in 1953, in English in 1955, caused a furore of outraged incomprehension. Subsequent

Beaulieu, Co. Louth. The symmetrical entrance front of the house, built in the 1660s.

Beckett, Samuel. A scene from a 1961 Paris revival of *Waiting for Godot*, first produced in 1953.

plays have become bleaker, barer – *Endgame* (1956), *Happy Days* (1961), a short sketch *Breath* (1969), and *Not I* (1972), performed by a mouth. Beckett writes compellingly for radio (*All that Fall*, 1957; *Words and Music*, 1962), for television (*Eh Joe*, 1965), and for cinema (*Film*, 1964). His philosophy offers little comfort, little choice; man's only heroism is his endurance displayed in the face of pain, futility and boredom.   BH

Deirdre Bair, *Samuel Beckett*, 1978; Raymond Federman and John Fletcher, *Samuel Beckett, His Works and his Critics*, 1970; Hugh Kenner, *Samuel Beckett: A Critical Study*, 1968; Vivien Mercier, *Beckett/Beckett*, 1977; John Pilling, *Samuel Beckett*, 1976.

(*Above*) **beehive hut.** One of the Early Christian corbelled stone huts at Skellig Michael, Co. Kerry.

(*Right*) **Behan, Brendan.** A scene from a production of *The Quare Fellow* at the Abbey Theatre, 1969.

beehive huts. Stone huts, found in considerable numbers in Co. Kerry, a few other examples being known elsewhere. The huts are usually round in shape both inside and out, though some (e.g. at SKELLIG MICHAEL) are squared on the inside. The huts are roofed in the corbel principle by means of stones being laid in circles of ever-decreasing diameters until the central aperture at the top can be closed by a single stone; they have only one door, and occasionally have corbels protruding from the walls inside – or outside (e.g. Skellig Michael) where they formed steps providing external access to the top of the building. Although the huts are often associated with small ecclesiastical (eremitical) sites, many of them on the Dingle Peninsula, sometimes in clusters, were presumably for secular use, perhaps in connection with transhumance activity known as booleying. While the ecclesiastical examples date from the Early Christian period, one much-ruined example (structure G at Reask, Co. Kerry) has been radiocarbon dated to the pre-Christian Iron Age. The huts' origins may therefore be prehistoric, yet one or two examples on the Dingle Peninsula may be less than a century old.   PH

Behan, Brendan Francis (1923–64). Writer; born in Dublin. As a result of IRA activities, he served sentences in an English Borstal at 16 and later in an Irish gaol, and these experiences inspired the vivid autobiographical prose narrative *Borstal Boy* (1958) and the fiercely comic play *The Quare Fellow* (1954). He translated his own Irish play *An Giall* (1958) into *The Hostage*, a *tour de force* of satire, rhetoric, song and dance built round an English soldier being held as hostage for an IRA man.   BH
C. Kearney, *The Writings of Brendan Behan*, 1977; U. O'Connor, *Brendan*, 1970; B. Behan with D. Hickey

and G. Smith, *My Life With Brendan*, 1973; D. Behan, *My Brother Brendan*, 1965.

Behy, Co. Mayo. A COURT TOMB at 150 m. (500 ft) above sea-level on the N Mayo coast on slopes of Maumakeogh, W of Ballycastle, excavated by De Valéra, Ó Nualláin and Herity, 1963–5. This double-trapezoid cairn, 28 m. (90 ft) long, with dry-walled revetment, has an enclosed mainly dry-walled court, 7·50 × 5 m. (25 × 16 ft), at the E end, opening from the megalithic façade onto a two-chambered megalithic burial-gallery; the gallery is segmented by parallel jambs and sill (quarried gritstone slabs), with a pair of matched transepts situated off the rear chamber.   MH
R. de Valéra and S. Ó. Nualláin, *Survey of the Megalithic Tombs of Ireland: vol. II, Co. Mayo*, 1964.

Beit Art Collection. The present art collection incorporates highly important Old Master paintings, mainly of the Dutch, Flemish and Spanish schools, and bronzes acquired by Alfred Beit (1853–1906), co-founder of the De Beers Diamond Co., and additions made by Sir Alfred Lane Beit (1903–   ) who, having acquired RUSSBOROUGH, Co. Wicklow, in 1952 and having restored the house, in 1976 transferred it and its magnificent contents – paintings, bronzes, porcelain, fine furniture, tapestries and carpets – to the Alfred Beit Foundation (a charitable and educational trust) for the benefit of the public.   B de B

Belfast Natural History & Philosophical Society. Learned society founded in 1821; ten years later its handsome museum by T. Jackson was built in College Square, where the Society met. It also publishes its *Proceedings*.   MC

Bellamont Forest. The Palladian villa designed by Sir Edward Lovett Pearce, *c.* 1730, showing the Doric entrance portico.

Belleek. Hard-paste porcelain vase with seashell decoration, by David McBirney & Co., *c.* 1865–70. Victoria and Albert Museum, London.

Bellamont Forest, Co. Cavan. One of the earliest and finest Palladian villas in Ireland, designed by Sir EDWARD LOVETT PEARCE, *c.* 1730. It is built of red brick, in the true Palladian manner, over a rusticated stone basement, and has a near-square plan and a Doric portico. Despite its deceptively simple external appearance, the house contains an intricate jig-saw of different spatial volumes and includes a number of superbly proportioned rooms with fine coffered ceilings. WG
Maurice Craig, 'Bellamont Forest, Co. Cavan', *Country Life*, vol. cxxxv, 1964, pp. 1258, 1330.

Belleek. Village in Co. Fermanagh, the name of which is synonymous with a type of highly glazed softpaste porcelain originally produced there and later copied in the USA. The venture was planned from 1857 and began production in 1863. The factory was the brain-child of the local landlord, John Caldwell Bloomfield; it was financed by David McBirney of Dublin, and the Art Director, to whom its initial success was mainly due, was Robert Williams Armstrong, an architect-civil engineer, inventor and ceramic historian.

Belleek had the advantage of excellent local porcelain clays, cheap water-power from the river Erne, an abundance of turf for the kiln, a convenient Atlantic port and, after 1866, a railway line. Financial security was due to winning a contract for supplying telegraph insulators, but the main product was earthenware which was sold by pedlars, at fairs and in shops. Earthenware, plain, or with transfer-printed or sponged decoration, was made for kitchen, dairy, bathroom and bedroom use.

Belleek's prestige ware was porcelain made in ivory or white, glazed or unglazed and plain or painted. Although the earliest products were based on commercially successful lines of the contemporary English potteries, Belleek produced its own designs, drawing inspiration from sea-shells and marine life,

from garden flowers and insects and from ceramic and ivory masterpieces of the past. Prestige orders for porcelain tea- and table-services for Queen Victoria, for Edward, Prince of Wales, and members of the nobility guaranteed a demand for Belleek porcelain. In the 19th century complimentary notices in the *Art Journal* and many prizes and recommendations for pieces displayed in major international exhibitions demonstrated the social and artistic approval bestowed on Belleek's designs. Armstrong also experimented with and produced other types of wares such as ointment boxes, wall tiles, pestles and mortars, sanitary services and fine stoneware.

McBirney and Armstrong died in 1882 and 1884 respectively, after which the Pottery was purchased by a local consortium which streamlined the business. In 1919 that company failed but the factory was saved by four Northern businessmen who formed The Belleek Pottery Ltd. In an attempt to improve the Belleek image this company introduced many new designs, particularly Celtic interlace and certain floral work. To survive the market restrictions of World War II they produced an extra range of glazed earthenware called Melvin Ware which was sold locally. Since 1947 the company has concentrated exclusively on the production of porcelain and since 1955 electric kilns have been used. MR
Richard K. Degenhardt, *Belleek, the Complete Collector's Guide and Illustrated Reference*, 1978; M. Reynolds, *Early Belleek Wares*, 1978.

Berkeley, George (1685–1753). Theologian and philosopher; born in Kilkenny, he was educated there and at Trinity College, Dublin. Elected a Fellow of the College in 1707, he was ordained a priest in the Church of Ireland in 1710 and consecrated Bishop of Cloyne in 1734. He spent the years 1728–31 in America in a frustrated mission to found a college in the Bermudas. Berkeley's *Theory of Vision* (1709), *Principles of Human Knowledge* (1710), and *Three Dialogues between Hylas and*

Berkeley, George. Portrait of the eminent theologian and philosopher by John Smibert, 1730. National Portrait Gallery, London.

Philonous (1713) contain the basis of his Immaterialism – the doctrine that matter exists only insofar as it is perceived. *Alciphron* (1732), written during his American venture, is his most substantial defence of orthodox Christianity against deism and atheism. Among Berkeley's miscellaneous writings are works on politics, the medicinal virtues of tar-water, and mathematics, to which last he made a notable contribution. *The Querist* (1735–7) is a collection of penetrating questions on the state of Ireland. Though far from easy, Berkeley is a philosopher of great lucidity and, in several works, of no little charm. *See* LITERATURE.   I C R
A. A. Luce, *The Life of George Berkeley, Bishop of Cloyne*, 1949; I. C. Tipton, *Berkeley, the Philosophy of Immaterialism*, 1974.

Bindon, Francis (*c.* 1690–1765). Painter and architect; son of David Bindon, M.P. for Ennis, Co. Clare. He was a gentleman-amateur, who practised first as a portrait painter and secondly as an architect. Bindon worked with RICHARD CASTLE on RUSSBOROUGH, Co. Wicklow, and Belan, Co. Kildare. His main identified works are Bessborough (*c.* 1744), Woodstock (1740) and Castle Morres, all in Co. Kilkenny; Dunsandle, Co. Galway, and the delightful brick house, New Hall, Co. Clare (*c.* 1745), are attributed to Bindon.   W G
The Knight of Glin, 'Francis Bindon', *IGS Bulletin*, 1967.

Blackshaw, Basil (1932–). Landscape and figurative painter; born at Glengormley, Co. Antrim, he studied at Belfast College of Art, won a CEMA travelling scholarship and studied in Paris for a year. In 1958 he was represented in the exhibition 'The Religious Theme' at the Tate Gallery, London. Since 1960 he has had a number of one-man shows, as well as exhibiting in various annual exhibitions in Ireland.   C MacG

Bodkin, Thomas (1887–1961). Lawyer and art historian; born in Dublin, he graduated from the Royal Irish University in 1908, and was called to the Irish Bar in 1911. He was Director of the National Gallery of Ireland 1927–35, subsequently Barber Professor of Fine Arts and first Director of the Barber Institute in Birmingham. A member of the Commission on Irish Coinage Design in 1926, he also took a leading part in the movement to secure for Dublin the art collection (then in London) made by Sir HUGH LANE, and was commissioned by the Free State Government to write the account of Lane and his collections, entitled *Hugh Lane and his Pictures* (Pegasus Press, 1932).

His report, *The Arts in Ireland* (1951), commissioned by the Irish Government, led to the establishment of the ARTS COUNCIL. Bodkin was also on the Committee of the National Museum of Ireland, and that for Art Education, as well as serving as a member of the Board of the National Gallery of Ireland; with Lord Moyne and Lord Pakenham, Bodkin was part of a team which successfully negotiated on behalf of the Irish Government terms for the return of the Lane Collection to Dublin.   C MacG

Bodley, Seoirse (1933–). Musician and composer; since 1959 he has taught at the National University of Ireland, where he became Associate Professor of Music at University College, Dublin, in 1981. The lucidity of his teaching reflects his wide musical interests and sense of commitment to the Gaelic heritage, while his broader studies have drawn him to Johann Nepomuk David in Stuttgart and to Darmstadt in its most influential period. His Symphony No. 1 (1959) relates to later Hindemith. Since that time he became the Irish composer most concerned with avant-garde techniques and in the following decade his music became increasingly complex in thought, but revealed a remarkable acuteness and fastidiousness of ear in exploring new worlds of sound. The Chamber Symphony (1964) is now widely accepted on its own terms, while 'Configurations' (1967) is more aloof and somewhat perplexing. Three works for voice and orchestra are essential to an understanding of his development: 'Never to have Lived is Best' (1965), a setting of YEATS; 'Meditations on Lines from Patrick Kavanagh' (1971); and a cycle (in Gaelic) of poems by Maire Mhac an tSaoi.

In his most recent work a new style has emerged in which sections in full traditional Irish ornamental style are amalgamated with avant-garde elements, producing a new stylistic totality. This phase begins with a work for two pianos, 'The Narrow Road to the Deep North' (1972), expands with the orchestral 'A Small White Cloud Drifts over Ireland', and leads through the five-movement 'Aisling' (1977) for piano, and the cycle of 22 songs, 'A Girl' (1978), to the triumphal première in January 1981 of his Symphony No. 2 (subtitled 'I have Loved the Land of Ireland'), dedicated to the memory of the patriot Padraic Pearse. The Symphony No. 3, for soloists, choir and orchestra, rapidly followed; it was played at the inauguration of the National Concert Hall in Dublin on 9 September 1981. AGH

Boland, Eavan (1945–). Poet; born in Dublin, she is currently the most distinguished female voice in Irish poetry. *New Territory* (1967) and *The War Horse* (1975) display superb technical skill. *In Her Own Image* (1980) constitutes a revolutionary experience in Irish poetry. T McC

bookbinding. Though elaborate bindings were certainly put on the books of Early Christian and Romanesque Ireland, they have not survived. A handful of book-satchels exist, but the story really begins with the appearance in the middle of the 17th century of gold-tooled bindings, in styles and using techniques derived from contemporary England and France. Though the great series of bindings on the manuscript journals of the Irish houses of lords and commons are dated from 1613 onwards, it seems unlikely that any of them were actually bound much before the close of that century. This splendid series of 149 large volumes constituted the core material of Irish bookbinding and was without parallel in the world. Their destruction in the Public Record Office (Four Courts) in June 1922 was a loss which so poor a country could ill afford. Fortunately, photographs of some, and rubbings of many more, had been taken by Sir Edward Sullivan (himself an amateur bookbinder) and from these it is possible to form some idea, though faint, of their unique magnificence. During the first three-quarters of the 18th century, and especially between 1730 and 1765, Irish, and more particularly Dublin, bookbinding attained world eminence, both in respect of the originality of its design and the accomplishment of its execution. Names are scarce: those of the contractors for the parliamentary bindings are known: 1692 Robert Thornton; 1705 Thornton again, but with Joseph Ray; 1718 Nicholas King; 1723 Samuel Fairbrother; 1749 Abraham Bradley; 1780 Abraham Bradley and his grandson Abraham Bradley King; 1784 onwards Abraham Bradley King. The sequence of styles can be traced from a kind of baroque with oriental elements (e.g. from carpet designs) before 1725, via a more rigid though very rich phase lasting till *c.* 1748–9, to the remarkable 'featherwork' style of the 1750s, which was followed by a more sober style lasting till *c.* 1770. After this the gradual assimilation to the international Neo-Classical style of Adam and his followers diluted the Irish character of the bindings and makes it increasingly difficult to distinguish Irish bindings from those of other countries, though the

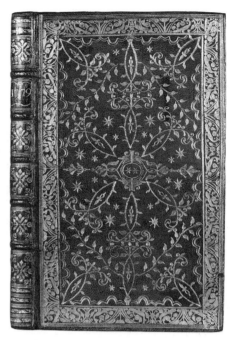

bookbinding. The elaborately decorated binding of *The Gentleman and Citizens Almanack*, Dublin, 1779. Victoria and Albert Museum, London.

quality remained high. The Union of 1800 brought to an end the need for parliamentary bindings, and quickly undermined the luxury market of private clients as well.

Eighteenth-century Irish decorated bindings are generally in morocco, unusually red, blue or green, and commonly relieved by white or cream inlays, often lozenge-shaped or oval and usually of paper or of fair calf. Vellum bindings are rare: sometimes the vellum is stained green. Towards the end of the century a few are signed, usually by ticket, e.g. that of William Mackenzie. In the early 19th century George Mullen of Dublin, influenced by Roger Payne of London, did many bindings for collectors in the romantic and the more severe styles. After his death in 1846 Irish binding is of little account until the modest revival of the 20th century. MC

Maurice Craig, *Irish Bookbindings 1600–1800*, 1954.

botanic gardens. Of the four botanic gardens established in Ireland between 1795 and 1827, only one remains today as a fully-fledged institution. In 1790, Dr Walter Wade, a Dublin botanist, presented a petition to the Irish House of Commons for the formation of a garden. The ground for it, at Glasnevin, near Dublin, was taken over in March 1795 by the DUBLIN SOCIETY and Wade was appointed the first professor. The second curator, Ninian Niven, revitalized the garden after 1834. Niven's successor, David Moore, and the latter's son Sir Frederick

(*Above*) **botanic gardens.** Palm House by Richard Turner in the Belfast gardens; the wings date from 1839–40, the central part from after 1852.

(*Right*) **botanical illustration.** The spring gentian (*Gentiana verna*) by Wendy Walsh, one of 48 illustrations reproduced in colour in *An Irish Florilegium*, 1983.

Moore, between them remained in control of the garden for 84 years, during which period it reached its zenith. The State assumed responsibility for the garden in 1877, after which it became known as the Royal Botanic Gardens until the foundation of the Free State in 1922, when the title National Botanic Gardens was adopted. The garden is now administered by the Department of Agriculture.

The Botanic Garden of Trinity College, Dublin, was re-established on 6½ acres at Ballsbridge in 1806, having gradually evolved from the physic garden formed by the Provost and Fellows in 1687. One of its curators, James Mackay, published *Flora Hibernica* (1836), but the collections reached their peak under F. W. Burbidge (1847–1905). The Ballsbridge site was sold in the 1950s. The Cork garden was started in 1809 by the Royal Cork Institution; James Drummond became its first and only curator, for it closed due to a shortage of money in 1829. In 1827 the Belfast Botanic and Horticultural Society started its garden, which moved to its present site in 1829. Thomas Drummond, J. F. Johnstone and C. S. McKim were the most distinguished of a long line of curators. Although it enjoyed the title 'Royal' from 1840, lack of funds forced it to broaden its scope into that of a public park, in which form it has continued since being taken over by Belfast Corporation in 1894. *See* also HORTICULTURE AND GARDEN DESIGN. PB

E. Charles Nelson, 'The Influence of Leiden on Botany in Dublin in the Early Eighteenth Century', *Huntia* 4 (2), 1982; T. P. C. Kirkpatrick, *History of the Medical Teaching in Trinity College Dublin and of the School of Physic in Ireland*, 1912; M. E. Mitchell, 'Irish Botany in the Seventeenth Century', *PRIA* 75(B), pp. 275–84.

botanical illustration. There lived in Ireland during the 18th century a number of representatives of the Dutch-influenced school of flower painters. Among them were: Philip Hussey (1713–83), a portrait painter also described as a 'botanist and florist', who frequently included in his pictures baskets of accurately depicted florists' flowers; and Samuel Dixon (fl. 1740–60), who painted flower pieces using a bas-relief technique.

The tradition of botanical illustration for scientific as well as for decorative purposes seems to have begun with the publication in 1729 of the earliest-known illustration in Ireland, which was by James Gwim (fl. 1720–69). A single plate (of henbane) survives from an illustrated flora of Dublin proposed in 1789 by Dr Walter Wade (*see* BOTANIC GARDENS), but the identity of the artist is unknown, as is also the case with a later illustration to an article by Wade in 1804. William Kilburn (1745–1818), a Dubliner better known for his floral designs for printed textiles, prepared at least 25 illustrations for William Curtis's *Flora Londiniensis* and *Botanical Magazine*.

At about the same period native plants were recorded by two amateur botanists, John Templeton (1766–1825) of Belfast, and Ellen Hutchins (1785–1815) of Ballylickey, Co. Kerry, followed later by a pupil of GEORGE PETRIE, George du Noyer (1817–69), who was recommended by Petrie to the Ordnance Survey (1837) as an illustrator.

During the 19th century examples of the plants of many distant countries were depicted by Irish artists: those of Ceylon by ANDREW NICHOLL; those of South Africa by William Harvey (1811–66); those of India and Burma by Lady Wheeler-Cuffe (1867–1967); and those of Jamaica by Lady Blake (1847–1926). Over 1,000 paintings of exotic orchids by Lydia Shackleton (1828–1914) survive among a total of nearly 1,500 extant works be her. These paintings were not done abroad but at the Glasnevin Botanic Gardens, under the patronage of its curator, Sir Frederick Moore.

In the present century the interest of Irish illustrators seems to have returned to the depiction of native plants. The Hon. Katherine Plunket (1820–1932) had painted those of Western Europe as well as those of Ireland. Sir John Langham (1894–1972) made water-colours of the flora and fungi of Co. Fermanagh. Rosamund Praeger (1897–1954) illustrated the works of her brother, R. Ll. Praeger, one of Ireland's greatest naturalists, and Violet Cusack (1874–1956) of Kinsealy painted the plants of north Co. Dublin. The present generation continues in this tradition. Raymond Piper has since 1958 concentrated on painting the many species of native orchid, and Wendy Walsh prepared 48 watercolours of native and cultivated plants for *An Irish Florilegium*, published in 1983.

Two Irishmen have been associated with outstanding works of botanical art which depict the plants of other countries: *The Civil and Natural History of Jamaica* (1756), by Dr Patrick Browne of Co. Mayo, was illustrated by G. D. Ehret, who was the dominant influence on botanic art in the 18th century; and *The Endemic Flora of Tasmania* (1967–78), illustrated by the Australian artist Margaret Stones, was sponsored by the late Lord Talbot de Malahide. PB
M. J. P. Scannell, 'Botanic art and some Irish artists', *Capuchin Annual*, Dublin 1976; Anne Crookshank and the Knight of Glin, *The Painters of Ireland*, 1978; E. C. Nelson and Aidan Brady (eds.), *Irish Gardening and Horticulture*, 1979; A. K. Longfield, 'Samuel Dixon', *IGS Bulletin*, vols. xviii and xxiii; ——, 'William Kilburn', op. cit., vol. xxiv.

Boucicault, Dion (1820/22–1890). Dramatist, actor, and man of the theatre; born in Dublin. His mastery of sentiment and melodramatic effects helped him achieve great popular success. His most famous plays, *The Colleen Bawn* (1860), *Arrah-na-Pogue* (1864–65), and *The Shaughraun* (1874), reverse the stereotype of the 'stage Irishman' by depicting Irish characters in a romantic and positive way. His work influenced that of such later dramatists as GEORGE BERNARD SHAW and SEÁN O'CASEY. BH
David Krause (ed.), *The Dolmen Boucicault*, 1964.

Bourke, Brian (1936–). Landscape, figurative and graphic artist; born in Dublin, he studied at the National College of Art, Dublin, St Martin's School of Art and Goldsmiths' College, London. He represented Ireland at the Paris Biennale, 1965, and also at the first Triennale of Contemporary World Art, New Delhi, 1968. From the early 1970s he turned to print-making and sculpture. He is represented in all public collections in Ireland. C MacG
The Art of Brian Bourke (Catalogue with Introduction by James White), 1981.

Bowen, Elizabeth Dorothea Cole (1900–73). Writer; born in Dublin, her early years were divided between Dublin and Cork, but she lived mainly in England after 1935. Her work included stories, novels, criticism, autobiography, and the history of her home, Bowen's Court in Co. Cork. Much of her fiction

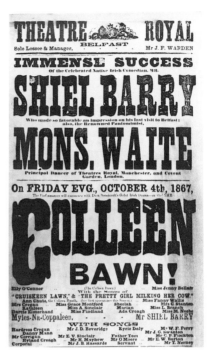

Boucicault, Dion. Detail of a playbill announcing a performance of *The Colleen Bawn* at the Theatre Royal, Belfast, 4 October 1867.

Bowen, Elizabeth. Studio portrait of the well-known Anglo-Irish author, *c.* 1950.

depends upon an English setting, as in *The Death of the Heart* (1938), a sensitive analysis of the disillusioning of an orphaned adolescent girl. *A World of Love* (1955), however, portrays provincial Irish life, and in *The Last September* (1929) her own Anglo-Irish heritage provides the 'Big House' as symbol, set against the revolutionary disturbances of the 1920s.   BH
Victoria Glendinning, *Elizabeth Bowen, Portrait of a Writer*, 1977; A. Allen, *Elizabeth Bowen*, 1971; W. Heath, *Elizabeth Bowen, an introduction*, 1961.

Boydell, Brian P. (1918–). Composer; born in Dublin, he was Professor of Music at Trinity College, Dublin (1962–82). Influenced by the thought if not the actual style of Bartók and Hindemith, his work shows a fondness for terse rhythmic patterns. His music is serious in tone and at times hieratic. The Violin Concerto of 1953 is perhaps his most melodious and approachable work, while 'Symphonic Inscapes' (1968), based to some extent on earlier film music, has a great concentration of thought and orchestral imagery; his three String Quartets are effective and eloquent.   AGH

Brandt, Muriel (1909–81). Landscape and figurative painter; born in Belfast, she trained at Belfast College of Art, and afterwards at the Royal College of Art, London. Noted for her portraits and especially those of children, she was elected RHA in 1962.   C MacG

Brenan, James (1837–1907). Landscape and figurative painter; born in Dublin, he was educated in Dublin and London. He taught in London and English provincial towns, and was Headmaster of Cork School of Art (1860–89) and of Dublin School of Art (1889–1904). He was elected RHA in 1878. Brenan encouraged the applied arts, especially lace-making. He is represented in the Crawford Municipal Gallery, Cork, by the *Prayer of the Penitent*, as well as in other public collections. He is not be confused with his contemporary, the portrait painter James Butler Brenan, RHA (1825–89), who also lived and worked in Cork.   C MacG

broadcasting. *See* RADIO; TELEVISION.

Broighter Hoard. A group of gold objects, found in 1896, near Limavady, Co. Derry, and sold to the British Museum; following a court action, however, the treasure was surrendered to the Crown and returned to Ireland in 1903 in conformity with Irish Treasure Trove practice. The hoard consisted of a tubular gold collar with lavish LA TÈNE ornament, a gold boat complete with oars, benches and mast, a gold bowl fitted with loops for suspension and two gold chains with clasps. The collar is probably of the 1st century BC and the chain is of Roman type, but the other objects are not closely datable. Recent research has suggested that the find may be a votive deposit of the early centuries of the Christian era.   MFR

Broighter Hoard. The gold boat with oars, from the hoard discovered in 1896; length of boat 18·5 cm. (7¼ in.). NMI.

Bronze Age. Ireland's rich deposits of copper and gold were exploited from *c.* 1800 BC on. Flat axeheads (some 2,000 are known) replaced the stone axeheads of the Neolithic, the earliest examples being manufactured in a one-piece stone mould. The rich copper ores of Kerry, west Cork and Tipperary apparently provided the raw material. Fourteen tanged daggers of west European type made by this simple casting process are related to the fine Beaker pottery characteristic of this earliest Bronze Age. LOUGH GUR yields evidence of habitation of this period.

Evidence of ancient copper-mining has been found at Mount Gabriel in Co. Cork, at Killarney in Co. Kerry and at Bonmahon in Co. Waterford: at Mount Gabriel 25 ancient mines were found, one reaching 9 m. (30 ft) into the rock face. Fire and stone mauls were used to loosen the ore, which was crushed with mauls outside.

Early gold ornaments related to Beaker pottery are ear-rings like that from Deehomed in Co. Down, with affinities in Iberia, and sun-discs (circular plates of gold apparently worn in pairs on the breast), with affinities in central Europe, found in Co. Monaghan, Donegal, Mayo, Roscommon, Cork and Wexford. Four Beaker vessels found in a WEDGE TOMB at MOYTIRRA in Co. Sligo are the best Irish examples of a type known in Atlantic Europe; 400 of these tombs are known. They are apparently related to the *allées couvertes* of Brittany, and Beaker pottery and barbed-and-tanged flint arrowheads are commonly found in them.

In this earlier phase of the Bronze Age (EBA), Ireland thus looks east across Britain to north and central Europe, while it also continues to receive influences from the Atlantic coast as far south as Iberia. This dual outlook is mirrored in Ireland in the presence of wedge tombs mainly in the west and in central Ulster, and in the presence of Beaker and cognate Food Vessel pottery with single burials in a mainly eastern area.

This earliest metalworking tradition continues with the manufacture of LUNULAE (sheet-gold neck ornaments), flat riveted daggers and flat axeheads of central European type. These probably overlap with the local Food Vessel pottery: thick-walled vessels of bowl or vase form decorated all over in impressed and slightly plastic techniques. These are found with the crouched single burial characteristic of Continental and south British Beakers, or with single cremations. They are found stratigraphically later than Beakers at Ballynagilly in Co. Tyrone and at LONGSTONE in Co. Tipperary; their beginnings may date to *c.* 1700 BC.

Later, casting in bivalve moulds made possible more sophisticated weapons; daggers with midribs and axes with cast flanges, some with stopridges. A new central European type, the halberd, is a curved dagger-like implement mounted at right-angles to a wooden haft. This weapon is frequently made of copper, possibly for its superior pliability. Modification of the single-burial ritual resulted in the introduction of the Cinerary Urn, of which some 400 examples are known, mainly in the eastern province; these urns were inverted over single cremations and are found in four styles – Collared, Cordoned, Encrusted and Enlarged Food Vessel. They are found side by side with Food Vessel burials in cists in MULTIPLE CIST CAIRNS such as KNOCKAST and TARA. The urns are found together with flat daggers and daggers with midrib, and also with a later type, the razor, found in male burials dating from *c.* 1400 BC.

The razor, together with the rapier, a fine example of which is known from Lissane in Co. Derry, and the socketed spearhead may belong to a separate Middle Bronze Age phase. The socketed spearhead requires the insertion of a plug into a bivalve mould, a significant advance in technology represented among the hoard of stone moulds from Killymaddy in Co. Antrim, which also provided for the casting of a sickle and a rapier. A development of the flat axe with stopridge, the palstave, also appears to date from this time. Gold is used in a restrained fashion to decorate the pommel of a dagger from Topped Mountain in Co. Fermanagh and the shaft of a spearhead from LOUGH GUR.

A Bishopsland phase with influences from northern Europe *c.* 1200 BC ushers in the Later Bronze Age (LBA): craftsmen's tools like the anvil, saw, hammer and punch are found for the first time, clay moulds are attested, the socketed axehead is introduced, and barbaric gold torcs like those from Tara become, with delicate twisted ear-rings of east Mediterranean inspiration, the fashionable gold ornaments. The sheer quantity of gold in these torques is overwhelming: the larger surviving torc from Tara weighs 839 g. (1 lb. 14 oz.); a hoard from Tipper, near Naas in Co. Kildare, had 1771 g. (almost 4 lb.) of gold.

The great flowering of bronze industry belongs to the Dowris phase beginning in the 8th century BC. Swords are found in great numbers (as at CULLEN), some circular shields are known, the socketed axehead, various forms of knives, sickles and metalworkers' tools. Sheet-metal working is common, buckets and cauldrons being made of riveted plates. For the first time,

Gold torc, *c.*1000 BC, found in Carrowmore Bog, Co. Mayo, diameter 16·9 cm. (6⅛ in.). Barber Institute of Fine Arts, Birmingham.

Tubular bronze goad with applied swans confronted by a pair of crows or ravens, from Dunaverney, Co. Antrim; Late Bronze Age, length 60·7 cm. (23⅞ in.). British Museum, London.

Decorated bronze axehead from Scrabo, Co. Down, *c.* 17th century BC; length 13·5 cm. (5¼ in.). NMI.

Decorated Food Vessel, *c.* 1600 BC, from a burial at Dunamase, Co. Laois; height 10·2 cm. (4 in.). NMI.

lead occurs as a significant constituent in bronze. Gold bowls are known from the Shannon estuary, and a great variety of personal ornaments of gold are decorated with gold leaf: gorgets, dress-fasteners, sleeve-fasteners, hair-rings, sunflower pins. Bronze ceremonial horns with a restricted musical range are known. Horse-trappings now attest the use of horses as draught animals. Plain woven cloth was found at Cromaghs in Co. Antrim, together with a woven belt of horsehair with tassels on the end.

For the first time since the beginning of the Bronze Age, good evidence of habitation is provided by lake-dwellings or CRANNÓGS at Ballinderry (Co. Offaly), Knocknalappa (Co. Clare), Lough Eskragh (Co. Tyrone) and LOUGH GARA. RATHGALL has yielded a great deal of evidence of the period, centred on a circular post-built house, 15 m. (50 ft) in diameter, within an enclosing ditch 35 m. (115 ft) in diameter. The earliest houses at EAMHAIN MACHA appear to be contemporary. *See* also IRON AGE.   M H

brooches, penannular and pseudo-penannular.

Penannular brooches. Used as ornamental cloak fastenings, they consist of a gapped hoop and a free-swivelling pin. The pin was stuck through folds of cloth and the hoop rotated underneath it. The drag of the cloth then tightened the pin on the ring, thus locking the brooch. Normally made of bronze, they were in vogue in Ireland in the period from about the 3rd century AD to the 10th although their ancestry lies in the later phase of the prehistoric era in Britain. The earlier forms – the zoomorphic type – are modelled so as to suggest animal heads and in the 6th and 7th centuries these are often elaborately enamelled and decorated with 'Ultimate La Tène' (*see* LA TÈNE) scrollwork. In the 9th century they became once again fashionable when a new type, the bossed silver penannular, emerged. These were elaborately decorated with engraved animal designs and domed bosses, and billeted lines were a feature of their design. In the 9th and 10th centuries a further type, the 'thistle' brooch, developed: penannular hoops with spherical terminals and pin-heads, often 'brambled', i.e. engraved so as to resemble the surface of a blackberry. Fragments of both 'thistle' brooches and bossed silver penannulars which have been cut up have been found in early 10th-century Viking hoards. Examples of both types have been found in areas of Viking settlement outside Ireland and their origins are somewhat controversial.

Pseudo-penannular brooches. In the 8th century a fashion for large brooches with completely closed rings developed. These, therefore, could not have functioned as locking devices in the manner of penannular brooches, the rings served both as a stop and as a field for the display of ornament. Decoration was often arranged in panels which clearly mimicked the form of penannular brooches, but a number of types of cloak fastener and pin may have contributed to their development.

This is a distinctive Irish type, of which more than twenty highly decorated silver examples are known, together with a number in gilt bronze. The 'TARA' BROOCH is the best known of the type made in the 8th century but the tradition is continued into the 9th by, for example, the two smaller brooches in the ARDAGH HOARD.   M F R

Brooke, Henry (*c.* 1703–83). Writer; born in Co. Cavan, the son of a clergyman, and educated at Trinity College, Dublin, he went to London to study law and there wrote an admired philosophical poem, *Universal Beauty* (1735) and a celebrated political drama, *Gustavus Vasa* (1739). His novels are *The Fool of Quality* (1765–70), a *roman à thèse* on education, and the sentimental *Juliet Grenville, or, The History of the Human Heart* (1774). He was a landowner in Co. Cavan, where he principally lived, and author of the *Farmer's Letters to*

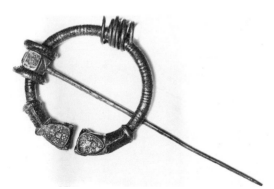

brooch. Penannular type, the bronze ring being decorated with incised patterns and the terminals with inlaid millefiori glass; 6th–7th century, from Ballinderry, Co. Offaly. Length of pin 18·7 cm. (7¼ in.). NMI.

(*Right*) Penannular 'thistle' brooch, silver, *c.* 10th century, from Ardagh, Co. Limerick; diameter of ring 7.6 cm. (3 in.). NMI

(*Opposite*) V **Cong, Cross of.** The 12th-century reliquary made for Turlough O'Connor, King of Connacht. A relic of the True Cross was set in the centre and protected by a translucent rock crystal; the surrounding panels of interlaced designs are of gilt bronze. NMI.

the Protestants of Ireland (1745) and other Irish writings. His daughter, Charlotte, produced the influential *Reliques of Irish Poetry* (1789).   ICR

Buchanan, George (1904–   ). Poet; an experimentalist in the tradition of McGreevy and Coffey. He has published prose as well as a unique body of poetry, which includes *Bodily Responses* (1958), *Conversation with Strangers* (1959) and *Minute-book of a City* (1972).   T McC

Buck, Adam (1759–1833). Painter; born in Cork, he practised mainly in Dublin and London, specializing in watercolour portraits and subject pictures which combine Neo-Classical elegance and Victorian sentimentality. His charming groups such as the Edgeworth and Kingston portraits were influenced by his knowledge of Greek vase painting.   AOC

Bunting, Edward (1773–1843). Musician and antiquarian, born in Armagh; he began his professional career as assistant organist at Belfast at the age of eleven. He travelled the country, collecting traditional airs, of which he published sixty-six in 1796 in a *General Collection of the Ancient Irish Music*, a further seventy-seven in 1809, and a further one hundred and twenty in 1840 in Dublin, where he was organist at St Stephen's and taught music.   B de B

Burgh, Thomas (1670–1730). Engineer and architect, son of the bishop of Ardagh. After serving in the military, some of that time as an engineer, he served under the Surveyor-General, Sir WILLIAM ROBINSON, to whose office he was appointed in 1700. He engaged in various improvements and projected improvements to existing buildings and was responsible for a number of fine Dublin buildings: the Royal Barracks, the old Custom House on Essex Quay, the library of Trinity College, Dr Steevens' Hospital (1721–33) and probably St Werburgh's Church, among others, as well as military buildings and fortifications in the country. His architectural style may be described as a sober and very restrained interpretation of the English Baroque tradition.   B de B

Burke, Edmund (1729–97). Political philosopher; born in Dublin, he was educated at Trinity College, Dublin, and the Middle Temple in London. He served in the British House of Commons 1765–94, and though never in the Cabinet was an influential M.P. as well as a distinguished orator. Though he was an Anglican, Burke's mother and wife were both Roman Catholics and in his Irish writings Burke argued on moral and pragmatic grounds against the Penal Laws. Famous in his twenties for his ironic *Vindication of Natural Society* (1756) and the aesthetic treatise *On the Sublime and Beautiful* (1757), he made significant contributions to the debate on the American colonies – *On American Taxation* (1774) and a *Letter to . . . the Sheriffs of Bristol, on the Affairs of America* (1777) – and, during the 1780s, on the British administration of India. The conservative *Reflections on the Revolution in France* (1790) provoked

Burke, Edmund. Statue by J. H. Foley, 1868, in College Green, Dublin.

many replies, among them Tom Paine's *The Rights of Man* (1791–2). In several respects – notably his ideas on party and his belief that a Member of Parliament is an elected representative, not a delegate – Burke's political philosophy has continuing practical consequences, as well as historical significance.   ICR
Philip Magnus, *Edmund Burke: A Life*, 1939; Gerald W. Chapman, *Edmund Burke: The Practical Imagination*, 1967; Thomas H. D. Mahoney, *Edmund Burke and Ireland*, 1960.

Butler, Mildred Anne (1858–1941). Painter; born at Kilmurry, Co. Kilkenny, she studied at Westminster School of Art, and with Frank Calderon. She also went to Newlyn and worked under Norman Garstin. She exhibited at the Royal Academy from 1889, and was elected an Associate of the Royal Watercolour Society in 1896, and a full member in 1937. In 1896 her work *A Morning Bath* was purchased by the Chantry Bequest and now hangs in the Tate Gallery, London. Her works, the bulk of which had remained in her family home at Kilmurry, were rescued from obscurity in two exhibitions held in Dublin and London, followed by the sale of a large number of watercolours, drawings and sketchbooks at Christie's in London, October 1981.   C MacG

(*Opposite*) VI **Durrow, Book of.** A 'carpet' page (folio 3v) from the 7th-century manuscript preserved in the library of Trinity College, Dublin.   53

Cahirguillamore, Co. Limerick. The site of collective and individual burials of the Late Neolithic/Early Bronze Age, discovered in 1948 in Rockbarton townland, W of Lough Gur. Between a slab-boulder and a rock-face there were at least thirteen burials, ten of adults, with pottery including Beakers, bone skewers (one of horse), two broken barbell bone toggles and four disc-beads. In the clay covering sealing this deposit was a single crouched burial with fragments of a decorated globular bowl and the butt of a polished stone axehead. Nearby was a Beaker with reed-stamped ornament.   MH
J. Hunt, 'Prehistoric Burials at Cahirguillamore, Co. Limerick', in E. Rynne (ed.), *North Munster Studies*, 20–42.

Campbell, George (1917–79). Landscape, figurative and abstract painter; born at Arklow, Co. Wicklow, the son of Gretta Bowen, painter. After leaving school he lived with his mother in Belfast and took up painting about 1942. Largely self-taught, he worked with DANIEL O'NEILL and GERARD DILLON, and had his first one-man show in 1946. His favourite places for painting were Connemara and Spain. Campbell also designed STAINED GLASS. Member of the RHA.   C MacG

Campbell, Joseph (1879–1944). Poet; born in Belfast, he was an Ulsterman who had a superb knowledge of Irish folklore. He published many collections of verse, including *The Garden of the Bees* (1905), *The Rushlight* (1906) and *The Mountainy Singer* (1909).   T McC

Carleton, William (1794–1869). Writer; born and raised among the Catholic peasantry of Co. Tyrone, he made his way to Dublin, where he came under the influence of the fanatic Protestant editor Caesar Otway, and for a time marred his work with proselytizing passages. Nevertheless, his *Traits and Stories of the Irish Peasantry* (1830–33), generally considered his best work, dates from this era. He also wrote several novels, including *Fardorougha the Miser* (1839), *Valentine McClutchy* (1845), and *The Black Prophet* (1847). His fiction is often unconvincing in plot and weak in form, but presents graphically the life and language of the common people of his day.   PLM
Benedict Kiely, *Poor Scholar*, 1948; Robert L. Wolff, *William Carleton, Irish Peasant Novelist*, 1980.

Carnfree (Carn Fraoich), Co. Roscommon. A small stone-faced cairn, 4·50 m. (14 ft 9 in.) across and 2·40 m. (5 ft 6 in.) high, standing at 120m. (400 ft) above sea-level, S of Tulsk, and near the SE edge of the complex of monuments at Crúachain (*see* RATHCROGHAN), is traditionally the inauguration-place

of the O'Connor kings of Connacht; it was so used as late as the 15th century. A stone with a 'footprint' was associated with the mound. Nearby to the SE is a burial-mound, probably early Bronze Age; 450 m. (490 yds) to the E is a ring-barrow, *c.* 40 m. (130 ft) in diameter, with a standing stone at the centre and a second, fallen, pillar nearby. Carnfree itself may be the site of a prehistoric burial mound.   MH

Carolan, Turlogh (1670–1738). Harper and composer; born at Nobber, Co. Meath, he later moved with his family to Co. Roscommon where they were befriended by the McDermott Roes and where he died. On losing his sight at the age of fourteen he was apprenticed for seven years to a harper, after which he travelled in Connacht and Ulster, composing and dedicating pieces to patrons, mostly the remnants of the old Irish aristocracy, who received him. About fifty of his compositions were published by EDWARD BUNTING in 1796.   B de B

carpet making. Until the end of the 16th century, the floors of great houses were strewn with straw and rushes. Later a thick woven fabric was introduced as a covering for floors, chairs and couches. Inventories of some great houses in the 17th century include imported Turkish carpets.
    In 1740 the DUBLIN SOCIETY offered premiums for carpet weavers; the first was one 'in imitation of Turkey carpets'. This premium was not offered again until 1752 and there were few claimants because the product was so costly to make and needed expensive looms.
    The Donegal carpet industry which flourishes today owes its origin to Alexander Morton. The Congested Districts Board, established in 1891 to help alleviate unemployment in the western counties, approached Morton, who settled at Killybegs, Co. Donegal, where he began carpet manufacture. There, the weavers sit side by side facing the warp on an upright loom.
    The DUN EMER GUILD developed a hand-knotted carpet industry, undertaking large commissions to original designs, one of which was the stair-carpet for Dáil Éireann. There are also beautiful examples in private houses. In the present century successful commerical carpet factories geared to mass production have been established at Navan, Co. Meath, Youghal, Co. Cork, and Newbridge, Co. Kildare.   HLM
A. K. Longfield, 'History of Carpet-making in Ireland in the 18th century', *JRSAI*, lxx, pt II, June 1940; Donegal Carpets Ltd (ed.), *A Short History of hand-knotted Carpet Manufacture in Ireland*, n.d.

Carr, Thomas (1909–). Painter; born in Belfast, he studied under Tonks at the Slade School of Art, London. First exhibited in London in 1936 with Victor Pasmore, Claude Rogers and the Euston Road School of painting; exhibited at the Royal Academy, London, and the Royal Hibernian Academy, and is a Member of the Royal Society of Watercolour Painters. His work is represented in many collections in Ireland and England, as well as the Royal Collection.   C MacG

Carolan. Monument to the bard by John Hogan, erected in 1824 in St Patrick's Cathedral, Dublin.

Carrowmore, Co. Sligo. A large cemetery of PASSAGE GRAVES, a great number of them built boldly and simply of local ice-boulders, sometimes split, near Sligo town and under Knocknarea (330 m.; 1,080 ft), on which there is also a small group of passage graves. Records by Beranger (1779) and PETRIE (1837) document the former existence of many tombs. Over 60 monuments are concentrated in a rough oval, 1,000 × 600 m. (1,100 × 650 yds) surrounding the slab-built Listoghil tomb (Petrie's No. 51), which overlooks them. The site has been investigated at various dates, yielding typical cremated remains, with mushroom-headed antler pins, beads and pendants, and Car-rowkeel Ware. Recent investigations (1978–80) by Burenhult supplement this evidence.   M H
M. Herity, *Irish Passage Graves*, 1974, pp. 264–71.

Carson, Ciarán (1948–   ). Poet; among the best of the new generation of Irish poets, his first collection is entitled *The New Estate* (1976).   T McC

cartography. Irish cartography in the strict sense begins no earlier than the 17th century. Before that, the mapping of Europe's outermost Atlantic fringe belongs to the history of other nations and other cultures, with the British Isles taking an inconspicuous place successively in Claudius Ptolemy's Alexandrian world map of the 2nd century AD, in the diagrammatic *mappaemundi* characteristic of early-medieval Christendom, and in the sea charts produced by Italian and Iberian navigators in the 14th century and after. Only from *c.* 1540 did Ireland assume a definite cartographic identity in the many English military and political maps that were the surveyors' and engineers' contribution to the forward policy pursued by Tudor Governments. In this connection the maps of Robert

Lythe (1567–71), the two John Brownes (uncle and nephew; 1583–90), Francis Jobson (1587–98) and Richard Bartlett (1601–2) are particularly notable, but none of these men became famous in Ireland or anywhere else. Much of their work remained shut away in government offices or private archives, though some was used without acknowledgment in the compilations of foreign cartographers like Gerhard Mercator (1564, 1595) and Abraham Ortelius (1573), and later in the maps of the Englishman John Speed (1611), whose version of Ireland found general acceptance for most of the 17th century.

War and the threat of war continued to inspire their own distinctive maps in Ireland as in other countries, but by Speed's time military campaigns were becoming a less important cartographic influence than the confiscation and redistribution of landed property. The emphasis now was on the admeasurement and plotting of numerous small territorial divisions at large scales. William Petty is pre-eminent among the organizers of these plantation surveys, not only in the magnitude of his Down Survey (1655–9) but also in the originality he showed by working up the results into an atlas of all the Irish provinces and counties. Though published in London, Petty's famous *Hiberniae delineatio* (1685) may be accepted as characteristically Irish in its evocation of the utilitarian character of plantation cartography. Its outline reappeared in most of the general maps of Ireland published by British and foreign cartographers between *c.* 1690 and the advent of the Ordnance Survey. Such longevity does little credit to Petty's successors. Once the supply of new plantation surveys dried up in 1703, few Irishmen were willing to carry out cartographic research for its own sake, a major exception being Daniel Beaufort, whose ecclesiastical map of Ireland (1792) was rightly admired as a masterpiece of careful scholarship.

Petty's real bequest to 18th-century Ireland was the country's flourishing class of land-surveyors. Some of them made maps of complete counties, including several that were engraved in Dublin, but their main interest was in the manuscript mapping of farms and estates. This remained an Irish preoccupation even after the visit to Dublin in 1754–60 of the celebrated Anglo-French cartographer John Rocque, who through his pupils (especially Bernard Scalé) exercized more influence in Ireland on estate surveying than on the kind of printed map that Rocque himself had specialized in. Certainly no cartographer of Irish extraction ever equalled the magnificent plan of Dublin which Rocque published in 1756.

Another generation of innovators, several of them Scotsmen or with Scottish connections, appeared in Ireland after the union of 1801 and were especially active in the mapping of roads, canals and harbours, exploiting new cartographic techniques and achieving new standards of accuracy. Prominent in this group were William Bald, Richard Griffith, William Duncan and William Edgeworth. Most of them spent some time practising as independent civil engineers, but their best work was done under either central or local government direction, particularly in surveys for the

Irish Bogs Commission of 1809–14 and in several county maps that were by-products of the bogs surveys. Some engineers, such as William Armstrong in Co. Armagh, tried to apply these improved standards of precision to the traditional subject-matter of Irish estate surveying, but their efforts were overtaken by the arrival of the Ordnance Survey, a large and efficient government map-making agency directed by officers of the Corps of Royal Engineers. The newcomers began by publishing maps of the whole of Ireland at the scale of six inches to one mile (1833–46), and then widened their range in the later 19th century to embrace almost every other kind of map. Today most new maps of Ireland are derived from the work of the Survey and of its two successors, the Ordnance Survey of Ireland (Dublin) and the Ordnance Survey of Northern Ireland (Belfast).　　　　　JHA

Carton, Co. Kildare. originally built in the 17th century, the house was reconstructed by RICHARD CASTLE for the 19th Earl of Kildare between 1739 and 1745. Castle added a storey to the house, plus colonnades and wings, while the FRANCINI brothers embellished the saloon with a Baroque ceiling. The 1st Duke of Leinster laid out the park in an informal manner with a lake, a bridge (1763) by THOMAS IVORY, a Gothick tower and a shell cottage. Major reconstruction of the house occurred in 1815 when the 3rd Duke employed the MORRISONS to extend the house; they removed the colonnades, added a sumptuous dining room and a delicate library.　　　　　WG

Cary, Joyce (1888–1957). Writer; born in Londonderry as Arthur Joyce Lunel Cary, he lived in England, Ireland and Africa, and wrote four political treatises, novels about Africa, novels of childhood, and 'chronicles'. Cary's two trilogies exhibit many different styles, and a fertile, rich, fantastic imagination: the first, a picaresque life of an artist, Gulley Jimson (*Herself Surprised*, 1941; *To Be A Pilgrim*, 1942; *The Horse's mouth*, 1944), the second political (*Prisoner of Grace*, 1952; *Except the Lord*, 1953; *Not Honour More*, 1955).　　　BH

Cashel, Rock of (Co. Tipperary). The Rock, which rises dramatically above the surrounding plain, served as a fortification of the Eoghanachta kings of Munster as early as the 4th century. According to the Tripartite Life, ST PATRICK came to the Rock on his missionary expedition through Munster in the 5th century and baptized the king there; subsequently it was the seat of a succession of king-bishops, of whom the most illustrious was CORMAC MAC CUILLEANÁIN. Brian Boroimhe (Boru) was crowned on the Rock in 977 and made Cashel his capital; his descendant, King Muirchertach, granted the Rock to the Church in 1101.

The earliest of the surviving structures on the Rock is the small Romanesque church, CORMAC'S CHAPEL, consecrated in 1134; the Round Tower was probably built in the 12th century also. The adjacent Cathedral, now in ruins, dates from the 13th century, the tower over the crossing being a 15th-century addition.　　　　　BdeB

Cashel, Rock of. Aerial view showing the principal buildings: Cormac's Chapel (left), the ruined Cathedral and the round tower.

Castle, Richard. The façade of Leinster House, Dublin (1745); engraving by James Malton, 1794.

Castle, Richard (*c.* 1690–1751). Architect; came apparently of a Huguenot family settled in Germany. His original surname is thought to have been Cassel, but his Irish will dated 11 August 1750 mentions his three brothers in Saxony all called de Richardi, and this may have been his own surname. Came to Ireland at the invitation of Sir Gustavus Hume to build Castle Hume, Co. Fermanagh, in 1729. He worked on the PARLIAMENT HOUSE and the Newry Canal under PEARCE and was recommended by Pearce to members of parliament as a country-house architect. In 1733 he married Jeanne Truphet in the French Church, Dublin, and after the death of Pearce in that year Castle became the most sought-after architect in

Ireland. He was a Palladian of the Pearce-Burlington-Kent school and enjoyed the 'masculine' effect of heavy mouldings and sculpted stonework. Westport, Co. Mayo (*c.* 1730), shows him in his muscular vein, while Ballyhaise, Co. Cavan (1733), which is Pearcian in plan, has the earliest oval room in Ireland. He developed a greater sense of depth at Powerscourt, Co. Wicklow (1741), and RUSSBOROUGH, Co. Wicklow (1741), while at CARTON, Co. Kildare (1739–45), and Bellinter, Co. Meath (*c.* 1750), there is an increased delicacy. In Dublin he designed the delightful Printing House (1734) in TRINITY COLLEGE, Clanwilliam House (1738), the first stone-faced town-house in Ireland, the ponderous Leinster House (1745), Tyrone House and the Rotunda Hospital. His name appears on the foundation stone of Leinster House, thereby proving the esteem in which he was held.   W G

The Knight of Glin, 'Richard Castle', *IGS Bulletin*, vol. VII, 1964.

Castlecoole, Co. Fermanagh. House, of Portland stone, built 1790–8; JAMES WYATT altered plans originally supplied by Richard Johnston (brother of FRANCIS JOHNSTON), to create a monumental Hellenistic essay which owes much to Stuart and Revett's *Antiquities of Athens.* Wyatt's great achievement at Castlecoole was twofold: to model the house in the round and to see the interiors as part of the sculptural whole.   W G

Castletown, Co. Kildare. Almost the first and undoubtedly the largest and most palatial 18th-century house in Ireland, Castletown was designed for the fabulously wealthy William Conolly, Speaker of the House of Commons, between 1722 and 1732 by the Florentine architect ALESSANDRO GALILEI and Sir EDWARD PEARCE. The central block is a Roman palazzo, faced with silvery limestone, and linked to service wings by curved colonnades of Ionic columns (the first in Ireland). The great staircase by Simon Vierpyl is dated 1760 and the plasterwork by the FRANCINI brothers is from the same period. The long gallery was decorated in the mid-1770s in the Pompeian manner under the direction of Lady Louisa Conolly, who also created the print room. The house was saved from probable decay and destruction and restored in the 1960s by the IRISH GEORGIAN SOCIETY. It is open to the public.   W G

Castletown, Co. Kilkenny. Sometimes distinguished as Castletown Cox, this house is the masterpiece of the Italian architect DUCART; it was built of dressed sandstone and unpolished Kilkenny marble *c.* 1767 for Michael Cox, Archbishop of Cashel. The seven-bay central block, three storeys over a vaulted basement, is flanked in the Palladian manner by service wings, here of two storeys on three sides to form a courtyard, with pavilions crowned by octagonal domes and cupolas at the east and west corners. The detailed accounts exist of the stuccodore, Patrick Osborne, dated 1774, for the magnificent Rococo PLASTERWORK in the main rooms.   B de B

Castlecoole. Part of the circular Saloon, planned by James Wyatt, *c.* 1795.

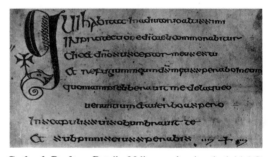

Cathach Psalter. Detail of folio 45r, showing the initial Q terminating in an animal head, *c.* 560. RIA.

Cathach Psalter. The 'Cathach' (battler or champion) reminds us of the place of the psalter in Irish monastic life. It is the oldest of the extant Irish illuminated mss., dated *c.* AD 560, and is thus contemporaneous with St Columba, and was perhaps written in Iona. It still exudes the air of the earliest days of Celtic Christianity. A total of 58 leaves survive, containing text of Psalm 31, v. 10, to Psalm 106. While colour, mostly yellow, is sparse, capitals formed of spirals, recalling metalwork, are lively, with freehand animal heads and crosses. Scarlet dots and rubrical headings outline and frame the clear semi-uncial script. Enshrined for a member of the O'Donnell family, relatives of St Columba, in the 11th century, it has been deposited in the RIA; the finely wrought Shrine of the Cathach (*see* SHRINES) is in the NMI. Tradition associates this ms. with St Columba's copyright controversy.   GOS

Céli Dé. A spiritual reform movement (Culdees) which flourished for about 150 years from its beginnings around Lismore, Co. Waterford, in the second quarter of the 8th century. Its aims were to combat monastic laxity, to promote monastic studies and to stress the Anchorite values of poverty, charity, self-denial and perseverance in endeavour. Thus the movement stimulated a prodigious literary activity, both religious and secular. CORMAC MAC CUILLENÁIN, an outstanding literary figure in Ireland in the 9th and 10th centuries, was educated in a monastic school. The best-known works issuing from the movement are *The Rule of Fethad* and *The Alphabet of Piety*, while its principal leader was Maelruain, whose monastery at Tallaght, Co. Dublin, and the monastery at Finglas, Co. Dublin, were important centres of the reform.   BdeB
P. O'Dwyer, O.C., *Céli Dé*, 1981.

Celtic Revival. A growing awareness of and pride in the special achievements of Irish artists of the Early Christian period combined with the general imitative or copyist tendency in 19th-century decorative art to produce the Celtic Revival – the revival of the various forms of early Irish or, as it came to be popularly known, 'Celtic' ornament. This revival was the most dominant force in Irish applied art from the 1880s to 1930s, though it started much earlier and was still in evidence after World War II (*see* pls. III, IV).

The revival started in antiquarian circles in Dublin in the 1840s. The Irish Archaeological Society had initial letters from the BOOK OF KELLS and other manuscripts engraved for use in its own publications of important texts and the Celtic Society used motifs from the BOOK OF DURROW and the CROSS OF CONG on its bindings. Later Margaret Stokes and then Helen D'Olier made coloured copies of various details from Irish illuminated mss., Stokes being the first person, in 1865, to complete an accurate copy of the famous Chi-Rho monogram page of the Book of Kells. This early phase of the Celtic Revival saw the rise in popularity of reproduction Irish jewellery and also the modern Celtic cross (*see* SILVERWORK). Waterhouse & Co. and West & Son were the first in the field of jewellery but were soon joined by other Dubliners, such as W. Acheson and R. & J. Gardener, and later Edmond Johnson who also made excellent facsimiles of the larger pieces of early Irish metalwork such as the Shrine of St Patrick's Bell (*see* SHRINES) and the silver Chalice in the ARDAGH HOARD.

By the end of the 19th century Celtic ornament had been put to many varied uses. In the 1880s the Donegal Industrial Fund, the Royal Irish School of Art Needlework and the Poor Clares Convent in Kenmare used it in embroidery; Marcus Ward & Co., T. J. Lynch and others used it in illuminated addresses; and the Clonkeen, Ahane, Stradbally, Bray and Terenure

Celtic Revival. Silver reproduction of the Clasp from the Ardagh Hoard by Hopkins & Hopkins, 1912; width 10·2 cm. (4 in.). Ulster Museum.

Carving Classes used it in woodwork. Charles Russell, RHA, used it in the decoration of ceramics in the 1880s, John Vinycomb used it in bookplates, and J. M. KAVANAGH used it in repoussé metalwork in the 1890s. It was fostered to some extent by the 'Gaelic movement' at the turn of the century, being used on medals and trophies, in stage settings and costumes for Irish plays and pageants, on Irish harps, and on the covers of Irish music festival programmes.

In the early 1900s a number of groups were specializing in Celtic ornament. The DUN EMER GUILD used it in embroidered vestments and hand-tufted carpets; the Youghal Art Metal Workers in repoussé copper and brass vases, frames and buckles; and the Irish Decorative Art Association of Belfast in a whole range of domestic furnishings, calendars and cards, as did the Cluna Studio in Dublin later in the 1920s. Some ecclesiastical art manufacturing firms also specialized in Celtic ornamental work, in particular Watson & Co. of Youghal, Co. Cork, in stained glass, and Egan & Sons of Cork in altar plate and in vestments.

While some highly original work was done in the 19th century, most designs then were of a derivative nature, with details culled from the various publications of J. O. Westwood, Henry O'Neill, and Margaret Stokes. The early 20th century, however, saw a growing number of artists and designers eschewing standard patterns and developing highly original and personal treatments of Celtic ornament. These included John Maxwell, WILLIAM SCOTT, Alice O'Rourke and ART O'MURNAGHAN of Dublin, Mícheál O'Riada of Killarney, and Eva McKee of Belfast.

The revival of Celtic ornament touched sculpture only slightly (as in the interlaced embellishments to some early 20th-century figured works by OLIVER SHEPPARD), and painting hardly at all (with the exception of some details in a few works by DANIEL MACLISE and F. W. Burton), but it did make an impact on architecture. A number of churches and other buildings were decorated in Celtic style.

In the course of the Revival some attempts were made at analysis of Celtic ornament, with the intention of working out systems for constructing new patterns: Thomas Cooke-Trench (who built St Michael's

Church, Clane, Co. Kildare) tried in the 1880s, as did the English antiquary J. Romilly Allen. In 1931 the Co. Cork art-teacher John G. Merne published *A Handbook of Celtic Ornament*, and later still, in 1945, George Bain, a Scot, published a series of instructional booklets. By then, however, the heyday of the Celtic Revival was over, although fine illuminated work was still being done by Michael O'Connor in Dublin and Maureen Collins-Ryan in Limerick as late as the 1960s.   PL

P. Larmour, 'The Celtic Revival and a National Style of Architecture' (Ph.D. thesis, The Queen's University of Belfast), 1977; ——, *Celtic Ornament*, 1981; E. Rynne, 'The Revival of Irish Art in the 19th and 20th century', *Topic*, 1972; J. Sheehy, *The Rediscovery of Ireland's Past: the Celtic Revival 1830–1930*, 1980.

censorship. *See* under LITERATURE: Literature from 1920 to the present.

ceramics. Probably the earliest pottery sherd known from Ireland is that found in a house site in Co. Tyrone and dated by the radiocarbon method to *c.* 3675 BC. From this Neolithic period onwards each successive incursion brought its own style of domestic and funerary pots to the country.

Change came with the introduction to Ireland of the potter's wheel by the Normans. Such new technology encouraged a specialization in pottery-making in urban areas. However, interest decreased over the following centuries until in the 15th century the principal product of Dublin potters was the chafing dish (a pottery portable oven), while rural potters made crude storage jars and cooking pots.

From Roman times wealthy Irish people had occasionally imported prestige pottery pieces. This practice increased in the late 17th century due to the improvement in communications and the growing fashion for display of Oriental porcelains in the new-style home. By the early 18th century Irish people, even those of modest means, aspired to own porcelain, a ware which was essential to the new symbol of social refinement, tea, coffee and chocolate-drinking.

With the manufacture of delftware (tin-glazed earthenware) in Belfast from *c.* 1688, production enters its industrial phase. Delftware factories were established also in Dublin, *c.* 1735; Rostrevor, *c.* 1742; Limerick, *c.* 1762; and possibly Youghal, Co. Cork. The Dublin pottery was started by John Chambers who imported trained workmen and built a 'White Pothouse' at the World's End on the North Strand. Manufacture was carried on there later by John Crisp and by David Davis. The ware produced shows that they copied the styles, decoration and shades of blue from contemporary Chinese porcelain. Although they claimed to produce delftware not only of equal standard to that imported, yet cheaper, the enterprises failed financially.

In their encouragement of native industries, the DUBLIN SOCIETY offered a premium 'for erecting a manufactory in imitation of Delft, Rouen and Burgundy ware'. The Society's challenge was met by

ceramics. Delftware plate, with painted landscape in imitation Chinese style, by Delamain's factory, Dublin, *c.* 1760. Victoria and Albert Museum, London.

Captain Henry Delamain, who took over Davis and Company's pottery, *c.* 1753. He added to the factory building; re-employed the more skilled workers, prepared to employ about forty families and sought Charter schoolboys and young girls as apprentices. Using clay from the Carrickfergus area of Co. Antrim, his factory produced delftware dinner services, spirit barrels, wall-fountains, fruit baskets and apothecary jars. Items were painted in strong blue or manganese with distinctive designs of traditional Chinese patterns, views of gentlemen's country seats, landscapes, floral designs or coats-of-arms. Delamain exported his wares to Germany, Spain, Portugal and the West Indies.

Like the master-potters of his day, Delamain spent much time in relevant scientific experimentation. His proudest boast was that he designed a kiln for firing delftware which used coal as fuel. His 'invention' was controversial but sufficiently successful for Liverpool potters to employ Delamain's factory-manager, William Stringfellow.

When Delamain died in 1757 the business was carried on by his wife and then by executors in trust for their sons. The industry failed. The reason offered was that war stopped the export trade to the Continent. When the workmen took over the factory *c.* 1769 it was becoming increasingly difficult for an Irish delftware factory to remain viable. By the 1760s European and Oriental porcelain was readily available in Dublin through china-merchants and public auctions. Irishmen attempted to compete by producing popular, less expensive, wares such as creamware and 'china'. The most successful of these was the Downshire Pottery near Ballymacarrett, Belfast, which won prizes for Queen's Ware from *c.* 1780. However, Irishmen played

ceramics. Ornamental delftware shoe decorated in dark blue, Belfast, 1724; length 15·2 cm. (6 in.). NMI.

major roles in ceramic production in Britain. Thomas Frye was the first to add bone-ash from calcined ox-bones to a porcelain paste as a flux and John Brooks was one of the first to develop transfer-printing for decorating ceramic wares.

The decline of the ceramic industry in Ireland signalled an increase in importance for merchants handling imported wares. James Donovan of George's Quay and Ringsend, Dublin, seems to have made transfer-printed pearlware *c.* 1780, but by the early 19th century Donovan concentrated on retailing English and Continental ceramics and used his muffle-kiln for decorating replacement pieces and for 'special orders'. Other firms such as Wedgwood, Thomas and Higginbotham, and Eardleys decorated occasional pieces on their premises.

Throughout the early 19th century scientists and patriots pointed to the 'abundance of porcelain earth and potter's clay in Ireland', and urged the establishment of ceramic industries which would use local clays, provide regular employment and reduce the country's dependence on imported wares. The only porcelain works to succeed were BELLEEK, and Coalisland, Co. Tyrone, after Belleek workers defected there. Plain and decorated glazed earthenware was made also at Belleek and at Larne, from *c,* 1850.

Although Ireland's fine ceramics always suffered from foreign competition, the country was mainly self-sufficient in 'coarse' ware. These products included a wide range of articles, for example, moulds, drips and crocks for sugar-refining; pan, ridge and floor tiles; glazed red ware for the dairy; building bricks and flower-pots (both plain and decorated); and the popular clay tobacco-pipe. Red clay, used since the 16th century for drainpipes and flower-pots, was available in many parts of the country. Potteries which existed because of that supply include Carley's Bridge, Co. Wexford, and Florencecourt, Co. Fermanagh, *c.* 1863–80, a number of potteries at Youghal, Co. Cork,

from at least the 18th century, and at Coalisland, Co. Tyrone, from *c.* 1835. Samuel Murland had a brick and tile works at Castle Espie near Comber, Co. Down, *c.* 1870–88. His factory also produced ornamental and tea-ware decorated with an agate-style glaze.

The pioneer of Irish art pottery, Frederick Vodrey, first worked with Herbert Cooper, the professor of ceramics at the Queen's Institute, Dublin. About 1874 Vodrey opened a pottery at the back of his Moore Street warehouse, employed English master-potters and commissioned designs from members of the Dublin Sketching Club, especially the talented Charles Russell. Vodrey's styles ranged from his early lead-glazed vases, with moulded arabesque-style decoration through moulded Celtic interlace design, to vases showing the influence of Japanese art. Vodrey's work won medals and prestige patronage but he remained financially dependent on the production of glazed white earthenware tea-ware with applied flowers and birds, and on his retail glass and china shop. The business was unsuccessful and Vodrey emigrated *c.* 1886.

Although samples of china and glazed earthenware were made from Irish clays for Government departments from *c.* 1850 to 1902, there was little progress until in 1928 an industrial pottery was established in Carrigaline, Co. Cork, to produce utilitarian, souvenir and art wares. Other industrial potteries which followed include: Arklow Pottery Ltd, established 1934; Royal Tara Ltd, Galway, established 1953; Ceramics Ltd, Kilrush, 1963; and Noritake Ireland Ltd, Arklow, Co. Wicklow, 1963.

Probably the greatest change in the present century has been the return to the individual artist-potter, made possible by the availability of the small electric kiln. The first such kiln was used in Dublin in the early 1930s by Kathleen Cox. Irish art pottery entered a new stage of vibrancy with the advent of potters such as Peter Brennan (from 1941), John Ffrench (from *c.* 1950) and Grattan Freyer (from 1952).   M R
M. S. D. Westropp, *General Guide to the Art Collections: Irish Pottery and Porcelain*, 1935; Michael Archer and Patrick Hickey, *Irish Delftware* (Rosc exhibition catalogue), Dublin 1971; M. Archer, *Irish Pottery and Porcelain* (Irish Heritage Series no. 27), 1979; Michael Kenny and Patrick Wallace, *Pottery in Ireland through the Ages*, NMI exhibition cataglogue, n.d. [*c.* 1978].

Chambers, Sir William (1723–96). Architect; born in Sweden and educated in Paris and Rome, he had a successful career in England (where he was allowed to use his Swedish knighthood). He introduced the Neo-Classical style to England, published the influential *Treatise on Civil Architecture* (1759) and is best known for Somerset House, London, which he commenced in 1775. He found the perfect patron in Lord Charlemont, for whom he designed in 1762 a town house in Dublin (now the Hugh Lane Municipal Gallery of Modern Art), and the exquisite Marino Casino, Clontarf, Co. Dublin. The Casino is a tiny pleasure house with the external appearance of a symmetrical temple and interior with finely proportioned rooms. It

Chambers, Sir William. The Marino Casino, begun in 1758; detail of an engraving published by T. Milton, 1783.

was built between 1758 and 1776 at the then phenomenal cost of £60,000, with stonework carved by Simon Vierpyl and sculpture by Joseph Wilton. This masterpiece in the Franco-Roman manner can only be compared with the Petit Trianon at Versailles. Chambers also supplied designs for the theatre and chapel in TRINITY COLLEGE. W G
John Harris, *Sir William Chambers, Knight of the Polar Star*, 1970

Chester Beatty Library, Dublin. The Library, formed by Sir Alfred Chester Beatty (1875–1968), is now held in trust for the nation. Born in New York, Sir Alfred was a philanthropist and art collector who, after a successful career as a mining engineer in many countries, developed an interest in Oriental manuscripts. On settling in Dublin in 1953, he had a library built in Shrewsbury Road to house his magnificent and extremely valuable collection of 13,000 books and manuscripts. B de B

Chomhairle Ealaíon, An. *See* ARTS COUNCIL.

Christian Brothers, The. Four Irish laymen dedicated to Roman Catholic education, and led by EDMUND IGNATIUS RICE, opened a school at Waterford in 1803 and lived an ordered religious life patterned on the rule of NANO NAGLE's Presentation Sisters; they were the nucleus of a Congregation formed in 1808. In 1827, Brothers in Cork separated themselves from the Institute and formed a separate diocesan congregation, the Presentation Brothers. At the time of Rice's death in 1844 there were no more than a hundred Christian Brothers, distributed among nineteen communities in England and Ireland, conducting 58 schools; and the whole educational enterprise in Ireland relied on private funding because in 1836 the Congregation had rejected participation in the National Schools system on the grounds that the restrictions it entailed were incompatible with the movement's ideal of Christian education.

Today, the Irish Christian Brothers number over 3,000, dispersed among some 500 communities in Ireland, Britain, the United States, Canada, Australia, New Zealand, Africa, India, the West Indies, the South Pacific and South America. Their cultural impact for more than a century through their schools has been enormous, not only in Ireland but among working-class Roman Catholics in the English-speaking world. While their dedication and their heroic contribution to popular education must be acknowledged, in assessing their influence it has also to be said that the narrow focus of their educational apostolate has led to a certain narrowness of cultural and intellectual vision. They have come to be associated with a predilection for corporal punishment and cramming, as well as a severely functional, exam-oriented approach in which the broader purposes of the educational process – the development of a capacity for critical reflection, of aesthetic sensibility and of moral autonomy – figure little, and this has affected the cultural outlook of generations of their pupils in Ireland.

The failure of the Brothers to achieve a more liberal conception of their educational role may be linked to their refusal in the 19th century to broaden the social range of their educational endeavours, a decision which was against the express advice and wishes of the founder. It resulted in the apostolate of the Brothers being confined to a working-class milieu in which the acquisition of the basic skills of literacy and numeracy and the exploitation of educational achievement for socio-economic betterment were paramount, and as the Brothers drew their recruits almost exclusively from the limited social milieu of their own schools it became increasingly difficult for them, as a body, to broaden their perspectives. *See* EDUCATION. B B

Christianity. Irish history is in large measure dominated by Anglo-Irish relations, and the history of Irish Christianity provides abundant evidence of this, traditionally beginning with the capture in the 5th century by Irish sea-raiders of PATRICK, whose father, a Roman citizen, was a deacon and decurion in an unidentified *vicus* in Britain, 'Bannaven Taberniae'. Carried by his captors into slavery in Ireland, Patrick (whose *Confessio* has survived to tell us something about him) eventually escaped, to return years later a bishop. While we may assert with confidence that Patrick did much to propagate and organize Christianity among the Irish, particularly in the north, it appears certain that small numbers of Christians were already scattered throughout the land. Nor was Patrick by any means the only evangelist of the Irish, though tradition has accorded him a primacy as 'Apostle of Ireland', and her patron saint.

In other parts of Europe ecclesiastical organization followed the pattern of civil administration, but Irish society, never having come under Roman influence, developed an organization less determined by territorial boundaries than by family or tribal influence, so that in a short space of time a distinctively Irish form of MONASTICISM became the ecclesiastical unit, following the model of the 'tuath', or tribal territory, under the protection and influence of the family, and with the leading figures (including the bishop) frequently members of that family, and indeed regarding their offices as hereditary. Ireland boasts three patrons: Patrick; Brigid, foundress of a women's community at Kildare; and Colum Cille (Columba), founder of several monasteries in Ireland, including Derry, and also of the monastic centre at Iona in Scotland. Others went further afield at a time when Continental Christianity was recovering from the effects of the disintegration of Roman imperialism – among them, Columbanus (to Burgundy and Italy), Fiachra (to Gaul), and Gall (to Switzerland). In many ways they represented the first waves of Irish emigration, preferring to be called 'exiles' rather than 'emigrants'. But the non-conformity of the Irish Church to the European norm in matters of organization and liturgical observance was a cause of unease to many of its leaders, and by the early 12th century a diocesan system was established, along lines that very largely obtain to the present day. This 12th-century reform movement, which began with the First Synod of Cashel (1101) and the Synods of Ráth Bresail (1111) and Kells (1152), received an impetus from the coming of the Normans to Ireland (1169), and culminated in the Second Synod of Cashel (1172) when a settlement was reached whereby the Irish Church would conform to European, and particularly English, usage.

The Norman (or Anglo-Norman) conquest of Ireland was not an event that can be represented by a single date; rather it was an unsteady process, experiencing many reverses, and remaining incomplete until the time of the Tudors. The Anglicization of the Church by preferment, order and liturgical rite was attempted simultaneously, and it was the policy of the Crown to restrict high office – in diocese, cathedral and the religious houses of monks and friars – to men of English birth. As early in the conquest as 1217 the king decreed that only Englishmen should be appointed to any office as bishop or in cathedrals, but this provision was only effective where the royal writ ran.

The several clauses of the Statute of Kilkenny (1366) reflect the deep anxiety of the conquerors that Gaelic influence was reviving, and it was found necessary to decree (with uneven results) that Irishmen should not hold office in the Church in those areas that were under English jurisdiction. The tension in the Church engendered by this racial factor served to exacerbate those symptoms of decay that mark so many reports on Church life in the immediate pre-Reformation period, when the Irish Church shared with the rest of Europe in a decline of standards both in administration and piety: plurality, absenteeism, a high incidence of hereditary succession to office by both secular and religious clergy, and great neglect of duty on the part of those who held such office. Abuses such as these, and many others, fuelled the Protestant Reformation in Germany and England, and when Henry VIII espoused the cause and the English Church was declared by legislation to be no longer subject to Rome, it was to be expected that similar legislation would seek to make the Irish Church, not only Anglicized, but 'Anglican'. An Irish parliament of 1536 extended to Ireland the laws governing the Church that already operated in England. Henry was declared 'supreme head of the Church of Ireland', and all office-holders in Church and State (and many others) had henceforth to swear to that fact by taking the Oath of Supremacy. No bishop refused to take the oath, so none was dismissed, and the Reformation in its initial stages seems to have provoked little opposition. In time, when theological and liturgical change became more dramatic (the Act of Uniformity prescribed the use of the Prayer Book in English), when the monasteries were suppressed, and when reforming bishops exercized their power with increased zeal, even the colonists of English blood felt a strain on their allegiance to the Crown, while the Gaelic Irish, already finding themselves and their land under pressure of conquest, viewed the ecclesiastical changes as further English aggression, and welcomed the emissaries of Rome who sought, with much success, to counter the Reformation in Ireland.

Under the Tudors considerable colonization of conquered Irish land took place both through personal initiative and by Crown 'plantation', thus much of the midlands and the south passed into English Protestant hands. Elizabeth I defeated the last of the powerful chiefs – O'Neill and O'Donnell – whose lands in Ulster were planted under James I by Anglicans and by Scots Presbyterians, giving that province a religious and cultural complexion quite different from that of the other three provinces.

Ulster, formerly the least Anglicized of the provinces, became (and remains) the region of Ireland that is (apart from cosmopolitan Dublin) culturally

Statue of St Patrick on Slieve Padraig, Saul, Co. Down.

most diverse. Present-day antagonisms in Northern Ireland are a fusion of political, cultural and social differences, rooted in past centuries, and fed by incompatible folk-memories, compounded on one side of confiscations, Penal Laws and subsequent deprivation, and on the other of the Siege of Derry, the Boyne, and an enduring experience of being beleaguered. No love was lost between Presbyterians and the Anglicans of the Established Church of Ireland (though both, where land tenure was concerned, regarded the Roman Catholics, whom they had largely dispossessed, as the common enemy). However, the term 'Protestant' tended to signify the Established (Anglican) Church whose leading members constituted that 'Protestant Ascendancy' – at once political, social and cultural – whose achievements are epitomized by Georgian Dublin, its architecture and its letters.

The Penal Laws of the early 18th century were directed at the Catholic population in particular by an insecure Anglican political and ecclesiastical establishment, but dissenters likewise suffered considerable social and economic disabilities, Presbyterians, Methodists, and Quakers alike, to the extent that the first Irish republican movement, Wolfe Tone's 'United Irishmen', drew much of its ideological impetus for political reform and religious equality from among Ulster Presbyterians fired with French revolutionary fervour, who figured largely in the 1798 insurrection. Catholics in the other provinces were more preoccupied with grievances against Protestant landlords (and sometimes tenants), thus giving, inevitably, a sectarian character to the struggle.

The failure of 1798 was compounded by the Act of Union, whereby the two kingdoms were united from 1801, and the two Established Churches (of England and Ireland) were joined. Most religious penalties had been lifted from the Catholic population by then, the one remaining disability being exclusion from political office. Daniel O'Connell's community leadership achieved total 'Catholic Emancipation' by 1829, and the Catholic Church entered upon a period of new-found confidence, closely in tune with aspects of European ultramontanism, as exemplified by the building of churches, cathedrals and schools on an unprecedented scale, their ornamentation expressing the current upsurge of popular devotion to the Sacred Heart and the Virgin Mary, their teaching heavily dependent on such formularies as the 'penny catechism', and by an upsurge of evangelism and personal piety at home and in the mission field. Nineteenth-century evangelicalism also invigorated the Protestant Churches, evangelistic sermons and hymns being the Protestant mode of expression. Proselytizing societies, some countenanced by the Established Church of Ireland, some positively discouraged, contributed to sectarian tensions that were already heightened by land and tithe agitation. The Established Church also experienced the effects of the tractarian Oxford Movement which proved timely when in 1870 the disestablishment of the Church of Ireland gave statutory endorsement to religious equality and Anglicans lost State support.

Daniel O'Connell, 'the Liberator' (1775–1847); portrait by G. J. Mulvany. NGI.

O'Connell's other ambition, to win repeal of the Act of Union, proved unattainable for half a century. When constitutional change came, in the 1920s, it took the form of a partitioned island, the several Churches spanning the border, the population of the Irish Free State (eventually Republic) 92·6% Catholic, and Northern Ireland 66·5% Protestant (1926 figures). In the formative years of the Free State social legislation (especially where matters of family planning, divorce and censorship were concerned) was strongly coloured by Catholic social teaching, while the majority Protestant population of the north was swept along – generally willingly – by the attitudes of the United Kingdom, culminating in the philosophy of the Welfare State. Such factors, combined with a policy of Gaelicization by the Free State, highlighted the cultural distinctiveness of the two parts of Ireland, though the Gaelic Revival and the Anglo-Irish literary and dramatic renaissance at the turn of the century, both major contributors to the nationalist movement, were heavily indebted to such Protestant figures as STANDISH O'GRADY, DOUGLAS HYDE, W. B. YEATS, J. M. SYNGE and SEÁN O'CASEY. With the 1960s and 1970s the communities of north and south found themselves impelled by external influences, notably the ecumenical movement (Vatican II in particular) and the movement towards European unity (especially membership of the EEC), to face major tasks of adjustment and reconciliation; some of these, as in the ecumenical field, were generally (if cautiously) welcomed, while others involving political considerations were more painful. Irish society still suffers from the strains imposed by the inter-relationship of religious and political issues, from the sense of identity with both islands that is deeply ingrained in most northern

Protestants, and from the aspiration of the northern Catholic minority to a closer political relationship with the rest of the island. The mainstream Irish Churches, more conscious than ever before of their common Christian tradition, yet mindful of their contribution to division in past years, are aware of the urgent need for ecumenical effort and have embarked on various schemes of joint action and serious dialogue to bridge a divide, part-political, part-religious, and manifestly social and cultural.   K M

cinema. The first public projection of a film was made in Ireland in 1896 at the Star Theatre of Varieties, Dublin, less than seven years after the first projections in England and the USA. In 1898 Dr R. A. Mitchell of Belfast became the first Irishman to make a film; his subject was a yacht race in Belfast Lough. The turn of the century saw the establishment of the first Irish company to exhibit and distribute films, the Irish Animated Pictures Co. Ltd; its projectionist, Louis de Clerq, made the first known Irish documentary film, *Life on the Great Southern and Western Railway* (1904). The Irish Animated Photo Co., the country's first film production company, filmed the consecration of the R.C. Cathedral at Armagh (1904). The Film Company of Ireland was founded in 1916 by James Mark Sullivan and his wife, both Irish-Americans, with John MacDonagh as its film director; this company produced the first feature-film to be made in Dublin, achieving remarkable success with their adaptation (1918) of Charles Kickham's *Knocknagow*, followed by a more ambitious film *Willie Reilly and his Colleen Bawn* (1919) derived from the work of BOUCICAULT. Norman Whitten, who had made newsreels, made and produced *In the Days of St. Patrick* (1919), with an original script. A feature film adapted from Donn Byrne's *Land of her Fathers* was shot in Ireland in 1924 with an Irish cast, mostly from the ABBEY THEATRE, but with an American director and cameraman. DENIS JOHNSTON directed and edited a silent feature film in 1933 adapted from FRANK O'CONNOR's short story *Guests of the Nation*; it had an Irish cast and was photographed in Ireland on 16-mm. reversal film-stock by John Manning and Jim Douglas. *The Dawn* (1937), an entirely Irish-financed 35-mm. sound feature film directed by Tom Cooper, enjoyed much popularity; it contains effective location sequences emotively and beautifully handled, but suffers from poor sound quality due to the use of out-of-date de Forest Photophone recording equipment.

Return to Glenascaul (1951), from a script by MICHEÁL MACLÍAMMÓIR and planned for both cinema and television release, was produced and directed by HILTON EDWARDS with a cast drawn from the Gate Theatre, Dublin. MacLíammóir-Edwards Productions made a documentary on the performance of *Hamlet* at Elsinore in 1952 and a second short feature-film, *From Time to Time* (1953), with a script by Hilton Edwards and George Morrison.

The successful *Mise Eire*, compiled, edited and directed by George Morrison and with a score for a full symphony orchestra by SEÁN O'RIADA, was sponsored with other films of the late 1950s by a non-profit making trust, Gael Linn; it had its première at the Cork Film Festival in 1959. Sponsorship, mainly by government departments, backed a number of short films in the 1960s. Two feature-length films were made in the late 1960s, Louis Marcus's *An Tine Bheo*, a colour documentary of the 1916 Rising, and Kieran Hickey's rostrum film using stills from the Lawrence Collection in the NATIONAL LIBRARY OF IRELAND, *The Light of Other Days*.

Louis Elliman and Emmet Dalton, who founded the Ardmore Film Studios in the 1950s, planned to film ABBEY THEATRE productions there but the film company soon collapsed and the studios changed hands several times. Films made at Ardmore over the next two decades were the result of foreign endeavour; these included such large-budget successes as *The Lion in Winter* and *The Spy Who Came in From the Cold*. While the studios functioned as a production facility for foreign companies making 35-mm. feature work, Irish film-makers were obliged by lack of funding to work with 16-mm. film. Nevertheless, stimulated by the script competition instituted by the ARTS COUNCIL, some good feature films were made under the direction of Kieran Hickey, Joe Comerford and Tom McArdle; Ciarin Scott, daughter of MICHAEL SCOTT, produced and directed a long documentary on the ROSC exhibitions; Bob Quinn left RTE to set up Cinegael, his own production and exhibition company in Connemara, which made two feature films and a number of short films of exceptional interest.

The establishment of the National Film Studios at Ardmore in 1975 did little to promote an indigenous Irish film industry. Due to lack of capital the studios continued to provide facilities for foreign companies and crews. Of over thirty major productions filmed in the National Film Studios between 1975 and 1980, only John Boorman's *Excalibur* could possibly be described as an 'Irish film'. Meanwhile film as an art and feature form survived in the productions by RTE for TELEVISION, one of which – *Strumpet City*, based on the novel by JAMES PLUNKETT – was sold abroad in forty countries.

Under the provisions of the Irish Film Board Act (1930) the Irish Film Board was established in 1981. Under the Board's loan and investment scheme Barry Blackmore's production of *Angel* (written and directed by NEIL JORDAN) received £100,000 but a much larger advance came from Britain's Channel 4 for television rights in this Irish feature film which must be considered a landmark in the history of the Irish film industry. In 1982 as many as 150 projects were before the Irish Film Board but the funds at its disposal were not sufficient to make even one full-length feature film. The decision of the Government in 1982 to sell the National Film Studio produced an atmosphere of further gloom and uncertainty concerning the prospects for the film-making industry in Ireland.   G M

Clarke, Austin (1896–1974). Poet, dramatist and novelist; born in Dublin, he was educated at Belvedere and University College, Dublin. A profoundly engaging poet and versatile man of letters, his first book was *The Vengeance of Fionn* (1917). His interest in Irish history and legend pervades his work from *Pilgrimage* (1929) to *A Sermon on Swift* (1968). Like Yeats, Clarke grew in wisdom and confidence as he got older. *Orphide* (1970) and *Tiresias* (1971) display a relaxed, mischievous sensuality. *See* POETRY.   T McC

Clarke, Harry (1889–1931). Illustrator and stained-glass designer; raised in his father's North Dublin church-decorating business, he studied stained glass at the Dublin School of Art and in London. In 1914 he married Margaret Crilley and in the same year a scholarship enabled him to study medieval stained glass before he embarked on his first and finest stained-glass commission, eleven windows for the HONAN CHAPEL, Cork, which established his reputation and revealed his rare technical and imaginative abilities: intriguing tiny figures and a wealth of arcane symbolism surround each of the sumptuously apparelled, androgynously beautiful saints depicted.

His book illustrations were complemented by minutely detailed stained-glass panels illustrating literary subjects. Two windows composed of a number of such panels illustrate contemporary Irish literature and Keats's *Eve of St Agnes* (Hugh Lane Municipal Gallery of Modern Art, Dublin). There are windows by Clarke throughout Ireland, as well as in England, Scotland and Wales.

When he took over the family business, he gave it as much inspiration as his own glass and graphic commissions. His prolific output was curbed by tuberculosis, from which he died at the age of 41. The Harry Clarke Stained Glass Studios Ltd, registered in 1930, continued to produce windows, often after his idiosyncratic style, until 1973.   NGB

Nicola Gordon Bowe, Catalogue and Monograph of the exhibition, *Harry Clarke*, the Douglas Hyde Gallery, Trinity College, Dublin, 1979; ——, 'The Life and Work of Harry Clarke' (unpublished Ph.D. thesis, Trinity College, Dublin), 1981; ——, *Harry Clarke, the Graphic Work*, 1981.

Clarke, Margaret (*née* Crilley; 1888–1961). Landscape and portrait painter; born at Newry, Co. Down, she studied art at Newry Technical School, and came to Dublin on a scholarship to the Metropolitan School of Art, where she studied under WILLIAM ORPEN. She married HARRY CLARKE in 1914; elected ARHA 1926 and RHA 1927, she was an early member of the IELA, established in 1943.   C MacG

Clonfert Cathedral, Co. Galway. The building is best known for its decorated west doorway, a culminating achievement of the late Hiberno-Romanesque style dating, apparently, from the close of the 12th century. The low-relief geometrical, plant and animal ornament of the inclined jambs, with their mask capitals, contrasts with the exuberant high-relief decoration of the arches. The pointed gable combines stylized and more naturalistic human heads. The innermost order of the doorway was a later insertion, added in the 15th century.   PH

Clarke, Harry. Window depicting St Gobnet, in the nave of the Honan Chapel, Cork.

Clonfert Cathedral. Hiberno-Romanesque west doorway, late 12th century.

(*Above*) **Clonmacnois.** Aerial view showing the layout of the monastery complex.

(*Right*) **Clonmacnois Crozier.** The bronze crook with elaborate silver and niello interlace ornament, *c.* 1100. NMI.

Clonmacnois, Co. Offaly. The tranquil monastery of Clonmacnois, one of the greatest artistic centres of early Ireland, was founded *c.* 545 by St Ciarán. In addition to the Cathedral, the site has five churches, including the beautiful 12th-century Nuns' Church to the east of the main enclosure, two ROUND TOWERS (one built into a church), as well as two complete HIGH CROSSES and fragments of a number of others.   P H

Clonmacnois Crozier. The 'Crozier of the Abbots of Clonmacnois', a short crozier of Irish type, probably dating from *c.* 1100, was either found at Clonmacnois in the 18th century or obtained from its hereditary keeper by Major Sirr, with whose collection it was acquired by the ROYAL IRISH ACADEMY; it is now in the National Museum. The crozier is constructed in the familiar Irish manner by encasing a wooden core in bronze plates. Its crook, knops and ferrule form fields for the display of ornament. The openwork crest of dog-like animals, each one biting the rump of that in front of it, and the cast animals on the bottom of the uppermost knop are especially noteworthy. The loose animal interlace on the crook is excuted in silver and niello inlay in a manner partaking of elements of both the Irish Urnes style and the Ringerike style (*see* METALWORK).   MFR

Coffey, Brian (1905–). Poet; the most cosmopolitan of Irish poets, his first book *Poems* (1930) was published with DENIS DEVLIN. His *Collected Poems* were published by Dolmen Press in 1964; in 1971 New Writers Press issued a selected edition of his work.   T McC

Collins, Patrick (1910–). Landscape and figurative painter; born at Dromore West, Co. Sligo, he is largely self-taught. He exhibits with the RHA and the IELA. He won the National Award at the Guggenheim Award Exhibition, New York, 1958. Collins went to live in Paris in 1971, but eventually returned to Dublin where he was given a retrospective exhibition by the ARTS COUNCIL, 1982. His work is represented in all major collections in Ireland.   C MacG

Frances Ruane, *Patrick Collins Retrospective*, Arts Council of Ireland, 1982.

Colum, Padraic (1881–1972). Writer and poet; born in Longford, he worked in Dublin for several years and became active in literary circles. His best work is found in a handful of poems (especially 'Wild Earth', published in 1907) and in the three dark, powerful plays that he contributed to the ABBEY THEATRE during its early years: *The Land* (perf. 1905), *The Fiddler's House* (perf. 1907), and *Thomas Muskerry* (perf. 1910). Beginning in 1914, he lived primarily in America and although he continued to publish voluminously, in many genres, he never fulfilled the promise of his early career.   PLM

Zack Bowen, *Padraic Colum*, 1970.

Cong, Cross of. A 12th-century cross, measuring 76·2 cm. × 47·9 cm. (2 ft 6 in. × 1 ft 6¾ in.), now in the National Museum of Ireland. It is made of wood, covered in bronze plates decorated in openwork interlaced animal designs in the Irish Urnes style and filigree (*see* METALWORK), and the edges are bound with a rounded binding strip. The sides are covered in silver foil. The outline of the cross takes the form of a series of elegant curves, the junctions between pairs of curves being emphasized by elaborately enamelled rivet heads. A central domed rock-crystal was designed to protect and display a fragment of the True Cross for which the object was made. An inscription on the side records that the cross was made at the behest of Turlough O'Connor, King of Connacht, by the craftsman Mael Isu: the work can be dated to between 1119 and 1123, when the annals record that relics of the True Cross were brought to Ireland and a portion retained and enshrined at the instance of Turlough in Roscommon. The cross was purchased in 1839 by Professor MacCullagh of Trinity College, Dublin, from the heir of a certain Fr Prendergast of Cong, Co. Galway, in whose possession it had been. (Little is known about Fr Prendergast – he is variously described as the last Augustinian abbot of Cong and as parish priest.) Professor MacCullagh presented the cross to the ROYAL IRISH ACADEMY, whose collections are now in the NMI. *See* pl. v.   MFR

Congreve, William (1670–1729). Playwright; born at Bardsey, near Leeds, he was taken to Ireland in 1674. He was SWIFT's contemporary at Kilkenny College and at Trinity College, Dublin. Leaving Ireland in 1688, he published a romance, *Incognita* (1692), before producing his first comedy, *The Old Bachelor* (1693). After *The Double Dealer* (1693), Congreve consolidated his reputation with *Love for Love* (1695), the tragedy *The Mourning Bride* (1697), and finally his masterpiece, *The Way of the World* (1700), which established him as the outstanding writer of the comedy of manners.   ICR

Congreve, William. Mr Foote as Fondlewife in Act IV of *The Old Bachelor*; engraving published in 1776.

Conor, William (1884–1968). Genre and narrative painter; born in Belfast, he attended the Belfast College of Art, then worked as a poster artist. He also studied in Dublin and in 1912 in Paris. During World War I, he was appointed by the Government to make pictorial records of the army and munitions workers. A regular exhibitor at the ROYAL HIBERNIAN ACADEMY Annual Exhibitions, he was elected ARHA 1939, RHA 1947; awarded the OBE 1952. In 1957 a retrospective exhibition of his work was held in the City Art Gallery, Belfast. A collection of fifty-three of his paintings and drawings are presented in the Conor Room in the Ulster Folk Museum, Holywood, Co. Down, as a visual commentary on the social and folk life of the area.   C MacG
Judith C. Wilson, *The Life and Work of an Ulster Artist*, 1981.

conservation. Conservation of Ireland's architectural heritage has not had a very happy past and it faces a somewhat uncertain future. This heritage includes medieval churches and castles and a great number of fine houses of the 18th and early 19th century (*see* ARCHITECTURE), but political troubles, neglect and indifference have all taken their toll over the years. Many 18th-century houses have been lost through a combination of the troubles of the 1920s, the decline of the landlord classes, neglect and fire. In recent years the pressures of urban development have had particularly devastating results.

In the Republic the Office of Public Works – a Government department – is charged with the care of national monuments, most of which date prior to the 18th century. Over 400 monuments are vested in the Commission of Public Works, while a further 417 are subject to preservation orders. However, much of Ireland's heritage is in private ownership and it is in this area that the struggles for survival have taken place. Some few private trusts have been set up with the object of preserving individual houses, such as the Alfred Beit Foundation at RUSSBOROUGH and the Castletown Trust (*see* CASTLETOWN, Co. Kildare).

The modern conservation movement started to grow in the 1960s; it was part of a wider European post-war concern. Awareness grew largely as a result of the demolition of some important 18th-century houses in Dublin. Conservation and amenity bodies came into being and existing organizations became stronger, These lead public opinion in their own individual ways and their impact has been considerable, especially in recent years. The National Trust for Ireland (AN TAISCE) and the IRISH GEORGIAN SOCIETY are country-wide, while smaller local groups such as the Cork Preservation Society and the Kildare Archaeological Society make their own distinctive contribution. These organizations hold lectures, seminars, publish booklets and conservation journals, all with the objective of focusing public attention on the country's heritage (*see* also ULSTER ARCHITECTURAL HERITAGE SOCIETY).

In 1967 An Taisce published its *Amenity Study of Dublin and Dun Laoghaire*, which is regarded as a milestone in the history of conservation. Many of its recommendations were included in Dublin Corporation's first Development Plan.

When 1975 was designated European Architectural Heritage Year by the Council of Europe, authority and impetus were given to the conservation movement. The popularity of the cause was demonstrated by the huge protest march in 1978 of 20,000 people against the erection of civic offices in Dublin on a Viking site at WOOD QUAY. While conservationists largely lost that particular battle, its impact on public opinion was very significant. Planning authorities know that in drawing up and administering their development plans under the planning legislation of 1963 and 1976 they cannot now neglect the local architectural heritage, and some developers now also have a more enlightened approach to conservation.

While there has been a considerable growth in public awareness, in the membership of voluntary organizations (e.g. the IRISH ARCHITECTURAL ARCHIVE) and in voluntary input to the cause of conservation in recent years, the situation is still far from satisfactory. Literally dozens of worthwhile buildings have been demolished in the last few years and this trend continues. There is no mandatory listing of important buildings.

The situation of many houses in private ownership is very difficult, since the costs of maintenance, repairs and insurance place a heavy burden on the owner. No satisfactory solution has yet been found in the area of tax concessions. The future of such buildings must therefore be regarded with real anxiety; this is one of the biggest challenges of the conservation movement in Ireland today. CO'C

Cooke, Barrie (1931-). Landscape painter, designer and environmental artist; born in Cheshire, England, he grew up in Jamaica and studied in the United States with Rattner and Levine. He had his first one-man show in New York in 1950 and came to

Cooke, Barrie. Portrait of the actress Siobhan McKenna. An Chomhairle Ealaion Collection, Dublin.

Ireland in 1954. He represented Ireland at the Paris Biennale in 1963. In 1971 he shared a retrospective with CAMILLE SOUTER. His work is semi-abstract in style, with a strong suggestion of physical presence, and is also much influenced by landscape, particularly of the Nore Valley and Clare.

Fascinated by anatomy, Cooke has produced in many of his works of the late 1970s and early 1980s assemblages in perspex boxes, dealing with the structural forms in humans and animals. His work is represented in the Hugh Lane Municipal Gallery of Modern Art, Dublin, the Crawford Municipal Gallery, Cork, and the ULSTER MUSEUM. C MacG

Cork Historical and Archaeological Society. Founded in 1892 and still active, the Society publishes a *Journal*. MC

Cork Royal Institution. Founded in 1803, the Institution acquired the Old Custom House in 1830; from 1834 onwards that building also housed the Cork Scientific and Literary Society, and now, after being enlarged by the Crawford family in 1885, houses the Crawford Municipal School of Art and the Art Gallery. MC

Corlona, Co. Leitrim. Here, in a small peat-bog, about 1 m. (3 ft) under the surface of the peat, was discovered a wooden trackway 1 km. (over $\frac{1}{2}$ mile) long. It was built in sections, each c. 2·25 m. (7 ft 6 in.) long, consisting of a main plank 45 cm. (18 in.) wide, flanked on either side by a narrower plank, the whole being 89 cm. (2 ft 11 in.) wide. At the west end of each section support was provided by two piles 1·55 m. (5 ft) long, driven obliquely into the bog and jointed to the outer planks by a mortice and tenon; at the east end each rested on a pile of brushwood. The site has been dated by radiocarbon to c. 1500 BC. MH
P. Tohall *et al.*, 'A trackway in Corlona Bog, Co. Leitrim', *JRSAI* 85 (1955), 77-83.

Cormac Mac Cuillenáin (836-908). King-Bishop of Munster, enthroned at Cashel in 902; the most outstanding literary figure in Ireland in the 9th-10th century, he was author of several poems and traditionally the author of *Sanas Cormaic* ('Cormac's Glossary'), the first etymological dictionary in a vernacular, valuable not only for its glossarial content but for the information it embodies regarding ancient customs and beliefs. Cormac studied in the monastic school of Dísert Diarmata which seems to have been founded under the auspices of the CÉLÍ DÉ reform; its principles are apparent in a work attributed to Cormac, 'The Rule of Cormac', which stresses the necessity of humility, abnegation, spiritual discipline and scriptural study. The Psalter of Cashel, also attributed to Cormac, included the part-prose, part-verse Book of Rights with genealogies and details of the rights of provincial monarchs. B de B

Cormac's Chapel, Cashel, Co. Tipperary. Standing on the ROCK OF CASHEL, this is considered to be the first

Cormac's Chapel. The south front of the Chapel, probably built 1127–34.

and most important of the Irish churches to have been decorated in the Romanesque style. It is normally equated with the church erected by Cormac MacCarthy between 1127 and 1134, though evidence for the equation is of comparatively recent date. The building consists of a nave and (slightly off-centre) chancel, with two flanking square towers at the junction, perhaps wrongly attributed to influence from Regensburg in Bavaria. Unusually, the church had three entrances, the most important of which faced north, and was emphasized by a pointed gable; it was, in addition, (secondarily?) provided with a carved tympanum. A second entrance (now blocked up) was through the north tower, suggesting the former presence of some important building (a palace?) to the north of the chapel. The chapel is the most richly decorated of all the Irish Romanesque churches, with blind arcading, carved capitals and many individual heads, and it was originally decorated with frescoes. The external walls have superimposed rows of arcading, and the chapel has a stone roof with a small croft above the barrel-vaulted nave and ogival-vaulted chancel. At the west end of the chapel the sarcophagus sculpted with ornamentation of Scandinavian origin, consisting of interlaced thin and fat serpents (*see* VIKINGS), is believed to be that of the founder, Cormac MacCarthy who died in 1138.   PH

costume. This article deals with types and styles of clothing from the 3rd century BC to the 19th century; for later developments *see* FASHION DESIGN.

Pre-Norman

Though examples of magnificent gold jewellery – GORGETS, LUNULAE, ear-rings and lock rings – survive from the BRONZE AGE, there is no extant evidence of contemporary garments, although the use of double fasteners presupposes the wearing of heavy ceremonial cloaks. When the Celtic tribes arrived in the 3rd century BC, they were clad in what approximated to a jacket and knee-length trews, covered with a woollen cloak secured by a brooch. The men were long-haired and bearded and both men and women of the upper classes wore fine, twisted gold torcs. Generally, women wore ankle-length linen tunics and cloaks similar to the men's. Shoes and sandals were mostly of leather, though some were composed of a leather sole and a linen upper. Later, certain Roman fashions fused with Celtic traditions, one notable example being the cloak-fastening known as a penannular BROOCH; examples survive from the 6th century AD and such brooches were still being made 400 years later.

The early Christian Irish, though far from isolated from European trends, adhered to two basic male fashions that altered only minimally from at least the 8th century until the mid-16th century, and which appear to be of very ancient origin. The simpler – though apparently the more prestigious – was the straight linen tunic (*léine*) fastened by a tablet-woven girdle (*crios*) and worn with an unshaped woollen mantle (*brat*). Those of lesser social standing wore a sleeved jacket, pulled on over the head, with close-fitting trews, either knee-length or secured by a strap under the instep. Many went barefoot from choice, though pointed leather shoes existed. The women continued in the *léine* and *brat*.

The VIKING raiders, who descended in the 9th century, wore garments resembling the jacket and trews, though the trousers were frequently short and baggy and they scorned bare feet. Their long cloaks, often hooded and fur-lined, were pinned at the left shoulder by a brooch, unlike the *brat* which was invariably worn over both arms. Their flowing hair was tied back with colourful headbands. The wealthy flaunted expensive jewellery, popularizing the use of silver in its manufacture. Their women wore a linen under-shift beneath a long full dress tied with a girdle and topped by a cloak or woollen shawl and all the jewellery they could afford.

Norman and medieval

The Norman invaders who landed in 1169 brought new ideas. Their knights were clad in a linen surcoat over a suit of chain-mail (which in turn was set on thickly-padded undergarments), with a flat-topped helmet over padded arming coifs. Their underlings fought in stout leather jerkins and padded breeches.

By the late 13th century, chain-mail was being replaced by plate armour worn over a less bulky padded jerkin, the aketon. Mail sabatons were sometimes replaced by leather shoes, and a distinctive helmet called a barbut developed, with a pointed crown and a rounded, T-shaped opening to clear eyes, nose and mouth. The Norman-Irish also preferred a

(*Above*) Tomb effigies of the 8th Earl of Ormond (d. 1539) and his wife (d. 1542), shown wearing the padded, horned head-dress, in St Canice's Cathedral, Kilkenny.

(*Right*) An Irish colleen wearing a typical hooded cloak.

large piscane to the aventail currently favoured in England.

The 14th century saw a merging of fashions, as some Norman lords affected Irish beards and moustaches and even the front-opening Irish mantle. By the mid-15th century a new style of armour, formed of iron hoops riveted together and known as a 'pair of plates', was widespread in Ireland, 50 years before it became common in Europe. The Norman-Irish retained it, virtually unaltered, until armour finally became obsolete. Non-military dress resembled that in England. It consisted of a long, full gown with a mantle secured at the neck by linked fibulae, a type of garb also worn by churchmen, with priests assuming canonicals for Mass. Up to the 15th-century, Gaelic bishops of the south and west used a French-style, high, triangular mitre with a decorative border to its lower edge.

Until *c.* 1350 Norman-Irish ladies followed current English fashions, but thereafter went attired in long, full kirtles over which were shorter gowns with pleated skirts, V-necklines and long, wide 'pudding sleeves', gathered at shoulder and wrist. The padded, horned and veiled head-dress had reached Ireland by 1450 and continued to be regarded as the insignia of great noblewomen right up to 1540.

The Gaelic Irish retained their own styles. In the late 14th century the bare-footed Ulster chieftains were wearing a low-necked, knee-length *léine* with a 'great hooded cloak'. They fought with an aketon under their armour and as late as 1359 might enter battle with one gold TORC worn on the head and another around the neck. The *galloglai* favoured a form of long, thickly-ribbed gambeson (*cotun*) and fought in boots or sabatons, whereas the kern still fought bare-footed. From the ancient *brat* there developed the flannel 'Shagg-Rugg' or 'Irish Mantell', shaped on the shoulders and with its gaily-dyed texture raised into a nap of thick curls and fringed all round with a double fringe at the neck. Worn by both sexes, all economic brackets and exported to England and Europe, these garments were in common use for some 800 years.

Tudor and Stuart

Officials and merchants brought smart Tudor fashions to Dublin, though Elizabethan farthingales proved unpopular amongst Irish ladies, who preferred rather straight-cut gowns with trailing sleeves and narrow neck-ruffs, below which hung a cross on a short chain. Early Tudor Gaelic and burgher women wore 'Irish mantells' and voluminous linen head-dresses of varying shapes. By the 1520s some of the kern had adopted single-strap sandals and might pull a long-sleeved loose jacket over their *léine*. By the 1580s the *léine* had been replaced, at least in Ulster, by a wrap-around jacket, closely pleated at the waist like a ruff and ending in a short skirt to mid-thigh, and with wide hanging sleeves. The Gaelic nobility wore a front-buttoning quilted leather jacket, tight trews and a tall domed hat of quilted leather. The lower classes went bare-headed, their hair hanging in 'glibs', while everybody resorted to the shaggy mantle. Gaelic women's dress altered little; the long, wide-sleeved *léine* being retained as an under-dress, covered by a woollen gown and either a fringed *brat* or a mantle. Their hair hung loose below the thick linen rolls of their head-dresses, whose shape varied from province to province.

The 17th century brought an increase in English-style clothing, though the old Gaelic fashions lingered on until Charles II's time. The ancient 'Irish mantell' finally expired about 1660, being replaced for upper-class females by the hooded cloak, and the population ceased to be divided racially by dress. The contrast was now between rich and poor, the rich – irrespective of origin – wearing 'English' garments and the poor 'Irish' garments.

The 18th century

Fashionable attire followed that in England fairly closely, with a few exceptions and several years' time-lag. The 1730s and 1740s brought unwonted extravagance, particularly among gentlemen, whose coats and waistcoats were lavishly embroidered and heavily trimmed with gold or silver braid, quite in excess of anything customary in England. The English vogue in the 1750s for ornamental aprons for ladies was never universal in Ireland. During the 1780s there was a marked preference in Munster for *brown* bouffant curled wigs. From the start of the century, hats for women replaced the old hooded cloaks. The fashion time-lag ended abruptly and for ever *c.* 1790.

Mid-18th-century farmers wore a plain frock-coat, waistcoat, breeches and boots, with either a three-cornered or a round-crowned hat. Very popular was a long, loose woollen overcoat called a 'trusty', a type which endured into the mid-19th century and even had its descendants up to the 1930s. By the 1790s caped coats were being used by coach-drivers and drovers. Country women were clad in either simple, full-skirted dresses or a bodice and petticoat, with a folded kerchief across their shoulders and an apron as protection for their skirt. The hooded cloak, introduced by 17th-century ladies, survived in common use by such as could afford it, often dyed bright red. Shoes were still precious and their useful life was prolonged by dint of the owner going barefoot whenever possible.

The 19th century

The farming classes adhered determinedly to the swallow-tailed, high-collared coat, breeches (often tied with string), boots and high-crowned hat; in Munster this was topped by the loose 'trusty', in Leinster by a more closely-fitting coat. In remote areas old men continued to wear wigs into the 1820s. Regional differences, both in cut and colours, became marked: in Co. Limerick and east Cork the women's hooded cloaks were bright red, in Kerry, west Cork and Galway they were blue or grey. In Galway red petticoats were usual, in Leinster they were apt to be green. By the 1840s large tartan shawls were replacing cloaks in Ulster and after the Famine fringed shawls gained general acceptance, the hooded cloak surviving only in Munster. Very handsome ornamental shawls were made for gala occasions, though everyday ones were mostly plain black.

The uniquely Irish forms of footwear remained in use: (1) knee-length sole-less stockings (triheens), secured by a hole through which the big toe fitted, which were worn for cold, wet work and are believed to have derived from the Celtic period; (2) the untanned leather pampooties, also for wet work, that survived in the Aran Islands (home also of distinctive patterns for fishermen's jerseys) into modern times.   R ff

court tomb. The remains of the cairn at Creevykeel, Co. Sligo, showing layout of court and adjacent chambers.

Craig, James Humbert. A characteristic landscape, *Cloud Shadows, Connemara.* Hugh Lane Municipal Gallery of Modern Art, Dublin.

Courts of Poetry (*Cuirt Eigse*). Term used to describe 18th-century gatherings of professional poets; the original 'poetry Workshop'. The activities of these Courts have been described by Daniel Corkery in his *Hidden Ireland* (1925). *See* POETRY.   T McC

court tomb. A trapezoidal cairn, of the Primary Neolithic (*c.* 3000 BC) and later, containing an oval court, off which is a burial gallery or galleries divided by jamb and sill into two or more chambers; 330 such tombs are known in Ireland. Three variant forms are known: single court, dual court and centre court. Finds include: Primary Neolithic pottery, flint lozenge arrowheads and hollow scrapers. *See* BALLYGLASS; BEHY; MALINMORE; STONE AGE.   MH

Craig, James Humbert (1878–1944). Landscape painter; born in Belfast, he was mainly self-taught; he exhibited at the ROYAL HIBERNIAN ACADEMY from 1915, and at the Royal Academy in London, as well as the

Glasgow Institute. His work was reproduced widely in the 1930s, and is now very popular with collectors.   C MacG

Cramillion, Bartholemew. Stuccodore; employed by Dr Bartholomew Mosse to decorate the ceiling of the Rotunda Hospital chapel, Dublin. The ceiling has four recesses, one for the organ, and the others for allegories of Faith, Hope and Charity. The figures are treated sculpturally, in high relief, and surrounded by angels and putti. Large panels on the ceiling were left empty for paintings by Cipriani which, however, were never executed. For his work at the hospital between 1755 and 1758 Cramillion was paid £585 9s. 9d. No other work by this outstanding stuccodore has been identified. *See* PLASTERWORK.   W G

crannóg. Aerial view showing Crannóg No. 83, on the edge of Lough Gara, Co. Sligo.

crochet. Collar with decoration of floral motifs.

crannóg. A late-dwelling; an artificially made island, usually circular, often made of wooden beams stabilized by piles and augmented by stone etc., and sited near the edge of the lake. Organic material is commonly preserved; hearths and houses are frequently found. These flourished from the late BRONZE AGE to medieval times. Examples are: LISNACROGHER, LOUGH GARA, Lagore (Co. Meath), Knocknalappa (Co. Clare), Moylarg (Co. Antrim), Lough Faughan (Co. Down).   M H

crochet. Closely allied to LACE-making and KNITTING, crochet is done with cotton thread and hook. Honoria NAGLE, a dedicated teacher who had studied in Paris, gained permission for four girls to enter the novitiate of the Ursuline nuns in Paris in 1769 so that they could be trained there and return to Cork to instruct the poor. Nuns taught the art of crochet to poverty-stricken men and women who could make a hook themselves. In 1841 it was reported that the crochet industry in Cork helped families to survive and also to earn the means to emigrate. To give employment in the famine years Mrs W. C. Roberts taught and organized crochet-making at Clones, Co. Monaghan. This artistic crochet work has been highly valued and modern fashion designers have sought it out to use for special features of their designs, such as hand-crochet collars, evening blouses etc.   H L M

Cronin, Anthony (1926–). Poet, novelist and essayist. His *Collected Poems* were published in 1973. More recently he has published a book of reminiscences (*Dead as Doornails*), a novel (*Identity Papers*) and a long poem (*Reductionist Poem*). His unique sojourn as a Government Advisor on the Arts will have long-term repercussions as he was responsible for setting up AOSDÁNA, for the benefit of writers and artists.   T McC

Crúachain. *See* RATHCROGHAN.

Cuala Press. The press, which had its origins in the Dun Emer Craft Centre (*see* DUN EMER GUILD), one of whose three main crafts was printing, produced its first book, *In the Seven Woods* by W. B. YEATS, in 1903. The press was later to produce prints and Christmas cards. The choice of what books were to be produced was in the hands of the editor, W. B. Yeats. The imprint of the company became 'The Cuala Press' after 1908, when Elizabeth Corbet (Lolly) Yeats and Susan Mary (Lily) Yeats took their side of the business to Churchtown and formed Cuala Industries. The Yeats sisters produced the printed material, beginning with *A Broadside* in 1908; the *Broadsides*, by their brother JACK B. YEATS, eventually changed into the *Broadsheets*, with poetry by various contributors and illustrations by contemporary Irish artists.   C MacG

Culdees. *See* CÉLÍ DÉ.

Cullen, Co. Tipperary. A village near which a small bog yielded many prehistoric antiquities, including gold objects, in the 18th and 19th centuries, as

recorded by Nash, Cleary, Armstrong, O'Halloran and O'Curry; it may have been the site of votive deposits. Many of the objects were late BRONZE AGE in type, and included some 300 swords; in 1753, thirteen of these were found, with a single purse-shaped scabbard chape. The 18th-century gold find made by John Damer (1744–76) of Shronell may have come from here. Nearby, on a hilltop to the SW, is the burial mound of LONGSTONE.   M H
T. Pownall, 'An Account of some Irish Antiquities', *Archaeologia* 3 (1775), 355–70.

cultural works of merit, tax exemption for. The Finance Act, 1969, enacted by Dáil Éireann provides that an individual who is resident in the Republic of Ireland and whose creative work – books, plays, musical compositions, paintings, sculptures etc. – is in the opinion of the Revenue Commissioners generally recognized as having cultural or artistic merit, shall, subject to approval, be entitled to have the profits or gains from the publication, production or sale of a work or works disregarded for all purposes of the Income Tax Acts.   C MacG

Cusack, Cyril (1910–   ). Actor; made his first stage appearance as a child in 1917. He joined the ABBEY THEATRE in 1932 and ran his own company, *c.* 1947–1961. Film appearances include *The Blue Veil, The Day of the Jackal, The Wild Heart* and *Jesus of Nazareth.* He has taken numerous leading roles in international theatres. He was awarded an honorary doctorate by the National University of Ireland in 1977.   C F-S

Cusack, Cyril. The well-known actor in the role of Conn, in a revival of Dion Boucicault's *The Shaughraun* at the Abbey Theatre, 1967.

Dagda. The father of the gods, his name means the 'Good God', and he is also known as Eochaid Ollathair ('Eochaid the great father') and In Ruad Rofhessa ('Ruad of Great Wisdom'). He is represented as a mighty warrior of huge size, possessed of a huge club and an inexhaustible cauldron. He is the god of Druidism and magic and lord of the Otherworld. *See* MYTHOLOGY.   DÓC

Daly, Padraig J. (1943–   ). Poet; born in Dungarvan, Co. Waterford. He has published two collections: *Nowhere But In Praise* (1978) and *That Day's Importance* (1981).   T McC

Daly, Richard (1758–1813). Actor, theatre manager and entrepreneur; born in Co. Westmeath, he was educated at Trinity College, Dublin. He purchased the Smock Alley Playhouse, Dublin, in 1788, but the venture did not flourish. He ran several provincial theatres and was manager of the Crow Street Theatre, Dublin, from 1788 until his retirement in 1798. *See* THEATRES.   CF-S

Danby, Francis (1793–1861). Painter; born at St John's near Killinick, Co. Wexford, he studied at the DUBLIN SOCIETY Schools. He never returned to Ireland after the visit he made to England with JAMES O'CONNOR and GEORGE PETRIE in 1813, settling first in Bristol and then, in 1824, in London. There for several years he had an enormously successful career, exhibiting landscapes, cataclysmic biblical scenes, and other subject pictures at the Royal Academy. After living in France and Switzerland for most of the 1830s he returned to England but never to the same success as before. In

Danby, Francis. A characteristic romantic landscape, *Liensfjord Lake in Norway,* oil on canvas, *c.* 1840. Victoria and Albert Museum, London.

1855 he won a prize, and great critical acclaim, for a seascape exhibited in the International Exposition in Paris. His romantic approach to nature had, however, been overtaken by a new, scientific and objective vision.　　　　　　　　　　　　　　　　　AOC
Eric Adams, *Francis Danby*, 1973.

Darley, Hugh Architect; he was a member of a quarry-owning family living in Co. Meath. He designed the ambitious St Peter's (Protestant) Church, Drogheda, Co. Louth, between 1749 and 1752, and in Dublin supervised the building of Theodore Jacobsen's west front of TRINITY COLLEGE. Also in Drogheda he designed the Mayoralty House in 1765, while a relation, George Darley, designed the Classical Tholsel (now a bank) in 1766. Frederick Darley, who built the new square in Trinity College and flourished in the 1820s and '30s, came from the same family.　　　WG

Davis, Thomas (1814–45). Poet and nationalist; born at Mallow, Co. Cork, he founded the extremely important newspaper *The Nation* in 1842. As leader of the Young Ireland Party, he was responsible for much of the flowery patriotism and starved verse characteristic of the pre-Yeats era. His *Poems* were published in 1846, and his *Essays and Poems* were republished (1946) in Dublin by Gill.　　　　　　　　　　　TMcC

Dawe, Gerald (1952–). Belfast poet; lived in Galway for some years. Published one volume of poems, *Sheltering Places* (1978), and a second collection is in preparation.　　　　　　　　　　　TMcC

Deane, Kearns. St Mary's (the Dominican church), Cork, showing the impressive Ionic portico, built 1832–9.

Deane, Seamus (1940–). Poet; an Ulsterman who teaches at University College, Dublin. A brilliant left-wing critic as well as a skilled poet, he has published two collections, *Gradual Wars* (1972) and *Rumours* (1977).　　　　　　　　　　　　　　　　TMcC

Deane and Woodward (architects). The Cork family of Deane was involved in architecture for more than a century. Thomas, later Sir Thomas, Deane (1792–1871) designed the Commercial Buildings, Cork (1811). He and his brother Kearns (d. 1847) designed the Savings Bank, Cork, while Kearns built St Mary's Church, Pope's Quay, Cork (1832–9). Sir Thomas built Dromore Castle, Co. Kerry, in the 1830s and the Tudor-Gothic University College, Cork (1845–9). His son, Sir Thomas Newenham Deane (1828–99) and Benjamin Woodward (1815–61) designed the Museum Building (now the Engineering School) in TRINITY COLLEGE in 1852, in the Venetian palazzo style, using the principles advocated by John Ruskin. Though the plan was that of John McCurdy, they experimented with structural polychromy and allowed their craftsmen (notably the O'Shea brothers) the liberty of individual expression. Deane and Woodward won the competition for the University Museum, Oxford, in 1854, and built St Anne's Schools, Molesworth Street, Dublin (1857–8), and the red-brick Kildare Street Club (1858–61). Other works include: Glandore, Monkstown, Co. Dublin; St Austin's Abbey, Carlow; and Brownsbarn, Co. Kilkenny. Sir T. N. Deane and Son designed Bray Town Hall, Co. Wicklow, in 1882 and Sir Thomas Manly Deane designed the NATIONAL MUSEUM and NATIONAL LIBRARY buildings (1884–90).　　WG

Delaney, Edward (1930–). Sculptor; born at Claremorris, Co. Mayo, he studied at the National College of Art and Design, Dublin, and in Germany. He has represented Ireland at the Paris Biennale, 1959, the New York World's Fair, 1965, and in Buenos Aires and Tokyo. He came to public notice in Ireland when he executed the memorial to Thomas Davis in College Green, Dublin, which gave rise to controversy. He was also responsible for the large public memorial to Wolfe Tone and the Famine in St Stephen's Green. His style has similarities to English sculpture of the 1950s, notably Armitage and Chadwick. He is at his best in smaller modelled and welded work with rich textural effects. His sculptures, which are consistently in a figurative idiom, show liveliness, imagination and often possess a distinctly romantic flavour.　　　JT
Irish Art 1943–1973, Rosc catalogue, Cork 1980.

delftware. *See* CERAMICS.

Derrynablaha, Co. Kerry. The site, 2 miles S of Ballaghbeama Gap on the Iveragh peninsula, of a series of fifteen carved rocks in three groups, comprising 320 BRONZE AGE rock-scribings; discovered in 1962, the carvings include concentric circles and ring-and-gutter devices. Some experts recognize among them a representation of a Late BRONZE AGE shield with a Vnotch of north European Herzsprung type, comparable to a wooden shield from Clonbrin, Co. Longford.   MH

E. G. Anati, 'New Petroglyphs at Derrynablaha, County Kerry, Ireland', *JCHAS* 68 (1963), 1–15.

Derrynaflan Hoard. A hoard, found in 1980 within the precincts of the ancient monastery of Derrynaflan, Co. Tipperary, consisting of a silver chalice, paten and its stand, a bronze strainer of ladle-like form and a bronze basin which had covered the other objects and was considerably decayed. The objects are now in the NMI. The date of burial of the hoard is unknown.

The paten, a large shallow silver dish with an elaborate foot, is decorated with stamped panels of interlace and Ultimate La Tène (*see* LA TÈNE) devices and glass and enamel settings; the upper surface is edged with a ring of gold filigree panels in gilt-bronze frames with, at intervals, elaborate studs of glass and enamel. The style is of the 8th century and compares closely with that of the silver Ardagh chalice (*see* ARDAGH HOARD) and the 'TARA' BROOCH. The chalice is of the large, two-handled ministerial type, strikingly similar in design to that from Ardagh. Its handles, handle-escutcheon, stem, foot and bowl-girdle bear elaborate patterns in a somewhat coarse filigree. The underside of the foot is decorated with cast interlace. Amber is used for the settings rather than glass. Resemblances to the decoration of certain 9th-century pseudo-penannular BROOCHES suggest a date of manufacture probably after 800.

The strainer is an elaborate version of the bronze ladles known in 8th/9th-century contexts, with the addition of a perforated sieve-plate to the bowl. It bears panels of stamped ornament, and glass studs with millefiori plaques. Its terminal has a domed rock-crystal backed by silver foil. The basin is of a type reasonably well-known in insular contexts.   MFR

de Vere, Sir Aubrey (1788–1846). Gentleman-poet; born Aubrey de Vere Hunt, at Curragh Chase, Co. Limerick. A man of mild emotions and author of milder sonnets, he was the father of the agitator-poet, Aubrey Thomas de Vere (1814–1902).   TMcC

Devlin, Denis (1908–59). Poet and diplomat; born at Greenock, Scotland, he brought an important internationalist voice to the parochial Irish atmosphere of the 1940s and '50s. Published three books of translation from St John Perse, *Rains* (1945), *Shows* (1945) and *Exile* (1949). He was appointed Irish Ambassador to Italy, 1958. His *Collected Poems* were published in 1964.   TMcC

Dillon, Gerard (1916–71). Painter, designer and graphic artist; born in Belfast, he studied art at Belfast Technical School. By 1936 he had taken up painting seriously, visiting Connemara. He joined the White Stag Group and, in 1943, the Dublin Painters Group and exhibited the following year at the IELA.

He visited Italy in 1947, and Spain about 1952, as well as living for a time on the island of Inishlacken off

Dillon, Gerard. *The Yellow Bungalow*, oil on canvas, *c.* 1950. Ulster Museum.

Roundstone, Co. Galway; he represented Ireland at the Guggenheim International (1958) and Great Britain at the Pittsburgh International Exhibition (1958). A retrospective exhibition of his work was held in Dublin and Belfast in 1972/3, jointly organized by the Arts Councils of Ireland and Northern Ireland.

Dillon also took up etching at the Dublin Graphic Studios. He is probably best known for his paper collage *Clown* pictures, as well as for his tapestries and murals.   CMacG

Dimma, Book of. A pocket gospel-book dating from *c.* mid-8th century, now in Trinity College, Dublin, library (A.IV.23 ms. no. 59). It consists of 74 folios, measuring 175 × 142 mm. (6⅞ × 5⅝ in.). Small and portable, it was written in cursive minuscule script, perhaps by three different scribes, using many abbreviations. the neatness of the writing and the compactness of the volume add to the charm of this ms. It is thought that the colophons, which include three separate mentions of the name 'Dimma', were contrived to link the writing to a contemporary of St Cronan (d. 665). The ms. was localized in Ireland at Roscrea, Co. Tipperary, from the 11th century. There are four coloured pages with portraits of the Evangelists Matthew, Mark, and Luke, and the eagle symbol of John; in style they are somewhat akin to the Echternach illuminations. The 'In [principio]' is decorated in St Gall style. The shrine made for the ms. is also in TCD library; dated *c.* 1150, it has silver-plated animal decoration, and was found in 1789 by boys hunting rabbits near Devil's Bit mountain.   GOS

Dixon, James. (1887–1970). Naive landscape painter; born on Tory Island, Co. Donegal, where he was inspired to paint by seeing the artist DEREK HILL at work. Much of his work is the narration of life on that storm-

Dixon, James. *West Town – Tory Island*, oil on paper. Private Collection.

girt island; gales at sea, coastal scenes, landscapes and the harvest all form part of his *oeuvre*. Although his work is much admired today, he did not have the success in his lifetime which another comparable painter, Alfred Wallis enjoyed in his. Works by Dixon can be seen in the Ulster Museum and the Hugh Lane Municipal Gallery of Modern Art, Dublin. C MacG

Donleavy, James Patrick (1926–). Writer; born in Brooklyn, N.Y., he has become an Irish citizen and lives in Co. Westmeath. His novels have Irish and American backgrounds: *The Ginger Man* (heavily censored in 1955 for its outspoken and comic lewdness), *A Singular Man* (1963), *The Saddest Summer of Samuel S.* (1966), *The Beastly Beatitudes of Balthazar B.* (1968), *A Fairy Tale of New York* (1973) – all of which he adapted for the stage – *The Destinies of Darcy Dancer, Gentleman* (1977) wholly set in Ireland, and *Schultz* (1980). BH

Dorsey (na Dóirse), Co. Armagh. Elongated fortified enclosure, measuring about 1,600 × 330 m. (1,750 × 360 yds), having its long axis aligned E–W. It consisted mainly of a double bank and ditch, 36 m. (39 yds) wide overall, the smaller bank outermost; the present top of the larger bank is 7·80 m. (25 ft 6 in.) above the original

bottom of the ditch. Along boggy stretches near the centre of each of the long sides, the rampart is continued by oak piling with horizontal beams. There are traces of a wooden guard-house at a break in the bank along the line of an old roadway in the SE sector.

Probably early IRON AGE in date; if so, it is the largest known fortification of the period in Ireland; its name (meaning 'the portals') may indicate that it lay on a roadway through the southern boundary of the territory of the Ulstermen. MH

Dowth, Co. Meath. Site of a group of PASSAGE GRAVES on a knoll 67 m. (220 ft) above sea-level at the E edge of the Boyne Valley cemetery. The large tumulus is 85 m. (280 ft) in diameter and 15 m. (49 ft) high, with a kerb of oblong boulders. Two tombs close together open from the W side; that on the N is cruciform, with a passage 8 m. (26 ft) long, chambers 6·50 m. (21 ft) wide and 3 m. (10 ft) high, with a unique L-shaped annexe off the right-hand side-chamber; that on the S has a passage 3·50 m. (11 ft 6 in.) long leading to a circular chamber 4·50 m. (14 ft 9 in.) across, with a single side-chamber on the S. There are several decorated stones in both tombs and kerb. A souterrain, apparently early IRON AGE and Early Christian in date, is incorporated into the W end of the mound.

The cairn had been dug into and its chambers exposed since before 1836. Frith made a large cutting into the tumulus from the E side in 1847, removing about 3,000 cu. m. (3,900 cu. yds) of material and discovering a narrow vertical shaft, 12 cm. (5 in.) in diameter and 10 m. (33 ft) high, at its centre. MH
M. Herity, *Irish Passage Graves*, 1974, pp. 247–50.

Dromore Castle, Co. Limerick. Built 1866–73 by the English architect E. W. Godwin (1833–86), the castle is a brilliant romantic creation based on original Irish material, including the ROCK OF CASHEL, a ROUND TOWER and local TOWER HOUSES. Its dramatic situation overlooking a lake emphasizes its jagged silhouette. WG

Dublin Metropolitan School. *See* NATIONAL COLLEGE OF ART AND DESIGN.

Dublin Society. Founded in 1731, the Society – which became the Royal Dublin Society in 1820 – is one of the oldest improvement societies in existence; its original aims were the encouragement of agriculture and industry, but in the 1740s the Society took over the drawing school run by the painter ROBERT WEST (*see* PAINTING); he continued to teach drawing there, while landscape and ornament were taught by James Mannin (or Manning). Later, *c.* 1765, THOMAS IVORY took charge of the new School of Architecture, and EDWARD SMYTH of the School of Modelling, 1811. Most leading artists received some of their training at the Society's Schools, which held annual exhibitions of students' work and awarded premiums. During its 250-year existence the Society has shown great adaptability: its offspring include the NATIONAL LIBRARY, the NATIONAL MUSEUM, the NATIONAL COLLEGE OF ART AND DESIGN, the BOTANIC GARDENS at Glasnevin, and the

Dowth. The large tumulus, rising to a height of 15 m. (50 ft) above the surrounding land.

Dromore Castle. The striking silhouette of E. W. Godwin's romantic castle, completed in 1873.

Ducart, Davis. The Custom House, Limerick, completed in 1769.

Veterinary College. At present it is best known for promoting the annual Horse Show at Ballsbridge (the Spring Show), for its chamber concerts and library, and for attention to applied science with special reference to agriculture. It has published *The Journal of Life Sciences* since 1978 and *The Journal of Earth Sciences* since 1977.   MC

James Meenan and Desmond Clarke (eds.), *The Royal Dublin Society 1731–1981*, 1981; H. F. Berry, *A History of the Royal Dublin Society*, 1915.

Ducart, Davis (d. *c.* 1786). Architect; the Piedmontese Daviso de Arcort, known in Ireland as Ducart, worked as an engineer on the Newry and Coalisland canals and subsequently in the south of Ireland as an architect. He created a house of Italianate warmth and gaiety at Kilshannig, Co. Cork (1765). He repeated the rear façade of Kilshannig at the Custom House, Limerick (1765), while the arcades and domed pavilions were used at his masterpiece, CASTLETOWN, Co. Kilkenny (*c.* 1767), and at Florencecourt, Co. Fermanagh (*c.* 1768). He also designed the Mansion House (now Mercy Hospital), Cork (1766), and Lota, Co. Cork (1768).   WG

Dún Aenghusa, Inishmore, Aran Islands. A multivallate stone fort on the 100 m. (330 ft) high cliff face in Kilmurvy townland. Originally there were four walls, the outer one enclosing 11 acres, and having its ends 400 m. (440 yds) apart at the cliff face. A *chevaux de frise*

Dún Aenghusa. Aerial view of the ancient stone fort in its cliff-top setting.

of limestone spikes 1 m. (3 ft) high, set upright or slanting outwards in fissures of the limestone, stands 9–24 m. (30–80 ft) wide outside the third wall from the centre of the original plan. The inner citadel, roughly semi-circular and 45 m. (150 ft) across, has walls 5 m. (16 ft) thick and 4 m. (13 ft) high, with a terraced wall with ladder-like steps and a single wall-chamber; the doorway, in the E side, has a stepped lintel. A square natural platform stands at the centre of the citadel. In 1839 an early Iron Age bronze bird-head fibula was found in its wall.   MH

T. J. Westropp, 'Aran Islands', *JRSAI* 25 (1895), 250–78.

Dun Emer Guild. One of the most enduring successes of the ARTS AND CRAFTS MOVEMENT, the Dun Emer Guild studio was founded in 1902 by Evelyn Gleeson (1855–1944) at Dundrum, Co. Dublin. A wide range of crafts was pursued, the foundress concentrating on carpets, rug-making and tapestry-weaving, with her associates – the Yeats sisters, Susan Mary (Lily) and Elizabeth Corbet – managing the embroidery and printing departments respectively. The aim of Dun Emer, expressed in their prospectus, was 'to find work for Irish hands in the making of beautiful things'. In 1908 the Yeats sisters took their side of the business to nearby Churchtown to form Cuala Industries (*see* CUALA PRESS), leaving Miss Gleeson to continue the work of the Guild, which was carried on in Dublin after her death by her niece and chief assistant, Katherine MacCormack, until the early 1960s. *See* CELTIC REVIVAL.   PL

Dun Emer Guild. An embroidery workshop, 1903.

Dunsany, Lord (Edward John Moreton Drax Plunkett, 18th Baron Dunsany; 1878–1957). Writer; born in London, Lord Dunsany's sympathies were strongly with the British Empire. He opposed Home Rule and remained at the periphery of the Irish Renaissance. The family seat is at Dunsany Castle, Co. Meath. Lord Dunsany published many volumes of stories and plays and achieved considerable popular success. His most characteristic works are fantasies with remote, exotic settings, written in poetic prose and embodying a personal mythology. Important volumes include *The Gods of Pegana* (1905), *The Sword of Welleran* (1908), and *Plays of Gods and Men* (1917).   BH

Mark Amory, *Lord Dunsany*, 1972.

Durcan, Paul (1944–). Poet; his prolific *oeuvre* is of immense value, combining humour, surrealism and acid commentary. He has published four main collections: *O Westport in the Light of Asia Minor* (1975); *Teresa's Bar* (1976); *Sam's Cross* (1978); and *Jesus, Break His Fall* (1980).   T McC

Durrow, Book of. The ms. (Trinity College, Dublin, library, A.IV.5, ms. no. 57), consisting of 248 folios, 245 × 145 mm. (9¾ × 5¾ in.), dates from the middle of the 7th century. It contains the four Gospels in Latin, with the usual introductory letter of Jerome, canon tables, prefaces, summaries, and glossary of proper names. There are 11 fully ornamented pages; 'carpet' pages – completely illustrated left-hand pages (cf. pl. VI) – of geometrical designs of exquisite precision and proportion include roundels, spirals, trumpet patterns, and panels of interlace in three dominant colours, yellow, green, and red. The 'biting animals' page with its rhythmical, lively interlace of great beauty, is of particular interest, recalling Saxon-style motifs similar to the Sutton Hoo decoration. The symbols of the four evangelists, man, eagle, calf, and lion – each deliberately stylized – are depicted on separate pages with coloured frames of outstanding beauty in the Old Latin order, although the gospel text is 'mixed' and largely Vulgate. Apart from discoloration on opening pages (one with a double 8-square cross and one with the symbols of the four evangelists grouped round a cross), the ornament retains a brilliant beauty gracing the formal, dignified designs. Mention is made of the book in the Annals of Clonmacnois (1627): Connell MacGeoghegan writes of Colum Cille (Columba; *see* MONASTICISM): 'he left a book to each of his churches in the kingdom, which bookes have a strange property, which is that if they or any of them had sunck to the bottom of the deepest waters they would not lose one letter, signe, or character of them, which I have seen partly myselfe of that book of them which is at Dorow in Ks County, for I saw the ignorant man that had the same in his custody, when sickness came upon cattle, for their remedy putt water on the book and suffered it to rest there awhile and saw alsoe cattle return to their former or pristin state and the book to receave no loss.'

The book remained in the monastery at Durrow, N of Tullamore, Co. Offaly, until it was placed by Bishop Henry Jones of Meath in Trinity College, Dublin, in

Durrow, Book of. Stylized Lion, symbol of St Mark; detail of a page from the 7th-century ms. TCD.

the 1660s. There was clearly a close connection between Northumbria and Ireland in the 7th century; Bede refers to Durrow as 'a noble monastery'. Adamnan mentions Durrow as an early foundation of Columba. However, the colophon which refers at the end of the ms to 'this little book' and 'Columba the writer who wrote this gospel for myself in the space of 12 days' is clearly a copy from another ms. and could not refer to Durrow's illuminated work.   GOS
Facsimile edition, *Evangeliorum Quattuor Codex Durmachensis* (2 vols.), 1960.

dyeing. From early times in Ireland cloth has been dyed to accommodate tastes in clothing (*see* COSTUME). Saffron-coloured clothing favoured in Gaelic society was among items forbidden by laws of 1536, intended to promote 'English Order, Habit and Language', but it is not known what dye was then used. There are two classes of dye: substantive dye gives colour directly to the material; adjective dye requires the use of a mordant to bring out the colour by preparing the fleece or yarn to take the dye. The earliest mordant used was mud and clay containing iron; leaves of the *fernog* (alder) were also used as a mordant, and later alum in the form of plant and mineral substances. Lichen dyes do not require a mordant. Of these the most popular have been *Parmelia omphalodes*, gathered from the rocks on the Donegal coast, and *Parmelia saxatilis* from the rocks of the Connemara coasts; both produce a tan-brown shade. A common plant, *Rubia peregrina*, which grows on the Burren coast and the Aran Islands, and *Rubia tinctorum* produce dye used for madder red, another popular tint. Blocks of imported indigo were used in Donegal, Mayo and Galway, prepared with urine to produce a blue dye. Mud-caked water-lily roots were used to dye black. Change began with the development of aniline dyes in 1826 and now well-tested chemical dyes have mostly replaced the traditional vegetable dyes.   HLM
Ethel Mairet, *Vegetable Dyes*, 1920.

Eamhain Macha (Navan Fort), Co. Armagh. A HILLFORT enclosing 18 acres, 3 miles W of Armagh. Excavations by D. M. Waterman in 1963–71 revealed three phases of construction under a mound 45 m. (150 ft) in diameter. A circular enclosure, 33 m. (110 ft) in diameter, defined by a broad, shallow ditch, had a palisade of spaced upright timbers; within was a series of eight consecutive circular houses, *c.* 12 m. (40 ft) in diameter, built of plank uprights set in wall trenches and with a porch fronting a cobbled area; this phase was dated by radiocarbon to *c.* 680–400 BC. In a second phase, three further consecutive round houses, each with two opposed entrances, were built on a different part of the same site. Artefacts from these phases were scarce; those found included lignite bracelets, glass beads, iron fragments, part of a Late Bronze Age socketed sickle, and coarse, flat-rimmed pottery. In a third phase, a massive circular timber structure, 39 m. (130 ft) in diameter, was built over the whole area; it had a gigantic central post, four concentric rows of posts set 3 m. (10 ft) apart and a double row of posts marking the way from the entrance at the W to the centre. This was apparently buried in the limestone cairn with an envelope of turves and soil, while the timbers were still standing *c.* 265 BC.
    The site was celebrated in Irish MYTHOLOGY as the seat of Concobhar Mac Neasa and the Red Branch Knights. Two fibulae of the 1st century AD are old finds from within the enclosure; a ceremonial horn found in the Loughnashade bog beside the hill can be dated to the 1st century BC.   MH
A. and W. Selkirk (eds.), 'Navan Fort', *Current Archaeology*, 2, No. 11 (Sept. 1970), 304–8.

Edgeworth, Maria (1768–1849). Writer; born in England in Oxfordshire, she accompanied her father, Richard Lovell Edgeworth, to his estate at Edgeworthstown in Co. Longford, where she mostly lived from 1782 until her death. Early children's stories were followed by *Practical Education* (1798), written with her father. *Castle Rackrent* (1800), her finest book, reveals the pressure of her Irish experience and the Enlightenment values she inherited from her father. Her friend, Sir Walter Scott, acknowledged the book's influence on his own work. Her other Irish fiction consists of *Ennui* (1809), *The Absentee* (1812), and *Ormond* (1817). Her other major and, to her, equally important work not concerned with Ireland ranges from *Belinda* (1801) through *Patronage* (1814) to *Helen* (1834). She also completed her father's *Memoirs*, published in 1820. *See* LITERATURE.   ICR
M. Butler, *Maria Edgeworth: A Literary Biography*, 1972.

education. Two distinct educational systems co-existed in Ireland from the Early Christian period until

79

the end of the Middle Ages: the BARDIC SCHOOLS – pagan and pre-Christian in origin but which survived as secular institutions after the defeat of the Druids and into the 17th century – and the MONASTIC SCHOOLS, the earliest of which were founded in the 5th century and which flourished until the latter part of the 12th century.

Following the ecclesiastical reforms of the 12th century, the introduction of monastic orders from the Continent and the Anglo-Norman invasion, some of the new monasteries maintained schools. It was reported in 1539 that six monasteries taught 'vertue, learnyng and . . . the English tonge and behavior'; these were: the Nunnery of Grace Dieu, Co. Dublin, for girls; and, for boys, St Mary's Abbey, Christ Church, and a house of the White Monks in Dublin, Greatconnell, Co. Kildare, and Jerpoint, Co. Kilkenny. Outside the PALE there were schools attached to the friaries of the Franciscan Third Order Regular, whose system was preferred in Ireland to the system of cathedral schools and chantry schools which existed in England and Scotland. There were, however, a few collegiate churches in Ireland prior to the Reformation: those at Drogheda, Co. Louth, and Kilmallock, Co. Limerick, were founded as early as the 13th century; Gowran, Co. Kilkenny, in 1312; Scattery Island, Co. Limerick, was confirmed in 1400; and Cashel was flourishing by 1440. Later collegiate churches were: Youghal, Co. Cork (1464); Athenry, Co. Galway, and Galway (1484); Slane, Co. Meath (1512), and Maynooth, Co. Kildare (1518). At Kilkenny a College for the Vicars Choral of the Cathedral, with a common hall and other buildings, was founded in the latter half of the 13th century. At Kildare Cathedral a College for the Dean and Chapter was founded c. 1500.

From the beginning of the 13th century there is record of Irish students of divinity at Oxford and Cambridge and of law at the London Inns of Court. In the 14th century Irish medical students began to go to France and Italy to advance or complete their studies.

After the Reformation, at the elementary level, Parish Schools were promoted by an Act of Parliament of 1537 which enjoined every clergyman to keep a school in his parish and to pay a schoolmaster to teach in English, but although this Act was reinforced by another in 1696, by the end of the 18th century only some 200 Parish Schools were operating. Efforts to increase the system were successful; by 1809, approximately 23,000 pupils were attending a total of 549 Parish Schools and by 1825 the number of these schools in operation had risen to 800.

Under various private enterprises, 65 so-called 'English Schools' were established in various parts of the country in the 18th century with a curriculum usually confined to reading, writing and arithmetic, although a few taught practical subjects also. Most of these privately founded schools were strictly Protestant in orientation but some did admit Roman Catholic pupils; the five Forkhill schools in Co. Armagh had Protestant teachers but a majority of Roman Catholic pupils. The school at Finglas, Co. Dublin, was intended for Roman Catholic children to be raised as Protestants. Drelincourt's Charity School for Girls brought all its pupils up in the Established Church and taught them reading, spelling, needlework and straw-plaiting.

The Charter Schools were founded in 1733 with the aim of accepting as boarders poor Roman Catholic children under ten years of age to raise them as Protestants and prepare them for apprenticeship. Over £1,000,000 of public funds, as well as private funds, were spent on this project and about sixty Charter Schools were built. However, as the pupils were obliged to work for several hours a day in farms or factories attached to the schools and were frequently poorly clothed and ill-fed, the system eventually attracted considerable adverse criticism from enlightened circles. In 1832 public funds were withdrawn, the system abandoned, and the schools used for Protestant pupils.

While a very few children of the Roman Catholic majority of the population did attend Parish and English Schools or were converted in the Charter Schools, most were instructed at elementary level, if at all, in the HEDGE SCHOOLS. The schools opened in Cork by NANO NAGLE in the 1750s operated in defiance of the law.

The Relief Act of 1782 finally opened the way for the establishment of Roman Catholic schools but the Established Church continued to see the school system as a vehicle for proselytization (which they regarded as a zealous duty). Therefore, when State-funded elementary education was introduced in 1832 it was strongly opposed by the Established Schools. The principle in the new National Schools was that no attempt should be made to disturb the religious beliefs of any sect or denomination of Christians in the schools. This idea of 'united education' was not approved by the Established Church, which deplored the exclusion of the Scriptures in the curriculum and the admission of Roman Catholic priests to the National Schools to give religious instruction to the Roman Catholic pupils. The Presbyterian Church, which maintained that the Bible should be the basis of elementary education, also opposed the State system. The majority of the Roman Catholic hierarchy approved the new State system, but Archbishop McHale of Tuam remained a vociferous opponent of it. Despite the difficulties, a non-denominational teacher-training college was set up in 1838 in Marlborough Street, Dublin, to which women were admitted in 1845. This was followed by Model Schools for early teacher training and, by the end of the century, by several denominational teacher-training colleges. The Established Church, the Roman Catholic Church and the Presbyterians were each represented on the Board of Commissioners of the National Schools, the representatives being nominated by the Lord Lieutenant. These Commissioners prescribed the textbooks to be used in the schools; these books were well printed, well illustrated and well bound. In necessitous cases they were provided gratis, but were normally purchased by pupils for a few pence; as the same textbooks remained in use for about 70 years, they were usually passed on in families. The literary material was selected with careful discrimination, but anything which tended to stimulate Irish nationalism was excluded. While the system and curriculum did have early inadequacies, it may best be judged by the fact that it reached a high enough level to cause even parents who could afford private education to send their children to National Schools, in a number of which extra-curricular subjects such as instrumental music, French and Latin were offered outside school hours.

Changes instituted in 1904 allowed for bilingual (English and Irish) programmes in the Gaeltacht regions. With Independence the desire for a central role for the IRISH LANGUAGE and an Irish emphasis in the teaching of other subjects influenced educational policies and the exigencies of cultural nationalism took precedence over other needed reforms. The programme framed in 1922 provided for the use in infant schools of Irish only and of Irish as the medium of instruction in the senior schools for history (which was to be exclusively the history of Ireland), geography, drill and singing. This programme was not easy to implement but it set the general pattern for the next fifty years and, although there were minor modifications, mastery of the Irish language and the promotion of a patriotic and Gaelic outlook remained paramount. A test in oral Irish was introduced for teachers in 1926. The new programme launched in 1971 was ideologically child-centred, allowing teachers a wide measure of freedom. Guidelines are provided but teachers are encouraged to adapt to the needs of the pupils and their environment in teaching a wide range of obligatory subjects including religion, Irish, English, mathematics, arts and crafts, social and environmental studies, civics, geography, history and music.

In 1982 more than 96% of primary education in the Irish Republic is State-aided. About one in six of the national schools (catering for about one-third of all pupils) are convent or monastery schools but all must comply with the rules and regulations of the Department of Education. Although below the compulsory age, 85% of children aged 4 and 5 attend school. The minimum school-leaving age is 15.

At secondary level, the Diocesan Schools were established under an Act of Parliament of 1570 which provided for one free school in the principal shire town of each diocese. However, by the end of the 18th century there were still only twelve such schools and when the last was opened, at Waterford in 1862, there were fifteen; they were discontinued following the disestablishment of the Church of Ireland in 1869. Royal Schools to provide free secondary education were planned with the Ulster Plantation schemes in the reign of James I, one each for the counties of Armagh, Cavan, Derry, Donegal, Fermanagh and Tyrone. Of these the Armagh Royal School and the one established in Co. Fermanagh in 1608 (now known as the Portora Royal School) were the most successful, with several distinguished alumni including OSCAR WILDE, who attended Portora.

There were also some privately endowed grammar

The foundress and educational pioneer Nano Nagle with pupils; engraving by Charles Turner published in 1809.

schools which took both fee-paying and non-paying pupils. One was founded at Kilkenny in 1538 by the Earl and Countess of Ormond. In the 1560s it was conducted by Peter White, a Roman Catholic priest who was an Oxford graduate and enjoyed a high reputation. At that time the school received both Roman Catholic and Protestant pupils, but in that respect it was an early exception to the strong bias of post-Reformation schools in Ireland at all levels in favour of the promulgation of the Protestant faith. The Kilkenny Grammar School preceded Kilkenny College (founded by the Duke of Ormonde in the following century), which is still in operation. Other grammar schools were founded in the 17th century. The one which became Foyle College dated from 1617; at Lifford, Co. Donegal, the school was founded in 1619; the Blue Coat School near Dublin, established by Royal Charter in 1671, is now King's Hospital School; Midleton School, Co. Cork, founded in 1696, survives as Midleton College. Exceptionally, in the school at Clonmel, Co. Tipperary, founded in 1685, trade and business subjects were taught at the request of parents, instead of the usual Classical curriculum. Erasmus Smith endowed grammar schools at Drogheda, Co. Louth, and in Galway and Tipperary, with the aim of propagating the Protestant faith. Smith's Royal Charter of 1669 ensured the Protestant allegiance not only of the masters of the schools but also of the ushers. Ennis Grammar School, Co. Clare, was funded later (1773) from a Smith endowment. Wilson's Hospital, a privately endowed Protestant school, still operates in the building constructed for it in 1759 near Multyfarnham, Co. Westmeath; it is now a secondary-level co-educational boarding school.

In 1881 there were fifteen privately funded grammar schools in Ireland. St Columba's College, Rathfarnham, which is now co-educational, was opened at Stackallan, Co. Meath, in 1843 to educate the sons of the Church of Ireland gentry. The Irish language was included in the college's curriculum until 1854. Alexandra College for young women opened in Dublin in 1866.

Following the Relief Act of 1782, the Presbyterians established secondary-level schools, beginning in 1786 with the Royal Academy, Belfast, to which was added a girls' school in 1901; it became co-educational in 1923. The Belfast Royal Academical Institution, founded by public subscription in 1810 principally to educate candidates for the Presbyterian ministry, also admitted candidates for the Roman Catholic priesthood who were preparing to study at Maynooth. St Andrew's College, a Presbyterian school in Dublin, was founded in 1894.

Two prominent non-conformist educational establishments were founded in the 19th century, one in 1845 – the Wesleyan Classical and Commercial School, Dublin, which became Wesley College – and one in 1865 – Methodist College, Belfast, which a hundred years later was, with nearly two thousand pupils, the largest school in Ireland.

The Society of Friends, who had started educational facilities in Quaker Meeting Houses in the latter years of the 17th century, established a number of schools in the 18th century. Their co-educational Newtown School at Waterford was founded in 1798.

At various times in the latter half of the 17th century Jesuits contrived to run schools at New Ross, Dublin, Armagh, Waterford, Cashel, Drogheda and Kilkenny. Little is known, however, of the fee-paying schools kept by Roman Catholic schoolmasters in the towns in defiance of the Penal Laws. In a letter of 1741 Brian O'Rourke, Roman Catholic Bishop of Killala, mentions the wide difference in the current method of teaching and that of fifty years before and the lack of proficient teachers; the diet and schooling of the Bishop's young kinsman in Sligo cost more than £8 per annum in 1741 and his curriculum included the Classics (Ovid) and grammar. EDMUND IGNATIUS RICE must have attended such a school at Kilkenny in the 1770s.

The first Roman Catholic ventures in secondary education following the Relief Act were diocesan colleges: in 1783 an academy at Kilkenny, which was to become the present St Kieran's College in 1839; in 1793, St Patrick's College, Carlow; and St Jarlath's College at Tuam, Co. Galway, which was to the fore in the promotion of the Irish language in education. Clongowes Wood College, where JAMES JOYCE and many other distinguished men were to be educated, was opened by Jesuits in 1814. Other religious orders followed suit: among the earliest were the Cistercians in 1845, the Holy Ghost Fathers with Blackrock College in 1860, and the Marists at Dundalk in 1861. The Benedictines, who did not return to stay until 1927, then established a distinguished school at Glenstal Abbey, Co. Limerick.

In the field of Roman Catholic education in the 19th century the CHRISTIAN BROTHERS (who became a religious society under Edmund Rice in 1808 and had already opened their first school in 1804), the Presentation Brothers, and the Congregation of the Brothers of St Patrick (who opened their first school at the beginning of the century in a disused chapel at Tullow, Co. Carlow), were all three extremely active and successful. Besides these Irish-founded congregations, Carmelites returned from banishment and c. 1813 started a school at Clondalkin. In 1820 the Franciscans opened schools in the Archdiocese of Tuam. Among the many other orders with schools are the Oblates of Mary Immaculate, the Dominicans and the Austin Friars. The De La Salle Brothers came in 1880.

The first order of nuns to open a school in Ireland after the Reformation were the Ursulines; they came to Cork from France to open their school in 1771. NANO NAGLE, who was responsible for their coming, founded an Irish congregation – the Presentation Sisters – who were pioneers in education for girls in Ireland, followed a few years later by two other Irish congregations, the Sisters of St Brigid (founded 1807) and the Irish Sisters of Charity (founded 1815). The Dominican sisters, who had contrived to maintain a clandestine presence in the 18th century, emerged to open convents and schools. The Sisters of Mercy, founded by CATHERINE MCAULEY, established no less than 150 schools, as well as orphanages, industrial schools and teacher-training colleges. The Loreto Sisters, who came to Ireland in 1822, opened schools for girls, as did the nuns of the Society of the Sacred Heart who came in 1842, and those of the Society of the Faithful Companions of Jesus, who came in 1844. Later arrivals who also opened schools were: the Sisters of Charity of St Vincent de Paul, who came 1855; the Daughters of the Heart of Mary, who came in 1856; the Sisters of St Louis, who came from France in 1859; the Sisters of the Sacred Heart of Mary, who came in 1870; and the Sisters of the Cross and Passion, whose first establishment in Ireland dates from 1878. Others followed, among them the Poor Servants of the Mother of God (an order founded in England) and Benedictine nuns from Ypres in Belgium, who established their abbey at Kylemore Castle, Co. Galway, in 1921 with a distinguished boarding school for girls.

Generally, secondary education in Ireland in the 19th century remained wedded to the English grammar-school tradition with a humanistic intellectual approach. First place was accorded to English language and literature and the Classics, with science and mathematics very much in second place. After Independence, State-funding to private secondary schools was increased and the teaching of Irish was introduced. A new programme came into operation in 1924; schools where Irish was the official language received an additional grant of 25%. Irish became an obligatory subject for the Intermediate Certificate in 1928 and for the Leaving Certificate from 1934 until 1973. Vocational schools were established following the Vocational Education Act of 1930. The first State-run comprehensive schools were opened in 1966 but were superseded by community schools. In the autumn of 1967 free post-primary education became available. The present curriculum requires Irish, English, history and geography, mathematics, science or a foreign language or a commerical business subject, and civics, plus physical education, singing and, for girls, home economics. In vocational, comprehensive and community schools other subjects may be substituted for history and geography – technical drawing, art, home economics or commerce. In the academic year 1978/9 there were 196,606 pupils attending secondary schools, while 68,120 were at vocational schools, 14,204 at community schools and 8,152 at comprehensive schools.

At the higher level of education after the Reformation, TRINITY COLLEGE, DUBLIN, founded in 1592, long remained Ireland's only university. In its early years some Roman Catholics studied there but from 1637 until 1793 Roman Catholics and Dissenters were debarred from taking degrees; Irish Presbyterians seeking a university education tended to go to Scotland to study, while Roman Catholics resorted to universities on the Continent. Young men destined for the priesthood were usually sent to the Irish colleges which had been established in France, Belgium, Spain and Italy, until Maynooth College was founded in 1795 by the Government for the education of future Roman Catholic priests in Ireland. Trinity, which enjoyed a high reputation in the teaching of Hebrew and the classical languages, counted many famous names among its alumni, including JAMES USSHER, BERKELEY, SWIFT, CONGREVE, GOLDSMITH, EDMUND BURKE, THOMAS MOORE, THOMAS DAVIS, OSCAR WILDE, the mathematician Sir William Rowan Hamilton, the patriots Robert Emmet and Wolfe Tone, and for centuries the majority of the clergy and bishops of the Church of Ireland. Trinity's monopoly of university-level education in Ireland lasted, save for Maynooth College, until the middle of the 19th century. The non-denominational Queen's Colleges at Belfast, Cork and Galway were set up following an Act of Parliament of 1845; in 1850 The Queen's University was created to unite the three and to hold examinations. As a result of the implacable opposition of the Roman Catholic hierarchy to the Queen's Colleges, the Catholic University was established in Dublin in 1854, with Cardinal Newman as its first Rector and reliant on voluntary aid alone. The Presbyterians established Magee College at Londonderry in 1865.

The University Education (Ireland) Act of 1879 dissolved the Queen's University and established the Royal University of Ireland as an examining institution and to confer degrees. Its thirty-two salaried fellowships were distributed among the professional staff of the Catholic University (which was restructured to become University College, Dublin, in 1882), the three Queen's Colleges and Magee College. A number of students from the new women's colleges also sat for the examinations of the Royal University and obtained degrees. Altogether during the twenty-nine years of its existence the Royal University provided an important stimulus to intellectual and educational development. It was dissolved in 1908 when the Government established in its place two State-endowed universities, the National University of Ireland (with constituent University Colleges in Dublin, Cork and Galway), and Queen's University, Belfast (in place of Queen's College, Belfast). The governing bodies of the two universities included representatives of both the Roman Catholic and Protestant hierarchy, professional men, businessmen and local politicians.

The NUI, which granted recognized status to Maynooth College in 1910, now has five other recognized colleges: St Patrick's College of Education and Our Lady of Mercy College of Education – both in Dublin – were recognized in 1974, as was Mary Immaculate College of Education in Limerick. The Royal College of Surgeons, Dublin, became a recognized college of the NUI in 1977, followed by St Angela's College, Sligo, in 1978.

A student-grant scheme linked to a means test was introduced in 1968 for third-level education. The Higher Education Authority set up in the same year was granted statutory powers in 1971; it is a body corporate with planning and budgetary authority, the funding agency for all the universities and other third-level institutions in the Republic. This includes those grouped as the Dublin Institute of Technology, Thomond College, Limerick, the NATIONAL COLLEGE OF ART AND DESIGN, the National Institutes for Higher Education (which opened to students at Limerick in 1972 and at Ballymun, Dublin, in 1980), Limerick Technical College, the Crawford Municipal School of Art and Cork School of Music, the School of Art at Dun Laoghaire, Co. Dublin, and the nine Regional Technical Colleges, the first five of which were opened in 1969.   B de B

Edwards, Hilton (1903–82). English actor and director; he came to Ireland to join Anew McMaster's company in 1928. He founded Dublin Gate Theatre with MÍCHEÁL MAC LÍAMMÓIR, and brought to Ireland a standard of stage presentation hitherto unknown, emphasizing techniques of lighting and movement inspired by contemporary European theatre. He directed over 300 productions at the Gate, and also in Britain, Europe, North America and the Near East. *See* THEATRES: Dublin.)   CF-S

Elvery, Beatrice Moss. *See* GLENAVY, LADY.

embroidery. The ancient stories of the Ulster Cycle relate that Emer, wife of Cuchulainn, was a famous embroideress, but no vestige of early Irish embroidery work remains. Indeed, the earliest known example in the country seems to be the Lennox quilt, embroidered with brilliant flowers and foliage by Martha Lennox in Belfast, signed and dated 1712; it is now in the Ulster Museum. In the 18th century white embroidery work was favoured for quilts and for christening robes which were handed down in families for generations. About 1825 at Mountmellick, Co. Laois, a town with a strong

embroidery. Two examples of 'Mountmellick work', using designs based on nature.

engraving. View from Carlisle Bridge, Dublin (detail), from *Coloured Views of Dublin*, 1820, by Henry Brocas.

Quaker establishment, Mrs Johanna Carter is credited with having started a thick style of stitch done with knitting cotton on white satin jean. This white padded embroidery, usually with designs based on nature, e.g. blackberries, foliage, acorns and wheat, is known as 'Mountmellick work'. In 1829, John Cochrane opened an embroidery branch at Donaghadee, Co. Down, where the work was known locally as 'sprigging' or 'flowering'. The articles came to the workers with the designs already stamped; wages were low but families worked together and women were able to do this skilled work at home.

Lily Yeats, one of the co-foundresses of the DUN EMER GUILD (1902) where she was in charge of the embroidery section, had worked in London under the influence of William Morris. The Guild's most important commission was for LOUGHREA CATHEDRAL, for which they embroidered superb sets of vestments and twenty-four banners, mostly depicting Irish saints, worked in silk and wool on linen with a needlepoint background to designs by JACK YEATS (brother of Lily) and his wife Mary Cottenham Yeats. Subsequently, in their next enterprise, Cuala Industries (*see* CUALA PRESS), Lily Yeats and her sister continued to produce embroidered baby garments, frocks, cot covers, christening robes and cloaks. The magnificent embroidered vestments for the HONAN CHAPEL, Cork, were designed by Ethel Josephine Scally (d. 1916) and made in the workshops of Barry M. Egan, Cork.   HLM
E. Boyle, *The Irish Flowerers*, 1971.

engraving. The earliest known print done in Ireland was engraved by Gaspar Huybrechts (1619–84) of Antwerp at Kilkenny in 1645. At the close of the 17th century Edwin Sandys was working as an engraver in Dublin, where he drew and engraved a portrait of Sir William Petty in 1685, maps of Londonderry (1693), and a view of the Giant's Causeway (1696); he died in

1708. The first known mezzotint engraver in the country was Thomas Beard, who came from London *c.* 1720 and worked in Dublin. Engravings by Philip Simms of Dublin were published from 1725 by George Faulkner and others; in 1728 Grierson published engravings by L. Dempsey and, from 1723, engravings by James Gwim, a native of Co. Kildare, originally a coach-painter, who later went to London where he worked as a designer in the Battersea Enamel works then under the management of John Brooks, who had himself left Dublin in 1746.

Brooks, a native of Dublin, had an engraving published there in 1730 by Fuller; subsequently he spent some time in London, where he gained experience with the Dutch engraver John Faber the Younger. On his return to Dublin, Brooks opened a studio where he was joined by a brilliant assistant, Andrew Miller, a Londoner who had also trained under Faber. Several illustrious engravers learned their art in Brooks's studio and with Miller, whose influence was considerable in Dublin, where he lived and worked until his death in 1763. The engravers trained by Brooks and Miller in Dublin mostly emigrated to London where they inaugurated the great 18th-century school of mezzotint engravers in England. Prominent among these Dublin-trained engravers were: JAMES MCARDELL; Richard Houston (1721–75), who followed Brooks to London where he executed excellent engravings after Rembrandt, a fine series of portraits of statesmen, and also painted miniatures; Charles Spooner, a native of Co. Wexford who settled in London, where he died in 1767; and Richard Purcell, who also settled in London, where he died *c.* 1766. Others who were probably also pupils of Brooks and/or Miller include: Edward Fisher, born in Dublin in 1722, who settled in London; Michael Jackson of Dublin, who engraved portraits there and also sold prints; and Michael Ford, who took over

Brooks's Dublin premises on Cork Hill. Thomas Chambers (*c.* 1724–1789), who left Dublin for London *c.* 1756 after practising for ten years in Ireland as a line engraver, had studied in the DUBLIN SOCIETY's Schools but may also have had instruction from Miller.

Despite the fact that Dublin's most proficient engravers went with their expertise to London to the benefit of the art there, a number of good engravers were trained in the Dublin Society's Schools in the latter half of the 18th century. Notable among these were: John Dixon, who engraved Rocque's map of Co. Dublin in 1760 but later settled in London, where he executed brilliant prints after Reynolds; James Watson, who went to London in 1764 to work with McArdell (his daughter Caroline, born 1760/1, became engraver to Queen Caroline); Benjamin Clayton, the progenitor of several generations of Dublin mezzotint and wood engravers, remained in Ireland, as did William Esdall (d. 1795) who entered the Society's Schools in 1765 and specialized in book illustration. In the next generation William Nelson Gardiner, George Gonne, John Mannin, Charles Henecy, William Paulet Carey and others had all studied in the Society's Schools. Henry Brocas (1762–1837), as well as painting landscapes, was a prolific engraver. John Logan (1750–1805), a native of Co. Waterford, excelled as a seal engraver, Edward Lyons (1726–1801) specialized in heraldic work, while the gentleman-amateur Captain William Baillie (1723–1810) began with etchings and later executed able mezzotint engravings of old master paintings. In Cork, Daniel Corbett engraved the plates for Smith's *History of Cork*, 1750. The prolific Dublin-born engraver Thomas Burke (1749–1815), a pupil of Dixon, settled in London where Angelica Kauffmann favoured him to engrave her work. Dublin also produced talented gem-engravers. John Debenham, an English engraver, settled in Dublin *c.* 1767 and worked there until the end of the century.

Numerous engravers of merit worked in Dublin in the 19th century, some, like Benjamin Clayton Jun. and Caroline Millard (*née* Clayton), worked principally in wood; Henry Brocas Jun. (*c.* 1798–1873) was also a landscape painter; Benjamin Clayton III was also a miniature painter. Erin Corr (1803–62) achieved fame as an engraver in France and Belgium where he lived and worked. BdeB

Ennis, John (1944–). Poet; a native of Westmeath, settled in Waterford City. Won the Patrick Kavanagh Award in 1975. Two years later he published *Dolmen Hill*, containing an amazing long poem 'Orpheus', which won the Listowel Writers' Week Award in 1977. T McC

Ensor, John (fl. 1750–70). Architect; an assistant of RICHARD CASTLE, he was involved with the development of Parnell Square, Dublin, in the 1750s. He laid out Merrion Square in 1762 and designed Antrim House at the east end of the Square. He built the Rotunda (beside the Rotunda Hospital) in 1764 though its external appearance was altered in 1786. WG

Fallon, Padraic (1905–74). Poet and playwright; born at Athenry, Co. Galway. He is better known for his plays *The Seventh Step* (1954) and *Sweet Love Till Morn* (1971) and radio plays than for his posthumously published poems. T McC

Fallon, Peter (1951–). Poet; his own poetry is much overshadowed by his enormous liveliness as a publisher. Fallon, like James Laughlin of *New Directions*, obscured his own creative talents while asssembling a comprehensive list of Irish poets – but his own work in *The First Affair* (1974) and *The Speaking Stones* (1978) deserves attention. T McC

Farquhar, George (1678–1707). Playwright; born in Derry, Farquhar attended Trinity College, Dublin, before commencing as an actor at the Smock Alley Playhouse. Abandoning the stage to write, he produced his first play in London in 1699, but wrote nothing of lasting value before *The Recruiting Officer* (1706) and *The Beaux' Stratagem* (1707), two fine late contributions to Restoration comedy. ICR
Eric Rothenstein, *George Farquhar*, 1967; Albert Farmer, *George Farquhar*, 1966.

Farrell, Michael (1940–). Painter and graphic artist; born in Kells, Co. Meath, he studied at St Martin's School of Art, London, and at the Colchester College of Art. He has exhibited in London from 1957 and has exhibited and worked in New York, Dallas and Paris. Represented Ireland at many of the international festivals and Biennale exhibitions. He was given a retrospective exhibition in the Douglas Hyde Gallery, Trinity College, Dublin, in 1979; his works can be seen in many public collections in Ireland, including the Hugh Lane Municipal Gallery of Modern Art, Dublin. CMacG
Michael Farrell retrospective, exhibition catalogue (Douglas Hyde Gallery, TCD), 1979.

fashion design. Modern Irish fashion, with sales figures which reached £159,000,000 (wholesale) in 1978, and currently employing over 20,000 people, had its origins both in Court dressmaking, which flourished in Dublin until the demise of the Vice-regal Lodge society after 1921, and in the traditional rural skills of handcraft in fabric and KNITTING. While these two traditions had co-existed to fulfil different requirements, they were to merge later and be transformed by the organized effort of a group of pioneer entrepreneurs who foresaw the commercial and aesthetic value of Irish fashion.

Although a menswear tailoring factory, the first in Europe, had been established in Limerick in 1851, it was only after the formation of the Irish Free State

fashion design. Matching berry-red suede blouse and Irish tweed pants, from the 1982 autumn collection of Ib Jorgensen.

that industrial development benefited from the protection policy adopted in the early 1930s, when family firms like Glen Abbey and Weartex, manufacturing women's and men's wear respectively, were founded.

During the 1920s and '30s the fashion trade in Dublin and in the major cities such as Cork and Galway was centred around the big stores: Switzer's, Brown Thomas, Arnott's, McBirney's, and Clery's in Dublin: Cash's and the Munster Arcade in Cork; the Munster House in Kilkenny; Cannock's Drapery Warehouse in Limerick; and Alexander Moon and Co. in Galway. In addition to their ready-to-wear lines, many of these and shops in smaller provincial towns, operated as 'costumiers', producing high-quality mantles and gowns made on the premises by their own tailors and dressmakers, while some also had their own milliners and furriers. Design guidance in these establishments came either from the well-known English pattern-book stylists, like Bell's of South Molton Street, London, or more exclusively from 'toiles' imported from France, this being the heyday of French *haute couture*, which dominated fashion all over Europe.

Outside the metropolitan areas, dressmakers working from their homes continued to cater for a local clientèle. Dressmaking then, as now, often ran in families, the skills being handed down from one generation to the next from mother to daughter, while country tailors provided a service for both men and women.

One of the most important aspects of modern Irish fashion, and a prime factor in its growth and development, must be the island's indigenous TEXTILES. The many fabrics included: handwoven tweeds and knits that were the result of an unbroken craft tradition; the black and white flecked tweed of Donegal; the unbleached cream tweed known as *bainin*: the fuchsia-dyed red flannel; and, in more sophisticated vein, Irish poplin, a fine crossweave of wool and silk. From Belfast came fine linens, and exquisite handmade LACE emerged from the cottages of Carrickmacross, Limerick and Killarney. Fine CROCHET was another popular and widespread skill. Designs in EMBROIDERY were fashionable, especially on linen underwear.

It is not surprising that by the late 1940s such a wealth of inspirational material stimulated the exploration and organization of an export market. The pioneer in this field was Jack Clarke who, using Irish fabrics, manufactured (under the label 'Countrywear') high-quality coats and suits for women; as early as 1948 he exported to the USA, where he opened his first account with the distinguished sportswear store, Abercrombie & Fitch of New York. Shortly after Clarke came Donald Davies, who became famous for his use of featherweight tweed woven in 'jewel' colours.

In 1953, Clarke's protégée Sybil Connolly emerged with the brilliant innovation of finely pleated Irish linen used as a textured fabric. She combined this with the use of traditional red flannel and with black woollen shawls, and thus the romantic Irish fashion legend was born.

The movement gained strength and momentum throughout the 1950s with designers like Irene Gilbert and Ib Jorgensen. Mary O'Donnell and Nelli Mulcahy utilized Irish crochet and tweeds. Maureen Evans transformed the traditional Aran knitwear into high fashion. From its traditional handcrafted past, knitwear has developed into a leading contribution to the fashion scene, as shown by designers Michelina Stacpoole (who came to Ireland from Italy), Jodi Knits, Pallas, and Cyril Cullen. While Dublin began to attract an international press to its fashion show, the export drive was building up until, under the auspices of the Irish Export Board, a major breakthrough was made in 1966; a group of manufacturers including Jimmy Hourihan and John Hegarty were successfully launched on the American market. The foray into the sterling market which began in 1958 has been steadily expanding.

Many Irish designers succeed in making a major impact outside Ireland: Digby Morton, John Cavanagh, Owen at Lachasse and, perhaps the most original and best known, Michael of London, all members of the Incorporated Society of British Fashion Designers, enjoyed considerable influence and success throughout the 1950s and '60s.

Many of the Irish designers who first became known in the 1950s are still successful. Ib Jorgensen, now established as Ireland's leading designer, shows collections twice yearly and sells in his shops in Dublin and London; Sybil Connolly has added textile design to her repertoire. Specialist designers are also prominent: T. Wolfangel, Richard Lewis and Pat Crowley, as well as an increasing number of ready-to-wear designers; most of these export, and specialize in the casual classics and sportswear characteristic of fashion trends in the 1980s. Also notable in this field are Peter Fitzsimon, Michael Jacobs, Patrick Howard, Brian Tucker, Jody Carr and Michael Mortell.

Increased professionalism and organization has placed the Irish fashion industry in the position of prominence it occupies in the country's economy today, its awareness of technology is evident not only in its production and construction techniques but also in its management structuring and its forward looking design policies. The Irish Export Board (formed in 1952), the Industrial Training Board (AnCO), and the Apparel Division of the Confederation of Irish Industries – all Government-sponsored organizations – have guided and encouraged industry by financial grants and training facilities, while the influence of the School of Fashion and Textiles and of the NATIONAL COLLEGE OF ART AND DESIGN is already remarkable. PJ

Fay, Frank (1871–1931) and **William George** (1872–1947). Actors; brothers, born in Dublin, they ran their own company in Dublin until joining the Irish Literary Theatre in 1902, where Willie was largely responsible for creating the economic style of production which was to become the hallmark of the ABBEY THEATRE; he created the parts of Christy in *The Playboy of the Western World*, Bartley in *Riders to the Sea*

Fay, William. Portrait by John Butler Yeats. Hugh Lane Municipal Gallery of Modern Art, Dublin.

and Martin in *The Well of the Saints*. Frank was noted for his verse-speaking; he created Naisi in *Deirdre*, Cuchulain in *On Baile's Strand*, Sean Keogh in *The Playboy of the Western World* and Hyacinth in *Hyacinth Halvey*. The Fays left the Abbey in 1908 following a disagreement and produced Irish plays in the USA. Willie went to London in 1914 and pursued a successful stage career there. CF-S

W. G. Fay, *The Fays of the Abbey Theatre*, 1935.

Ferguson, Sir Samuel (1810–86). Poet and antiquary; born in Belfast, he became immensely important as a translator of old Irish poems and sagas. A lawyer by profession, he was appointed Q.C., and was the first Deputy-Keeper of the Public Records in Ireland; he was knighted in 1878 in recognition of his services in organizing that department. He became President of the Royal Irish Academy in 1882, and his Dublin house was frequented by scholars and patrons of literature, music, archaeology and art. Ferguson's principal antiquarian work, a collection of all the known OGHAM inscriptions in Ireland, was edited by his widow, Lady Ferguson (*née* Mary Catherine Guinness), and published posthumously in 1887. Ferguson published his *Congal: A Poem in Five Books* in 1872 and *Deirdre* in 1880; his poems were edited by Padraic Colum and were published in 1963. TMcC/BdeB

Lady Ferguson, *Sir Samuel Ferguson in the Ireland of His Day*, 2 vols., 1896; Robert O'Driscoll, *An Ascendancy of the Heart: Ferguson and the Beginnings of Modern Irish Literature in English*, 1976.

Feritear, Piaras (c. 1600–1653). Poet; one of the great Irish poets of the 17th century, he was a minor aristocrat in the Dingle peninsula of Co. Kerry. He was hanged by the Elizabethan Colonists in Killarney for his part in a native rebellion. As a writer he was at his best in the courtly lyric of wit and passion such as 'Leig Dhiot Th'Airm, A Mhacaoimh Mna' ('Lay Down Your Weapons, Young Lady'). TMcC

Ferran, Brian (1940–). Painter; born in Derry, he was educated in Belfast, where he studied painting 1959–63. He won the Douglas Hyde Gold Medal (awarded by the Irish ARTS COUNCIL) for an historical subject in 1965; he had his first one-man show in Derry, 1966; in 1969 he won the Leverhulme European Award to study communication in the visual arts at the Brera Academy, Milan. Ferran has had one-man shows in Ireland, Europe, Scandinavia and the USA. He is Art Director of the Arts Council of Northern Ireland. CMacG

Fiacc, Padraig (1924–). Poet; born in Belfast, he won the A.E. Memorial Award for poetry, 1957. Three published collections are: *By the Black Stream* (1969); *Odour of Blood* (1973); and *Nights in the Bad Place* (1977). He edited a major anthology, *The Wearing of the Black*, in 1974. TMcC

Field, John (1782–1837). Composer; born in Dublin, he was taught music there by his father, a theatre

Field, John. The Dublin-born composer and pianist portrayed in a steel engraving by Carl Mayer, Nuremberg.

violinist, and his grandfather, an organist, and studied under Tommaso Giordani. He made his début at the age of nine; two years later he went to London where he was apprenticed to Muzio Clementi (1752–1832), with whom he visited France, Germany and Austria, before settling in St Petersburg in 1803. He developed a personal keyboard style, subsequently expanded by Chopin, Schumann, Liszt and many lesser composers. Two of his seven piano concertos were in the repertoire of the finest pianists of the 19th century. He was the originator of the Piano Nocturne, a serene dreaming melody decorated with some ornate figuration floated by the sustaining pedal over an arpeggiated harmonic bass; of the eighteen that he wrote, many are familiar to this day. Field died in Moscow.   A G H

Finn or **Finn mac Cumaill.** Originally a Celtic god, Finn is the hero of much medieval and early modern Irish story-telling and song. His name comes from Celtic *Vindos* (which gives Welsh Gwyn and the Gaulish god-name Vindonnus) and means 'fair, bright'. The Continental place-names which derive from it – Vienna, Windisch, Vendresse and others – point to the widespread cult of Finn amongst the continental Celts. Scholars have argued that Finn and another deity, LUG, are ultimately identical. *See* MYTHOLOGY.   D Ó C

Fitzgerald, Barry. Stage name of William Joseph Shields (1888–1961), character actor; born in Dublin, he acted part-time at the ABBEY THEATRE 1918–29, after which he joined the company permanently. Created the parts of Boyle in *Juno and the Paycock*, Fluther in *The Plough and the Stars*, Paul in *Paul Twining*, St Leger in *The Big House*, etc. From 1937 he played chiefly in

films, including *Going My Way* and *The Quiet Man*, and almost always in Irish roles. *See* pl. VII.   CF-S

Fitzmaurice, George (1877–1963). Playwright; although his plays derive from his Kerry background, which is reflected not only in their subjects and angle of vision but also in a rich, poetic prose (distinct from but comparable to that of J. M. SYNGE), he spent most of his working life in the civil service in Dublin. The ABBEY THEATRE produced his realistic comedy *The Country Dressmaker* in 1907, and it became one of the most popular plays in the repertoire. Unfortunately theatre audiences were puzzled by the elements of the fantastic and grotesque in *The Pie-Dish* (perf. 1908) and *The Magic Glasses* (perf. 1913), and Fitzmaurice worked largely in isolation and obscurity until his death. Recently there has been a revival of interest in his plays and he has been compared with JAMES STEPHENS as a master of fantasy.   PLM
Arthur E. McGuinness, *George Fitzmaurice*, 1975.

Flanagan, T. P. (1929–   ). Landscape painter; born in Enniskillen, Co. Fermanagh, he attended Belfast College of Art. He held his first one-man show in Belfast in 1961, and was elected Royal Ulster Academician in 1964. His works are in public collections in Ireland, Great Britain and the USA. He is noted for his watercolour scenes of historical and literary landscapes, which are painted with great delicacy and fluency.   C MacG

Fleischmann, Aloys (1910–   ). Composer; born in Germany, he studied in Munich. He was Professor of Music at University College, Cork, 1934–80. His music is rich in harmonic texture, strongly romantic in feeling, with colourful orchestration. *Clare's Dragoons* (1944) for soloists, chorus and orchestra, and his overture *The Four Masters* (1948) have a sense of sweeping pageantry. *Songs of Colmcille* (1964) show his sensitivity in setting words to descriptive effect. His long association with BALLET has inspired *Golden Bell of Ko* (1948); *An Coitin Dearg* ('The Red Petticoat'; 1951), *Macha Ruadh* (1955), and most recently *An Táin* (1981) which features elements of traditional Irish dances.   AGH

Foley, John Henry (1818–74). Sculptor; born in Dublin into a family with sculptural traditions, he received his early art education at the DUBLIN SOCIETY's modelling school, where he won many prizes. He moved to the Royal Academy Schools, London, in 1835 and exhibited at the Academy for the first time in 1839. He lived in London for the remainder of his life. His early ideal subjects were natural and graceful in the conventional idiom of the day. The turning point of his career came in 1844 when he won recognition at the Westminster Palace competitions which led to many British Government commissions. He became known for his commemorative statues of the 'heroic dead'. There are numerous examples, in Ireland, the UK and India, of his ability to conjure up a spirited conception of each subject, shown in a characteristic pose. He

rejected Neo-Classical draperies, and like Chantrey, his mentor, favoured contemporary dress and dynamic poses which are most evident in his superb equestrian statues. His portrait busts were equally lively. He reached the summit of his profession in England with his statue of the Prince and the *Asia* group on the Albert Memorial. He was a very able and fastidiously painstaking modeller who believed in naturalism, tempered by idealization of form.   J T
B. Read, 'John Henry Foley'. *The Connoisseur*, clxxxvi (1974), pp. 262–71; J. Turpin, 'The Career and Achievements of J. H. Foley', *Dublin Historical Record*, xxxii, nos. 2 and 3 (1979), which includes a catalogue.

Francini, Philip and **Paul.** Italian stuccodores; the Francini brothers worked for James Gibbs, in England, in 1731 and 1736. About 1739 they decorated the dining-room walls at Riverstown, Co. Cork, with framed allegorical figures and executed a ceiling decoration based on Poussin's *Time rescuing Truth from the assaults of Discord and Envy*. In 1739, working under RICHARD CASTLE, they decorated the ceiling of the saloon at CARTON: in the *Courtship of the Gods* (pl. XVII) the gods are shown sitting on clouds amid garlands and putti swinging on festoons. In Dublin they worked at 85 St Stephen's Green (a variant of Carton) in 1739–40 and at Tyrone House in 1740; also at RUSSBOROUGH, Co. Wicklow, in the 1740s. The Francinis worked in England in the 1740s and 1750s, where they decorated Wallington, Northumberland; Lumley Castle, Durham; and Northumberland House, London. They returned to Ireland in the 1760s and executed splendid plasterwork in 9 St Stephen's Green, Dublin, and CASTLETOWN, Co. Kildare. Their last known work is at Kilshannig, Co. Cork, dating from the 1760s. While their early work has a strong Baroque massing, their later work, after their sojourn in England, took on a graceful Rococo lightness. *See* PLASTERWORK.   W G

French, William Percy (1854–1920). Painter; born at Cloonyquin, Co. Roscommon, he was educated at Trinity College, Dublin, where he graduated as a civil engineer. A talented watercolourist, as a young engineer he spent his spare time painting the scenery of the Irish Midlands. His work is much in demand by collectors. He was also a talented song-writer; his most popular song was *The Mountains of Mourne*.   C MacG

Friel, Brian (1929–   ). Writer; born in Omagh, Co. Tyrone, he now lives in Donegal. He was a teacher until he was offered a contract from *The New Yorker* in 1960 for his short stories; they have since been published in several collections, the first *A Saucer of Larks* (1962). His major contribution has been to the theatre, starting with the brilliant *Philadelphia Here I Come* (1964), in which two actors represent the divided mind of the hero, a reluctant emigrant. *Freedom of the City* (1973) dramatizes the Ulster troubles by flashback technique. *Translations* (1979) explores the loss of identity entailed in the loss of a language, centred on the 19th-century Ordnance Survey's anglicization of Irish place-names.   B H

Foley, John Henry. Symbolic and historical figures in bronze, surrounding the base of the monument to the statesman Daniel O'Connell in Dublin, *c.* 1870.

Fuller, James Franklin (1835–1924). Architect; born in Co. Kerry, he was trained by Alfred Waterhouse and commenced his Irish practice in 1862. Fuller's houses include the Classical Annaghmore, Co. Sligo (*c.* 1865); extensions to Ashford, Co. Galway (1870s) in the baronial style, and St Anne's, Raheny, Co. Dublin, for Lord Ardilaun; Mount Falcon, Co. Mayo (1876); Ballyburley, Co. Offaly (1887); and Baronstown, Co. Westmeath (1903). His churches include Clover Hill, Co. Cavan (*c.* 1865), and Syddan, Co. Meath (1881), in the French Gothic style; while those at Rathdaire, Co. Laois (1880), with its façade based on St Cronan's church, Roscrea, at Clane, Co. Kildare (1882), and at Carnalway, Co. Kildare (1890), are in a vigorous Hiberno-Romanesque style. He wrote an anecdotal biography, *Omniana*, in 1916.   W G

furniture (17th–19th centuries). The survival of furnishings in Ireland is a considerable rarity before the 18th century owing to the country having been in a constant melting pot of wars, rebellions, and land resettlement. The castles and fortified houses of the 17th century were frequently burnt and looted. Inventories, wills and diaries are the chief source of information about what had once existed.

Fynes Moryson's (*c.* 1610) and Luke Gernon's (1620) descriptions of the country would lead one to believe that feather beds, sheets and even tables should not be expected, but while it is likely that in the average castle or tower house living conditions were rough and furniture very rudimentary, the writers probably exaggerated the case with typical English prejudice. This is borne out by the earliest known Irish inventory, that of Maynooth Castle, Co. Kildare, recording the goods of the 11th Earl of Kildare; it is dated 10 May 1578. Considerable luxury is shown: there are listed tapestry and arras hangings, many feather beds, some with testers of velvet and taffeta, and chairs and stools upholstered in velvet and crewel-work, with an assortment of cushions and rugs. Between 1613 and 1641 the diaries of the great Earl of Cork are replete with references to the buying of furniture and the decoration of his and his family's many houses. Some of his bedsteads, imported from Bristol, had elaborate hangings, and he records many of his purchases in Ireland, such as that on 22 January 1620 when he bought from a merchant, Randall Brian, two embroidered chairs, four high stools, two low stools of red, all embroidered with appliqué black velvet. Materials for upholstery and apparel were frequent and expensive items. In February 1624 Thomas Smyth of Dublin, 'upholsterer', supplied a red-velvet chair, stools and long cushions, and four months later a gilt bedstead and an Indian gilt table; this last must be an early reference to lacquer. Smyth is the first known named Irish craftsman in the furniture trade. An inventory of Cork House in Dublin taken in 1645, two years after Lord Cork's death, lists tapestry hangings, window curtains, elaborate state beds and carpets. The bed was the chief symbol of wealth and status in any house; it and costly tapestry hangings figure as the most expensive items in all the inventories of the period, such as those of Francis Aungier; Lord Longford's Dublin house (28 November 1628); John Skiddy, both father and son, merchants of Waterford (1640); Sir Hardress Waller of Castletown, Co. Limerick (1642); the Earl of Kildare's Dublin house (11 October 1656); the Earl of Orrery at Castlemartyr (1677); the Earl of Meath in Dublin (21 December 1685); Sir John Percival, Burton, Co. Cork (31 May 1686); Viscount Lanesborough, Rathcline, Co. Longford (10 April 1688); and finally and most importantly the incredibly elaborate inventories of the Restoration Viceroy, the great Duke of Ormonde, and his son, the attainted 2nd Duke, at Kilkenny Castle, at Dunmore, Co. Kilkenny, and at Dublin Castle (1647–1707). The splendours of Kilkenny Castle, with its tables and candle-stands embossed with silver, crystal chandeliers, silver sconces and andirons, lacquer cabinets, Turkey-work carpets and Flemish tapestries, must have rivalled the Restoration glories of Windsor, Knole, and Ham. The Cromwellian and Williamite wars and later neglect and bankruptcy left but one traceable item from all these inventories: a large 17th-century Japanese blacklacquer chest on a later 18th-century gilt stand, now again at Kilkenny Castle.

Surviving woodwork of the period up to the Restoration consists of the famous Armada table at Bunratty Castle, probably made up in Ireland *c.* 1600 with the heraldic lions, and figures of Hope and Charity that had formed some part of the decoration of a wrecked Spanish Armada galleon; also a few oak chairs such as those at St Patrick's Cathedral, Armagh, and two oak chimneypieces at CARTON, Co. Kildare, and at the college at Youghal, which complete the meagre list.

The Carolean period saw about a dozen turners and upholsterers admitted to the Freedom of the City of Dublin and at least seventeen watch and clock makers were then working in Dublin. A resurgence of building took place and unfortified houses such as BEAULIEU, Co. Louth, and Eyrecourt, Co. Galway, possessed elaborate interiors and carved decoration. The great oak 'imperial' staircase at Eyrecourt (now stored in the Detroit Institute of Fine Arts) is the most exciting piece of surviving woodwork; its strapwork, exuberant acanthus, and bizarre grotesque masks all suggest a Dutch or German origin, and tradition implies that the staircase was imported piecemeal from Holland. An immigrant French craftsman, James Tabary, is the author of the grandest remaining 17th-century work in Ireland – the chapel woodwork and altarpiece of Sir WILLIAM ROBINSON's Royal Hospital, KILMAINHAM. Tabary's oak carving, including the altar table itself, is monumentally classical and sober in contrast to the rioting Eyrecourt work. Tabary, a French Huguenot refugee, and other craftsmen were paid £809.12s.1d. in January 1687 for their work. The swags of fruit and flowers, trophies, palm-tree fronds and cherubs show a clarity and sureness of touch unequalled till then in Irish woodwork. Tabary's influence can be shown in the trophied overdoors in the hall at BEAULIEU, Co. Louth, and on the organ case of St Mary's church, Dublin (1697).

By the turn of the century Ireland had settled down to a period of peace, and prosperity slowly followed. As Dublin expanded, the climate for luxury items became more favourable, and the country saw a flowering of the decorative arts which was to increase as the years went by. It was not a simple process, as trade and industry suffered under the Navigation Acts which put a heavy embargo on Irish exports. As a result, a doctrine of self-sufficiency was preached by the more enlightened members of the Irish House of Commons and such thinkers as JONATHAN SWIFT, Bishop GEORGE BERKELEY, Thomas Prior and Samuel Madden wrote many pamphlets to encourage the nobility and gentry of Ireland to spend their money in their native country and to encourage the manufacture of, among other things, Irish textiles and furniture.

Furniture shown in inventories and accounts of the first half of the 18th century can be illustrated by three examples. Firstly, John Mahon at Strokestown, Co. Roscommon, whose inventory of 3 July 1708 shows that the beds with their curtains, and the table linen, were the most expensive items. It does not specify the types of wood the various chests and desks were made of, but we can presume they were of oak. There was no lacquer. Cane chairs and tables were mentioned and three looking-glasses were valued at 15 shillings. Secondly, a few years later (December 1715), we find walnut and japanned furniture being bought by Colonel Flower at Castledurrow, Co. Laois, and thirdly the very full inventory of the 6th Earl of Fingall at Killeen, Co. Meath (23 March 1736), frequently mentions japanned furniture, oak chairs veneered with walnut, and a walnut desk. Some of the more important reception rooms had sconces with glass

Writing cabinet in walnut with marquetry of holly, *c.*
1720–30; four other similar pieces are known, one having a
swan-necked pediment. Art Institute of Chicago.

coration on the aprons backed by a criss-cross diaper
pattern. The exaggerated leaves on the cabriole legs
leading down to divided panels terminating in heavy
paw-feet are typical of Irish work of the 1720s. Another
example is the trifid footed stand with *Régence* basket of
flowers and shells that supports a 17th-century Flemish
nest of boxes.

Oak was used frequently for mirror- and picture-
frames, as well as for architectural work. The quality of
this carving was often very high, as is exemplified in the
musical trophy and the organ case of St Michan's
church, Dublin. The carving here is documented as
being almost certainly by the hand of Henry Houghton
in 1724. He was probably the brother of John
Houghton, a carver and gilder who was paid £18.13s.
for the frame for the full-length portrait by BINDON of
Dean Swift in St Patrick's Deanery in Dublin.
Obviously John Houghton was also responsible for the
parcel-gilt frame of the Weavers' Hall tapestry portrait
of George II (Metropolitan Museum of Art, New
York) and an oak mirror-frame of great delicacy, with
birds perching in the pierced acanthus detail. The
flatness of the carving on all these pieces is typical of
Dublin craftsmanship in the 1730s and 1740s, and the
influence of Tabary is still strong. John Houghton also
worked in stone on the PARLIAMENT HOUSE and executed
church monuments and possibly chimneypieces, as did
his pupil John Kelly who made Doctor Moss's
mahogany four-poster bed in 1759 and carved doorcases for his house in Cavendish Row, all executed with
consummate skill. Thomas Oldham is another craftsman who worked on the Parliament House, finishing
the oak chimneypiece in the House of Lords in 1748/9.
Both these craftsmen could well have carved furniture,
though we have no record of it.

The Irish Parliament House was designed by Sir
EDWARD LOVETT PEARCE in 1729 and it is his Palladianism
with its Kentian interior decoration that was soon to
become the fashion in Dublin and in the country. It
was in this decoration that we find the masks, festoons,
swags, and side-tables and cabinets that furnished
these rooms, with their coffered ceilings and
tabernacle-framed walls. The designs of Inigo Jones
and William Kent were influential in the detailing of
the House of Lords and in some of Pearce's houses in
Henrietta Street, and these are the basis with a number
of other contemporary pattern books for the Baroque
style in Irish carving. Gilded pine tables in this style
were popular, such as those at Malahide Castle, but
from the 1730s mahogany takes over.

Mahogany was first imported from the West Indies
in 1725 as ballast, though large quantities did not begin
to arrive until the 1740s; it is a hard wood ideal for the
carver and it takes a fine polish. The inventories of
William Smyth of Barbavilla, Co. Westmeath (March
1742), of Lord Howth's Dublin house (23 April 1751)
and of Earl Grandison at Dromana, Co. Waterford (12
August 1756), all list many mahogany furnishings such
as marble-topped tables, sets of chairs, and desks,
among the walnut, oak and gilded work. The Irish
carvers working in the Kentian Baroque tradition
varied their style with all sorts of quirks and oddities.

candlebranches. Practically all the main rooms except
the dining room contained a bed hung with 'paragon'
– a ribbed, often watered, worsted cloth; in some rooms
they were described as 'field beds' and obviously could
be put up and down at will, and in others they are
termed 'couch beds' and were used as a day bed or sofa.
Though the inventory is dated 1736, it represents the
state of the house in the 5th Earl of Fingall's time. A
cousin of the 6th Earl, he had died young and without a
direct heir, only three years after his marriage in 1731.
Thus the inventory reflects the fashions of the 1720s
and early 1730s and this explains why there is no
mention of any mahogany in the house.

Surviving oak, walnut, japanned, and gilt furniture
in Ireland shows much of it to have been very similar to
English styles. There are exceptions, however, such as a
group of extremely elaborate and quirkish inlaid
walnut writing cabinets. One of these (now in the
Victoria and Albert Museum) is said to have belonged
to JONATHAN SWIFT. Although they all show much more
Dutch influence, they are demonstrably of Irish
manufacture. Their marquetry inlay includes spiral
decorated volutes for candlebranches flanking the
upper mirrored stage; the use of the spiral has a long
history as a feature of Irish decoration. Other individually Irish walnut pieces can be typified by a
richly carved marble-topped side-table with its de-

A bottle stand in mahogany, *c.* 1740–50; the flatly carved acanthus decoration and heavy square-shaped paw-feet are typical of Irish workmanship. Victoria and Albert Museum, London.

The resulting furniture is often heavy and overloaded with carved ornament, as well as being somewhat stiff and awkward in shape – qualities which give the pieces a marvellously naive but somewhat provincial appearance.

The peculiarities of Irish furniture of this date can be summed up thus: the carving on the aprons of card-, silver-, and side-tables, stools, blanket chests and bottle stands has low-relief foliated detail which often incorporates eagles' heads, winged birds, rosettes, oak-leaved festoons and tassels, usually centred on grotesque lion's-head masks, goblin heads, baskets of flowers, and scallop shells. These details are in relief against a ground, incised with a large-meshed trellis or diamond pattern that is often punched in the centre. Solid background punching such as usually appears on gesso work is also often found. Cabriole legs are frequently emphasized by further masks, acanthus leaves, cabochons or sea-shells. The shell motif is particularly common on chairs and settees. Chairs are often found with their backs and seat rails of oak, veneered with mahogany, and stretchers were usual even when they had gone out of date in England. The flat serpentine stretcher is very similar to those found on Philadelphia chairs. All this furniture seems to treasure the motifs of Queen Anne's reign and its *retardataire* quality which, coupled with the often bizarre carving, gives it an almost sinister animal life. As if to further emphasize the animal nature of this furniture, one of its chief characteristics is the muscle or hock just above the square-shaped paw or webbed claw-and-ball foot. Sometimes this little bulge is acanthus-decorated and frequently the leaf crawls further up the leg. Stylized hairs or scales occasionally take the place of the acanthus.

By no means all Irish furniture of this date shows such elaboration; a plainer and often more elegant type existed concurrently. A long sideboard with its shaped apron having a shell at the centre might be embellished further with only corner fretwork and plain straight legs. Neat little tea-tables with dished tops and prettily varied shaped aprons are supported by trifid slipper or club feet. Some of these are superbly springy; essays in delicate curves. A number of armchairs with serpentine stretchers, curved back, and curved voluted arms indicate that the maker must have been influenced by Hogarth's 'line of beauty'. Plain card-tables with flowing cabriole legs also fall into this category, the commonest type being decorated with a shell and incorporating a little drawer for counters on the apron; others are semi-circular with three folding leaves. The most ingenious has a reversible top with an interior hiding a backgammon board; on the outside of the top is a chess board 'drawer' and candle slides.

All this furniture is, however, anonymous, as none of it is ever stamped or identified by a maker's label, the only exceptions being mirror-makers and picture-framers. The most important craftsman in this line to be identified so far are the firm of Francis and John Booker of Essex Bridge, Dublin, who carried on a business started by their father in 1725 and which continued until 1775; many of their pedimented architectural mirrors bear their label. Their design is heavily indebted to the church monuments of the most prolific early 18th-century mason-sculptor working in Ireland, William Kidwell. Occasionally their mirrors are signed in script, such as one in the Cork County Club which bears Francis Booker's name and the date 1756. The firm also made smaller oval girandoles and one at least of their dressing-table mirrors is signed inside the casing of the back. Later in the century plainer and more delicate Neo-Classical mirrors appear, with the Dublin trade labels of William Partridge, Parliament Street, the Jacksons of Essex Bridge, and Kearney of Henry Street. One of the most important craftsmen was Richard Cranfield of Church Lane, who carved the highly Italianate presiding member's chair of the DUBLIN SOCIETY in 1769 (much of the good design shown by Irish craftsmen of this period was because so many of them went through the progressive Dublin Society drawing schools under the French-educated ROBERT WEST and James Mannin). Cranfield was paid £100 for work at CASTLETOWN, Co. Kildare, in 1765; this probably represents payment for the series of mirrors in the house. In 1771 he was at work on the Provost's House in Trinity College, Dublin, executing carved work and chimneypieces, and no doubt was responsible for the set of four superb gilt lion-masked brackets that still decorate the Saloon.

Though the influence of the English Rococo designers such as Thomas Chippendale and Thomas Johnson gave many a new item of decorative vocabulary to Irish craftsmen, it was Neo-Classicism that smothered the individuality and liveliness shown in the mahogany carved work reviewed here. William Moore, who had served with the fashionable London firm of Ince and Mayhew, settled in Dublin in 1782. Moore's satinwood semi-circular commodes, corner cupboards and elliptical side-tables, with their inlay of various other woods in the Adam style, furnished rooms decorated with plaster 'antique' ceilings by MICHAEL STAPLETON. Plainer mahogany furniture of this date is typified by the so-called oval, hunt, or coffin table, with its deep flaps, and the serpentine fluted friezed serving table so commonly found in Irish dining rooms. The published works of Sheraton and Hepplewhite continued to produce a simpler, lighter and more elegant style in comparison to the sometimes heavy solidity of the furniture of the previous generation.

The Act of Union of 1800 removed Ireland's Parliament to London and with it much aristocratic patronage. However, many of the craftsmen worked on in Dublin, and some splendid furniture dates from the two decades of the new century. The most magnificent documented work of the period survives at CASTLECOOLE, Co. Fermanagh, where John Preston of Henry Street, Dublin, supplied £17,000 worth of 'Grecian' furnishings in the 1820s. A pair of massive round tables have exquisite engraved brass borders decorated with bears and herms in 'parti' and 'contre parti' (brass inlay seems to have been particularly common in Dublin at this time). The elegant gilt sofa-tables and couches cost £186 and £490 respectively per pair and the heavily draped State bed (put up in expectation of a visit by George IV) cost Lord Belmore £345. These furnishings show the extraordinarily high quality of Dublin work. Labels become more common and, as in the 18th century, usually appear on the products of mirror-makers and picture-framers. Labelled items survive of William Telford (later to build organs), Murray of Dawson Street, Dublin, Peter D. Machey, Skinners Row and Cornelius Callaghan, Clare Street. The immigrant Italian, James del Vecchio, and his sons were in business in a big way in Westmoreland Street; a number of elaborate gilded pine and plaster console-tables have their names inscribed on the back or bear their trade-cards. The del Vecchio firm flourished between 1790 and 1853 and had relations and contacts ranging from Leghorn to the United States. Gilded plaster was now frequently taking the place of carved work and the mass production of the Victorian age was soon to threaten the old firms. Soon machine-made furniture was being imported from England, inevitably bringing a lowering of standards. Good solid pieces were still being made in Dublin in the 1840s. Williams and Gibton (later Mack, Williams and Gibton) of Strafford Street frequently stamped their chairs and console tables. A large three-pod mahogany dining table bearing their trade-label is recorded. Most ingeniously, they signed a mahogany revolving bookcase with their names as the authors of one of the dummy books that formed its partitions. The Butler family had a strong line in reproducing very skilfully the carved sideboards and balloon-seated Queen Anne style Irish chairs of the previous century; they also dealt in antique furniture, and the firm survives to this day on the Dublin quays. Robert Strachan of Henry Street, Dublin, and Arthur Jones of St Stephen's Green were two of the most frequent exhibitors in the series of exhibitions devoted to art and industry that were held in London, Dublin

A splat-backed armchair, c. 1730; the carved scallop shell on the seat rail is an unusual feature. Glin Castle, Co. Limerick.

and Cork from 1851 onwards. Jones published an elaborately illustrated pamphlet on his bog yew furniture, reviving the glories of 'ancient' Ireland in 1853. J. Kerr and Patrick Beakey both of Strafford Street, Dublin, worked in a similar IRISH REVIVAL vein and the latter's table made for Daniel O'Connell at Derrynane Abbey, Co. Kerry, with its base composed of round tower, wolf hounds and harps, sums up the patriotic nostalgia of the age. Killarney-work furniture, boxes and mementos of arbutus and bog oak were also extremely popular. J. Egan and Jeremiah O'Connor were the leading manufacturers of these charming, though somewhat naive, productions decorated with shamrocks, harps, and little views of well-known Killarney buildings.

By the end of the century a mass of imported Boule-embellished walnut whatnots, occasional tables, Chippendale-revival cabinets, and fancy foreign wares seem to stifle the rooms of the period. The fine craftsmanship of James Hicks stands out clearly through all these rather flimsy products. He revived the Adam-style satinwood of James Moore and carved many a Baroque sideboard. His is the last great name in the history of Irish furniture.   KtG

The Knight of Glin, *Irish Furniture* (Irish Heritage Series, no. 16), 1978; R. W. Symonds, *The Present State of Old English Furniture*, 1921; Geoffrey Wills, *English Furniture 1710–1910*, 1971; *see* also inventories of furnishings in *The Irish Ancestor* 1973 (no. 2), 1977 (no. 2), 1978 (nos. 1 and 2), 1979 (no. 2) and 1981 (no. 2).

Gaelic Athletic Association (Cumann Lúithchleas Gael). The Association (GAA) was founded at Thurles, Co. Tipperary, in November 1884, its principal founder being Michael Cusack, a forthright advocate of cultural nationalism and 'The Citizen' of James Joyce's ULYSSES. Its first patron was Archbishop Croke of Cashel. The aim of the GAA was to foster Irish traditional games – hurling, Gaelic football and handball – as part of a general movement to halt the spread of anglicizing influences in Ireland. From the beginning, the GAA had links with advanced political nationalism, especially the Fenians, and the Association's revival of native Irish games involved a hostile attitude towards what were termed 'foreign' games. However, the ban on the playing of such games by members of the GAA was lifted in recent years. The GAA remains a powerful factor in the life of rural Ireland and, to a lesser extent, in the cities. Competitions based on counties have contributed to the creation of a strong sense of county, as well as of national, identity. KBN

Gaelic League (Conradh na Gaeilge). The League was founded in 1893 to preserve the IRISH LANGUAGE in those areas where it was still spoken, and to encourage the use of the language elsewhere in Ireland. It also sought to stimulate interest in literary works in the Irish language. The two most important figures associated with the foundation of the League were Eoin MacNeill, the historian and later Chief of Staff of the Irish Volunteers, and DOUGLAS HYDE, Gaelic scholar and subsequently first President of Ireland, 1937–45. The League was originally non-political and non-sectarian, but from 1915 onwards it developed close links with the advanced nationalist movement. The vehicle of a cultural nationalism, the League succeeded in having the Irish language introduced into the schools (see EDUCATION), and a knowledge of the language was made a requirement for admission to the National University of Ireland. In its aim to spread the use of the language in everyday life, the League achieved only very limited results. With the establishment of the Irish Free State in 1922, the task of encouraging the use of Irish was taken over, to a considerable extent, by the new State but with equally limited results. KBN

Galilei, Alessandro (1691–1737). Florentine architect who, on a visit to Ireland in 1718, designed the exterior of CASTLETOWN, Co. Kildare, for Speaker Conolly; after his return to Italy he remained in contact with Sir EDWARD LOVETT PEARCE who continued that building. BdeB

Gallarus Oratory, Co. Kerry. Standing on the Dingle Peninsula, this is the largest and best-preserved

Gallarus Oratory. The largest surviving stone oratory built on the corbel principle; 8th–12th century.

example of a stone oratory built on the corbel principle. The sloping side-walls merge imperceptibly with the curve of the roof, suggesting the shape of an upturned boat. The west doorway slopes inwards towards the top. The oratory may date from any time between the 8th and the 12th century. Rectangular in plan, the building measures internally about 4·60 × 2·50 m. (15 × 8 ft) and reaches a height of c. 4·90 m. (16 ft); its external height is c. 5·20 m. (17 ft) and the walls c. 1·20 m. (4 ft) thick at the lowest point of the structure. PH

Galvin, Patrick (1930–). Poet and playwright; his genius is inseparable from the atmosphere and pieties of his birthplace, Cork City. His major collections are *Christ in London* (1960), *The Wood Burners* (1973) and *Man Lying on a Porch* (Selected Poems, published 1980). TMcC

Galway, James (1939–). Flautist; born in Belfast, he studied in London and Paris. Principal flautist with the London Symphony Orchestra, the Royal Philharmonic Orchestra and the Berlin Philharmonic Orchestra 1969–75; subsequently internationally renowned as a soloist. BdeB

Gandon, James (1743–1823). Architect; born in London, he was a pupil of Sir WILLIAM CHAMBERS and continued his style of Franco-Roman Neo-Classicism. He and the Irish architect John Woolfe extended Campbell's *Vitruvius Britannicus*, publishing two further volumes in 1767 and 1771. He turned down an invitation to St Petersburg and accepted that of the Rt Hon. John Beresford to settle in Dublin. Gandon's first Dublin building was the Custom House (1781), which displays his mastery of planning, understanding of materials and deployment of detail. The building is embellished with sculpture by EDWARD SMYTH, whom Gandon employed on all his Dublin buildings. The Four Courts, Dublin, begun in 1786, exploits the riverside site with a dramatic cliff of masonry and a massive drum and dome which dominate the area. His other Dublin works include the King's Inns, additions to the PARLIAMENT HOUSE, O'Connell (formerly Carlisle) Bridge and additions to the Rotunda Hospital. Gandon designed a great mansion at Emo, Co. Laois, for Lord Portarlington, stables at Carriglass, Co. Longford, and a few small villas with internal spaces ingeniously fitted together.   W G

garden design. *See* HORTICULTURE AND GARDEN DESIGN.

Geddes, Wilhelmina Margaret (1887–1955). Stained-glass designer; born in Leitrim, she was educated in Belfast and at the Dublin Art School before joining AN TÚR GLOINE *c.* 1912. As early as 1911 her panels depicting the *Life of St. Colman Macduagh* (Hugh Lane Municipal Gallery of Modern Art, Dublin) manifested her strong, expressive drawing, subtly dramatic simplification of line, and solemn and spiritual intensity, relieved by deeply glowing colour. She took as much trouble over choosing each piece of the rich, smouldering coloured glass she favoured as she did over painting and leading it up.

In 1925 she moved to Lowndes & Drury's Glass House in London, where she instructed EVIE HONE in the craft and rented a studio until her death.

Whether in Ireland, England, Canada (the Duke of Connaught's window dedicated to his Canadian staff, Ottawa, 1919) or Belgium (a memorial window to the King of the Belgians at Ypres, 1938), her powerful, evocative work warrants considerably more attention than it has hitherto received. A number of her small-scale graphic designs were worked in embroidery by her sister.   N G B
Stephen Gwynn, 'The Art of Miss W. M. Geddes', *The Studio*, vol. 84, October 1922; Nicola Gordon Bowe, 'Wilhelmina Geddes', *Stained Glass* (quarterly of the Stained Glass Association of America), vol. 76, no. 1, Spring 1981.

Giant's Ring, Ballynahatty, Co. Down. A circular earthen-banked enclosure 180 m. (197 yds) across, on a gravel terrace overlooking the River Lagan. The bank, which has five gaps, is 18–20 m. (60–68 ft) wide and 3·60 m. (12 ft) high; it consists of gravel material from the enclosed area. It is probably Late Neolithic or Early Bronze Age in date. Near the centre is a denuded simple boulder-built PASSAGE GRAVE in which cremated bones were found. The site (used as a racecourse until the 18th century) was excavated by Collins in 1954.   M H
A. E. P. Collins, 'Excavations at the Giant's Ring, Ballynahatty', *UJA* 20 (1957), 44–50.

Gibbon, Monk (1896–   ). Poet; although primarily a writer of poetry, his prose also makes excellent reading. His poetry collections include *The Tremulous String* (1926), *For Daws to Peck At* (1929), *Seventeen Sonnets* (1932) and *Collected Poems* (1951). His autobiographical work, *Inglorious Soldier* (1968), is a beautiful piece of writing.   T McC

Gandon, James. The Four Courts, Dublin, begun in 1786, seen from the Merchant's Quay.

glass. Glass beads, inlaid with colour, were made in Ireland in the early IRON AGE. Throughout the Early Christian period coloured-glass studs and millefiori were used in decorating metalwork, including such masterpieces as the Ardagh Chalice (*see* ARDAGH HOARD) and the Moylough Belt Shrine (*see* SHRINES).

From 1258 glaziers are named who made clear glass and STAINED GLASS. Although licences to make table and window glass were granted to English and Continental entrepreneurs in the late 16th century, it seems that George Longe was, in 1597, the first man able to claim to have maintained a glass-house. This was in Drumfenning woods, probably near Curryglass, Co. Cork. Other early glass-houses include Ballynegary near Ardmore, Co. Waterford; Birr, Co. Offaly; and Portarlington, Co. Laois. Soda glass (i.e. glass having soda as its alkali constituent, rather than potash) was manufactured in Dublin from about the early 17th century, but a patent was granted to Sir Philip Lloyd and others to make flint glass (i.e. lead glass using ground flint as the source of silica) in the St Michan's area in 1675, a year after George Ravenscroft obtained his first patent for flint-glass manufacture in London. Captain Philip Roche, who established the Round Glass House in the St Mary's Abbey district in the 1690s was the first in Ireland to set the flint-glass manufactory on an industrial footing. By 1729 Dublin glass-houses sold 'all sorts of fine flint drinking glasses, salvers, baskets for desserts, salts ground and polished, decanters, lamps etc.' Apart from fine tableware, Dublin glass-houses also made apothecaries' bottles, tubes for scientific experiments and spun-glass ornaments.

The growth of Ireland's glass industry was affected by punitive Acts of the English Parliament. An Act of 1746 forbade the export of any glass from Ireland and the import of any glass to Ireland except English. This forced Irish glass-makers to cater solely for domestic needs and it killed the incentive for development for almost forty years, but when Britain crippled its own industry with extra taxes in 1777 and 1781, Ireland won respite through free trade and entered a glorious phase in glass production. Skilled craftsmen came from Bristol and Stourbridge, Irish people learnt the craft and, soon, Irish glass was being exported to the USA, Canada, the West Indies, Madeira, Portugal, Spain, France, Denmark, Italy and Africa. In 1825 excise duty was levied on flint glass according to the weight of its metal. So cumbersome was the method of tax assessment that it hampered manufacture and the industry declined. However, glass production continued in Cork until 1835, Waterford until 1851, Belfast until 1868 and Dublin until 1893, where THOMAS and RICHARD PUGH were active from c. 1855. For further information on Belfast, Cork and Waterford glass, see below.

Irish glass usually complied with the shapes, cuts, designs, weight and colour expected by the London market. Irish cut designs are famous; these usually progressed from large flat diamonds, horizontal and upright bands and leaf-wreaths to an overall pattern of small sharp diamonds. From at least the early 18th century glass was engraved in Ireland. Enamelling and gilding were used, particularly in the late 18th century. Coloured glass was made in Waterford and by other glass-houses from the early 18th century.

It is probable that glass bottles were made from the 16th century in Ireland. As well as bottles, wares produced included: window glass, glass garden bells, snuff bottles, apothecary and chemical glasses, pickle and preserving jars, tavern glasses and decanters. Ireland was almost self-sufficient in bottles by 1761 and two decades later exported bottles from Cork, Dublin and Belfast. Bottle glass was made in Gurteens, Co. Waterford, 1729; Ballycastle, Co. Antrim, 1754–82; by Smylie & Co., Belfast, 1786–1800, and by numerous houses in Dublin, where manufacture still continues in one of the traditional bottle-making areas, Ringsend.

Moulded table glass was also made. Fully moulded glass bottles, decanters, celery glasses, salts and dishes were made, especially in the early 19th century. These were decorated with printies, fluting and diamond patterns.

In the late-18th/early-19th century some of the cheaper wares of the major factories were partly moulded. Goblets, bowls and pickle jars were occasionally made by adding a blown bowl to a moulded foot and stem. Decanters, jugs, butter coolers, wine-glass coolers etc., were made by blowing the glass into a shallow iron mould which impressed a decoration of flutes on side and base and the maker's name on the base; the piece was then taken from the mould and blown to its full size. The names of manufacturers which occur in this way are Penrose, Waterford; B. Edwards, Belfast; Cork Glass Co.; Waterloo Co., Cork. Similarly, the names of Dublin retailers which occur are 'CM&CO' (Charles Mulvany & Co.); Francis Collins, Dublin; Armstrong, Ormond Quay; Mary Carter & Son, Grafton Street, Dublin; and 'JDA' (John D. Ayckboum).

Since the early 18th century Irish glass has been engraved to commemorate events, people and causes.

Such glass usually carries a motto, toast or slogan, together with a heraldic device, military insignia, emblem or portrait. As special care was taken with commissioned pieces, such commemorative glass usually shows the highes standards of engraving and of workmanship. Political activity and associated banqueting throughout the 18th and early 19th centuries ensured a steady demand for this ware, but specially engraved glass pieces were still being ordered in the late 19th century. The earliest reference in a Dublin newspaper to engraving glass with 'Arms, Crests, Words, Letters or Figures' occurs in 1735, but there is evidence to suggest that engravers worked there earlier. Most Irish glass was wheel-engraved, but diamond-point was also used. The finest commemorative examples seem to date to that part of the 18th century before Irish cut glass was produced on a large scale, and to the late 19th century. The principal categories of Irish commemorative glass are Williamite and Volunteer.

The triumph of William III at the Boyne in 1690 was subsequently toasted at banquets commemorating the battle (1 July) and his birthday (4 November); Possibly the earliest Irish glass made to drink his health was commissioned by William King, Lord Archbishop of Dublin, in 1715, about the time of the defeat of the Stuarts at Preston. The 50th anniversary of the Boyne, in 1740, and the final defeat of the Stuarts at Culloden in 1746 started a new era of enthusiastic celebrations in Orange drinking societies. Engraved mammoth goblets were commissioned. Later wine and cordial glasses, decanters, claret jugs and bowls were engraved with stereotyped illustrations and the loyal toast. Caution must be exercised in dating Williamite glass; loyal supporters showed respect for the annual celebration by having glasses made to order in the 19th century but in a much earlier style, or by having old glasses engraved at a later date for some special occasion.

Associated with Williamite glass are pieces commemorating the siege of Derry, 1688. Examples which survive seem to have been made after the foundation of the Apprentice Boys of Derry Club in 1814. Reputedly to defend Ireland against invaders, volunteer corps were formed throughout the country. Engraved glassware was required by these Volunteers for their formal banquets held after military exercises. Their glass is important now because it documents the ware made especially in the years 1779–93 in Dublin, Drumrea and Belfast; it shows the high standard of table glass then produced, the quality of the engraving, the variety of stems (including plain, air-twist and enamel-twist), and the use of oil-gilding decoration. Surviving examples of Volunteer glass include wine, ale and cordial glasses, decanters and water jugs. Engraved decoration was based usually on the corps' military insignia and the legend was usually the corps' motto or a Volunteer toast. Irish glass was also engraved to commemorate the Union and various trade or political events; for use at Masonic Lodge dinners, local authority dinners; or to record family events.

Definite attribution of items to particular Irish glass-houses is difficult except in the case of mould-blown

Cut-glass hyacinth vase (*left*), height 17·5 cm. (6 in.), probably from Cork, *c*. 1800–10 (Private Collection); and decanters with (*centre*) mushroom stopper by Penrose of Waterford, early 19th century, and (*right*) wheel-engraved design and inscription 'Success to the Waterford Volunteers 1782' (both Victoria and Albert Museum, London).

items which have a factory name impressed on the base. The only Irish glass-house pattern books which survive today are those, dated *c*. 1830, of Samuel Miller, a foreman cutter in Waterford, and of John Fitzgibbon of the Cork Glass House Company (see below). Internal evidence in these books suggests that Irish glass cutters of that period copied and adapted commercially successful patterns used in other glass-houses in Scotland, England and Ireland.

Some glass forms evolved after *c*. 1790 which are now considered as being characteristically Irish. The piggin, or stave-built wooden pail, was interpreted in glass. Large fruit or salad bowls or miniature versions for salt were made with moulded stem and foot combined with a handsomely cut bowl. These were either boat-shaped bowls decorated with scalloped rims and cut festoons or round bowls with turn-over rim. Attractive late 18th-century wall mirrors are oval in shape and have a frame of a single or double row of faceted glass cubes of clear, dark-blue, green or opaque glass laid on silver or gilt foil; a cut-glass candelabra would be suspended in front of the mirror.

Belfast glass. Benjamin Edwards was superintendent of a glass-house in Drumrea, near Dungannon, 1771–3, and in Belfast from 1776. He later had a warehouse in Newry. In spite of the company changing hands on occasions and of threatened bankruptcies, flint-glass manufacture continued in Belfast until *c*. 1868. Early Belfast glass was influenced by Bristol styles, from which city Edwards emanated. Belfast decanters are usually of pyriform shape with two or three plain neck rings, or of triangular section, with a narrow lip and target stopper having moulded or bevelled edges or decorated with a cut central six-point star. Belfast glass decoration is usually light, with simple flat vertical fluting, incised pendants, stars and hollow facets. Engraving includes foliate and floral motifs and the crowned harp.

Cork glass. There were three glass-houses in Cork; the Cork Glass House Company in Hanover Street, 1783–1818; the Waterloo Glass House Company, 1815–35; and the Terrace Glass Works, 1818–41. Decanters exist with the names of the first two companies moulded on the base. However, caution should be exercised in dating these decanters, as excellent marked copies have been made in recent years.

Typical Cork Glass House Company decanters are mallet-shaped with two or three plain round, triple or feathered neck-rings, a medium-size lip and bull's-eye stopper. The Waterloo Company decanters are often of Waterford type (see below), with barrel-shaped body, three triple neck-rings and a mushroom-shaped stopper with moulded radial flutes. The Terrace Glass Works is noted particularly for sharp diamond cutting.

Cork glass is noted for the grace and variety of its designs. Distinctive patterns include the Cork Glass House Company's band of filled vesicae or lozenge-shapes, either joined point to point or separated by a star or bow-knot. To celebrate the passing of the Act of Union this house engraved some decanters with the legend 'The Land we Live in'. Other favourite Cork designs include engraved stars, festoons and cross-hatched daisies. Pieces were cut with large flat diamonds and with notched edges.

Waterford glass. Glass-houses existed in the Waterford area from the early 18th century but the celebrated factory there was set up by George and William Penrose only in 1783. The first manager was John Hill from Stourbridge. Jonathan Gatchell succeeded Hill in 1786 and the Gatchell family remained associated with the company until 1851.

The outstanding qualities of Waterford glass are its clarity and the precise cutting of the decoration. A typical early Waterford decanter is barrel-shaped, has three or four triple neck-rings and a wide flat lip. Stoppers are almost invariably mushroom-shaped with a rounded knop below the stopper neck. Common early 19th-century Waterford motifs include stars, pillar and arch, and bands of semi-circles filled with fine diamond cutting. The Samuel Miller pattern books show that *c.* 1830 Waterford appreciated a thick body deeply cut with wide pillar flutes, printies, hollow prisms and strawberry diamonds. Bases were star-cut and rims fan-edged. M R

M. S. D. Westropp, *Irish Glass* (rev. ed. with additional text etc., edited by Mary Boydell), 1978; W. A. Thorpe, *A History of English and Irish Glass*, vols. I and II, 1929; Phelps Warren, *Irish Glass*, 1970; Derek C. Davis, *English and Irish Antique Glass*, 1964; Catriona MacLeod, *Irish Glass*, n.d. [*c.* 1980].

Glenavy, Lady (*née* Beatrice Moss Elvery; 1883–1968). Designer, stained-glass artist, genre and narrative painter; born in Dublin of a musical and artistic family, she entered the Metropolitan School of Art in 1896 to study sculpture under JOHN HUGHES; she studied at Colarossi's in Paris, 1904, and afterwards in London at the Slade under Tonks and Steer. A protégée of SARAH PURSER, she did work for AN TÚR GLOINE, illustrated books, and designed prints for the CUALA PRESS. Elected RHA 1933. In 1912 she married Charles Henry Gordon Campbell, later 2nd Baron Glenavy, and settled in London where she knew many of the Bloomsbury group. She was the mother of the humorist, Patrick Gordon Campbell (3rd Baron Glenavy), and of the author, Michael Mussen Campbell (4th Baron Glenavy).

Her own account of her life in Dublin, London and Paris, *Today We Will Only Gossip* (1964), gives a vivid impression of Dublin at the turn of the century. C MacG

Glendalough, Co. Wicklow. Monastic site in a hauntingly beautiful valley in the Wicklow Hills; the entire complex was presumably expanded around the grave of its founder, St Kevin, who died in 618. The buildings include: a fine ROUND TOWER, a Cathedral, the widest surviving Irish Early Christian church, 14·63 × 9·14 m. (48 × 30 ft) internally; the stone-roofed St Kevin's Church, measuring 6·90 × 4·44 m. (22 ft 8 in. × 14 ft 6 in.) internally, near the Lower Lake; Reefert Church and Temple-na-Skellig near the Upper Lake; and the Romanesque St Saviour's church. P H

Glendalough. Part of the monastic site, showing the well-preserved round tower.

Glenree, Co. Mayo. Valley in the western foothills of the Ox Mountains, 7 miles E of Ballina. A Bronze Age farmstead with a small round hut, 5 m. across, in Carrownaglogh townland, was investigated by M. Herity in 1970–81; this yielded the first modern evidence of prehistoric cultivation in ridges made with the spade. The cultivated areas were bounded by stone walls; some had been cultivated more than once and apparently wheat was grown. The primary area was enlarged on all sides, particularly to the S and W, in successive expansions. The final stone wall, an expertly built construction to replace the earlier fences in a grassland phase, was never finished. Radiocarbon determinations and a flint knife found in the wall indicate a date in the 2nd millennium BC. M H

M. Herity, 'A Bronze Age Farmstead at Glenree, Co. Mayo', *Popular Archaeology*, March 1981, 36–7.

Gogarty, Oliver St John (1878–1957). Surgeon, wit and writer; born in Dublin, he was an excellent poet who had the misfortune to know James Joyce, thus becoming Buck Mulligan in ULYSSES. Ulick O'Connor's biography of Gogarty gives one an idea of the full range of the qualities of this flamboyant, witty but sensitive man. T McC

Goibniu. The Celtic god of iron-working; later known as Goibnenn and Gaibhneann, he is identical with the Welsh deity Govannon, and is well-attested amongst the Continental Celts. He and his fellow-craftsmen, Crédne the bronze-worker and Luchta the wright, provide the Tuatha Dé Danann with their magic weapons at Cath Maige Tuired. He survives in Irish tradition as Gobbán Saor, the cunning master-craftsman of folklore. St Gobnait of Ballyvourney, whose site proved on excavation to be an important centre of iron-working, may well be his Christianized female equivalent. *See* MYTHOLOGY. D Ó C

gold- and silverwork. *See* SILVERWORK.

Goldsmith, Oliver (1728?–1774). Writer; the son of Rev. Charles Goldsmith (Curate and later Rector of the parish of Kilkenny West, Co. Westmeath), he grew up at Lissoy, Co. Westmeath, and was educated at Trinity College, Dublin, and the University of Edinburgh. A two-year tour of Europe, undertaken in penury, and a hated spell as an assistant master at a London school preceded Goldsmith's immersion in the London literary world. The periodical essays, supposedly from a Chinese philosopher in London, collected as *The Citizen of the World*, brought him fame in 1760–1. His major productions – *The Traveller* (1764) and *The Deserted Village* (1770), *The Vicar of Wakefield* (1766), *The Good Natur'd Man* (1768) and *She Stoops to Conquer* (1774) – show his varied talents in verse, prose and drama. His last work was the ambitious *History of the Earth and Animated Nature* in 8 volumes.   ICR

Robert Hopkins, *The True Genius of Oliver Goldsmith*, 1969; A. Lytton Sells, *Oliver Goldsmith, His Life and Works*, 1974.

'gorget' (later Bronze Age). Some confusion surrounds the use of this term borrowed from 18th-century military dress; then officers wore on the breast inscribed crescentic metal plates suspended on chains – a memory of earlier days when armour was worn. Initially the term was applied to those solid, one-piece crescentic gold collars in the Great Clare Gold find from Mooghaun North, discovered during railway construction in 1854. Nowadays the term is applied loosely to the great composite gold collars consisting of a ribbed crescentic plate and stitched-on disc terminals such as that from Gleninsheen, Co. Clare. Of eight recorded examples, six were found in the area of the Shannon Estuary. Gold discs and other fragments in the possession of the NMI may be portions of other examples.   MFR

Graves, Alfred Percival (1846–1931). Poet; born in Dublin, he was the son of the Bishop of Limerick. A prolific writer of popular poems that employed Irish material, his work includes *Songs of Killarney* (1837), *Father O'Flynn and Other Irish Lyrics* (1889), *An Irish Faery Book* (1909), as well as a surprisingly good anthology, *The Book of Irish Poetry* (1914).   T McC

Greacan, Robert (1920–). Poet; born in Derry City, he had a central place in Ulster literary circles during World War II. He edited an anthology, *Northern Harvest*, in 1944. His work includes *A Garland for Captain Fox* 1975 .   T McC

Greevy, Bernadette (19–). Singer; born in Dublin, she studied in Dublin and London. As a mezzo-soprano she has sung throughout Europe, North America and in New Zealand and Hong Kong. A frequent visitor at the London Promenade Concerts, she is especially associated with Elgar and Mahler. She has also sung in opera in Dublin, Wexford, Glasgow and London. She has recorded opera and oratorio.   AGH

Goldsmith, Oliver. Statue by John Henry Foley, 1861, in College Green, Dublin.

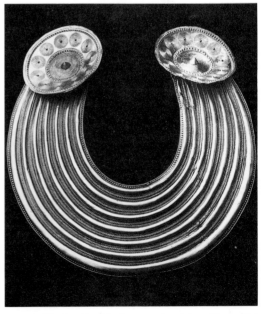

gorget. Sheet-gold ribbed crescentic plate with applied terminals, 8th century BC, from Gleninsheen, Co. Clare. NMI.

Gregory, Lady. A scene from her play *Hyacinth Halvey*, performed at the Abbey Theatre, 1906.

Grogan, Nathaniel. *North Gate, Cork. Lord Barrymore's carriage and pair.* Private Collection.

Gregory, Lady (*née* Isabella Augusta Persse; 1852–1932). Playwright and folklorist; born at Roxborough, Co. Galway, she grew up in a Protestant, 'Big House' environment, but after being widowed in 1892 she involved herself in nationalist political activities, learned Irish, and began collecting folklore. In an English coloured by Irish syntax she retold the traditional heroic and mythic tales in *Cuchulain of Muirthemne* (1902) and *Gods and Fighting Men* (1904). With W. B. YEATS and EDWARD MARTYN she initiated the Irish theatre movement, and as co-director of the ABBEY THEATRE played a crucial role in policy-making and in the practical aspects of theatre management. She was one of the few writers with whom Yeats could collaborate; he was indebted to her for ideas, scenarios, and peasant dialogue in several plays. Moreover, when the Theatre was in need of more plays she turned her hand to writing them, with considerable success. Generally using the same 'Kiltartan' dialect as in her collections of tales, she produced comedies, 'folk-history' plays, tragedies and even mystery plays and translations of Molière. *Spreading the News* (perf. 1904), *The Rising of the Moon* (pub. 1903, perf. 1907), *The Gaol Gate* (perf. 1906), *Hyacinth Halvey* (perf. 1906), and *Grania* (pub. 1912) are representative of her best work.

Coole Park, her Galway estate, incarnated a rapidly vanishing aristocratic culture and served as a haven for many Irish writers and artists. However, her later years were darkened by the violence of the Troubles; by the death of her only child, Robert Gregory, in World War I; and by the British Government's refusal to return the great collection of paintings her nephew Sir HUGH LANE had intended for Dublin. Yeats's moving elegy 'Coole Park and Ballylee, 1931' recognizes the centrality of Lady Gregory's contributions to modern Ireland. PLM

Elizabeth Coxhead, *Lady Gregory: A Literary Portrait*, rev. ed. 1966; Ann Saddlemyer, *In Defence of Lady Gregory, Playwright*, Dublin 1966.

Grogan, Nathaniel (*c.* 1740–1807). Soldier and painter; born in Cork, he spent his youth in the army in America and the West Indies, returning *c.* 1780. He settled in Cork and had little, if any, contact with his fellow-artists in Dublin. The main influence on his work was Dutch and, despite his lack of conventional training, he was a superb figure painter. This, coupled with his sense of character and humour, gives his work a unique flavour. His scenes of Irish country life are vividly real, the figures packed into dark, low rooms, and his landscapes are peopled with real workers who give point and animation to his river scenes. AOC

Guinness, May (1863–1955). Abstract painter and art collector; born in Dublin of the famous brewing family, she studied in Paris in 1910 with André Lhote and had a heroic career during World War I as a nurse, being decorated for bravery afterwards by the French Government. She left an interesting collection of sketchbooks and other records of this period. She exhibited continuously during her life, as well as collecting works by Picasso, Bonnard, Rouault, Matisse, Dufy and others. A memorial exhibition of her work was held in Dublin in 1956. CMacG

Guthrie, Sir Tyrone (1900–71). Theatrical director; born at Tunbridge Wells, Kent, he was a great-grandson of TYRONE POWER. He was one of the earliest producers for the BBC in Belfast. He took a lifelong interest in the theatre in Northern Ireland. From 1933 to 1952 he was chiefly connected with Sadler's Wells and the Old Vic, London, directing a prodigious number of operas and theatre classics. His *forte* was directing pageantry and farce. Guthrie was the first director at the Stratford, Ontario, Festival, and at the theatre which commemorates him in Minneapolis. His greatest technical contribution was the development of the thrust stage. He left his home to the Irish nation as a retreat for artists. CF-S

VII **Fitzgerald, Barry.** The actor in the role of the King, in Lady Gregory's *The Golden Apple* at the Abbey Theatre; oil on canvas by Dermod O'Brien. Abbey Theatre Collection.

VIII **Hamilton, Hugh Douglas.** *Cupid and Psyche in the Nuptial Bower*, 198 × 151 cm. (78 × 59½ in.), exhibited 1800. NGI.

Hamilton, Hugh Douglas (1739–1808). Painter;
born in Dublin, he attended the DUBLIN SOCIETY
Schools. He started his career drawing small, oval,
pastel, head-and-shoulder portraits, and in 1764 he
went to London where he was equally successful with
similar works, occasionally drawing small conversation
pieces, also in pastel. He spent twelve years in Italy,
1778–91, and while there, under the influence of
Flaxman, he was encouraged to turn to oil painting,
both portraits and subject pictures. His Roman
masterpiece was, however, in pastel – a portrait of
*Henry Tresham and Canova looking at Canova's 'Cupid and
Psyche'*. After his return to Ireland he was the principal
portrait painter in Dublin; painting in oils, he executed
splendid, Neo-Classical, full-length works, as well as
head-and-shoulder portraits, distinguished by their
excellent composition and quiet colouring.   AOC

Hamilton, Laetitia Mary (1878–1964). Landscape
and figurative painter; born at Hamwood, Co. Meath,
she studied at the Metropolitan School of Art, Dublin,
under WILLIAM ORPEN. She first exhibited at the Royal
Hibernian Academy in 1909, and was a founder-member of the Dublin Painters Group. Elected RHA in
1944.   C MacG

Hand, Richard (d. 1816). Painter; from 1775 he
studied at the Drawing School of the DUBLIN SOCIETY,
which supported his experiments in glass painting.
Little of his work remains either in Ireland or England,
where he settled early in the 19th century and worked
for distinguished patrons at Carlton House, Arundel
Castle and Donington Hall, as well as painting small
genre panels. He died in London.   NGB
Michael Wynne, 'Stained Glass in Ireland: principally
Irish Stained Glass 1760–1963' (unpublished Ph.D.
thesis, Trinity College, Dublin), 1975; Michael
Wynne, catalogue entry on R.H. in *Das Bild in Glas: von
der europäischen Kabinettscheibe zum Neu– Glas*, 1979.

Hanlon, Rev. Jack (1913–68). Landscape and
subject painter; born in Dublin, he was ordained a
priest and served in the Dublin archdiocese. He studied
under André Lhote, and was a founder-member of the
Irish Exhibition of Living Art (1943). Hanlon was at
his best in the watercolour compositions painted in thin
washes, and tending towards the Cubist formula. A
decorative painter of considerable charm, he also
formed a good collection of avant-garde painting of the
École de Paris. This collection was dispersed after his
death. Examples of his own works are in most of the
public collections in Ireland.   C MacG

harp. The skills of Irish harpers were described as
early as 1183–5 by Giraldus Cambrensis, but the oldest

Hamilton, Hugh Douglas. *Henry Tresham, R.A., and Canova
looking at Canova's 'Cupid and Psyche'*, pastel on paper, *c*.1790.
H. Farmer Collection. Cf. colour pl. VIII.

harp. The oldest surviving Irish harp, known as 'Brian Boru's
Harp', dating from the 14th century. TCD.

surviving Irish harp, one of the treasures of Trinity
College, Dublin, dates from the 14th century. The
distinctive features of the Irish harp are its sounding
box hollowed from a single block of willow; the sturdy
fore-pillar is T-shaped and curves outwards. The neck,
deep and heavy, was bound on either side by a metal
band. The strings were of thick brass held by metal pins
on 'the left-hand side of the neck, twisted round the
wooden pegs inside the sound box. The Irish harp was

held on the player's left shoulder and the strings were plucked with long fingernails. This style of playing persisted until the end of the 18th century. The harpers were greatly honoured in Gaelic society. In the period of their decline they travelled between houses of the new gentry, seeking hospitality. The harp, which is the national emblem of the Republic of Ireland, appears on the country's coinage. All told, some fourteen early instruments of different periods survive.　　AGH
Joan Rimmer, *The Irish Harp*, 2nd ed., 1977.

Harrison, Sarah Cecilia (1863–1941). Figurative, genre and miniature painter; born at Holywood, Co. Down, she studied at the Slade School under Alphonse Legros, and moved to Dublin in the late 1880s. There, she was a regular exhibitor at the Royal Hibernian Academy until shortly before her death. An intimate friend of Sir HUGH LANE, she was an aide in his plans for the Modern Art Gallery in Dublin. Her works are in the collections of the Hugh Lane Municipal Gallery of Modern Art, Dublin, and the NGI.　　CMacG

Hartnett, Michael. *See* Ó HAIRTNEIDE, MÍCHEÁL.

Harty, Sir (Herbert) Hamilton (1879–1941). Conductor and composer; born at Hillsborough, Co. Down. First noted as an accompanist, he soon became a celebrated conductor. He frequently visited the USA, and in the inter-war years was associated with the Hallé Orchestra in Manchester and the London Symphony Orchestra. His orchestral music reveals a full-blooded romantic virtuosity, his 'Irish Symphony' being the most effective of this genre. Harty tackled historical subjects in such works as his symphonic poem 'With the Wild Geese'. He wrote concertos for piano and for violin. His impressive setting, for soprano and orchestra, of Keats's 'Ode to a Nightingale' is occasionally performed. His songs, rich in feeling, at times echo the idioms of traditional singers.　　AGH

Healy, Michael (1873–1941). Painter and stained-glass designer; a native of Dublin, he spent two years in business before attending the Dublin School of Art, the Royal Hibernian Academy Schools and the Istituto di Belle Arti in Florence. In 1903, he joined AN TÚR GLOINE, where he worked until his death. His skilful, at times academic, draughtsmanship is evident in his earliest window, *St Simeon* (1904), in LOUGHREA CATHEDRAL, Co. Galway, as is a powerful, deeply spiritual characterization and willingness to experiment, well illustrated by his subsequent work (1904–40) there.

The rare majesty and poignant simplicity of his work is manifested at Bridge-a-Crin, Co. Louth, and in Dublin at the Catholic Church, Donnybrook, the Protestant Church, Donore Avenue, and the Augustinian Church, Thomas Street. His watercolour studies of Dublin street scenes are, however, generally better known than his stained glass.　　NGB
C. P. Curran, 'Michael Healy, Stained Glass Worker', *Studies*, vol. 31 (March), Dublin 1942; James White and Michael Wynne, *Irish Stained Glass*, 1963; Michael Wynne, *Irish Stained Glass*, 1980.

Healy, Robert. *Tom Conolly and his friends skating*, grisaille, Castletown 1768. Hon. Desmond Guinness Collection.

Heaney, Seamus. Portrait of the poet (detail) by Edward McGuire, oil on canvas, 1974. Ulster Museum.

Healy, Robert (d. 1771). Painter; a pupil of the DUBLIN SOCIETY Schools, he is best known for his series of pastels of the Conolly family and their friends skating, walking, shooting and hunting at CASTLETOWN, Co. Kildare. These were done in February 1768. His surviving pastels are all in grisaille and include some life-size heads as well as the more usual whole-length portraits on a smaller scale. He was famed for his pictures of horses, though only the Castletown groups are now known. He died at Dangan, where he had been drawing animals for Lord Mornington.　　AOC

Heaney, Seamus (1939–). Poet; born in Co. Derry, he is the best loved and most widely known of contemporary Irish poets. He has published five major collections, *Death of a Naturalist* (1966), *Door into the Dark* (1969), *Wintering Out* (1972), *North* (1975) and

Field Work (1979), as well as a book of prose, *Preoccupations* (1980). His first two books dealt with childhood on a farm, while *Wintering Out* marked the watershed in his development as it dealt with the problems of human relationships, the poet's pre-occupation with the power of words, and revealed the for him highly significant symbolism of bogland. In later poems like 'Triptych' and 'The Singer's House' (from *Field Work*) the poet opens out into pure confident statement rather than the sidelong or implied commentary which is a typical feature of his earlier work. TMcC

Blake Morrison, *Seamus Heaney*, 1982.

Hedge Schools. Schools operating in Ireland from the 18th century and so called because, operating in defiance of the law, the master convened his pupils clandestinely in a secluded field under the sunny side of a hedge. In the course of the 18th century as the Penal Laws restricting education were relaxed or not implemented, the Hedge Schools came to operate in farmhouses and barns, in the schoolmaster's house if he had a sizable room, or in a rough hut thrown up for the purpose by the parents. WILLIAM CARLETON was educated in such a school and became the master of one. Usually only reading, writing and arithmetic were taught in these schools, which provided the only elementary education available to the majority of the population. Oral repetition was the prevalent teaching method because the schools were financially self-supporting and books and materials were costly and scarce. In the 18th century there was a fine tradition of learning in the Hedge Schools of Co. Kerry, where classical education was included, but inevitably the standard of teaching and the curriculum varied considerably from school to school throughout the country. When State elementary education was introduced in Ireland in 1832 the total number of Hedge Schools operating was about 9,000. *See* EDUCATION. BdeB

Hennessy, Patrick (1915–80). Figurative painter; born in Cork, he was educated in Scotland and graduated from Dundee College of Art, after which he went to Paris and Rome. He divided his time between Morocco and Continental Europe. He is best known for his surrealistic effects and a formula of absolute realism, especially in painting roses. Examples of his work are in many public collections in Ireland, the UK and the USA. He was elected ARHA 1948, and RHA 1949. CMacG

Henry, Grace (*née* Mitchell; 1868–1953). Landscape and still-life painter; born in Aberdeenshire, Scotland, she studied in France under L. R. Garrido and at Delacluse's Académie, as well as with André Lhote and François Quelvec. She married the painter PAUL HENRY. Elected ARHA 1949; she is represented in many public collections in Ireland. CMacG

Henry, Paul (1876–1958). Landscape and figurative painter; born in Belfast, he studied at Belfast School of

Henry, Paul. *Launching the Currach*, oil on canvas. NGI.

Hewetson, Christopher. Memorial monument to Provost Baldwin, erected in Trinity College, Dublin, in 1784; the figures are of Carrara marble.

Art, the Académie Julian, Paris, 1898, and at Whistler's studio. In 1912 he moved to Achill, Co. Mayo, where he painted for about seven years. In 1917 he held the first of a series of exhibitions with his wife GRACE HENRY; together with his wife and others he founded the Dublin Painters Group. He is best known to a wide audience through his works which were reproduced for the London, Midland and Scottish Railway. Elected RHA 1929. CMacG

Paul Henry, *An Irish Portrait*, 1951; *Further Reminiscences*, 1973.

Hewetson, Christopher (*c.* 1739–1798). Sculptor; born in Kilkenny, he studied at Kilkenny College and in Dublin before settling in Rome by 1765, where he remained until his death. He sculpted highly accomplished portrait busts in marble, terracotta and bronze,

including two of Pope Clement XIV (1772), the future Tsarina Maria Fedorovna (1784), Gawin Hamilton (exhibited at the Royal Academy, 1784), the Earl-Bishop of Derry, the artist Anton Rafael Mengs (1779) – Mengs painted Hewetson at work on the Hamilton bust, and a colossal marble bust of Leibniz erected at Hanover by public subscription (1789/90). His best-known work is the memorial to Provost Baldwin executed for TRINITY COLLEGE, Dublin, where it arrived from Rome in 1784. BdeB
Terence Hodgkinson, 'Christopher Hewetson, An Irish Sculptor in Rome', *The Walpole Society*, vol. xxxiv (1952–4), pp. 42–54.

Hewitt, John (1907–   ). Poet; he helped younger Ulster poets by providing them with board, lodging and advice during the dark days of the 1940s and '50s. His collected poems were published in 1968; individual collections include *Conacre* (1943), *Those Swans Remember* (1956), *Out of My Time* (1974) and *Kites in Spring* (1980). T McC

Hickey, Patrick (1927–   ). Landscape painter and graphic artist; born in India, he came to Ireland in 1948, qualified as an architect at University College, Dublin, and studied etching and lithography in Italy at the Scuola del Libro, Urbino. He held his first one-man exhibition in Dublin in 1961, and his first one-man exhibition of graphics, Dublin 1965. Founded the Graphic Studio, Dublin, 1961. His etchings for the Stations of the Cross were purchased by the National Archives in Paris. CMacG

Higgins, Aidan (1927–   ). Writer; from his birthplace, Celbridge, Co. Kildare, Higgins has created the memorable novel of a house in decline: *Langrishe Go Down* (1966). His first collection, *Felo de Se* (1960; later called *Asylum*), includes heavily, unjoyously sexual tales like 'Winter Offensive'. His work is Baroque in style, disturbing in content, as in his novels *Balcony of Europe* (1972) and *Scenes from a Receding Past* (1977). BH
B. M. Beja, 'Felons of Our Selves: The Fiction of Aidan Higgins', *Irish University Review*, vol. 3 (Autumn 1973), pp. 163–78.

Higgins, Frederick Robert (1896–1941). Poet; born at Foxford, Co. Mayo, he was a very gifted poet who fell under the shadow of W. B. YEATS. His books include *Island Blood* (1925), *The Gap of Brightness* (1940) and *Arable Holdings* (1927). At his best he was a rustic poet as accomplished as PADRAIC COLUM or JOSEPH CAMPBELL, though his efforts to break away from mere rural poetry never succeeded. T McC

high crosses. Probably the most important achievements in the entire history of Irish SCULPTURE, these crosses are identifiable by a large stone circle intersecting the arms and the upright shaft. From the earliest days of Irish Christianity, crosses had been set in slabs as symbols of the faith and erected in monastic settlements. The progenitors of the Irish crosses were

high cross. The Cross of SS. Patrick and Columba at Kells, Co. Meath, decorated with biblical scenes; early 9th century.

probably the stone crosses erected in Northumbria in the late 7th century. There was also an indigenous origin because it is clear that in early examples, such as the North Cross, Ahenny, Co. Tipperary (late 8th century), the abstract geometric ornament on the shaft and ring is derived from earlier METALWORK; the ornamental studs and cylindrical angle mouldings are clear copies of metal executed in stone. Portable wooden processional crosses decorated with metal panels were probably the direct ancestors of the high cross. The Moylough belt (*see* SHRINES) also displays a cross in a circle.

Figured sculpture which had hitherto been so rare in Irish stone carving became a major element of these crosses. In the early examples, hunting scenes, presumably with moral significance, appeared only on the substantial bases, as at Ahenny. In the transitional style, shafts became covered with relief panels as in the South Cross, CLONMACNOIS. Two shafts at Clonmacnois and others at Bealin and Banagher (*c.* 800) show non-scriptural hunting scenes. The South Cross at Clonmacnois is transitional in its proportions, 'studs' and abstract ornament, but a figured panel of the Crucifixion has been introduced which points to the central group of major high crosses. The use of the human figure on the Irish crosses may have been influenced by English ivories. The Columban Monastery of KELLS, Co. Meath, has another transitional cross, that of SS. Patrick and Columba (early 9th century) which carries a number of biblical scenes; some others in the Meath area are similar. The Kells area appears to have been crucial in the development of later high crosses in eastern and northern Ireland.

The central group of scriptural high crosses have a coherent religious subject-scheme based on the themes of God's grace to man and the parallels between events in the Old and New Testaments, ideas which relate to the Reformist CÉLÍ DÉ movement, with its renewed interest in the Scriptures. These great crosses look forward to Irish Romanesque art. The finest examples are the Cross of Muiredach (probably mid-9th century) and the West Cross at Monasterboice, Co. Louth; also the Cross of the Scriptures at Clonmacnois (probably mid-9th century); all these are cut in sandstone. Figured panels occupy the broad faces of the shaft, and ornamental panels the narrow faces. Usually there is a Crucifixion on one side with New Testament scenes in panels beneath; on the other face is the Last Judgment and Old Testament scenes. Contemporary with the Midland Scripture crosses and displaying similar subjects is a distinct group in the Barrow Valley in Co. Kildare, especially at Moone and Castledermot; they are carved in granite, not sandstone, and consequently the description is much more stylized and diagrammatic.

The renewed VIKING attacks appear to have halted the carving of High Crosses in the south of Ireland and later crosses appear mostly in the northern half. These are more elongated, e.g. West Cross of Monasterboice. In these examples in Counties Tyrone, Derry, Monaghan, Fermanagh and Sligo, the quality of the carving declines. In the late examples of the early 11th century abstract ornament is again pervasive, as if a deeply seated Irish tradition was asserting itself. The final episode in the development of the high cross is seen in the late and very different crosses of the 12th century, usually decorated with two large simple figures, e.g. Dysert O'Dea.   JT
F. Henry, *Irish High Crosses*, 1964; and numerous articles by H. M. Roe.

Hill, Derek (1916–   ). Landscape and portrait painter; born in England, he settled in Donegal. In 1981 he gave his house there and his collection to the Irish nation. He has exhibited all over the world, and is noted for his portraits and landscapes, many of which can be found in public and major private collections in Great Britain and Ireland. Hill introduced the Irish public to the Tory Island Naive painters. He was awarded a major retrospective at the Hugh Lane Municipal Gallery of Modern Art, Dublin, and in Belfast, and he held a retrospective exhibition at Wexford, 1982.   C MacG

Hill, Derek. *Tory Island from Tor More*, oil on canvas, c. 1960. Ulster Museum.

hillfort. An enclosed site, usually of several acres, consisting of one or more than one bank and ditch surrounding a hilltop, often following the contours of the land; found throughout the Celtic west, at least 50 examples are known in Ireland. Those classed as univallate are found mainly in the east and north, sometimes on sites which enclose earlier burial cairns and are often denoted as royal sites in history and MYTHOLOGY; the multivallate type occurs mainly in the west and south. *See* DÚN AENGHUSA; EAMHAIN MACHA; RATHGALL; TARA; IRON AGE, EARLY.   M H

Hogan, Desmond (1951–   ). Writer; born in Ballinasloe, Co. Galway, he has written short stories, plays and novels, of which the first, *The Ikon Maker* (1976), is a perceptive, troubling study of the disintegration of the relationship between a mother and son in a society that is itself disintegrating.   BH

Hogan, John (1800–58). Sculptor; born at Tallow, Co. Waterford, he was reared in Cork where he received his art education at the then newly opened School of Art. He was employed as a wood-carver by

Hogan, John. Bust of Thomas Steele (a follower of Daniel O'Connell), c. 1840. NMI.

Thomas Deane (*see* DEANE AND WOODWARD). On the strength of a subscription promoted by W. P. Carey, he went o to Rome in 1824. There, under the influence Gibson and Thorwaldsen, he was converted to Neo-Classicism. At first he sought to emulate the mythological subjects of his Roman contemporaries, but the bulk of his output, notably his fine religious statues, was in response to commissions from his Irish patrons. He made many funerary monuments, commemorative statues and busts of important Irishmen, which reflects his ardent nationalism and zealous Catholicism. He revisited Ireland many times, before he returned permanently in 1849 hoping for additional patronage; he misjudged post-famine Ireland and died a disappointed man. Despite his complaints, he was in fact appreciated by both Unionist and Nationalist alike, notably by Lord Cloncurry and Daniel O'Connell. Technically able, his achievement was that he harnessed the international Neo-Classical style to commissions arising from resurgent Irish Catholicism and nationalism. Although severely Neo-Classical, his style was infused with sentiment – so much a feature of the sculpture of his day.   JT

J. Turpin, 'John Hogan, Neoclassical Sculptor in Rome', *Apollo*, August 1981; ——, *John Hogan, Irish Neo-Classical Sculptor in Rome*, 1982 (with bibliography).

Holy Cross Abbey, Co. Tipperary. A Cistercian foundation, the Abbey became a popular place of pilgrimage in the 15th century because a relic of the True Cross was kept there. The wealth accruing to the monastery from this source permitted the building, in the first quarter of the 15th century, of what may be considered the finest church of that century in Ireland. Certainly the chancel must be the most excellent Irish architectural work of the period, with exquisitely executed ribbed vaulting and a beautiful reticulated

Holy Cross Abbey. The 15th-century church seen from across the River Suir.

east window. In the chancel is a richly carved sedilia with the Butler Armorial bearings and those borne by the English Sovereign between 1413 and 1461. The superbly carved vaulted structure between the chapels in the south transept was probably the shrine where the revered relic was kept, but is known as the 'Monks' Waking Place'. The Abbey was expertly restored in the 1970s under the direction of Percy Le Clerc and the church is again in use   B de B

Geraldine Carville, *The Heritage of Holy Cross*, 1973; W. J. Hayes, *Holy Cross Abbey*, 1976.

Honan Chapel, Cork. The Hiberno-Romanesque Revival Chapel of St Finnbarr, within the University's grounds, was completed in 1917. Sir John O'Connell, the legal trustee of the Honan family bequest, was largely responsible for ensuring that it would be a simple but characteristic expression of the best contemporary Irish workmanship, revealing a 'thought-out scheme based on one recognized and guiding ideal'.

From James F. McMullen's design, based on St Cronan's Oratory at Roscrea, local builders erected a deliberately restrained essay largely in local cut limestone. The foundation stone was laid in May 1915 and the Chapel dedicated in November 1916.

All but the mosaic floor and opus sectile *Stations of the Cross* were made in Ireland. OLIVER SHEPPARD's statue of St Finnbarr and WILLIAM SCOTT's wrought-iron CELTIC REVIVAL grille, made by McGloughlin's of Dublin, adorned the west door. Inside, Henry Emery and his Technical School apprentices carved the ornamented stone; Edmond Johnson made the sanctuary lamp, altar cruets and candles, processional cross and monstrance (all from Professor Scott's designs). Of the twelve Munster Saints represented in the stained-glass windows of the nave, six are by HARRY CLARKE and six by AN TÚR GLOINE, which also made the *Our Lord* and *St John* windows in the chancel. The three west-end *Wonder-Working Saints* and chancel *Joseph* and *Our Lady* are by Clarke. The unity of this scheme is rare. Evelyn Gleeson, Katherine McCormack and the DUN EMER GUILD made the dossal (*see* pl. III) and antependium, the hand-knotted sanctuary carpets and the woven banner. The vestments, including the cloth-of-gold cope, chasuble and dalmatics for High Mass, as well as some of the altar plate, were designed and made by Barry Egan's Cork workshops; Eleanor Kelly tooled the missal bindings, Joseph Tierney illuminated the altar cards and OSWALD REEVES enamelled the tabernacle door. The Chapel constitutes a unique record of the best Celtic Revival craftsmanship.   NGB

J. R. O'Connell, *The Honan Hostel Chapel, Cork – Some Notes on the Building and the Ideals which inspired it*, 1916; Jeanne Sheehy, *The Rediscovery of Ireland's Past: the Celtic Revival 1830–1930*, 1978.

Hone, David (1929–   ). Landscape and portrait painter; born in Dublin of the famous family of artists, he studied at the National College of Art, and subsequently in Italy. He is best known for his intimate landscapes. PRHA.   C MacG

Honan Chapel. Altar card illuminated by Joseph Tierney and set in a frame of silver, silver gilt, enamel and inset crystals.

Hone, Evie. *The Crucifixion and Last Supper*, study in gouache, 30·5 × 21·0 cm. (12 × 8¼ in.), for the east window in Eton College Chapel, *c.* 1949. Tate Gallery, London.

Hone, Evie (1894–1955). Painter and stained-glass designer; born in Dublin of the famous family of artists, she trained at the Byam Shaw School of Art, and briefly in 1918 under Walter Sickert, and with Bernard Meninsky. She went to Paris in 1920 to study under André Lhote, where she was joined by MAINIE JELLETT. In 1921 they persuaded Albert Gleizes to take them as pupils and they worked with him for part of each year until 1931. An involvement with abstraction, pure colour and the work of Georges Rouault preceded her interest in STAINED GLASS. In 1933, aided by WILHELMINA GEDDES, she designed her first window, an *Annunciation* for St Naithi's, Dundrum, Co. Dublin, composed of three medievally-inspired panels, a deeply coloured, semi-abstract patchwork of antique pot metals. She worked at AN TÚR GLOINE, 1935–44, and thereafter from her studio at Marlay Grange, Rathfarnham, completing about 48 glass commissions, the most famous of which is her huge *Crucifixion* and *Last Supper* window in Eton College Chapel (1942–52), the designs for which are lodged in the NGI. She was a founder-member of the IELA. A memorial exhibition of her work was held in University College, Dublin, 1958. NGB

C. P. Curran, 'Evie Hone: Stained Glass Worker 1894–1955', *Studies*, vol. 44 (Summer), Dublin 1955; Stella Frost (ed.), *Evie Hone*, 1958.

Hone, Nathaniel (the Elder; 1718–84). Painter; born in Dublin, he probably trained there, but went to England before 1742. Though he always painted in oils, he was best known in his youth as an enamel miniaturist. He was an admirer and follower of Dutch art, using strong, Rembrandtesque chiaroscuro. In London he became a founder Royal Academician, but after his famous satire on Reynolds in 1775, *The Conjuror* (now NGI; pl. IX), in which he ridiculed the contemporary taste for Italian art, he quarrelled with, and left, the Royal Academy. He then held one of the earliest recorded one-man shows. His self-portraits and portraits of his children are justly famous. AOC

Hone, Nathaniel (the Younger; 1831–1917). Landscape painter; born in Dublin, he was related to NATHANIEL HONE the Elder. He studied engineering at Trinity College, Dublin, and began painting in 1853; he studied under Yvon and Couture in Paris, and went to Barbizon in 1855 where he remained for seventeen years. Natural realism combined with *plein-air* painting served him well for the duration of his long active career.

Hone's methods of composition and notions of colour harmony were largely derived from the influence of Jean-Baptiste Corot, Jean-François Millet and Henri Harpignies, adapted to an Irish environment when he returned to live on his estates in North County Dublin after 1875. He remained in rather splendid isolation from the Irish artistic world, wintering on board his yacht *Magda* (named after his wealthy wife) in the harbour in Monte Carlo.

Many of Hone's best pictures were painted in and around Malahide. Elected ARHA in 1890, he was Professor of Painting in the RHA Schools 1894–1917. He exhibited with JOHN BUTLER YEATS at 7 St Stephen's Green, Dublin, in 1901. His widow presented over 500 of his oil paintings and some 900 watercolours and drawings to the NGI. C MacG

Thomas Bodkin, *Four Irish Landscape Painters*, 1920.

horse racing. Horse racing has been popular in Ireland for many centuries. By the 1500s Irish horses, called 'Hobbies', were even raced in England against the King's horses, as witnessed by Privy Purse accounts of King Henry VIII for 1532. The Curragh of Kildare has traditionally been the focus of Irish racing and in the 17th century King Charles II presented two plates for competition there; it is the headquarters of the Irish Turf Club and of the Irish National Hunt Steeplechase Committee.

Racing features in the writings of many authors, including SOMERVILLE AND ROSS, Don Byrne and John Welcome. Artists have depicted racehorses and racing scenes since at least the 18th century. They include D. Quigley's painting of the match between *Paoli* and *Hero* on The Curragh in 1764, J. F. Herring's portrait of *Faugh-a-Ballagh*, winner of the 1844 St Leger in England, Michaelangelo Hayes's *The Corinthian Cup at Punchestown 1854* and, recently, Teresa Byrne's study of *Monksfield* and Lucilla Jones's *Le Moss at Ascot* and *Cairn Rouge winning at The Curragh*. The statue of *Arkle* at Cheltenham and Susan Crawford's painting of *Red Rum* immortalize two of the most famous of all Irish-bred steeplechasers. CAL

horse racing. *A Bay Racehorse with Jockey* by D. Quigley, oil on canvas, *c.* 1773. NGI.

horticulture and garden design. 'Ireland is far more favoured than Britain by latitude, and by its mild and healthy climate . . . no need to store hay in winter . . . snow rarely lies more than three days . . . milk and honey . . . no lack of vines', wrote the Venerable Bede (673–735) of Ireland's mild, maritime climate which continues to be the most important influence on the character of its horticultural activity.

Although the Celts began the identification and classification of plants according to their utility, a systematic art of gardening was not established until the arrival of the Roman-educated followers of St Patrick, post AD 432. The Early Fathers cultivated some root vegetables, herbs, apples and vines. The manors of the Norman knights, after their arrival in 1170, grew into complex agricultural and horticultural systems in which deer ran, rabbit warrens teemed, peacocks strutted, doves flew, gardens produced leeks and herbs, orchards apples and pears, and vineyards grapes. They were frequently outdone by the monastic demesnes, in whose gardens were also grown roses and lilies for use in sacred decorations. By the middle of the 16th century, the manors of the old Gaelic and Norman nobles and the gardens of the wealthy merchants in the towns boasted an impressive variety of flowers, vegetables, herbs, fruit and nuts.

With the advent of the Elizabethan era the import of plants from the New World began. Sir Walter Raleigh is credited with the introduction to his estate near Youghal, Co. Cork, of the cherry, the myrtle, the tobacco plant and, most important, the potato. His successor as owner of the estates of Youghal, the Great Earl of Cork, was foremost in laying out a formal pleasure garden in the Renaissance style with fountains, terraces and roses. Such gardens advanced in sophistication during the succeeding Jacobean reign. The ornamental courts around PORTUMNA CASTLE, Co. Galway, and Lismore Castle, Co. Waterford, are the most impressive surviving examples.

The Restoration of the Monarchy under Charles II in 1660 ushered in a glittering period of Irish gardening, for the King and his court, which included the Duke of Ormonde, had assimilated the influence of Le Nôtre during their exile at Versailles. Of the gardens created by the Restoration grandees, only those at Kilruddery, Co. Wicklow, and Antrim Castle survive as a vestige of their former selves. Rapid strides were also made in botany. The Earl of Longford and Sir Arthur Rawdon of Moira, Co. Down, raised glasshouses to shelter collections of exotic plants. The improved horticultural techniques of the Dutch were introduced by immigrants from that country after the victory of William of Orange over the Stuart dynasty in 1690. The horticultural explosion was tempered in the subsequent reigns of Queen Anne and George I, when a formal landscape of avenue, vista and pond – as may yet be experienced at CASTLETOWN, Co. Kildare – supplanted the garden as the favoured setting for a mansion. The Baroque formality of this style had been softened by the 1730s into the whimsical Rococo of the gardens wrought by literati such as DEAN SWIFT, and Dean and Mrs Delany, of which none now remain.

The agricultural revolution then about to take place was to transform the landscape of Ireland into a geometrical patchwork of field and hedgerow. This offended the sensibilities of those who appreciated the beauty of the landscape in its former state, so that they determined on retaining a vestige of naturalism around their houses in the form of a landscape park. The first model adopted by these aesthetes was the arcadian landscape of Italy, as reverentially painted by Claude Lorrain, so that the early parks, such as that laid out *c.* 1750 by Matthew Peters for the Earl of Charlemont at Marino, Co. Dublin, were after this Neo-Classical model. Its influence was soon supplanted, however, by that of the work of the English landscape gardener, Capability Brown, which was more adaptable to the Irish landscape and climate. Soon, there were no fewer than three landscape gardeners in Ireland working in his manner: W. King, Thomas Leggett and Peter Shanley, whose principal surviving creations are at Florence Court, Co. Fermanagh, Marley Park, Co. Dublin, and Avondale, Co. Wicklow, respectively. Their efforts were soon overshadowed by those of the prolific John Sutherland (1745–1826), whose elegant taste was widely employed and whose parks at Slane Castle, Co. Meath, Rockingham, Co. Roscommon, and Shane's Castle, Co. Antrim, are among those which survive to testify to his genius. Before his death, however, a new direction in landscape gardening, called the Picturesque movement, had arisen. It decried the Brownian style as being ill-adapted to the Irish landscape and called for a new native-born style. Its principal exponents were Hely Dutton, whose park and lake at Mount Bellew, Co. Galway, are now sadly derelict, and Edmund Murphy, who created the setting for the waterfall in Powerscourt demesne, Co. Wicklow.

By 1810, the English encyclopaedist, J. C. Loudon, had succeeded in reorientating the interest of the gardening world away from the wider reaches of the landscape park back to the confines of the garden proper and its plants. This movement, known as the 'gardenesque', was given currency in Ireland by his pupil, Alexander McLeish, whose major design was at Headfort, Co. Meath. The reactivation of interest in horticulture resulted in the foundation of the Royal Horticultural Society of Ireland in 1816 and no fewer than four BOTANIC GARDENS during this period. Such interest in plants for their own sakes often led to a neglect of the garden's overall design, a defect which was remedied during the 1840s by the incursion into garden design of architects such as Daniel Robertson (fl. 1821–43), the original designer of the garden at Powerscourt. From a happy combination of architect and plantsman grew the formal gardens of the Victorian age. James Fraser (1793–1863), who laid out the gardens at Curraghmore, Co. Waterford, exemplified this combined approach, as did Ninian Niven (1799–1879), the outstanding figure of the period, whose gardens at Aras an Uachtaráin (then the Viceregal Lodge), the reorganized Botanic Gardens, Glasnevin, and Iveagh Gardens, Dublin, survive in essence if not in all of their original elaboration. The

horticulture and garden design. Carton, Co. Kildare, before 1738, by Willem van der Hagen; detail showing the formal layout of the park as it existed at that time. Powerscreen Ltd, Carton.

Victorian garden required other specialist skills to realize some of its main features, none of which was more outstanding in Ireland than that of ironmasters such as Richard Turner of Dublin, whose work may be observed in the palm houses of the Royal Botanic Gardens, Kew, the Belfast Botanic Gardens and the Curvilinear Range at the National Botanic Gardens, Dublin.

The complexity of these gardens seemed to some to have reached a point of absurdity. One such was William Robinson, an Irishman and author of *The Wild Garden* (1870), who invigorated garden design with a new naturalism based on a close observation of the landscape and of plants themselves. Ireland possesses a unique and famous complement of gardens in the Robinsonian style – Mount Usher, Co. Wicklow, Annes Grove, Co. Cork, Rowallane, Co. Down, Rossdohan and Derreen, Co. Kerry. The four great gardens of Mount Congreve, Co. Waterford, Glenveagh, Co. Donegal, Malahide Castle, Co. Dublin, and Birr Castle, Co. Offaly, all laid out since World War II, demonstrate the continuing prevalence of this style.

These are large gardens, however, and present no answer to the problem presented by the compact size of the typical 20th-century garden. This challenge was first met by the development of a cellular layout of small formal compartments, the very small garden comprising one such compartment whereas the large garden would be multi-cellular in scope. Although its outstanding English innovators, Sir Edwin Lutyens and Gertrude Jekyll were employed in Ireland (their garden on Lambay Island, Co. Dublin, is the most

horticulture and garden design. The intimate Japanese gardens at the National Stud, Tully, Co. Kildare.

Hughes, John. The Victoria Memorial, completed 1906, in its original position outside Leinster House, Dublin.

complete), the best maintained of the many-compartmented creations are at Mount Stewart, Co. Down, made by Edith, Marchioness of Londonderry, and at Ilnacullin, Co. Cork, designed by Harold Peto.

After World War II, the style of the miniature landscape, the origins of which lay in the natural rock gardens and Japanese gardens popular in the early years of the century – the Japanese Gardens at Tully, Co. Kildare (1906), being the best example in Ireland – was adopted as allowing the creation of a natural design within a restricted, often urban, setting. Such gardens as Lucy's Wood, Bunclody, Co. Wexford, and Ballykilty, Malahide, Co. Dublin, contain many thousands of dwarf and small species, allowing great freedom of individual expression within a small space.

The history of gardening in Ireland is representative of all of the great periods of European gardening, adapted though they were to the island's unique climate and landscape. Examples of most types survive to this day, many being open to the public.   P B
Edward Malins and the Knight of Glin, *Lost Demesnes: Irish Landscape Gardening 1660–1845*, 1976; Edward Malins and Patrick Bowe, *Irish Gardens and Demesnes after 1830*, 1980.

Hughes, John (1865–1941). Sculptor; born in Dublin, the son of a carpenter, he was educated by the CHRISTIAN BROTHERS and in 1878 entered the Metropolitan School of Art, Dublin, where he was a part-time student for the next ten years. In 1890, he went to the Central Art Training School, South Kensington, where he studied under Edouard Lanteri. Subsequently, he went to Paris on a scholarship, and studied at Académie Julian; from there he went to Italy where he was deeply influenced by Renaissance sculpture. In 1893 he taught at Plymouth Technical School and in 1894 became Instructor in modelling at the Metropolitan School of Art, Dublin, and Professor

of Sculpture at the Royal Hibernian Academy. He was linked to the Revivalist movement in Irish art through his fine bronze altar reliefs for LOUGHREA CATHEDRAL. He gave up his professorship when he was commissioned to make the Victoria Memorial, outside Leinster House, 1903–6 (subsequently removed to the Royal Hospital, KILMAINHAM). He settled in Paris in 1903 and exhibited there. In the 1920s he lived in Florence. His work reflects the influence of French realistic modelling, e.g. Aimé-Jules Dalou (1838–1902), and the smooth surfaces of Renaissance marble sculptures.   J T
A. Denson, *John Hughes 1865–1941*, 1970.

Humewood Castle, Co. Wicklow. Built in part, 1866–70, by William White (1825–1900), finished by James Brooks, the castle is a superbly muscular Gothic house built on the western slopes of the Wicklow Hills. White used massive blocks of granite, and combined stepped gables, pylon stacks and crenellated towers to create an extravagant overall composition.   W G

Hunter, Robert (fl. 1750–1803). Painter; born in Ulster, he became the principal portrait painter in Dublin from *c.* 1750 to the late 1780s. In 1792 he held one of the earliest one-man shows in Dublin. His manner varies from the Rococo of his early works, through the elegance of portraits like that of Lord Newbattle (1762) to the chiaroscuro of his later pictures.   A O C

hunting. The chase has often provided a source of inspiration for sculptors, poets, writers, painters and musicians; HIGH CROSSES dating from as early as the 9th century depict hunting scenes. Irish heroic poems of the first millennium AD name hounds and describe hunts. A 15th-century mural in Holy Cross Abbey, Co. Tipperary, shows a hunting scene, and hounds feature on 16th-century tomb sculptures, as in Kilkenny

hunting. One of Robert Healy's well-known studies in grisaille, *Tom Conolly and his hounds*, executed at Castletown in 1768.

Cathedral. In the 17th century Seán O Duibhir an Ghleanna and other poets described, in Irish, the thrills of foxhunting, as did BRIAN MERRIMAN in the 18th century. In 1714 Arthur Stringer produced *The experienced huntsman*. Among 19th- and 20th-century writers, MARIA EDGEWORTH, LORD DUNSANY, Donn Byrne and, greatest of all, SOMERVILLE AND ROSS, described the thrills and intrigues of the hunting field. Traditional musicians composed reels and other tunes that suggest hunting sounds, while Mozeen and Bray's song of 1744, 'The Kilruddery Hunt', is still sung. Stanislaus Lynch's poems record modern hunting.

By the 1700s many painters were recording hunting scenes, *The Kilruddery Hunt* being among the earliest. Far more splendid is that of *Lord Carbery and his hounds*, of the 1740s. Hounds are included in VAN DER HAGEN's *Carton before 1738* and Joseph Tudor's *Prospect of Blessingtown*. In 1768 ROBERT HEALY produced his masterly *Tom Conolly and his hounds*; thereafter innumerable artists immortalized hunting, including William Sadler II, George Nairn, William Osborne, J. W. Baldock, Sir A. Munnings and Lionel Edwards. *See also* HORSE RACING.   CAL

C. A. Lewis, *Hunting in Ireland*, 1975.

Hutchinson, Pearse (1927–   ). Poet and broadcaster; he writes equally well in Irish and English, with passion and a commitment to left-wing attitudes. His published collections include *Tongue Without Hands* (1963), *Expansions* (1969) and *The Frost is All Over* (1975).   TMcC

Hyde, Douglas (1860–1949). Poet, scholar, translator and the first President of Ireland, 1937–45; born at Frenchpark, Co. Roscommon, he was the founder of the GAELIC LEAGUE. His fame as a translator-poet rests on the publication of *Love Songs of Connaught* (1893).   TMcC

illuminated manuscripts. Outstanding among the surviving illuminated mss. of a golden age of faith, culture, and learning in Ireland (6th–9th century) are the following: the Books of DURROW, DIMMA, Mulling, KELLS, and ARMAGH (in the library of Trinity College, Dublin); also the CATHACH PSALTER and the STOWE MANUSCRIPT (missal and gospel of St John; in the Royal Irish Academy, Dublin). Other so-called 'Insular' decorated mss., with their origins in Iona, Ireland, and Northumbria (all monastic centres), inspired by Colum Cille (Columba; 521–97), closely associated and frequently influencing one another, are now abroad, in what might be called 'a greater Ireland of art and culture'. The impressive and colourful list – the result of a remarkable series of missionary enterprises – includes: the Lindisfarne Gospels (London, British Library); the Durham Cathedral Gospels; the St Chad Gospels (Lichfield); the Hereford Gospels; the Mac Regol or Birr Gospels (Oxford), the Corpus Christi Gospel (Cambridge), the Echternach or Willibrord Gospels (Paris); the Bobbio or Irish Gospels (Milan); the St Gall Gospels (Switzerland); and many other *libri scottice scripti*.

A study of these extant mss. reveals the development of the art of writing and ornamentation during this period. There is something distinctively Irish in the style of the well-rounded, semi-uncial, boldly legible script which emerged from the compressed, cramped minuscule typical of the smaller, 'pocket', gospels. The colour-design which decorated the writing, and often, in particular, initial letters of graceful beauty and

illuminated manuscripts. Page from the 7th-century St Chad Gospels, preserved in Lichfield Cathedral, showing the symbols of the four Evangelists.

illuminated manuscripts. Page from the St Gall Gospels, showing the evangelist St Luke, accompanied by his symbol, the winged ox.

fascinating intricacy, displays the influence of many styles of art, including Coptic and Syrian, as well as Anglo-Saxon, Pictish, and LA TÈNE-style ornament from the European continent. The illuminators, as they designed and painted, did not, on the whole, create new forms; they copied and borrowed from other forms of art, in their own distinctive style. The purpose of the decoration appeared to have been twofold: (1) for the instruction of the illiterate, to quote Gregory the Great (590–604) – 'painting can do for the illiterate what writing does for those who read'; and (2) for beautifying the sacred text, for use in the liturgy, for the glory of God. This high aim seems to have been appreciated by Gerald of Wales who wrote of his visit to Ireland in 1185, and described a ms. (untraced and presumed lost) called the Book of Kildare in these terms: '. . . fine craftsmanship is all about you, but you might not notice it. Look more keenly at it and you will penetrate to the very shrine of art.' Such was the artist's skill in producing work of the finest detail, while keeping in view, with a rare patience and control, the overall design.

The ornament included many varieties of interlace: thread, ribbon and spiral abstract designs were enriched with the interlacing of writhing, supple animal bodies, and intertwining foliage of plants and tendrils of the vine. Compass-drawn circles and free-hand curvilinear rhythmical patterns brought lively movement to the richly ornamented pages. Oriental key-patterns, more formal than the imaginative Irish meanderings, were intermingled. Whole-page illustrations, frequently with portraits of evangelists and their symbols (man, lion, ox, and eagle), together with the *chi rho* (Christ) motif, emphasized the incarnate life of the Saviour and the unity of the faith. The scribes with fascinating skill turned the dead letters of the text into living truth.

Vellum, of calf or other animal skin, was used as material for the folios. The skins were pumiced and polished, the hair having been removed, then folded; margins were outlined with prickings and lines ruled to guide the writing. The scriptorium (writing office) would be equipped with quill, ink-horn, knife, compasses, sponge, and the coloured paints, if, as was often the case, artist and scribe were one and the same person. The colours included: tomato-red lead, often used for rubrical directions and accents, as well as in major illustrations; emerald green, from copper, verdigris; orpiment, producing a yellow-gold sheen; ultramarine, from lapis lazuli; shades of purple from folium; white lead to tint the human figures' faces, hands and feet. These colours, in many cases, retain their luminosity with surprising freshness and light up the grey of the parchment and the blackness of the ink.

Many mss. were destroyed at the time of the VIKING invasions. The biblical and liturgical books probably received more protection than the secular books, which suffered greater losses still. There is much discussion about the places of origin of the mss. It is recognized that books travelled widely. Colophons, which might be expected to throw light on authorship, in their concluding sentences, were notoriously unreliable and misleading. Sometimes the text of the Latin version of the scriptures provides evidence about the origins of the ms. The Irish versions were often a mixture of old Latin, pre-Jerome versions and the Vulgate, Jerome version. The colourful gospel symbols have played a part in revealing the old Latin order of the four Gospels – Matthew, John, Luke, Mark – while the Vulgate text has the more familiar order in the script. It is difficult to know how long these mss. were in the making. A workday of six hours, as in the Benedictine rule, with one full line written in $1\frac{1}{2}$ minutes and with decoration taking, in some of the more elaborate mss., three or four times as long, are conditions which suggest several years for the completion of a codex. Marginal comments in some of the mss. reveal with delicious touches of humour the dedicated approach of the scribe to his labour of love, as 'hunting words he sits all night'. G O S

F. Henry, *Irish Art in the Early Christian Period to 800*, 1965; G. L. Micheli, *L'enluminure du haut moyen âge et les influences irlandaises*, 1939; C. Nordenfalk, *Celtic and Anglo-Saxon Painting*, 1977.

interior decoration. *See* FURNITURE; PLASTERWORK.

Iremonger, Valentin (1918–). Poet and diplomat; he won the A.E. Memorial Award in 1945. His first book was *Reservations*, published in 1950; *Horan's Field and Other Reservations* appeared in 1972. T McC

Irish Academy of Letters. The Academy was established (with the special objective of promoting creative literary endeavour in Ireland) by GEORGE BERNARD SHAW, who hoped it would also be a vehicle to provide recognition for writers and to combat the oppression of censorship (*see* LITERATURE, p. 138), and YEATS; they were elected respectively President and Vice-President at its first meeting in 1932, at which Yeats, F. R. HIGGINS, Seumas O'Sullivan, FRANK O'CONNOR, LENNOX ROBINSON and A.E. were present. Originally the Academy was to have twenty-five academicians and ten associates, but there were less as JAMES JOYCE, DOUGLAS HYDE, Daniel Corkery, SEÁN O'CASEY, GEORGE MOORE, Stephen McKenna and LORD DUNSANY declined the invitation to participate, while AUSTIN CLARKE, JAMES STEPHENS, St John Ervine, Brinsley Macnamara, SEÁN O'FAOLAIN, EDITH SOMERVILLE, Peadar O'Donnell, LIAM O'FLAHERTY, PADRAIC COLUM, Forrest Reid, FRANCIS STUART, T. C. Murray and OLIVER ST JOHN GOGARTY accepted to become academicians, along with Shaw and the six others present at the first meeting; Dunsany later changed his mind and entered the Academy.

The Academy awarded the Harmsworth Prize of £100 for fiction annually from 1934 to 1938, the Casement Award of £50 for poetry or drama annually from 1934 to 1939 and, in those years, an annual prize of £50 for work in the IRISH LANGUAGE. No further awards could be made until the Academy received

financial help from the ARTS COUNCIL in 1969 and was able to establish prizes of £250 each for writing in English and Irish. Subsequently with help from Allied Irish Banks the Academy was able to award a prize for a contribution to literature, which amounted to £2,000 in 1982, and an award of £1,000 for a young writer. In 1982 the Academy had twenty-nine members with BENEDICT KIELY as its President. B de B

Irish Architectural Archive. Ireland's rich architectural heritage reflects more than a thousand years of artistic endeavour and constructional effort. It is one of the country's principal cultural assets and constitutes one of its foremost contributions to the visual arts. However, official policy for management of the Irish architectural heritage has been slow to evolve. Ireland has no State agency to record the full range of its notable buildings, both historic and modern (*see* CONSERVATION).

Against this background the Archive was established, through voluntary initiative, in 1976; the nucleus of a national collection of architectural records has now been assembled and the organization has become recognized as a natural starting-point for anyone seeking information on Irish buildings. The Archive is almost wholly privately funded and its work – being separate from conservation debate – is non-controversial. It answers a growing number of enquiries from architects, planners, and writers of books and articles, who seek information both in person and by letter, and has already contributed illustrations and historical data to a number of published studies of Irish architecture. In addition it replies to queries from members of the public and provides facilities for student seminars.

The Archive is active in both the commissioning and collecting of architectural records. The most important of its tasks is to record photographically – and in certain cases by measured drawings also – notable buildings which are about to disappear, whether through demolition or dereliction. The historical significance of these records is economic and social as well as architectural, and in 1981 fieldwork surveys ranged from a thatched farmstead and water-mill in Co. Louth to an entire 18th-century street in Dublin. The photographic library comprises some 30,000 photographs, and contains major collections acquired from An Foras Forbartha (the National Institute for Physical Planning and Construction Research) and the IRISH GEORGIAN SOCIETY. In addition to photographs, a collection of over 20,000 architectural drawings has been assembled which documents through detailed designs and surveys many important buildings of the last 250 years. In cases where original photographs or drawings cannot be transferred, temporary loan facilities for copy photography are negotiated. A reference library of over 2,000 titles has been established and extensive biographical files relating to the work of Irish architects, compiled by the late Alfred Jones, are housed on loan. In addition, there are substantial holdings of manuscripts, and magazine and newspaper articles.

As a non-profit-making company with a director and a small professional staff, the Archive benefits from the strong voluntary support it receives from the members of its board and from the members of its finance and accessions committees. Its premises at 63 Merrion Square, Dublin, are open to the public on weekdays. **N S**

Irish Christian Brothers. *See* CHRISTIAN BROTHERS.

Irish Georgian Society. Founded in 1958 by the Hon. Desmond Guinness, the Society has been one of the most influential CONSERVATION groups in recent years. One of its finest achievements has been the preservation of CASTLETOWN, Co. Kildare, Ireland's largest 18th-century mansion. The Society has about 4,000 members, half of whom live abroad, mostly in the USA. It seeks to protect buildings of architectural merit in Ireland, particularly those of the 18th century, and also seeks to stimulate an interest in art and architecture of this period. It engages in research on furniture, silver, paintings etc. and organizes seminars, lectures and field trips. It also publishes a scholarly periodical, *Irish Georgian Society Bulletin*. The Society also leases Longfield House, Co. Tipperary, Damer House in Roscrea, and Doneraile in Co. Cork, and owns Roundwood in Co. Laois. **CÓC**

Irish language. Irish belongs to the great Indo-European family of languages. Its nearest affinities are to Scottish Gaelic and Manx, with less close ones to Welsh, Cornish and Breton; all these belong to the Celtic sub-group among the Indo-European languages.

Exactly when the first speakers of Irish or any other Celtic language reached Ireland is a matter of dispute among scholars, as is the question of the influence, if any, upon Irish of the language that was spoken there before. Our earliest sources, *c*. 3rd century, are written in the so-called OGHAM alphabet, a writing system using symbols independent of the shape of the letters of the Latin alphabet but with an internal arrangement based on one used by Latin grammarians. Where Ogham was employed, it reveals a state of the language when the reduction of internal and final syllables had not yet taken place.

The first documents that still survive of Irish written in the Latin alphabet date from the 8th century, but the adaptation seems to have taken place at least a hundred years earlier. The traditional so-called 'Gaelic fount', used fairly widely for writing Irish until the 1960s, is based on the half-uncial alphabet used in early medieval Latin and vernacular manuscripts.

As far as our sources allow us to judge, Irish had established itself as the only language of Ireland before the beginning of recorded history, but the influence of Latin is evident from the earliest period. Later, Norse, Norman French and finally English came in to a lesser or larger extent, together with outside political dominance over varying parts of the country. Gradually, English replaced Irish as the main spoken language in Ireland, first among the upper classes, as most of the native nobility were suppressed by the end of the 17th century. However, it was only in the 19th century that English replaced Irish as the majority language, the change then taking place rather rapidly, due to factors such as the lack of interest in the language shown at that time by the Roman Catholic Church, the Great Famine and the establishment of English-medium primary schools all over Ireland.

The presence of the language as a national symbol was an important factor in the founding of the independent Irish State in the 20th century. The new State certainly helped to prevent Irish from dying out completely, as it might otherwise have done during the first part of this century; Irish was given a firmly entrenched position in the country's educational system, which it retains today (*see* EDUCATION). On the other hand, the advent of modern communications media, especially television, has changed the situation in a serious way. Official policy remains in favour of supporting the language, but in fact it seems that if broadcasting policies are not fundamentally altered reasonably soon, they may cause the remaining – hardly more than 30,000 – genuine native speakers of Irish to abandon their language for ever.

It is usual to divide the history of Irish into periods: (a) that of Ogham inscriptions, 200/350–600; (b) Old Irish, 600–900; (c) Middle Irish, 900–1200; (d) Classical Modern Irish, 1200–1600; (e) Modern Irish proper, 1600 to the present.

Irish has a number of peculiarities not shared by other European languages. At the phonological level, the initial mutations must be mentioned. Irish has two of these: lenition, sometimes called 'aspiration' by native grammarians, changes a stop, for instance, into the corresponding spirant and occurs in certain grammatically defined contexts. Thus, the word meaning 'woman' is *bean* which, with the definite article, becomes *an bhean* (*bh* is pronounced *v*), 'the woman'. Historically speaking, this is found where a consonant originally stood between two vowels, both inside a word and, as in the example above, between two closely connected words. The other mutation is nasalization, also known as 'eclipsis', whereby a lost nasal at the end of one word causes the beginning of the next to change, as when *Páras* (Paris) with the preposition *i* (in) becomes *i bPáras* (*bP* is pronounced *b*). Similar mutations exist in the other insular Celtic languages. Where they occur in some Italian dialects, their grammatical function is, however, rather marginal. Another phonological feature of Irish is that known as palatalization, whereby all consonants can be either palatalized or not, according to the quality of the following vowel, whether it is preserved or lost. In the latter case, this distinction becomes grammatically significant, as in the word *ball* (member) and its plural *baill* (members), where the *i* serves only to indicate that *ll* is pronounced as in English 'million' rather than as in 'hull'. This distinction, known in grammars as that between 'broad' and 'slender' consonants, is very similar to that found in Russian between so-called 'hard' and 'soft' consonants. The origins of these phonological features are to be found in the sharp reduction in the number of syllables that took place around the 5th century, as a result of the introduction of very strong stress on initial syllables at some stage before that.

Although superficially quite different from that of Latin, for instance, the morphology of Old Irish can easily be compared with that of other ancient Indo-European languages, once the rules governing the phonology are known. Thus, Old Irish preserves the same number – five – of nominal cases as Greek and, in the verbal system, a deponent verb fairly similar to that of Latin. For the pronoun, however, the stress changes mentioned have had serious consequences, resulting in object pronouns being attached to verbs in one single stress group, much like the usage in present-day French.

In Modern Irish, the case system has been simplified a great deal, with the distinction now being almost obliterated in some of the less conservative of the modern dialects. The verbal system underwent a major change in Middle Irish, with few of the regular complexities of the Old Irish verb surviving, except in some few very commonly used irregular verbs. The suffixed and infixed pronouns have disappeared completely, giving way to fully stressed independent pronouns.

The main feature of Irish syntax at all periods is that – like the other insular Celtic ones, but unlike all other European languages – the verb occupies the first place in the sentence. The distinction between the copula *is* and the substantive verb *tá*, similar to that between Spanish *ser* and *estar*, may also be mentioned; the etymological connection is obvious. Due to the importance of alternations such as those caused by initial mutations, Irish has acquired a morpho-phonemic spelling system, one that tries to show not only the actual pronunciation in any given case, but also what the radical forms look like, as in the example already quoted: *i bPáras*, where the *b* shows the actual pronunciation and *P* the radical. Given the large number of distinct sounds or phonemes that Irish has, and the relative complexity of alternations to be shown, Irish spelling is remarkably well suited to the language, in spite of certain combinations of letters that may initially strike users of other orthographies as somewhat odd.   A A

G. B. Adams, 'Language and Man in Ireland', *Ulster Folklife* 15/16 (1970), 140–71; D. Greene, *The Irish Language*, 1966; N. Ó Cuív (ed.), *A View of the Irish Language*, 1969; R. Thurneysen, *A Grammar of Old Irish*, 1946.

Irish Revival (1830s–1930s). Part of the self-conscious attempt to regenerate Ireland spiritually and physically, this cultural phenomenon embraced all the arts and even extended to industry. It incorporated the growth of a 'Celtic consciousness'; the revival of distinctly Irish forms in architecture; the revival of Celtic ornament in the decorative arts; the use of traditional national symbols such as the wolf-hound, HARP, shamrock and Irish ROUND TOWER motif; the turning to Irish subject-matter in paintings, poems,

Irish Revival. The customary symbolic device used by the Abbey Theatre, Dublin.

and plays; the efforts of the 'language movement'; the insistence on the use of Irish materials or manufactures in the building, clothing and other trades; and the adoption of an Irish National Trade Mark, the first to be instituted in any country. Designed by W. Buckley in 1906, the mark consisted of a Celtic interlaced motif within a letter *E* bearing the words 'Déanta i nEirinn'.   P L

Irish Theatre Company. The Company was founded in 1975 to bring professional theatre to provincial centres, and give an annual season at the ABBEY THEATRE. Productions include works by Anouilh, BOUCICAULT, GOLDSMITH, Ibsen, Molière, O'CASEY, Orton, Priestley, SYNGE, Shakespeare, SHAW and WILDE; contemporary Irish writers performed include SAMUEL BECKETT, Wesley Burrowes, THOMAS KILROY, HUGH LEONARD, JOHN B. KEANE and THOMAS MURPHY. Artistic directors have been Phyllis Ryan, Godfrey Quigley, Joe Dowling, Edward Golden and Christopher Fitz-Simon. The ITC has also performed in England, Scotland and Wales.   C F-S

Iron Age, Early. Though the knowledge of iron, simple to work and keeping a sharper edge than bronze, was known to the Hittites in Asia Minor as early as 1400 BC, the secret did not reach the Celts in Bohemia, south Germany and Austria till 700 BC. Archaeologists recognize from then on an Early Iron Age (EIA) in Europe, with an earlier Hallstatt tradition named from a cemetery in Austria, which is poorly represented in Ireland, and a later LA TÈNE tradition from 450 BC, named after a lakeshore site in Switzerland; good evidence of an insular version of this

Staigue Fort, Co. Kerry, with outer stone walls 5 m. (16 ft 6 in.) thick at the base.

Bronze trumpet from Lough-na-Shade, Co. Armagh, 2nd–1st century BC. NMI

Carved stone double-headed figure on Boa Island in Lough Erne, Co. Fermanagh.

tradition exists in Ireland from 300 BC on. The sites of Rathtinaun in LOUGH GARA, of EAMHAIN MACHA and RATHGALL provide some evidence of continuity from the late BRONZE AGE into this EIA phase.

Other CRANNÓGS were probably continuously inhabited through the EIA, as were ringforts like that at Feerwore in Co. Galway, beside which the TUROE STONE stood. Subsistence was based largely on cattle, as both archaeology and the TÁIN myth attest; rotary querns, a Celtic innovation, document grain-growing and are introduced in the form of the beehive type from

northern Britain, replacing the older saddle type. These appear on open, undefended sites; a small number of them, like examples at CLONMACNOIS in Co. Offaly and Ticooly O'Kelly in Co. Galway, being decorated with typical La Tène curves. They are found in the northern half of the country, as is the greater part of Irish decorated La Tène material. There is reason to believe that impulses, into the southern and SW parts of the country, represented by ringforts, came direct from the Continent, thus complementing the northern La Tène material, including these querns.

The heroic society celebrated in Celtic myth is reflected in archaeological remains. Short double-edged iron swords are found with decorated quillons of bronze, occasionally accompanied by scabbards; spear-heads with doorknob spear-butts were also part of a warrior's armament, as the evidence from LISNACROGHER attests. A single rectangular Celtic shield, made of leather and found at Littleton Bog in Co. Tipperary, is known; bronze shields have been found at Lambay. The horse is important in the EIA; horse-bits and Y-shaped trappings being decorated with stylized human faces and sometimes in a bird's-head shape. Chariots, famous in myth and attested from chariot-burials in the Marne and in Yorkshire, have not yet been found in Ireland, but paired horse-bits, like those from Attymon in Co. Galway, suggest that chariots did exist in Ireland. A bronze ceremonial horn, like the *carnyx* of the Romans, decorated at the mouth, was found with three others at Loughnashade near EAMHAIN MACHA, and may be a votive deposit.

It appears from the mythology that TARA was an inauguration site; this tradition also applies to CARNFREE, at the edge of the complex of monuments at RATHCROGHAN (Crúachain). Also HILLFORTS, as at Eamhain, Tara, Rathgall and Dún Ailinne, were apparently tribal and religious centres. Coastal forts of very large size like Loughshinny, north of Dublin, and DÚN AENGHUSA, with its *chevaux-de-frise* defences, may have had a more directly defensive function.

The La Tène objects of this period, though relatively few in number, speak of schools of the highest accomplishment: the Bann disc, PETRIE CROWN, Kesh-carrigan Bowl, a tankard from Carrickfergus and the famous Lisnacrogher assemblage. We are fortunate in having thousands of bone pattern-pieces and the remains of iron compasses from Cairn H at LOUGHCREW in Co. Meath, a prehistoric PASSAGE GRAVE, in which an EIA artist had made his *atelier*. One of these bone slips is depicted on the Irish £1 note.

Many of these art objects were for personal adornment, like coloured glass beads, decorated safety pins, bronze armlets and the gold collars from BROIGHTER and Clonmacnois, insular versions of the typical neck-ornament of the Continental Celts. A polished iron mirror from Ballymoney in Co. Antrim is decorated on the bronze handle with bird's-head designs; a plainer iron example was found at Lambay.

Some shadowy evidence exists of Celtic religion: the three-faced stone head from near Corleck in Co. Cavan, apparently part of a composite effigy; the stone idols and animal figures found under Armagh Cathed-

IX **Hone, Nathaniel** (the Elder). *The Conjuror*, 145 × 173 cm. (57 × 68 in.), 1775. NGI.

ral; the two-faced Boa Island effigy from Co. Fermanagh and an effigy from Lustymore nearby; and the phallic stone standing at TUROE in Co. Galway. The rich Lisnacrogher find may have been a votive deposit in a lake or marsh following a LBA custom represented in the finds from CULLEN. Burials are few, apparently cremated and sometimes deposited in a low circular mound, as at Cush (Co. Limerick), Carrowjames (Co. Mayo), Oran beg (Co. Galway) and Mullaghmore (Co. Down). Mounds at Rathcroghan and Rathbeg may be EIA burial mounds, as may be Ráth Gráinne and the two Sloping Trenches at Tara. Burials at Lambay Island and near Donaghadee appear to belong to the Roman period: the latter had 150 glass beads, a bronze brooch, a pair of bronze tweezers, glass bracelets and a bronze finger-ring.

In this Roman period Agricola looked enviously at Ireland from Scotland, while Ptolemy of Alexandria noted the names of rivers, tribes and tribal centres in his Geography, written in the 2nd century AD and based on earlier work by Philemon and Marinus of Tyre. Romans were buried near Bray Head in Co. Wicklow, coins were left by Roman visitors to NEWGRANGE, and Roman *terra sigillata* pottery is found at many Irish sites. At Tara, a lead seal, a piece of Roman glass and *terra sigillata* were found at the Rath of the Synods, attesting contacts between this royal site and the Roman world in the 2nd to 4th centuries AD. CHRISTIANITY arrived in Ireland soon afterwards. MH

Ivory, Thomas (*c.* 1730–1786), Architect; probably born in Cork, he was a superb draughtsman, and in 1759 was appointed to teach architectural drawing at the DUBLIN SOCIETY's Schools. He designed: the Blue Coat School (1773), with a Palladian plan, while incorporating Neo-Classical motifs; Newcomen's Bank (1781) Dublin, with its subtle recessed planes; and Kilcarty, Co. Meath (1770s), which is one of the most ingeniously thought-out houses built in Ireland in the 18th century. WG
E. McParland, *Thomas Ivory, Architect*, 1973.

Jellett, Mainie (1897–1944). Painter and Cubist theorist; born in Dublin, she attended the Metropolitan School of Art, 1914, transferred to the Westminster School, London, 1917, studied under Walter Sickert and won the Taylor Art Scholarship, 1920; she also studied in Paris, first with André Lhote and (together with EVIE HONE) under Albert Gleizes.

A vigorous propagandist for Abstract and Cubist art, she adapted many of its forms to human representation and religious subject-matters and wrote and lectured extensively on the subject. She was the first Chairman of the IELA (1943). She is well represented in the NGI and the Hugh Lane Municipal Gallery of Modern Art, Dublin. CMacG
Bruce Arnold, *Mainie Jellett 1897–1944*, 1954; Eileen MacCarvill (ed.), *Mainie Jellett, The Artist's Vision*, 1958.

Jerpoint Abbey, Co. Kilkenny. The remains of this 12th-century foundation could be considered the most interesting of the Cistercian monastic ruins in Ireland; while less magnificent than Boyle Abbey, Co. Roscommon, or Duiske Abbey, Graiguenamanagh, Co. Kilkenny, the layout is more complete and illuminates the characteristic plan of the Order. The church, built at the close of the 12th century, reveals changing stylistic influences of the period; the pillars of the nave vary from round to rectangular to polygonal, with some good Romanesque carving on the capitals. The east window is a 14th-century insertion and the tower over the crossing was added in the 15th. The sacristy, chapter-house, parlour and day-room to the east are relatively complete and the outline of the monastic buildings to the south is clear. The beautiful 15th-century cloister has some interesting figure sculpture

Ivory, Thomas. The Blue Coat School, Dublin, 1773–80; watercolour by James Malton, showing the unexecuted central tower (based on the architect's designs). NGI.

Jerpoint Abbey. Part of the church nave (12th century) and tower over the crossing (15th century) seen through the arcade of the 15th-century cloister.

(*Opposite*) X **Kells, Book of.** The Virgin and Child page (folio 7v) from the 9th-century gospel book in the library of Trinity College, Dublin.

between the columns. There are some finely sculpted tombs by masons of the Callan school.   B de B

Jervais, Thomas (d. 1799). Glass painter; born in Dublin, he was one of the best-known artists in this field in England, translating Sir Joshua Reynolds's cartoon to *The Nativity* window in New College ante-chapel, Oxford (1785), and Benjamin West's *Resurrection* to the east window in St George's Chapel, Windsor (1787–90). His delicate oil paintings on glass, whether on a large scale or as highly popular cabinet panels depicting copies of Old Masters, negate the true functions of leaded stained glass, but led to important commissions in Ireland for the Duke of Leinster, the Loftus, La Touche and Wellesley families and Lord Charlemont. In 1770, the latter recommended that he go to London, where he was well established by 1891. He died in Windsor.   N G B
Michael Wynne, 'Stained Glass in Ireland: principally Irish Stained Glass 1760–1963' (unpublished Ph.D thesis, Trinity College, Dublin), 1975.

Jervas, Charles (*c.* 1675–1739). Painter; the son of John Jervas of Clonliske, Shinrone, Co. Offaly, he studied at Kneller's Academy in London, 1694–5, before going to Rome. He returned to London in 1709 becoming, on the death of Kneller, Painter to the King in 1723. He paid frequent, long visits to Ireland where he painted many fine, realist portraits, though his work is sometimes lifeless, possibly because he usually painted several versions of each portrait. He made a notable collection of Old Masters and was a friend of the great literary men of his day, including SWIFT and Pope, both of whose portraits he painted.   A O C

jewellery. *See* COSTUME; BROOCHES; METALWORK; SILVERWORK.

Jigginstown, near Naas, Co. Kildare. This ambitious, palatial red-brick mansion with a 380-ft (115·82 m.) frontage was built *c.* 1636 for Viscount Wentworth (afterwards Earl of Strafford), Lord-Deputy of Ireland; according to a later report by John Allen, but certainly with the Rev. John Johnson acting as overseer and engineer. After the Restoration it fell into decay and only some walls and the basement remain. In the 18th century Sir EDWARD LOVETT PEARCE drew a reconstruction, now at Chatsworth, of the ruins. The grandiose house appears to have had one principal storey above a high brick-vaulted, stone-faced basement. Projecting towers or pavilions flanked the long central block.   B de B
Maurice Craig, 'New Light on Jigginstown', *UJA*, vol. 33 (1970), 107–10.

Johnson, Neville (1911–   ). Painter and designer; born in England, he eventually settled in the north of Ireland. He exhibited with the Irish Exhibition of Living Art, and in London. He has exerted a considerable influence on many younger Irish painters, such as CECIL KING, ANNE YEATS, Leslie Macweeney and Theo Macnab. He has also designed textiles and stage sets, as well as being interested in photography.   C MacG

Johnston, Francis (1760–1829). Architect; son of William Johnston, architect, of Armagh, he worked for Primate Robinson, under Thomas Cooley, at Armagh, and at Rokeby and Ballymakenny, Co. Louth. He worked in Drogheda, Co. Louth, in the 1790s and built his masterful Neo-Greek country house, Townley Hall, nearby in 1794. He built the spectacular Charleville Forest, Co. Offaly (1801), and several other castles symmetrical in plan. His Classical houses include Farnham, Co. Cavan (1802), Corbalton Hall (1801) and Galtrim (*c.* 1802), Co. Meath. In Dublin he reconstructed the PARLIAMENT HOUSE for the Bank of Ireland (1804), resolving the work of former architects. He designed St George's church (1802), the Chapel Royal, Dublin Castle (1807–14), and the General Post

Jigginstown. Some of the massive square pillars and vaulting of the basement crypt which runs the full extent of the building.

Johnston, Francis. The picturesque Gothick essay, Charleville Forest, Co. Offaly, begun in 1801, featuring towers and battlements.

Office (1812–18). As architect to the Board of Works, he designed a large number of penitentiaries and lunatic asylums. Stylistically, Johnston was inspired by JAMES WYATT, though his work was firmly based on geometric form and strict attention to structural detail.   WG

E. McParland, 'Francis Johnston, Architect', *IGS Bulletin*, vol. xii, 1969.

Johnston, Jennifer Prudence (1930–   ). Writer; born in Dublin, she is the daughter of dramatist (WILLIAM) DENIS JOHNSTON and actress-director SHELAH RICHARDS. Now living in Derry, she has drawn from events in embattled Ulster the moving novel *Shadows on our Skin* (1977); from World War I, *How Many Miles to Babylon?* (1974); from the aftermath of the Troubles, *The Old Jest* (1979), poignantly told from the viewpoint of an eighteen-year old girl in a declining Ascendancy family near Dublin in the 1920s.   BH

Johnston, William Denis (1901–   ). Actor and writer; born in Dublin, he first became a lawyer, before turning to the theatre, as an actor, dramatic critic, writer and director (at the Gate and ABBEY theatres and for BBC radio and television). His first play, *The Old Lady Says No!*, rejected by the Abbey and produced by the Gate in 1929, is an Expressionist satire on romantic patriotism, the dreamed wanderings around modern Dublin of an actor playing – or living – the part of Robert Emmet. *The Moon in the Yellow River* (1931) is based on IRA plots to blow up a powerhouse built by the Free State Government. *A Bride for the Unicorn* (1933) is a 'quest' parable about the life of man. *Storm Song* (1934) uses film-making to satirize attitudes to art; *The Dreaming Dust* (1940) is a stylized drama about Swift; *The Scythe and the Sunset* (1958) is concerned with the Easter Rising. Johnston is always technically innovative, using song, concerted speech, poetry, rhetoric and burlesque.   BH

G. A. Barnett, *Denis Johnston*, 1978; H. Ferrar, *Denis Johnston's Irish Theatre*, 1973; R. Hogan, 'The Adult Theatre of Denis Johnston', in *After the Irish Renaissance*, 1967, pp. 133–46.

Johnstone, Charles (?1719–?1800). Writer; born at Carrigogunnel, Co. Limerick, Johnstone studied at Trinity College, Dublin. His first and most successful novel, *Chrysal, or the Adventures of a Guinea* (1760, 1765), started a vogue for narratives supposedly related by inanimate objects. Johnstone also wrote *The Reverie, or, a Flight to the Paradise of Fools* (1762); an oriental tale, *Arsaces, Prince of Betlis* (1774); *John Juniper* (1781); and *Anthony Varnish* (1786). He went as a journalist to India in 1782 and died at Calcutta.   ICR

Jordan, Neil (1950–   ). Writer; born in Sligo, he moved to Dublin as a child. After graduating from University College, Dublin, he produced a remarkable first collection, *Night in Tunisia and other Stories* (1976), in which petty lives are significantly chronicled, with precise details and memorable images, as in 'Last Rites'.   BH

Joyce, James. Portrait drawing by Seán O'Sullivan, signed and dated 1935. NGI.

Joyce, James A. (1882–1941). Writer; born in Dublin, he was educated in Catholic schools, and graduated from University College, Dublin, in 1902. Although as a youth he abandoned religious orthodoxy, Catholicism left a permanent imprint upon his vision of experience. He found Ireland uncongenial to art, and from 1904 lived on the Continent, but made his homeland the setting for, and to a considerable extent the subject of, all his fiction. Assimilating the lessons of such cosmopolitan masters as Ibsen and Flaubert, he developed great technical sophistication and became increasingly radical in his experiments with form and language. *Dubliners* (1914) presented – through a sequence of fifteen stories linked primarily by situation, atmosphere, and symbol – a predominantly negative view of the modern metropolis. In his highly autobiographical *A Portrait of the Artist as a Young Man* (1916), begun like *Dubliners* in 1904, he depicted the nascent conscience of the artist struggling to develop in those hostile surroundings. His *tour de force* ULYSSES (1922) juxtaposed present and past through extended parallels with, among other works, *The Odyssey*, *The Divine Comedy*, *Hamlet*, and the Bible. Carrying this universalizing tendency to its extreme limits, *Finnegans Wake*, perhaps the most affirmative of all his books, dramatized the archetypes of universal history in a kaleidoscopic dream with correspondingly polyglot language. Joyce's commitment to his art sustained him through frequent poverty, severe eye problems, war, formal and informal censorship, uncomprehending readers and hostile critics. All the while, however, his work was exerting a powerful influence upon such figures as T. S. Eliot, Ezra Pound, William Faulkner, Vladimir Nabokov, and the Irish novelist Flann O'Brien (*see* O'NOLAN); and today his place among the greatest of the moderns is secure. *See* LITERATURE.   PLM

Richard Ellmann, *James Joyce*, revised ed. 1982, A. Walton Litz, *James Joyce*, 1966.

Kavanagh, Joseph Malachy (1856–1918). Landscape painter; born in Dublin, he attended the Royal Hibernian Academy Schools, and first exhibited at the RHA in 1878. In 1882 he went to Antwerp and studied under Verlat; became one of a group of Irish painters, the Antwerp School, which also included WALTER OSBORNE and DERMOD O'BRIEN. Kavanagh moved to Brittany in 1885, but returned to teach in the RHA Schools in 1887; elected ARHA 1889 and RHA 1892, he became Keeper of the RHA in 1910. During the Rising of 1916 when the Academy House in Abbey Street was set on fire, Kavanagh escaped with the Academy's insignia and some of the account books, braving shots from British soldiers manning a barricade at Butt Bridge; however, the Academy House and all its contents, including the Annual Exhibition, were destroyed.

Kavanagh suffered from nervous shock, and his death two years later was a direct result of this experience. He is probably best known today for a series of paintings and related studies painted around Dublin Bay and called *The Cockle Pickers*.   C MacG

Kavanagh, Patrick (1905–67). Poet; born in Co. Monaghan. His first book, *Ploughman and Other Poems*, was published in 1936. *The Green Fool* (1938) established him as a realistic rural voice and *The Great Hunger* (1942), *A Soul for Sale* (1947) and *Terry Flynn* (1948) consolidated his reputation. More important work came with *Recent Poems* (1958) and *Come Dance with Kitty Stobling* (1960). The quality of poems like 'Canal Bank Walk' and 'Lines Written on a Seat on the Grand Canal' is superlative. *See* POETRY.   T McC

Keane, John B. (1928–   ). Writer; born at Listowel, Co. Kerry. His work dramatizes the emotional undercurrents in rural society, as in his enormously successful first play, *Sive* (1959), about matchmaking and the forced marriage of a young girl to an old man, and in *The Field* (1965).   B H

Keating, Geoffrey (*c.* 1570–*c.* 1650?). Writer of prose and poetry in Irish; born at Burges, near Clonmel, Co. Tipperary, he became a Doctor of Divinity. His main works are: *Foras Feasa ar Éirinn* ('Basis of Knowledge about Ireland'; historical, *c.* 1633); and *Trí Bhior-Ghaoithe an Bháis* ('The Three Shafts of Death'; devotional, 1631).   A A

Keating, Seán (1889–1978). Landscape and figurative painter; born at Limerick, he studied at Limerick Technical School, and was awarded a scholarship to the Metropolitan School of Art, Dublin, 1911; he studied under WILLIAM ORPEN, and afterwards worked as an assistant in Orpen's London studio. His best-known work, *Men of the West*, which evokes the romantic stoicism of the west of Ireland, is now in the Hugh Lane Municipal Gallery of Modern Art, Dublin; it was first exhibited at the RHA in 1915. He was appointed a teacher at the Metropolitan School of Art in 1918, eventually becoming Professor of Painting there. Elected RHA in 1919, he was President, 1948–62; he was also an Honorary Member of the Royal Academy, London, and of the Royal Scottish Academy, Edinburgh.   C MacG

Kells, Co. Meath. Probably first founded from Iona early in the 9th century, Kells was for centuries the home of the BOOK OF KELLS. Here, four HIGH CROSSES, a

Keating, Seán. *Men of the West*, oil on canvas, 1915. Hugh Lane Municipal Gallery of Modern Art, Dublin.

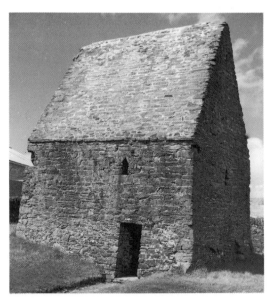

Kells. St Columb's House, a stone structure probably dating from the 12th century.

ROUND TOWER, and the stone-roofed church known as 'St Columb's House' all survive to remind us of the artistic and architectural ingenuity and vitality of the monks of this Columban foundation. 'St Columb's House' has sometimes been equated with a church known to have been built at Kells in 814, but it dates, more probably, from the 12th century.   P H

Kells, Book of. The Book of Kells (Trinity College, Dublin, library A.I.6, ms. no. 58) consists of 340 folios measuring 330 × 250 mm. (13 × 10 in.). It dates from the early 9th century and is famous for the wealth and variety of its designs (*see* pl. x); it includes colour ornament on every page except two. The origin of this Latin gospel book *de luxe* is uncertain. It may have had its beginnings in Iona, continued at KELLS, Co. Meath, after invading Vikings drove the Abbot of Iona with his monks to their new home in Ireland. The book is probably the one referred to in the *Annals of Ulster* (under the year 1006–7), which record that 'the great gospel of Colm-Cille [Columba] was stolen from the western sacristy of the great stone church at Cenannas [Kells] on account of its wrought shrine [*cumtach*]'. Happily, most of the folios were rescued, although the original golden cover was never found. The book has been in Trinity College Library since Bishop Henry Jones of Meath donated it, together with the BOOK OF DURROW, in the second half of the 17th century; it is now bound in four volumes.

Full-page illustrations depict the nativity of Christ, his temptation and arrest; there are portraits of Christ and two of the evangelists, the 8-Circle Cross, and the colourful Chi-Rho page. The Crucifixion and Ascension pages are movingly symbolic rather than representational. A series of elaborately ornamented canon-table pages and many varied artistic treatments of the symbols of the evangelists (man, lion, ox and eagle) provide examples of the mixture of the grotesque, the mysterious, and the unpredictable in the ornament. Initial letters, of anthropomorphic, zoomorphic, phyllomorphic, geometric designs abound in great variety, notable examples being the dignified ornamentation of the Beatitudes, Paternoster, Magnificat, and the Prodigal son. There is a wide range of colours – red, blue, green, yellow, mauve of varying shades. Charming little animals frequent the pages throughout, filling gaps and serving as brackets, as words spill over the margin: dogs, cats, kittens, mice, fish, hare, butterfly, poultry, horses, and gaily coloured peacocks all bring life and joyfulness to many a page. Their supple shapes mingle the humorous with the terrifying. Differing styles suggest a team of artists. Several hands are thought to have worked on the well-rounded semi-uncial letters of great beauty and characteristically Irish shaping. Abbreviations are few, save for the sacred names, such as 'ihs' (Jesus), 'xps' (Christus), 'ds' (deus). The overall artistic plan subtly weaves the four gospels into a unity and presents the ms. as a single life of Christ. The inclusion of seven legal documents in the IRISH LANGUAGE on pages originally left blank points to Kells as the home of the ms. in 11th and 12th centuries. There is no colophon; the beginning and end of the ms.

are missing, but the surviving leaves have deservedly been classed among the most wonderful books of the world.   G O S
Françoise Henry (ed.), *The Book of Kells*, 1974; Sir E. Sullivan, *The Book of Kells*, 1914; facsimile edition, *Evangeliorum Quattuor Codex Cenannensis* (2 vols.), 1950–1.

Kelly, Hugh (1739–77). Writer; born in Killarney, he found success in the London theatre with his first comedy, *False Delicacy* (1768), put on to rival Goldsmith's *The Good Natur'd Man*. The best of his subsequent plays is *The School for Wives* (1773). A journalist and lawyer, Kelly was also author of the popular sentimental novel, *Memoirs of a Magdalen* (1767).   I C R

Kelly, Oisin (1915–81). Sculptor; born in Dublin, he took a degree in French and Irish at Trinity College, Dublin. In Frankfurt in 1937, while on a language scholarship, he became interested in Barlach and German Expressionism. He attended evening classes at the National College of Art, Dublin, and at the Waterford School of Art, and became a teacher at St Columba's, Rathfarnham, 1946–64. He spent two terms at Chelsea Polytechnic working under Henry Moore. He exhibited at An t-Óireachtas in 1946 and subsequently at the IELA and the ROYAL HIBERNIAN ACADEMY, to which he was elected in 1965. He also designed for the KILKENNY DESIGN WORKSHOPS for several years. He worked on a number of church commissions and was a leading practitioner of religious art. He executed several outdoor monuments in Dublin and Cork. On a smaller scale he executed many sculptures of birds and animals. Traditional in subject, with many echoes of an Irish nature, Kelly was equally skilled in wood and metal, showing great sensitivity of observation and delicacy of feeling.   J T
The Works of Oisin Kelly, Sculptor (exhibition catalogue), Dublin, Belfast, Cork 1978.

Kelly, Oisin. Carved decoration on the front of St Theresa's church, Sion Mills, Co. Tyrone, completed in 1966.

Kennelly, Brendan (1936–). Poet; born in Co. Kerry, he is the senior bard of Munster, a writer whose modesty has deflected critical attention from his work. He is happiest when handling the great themes of poetry – love, death and betrayal. Books like *My Dark Fathers* (1965) and *Islandman* (1977) pursue those themes, and areas of loneliness and stolen passions. T McC

Kenny, Seán (1933–73). Stage designer; born at Portroe, Co. Tipperary, his earliest major success was the Theatre Workshop (London) production of BEHAN's *The Hostage* (1958), and most popular was the London production of the musical *Oliver*. He redesigned the Old Vic for use by the National Theatre pending the construction of a permanent purpose-built theatre complex on the South Bank of the Thames. C F-S

Kernoff, Harry (1900–74). Landscape, genre and narrative painter; born in London, he moved to Dublin in 1914, and there attended night classes at the Metropolitan School of Art. He won the Taylor Art Scholarship in 1923, and was elected RHA in 1936. A memorial exhibition was held in the Hugh Lane Municipal Gallery of Modern Art, Dublin, in 1976. Kernoff is best known for his paintings of Dublin characters and for his books of woodcuts. C MacG

Kiely, Benedict (1919–). Writer; born in Co. Tyrone, he entered the Jesuit novitiate but abandoned it and studied at the National University of Ireland. From 1946 he worked as a journalist on the *Irish Independent* and *Irish Press*. He has combined writing fiction with excellent journalism (for press, radio and television) and criticism (his *Poor Scholar. A Study of William Carleton*, 1948, and *Modern Irish Fiction*, 1950, were seminal works). His short stories appear regularly in *The New Yorker* and in collections such as *A Ball of Malt and Madame Butterfly* (1973). Of his novels, *Dogs enjoy the Morning* (1968) is the most racy and rakish, *Proxopera* (1977) the most disturbing, recounting the effect of the IRA upon ordinary life in the North. Kiely has both an acute eye for character and detail and an acute ear for dialect and comedy. B H
D. J. Casey, *Benedict Kiely*, 1974; G. Eckley, *Benedict Kiely*, 1975.

Kilkenny Design Workshops. In 1960 Córas Tráchtála, the Irish Export Board, obtained administrative responsibility for the promotion of industrial design from the ARTS COUNCIL, and invited a group of eminent Scandinavian designers to tour Ireland and assess the state of affairs. The group's report, *Design in Ireland*, was published in April 1961 and, for a document of only 55 pages, ranged with remarkable authority and insight over many aspects of the subject.
Within a year Córas Tráchtála had set up a committee of designers, artists and exporters to look into the idea – the main recommendation of the report for an 'Irish Institute of the Visual Arts'. In 1964 an autonomous company, Kilkenny Design Workshops, was set up to give practical help to manufacturers in industrial design, as well as to foster public taste and interest.

The new company bought and converted the abandoned 18th-century stables and coach-house of Kilkenny Castle, 75 miles from Dublin, and installed designers and skilled craftsmen in departments concerned with textiles (woven and printed), ceramics, precious metals, woodwork and other craft-based disciplines. The idea was that a community of designers alone might have difficulty in making an impact upon Irish industry, but if they had sufficient means of production they could produce prototypes which would be convincing demonstration of the practicality and sales appeal of their work.

The Workshops, in response to the perceived needs of industry, have since grown, providing design services also for engineering-based manufacture, furniture, print and packaging and many other products. The Workshops have been given responsibility by the Department of Industry and Energy for the advancement of industrial design in Ireland and have had a remarkable influence on public appreciation of, and demand for, higher standards of design, achieved through exhibitions and through the Kilkenny Shops (in Dublin and Kilkenny) which exhibit and sell 'the best of Irish workmanship and design in familiar things'.

Among other related activities, the Workshops have particularly fostered professionalism among young Irish designers through a Designer Development Programme and award schemes, as well as arranging exchanges between Irish and overseas designers and by representing the design needs of industry to the educational authorities.

Now with 120 employees and an annual budget of £2 million (1981), of which over two-thirds was earned from design fees and sales, the organization continues to grow and change to meet new demands of Irish industry. However, its early commitment to the crafts and craft-based industries is by no means neglected and it can be argued that the tradition of design integrity and concern for high qualities of workmanship thus established in the 1960s is standing it in good stead as it seeks to uphold standards amid the technology and consumerism of the 1980s. G T

Killaloe Cathedral, Co. Clare. This fine early 13th-century building houses a 12th-century HIGH CROSS from Kilfenora, and has an inserted late Romanesque doorway with carving in bold relief which ranks with CLONFERT, Co. Galway, as being among the best examples in the country. The Cathedral itself has a fine three-light east window, and curiously carved capitals. Beside the Cathedral is St Flannan's Oratory, a small rectangular stone-roofed edifice, its nave measuring 8·78 × 5·33 m. (28 ft 9 in. × 17 ft 6 in.); its chancel has been demolished. P H

Kilmainham, Co. Dublin. The Royal Hospital, Kilmainham, Ireland's most distinguished 17th-century building in the Classical style that was more

Killaloe Cathedral. The restored interior, showing the chancel and east window.

Kilmainham. The façade of the Royal Hospital, showing the overall symmetry of Sir William Robinson's design.

popular in France and the Netherlands than in England, was the work of the Irish Surveyor-General, Sir WILLIAM ROBINSON. Begun in 1680, it was in use by 1684; the chapel was consecrated in 1687 and the tower added in 1701. A royal commission of Charles II, it was built to accommodate 300 military pensioners on three floors around a closed courtyard with a ground-floor loggia. It seems that Robinson was influenced in his plan and design by the Hôtel des Invalides, Paris, which had recently been inaugurated for the same purpose and which, there is reason to believe, he could have seen; his design is also imbued with the Renaissance respect for symmetry. 	B de B

Kilroy, Thomas (1934–). Playwright; born at Callan, Co. Kilkenny, he is now Professor of Modern English at University College, Galway. Although he has written novels, such as *The Big Chapel* (a study of religious intolerance), 1971, he is best known as a playwright; his plays include *The Death and Resurrection of Mr. Roche*; *The O'Neill*; *Tea, Sex and Shakespeare*; and the expressionist *Talbot's Box* (1977), about the working-class mystic Matt Talbot. 	BH

King, Cecil (1921–). Abstract painter and collector; born at Rathdrum, Co. Wicklow, of a prosperous business family, he began painting in the 1950s after he had begun his own collection of paintings. He worked with Barbara Warren and NEVILLE JOHNSON; he exhibits in Dublin, as well as in Scottish, English, American and Spanish galleries. An exhibition of both his own works and works in his collection was held in the Hugh Lane Municipal Gallery of Modern Art, Dublin, 1981. 	C MacG

King, Cecil. Abstract study in black, grey and white, *Painting 1968*. An Chomhairle Ealaíon Collection, Dublin.

Kinsella, Thomas (1928–). Poet; born in Dublin, he was educated at University College, Dublin. He spent sixteen years in the Irish Civil Service before moving to the USA to become writer in residence at the University of Southern Illinois in 1965. He is Professor of English at Temple University, Philadelphia.

His own poetic work has moved from personal awareness in *Another September* (1958), to public statement in *Nightwalker and Other Poems* (1968), to psychological savagery in *Notes from the Land of the Dead* (1972). He had extended his search in two ways: towards the psychological process, and towards the Irish past in *The Táin* (1970) and *Poems of the Dispossessed* (1981), a translation of Gaelic poems from 1600 to 1900. Kinsella's quest is the repossession in full of the Irish past, the healing of a cultural schizophrenia which began in the 18th century.   T McC

knitting. The technique seems to have been known in Ireland at a very early period. The famous Chalice in the ARDAGH HOARD is decorated with knit wire which appears to have been made on a simple mechanical device, and with wire-knit filigree around its rims.

On the Aran Islands, where the men wear hand-spun and hand-woven jackets and trousers, a *crois* (or woven belt of bright colours) and knitted jerseys, knitting reached a high standard. The women use intricate stitches, Cables (representing fishermen's ropes), Diamonds (after the mesh of the fishing net), Honeycomb, Moss-stitch, Trellis, Zigzag, Tree of Life, Fern, and Trinity (the three last of religious significance), and plaited patterns which relate strongly to carved designs found on prehistoric stone slabs and early Irish crosses. The knitting patterns are not written down but are passed on from mother to daughter, each family having its own unique design. Aran-style knitting is now widely imitated.   H L M
B. Norwick, *The Origin of Knits. The Ardagh Chalice and Wire Knitting*, 1977; G. Thompson, *Patterns for Guernseys, Jerseys and Arans*, 1971.

Knockast, Co. Westmeath. Site of a MULTIPLE CIST CAIRN, 8 km. (5 miles) NE of Moate; 18 m. (59 ft) in diameter, it is situated on a hilltop, 200 m. (650 ft) above sea-level. The site was excavated by the Harvard Expedition in 1932: 43 burials, including 39 cremations and 3 adult male inhumations were found. Male burials also predominated among the cremations; some were in cists, some accompanied by Food Vessels, some in Cordoned or Encrusted Urns; most were found near the eastern half of the cairn. In the old surface were three pits containing bones of ox, sheep or goat, and horse. The grave-goods included a bronze dagger, a razor, an eyed pin of bone, a flint knife and parts of five bone cylinders presumably used as inlays for a haft like that of the Bush Barrow 'sceptre' from Somerset, England.   M H
H. O'N. Hencken and H. L. Movius, 'The Cemetery Cairn of Knockast', *PRIA* 41 (1934), 232–84.

Knowth, Co. Meath. Site of a PASSAGE GRAVE cemetery of 18 tombs, tightly grouped on a knoll, 76 m. (250 ft) above sea-level, at the NW end of Boyne cemetery; it has been under investigation by G. Eogan since 1964. The large tumulus, 78 × 90 m. (256 × 295 ft) has opposed passage graves opening from E and W. The western tomb 34 m. (112 ft) long, with a slightly angled passage and a box-like end-chamber, has a stone basin and highly accomplished decoration. The eastern tomb is cruciform, slightly larger than NEWGRANGE; it is 33 m. (108 ft) long, and the chamber is 8 m. (26 ft 3 in.) wide and 7·75 m. (25 ft 5 in.) high, with a carved stone basin in a recess on the north side. The kerbstones of this tumulus are boldly carved in an individual and accomplished abstract style.   M H

(*Above*) **Knowth.** Passage in the large tumulus, showing upright stones supporting lintels with incised decoration.

(*Left*) **knitting.** Aran sweater featuring characteristic traditional patterns.

lace. Irish lace is mainly of the 19th century; 'Limerick lace' was, however, not true lace, but was embroidered on machine net made at Limerick and other centres. In 'Limerick lace' the solid areas are achieved either by darning or by tambour work, a chain stitch worked with a special hooked tambour needle resembling a crochet hook. Mrs Vere O'Brien did much to revive this kind of work.

In 1852 the Royal Dublin Society (*see* DUBLIN SOCIETY) gave awards for artistic talent at Carrickmacross, Co. Monaghan, where desperate conditions were widespread after the famine. In 'Carrickmacross lace' the solid areas are of applied fabric; originally this was muslin or cambric but organdie was introduced as a substitute in the first half of the 20th century and after World War II the cotton net was replaced by nylon net.

Pillow (bobbin) lace is made on a bolster-like little pillow on which the pricked-out paper bearing the design is placed and where the pins, which are manipulated to twist and plait the threads according to the design, are firmly held.

Needlepoint is in the true lace tradition; an example, designed in 1911 by a member of the Community of Poor Clares and worked at Kenmare, Co. Kerry, may be seen in the National Museum, Dublin. It is a tabernacle veil with a central panel showing the figure of Christ between two angels; the centre is in flat point and the borders are in a coarser raised point.

From 1878 great efforts were made to improve standards of design and the Schools of Art in Cork, Waterford, Limerick and Dublin were encouraged to produce lace designs of quality. HLM
E. Boyle, *The Irish Flowerers*, 1971; A. K. Longfield, Catalogue to the Collection of Lace, National Museum of Ireland.

lace. An example of 19th-century 'Carrickmacross lace' with a floral pattern.

Lane, Sir Hugh Percy (1875–1915). Art collector; born at Ballybrack, Co. Cork, he was the youngest child of Rev. J. M. Lane and his wife Adelaide (*née* Persse), an older sister of LADY GREGORY. When still in his teens he worked for several art dealers in London, and then established himself in business.

Introduced by SARAH PURSER to the works of JOHN BUTLER YEATS and NATHANIEL HONE the Younger in 1901 at an exhibition in 7 St Stephen's Green, Dublin, he became interested in assisting Irish art and commissioned Yeats to paint a series of portraits of contemporary Irish figures; this commission was completed by WILLIAM ORPEN, a distant cousin of Lane's, with whom he shared rooms in London for some years.

Lane also organized several exhibitions of the visual arts in Ireland during the early years of the century, culminating in the foundation of the Municipal Gallery of Modern Art in Dublin. He gave and loaned

Lane, Sir Hugh. Portrait drawing by John Butler Yeats, signed and dated August 1905. NGI.

large numbers of works by modern painters to this gallery, then he commissioned Lutyens to design a gallery spanning the River Liffey to house this collection. The project met with great hostility and bitter criticism. It came to nothing, and so the first exhibition was opened in temporary premises leased by Lane in Clonmel House, Harcourt Street, and part of it remained there until the present gallery was opened in 1933 in Charlemont House.

Following many difficulties with Irish public opinion and the Dublin City Authorities, Lane moved the major part of his loan collection to London in 1913. In 1909 he was knighted for his services to Irish art and in 1914 became Director of the NGI.

While returning to Ireland from America on the *Lusitania* he was drowned when that ship was torpedoed off the Old Head of Kinsale on 7 May 1915; his body was never recovered. In his will he bequeathed his collection to London, but by an unsigned codicil he intended the return of the disputed Modern Collection, already in London, to Dublin.

A controversy raged over the terms of Lane's will and its codicil until 1959, when an agreement to stand for twenty years was reached between the Irish and British Governments, whereby the two parts of the collection should be rotated every five years between Dublin and London. In 1980 the agreement was renewed for a further fourteen years.

Charlemont House now contains the collection begun by Lane. Despite Lane's own request that it should not happen, the gallery has nevertheless been renamed the Hugh Lane Municipal Gallery of Modern Art. CMacG

Thomas Bodkin, *Hugh Lane and his Pictures*, 2nd ed. 1956; *Tribute to Sir Hugh Lane* (catalogue of the pictures bequeathed by Lane to the National Gallery of Ireland), 1961.

Lanyon, Sir Charles (1813–89). Architect; born in England at Eastbourne, he was apprenticed to Jacob Owen, supervisor of the Irish Board of Works, married his daughter and became County Surveyor of Antrim in 1835. For the Belfast Bank he remodelled the Market House, Belfast (1839), in the Italianate style which was to become his hallmark; yet he designed the Queen's College, Belfast (1847–49), and many churches in the neighbourhood of Belfast in the Gothic style. He designed several other buildings in Belfast: the Court House (1850), the Northern Bank (1852), and the Custom House (1857); also the Prince of Wales Terrace, Bray, Co. Wicklow (1861); a number of country houses, including Drenagh, Co. Derry (1837), Ballywalter, Co. Down (1846), Dundarave, Co. Antrim (1846), and Stradbally, Co. Laois (1866), which last he remodelled. He was in partnership with W. H. LYNN from 1854 to 1878 and was knighted for political services in 1868. WG

Lanyon, Sir Charles. The Custom House, Belfast, a notable example of civic architecture of the mid-19th century.

La Tène. Detail of the Keshcarrigan Bowl, showing bronze handle in the form of a duck's head.

La Tène. This name is given to the second major culture of the Continental Celts from 430 BC to the time of Christ; it derives from the finds at lake-dwellings on the east shore of Lake Neuchâtel in Switzerland, discovered by Col. Friedrich Schwab in 1857. Many of the objects found at this site are decorated in a characteristic manner marked by a love of abstraction and great subtlety. The La Tène style is represented by a variety of curvilinear and other motifs which include stylized animal, bird, and human forms, its hallmark being the thick-lobed spiral and trumpet curve. In Ireland the bird's head is found on the Keshcarrigan Bowl and the PETRIE CROWN. The La Tène style was introduced to Ireland probably in the 3rd century BC; it was employed in Ireland in the IRON AGE, most frequently on horse-bits and Y-shaped horse-trappings, on weaponry like swords, scabbards and spear-heads (*see* LISNACROGHER), on personal ornaments like armlets, fibulae (dress-fasteners), ring-headed pins and gold collars such as those in the BROIGHTER HOARD and from CLONMACNOIS; it also occurs on stones like the phallic TUROE STONE and on querns of beehive shape, all of them from the northern half of the country. The La Tène style survived in Ireland, refreshed, it seems, from sources in Western Britain, into the Early Christian period, when it is referred to as 'Ultimate La Tène' and occurs on such objects as the Ardagh Chalice (*see* ARDAGH HOARD) and 'TARA' BROOCH, in ILLUMINATED MANUSCRIPTS and on HIGH CROSSES. MFR/MH

Latham, James (1696–1747). Painter; probably born in Co. Tipperary. No details of his early education are known, but in 1724 he was a student in the Antwerp Academy, and as he shows a knowledge of

(*Above*) **Latham, James.** *Bishop Clayton and his Wife,* a notable example of the artist's formal portraits of public figures. NGI (on loan from the Representative Church Body).

(*Right*) **Lavery, Sir John.** *Lady Lavery as Cathleen ni Houlihan,* a portrait of the artist's wife, with harp, painted in 1923 for use on Irish paper currency. Bank of Ireland Collection.

both French and English art, he probably journeyed via London and Paris. He returned to Dublin before 1730 and painted portraits of most of the Establishment figures in Ireland: MPs, generals, bishops, municipal office holders, as well as society figures. His full-length portraits are not as successful as his three-quarter length likenesses or his excellent double portraits. His beautiful, silvery, colouring enhances the costumes of his sitters, and his easy brushwork builds up convincing, realistic, likenesses. A O C

Lavery, Sir John (1856–1941). Landscape and portrait painter; born in Belfast, he settled in Scotland where he made his name as a leader of the Glasgow School. He later had a considerable practice as a fashionable portrait painter in London. He was President of the Royal Society of Portrait Painters; Member of the Royal Academy, London, and of the Royal Hibernian Academy, Dublin, of the Royal Scottish Academy, Edinburgh, and also of the Academies of Rome, Antwerp, Milan, Brussels, and Stockholm. He was knighted in 1918. In 1940, at the age of 84, he published his autobiography, *The Life of a Painter.*

Sympathetic to the movement for Irish Independence, Lavery painted dramatic pictures of the trial of Sir Roger Casement and the lying-in-state of Terence MacSwiney. He was commissioned by the Government to design the new paper currency for the Irish Free State in 1923; the emblematic figure of Ireland on the notes is in fact a portrait of his American wife, Hazel. Lavery returned to live in Ireland and died near Kilmoganny, Co. Kilkenny. C MacG
Walter Shaw-Sparrow, *John Lavery and his Work,* 1911.

Lavin, Mary (1912–). Writer; born at East Walpole, Mass., she moved to Ireland at the age of nine, and her acute perception of the different world she then entered has never left her. She has said 'I would not place my characters in any setting other than Ireland'. Encouraged to write by LORD DUNSANY, her first collection of stories was *Tales from Bective Bridge* (1942). After her first husband died, leaving her with three children and a farm to run, her widowhood provided material for several stories, the most intriguing of which was 'In a Café'. In 1969 she remarried and divides her life beteen Dublin and Meath. To her, 'story writing is looking deeper than usual into the human heart'; in the process she writes perceptively about families and marriage, about social and religious conventions, about love and loneliness, ranging from the life of peasants and fishermen ('The Great Wave') to the prosperous middle classes ('The Becker Wives'). She is particularly skilled in catching shifts of perception ('Happiness', 'Lilacs') or of relationship ('A Memory'). She has also written two novels, *The House in Clewe Street* (1945) and *Mary O'Grady* (1950). Her latest collection is *The Shrine and other Stories* (1977). B H
A. A. Kelly, *Mary Lavin: A Study of the Short Stories,* 1980; Z. Bowen, *Mary Lavin,* 1975; R. Peterson, *Mary Lavin,* 1978.

Le Brocquy, Louis (1916–). Painter, designer and graphic artist; born in Dublin, he is largely self-taught. He was one of the founder-member of the IELA, 1943; elected RHA in 1949, he taught at the Central School of Art and Design, London. In 1947 he was represented in the British Council's exhibition 'Twelve

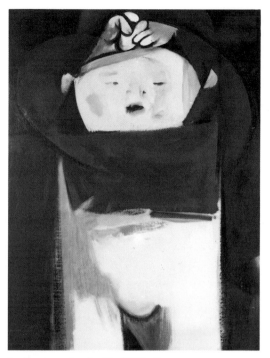

Le Brocquy, Louis. *Tired Child*, oil on canvas, 1954. Ulster Museum.

Leech, William John. *A Convent Garden, Brittany*, oil on canvas. NGI.

British Painters' and in the exhibition of Contemporary Irish Painting in New York; he represented Ireland at the Venice Biennale 1956, and has since then consistently represented Ireland abroad. He served on the board of KILKENNY DESIGN WORKSHOPS, 1965–79, and was appointed a Chevalier of the French Legion of Honour, 1975. Tinkers, children and the famous series of the TÁIN epic, textile and carpet designs, as well as illustrations for books, tapestries, mosaics, and the internationally famous series of evoked heads of literary and poetic figures (YEATS, Bacon, BECKETT, JOYCE and Lorca), together represent the huge output of this artist. His work can be seen in many leading museums, both in Ireland and elsewhere. He was awarded a major retrospective exhibition in Dublin and Belfast, 1966, and an exhibition 'Louis Le Brocquy and The Irish Head Image' was held at the New York State Museum, Albany, in 1981. C MacG

Dorothy Walker, *Louis Le Brocquy*, 1981.

Ledwidge, Francis (1891–1917). Poet, soldier and farm labourer; born at Slane, Co. Meath, his first published work appeared in 1916, and he was killed in action in Belgium the following year. Alice Curtayne edited his *Complete Poems*, published in 1974. T McC

Leech, William John (1881–1968). Landscape and figurative painter; born in Dublin, he was educated at the Metropolitan School of Art, Dublin, before attending, from 1899 to 1901, the RHA Schools under WALTER OSBORNE, and the Académie Julian, Paris, 1901. He was elected ARHA in 1907, and RHA in 1910. Leech lived in Brittany, 1903–16, and thereafter in England, save for returning to France to paint in Concarneau and Quimperle. Amongst his best-known works are *A Convent Garden, Brittany*, *The Parasol*, and *Goose Girl, Quimperle*, all now in the National Gallery of Ireland. The catalogue of his works produced by Alan Denson contains a useful list of his works and their datings. C MacG

A. Denson, *An Irish Artist, W. J. Leech RHA (1881–1968)*, 2 vols., 1968–9.

Leitch, Maurice (1933–). Writer; born in Co. Antrim, he worked as a schoolteacher and for the BBC. His novels *The Liberty Lad* and *Poor Lazarus* appeared in 1965 and 1969 respectively, and *Stamping Ground* (1975) uses an intriguing narrative technique to lay bare the violence of rural life. B H

Leonard, Hugh (pseudonym of John Keyes Byrne; 1926–). Playwright; born and brought up in Dalkey, Co. Dublin, by foster-parents, he worked as a civil servant in the Land Commission until 1959, then became a scriptwriter for the BBC. His early plays *The Big Birthday*, *A Leap in the Dark* and *Madigan's Lock*, were produced in 1956, 1957 and 1958 respectively. He is also remarkable for excellent stage adaptations, such as *The Passion of Peter Ginty* (1961) from Ibsen's *Peer Gynt*,

Stephen D (1962) from JAMES JOYCE, and *When the Saints Go Cycling In* (1965) from *The Dalkey Archive* by Flann O'Brien (*see* O'NOLAN). He is a prolific and talented writer for films and television, and has also published his autobiography, *Home Before Dark* (1975).   BH

Lever, Charles James (1806–72). Writer; born in Dublin, he was educated at Trinity College, but spent most of his later life on the Continent. A prolific novelist with a gift for comedy, he was very popular with English audiences, but he has frequently been condemned by Irish readers for not taking his fellow-countrymen seriously enough. He has been praised, on the other hand, as a shrewd observer of manners and politics. Among his best-known books are *The Confessions of Harry Lorrequer* (1839), *Charles O'Malley, the Irish Dragoon* (1841), *The Martins of Cro' Martin* (1856), and *Lord Kilgobbin* (1872).   PLM
Lionel Stevenson, *Dr. Quicksilver: the Life of Charles Lever*, 1939.

Liddy, James (1934–   ). Poet; born in Co. Clare. A writer of genius, he has published many collections: *In a Blue Smoke* (1964), *Blue Mountain* (1968), *Orpheus in the Ice-Cream Parlour* (1975) and *Corca Bascinn* (1977). He has edited *Arena* and served on the editorial board of *Poetry Ireland*.   TMcC

Linenhall Library, Belfast. This, the oldest learned institution in the city, was founded in 1788 as the Belfast Society for Promoting Knowledge, or the 'Belfast Reading Society', in the old White Linen Hall. It moved in 1896 to a site close by, where its rich collection of Irish material, studiously kept up to date, co-exists with a conventional lending library.   MC

Linkardstown, Co. Carlow. Site of a tumulus of the Late Neolithic; in the central cist, $2 \cdot 30 \times 2$ m. (7 ft 6 in. × 6 ft 6 in.), was the burial of an adult with several ancient fractures of the skull. With it were sherds of four decorated vessels, one necked and one broad-rimmed, together with a plain Neolithic sherd and a polished stone axe-head with the shadow of the haft still visible on its surface. The cist was excavated in a mound of yellow clay, 25 m. (80 ft) in diameter, on the slope of a hill about 110 m. (350 ft) above sea-level.   MH
J. Raftery, 'A Neolithic Burial in Co. Carlow', *JRSAI* 74 (1944), 61–2.

Lismore Crozier. This crozier, found in 1814, together with the Book of Lismore, in the wall of a tower of Lismore Castle, Co. Waterford, is one of the finest objects of the renaissance of the arts in Ireland which occurred in the late 11th–early 12th century. Now in the NMI, it is made of plates of bronze enclosing a wooden core; its crook, decorative knops and glass studs are magnificently ornamented. Its openwork crest of cast animals, human figures and Irish 'Urnes'-style animal ornaments are especially noteworthy. Many of its frames for ornament are now empty and only traces can be detected of the gold foil which originally covered the surviving motifs. An inscription in Irish attributes the crozier to the craftsman Nectan, working under the patronage of Niall Mac Meic Aeducaín, Abbot of Lismore 1090–1113.   MFR

Lisnacrogher, Co. Antrim. Archaeological material discovered during peat-cutting at this townland near Broughshane was first described in 1884. Worked oak timbers, now completely removed, and a large complex of metal objects were collected by Grainger and noted by Wakeman, Wood-Martin and Munro. The timbers suggest that a CRANNÓG existed here but the metalwork cannot certainly be linked with this; it may belong to nearby votive deposits.
   The material – now in the NMI, the Ulster Museum and the British Museum – comprises the finest LA TÈNE collection from Ireland: three scabbard-plates of bronze, lavishly decorated, a complete plain scabbard with its chape and the corroded remains of a sword-blade, two long iron spear-heads, over twenty knobbed spear-butts of insular type, one with a wooden shaft $2 \cdot 45$ m. (8 ft) long, five phalerae (horse-trappings), two ring-headed pins with enamelled decoration, and a bird's-head mount.   MH
W. G. Wood-Martin, *The Lake Dwellings of Ireland*, 1888.

literature (English language). This general history of English-language prose and drama in Ireland is divided into three major chronological sections. There are separate articles POETRY and LITERATURE (IRISH LANGUAGE); *see* also THEATRE. In this article the three chronological sections are: literature before 1820; literature from 1820 to 1920; and literature from 1920 to the present.

Literature before 1820
To determine precisely when a distinctively Irish literature in English emerged is no easy task. Nor is it much easier to decide who is, exactly, an 'Irish' writer. Should we – to go no further back – look to the 16th century and EDMUND SPENSER, who went to Ireland on a political mission, settled at Kilcolman in Co. Cork, and wrote there *A View of the Present State of Ireland*? Or should we prefer the 17th century which produced, among other Irish-born writers, the poet Sir John Denham, the critic LORD ROSCOMMON, and the playwright and Poet Laureate NAHUM TATE? If we opt for the 18th century, do we admit a writer such as LAURENCE STERNE who, born in Ireland by chance, left the island at the age of ten, never to return, yet whom JAMES JOYCE could call 'my fellow-countryman'?
   It is perhaps best to accept that family background, birth, and education must each play a part in any definition, as must some greater or lesser degree of engagement with Irish issues or Irish subject-matter. It is no coincidence that the emergence of major Irish-born writers was contemporaneous with the first serious attempts at self-definition in national and political terms by the English-speaking Protestants of Ireland. The 1690s saw not only the establishment of the Protestant Ascendancy – by means of the Penal

Jonathan Swift (1667–1745), portrait by Charles Jervas, c. 1718. National Portrait Gallery, London.

Laws – but also the publication of *The Case of Ireland's being bound . . . stated* (1698) by William Molyneux (1656–98), who argued for Ireland's right to legislative independence from England. With few exceptions, Anglo-Irish writers of the 18th century were members of the Protestant nation, linked by shared social and educational backgrounds and their common religious and political assumptions.

The 18th century, though, was a cosmopolitan age and the Enlightenment – to whose values many writers gave allegiance – a European phenomenon. Throughout the century national concerns were placed within wider literary and intellectual contexts. The result was a sense of confidence which, however, Anglo-Irish literature began to lose soon after 1800 and did not regain until the beginning of the present century.

No writer of the period engaged more energetically in Irish affairs than JONATHAN SWIFT, who suggested means of economic improvement in *A Proposal for the Universal Use of Irish Manufacture* (1720), defended Ireland from English exploitation in *The Drapier's Letters* (1724), and savagely taunted the nation's failure to respond to his ideas in *A Modest Proposal* (1729). In his best-known works, though, Swift transcends purely Irish themes. *A Tale of a Tub* (1704, 1710) reveals its author as an Augustan humanist taking up arms against modern philosophy and weighing the rival claims of tradition and individual experience as means of attaining true knowledge. In *Gulliver's Travels* (1726), Swift subordinates his manifold concerns to an overriding preoccupation with human nature itself. The Book IV account of Lemuel Gulliver, caught midway between the rational, horse-like Houyhnhnms whom he admires, and the instinctive, ape-like Yahoos from whom he recoils, suggests the tough-minded conviction that Man is not, as Swift wrote elsewhere, '*animal rationale*' but only '*rationis capax*'.

Throughout the early 18th century, philosophy flourished in Ireland; among notable Irish philosophers were William King (1650–1729), JOHN TOLAND, GEORGE BERKELEY, and Francis Hutcheson (1694–1746). Adapting the epistemology of John Locke to theological ends, Toland became notorious when he published the deistical *Christianity not Mysterious* (1696), which argued that religion depended not on revelation but on reason alone. Also taking Locke as a starting point, Berkeley combined his own acute awareness of the anti-religious implications of much contemporary philosophy with Christian orthodoxy. His early and most original works, *An Essay towards a New Theory of Vision* (1709), *A Treatise Concerning the Principles of Human Knowledge* (1710), and the *Three Dialogues between Hylas and Philonous* (1713), reveal a developing concern with his fundamental notion – '*esse est percipi*' – to be is to be perceived. From this philosophical principle Berkeley the theologian moved directly to argue for the necessary existence of God. Objects cannot, in Berkeley's terms, be known to exist when not perceived, and in order to avoid the belief – repugnant to common sense – that all objects in the material world cease to exist when not perceived by the finite minds of men, it is necessary to posit an infinite mind – God – which guarantees the continuity of the physical world. Berkeley's concern with literary style, especially evident in the elegance of his *Three Dialogues*, may be seen also in his later works, *Alciphron, or the Minute Philosopher* (1732) and *Siris* (1744), a curious treatise advocating the virtues of tar-water as a panacea. Berkeley's interest in Ireland's political, social, and economic problems is most evident in an ingenious compilation of several hundred interrogations published as *The Querist* (1735–37).

The Irish writings of EDMUND BURKE are much more extensive. In such works as his *Letter to a Peer of Ireland* (1782) or the *Letter to Sir Hercules Langrishe on the Subject of the Roman Catholics of Ireland* (1792), Burke considers with characteristically studied eloquence the injustices perpetrated under the Penal Laws, which he attributed to Anglo-Irish 'pride, arrogance, and a spirit of domination', and how they might be remedied. Burke, however, also contained his particular interest in Ireland within wider concerns, political and literary. He first came to notice with *A Vindication of Natural Society* (1756) and the *Enquiry into the Origin of Our Ideas of the Sublime and Beautiful* (1757), an aesthetic treatise of seminal importance to developing Romanticism. Burke's other principal writings, like the famous *Reflections on the Revolution in France* (1790), are political and he concerned himself notably with the American colonies and the administration of India. The founding father of modern conservatism, he argued that while change is the first law of nature, and perhaps its means of survival, human wisdom must provide that change proceed by 'insensible degrees'.

The dramatist John O'Keeffe (1747–1833), portrait by Thomas Lawranson, 1786. National Portrait Gallery, London.

An allegiance to values which transcended national or sectarian boundaries, common to so many writers, was forcefully expressed by OLIVER GOLDSMITH, who declared 'I should prefer the title of the ancient philosopher, viz. a Citizen of the World, to that of an Englishman, a Frenchman, an European, or to any other appellation whatever'. Goldsmith's literary allegiances were similarly comprehensive: he made notable contributions to poetry, the essay, history, the novel, and drama. As a playwright, Goldsmith was one of many Irish writers who contributed significantly to 18th-century drama, among them GEORGE FARQUHAR, CHARLES MACKLIN, Arthur Murphy (1727–1805), HUGH KELLY, John O'Keeffe (1747–1833), and RICHARD BRINSLEY SHERIDAN. Goldsmith's most famous play, *She Stoops to Conquer* (1773), remains, like Sheridan's *The Rivals* (1775) or *The School for Scandal* (1777), one of very few 18th-century plays to be regularly revived. Both Goldsmith and Sheridan wrote – in Goldsmith's own distinction – 'laughing comedy', looking back to the satirical comedy of the Restoration, rather than to 'sentimental comedy', which invited sympathetic tears more readily than mirth.

Neither dramatist, nor the earlier Farquhar, whose *The Recruiting Officer* (1706) and *The Beaux' Stratagem* (1707) are also revived with success, wrote 'Irish' plays, if by that is meant plays set in Ireland or dealing principally with Irish characters. Such plays did exist – especially on the lively Dublin stage – but in general the more local such plays were, the less successful. The typical 'stage Irishman' – the belligerent, brogue-ridden, impecunious braggart – was well known, however. Farquhar had used him and so did Macklin,

Murphy, and Sheridan. But in *The School for Wives* (1774) Hugh Kelly attempted an Irish character, Connolly, who went entirely against the type, while Arthur Murphy, in the prologue to *Know Your Own Mind* (1777), rejected all national types: Scottish and Welsh, as well as Irish.

The attitudes informing drama were generally present in prose fiction also. Early fiction substantially set in Ireland includes the picaresque *The History of Jack Connor* (1752) by William Chaigneau (1709–81) and the compendium novel, *The Life of John Buncle, Esq.* (1756, 1766), by Thomas Amory (?1691–1789), besides *The History of John Juniper* (1781) and *The Adventures of Anthony Varnish* (1786) by CHARLES JOHNSTONE. Most Irish fiction, however, tended to subordinate specifically Irish themes to wider interests. Charles Johnstone's influential *Chrysal, or the Adventures of a Guinea* (1760, 1765), a contemporary *succès de scandale*, is only marginally concerned with Ireland. So too is *The Fool of Quality* (1765–70), a thesis novel on education after Rousseau's *Émile*, by HENRY BROOKE. Leading writers of popular sentimental fiction included Richard (?1714–88) and Elizabeth (?1720–93) Griffith, Hugh Kelly, and FRANCES SHERIDAN whose *Memoirs of Miss Sidney Bidulph* (1761), a study of virtue under stress, is a fine novel. Mrs Sheridan's *Nourjahad* (1767) is an oriental tale which ranked second only to *Rasselas* in contemporary esteem. Goldsmith's gently ironic *The Vicar of Wakefield* (1766) remains widely read and admired.

The last three decades of the 18th century saw a clutch of novels with such pointedly national titles as *The Irish Guardian* (1776), *The Fair Hibernian* (1789), or *The Irish Heiress* (1797), but throughout the century the best fiction was written by those most in tune with contemporary European culture. So the greatest Irish novel of the period, *Castle Rackrent* (1800), was 'An Hibernian Tale' but one written by an author, MARIA EDGEWORTH, who had absorbed Enlightenment values and interests from her father. If the comic tale of the downfall of the hard-drinking, litigious, prodigal Rackrent family, recounted by the 'illiterate old steward' Thady Quirk, finally becomes a celebration of an age and way of life its author believed were past, it does so in spite of Edgeworth's conscious values. The Act of Union, she believed, would only confirm the tendency towards a more sober, prudent, and industrious way of life in Ireland, a view repeated in her other Irish fictions, *Ennui* (1809), *The Absentee* (1812), and *Ormond* (1817). Edgeworth's influence on the development of a specifically national fiction was great, as Sir Walter Scott allowed. Like her predecessors, though, she did not write on Irish matters alone and in such novels as *Belinda* (1801), *Patronage* (1814), and *Helen* (1834) eschewed them completely.

Maria Edgeworth wrote of the Anglo-Ireland she knew; when she looked at Gaelic society – as in *Ormond* – it was with evident unease. LADY MORGAN (Sydney Owenson), by contrast, revelled in the Gaelic world or, more accurately, her own Romantic view of it. *The Wild Irish Girl* (1806) brought her immediate fame but, unfortunately, her ambitions – most evident in *The*

Lady Morgan (Sydney Owenson; 1776–1859), the novelist; engraving. NLI.

O'Briens and the O'Flahertys (1827) – generally outstripped her talents.

As Irish fiction became more self-consciously nationalistic in the early 19th century it was increasingly distinguished by an uncertainty as to audience and direction. CHARLES ROBERT MATURIN produced in *Melmoth the Wanderer* (1820) the greatest Irish novel between *Castle Rackrent* and *Ulysses*. Yet Maturin had previously attempted with little success four novels of very different kinds – imitation Lady Morgan, rationalized Gothic, and a largely realistic study of lower-middle class Calvinist circles in contemporary Dublin. Only in *Melmoth*, a terror tale enthusiastically admired by Baudelaire, Balzac, and Poe, was Maturin successful, adroitly combining problems of cultural identity in Ireland at the beginning of the century with European legends – Faust, the Wandering Jew, the Ancient Mariner – in a narrative of extraordinary complexity.

By the 1820s, the confidence of the 18th-century Irish writers had become something of the past. For the remainder of the 19th century, Irish novelists were to search for a voice to explain themselves and their country to a willing but largely uncomprehending audience overseas.   ICR

Literature from 1820 to 1920

Maria Edgeworth, whose last significant Irish novel had appeared in 1817, was to write in O'Connell's time that 'it is impossible to draw Ireland as she now is in a book of fiction – realities are too strong, party passions too violent to bear to see, or care to look at their faces in the looking-glass. . . . We are in too perilous a case to laugh, humour would be out of season, worse than bad taste.' However, the challenge was taken up by others and, although the dominant mood was a dark one, humour was not entirely absent. The third decade of the 19th century saw the publication of works by John Banim (1798–1842), assisted by his brother Michael

(1796–1874), who experimented with the historical novel – a natural impulse in a country where the past loomed so large in the imagination of the people – and Gerald Griffin (1803–40), whose *The Collegians* (1829) was based on a contemporary murder case but had as its real subject the culture in which the deed had taken place. In the next decade WILLIAM CARLETON, a peasant from Co. Tyrone, began giving vivid portraits of his people in *Traits and Stories of the Irish Peasantry*.

As there had been no native tradition of fiction, all these writers had had to explore for themselves the problem of what an *Irish* novel should be. Realistic depiction of Irish life was one prominent goal, and Carleton, for example, called himself a 'historian' of the habits and manners of his time. On the other hand, Ireland had only a small reading public, and the primary audience was English. In offering to illustrate and explain the life of their nation, the novelists often yielded to propagandistic motives or catered to readers' tastes and biases in ways that worked counter to the realistic motive. Thus, for example, CHARLES JAMES LEVER and SAMUEL LOVER, both very popular, have often been criticized for a condescending treatment of their Irish characters; and Carleton, even when writing for his own countrymen, turned some of his novels into temperance tracts and political dissertations. The formal problem suggested by such mutations was also crucial. The conventions of English fiction were not equally relevant to the Irish novelists, and aesthetic motives often came into conflict with national ones. The result was a great unevenness in most of the fiction of the time, with memorable scenes and absurdly weak ones intermingled. With all its faults, however, the work of this era often had great power: looking back at it near the end of the century, the young W. B. YEATS was to praise Banim and Carleton especially as writers who 'tried to make one see life plainly but all written down in a kind of fiery shorthand that it might never be forgotten'.

After the Great Famine and the abortive rising of 1848 – perhaps at least in part because of those events – came a period of nearly 40 years during which the general quality of Irish fiction was unimpressive. There were noteworthy individual volumes, including *The House by the Churchyard* (1863) by Joseph Sheridan LeFanu, a famous writer of Gothic tales, and the Fenian leader Charles Kickham's tremendously popular *Knocknagow* (1879). STANDISH JAMES O'GRADY had discovered the epics and myths of early Ireland and his retellings of them in modern English were a major source of inspiration to the young writers of the Irish Renaissance, but in form his books hovered uncomfortably between romance and history. Thus it was only with GEORGE MOORE in the mid-1880s that fiction in Ireland showed a significant new development.

Moore, who had spent several years in Paris, brought from France not only the naturalists' fidelity to experience but also a commitment to artistic craftsmanship; the result, *A Drama in Muslin* (1886), is one of the most vivid and penetrating novels of the century. Even better, perhaps, was *The Real Charlotte* (1894), by SOMERVILLE AND ROSS. This novel, like *Castle*

Rackrent a century earlier, chronicles the decline of the gentry and the rise of more sordid elements in Irish society; and it, too, displays that subtlety and control of form so uncommon in Irish fiction between Edgeworth and Moore. Their collection of linked comic stories published in 1899 as *Some Experiences of an Irish R.M.* had a great popular success but alienated many nationalistic readers, who saw it as a recrudescence of Lever, Lover, and the 'stage Irishman'. During the same period, however, Moore once again returned to his homeland and soon produced three first-rate works of fiction: *The Untilled Field* (1903), *The Lake* (1905), and *Hail and Farewell* (1911–14).

Nor were these authors solitary voices. They were part of a burgeoning of Irish fiction surpassing that of the period preceding the Famine. It was the period of Gerald O'Donovan's *Father Ralph* (1913), a grim picture of Catholic clerical life seen from the inside; and of Seumas O'Kelly's 'The Weaver's Grave' (1919), which has often been called the greatest of Irish short stories. Also at this time JAMES STEPHENS began to write those novels in which the Irish genius for fantasy found full expression – *The Charwoman's Daughter* (1912), *The Crock of Gold* (1912), and *The Demi-Gods* (1914). Above all, there was JAMES JOYCE, who turned his back on the native tradition in fiction and yet represents its culmination.

In comparison with Joyce, who was influenced by some of the great Continental writers of the 19th century, the Irish novelists of that era seemed parochial in their concerns and woefully inadequate in technical skill; Joyce's *persona* Stephen Dedalus dismissed their work, in a phrase recalling Maria Edgeworth, as 'the cracked looking glass of a servant'; Joyce spoke scornfully even of Moore, who had anticipated his *Dubliners* (1914) and *A Portrait of the Artist as a Young Man* (1916). But once he had escaped from what he considered the constricting atmosphere of his native country, he turned his attention to giving that country life in his art. In a letter he actually called *Dubliners* a 'nicely polished looking-glass' for the citizens of the metropolis, and in ULYSSES (1922) he pushed the realistic vein in Irish fiction as far as it could go (then moved beyond, and perhaps intentionally undercut, the realism of his own novel). Furthermore, *Ulysses* offered an essentially comic vision of his country that, despite its elements of hostility, bore no trace of condescension; and proved that a universal master-piece could be rooted, without apology, in Irish soil.

The development of a viable native tradition in fiction had its parallel in the field of drama, but there the *pattern* of development was quite different. From CONGREVE and SHERIDAN in the 18th century to OSCAR WILDE and GEORGE BERNARD SHAW in the 20th, Irish dramatists experienced many brilliant successes on the London stage; Irish characters were included in many plays by English and by Irish authors; Ireland produced more than its share of leading actors and actresses; and a theatre had been opened in Dublin as early as 1635 – yet there was no significant indigenous Irish dramatic movement until the end of the 19th century. Earlier in that century DION BOUCICAULT had

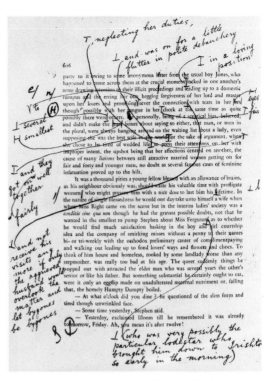

A page proof of James Joyce's *Ulysses* with the author's corrections. British Museum (on loan from the Society of Authors).

written some successful Irish melodramas, but he was more an entertainer than an artist and though in fact his plays have greater merit than they have been credited with and had a tangible influence on later, greater writers, their association with the image of the 'stage Irishman' made them difficult to assimilate to the patriotic concept of *national* literature that was emerging in the same era. Thus, when in 1897 W. B. YEATS, LADY GREGORY, and EDWARD MARTYN laid the groundwork for an Irish theatre (*see* ABBEY THEATRE), the prospectus they issued promised that the new dramatists would show that 'Ireland is not the home of buffoonery and of easy sentiment, as it has been represented, but the home of an ancient idealism'.

It was, undoubtedly, Yeats who had been primarily responsible for the reference to 'ancient idealism'. To him the Gaelic past offered spiritual and heroic ideals that, embodied in poetic, symbolic plays, might shape the future of the decidedly unheroic Ireland of the years following the death of Parnell. His own *The Countess Cathleen*, in which the aristocratic heroine sells her soul in order to redeem the souls of her people, was such a play; and it formed part of the inaugural programme in 1899. But the play with which it shared this distinction, Martyn's *The Heather Field*, reflected a quite different dramatic philosophy. Martyn, an enthusiastic Ibsenite, wanted realistic drama that dealt directly with problems of contemporary Irish life.

Although Yeats was to be the most powerful figure in the history of the Irish theatre, the movement itself developed along lines closer to those championed by Martyn.

Yeats himself had written peasant plays, usually in collaboration with Lady Gregory; her own dramatic work was dominated by folk characters and themes; and their associate JOHN MILLINGTON SYNGE found his inspiration in the life of the Wicklow glens and the rugged western coast. The language of all three playwrights was poetic, however, and the atmosphere, even in their darkest moments, tinged with lyric beauty. Synge's *The Playboy of the Western World* (1907), for example, though concerned with the debilitating effects of emigration, dramatized them in an Irish English that was joyous and 'as fully flavoured as a nut or apple'. But in the work of other dramatists, sordid aspects of the modern nation were presented with a grimness virtually unrelieved by lyricism. The early plays of PADRAIC COLUM exemplified this approach, as did the work of the so-called 'Cork Realists', LENNOX ROBINSON, T. C. Murray, and R. J. Ray. Robinson, in describing the vision they shared, clearly revealed the tension between that vision and Yeats's: 'We young men . . . didn't see [Ireland] as a queen, . . . we loved her as truly as Yeats . . . maybe we loved her more deeply, but just because we loved her so deeply her faults were clear to us. Perhaps we realists saw her faults too clearly, perhaps we saw her too often as a grasping, middle-aged hag. She was avaricious, she was mean, for family pride she would force a son into the Church against his will, she would commit arson, she would lie, she would cheat, she would murder and yet we would write all our terrible words about her out of our love.' Such criticism reflected a misunderstanding of Yeats's aesthetics: he felt as deeply as the realists that romantic Ireland was dead and gone, but thought that a drama of ideal images would be more effective than direct criticism or satire mirroring contemporary faults in preparing for its return.

Synge died in 1909, and the strange, fantastic plays of the Kerry author GEORGE FITZMAURICE failed to find an appreciative audience; but Yeats and Lady Gregory continued to produce new work and helped give the dramatic movement a valuable diversity. An effort was even made to counteract parochialism through the performance of Continental masterpieces. Nevertheless, the movement seems to have lost some of its intensity in the second decade of the 20th century and might have become a spent force had not its next great genius appeared in the person of SEÁN O'CASEY. He, like Joyce, was to become an 'exile' deeply at odds with his country; but his vigorous plays, which combined elements drawn from the realists, Synge, and even Boucicault, brought new energy and excitement to the theatre and constitute a triumph for the native dramatic tradition comparable to that represented for Irish fiction by *Ulysses*.　　　　　PLM

Literature from 1920 to the present
Whatever the political difficulties in establishing an Irish identity after 1922, when the Irish Free State began its tentative and turbulent existence, an Irish literary identity was already in being, and had been presented to the world by the internationally known figures of the Irish Literary Renaissance. The artists' task henceforth was to explore and extend that identity. Not all wished it to be bounded by a Yeatsian Celtic Twilight or by ABBEY THEATRE realism.

Censorship, however, became a major and often acrimonious subject of debate in the Irish Free State after 1922. Following the appointment of a Committee on Evil Literature in 1926, The Censorship Act of 1929 was passed. In England, and in Ireland until that date, legal controls affected 'corruptive' material already on sale; its vendors could be prosecuted. The new Irish censorship laws were aimed at *preventing the importation* of such material. The main criteria were that literature should not be 'indecent or obscene', nor advocate the unnatural prevention of conception or the procurement of abortion.

Certain forms of censorship are of course inherent in an organized society, and some defence was necessary against the spread of cheap pornographic books and periodicals in the 1920s, but the point at issue in Ireland was the systematic literary censorship carried out by the five-man Censorship Board, with its Register of banned books and periodicals (many of literary merit), and the use of Customs officials as 'watchdogs'. Irish censorship was thought by some to be too dependent on Roman Catholic doctrine, and too isolationist, based on narrowly nationalist standards; there was, for example, much controversy about what constituted obscenity, about the banning of KATE O'BRIEN'S *The Land of Spices* for two lines about homosexuality, and Eric Cross's *The Tailor and Ansty* (1942) for its inclusion of earthy language. SEÁN O'FAOLAIN vigorously combated official censorship in *The Bell*, the magazine which he founded and edited from 1940 to 1946, arguing that the 'cultural protectionism' of a narrow censorship was preventing Ireland from becoming a modern nation. In November 1942 the Council of Action on Censorship suggested improvements, some of which, including that of setting up an Appeal Board, became effective in 1946. In 1957 resignations and new appointments resulted in a more broadminded Censorship Board: in 1967 a new Censorship Bill was passed, allowing removal of a ban on a book after 20 years (later reduced to 12 years), freeing 5,000 banned volumes, and making standards of censorship less restrictive.

Two streams can be said to have evolved in Irish drama in the 20th century: the naturalist or realist school directly in that Abbey tradition, and the surreal, expressionist stream which gave vent to the rich fantasy of the Irish imagination, and became associated with the Gate and later the Peacock and the Pike Theatres. When, after staging SEÁN O'CASEY's apparently realist Dublin trilogy (1923–26), the Abbey rejected his expressionist *Silver Tassie* in 1928, and when it also rejected DENIS JOHNSTON's surrealist satire *The Old Lady Says No!* in 1929, it was setting itself on a course in which it could be accused of unvarying peasant realism. There were however, many fine writers in that genre: LENNOX ROBINSON, Paul Vincent Carrol (b. 1900), WALTER MACKEN, Michael Molloy (b. 1912) and JOHN B. KEANE, whose *Sive* and *The Field* draw universal truth from Irish peasant life. In the 1970s and 1980s, the urban South, too, has its chronicles, such as Heno Magee's *Hatchet* (1972) and Sé Sheridan's *Mobile Homes* (1976).

In the expressionist mode, O'Casey in exile produced stylized, symbolic message-plays, and satirical comedies with elements of farce, music hall, circus and concert: in *The Drums of Father Ned* (1958), commissioned for Dublin's An Tostal theatre festival, the drums symbolize love, life and joy (the play was censored – a recurring hazard in the Irish literary scene). Denis Johnston, too, continued to use fantasy, burlesque, chorus, symbol (*A Bride for the Unicorn*, 1933) and masque (*The Dreaming Dust*, 1940). It is of course this surreal line that goes to SAMUEL BECKETT, whose plays avoid stage reality, the better to chart the bleak and enigmatic reality of existence: the ever-waiting tramps, 'A country road. A tree.', of *Waiting for Godot* (1953); Nagg and Nell entombed in their dustbins in *Endgame* (1957); Winnie buried in sand in *Happy Days* (1961); the disembodied, unidentified mouth of *Not I* (1973). Other expressionist dramatists include: THOMAS KILROY, author of *Talbot's Box* (1977), whose actual box is 'part prison, part sanctuary, part active space'; THOMAS MURPHY, in whose *A Crucial Week in the Life of a Grocer's Assistant* (1978) dream alternates with reality; and BRIAN FRIEL, particularly in *Translations* (1979), where language itself becomes symbol, and the very roots of identity are examined by its light.

In prose fiction too, one can generalize to a realist and a surrealist mode, the 'realist' novelists including writers as different as LIAM O'FLAHERTY, JOHN MCGAHERN, EDNA O'BRIEN and JENNIFER JOHNSTON; the surrealist Flann O'Brien (*see* O'NOLAN), Samuel Beckett, JOHN BÁNVILLE, FRANCIS STUART. Stuart's self-figure 'H' in his supra-real autobiography *Black List Section H* expresses the particular problem of Irish novelists after Joyce: 'Ulysses, far from being a novel to end the novel, as some claimed, was a revelation of the form's possibilities. Post-Joycean fiction had had two paths to choose between and it seemed to be taking the old, well-tried one, with its practitioners producing novels and stories easily recognizable as realistic portrayals of local character and situation. No great risks were being taken, the pitfalls were being safely avoided, no imagination had been set alight by Joyce's smoky torch. A few tricks had been learned from him, but his obsessive kind of writing was not inspiring any of H's contemporaries to delve deeper into themselves. And so there was little to haunt, disturb, offend, or affect in any significant way.' Whereas Stuart (or 'H') is here dealing harshly with the greatest of the realist writers, the pitfalls of the Joycean path are apparent.

Those who did extend the novel even further were Stuart himself, whose haunting tales of underground man in wartime of post-war Europe expand the novel's philosophic perimeter, forging it from his own life, the life of the soul, of the heart, of the intellect; Beckett, for whom also art must be based on 'self-

Seán O'Casey (1880–1964), drawing by Harry Kernoff, 1930. NGI.

perception', created a disturbing juxtaposition of the abstract and the painfully concrete in his trilogy *Molloy, Malone Dies* and *The Unnamable* (1951–3); and Banville, who extends and develops the structure of the novel in opposition to the conventional forms. All embed the artistic experience at the very core of the novel.

Many, however, would consider Joyce's true heir to by Brian O'Nolan, for the Joycean density of Irish locality, the acutely observed transcription of speech, the linking of parody and philosophy, the fusing of the absolute and the absurd, apparent in novels such as *At Swim-Two-Birds* (1939) and *The Third Policeman* (written in 1940, published in 1966).

To use Stuart's phrase, 'Realistic portrayals of local character and situation' have figured large in 20th-century Irish prose, and the finest of these have a universal validity, and an extra dimension beyond their realism. The novels of Liam O'Flaherty, for example, are firmly rooted in their Irish locality, but the elemental violence and struggle for life in such novels as *Skerrett* (1932) and *Famine* (1937) raise them to epic levels. The novels of John McGahern depend very much on their stifling provincial setting, but rise above any purely local significance (*The Barracks*, 1963, *The Dark*, 1965). Edna O'Brien has moved from the naturalism of her first novels, *The Country Girls* (1960), *The Lonely Girls* (1962) and *Girls in Their Married Bliss* (1964), to a more experimental style, then back. Jennifer Johnston uses a variety of Irish settings, ranging from World War I to the present day, to express a sense of loss that is personal, national and universal. Nor need the novelist write purely about Irish locality: ELIZABETH BOWEN more usually chooses the English scene, and has been praised for her clear-sighted detachment from it; BRIAN MOORE writes equally convincingly with a North American or a Northern Irish setting. Nor indeed need a writer be Irish – J. P. DONLEAVY, an American, has written, in *The Ginger Man* (1956), a riotously 'Irish' novel that breathes Dublin in every paragraph. There is also a tributary stream to the realist novel which is the historical novel – one might instance the work of Walter Macken and Eilis Dillon who cover a range of periods, or JAMES PLUNKETT, whose *Strumpet City* is Dublin in the 1920s.

The prose form that has since 1920 consistently exhibited the best of the Irish writer in English is that of the short story: in the 1920s and 1930s (Liam O'Flaherty, Elizabeth Bowen; FRANK O'CONNOR, SEÁN O'FAOLAIN), in the 1940s and 1950s (MARY LAVIN, Michael McLaverty; BENEDICT KIELY, Val Mulkerns); in the 1960s and 1970s (WILLIAM TREVOR, AIDAN HIGGINS; NEIL JORDAN, Julia O'Faolain). Happily, for decades after these starting dates, these writers continued to write sensitive, revealing and satisfying stories; in fact all but Bowen and O'Connor are still writing. The sense of place is often of great assistance to the short-story writer if it can be quickly and convincingly transmitted; the Irish landscape seems particularly fertile in that sense, as well as being productive of what Seán O'Faolain calls 'significant incident'. To early peasant tales has been added a body of urban and suburban stories, with the growth of the little 'bright box in the suburbs' (Val Mulkerns).

The family and the Church, dominant in Irish life, are also dominant features in the short story, the novel, the play. But if one wished to select one particularly fruitful theme, it would still probably be that of the Ascendancy house in decline, chosen by so many Irish writers and encapsulating the regrouping of Irish life, the breaking down of an old social structure. Aidan Higgins's *Langrishe, Go Down*, Jennifer Johnston's *The Old Jest*, Mary Lavin's 'A Single Lady', William Trevor's 'The Distant Past'. Brian Friel's play *Aristocrats* and his story 'The Foundry House' all use the moribund house, whether of Protestant Ascendancy or Catholic aristocracy, as emblematic of a changing Ireland, her history and her loss. (This theme is also explored by Molly Keane [M. J. Farrell] in *Good Behaviour*, 1981, a remarkable artistic resurgence after forty years of silence.)

It would be false to classify 20th-century Irish writers in English as in any way a 'group'. Yet there are certain stimuli common to them which are not those of the English writer, for example, and which have naturally generated a distinctive literature: the struggle for freedom, the Civil War, the post-colonial trauma, the dislocation of life in the North. The exploration of identity entails both a healthy introspection and a looking outwards – not merely for an audience but for a point of reference. The finest of these writers have achieved both, and in doing so have produced a firmly grounded literature that transcends the local, illuminating a human identity beyond the national.   BH

Richard Fallis, *The Irish Renaissance; An Introduction to Anglo-Irish Literature*, 1973; Frank O'Connor, *The Backward Look. A Survey of Irish Literature*, 1967; Stephen Gwynn, *Irish Literature and Drama*, 1936; Vivian Mercier, *The Irish Comic Tradition*, 1962; E. A. Boyd, *Ireland's Literary Renaissance*, 1916 (rev. ed. 1922, reprinted 1969); Herbert Howarth, *The Irish Writers 1880–1940*, 1958; A. E. Malone, *The Irish Drama*, 1929; Mícheál Ó hAodha, *Theatre in Ireland*, 1971; Robert Hogan, *After the Irish Renaissance*, 1967; Benedict Kiely, *Modern Irish Fiction, A Critique*, 1950; Patrick Rafroidi and Maurice Harmon, *The Irish Novel in Our Time*, 1976; Thomas Flanagan, *The Irish Novelists, 1800–1850*, 1959; Robert Hogan and James Kilroy, *The Irish Literary Theatre*, 1975; Robert Hogan et al., *The Modern Irish Drama: a Documentary History*, 1975 et seq. (in progress).

literature (Irish language). In early period, literature in the IRISH LANGUAGE represents a mingling of two streams. The native one derived directly from the pagan Indo-European and Celtic past, whereas outside influence is mainly represented by the Christian tradition, which became quite powerful very early on, without displacing the native elements as ruthlessly as, for instance, in medieval Sweden.

The prose material in Irish in the earliest ILLUMINATED MANUSCRIPTS, dating from the 8th and 9th centuries, is not of literary value, consisting as it does mainly of glosses on Latin texts such as the Psalms, parts of the New Testament, and Priscian. However, it must be pointed out that as yet this material has not been studied closely for its content, but rather for its linguistic forms. Later mss. on the other hand, contain much early material of great literary interest, some of which can be dated as far back as the beginning of the 7th century; most of this is legal and is of considerable historic and linguistic importance as it preserves much about the Indo-European past, including certain concepts only found elsewhere among the Indo-Europeans in the extreme east of that world, i.e. in India.

Good editions exist of some important texts, such as the tract on legal status and social stratification, *Críth Gablach*, or that giving the old judge Morann's parting words or testament to a young king, *Audacht Morainn*. Although best preserved in a manuscript written as late as 1575, this text is important in that it is one of the oldest extant documents of pre-Christian Ireland; it provides, in language that is sometimes very archaic, a remarkably clear picture of a rather peaceful rural and pagan society.

The monument of the Old Irish epic is TÁIN BÓ CUALNGE ('The Cattle-Raid of Cooley'), a fairly long text, which has come down in several recensions. Another important setting for early story-telling is Leinster, where *Tochmarc Étaíne* ('The Wooing of Étaín') and *Togail Bruidne Da Derga* ('The Destruction of Da Derga's Hostel') take place. The mythological aspect is rather more marked here than in the Ulster cycle, as shown by Étaín's numerous reincarnations through supernatural re-births and her unions with supernatural and divine husbands. She is one of the ancestors of Conaire Mór, the tragic central character of the second story, the good king who is doomed to total destruction from the moment he commits one single unjust deed, that destruction being brought about as he is forced by circumstances to break the taboos, or *gesa*, affecting his reign. This text does much towards explicating the nature of early Irish sacral kingship, but it is also of interest from a purely literary point of view. Most of the action is narrated indirectly, by the device of a scout telling Conaire's main enemy what is happening and, moreover, what will happen in the hostel where Conaire has taken refuge, so that, by the time the action actually starts, its outcome is already known. This fairly complex device contributes towards keeping the narrative together, telling the story without, as it were, wishing to appear to do so.

Another stylistic feature of this, and of many other early Irish tales, is the mingling of prose and verse, a feature that sometimes has been considered archaic and even compared to a similar feature as found in early Indian literature. As in most other early literatures, the distinction between narrative and other prose in early Irish writings is not always as clear cut as it would be nowadays. Thus, the laws, for instance, sometimes include pieces of narrative to illustrate legal points.

Religious literature starts early, with texts such as the Cambray Homily and the *Apgitir Chrábaid* (or 'Alphabet of Piety'), but the most noteworthy example representative of this genre is probably *Fís Adamnáin*, with its very imaginative and colourful descriptions of Heaven and Hell. Also, there is a large collection of saints' lives, both in Irish and in Latin.

Secular history is represented by the *Lebor Gabála* ('Book of Invasions'), which purports to give a history of the various population-groups believed to have reached Ireland. Unfortunately, the manuscript tradition is a particularly difficult one, not yet adequately understood by scholars, so that the establishment of a definitive text still seems far away, as does the correct evaluation of how much of the accounts given is to be believed. The annalistic material has been studied more and it is at times very useful, even if a quantity of fake or 'synthetic' history must be reckoned with.

The nature of poetry was an obvious concern to a society in which the poet enjoyed a very high social status, comparable to that of the tribal kings. The so-called 'Caldron of Poesy', to use a probably rather inaccurate but by now almost traditional rendering of whatever the title *Coire Goriath* may have meant, has been studied quite intensively of late, which is perhaps not surprising, since it deals with the very nature of poetic inspiration.

Latin grammar was studied and known very early in Ireland and the interaction between the two cultures can be observed quite clearly in the *Auraicept na nÉces* ('The Scholars' Primer'), a text that deals mainly with various grammatical matters in the two languages, but also with the origin of the Irish language. It is worthy of note that the author endeavours to demonstrate the superiority of Irish over Latin, a thought the like of which would hardly have entered the minds of speakers of other European vernaculars at the time.

Even that which survives of Irish literature of the early period constitutes a much vaster body than can be described adequately here and represents what appears to be only a small portion of what may once have existed, as one may be led to suppose from the gaps in the manuscript tradition of known texts, and especially from the many textual references to manuscripts and texts we do not have. The picture one gets is varied, but there are some unifying characteristics, the principal one being the vividness and the sharpness of descriptive passages: one senses bright and clear colours rather than grey and muted ones. Also, the focus is on one episode at a time, so that the perception is of a series of 'still pictures' of individual episodes rather than the epic spread of a unitary story with one sequence of 'moving pictures' rolling into another.

The Middle Period

A clear distinction between the early and the middle period cannot be made. While much of the early literature survives only in versions belonging to the middle period, some distinguishing characteristics may be observed. It is quite clear that there is a difference in style; the taste for sharp and concise modes of expression gives way to a liking for prolixity, a copious use of synonyms, sometimes even degenerating into meaningless bombast. This can be seen if one compares the early version of the TÁIN BÓ CUALNGE with the later Recension II. Although the latter has the virtue of removing many of the inconsistencies that mar Recension I, it includes so many unnecessary added words that a modern reader must at times find the text rather tedious. However, it is not without flashes of humour, as in the introductory dialogue between Medb (Maeve) and her husband Ailill: the usual banter between husband and wife develops into a quarrel about who owns more, finally providing a reason for the Cattle-raid itself. Also, one finds this in a text like *Tromdam Guaire* ('The Heavy Retinue of Guaire'), which satirizes the very high status acquired by some poets, showing how Guaire forces them to cease making excessive claims on his hospitality by requesting that the entire *Táin* should be recited to him, although it had by then been forgotten. This text also illustrates the process of accretion so typical of manuscripts of this period. It is fortunate that we have sources showing how the story has grown around a nucleus consisting only of the legend about how the *Táin* was found again.

Another humorous text, *Aislinge Meic Con Glinne* ('The Dream of Mac Con Glinne'), describing the progress of a gluttonous monk, is a powerful satire of religious life. On the other hand, the genuine religious literature of this period is quite serious in content, notably so in the case of the large collection of *Passions and Homilies*. These are of great value to the linguist, in that they show the evolution of fairly ordinary language during a difficult period.

The same seriousness is manifest in the most important collection of narrative literature from this period, *Acallam na Senórach* ('The Conversation of the Old Men'), in which the adventures of Oisín, Caílte and especially Finn are told, together with material about St Patrick. The style is usually quite similar to that of the later recensions of the *Táin*, but there is a strong folklore element here, which makes it quite likely that many of these stories had formed part of an oral tradition long before being written down.

There is also a certain amount of historical and pseudo-historical writing, such as *Caithréim Cellaig* ('Cellach's Martial Career'), which has hagiographical touches. Like the *Acallam*, it is written in a language that may well be described as Early Modern Irish, as is that of the perhaps most important body of literature of this period, namely the Bardic Poetry.

The Modern Period
With the collapse of the native nobility in the 16th and 17th centuries an important and on the whole successful attempt to record what was left of native learning was made by Franciscan friars, who produced, among other works, the *Annals of the Four Masters*. Much of this work was carried out at Louvain, due to religious persecution in Ireland. In this context, GEOFFREY KEATING must be mentioned, mainly for his history of Ireland, *Foras Feasa ar Éirinn*, but also for his devotional works. Had it not been for the tradition breaking down so thoroughly in the 17th century, it seems more than likely that Keating's clear and simple, yet sufficiently elevated, style would have served as the model that Irish so badly needed during the 19th-century revival period.

Later prose reflects the difficult social conditions, as in the Parliament texts (*Páirlement Chloinne Tomáis* and *P. na mBan*), which describe assemblies of people deploring the brutishness etc. of the age; the foreign elements in these texts are quite noticeable. At the same time, native folklore survives, occasionally surfacing in paper mss. of the 18th and 19th centuries, which also continue the Fenian tradition.

A valuable document of early 19th-century life in Co. Kilkenny is provided by Humphrey O'Sullivan's diary, *Cín Lae Amhlaoibh*. During the same period, much antiquarian interest emerged for the language and the literature and, with the political awakening, one may begin to talk about the revival literature.

The links with Early Modern Irish prose having been broken, it was necessary to evolve a new standard language, for which the remaining dialects were used, at first individually and later together when the *Caighdeán Oifigiúil* ('Official Standard') was put together. Its impact on real literature has been confined to matters of spelling.

The first dialect to be used as a medium for written literature during the revival period was that of Munster, under the influence, to a large extent, of Canon Peter O'Leary who wrote, around the turn of the century, many stories, translations etc.

Somewhat later, international folklore scholars turned their attention to Ireland, which then still had preserved more folklore than any other European country, with the possible exception of Finland. This led to the production of some outstanding works of literature, notably from the Blasket Islands of Kerry, by TOMÁS Ó CRIOMHTHAIN, PEIG SAYERS and MUIRIS Ó SÚILLEABHÁIN.

One of the first of the Connacht writers was PÁDRAIG Ó CONAIRE but the outstanding one was MÁIRTÍN Ó CADHAIN, who attempted to create a new prose by welding his deep knowledge of European literature into the folklore tradition, using for this purpose a rather enriched form of his own Connemara Irish. He published several collections of short stories and a novel *Cré na Cille* ('The Dust of the Cemetery'), which has been justly acclaimed.

In Ulster, the best writing was by the brothers Séamus Ó Grianna (writing under the pseudonym Máire) and Seosamh Mac Grianna.

Writers of Irish today work in very difficult circumstances, the audience being severely limited. Consequently the most disappointing feature of revival literature is not surprising, namely the scarcity of novels for the general public, especially the committed urban speakers of Irish. The short story has fared rather better, with some notable success by Ó Cadhain in adapting his craft to the urban milieu.

Non-fiction literature is reasonably well represented, especially in the domain of biography, where L. Ó Broin, among others, has produced some fine books. More technical literature exists in various fields, such as dialectology, geography, history and chemistry, showing quite clearly that Irish can be used as a medium of communication in the modern world, not least because of the enormous progress made in Irish lexicography over the last quarter of a century.

As far as the international scholarly community is concerned, there are two areas of Irish literature that seem likely, more than others, to attract the attention of students, namely the early literature and the folklore material, but it is probably true to say that this simply reflects on the very difficult circumstances Irish writers have been forced to work in ever since the Middle Ages.   AA

A. de Blácam, *Gaelic Literature Surveyed*, 2nd ed., 1973; M. Dillon, *Early Irish Literature*, 1948; R. Flower, *The Irish Tradition*, 1947; F. O'Connor, *The Backward Look*, 1967.

Longley, Michael (1939–). Poet and critic; one of Ireland's finest poets, he is a meticulous craftsman and an ambitious worker in verse. He has published four collections: *No Continuing City* (1969), *An Exploded View* (1973), *Man Lying On A Wall* (1976) and *The Echo-Gate* (1980). The last of these, with its assembly of victims of civil strife and its superb poem 'Peace', is one of the best books to have come out of Ulster in recent years.   T McC

Longstone, Co. Tipperary. A complex multi-period archaeological site with burials excavated by P. Danaher 1973–76. There is an early Bronze Age burial mound, with three central stone cists containing cremated burials, a whetstone and piece of bronze, built over a Beaker habitation layer that yielded a bronze awl. The mound was later used as a MULTIPLE-CIST CAIRN for burials accompanied by Food Vessels, Cordoned and Encrusted Urns, and a Pygmy Cup; associated items were a jet spacer-bead and a bronze razor. On the SE side was placed an Iron Age ring-barrow which contained a cremated burial, a bone bead and iron objects. A circular enclosure of more recent date, with bank and ditch *c.* 70 m. (225 ft) in diameter and containing 20–30 cremations in pits, surrounded the original burial mound. In a final phase, a platform ringfort covered the site in the first millennium AD. The site takes its name from a standing stone which stood 2·5 m. (8 ft) high above the primary mound. *See* CULLEN.   MH

Loughcrew, Co. Meath. A PASSAGE GRAVE cemetery, originally with over 50 monuments, on three adjacent hilltops *c.* 275 m. (900 ft) above sea-level south of Oldcastle, discovered *c.* 1860 and described by E. A. Conwell, a schools inspector. On the summit of Carnbane East, a group of tombs are arranged around the largest, Cairn T, sited at the focus; on Carnbane West two groups are similarly arranged around the large, focal tombs, Cairns L and D. Many tombs are ornamented in characteristic fashion; they have yielded a rich assemblage of typical finds, particularly the small Cairn R2 on Carnbane East.   MH
M. Herity, *Irish Passage Graves,* 1974, pp. 233–44.

Lough Gara, Co. Roscommon and Co. Sligo. In this small lake, 6 miles west of Boyle, over 300 CRANNÓGS have been revealed since drainage works were carried out in 1952; two were excavated by J. Raftery, 1953–55. Crannóg 61, in Rathtinaun, Co. Sligo, was built of brushwood stabilized by piles. Ten houses, each with a hearth of wicker and clay, yielded Later Bronze Age objects, including amber beads and flat-rimmed pottery, immediately followed by Early Iron Age objects. A hoard of personal ornaments (boars' tusks, bronze and tin bracelets, amber beads, a bronze tweezers and gold-plated lead pendants) was found in a wooden box. A large circular house, dating from the dawn of the Early Christian period, and built on top of this crannóg, yielded pins, spindle-whorls, rotary querns and leather and textiles.   MH

Lough Gur, Co. Limerick. A tiny lake near Herbertstown which gives its name to a concentration of prehistoric monuments and sites on and near its shores and on the promontory of Knockadoon and in the nearby townlands of Grange and Rockbarton; dating from Late Neolithic times, the area was investigated mainly by Ó Riordáin from 1939 on.

The principal Late Neolithic/Early Bronze Age habitations were on Knockadoon: Site A had a rectangular post-built house measuring 9·80 × 5·60 m. (32 ft × 18 ft 4 in.) internally; Site C had three post-built houses, *c.* 5 m. (16 ft 6 in.) in diameter, yielding a mixture of the individual local Neolithic wares mixed with Beaker and Food Vessel pottery, pins of Unetice

type, bronze blades and whetstones. The animal bones preserved were predominantly of ox (95%), with some traces of horse, and proportionately few remains of hunted animals.   MH
S. P. Ó Ríordáin, 'Lough Gur Excavations: Neolithic and Bronze Age Houses on Knockadoon', *PRIA* 56c (1954), 297–459.

Loughrea Cathedral, Co. Galway. St Brendan's Roman Catholic Cathedral at Loughrea was designed in the Gothic Revival style by W. H. Byrne and completed in 1902 by Professor WILLIAM SCOTT; EDWARD MARTYN was responsible for ensuring that the building would contain work by the finest native craftsmen and women, rather than the ubiquitous commercially produced foreign clutter, and it thus became the first shrine to champion the Irish ARTS AND CRAFTS MOVEMENT.

AN TÚR GLOINE's inaugural commission led to a remarkable succession of work, representing most of the Co-operative's stained-glass workers, from A. E. Child's *Annunciation* window (1903) to EVIE HONE's *Creation* rose window (1950), with remarkable work by MICHAEL HEALY in his varying phases (1904–40), Hubert McGoldrick's fine *St Margaret Mary* window (1925) and Ethel Rhind's opus-sectile Stations of the Cross. Evelyn Gleeson's newly formed DUN EMER GUILD designed and embroidered a fine set of vestments and banners in silk and wool on linen; Michael Shortall (d.

Loughrea Cathedral. One of the banners designed by Jack B. Yeats and his wife and embroidered by the Dun Emer Guild; St Colum Cille (Columba) is shown writing – his bookmark being in the form of a Celtic cross.

1951) carved the font, corbels and nave capitals; William Scott designed the metalwork, woodwork and side-altars and JOHN HUGHES sculpted a white marble Madonna and Child and a bronze altar-relief.　　　　　　　　　　　　　　　　　NGB

Thomas MacGreevey, 'St. Brendan's Cathedral, Loughrea 1897–1949', *The Capuchin Annual*, Dublin 1946–7; Jeanne Sheehy, *The Rediscovery of Ireland's Past: the Celtic Revival 1830–1930*, 1978; David Caron, unpublished thesis, National College of Art and Design, Dublin 1982.

Lover, Samuel (1797–1868). Writer; born in Dublin of middle-class Protestant parents, he moved to London in 1835. He possessed considerable talent in both music and painting. Like many other writers of the day, he was astonishingly prolific, and published popular work in several genres. Today he is remembered primarily for the novel *Handy Andy* (1842), admired for its comic gusto but offensive to many readers, who (perhaps unjustly) detect a patronizing tone towards the Irish and associate its title character with the stereotype of the 'stage Irishman'.　　PLM

Lucy, Seán (1931–). Poet, critic and Professor of Modern English at University College, Cork. His first major selection of poems appeared in *Five Irish Poets* (1970), and his first solo collection, *Unfinished Sequence*, was published in 1980.　　　　　　　　　　　T McC

Lug. The Celtic and Old Irish deity who is called *Samildánach* ('skilled in all arts'). Julius Caesar, who describes him as 'the inventor of all the arts, a guide on roads and on journeys . . . the most influential in money-making and commerce', identified him with the Roman god, Mercury. The name Lug is cognate with Latin *lux* ('light'), and the name may mean 'the shining [resplendent] one'. The cult of Lug was widespread in the Celtic lands and this is reflected in various place names (Lyons, Laon, Leyden, Carlisle and many others). Many Irish tribes and dynasties claimed descent from him, including the Luigne and the Lugna, who gave their names to the baronies of Leyney in Sligo and Lune in Meath. Lugnasad (Lúnasa), the great harvest feast at the beginning of August, was the feast of Lug and it was celebrated at some two hundred sites in Ireland down to recent times. Lug is of course a major figure in early Irish literature and genealogy, especially in *Cath Maige Tuired*. *See* MYTHOLOGY.　　　　　　　　　DÓC

lunulae. Crescent-shaped ornaments of sheet gold of the early BRONZE AGE, possibly worn around the neck or in the hair. The decoration, mostly incised, is based on the ornamental patterns of Beaker pottery. It is usually geometric and confined to the horns or tips. Of 96 recorded finds, 81 examples have been found in Ireland. There is evidence to indicate that gold from Co. Wicklow was used in the manufacture of some of them. Although occasionally found in hoards as at Banemore, Co. Kerry, none has ever been found in a grave.　　　　　　　　　　　　　　　　　MFR

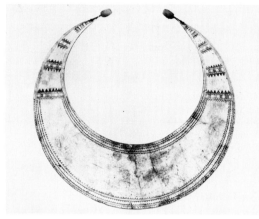

lunula. Sheet gold, with engraved decoration, *c*. 1800–1500 BC; found near Ross, Co. Westmeath. NMI.

Lyles Hill, Co. Antrim. An area of 5 hectares (12½ acres) which was enclosed by an earthen bank 6 m. (20 ft) wide on the 700 ft (213 m.) contour of this hill, probably in Neolithic times; local fine Neolithic pottery was found in quantity at a hearth inside the enclosure.

A robbed tumulus on the hilltop (753 ft; 230 m.) had a central cist and cairn core, apparently Late Neolithic and of Individual Burial type (*see* LINKARDSTOWN). Underneath was a black layer, the result of a great fire, up to 18 cm. (7 in.) deep and over 4 × 3 m. (13 × 10 ft) in extent, yielding charcoal and hazelnuts; small fragments of burnt bone, including human, were found in this layer and in the cairn. Among the finds were flint and stone objects including arrowheads, axeheads and a hone, four greenstone beads, and remains of possibly 1,000 pottery vessels, 80% of these in distinctive shouldered style. There were 14 sherds or vessels of decorated wares in distinctive Late Neolithic styles.　　　　　　　　　　　　　　　　　MH

E. E. Evans, *Lyles Hill, A Late Neolithic Site in County Antrim*, 1953.

Lynn, William Henry (1829–1915). Architect; after becoming a partner of CHARLES LANYON at the age of 24, he concentrated on the Gothic Revival side of the partnership. He ventured into Venetian Gothic with the Belfast Bank, Newtownards, Co. Down (1854), but afterwards worked in the muscular High Victorian Gothic style. His buildings include St Andrew's church, Dublin (1860), the Unitarian church, Dublin (1861), Old Conna, Bray, Co. Wicklow (1860), Glaslough, Co. Monaghan (*c*. 1865–72) and Belfast Castle (1865) – the last two in a baronial style – while the scholastic Jordanstown church, Co. Antrim (1865), is an important landmark in the revival of ancient Irish architecture. After 1872 he worked on his own and his output fell in quantity and quality.　　　　WG

Hugh Dixon, 'William Henry Lynn', *IGS Bulletin*, XVII (1974).

Mac An Tsaoi, Maire (1922–).

Poet; one of the major poets of her generation of Irish-language writers, she is a scholar of the highest calibre. She worked on the editorial board of the *English-Irish Dictionary*, as well as at the Institute of Advanced Studies in Dublin. Her poetry is of deliberate and deceptively simple construction.   T McC

McArdell, James (1728/9–1765).

Mezzotint engraver; born in Dublin, he was apprenticed in the art of ENGRAVING to John Brooks when Andrew Miller was associated with Brooks's Dublin workshop. At the age of eighteen he accompanied Brooks to London, and there gained a reputation as the finest mezzotint engraver in the country. He executed more than two hundred mezzotint portraits of the highest artistic quality, including many after paintings by Reynolds, Hudson, Ramsay and Gainsborough, before his early death when he was at the height of his career.   B de B

McAuley, Catherine (1778–1841).

Foundress and educator; born in Co. Dublin, she began charitable work in her early forties after inheriting a fortune from her foster-father. She opened a school for poor children and a home for destitute women in Dublin; and in 1831, with two companions, founded the Order of Mercy, one of the principal aims of which was to educate poor girls. The Order grew to be the largest religious congregation founded in the English-speaking world, and the cultural influence of the Irish Sisters of Mercy through their schools has been remarkable, not only in Ireland where they have 150 schools and two teacher-training colleges, but also in Britain, Australia, New Zealand, South Africa and the USA.   B de B

McCabe, Eugene (1930–).

Playwright; born in Glasgow, he was educated in Dublin and Cork, and was a farmer before becoming a playwright. His *King of the Castle* (1964) explicitly tackles sexual mores in a rural community; Patrick Pearse, one of the signatories of the proclamation of the Republic in 1916, is the major character in *Pull Down a Horseman* (1966) and *Gale Day* (1979). McCabe has written a television trilogy about present-day Ulster (*Cancer*, *Heritage* and *Siege*) and a novel, *Victims*.   BH

Mac Cana, Somhairle (1901–75).

Painter and designer; born in Belfast, he trained at Belfast College of Art, and the Royal College of Art in London. He became Principal of the Cork School of Art. He designed textiles and then metalwork, and illustrated books and periodicals in the 1930s and 1940s. His work, which seldom appears at auction sales, is much sought after by collectors; the best of it can be seen in the Crawford Municipal Gallery, Cork.   C MacG

Mac Cana, Somhairle. *The Galway Fish Market.* Crawford Municipal Art Gallery, Cork.

McCarthy, J. J. St Patrick's Roman Catholic Cathedral, Armagh; the 19th-century building was completed by McCarthy in Decorated Gothic style.

McCarthy, James Joseph (1817–82).

Architect; born in Dublin. His first church, Glendalough (1846), is – apart from A. W. N. PUGIN's churches – the earliest church in Ireland to be designed on ecclesiological principles. With the exception of Cahirmoyle, Co. Limerick (1870), and some work on Castle Forbes, Co. Longford, he was essentially a designer of religious buildings, including convents and 80 churches. These include Ballinasloe, Co. Galway (1846, started 1852), Kilskyre, Co. Meath (1847), Armagh Cathedral (started 1838 by Thomas Duff and completed by

McCarthy, 1853–73), St Saviour's, Dominick Street, Dublin (1852), Tramore, Co. Waterford (1857), Thomastown, Co. Kilkenny (1858), Killenaule, Co. Tipperary (1858), Monaghan Cathedral (1861), College Chapel, Maynooth, Co. Kildare (1875), and Kilmallock, Co. Limerick (1878). He contributed to Duffy's *Irish Catholic Magazine* (1847) and wrote *Some Suggestions on the Arrangement and Characteristics of Parish Churches* (1851).   W G

Jeanne Sheehy, *J. J. McCarthy and the Gothic Revival in Ireland*, 1977.

McCarthy, Thomas (1954–). Poet; born in Co. Waterford. Winner of the Patrick Kavanagh Award, 1977. The *First Convention* (1978) deals with political themes out of a personal mythology. His second book, *The Sorrow-Garden*, published in 1981, won the Alice Hunt Bartlett Award.   T McC

McCormack, John (1884–1945). Singer; born in Athlone, Co. Westmeath. At the age of 18 he won a gold medal at an Irish National Festival. Subsequent study in Italy resulted in his début there in opera in 1906; the following year he sang the role of Turiddù in *Cavalleria Rusticana* at Covent Garden. In the role of Alfredo in *La Traviata* he made his début at the Manhattan Opera in 1909 and at the Metropolitan Opera House, New York, in 1910. After 1914 he devoted his career to concerts and recitals, specializing in Irish ballads and *Lieder*, and was acclaimed as the greatest lyric tenor of his day. He was created a Papal Count in 1928.   B de B

McCormick, F. J. (stage name of Peter Judge; 1889–1947). Character actor; born at Skerries, Co. Dublin, he joined the ABBEY THEATRE in 1918, playing in some 500 productions. He created the parts of Seumas Shields in *The Shadow of a Gunman*, Joxer in *Juno and the Paycock*, Jack in *The Plough and the Stars*, Tim in *Professor Tim*, and Oedipus in YEATS's version of Sophocles's tragedy. He also acted in several films, including *Odd Man Out*.   C F-S

MacCuarta, Seán Dall (*c.* 1645–1733). Gaelic poet; from Co. Louth, he combined both classical and popular techniques in the composition of his work. Although partly blind, he nevertheless made a precarious living from his writings. His best-known poems are 'An Lon Dubh Baite' ('The Drowned Blackbird') and 'Fáilte don Ean' ('Welcome to the Bird').   T McC

MacFheorais, Séamus (1915–). Gaelic poet. Two collections of his work have been published, *Gearrcaigh na hOiche* and *Leargas*.   T McC

McGahern, John (1935–). Writer; born in Dublin, he was raised in the west of Ireland, and his work chronicles the claustrophobic nature of provincial life. His first novel, *The Barracks* (1963), finds tragedy and bitter comedy as a policeman's wife dies of cancer; his second, *The Dark* (1965), depicts a motherless boy with

a sadistic yet pitiful father, trapped between the conflicting pressures of education for the priesthood and of his emergent sexuality. This masterly novel was banned by the censorship board, causing its author to lose his job as a schoolteacher. McGahern's later work includes *The Leavetaking* (1974) and the short-story collections *Nightlines* (1970) and *Getting Through* (1978).   B H

MacGonigal, Maurice (1900–79). Landscape and figurative painter, born in Dublin; after early training as a STAINED-GLASS painter in the studios of his uncle, Joshua Clarke, he joined Na Fianna and the IRA in 1917. He was arrested and interned in Kilmainham Jail and Ballykinlar Camp. Having turned his back upon politics, he returned to the Clarke Studios, where he received much encouragement from his cousin HARRY CLARKE and became a junior partner. He left to enter the Metropolitan School of Art, Dublin in 1923; elected ARHA 1932 and RHA 1933, he was Professor of Painting to the Royal Hibernian Academy, and became Keeper in 1950; he was appointed PRHA in 1962. He signed his work 'MacCongail'. He was an Honorary Member of the Royal Academy of Arts, London and of the Royal Scottish Academy, Edinburgh, and received an Hon. LL.D. at the National University of Ireland in 1970. His work is represented in public collections in Ireland, Great Britain, the USA and the USSR.   C MacG

Maurice MacGonigal 1900–1979 (catalogue), Taylor Galleries, Dublin, with an introduction by Mervyn Wall 1979; *Maurice MacGonigal* (catalogue), Taylor Galleries, Dublin, with an introduction by Ciarán MacGonigal, 1981.

MacGreevy, Thomas (1893–1967). Poet; born at Tarbert, Co. Kerry, he lived for some years in Paris before returning to London in 1935. In 1940 he moved to Dublin and eventually became Director of the National Gallery of Ireland. His *Poems* were published in 1934 and *Collected Poems* in 1971.   T McC

McGuinness, Norah (1903–80). Cubist landscape and subject painter; born in Derry, she studied at Derry Technical School, and entered the Metropolitan School of Art, Dublin, in 1921. There she studied under PATRICK TUOHY, HARRY CLARKE and the designer OSWALD REEVES, and subsequently was much influenced by a period of study in Paris under André Lhote. She was a founder-member of the Irish Exhibition of Living Art in 1943 and on the death of MAINIE JELLETT became its President; she was elected HRHA, 1957. A retrospective exhibition of her work was held in Dublin in 1968. She was also famous for the designs she made for the Dublin retail store of Brown Thomas, for her designs for the stage and for illustrations to works by YEATS and Ethel Mannin. Her work is represented in many public collections in Ireland.   C MacG

Macken, Walter (1916–67). Playwright and novelist; born in Galway. Many of his plays, such as *Mungo's Mansion* (1946), and novels, such as *Quench the*

Moon (1948), are firmly rooted in Connemara life. His historical novels are set in a variety of periods: *Seek the Fair Land* (1959) in 17th-century Ireland under Cromwell; *The Silent People* (1962) in the Famine.   BH

MacKenna, Siobhán (1923–). Actress.; born in Belfast, she was educated at St Louis, Monaghan, and University College, Galway. Her early stage experience was with Taibhdhearc na Gaillimhe (*see* THEATRE), where she translated and played Shaw's *St Joan* in Irish. She has acted with all the principal Irish companies and with her own production company in Ireland and abroad, and has had a large number of Broadway and London West End roles, as well as appearing in films.   CF-S

Macklin, Charles (*c.* 1697–1797). Actor and playwright; born Charles MacLoughlin, probably in either Co. Donegal or Co. Derry. All his life he alternated between Dublin and London, as one of the most celebrated, and most irascible, actors of the century. His most famous role was Shylock. He also wrote several comedies, in which he also appeared: as Sir Archy MacSarcasm in *Love à la Mode* (1759), as O'Dogherty in *The True-Born Irishman* (1763), and as Sir Pertinax MacSycophant in *The Man of the World* (1781). He continued acting until 1789.   CF-S/ICR

MacLíammóir, Mícheál (*né* Wilmore; 1899–1978).. Actor, stage designer, wit and playwright; born in Cork. He created leading roles in Irish plays from 1928 to *c.* 1960, having founded the Dublin Gate Theatre with HILTON EDWARDS. He excelled in romantic, and later in character, parts. His solo performances in *The Importance of Being Oscar* (1960) and *I Must Be Talking to my Friends* (1963) toured internationally. His stage designs, influenced chiefly by Bakst and Beardsley, helped to create the avant garde image of the Gate in the 1920s–30s. His plays include *Where Stars Walk, Ill Met by Moonlight, Diarmuid and Gráinne*, etc.   CF-S

McKenna, Siobhán. The leading actress in the title role of Shaw's *St Joan*.

Macklin, Charles. The actor portrayed by Johan Zoffany as Shylock in Act III of *The Merchant of Venice*, Covent Garden 1767–8; on permanent display in the foyer of the National Theatre, London.

MacLíammóir, Micheál. The eminent actor and playwright at work on one of his stage designs.

Maclise, Daniel. Detail from *The Marriage of Strongbow and Eva* (exhibited 1854), showing the bard as a symbol of the Celts' departed glory. NGI.

Maclise, Daniel (1806–70). Painter; born in Cork, he studied at the School of Art there and became a fine portrait draughtsman. He went to the Royal Academy Schools in 1828, and soon afterwards became famous for his literary, biblical and historical scenes, painting a fresco for the Prince Consort in 1843, and many subjects for the Palace of Westminster, commissions which kept him busy till the end of his life. His style varies considerably, from Italian Renaissance grandeur to the intimacy of Dutch genre. His output was large, and included a few very fine portraits. He retained contacts with Ireland throughout his career and his emotional painting *The Marriage of Strongbow and Eva* shows his nationalist feelings and knowledge of ancient, Irish, civilization. AOC
W. J. O'Driscoll, *A Memoir of Daniel Maclise R.A.*, 1871; Richard Ormond and John Turpin, *Daniel Maclise 1806–1870* (exhibition catalogue), 1972.

MacMahon, Bryan (1909–). Writer; born at Listowel, Co. Kerry, he wrote plays, novels, children's books, short stories (collected in *The Lion Tamer*, 1948), and *The Red Petticoat* (1955). His finest work, *The Honey Spike* (a play in 1961, a novel in 1967), describes tragicomically the violent journey of a tinker and his pregnant wife down the whole length of Ireland to Kerry for the birth of her baby. BH
G. Henderson, 'An Interview with Bryan MacMahon' in *Journal of Irish Literature*, vol. 3, Sep. 1974, pp. 3–23; J. L. Henderson, 'Four Kerry Writers', in *JIL*, vol. 1, May 1972, pp. 112–8.

McMaster, Anew (1894–1962). Actor and producer; born in Co. Monaghan, he toured extensively in Britain and Australia before founding his own company in 1925 to tour Ireland, mainly performing works by Shakespeare. He played Hamlet at Stratford-on-Avon, and James Tyrone in *Long Day's Journey into Night* all over America. His most successful roles were Othello, Lear, Shylock, Coriolanus, Svengali in *Trilby* and Mathias in *The Bells*. CF-S

MacNeice, Louis (1907–63). Poet and broadcaster; born in Belfast, he was educated in England. His youthful exposure to the disciplines of philosophy and the classics is reflected in the controlled emotions and melancholy of his writing. He first came to prominence in the 1930s (*see* POETRY) and in his lifetime published sixteen collections of verse. His *Collected Poems* appeared posthumously in 1966. His best-known book, *Autumn Journal* (1938), is a valediction on Irish affairs and a celebration of memory. His care as a craftsman has influenced the best modern Irish poets. TMcC

McWilliam, F. E. (1909–). Sculptor; born at Banbridge, Co. Down, he studied first at the Belfast School of Art, then left Ireland in 1928 to study painting in London at the Slade until 1931, when he turned to sculpture and won the Ross Leaving Scholarship. He worked in Paris (1931–32) where he came in contact with Brancusi. He was involved with British Surrealism in the later 1930s and exhibited in London. During World War II he served with the

McWilliam, F. E. *Women of Belfast*, 7, bronze, height 35 cm. (13¾ in.) 1972, Ulster Museum.

RAF. He was a staff member at the Slade (1947–8) and served on the Arts Panel of the U.K. Arts Council (1962–8). He exhibited extremely widely after the war – in Sweden, Battersea Park (Festival of Britain), Irish Exhibition of Living Art, Tate Gallery, São Paulo etc., and had several one-man shows in Belfast, London and Dublin. He has worked in a variety of materials, notably wood and metal. His early work is within the organic tradition of Brancusi, Hepworth and Arp; he then took up the playful biomorphic forms of Surrealism, and in the 1950s moved towards welded figures. Although occasionally highly abstracted, his sculpture has in general remained figurative, with a recurring Surrealist element. In reaction to the Northern political troubles, he created a highly expressive series of the *Women of Belfast*; he has always maintained his links with Ireland, despite his residence abroad.   JT
G. McCann, 'F. E. McWilliam', in *Threshold*, no. 21 (Summer 1967); *F. E. McWilliam* (exhibition catalogue, The Arts Council of N. Ireland and An Chomhairle Ealaíon, Belfast, Dublin, Cork) 1981.

Madden, Anne (1932–). Painter and sculptor; born in London, she came to live in Ireland as a child. She studied at the Chelsea School of Art, London, and has exhibited at the Royal Hibernian Academy and Irish Exhibition of Living Art. In 1958 she married the painter LOUIS LE BROCQUY, and since then has lived mainly in France. As well as painting, she has produced various sculptures and perspex seriographs;

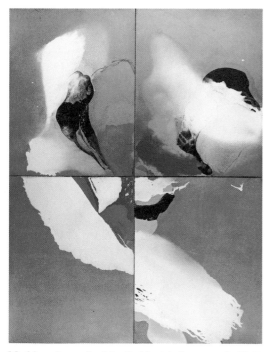

Madden, Anne. *Quadripartite Mountain Sequence, 1967 (Red)*, oil on canvas. An Chomhairle Ealaíon Collection, Dublin.

she held a retrospective exhibition at the Ulster Museum, 1974. Her work can be seen in the Fondation Maeght, France, the Gulbenkian Foundation, and the Hirshhorn Collection in Washington.   C MacG

Mahon, Derek (1941–). Poet; he has published four books – *Night-Crossing* (1968), *Lives* (1972), *The Snow Party* (1975) and *Poems: 1962–1978*. He is a versatile craftsman whose range is immense, from the *haiku*-like 'Light-Music' to the long existentialist treatise of 'A Disused Shed in Co. Wexford'.   T McC

Malinmore, Co. Donegal. A valley, to the south of Glencolumbkille, rich in megalithic tombs. Near the W, seaward, end is a pair of very large PORTAL TOMBS, 90 m. (100 yds) apart, with four smaller subsidiary structures between, which were apparently enclosed in antiquity in a long cairn.
Near the head of the valley is Cloghanmore, a fine double-trapezoid COURT TOMB, 40 m. (43 yds) long, excavated from the peat in the 19th century. This has a large full court opening from the E, with a pair of parallel two-chambered burial galleries at the W end and a pair of single-chambered subsidiaries opening off the NE and SE faces of the court; beside the entrance to each of these is a single jamb in the court façade with carved ornament.   M H
R. de Valéra, 'The Court Cairns of Ireland', *PRIA* 60c (1960), 108.

M'Allister, George (1786–1812). Stained-glass designer; the only son of the head porter at Trinity College, Dublin, he was educated at the Dublin Society Schools. From 1807 he exhibited glass and worked on Irish commissions with his three sisters in Dublin; five of their largely decorative windows survive in TUAM Cathedral.   NGB
Michael Wynne, 'Stained Glass in Ireland: principally Irish Stained Glass 1760–1963' (unpublished Ph.D. thesis, Trinity College, Dublin), 1975.

Marsh's Library, Dublin. This, the oldest public library in Ireland, was founded in 1707 by Archbishop Narcissus Marsh who had in 1704 bought the important library of Edward Stillingfleet, Bishop of Worcester. It still occupies the building designed for it by Sir WILLIAM ROBINSON, the Surveyor-General, in 1706.   M C

Martin, Violet Florence. *See* SOMERVILLE AND ROSS.

Martyn, Edward (1859–1923). Playwright and key figure in the Irish Revival; born at Tullira Castle, Co. Galway, he was a co-founder of the Irish Literary Theatre (*see* ABBEY THEATRE), where his best play, *The Heather Field*, was given in the inaugural season, 1899. He passionately supported the restoration of the IRISH LANGUAGE, sacred music and church art. A series of vehement articles attacking the cheap, commercial 'sham' readily imported into Irish churches by ill-educated clergy led to his inviting Christopher Whall (1849–1914), the pioneering English stained-glass

Martyn, Edward. Portrait by Norman McLachlan (d. 1978). NGI.

artist-craftsman, to produce windows for his family church at Ardrahan, Co. Galway, and to inaugurate stained-glass classes at the newly re-organized Metropolitan School of Art in Dublin, and thus train native artist-craftsmen and women in the art he felt had suffered such indignities. After visiting Co. Galway in 1901, Whall sent Martyn, A. E. Child and a glazier to set up classes and run a studio of native glass-workers (AN TÚR GLOINE) whose first commission, engineered by Martyn, was at LOUGHREA CATHEDRAL. The failure of many of his dreams, however, left him increasingly bitter and he died a frustrated man.   N G B
Denis Gwynn, *Edward Martyn and the Irish Revival*, 1930; Sr Marie-Thérèse Courtney, *Edward Martyn and the Irish Theater*, 1956.

Mathews, Aidan Carl (1956–). Poet; his *Windfalls* (1979) won the Macauley Fellowship (awarded by the Arts Council). Another book, *Minding Ruth*, is in preparation.   T McC

Maturin, Charles Robert (1782–1824). Writer; born in Dublin, where he was educated at TCD, and took holy orders in the Church of Ireland in 1803, revealing strong Calvinist leanings. Despite his persistent unease about combining the roles of author and clergyman, Maturin was forced by financial necessity to write, finally gaining success with a verse tragedy, *Bertram* (1816). His fiction includes *Fatal Revenge* (1807), *The Wild Irish Boy* (1808), *The Milesian Chief* (1812), *Women, or, Pour et Contre* (1818), and *The Albigenses* (1824). His Gothic masterpiece, *Melmoth the*

Wanderer (1820), made a great impact on such writers as Balzac, Baudelaire, and Poe.   I C R
Niilo Idman, *Charles Robert Maturin: His Life and Works*, 1923; Dale Kramer, *Charles Robert Maturin*, 1973; Robert E. Lougy, *Charles Robert Maturin*, 1975.

Maxton, Hugh (1947–). Poet and critic; his meticulous craftsmanship is reflected in his work published in two books, *Stones* (1970) and *The Noise of the Fields* (1976), the latter being a Poetry Book Society Choice.   T McC

Merriman, Brian (c. 1750–1803). Gaelic poet; born near Ennistymon, Co. Clare, he was reputedly the illegitimate son of a country gentleman. He was a schoolmaster, musician and mathematician, as well as the author of 'Cuirt an Mhean Oiche' ('The Midnight Court'), one of the greatest poems of the Irish language (*see* POETRY).   T McC

metalwork, Early Christian. Writing in the 7th century, the monk Tirechán refers to Assicus, the metalworker and companion of St Patrick, examples of whose craft he had seen in three churches – Elphin, Saul and Armagh. The remarks are instructive, perhaps more for the 7th century than for the 5th, the time of the Patrician Mission. From them we can deduce a tradition of craftsmanship in making liturgical objects, the wide distribution of the work of one artist and the fact that it did not appear strange to Tirechán that a churchman should engage in metalwork. We do not, however, learn what practical arrangements existed. Were objects fabricated in central workshops or were they made to order on site by itinerant craftsmen? Archaeological excavation has produced evidence for fine metalworking and other, more functional, decorative work at several sites. It is not, however, to be expected that strong physical evidence for goldsmiths' or silversmiths' workshops will ever be found, because the specialized equipment would be difficult to recognize as such in excavations – a furnace, a small portable kit of gravers, hammers etc. and some wooden gear are all that are really necessary for the production of metalwork of high quality. In some cases, where toxic materials were used – such as mercury for gilding – an enclosed building, with consequent ventilation problems, would have been a downright disadvantage. It is likely therefore that the main evidence for the history of Early Christian metalwork will remain whatever can be deduced from the objects themselves.

The art-historical record for the two centuries or so following the introduction of Christianity is patchy. The development of metalwork can only faintly be traced in personal ornaments, mostly cloak-fastenings, in particular penannular BROOCHES but also other types, such as the so-called 'hand pins' (stick pins with terminals recalling the shape of a human hand) and 'latchets' (discs with sinuous extensions often elaborately decorated). Influences from late- and post-Roman Britain can be detected. An increase in the use of *champlevé* enamel combined with curvilinear patterns

Dress fastening of enamelled bronze with curvilinear decoration, of the type known as a 'latchet', *c.* 6th century; length overall 16·5 cm. (6½ in.). NMI.

Gilt-bronze Crucifixion plaque from St John's, Rinnagan, Co. Roscommon, late 7th century. NMI.

of Ultimate La Tène (*see* LA TÈNE) style can be seen in objects which can tentatively be dated to the 6th and 7th centuries. Platelets of millefiori glass are often employed with enamel as, for example, on the brooch from Ballinderry Crannóg, No. 2, Co. Offaly, which probably dates to the early 7th century. Ornaments of this period were usually made of bronze but a small number of silver objects are known.

No specifically ecclesiastical example of metalwork of Irish manufacture survives from the earliest Christian period in Ireland. Objects such as chalices, patens, bells and basins would all have been necessary for the celebration of the liturgy, but no examples survive from before the 8th century. At that time, Ireland saw the beginning of a period of astonishing creativity in the visual arts, not least in the field of metalwork. New techniques, perhaps borrowed in the late 7th century mainly from Saxon England: filigree, 'kerbschnitt' (deeply faceted engraving) – in Ireland often mimicked by casting – and gilding. New materials were employed – mercury for gilding, crystal and silver appear much more frequently. Amber, too, makes an appearance but it is much more common later. Older methods were developed to satisfy new tastes – enamelling began to imitate the angular cloisonné garnet settings of Saxon and other Germanic jewellery, and casting in bronze became more ambitious. New motifs were adopted: some, such as the interlace, were no doubt transmitted by the circulation of illuminated mss. from overseas; animal designs became especially common – a beast, part-fabulous, part-credible, predominates, while snake-like forms and birds are known. Curvilinear designs of Ultimate La Tène style are important intially but occur less and less frequently on later objects. The chief effect of the metalwork is one of colour and great variety achieved by a superb technical mastery. Chief among the 8th-century liturgical objects are the great silver chalice from the ARDAGH HOARD, Co. Limerick, and the paten from the DERRYNAFLAN HOARD, Co. Tipperary.

While surviving sacred vessels and other utensils of this period are rare, fragments of SHRINES, as well as complete examples, are rather more frequent. House-shaped shrines were made to preserve the relics of saints, other types may be guessed at from the numerous fragments of bronze mounts which survive, and book coverings are probably represented by the Crucifixion plaque from St John's Rinnagan, Co. Roscommon. Shrines which take their shape from the objects they enclose are known, for example the Moylough Belt Shrine, and, from the end of the 8th or early 9th century, a portion of a bell shrine formerly at Killua Castle, Co. Westmeath.

Personal ornaments, such as the 'TARA' BROOCH and other pseudo-penannular brooches, are important also. Some of those which survive are sumptuously decorated with gold filigree, gilding, chip-carved ornament, glass and enamel. Whether worn by clerics or laymen, these pieces were obviously symbols of high social status.

Early texts speak of the beautiful decoration of churches and their altar-furniture and lamps, and there can be little doubt of the great efforts devoted to beautifying the liturgy. Ninth-century graves in Norway contain numerous objects of Irish manufacture, some evidently having been torn from shrines, book-mounts and other ecclesiastical objects. The loss sustained in the early VIKING raids must have been substantial, but it was by no means catastrophic since there is evidence that fine metalworking continued during the 9th century – for example the Derrynaflan chalice and several pseudo-penannular brooches. The tradition of making large brooches continued and the penannular form enjoyed a renewed vogue, this time

metalwork. Panel from the Soiscel Molaise, an important book-shrine of the 11th century. NMI.

mether. Wooden drinking vessel, from Corran, Co. Armagh, 17th century. NMI.

in silver with elaborate animal designs and other traits of Saxon inspiration. Inscriptions of any kind are rare on objects of 8th–10th century date. The history of metalwork in the 9th and 10th centuries is as yet poorly understood but at least one major piece – the lost shrine of the BOOK OF DURROW – was made late in the 9th century, as its inscription implied. In the period after the year 1000 a number of reliquaries were fabricated, often at the instance of an important lay patron. Some of these, for example the book shrine, the Soiscel Molaise, were re-modellings of earlier shrines, while others were entirely new. Often they show clear influence from Viking art styles and in one case – the Shrine of the Cathach – the craftsman's name is composed of both Irish and Scandinavian elements. There can be little doubt that the Viking town of Dublin was an important centre of metalwork production in the 11th and 12th centuries.

In the late 11th and early 12th century there was a renaissance in Irish art, inspired probably by the reform of the Church. Metalwork objects, often paid for by leading kings such as Domhnall O'Lochlann and Turlough O'Connor, were commissioned. Decorated normally in the Irish version of the Scandinavian Urnes style, outstanding pieces include the Shrine of St Patrick's Bell, the CROSS OF CONG, the Shrine of St Lachtin's Arm, the LISMORE and CLONMACNOIS CROZIERS and St Manchan's Shrine. Although not as spectacular as many objects of the 8th century, the metalwork of the late 11th/early 12th century does show a fine technical skill and sense of design, as well as an awareness of artistic developments, both in contemporary northern and southern Europe. This phase represents the last great period of native expression in the visual arts before the competition of the great quasi-industrial centres of Europe began to supply Ireland with relatively cheap metalwork, to the detriment of local schools. For later developments in metalwork *see* SILVERWORK.   M F R

mether. A name given by 19th-century scholars to a type of wooden cup found occasionally in bogs, based on the assumption that such cups were used for drinking mead. Ranging in height from 15 cm. to about 30 cm. (6–12 in.) methers are generally made from two pieces of wood. The main body (including handles) is usually carved from one piece, with a base separately fitted into a groove or croze. There may be one, two or three handles; on some examples, the handles extend below the base to form feet. Generally four-sided at the mouth, the body usually tapers towards a rounded base; there are normally rudimentary spouts at the corners. Some methers bear simple incised designs, and examples with inscriptions suggesting a 16th-century date are known. The arrangement of the handles is not unlike that of some post-medieval Staffordshire pottery and it is reasonable to suggest, therefore, that Irish methers are a rendering in traditional methods and materials of a borrowed fashion.   M F R

Metropolitan School of Art, Dublin. *See* NATIONAL COLLEGE OF ART AND DESIGN.

Meyer, Kuno. Portrait of the German-born Celtic scholar by Augustus John, oil on canvas. NGI.

Meyer, Kuno (1858–1919). Celtic scholar and translator of Gaelic legends and poetry; born in Hamburg, Germany, he founded the School of Irish Learning, 1903, and the seminal journal *Eriu*, 1904. Among his publications are *The Voyage of Bran* (1895), *Four Old Irish Songs of Summer and Winter* (1903) and *Selections from Ancient Irish Poetry* (1911). He was appointed Professor of Celtic Studies at Berlin University, 1911.   T McC

Middleton, Colin (1910–). Designer and painter; born in Belfast, he trained at Belfast College of Art; he exhibits with the Royal Hibernian Academy, the Irish Exhibition of Living Art and other groups, and at Irish annual exhibitions; he has also had retrospective exhibitions in Belfast, Glasgow, Edinburgh, and Dublin. He was elected RHA in 1969. Examples of his work are to be found in all public collections in Ireland.   C MacG

Milne, Ewart (1903–). Poet and man of letters; he is the author of at least fourteen books of poetry, his best-known works being *Letter from Ireland* (1940), *Selected Poems* (1953) and *A Garland for the Green* (1962).   T McC

monasticism. In technical ecclesiastical usage, monasticism has come to be defined in terms of its contemplative orientation, in terms of the monk's function of divine adoration through the liturgy and personal prayer. Hence the monastic vocation is generally distinguished from a religious vocation, i.e. to the active apostolate, either as a mendicant friar or as a

member of one of the modern religious societies (for which the Jesuits provided the prototype).

The Irish monastic tradition does not, however, lend itself to such a distinction. It already had half a millennium of history behind it, including a splendid golden age, before the distinction began to be perceived in the High Middle Ages in the contrasting life-styles of the (contemplative) Cistercians and the (active) mendicants. Besides, the distinction has little meaning for Irish Catholics today – the members of a religious institute as committed to the active apostolate as the CHRISTIAN BROTHERS are referred to colloquially as 'the monks'. In the present context, therefore, monasticism is considered not in the strict technical sense, but as the cenobitic tradition in Ireland more generally, the tradition moulded by the response of succeeding generations of Irish men and women to the gospel call to worldly renunciation and to the more perfect following of Christ in poverty, chastity and obedience.

It can be claimed that the cenobitic tradition in Ireland is as old as CHRISTIANITY itself. A reference in St PATRICK's *Confessio* indicates that already within his own lifetime the quest for perfection through a life of virginity and of worldly renunciation had become a feature of the nascent Irish Church. Scarcely more than a generation separates the *floruit* of Patrick and that of St Brigid, foundress of the monastic movement associated with Kildare, and less than a generation separates Brigid from the heyday of St Finnian's, Clonard, a veritable school for monastic Founders, including the great Colum Cille (Columba). By the late 6th century the Irish monastic movement had extended to the neighbouring island and by the early 7th century it was propagating itself on the European continent under the inspiration of that intrepid 'traveller for Christ', St Columbanus. By then the progress of the monastic movement in Ireland itself had produced the unique example of a local Church organized and administered under a monastic system rather than under the diocesan-episcopal system of the universal Church.

It was under the aegis of this monastically organized Church that the pagan Celtic culture and the Christian Latin one blended to produce the glories that are identified with Ireland's golden age. Its outstanding ILLUMINATED MANUSCRIPTS, most nobly preserved in the BOOK OF KELLS, continue to be a wonder of the world. The same combination of ingenious craftsmanship, artistic delicacy and spiritual power is reflected in the METALWORK of the period, e.g. the silver Chalice in the ARDAGH HOARD and the CROSS OF CONG, and in its sculpture in stone, e.g. the Monasterboice, Moone and Drumcliff HIGH CROSSES. In architecture the development of a solemn yet simple and fluid style can be seen in the contrast between the tiny GALLARUS ORATORY in Co. Kerry and the haunting beauty of such monastic sites as CLONMACNOIS and GLENDALOUGH – a development that culminated fittingly in such gems as CORMAC'S CHAPEL at Cashel and St Brendan's Cathedral at Ardfert. Though less well known nowadays, the achievements of the period in scholarship and literature are scarcely less remarkable. The openness of the

Part of the 12th-century cloister and the lavabo at Mellifont, Co. Louth, the first Irish abbey of the Cistercian Order.

monks to the native oral culture and their determination to assimilate it within the Christian tradition resulted in the first development of Irish historical scholarship and in the creation of a vernacular literature in prose (the sagas) and lyric poetry which, as KUNO MEYER has commented, 'occupies a unique position in the literature of the world'.

Monastic Ireland's extended Hiberno-Romanesque phase, as it may be termed, was brought to a close not by the coming of the VIKINGS in the 8th century but by the coming of the Normans in the 12th. Already before that time the Celtic Church had been 'normalized' through the ecclesiastical reform of the 12th century which St Malachy, himself an abbot in the Celtic tradition, did so much to promote. Normalization had two main effects: the episcopal-diocesan system replaced the monastic one as the institutional framework of the local Church; and secondly, the Irish cenobitic movement was transformed by the introduction of the Continental religious orders. Cistercians, Benedictines, and Augustinian Canons in the 12th century were followed by the mendicant friars – Franciscans, Dominicans, Augustinians and Carmelites – in the 13th. Thus reformed, the cenobitic movement continued to play a major role in the Irish Church. It has maintained a prominent place ever since; despite the vicissitudes of the Reformation era, the dissolution of the religious orders by parliamentary statute under Henry VIII (1536–7), and recurring pogroms, perpetrated in every reign from Elizabeth I to George II, the cenobitic movement survived in Ireland. Indeed, for much of the 17th century it flourished, revitalized by the newly introduced Counter Reformation orders, Jesuits and Capuchins, and even more so by the ever-reforming Conventual Franciscans, operating from their renowned expatriate convents of St Isidore's (Rome) and St Anthony's (Louvain).

Catholic Emancipation (1829) created new opportunities which were speedily seized, even anticipated. One was the opportunity to re-establish the contemplative orders whose mode of life had proved impossible to sustain in the period of persecution. The Cistercians settled at Mount Mellaray near Cappoquin, Co. Waterford, in 1833 and gradually expanded. The Benedictines established themselves at Glenstal, Co. Limerick, in 1927, thereby realizing within four years of his death, the unfulfilled ambition of the famous Irish abbot of Maredsous, Dom Columba Marmion. Meanwhile communities of enclosed nuns multiplied (Poor Clares, Carmelites, Reparation Sisters etc.). At the same time recently founded missionary congregations from the Continent (Vincentians, Holy Ghost Fathers, Redemptorists, Passionists, and Marists) established themselves in Ireland, much attracted by the rich promise of vocations. In Ireland itself urgently needed religious brotherhoods and sisterhoods sprang up to serve the social apostolate (Christian, Presentation and Patrician Brothers; Sisters of Charity, of Mercy, of the Presentation). These latter were generously supplemented by Continental congregations of a similar kind (Salesians, Little Sisters of the Poor, Good Shepherd Sisters etc.). Towards the end of the century the renewal of the tradition of the *peregrinatio* was signalized in the formation of Irish missionary societies (Columban, Kiltegan, Maynooth). Mother Mary Martin's highly effective Medical Missionaries of Mary were established as recently as 1937.

The religious communities in modern Ireland therefore, may claim continuity with a cenobitic tradition that stretches back to the earliest centuries of the Irish Church. However, that claim must be qualified, and the qualifications are no less significant than the fact that the claim can be made. For in the course of transmission the tradition lost some of its most vital elements. In this connection three radical historical disjunctures may be noted. The first was the reform of the 12th century. The price paid for drawing Irish monasticism into the mainstream cenobitic tradition of Western Christianity was to jettison the distinctively native tradition, at least in its formal aspect. Henceforth, for better or for worse – a recent commentator described the *Regula S. Columbani* as brutal – the quest for perfection by means of evangelical renunciation was guided in Ireland not by the rules and usages that had produced the saints and scholars of the early Irish Church but by those of the great architects of the Continental cenobitic tradition, Benedict, Augustine, Francis, Ignatius. The second disjuncture was occasioned by the introduction of the English Reformation in the 16th century. Although the religious continued to function despite the statutory dissolution of their foundations, they were forced to abandon their historic centres which passed into lay ownership. These were never regained. Nowadays the remnants of the ancient buildings provide charming specimens of that ubiquitous feature of the Irish countryside, the ruin. The upshot is that the religious communities of modern Ireland have lost contact with the hallowed centres in which the cenobitic tradition was moulded in Ireland throughout the millennium of the Middle Ages, in contrast with their Continental counterparts where the religious may continue to draw inspiration from contact with the living sources of their tradition at such hallowed sites as Subiaco, Monte Cassino, Cîteaux, Assisi, Manresa etc.

The third disjuncture is located in the transition from the 18th-century phase of penal repression to the 19th-century revival. The transition is marked by a puzzling feature that has yet to be adequately explored, intellectual and cultural regression. It is not merely that the cenobitic movement in the modern period has failed to emulate the near-miraculous achievements of early Irish monasticism, in scholarship and literature, in art and architecture; it has also failed to match the best achievements in these areas of any other phase. In literature it has failed to produce a creative writer worthy of a place beside the Franciscan bardic poet Tadhg Bocht Ó Huiginn or his 17th-century brethren Aodh Mac an Aingil and Pádraigín Haicéad. In scholarship its dwindling crop of university teachers has made no contribution to learning to compare with the crucial work of textual compilation, redaction and conservation undertaken by the medieval monasteries, or with the massive antiquarian projects of the 17th-century friars which produced, amongst much else, the *Annals of the Four Masters*. In the sphere of ecclesiastical scholarship there it little of significance or originality to show either. The modern scholasticates have generated a theological literature of a text-book and cathechetical kind, much of it highly competent but derivative – nothing to compare with the contribution to the revival of Scotism in the 17th century made by the Irish Franciscans, who, as well as much expository writing, produced an edition of Scotus's *opera omnia* in 1639. In ARCHITECTURE the record is, perhaps, most dismal of all, because of the missed opportunity provided by the massive building programme that followed Emancipation. The bleak barracks which the modern communities provided for themselves in a variety of imitative styles – Neo-Classical, Neo-Gothic, Neo-Hiberno-Romanesque – appear all the less appropriate by comparison with the structures built by their predecessors which seem so well attuned to the spirituality of the builders, as seen in the austere solemnity of the Cistercian abbeys, the simplicity and harmony of the Observants' convents – at harmony within themselves and with their environment – and the alternating stark (SKELLIG MICHAEL) and exuberant (CLONMACNOIS) beauty of the early monastic settlements. Further, when, in the early decades of the present century, the religious came into possession of many of the former stately homes of the Ascendancy, the brutal insensitivity of their renovations provided a kind of ironic revenge for the desecrations perpetrated on the medieval religious foundations by the lay expropriators of the Reformation period.

However, in the one thing that ultimately matters, the modern cenobitic movement in Ireland can claim continuity with the ancient tradition: in fidelity to the ascetic ideal of the gospel. That ideal was summed up by the old Irish monks in the phrase *bán mairtíreacht* ('white martyrdom'), by which was meant a witnessing to Christ by prayer and penance as heroic as the bloody witness provided by the martyrs. The spiritual vitality

A Franciscan of the Strict Observance; engraving from *History of the Antiquities of Ireland* (an English translation of Sir James Ware's Latin text), 1764.

of the Irish cenobitic tradition has always derived from this quest for personal sanctification through prayer and penance, undertaken in a spirit of witness, i.e. of apostolic service. Hence the prominence in the history of the cenobitic tradition in Ireland of communities of a strongly ascetical character, from the Culdees (*see* CÉLÍ DÉ) in the 9th century to the Cistercians and other 'strict-observance' communities at the present time. Another striking example of the continuity of the tradition is provided by the magnificent response of the modern Irish religious to the Church's missionary need; a response prompted, it is clear, by the conviction, shared by the missionaries of the early Irish Church, that 'exile for Christ' represented the ultimate act of self-renunciation short of death.

The future of the cenobitic tradition in Ireland seems less assured at the present time than at any other time since Catholic Emancipation. The religious communities were beset by a crisis of vocations in the mid-1960s which still continues. One interpretation relates this crisis to the modernization of Irish society, to the changing socio-economic structures and values brought about by Ireland's belated entry into the industrialized, urbanized, affluent and permissive society of the developed West. This analysis may, however, be questioned since the vocation crisis hit the already modernized cultures of Europe and the USA in the same way and at the same time as it hit modernizing Ireland. An alternative explanation is provided by the onset of modernization within the Church itself. The effect of the Second Vatican Council has been to release a dynamic impulse towards reform and adaptation, while at the same time precipitating an ecclesiastical crisis of profound dimensions, one symptom of which is an acute crisis of identity among priests and those dedicated to the religious life. Confidence has been sapped by the undermining of the sacralized conception of these roles through the humanistic theology of Vatican II which has fostered a cult of the laity and of the married state. In short, the ideological climate within the Church in the immediate aftermath of Vatican II has not been propitious for the cenobitic movement generally. On the other hand, this may be regarded as a temporary phenomenon, to be followed, as these ancient institutions adapt themselves to the new climate, by the re-establishment of stability and growth. The way in which the visit of Pope John Paul II in 1979 caught the imagination of the young people of Ireland, as no visit of a cult figure in secular life has done, may point in this direction. Again the success of the charismatic movement in tapping latent sources of spiritual enthusiasm, especially among the young, would suggest that the people of Ireland retain that sharp appetite for the spiritual and the transcendant which has sustained the cenobitic tradition since the days of Patrick.   BB

Kathleen Hughes, *The Church in Early Irish Society*, 1966; ——, *Early Christian Ireland*, 1972; P. J. Corish (ed.), *A History of Irish Catholicism*, 1967; John Watt, *The Church and the Two Nations in Medieval Ireland*, 1970; Brendan Bradshaw, *The Dissolution of the Religious Orders in Ireland under Henry VIII*, 1974; Brian de Breffny and George Mott, *The Churches and Abbeys of Ireland*, 1976.

monastic schools. The school of the monastery at Armagh claimed to have been founded by St Patrick himself in the 5th century. Among the alumni of the celebrated monastic school established by St Enda in the 5th century on the Aran Island of Inishmore were the founders of most of the other important monastic schools in Ireland: Bangor, Co. Down; Clonard, Co. Meath; Lismore, Co. Waterford; Monasterboice, Co. Louth; Mungret, Co. Limerick; and, most famous of all, Clonmacnois, Co. Offaly, founded in 544 by St Ciarán the Younger. By the end of the 7th century there were 45 monastic schools in Ireland. Grammar was considered important in these schools and in many the teachers compiled Latin grammatical treatises for the use of their students. St Isidore of Seville's *Etymologiae*, an encyclopaedia of human and divine subjects, was one of the works copied in monastic scriptoria for the students.

Many students from Britain and the Continent were instructed in these schools, as well as the native Irish (some of whom, as monks, went out to found monasteries and spread their faith and learning throughout western Europe – Irish monks, for example, taught in the schools of the court of Charlemagne). The Irish monastic schools suffered during the VIKING raids; their wonderful libraries and treasuries were plundered. While this may have contributed to their decline, it was the ecclesiastical reforms of the 12th century, the establishment in Ireland of the Benedictine, Cistercian and Augustinian orders, and finally the Anglo-Norman occupation which hastened the eclipse of the old monastic system and its schools (*see* MONASTICISM). In 1162 the Synod of Clane decreed that no one could hold the rank of *fer léiginn* (chief professor) in any Irish monastic school unless he had qualified in the school at Armagh, yet nothing more is heard of that school after 1188 following the Anglo-Norman occupation and plundering of that city. *See* EDUCATION.   B de B

Montague, John (1929–   ). Poet; an exceptionally gifted writer, he is one of the last carriers of that sense of the undiluted *heroic* strain in Irish poetry. He has published widely and consistently, from *Forms of Exile* (1958) to *The Great Cloak* (1978). His book-length poem *The Rough Field* (1972) was widely acclaimed as a major political exploration. A new collection, *The Dead Kingdom*, is in preparation.   T McC

Moore, Brian (1921–   ). Writer; born in Belfast, he emigrated to Canada in 1948. He writes equally perceptively about America (*Answer from Limbo*, 1960; *I am Mary Dunne*, 1968) and Ireland (*Judith Hearne*, 1955, about a frustrated Belfast spinster, and *The Emperor of Ice Cream*, 1965, about a young Belfast man in World War II). His novella *Catholics* (1972) is a fantasy set in Co. Kerry. Moore's themes are estrangement, alienation, loneliness and failure.   BH

H. Dahlie, *Brian Moore*, 1969; J. Flood, *Brian Moore*, 1974.

Moore, George (1852–1933). Writer; born in Co. Mayo, he was the son of a Catholic landlord. As a young man, however, he found Ireland less appealing than Paris, where he studied painting and discovered Zola and other French writers and artists. His early novels, such as *A Mummer's Wife* (1885), were written under the influence of French naturalism. A visit to Ireland provided the material for *A Drama in Muslin* (1886), a brilliant fictional study of contemporary social and political conditions; however, he made London his base of operations until the end of the century. At that point he became involved with the budding dramatic movement, and lived in Dublin from 1901 to 1910. His work for the theatre was only moderately successful, but during this period he wrote the powerful short stories of *The Untilled Field* (1903) and the symbolic novel *The Lake* (1905), both of which anticipated and may have influenced the fiction of JAMES JOYCE. Moore soon became discouraged about the prospects for a cultural rebirth in Ireland, where the Church (which he now ostentatiously renounced) seemed so powerful, and returned to London in 1911. He related his experiences and presented a comic but perceptive 'history' of the Revival in the three volumes of *Hail and Farewell* (1911–14). Moore had long been an almost obsessive reviser of his books and a dedicated

Moore, George. Portrait in oils by John Butler Yeats, 1905. NGI.

Morphey, Garret. Portrait of Oliver Plunkett (1629–81). Roman Catholic Archbishop of Armagh. NGI.

experimenter in fiction, and continued to be throughout the rest of his career; but his late work, though revealing great mastery of language and form, has not retained its original popularity.   PLM
Joseph Hone, *The Life of George Moore*, 1936; J. C. Noel, *George Moore*, 1966.

Moore, Thomas (1779–1852). Poet, musician and editor; born in Dublin, he studied at Trinity College, but was self-taught musically. Moore is best known for his *Irish Melodies*. His writing contains very little poetry, but has been of vital importance because it was, as FRANK O'CONNOR remarked, one of the few civilizing influences in the lives of the 19th-century poor. Among the most famous of his songs, 'The Last Rose of Summer', 'The Harp that Once in Tara's Halls' and 'The Minstrel Boy', with traditional tunes, have retained their popularity. His *Lalla Rookh* (1817) provided inspiration for work by Spontini and Schumann and Stanford (*see* MUSIC), and his lyrics were set by such distinguished composers as Weber, Mendelssohn, Berlioz, Rubinstein, Duparc and Hindemith.   T McC/B de B

Morgan, Lady (*née* Sydney Owenson; 1776–1859). Writer; born in Dublin, the daughter of the theatrical manager, ROBERT OWENSON, she first worked as a governess. Her third novel, *The Wild Irish Girl* (1806), was enormously successful and made her reputation. A romanticized view of Gaelic life, especially in Connacht, continued to dominate her fiction, including *O'Donnel* (1814), *Florence Macarthy* (1818), and *The O'Briens and the O'Flahertys* (1827), but though her work had considerable impact on contemporary English views of Ireland, her talents as a novelist did not always match her ambitions. She wrote two fine travel books, *France* (1817) and *Italy* (1821). She married the surgeon, Sir Thomas Morgan, in 1812.   ICR

Morphey, Garret (*c.* 1650–1716). Painter; first heard of in London in 1673 as a fellow-student with William Gandy at an Academy, where he was probably taught by Gaspar Smitz. He was painting in Dublin in the late 1670s, and in 1681 was in London where he made several versions of his portrait of the martyred St Oliver Plunkett. He may have visited the Low Countries soon afterwards, for his first small whole-length portraits (painted in the manner of Netscher) date from 1685–8 when he was in England, working mostly in Yorkshire. He returned to Ireland in 1688 or 1689 when he painted many Jacobites. After the Boyne he continued to paint in Ireland until his death. He was the first painter to use elements of European and English art, including symbolism, in his work, and he is the first professional Irish painter now known. He uses rich colours and is notable for his beautiful lace painting and his mannerism of depicting hands with long, thin fingers.   AOC

Morrison, Sir Richard (1767–1849) and **William Vitruvius** (1794–1838). Architects. Sir Richard, son of the architect John Morrison, was born at Midleton,

Co. Cork, and was a pupil of JAMES GANDON. He finished the Church of Ireland Cathedral, Cashel, Co. Tipperary, in 1788 and published *Useful and Ornamental Designs in Architecture* in 1793. He designed a number of intricately planned villas in the first two decades of the 19th century, of which Castlegar (1803) and St Clerans (1811), both in Co. Galway, are the most successful. He rebuilt Lyons, Co. Kildare (*c.* 1810), for the antiquary Lord Cloncurry, and remodelled CARTON, Co. Kildare (*c.* 1815), for the Duke of Leinster.

His son William Vitruvius Morrison, born at Clonmel, Co. Tipperary, was sent to visit Rome and Paris. On his return, father and son collaborated on a number of large country houses, including Kilruddery, Co. Wicklow (pl. II); Ballyfin, Co. Laois; Fota, Co. Cork; Borris, Co. Carlow; and Glenarm, Co. Antrim. William Vitruvius is credited with the introduction of Tudor Revival to Ireland, but more to his credit are the flamboyant interiors of Kilruddery, Ballyfin and Fota. In the late 1820s he developed an independent career, remodelling Baronscourt, Co. Tyrone, and building Oak Park, Co. Carlow, Clontarf, Co. Dublin, and Ballygiblin, Co. Cork. He also designed two of Ireland's finest courthouses: at Carlow (1830) and Tralee, Co. Kerry.   W G
E. McParland, 'Sir Richard Morrison's Country Houses', *Country Life*, 24 and 31 May 1973.

Mossop, Henry (1727/8–1774). Actor-manager; born in Co. Galway, the son of a clergyman, he was educated at Trinity College, Dublin. He first appeared at the Smock Alley theatre in Dublin in 1749; two years later he was invited by Garrick to London, where he remained till 1758, returning first to Crow Street and then to Smock Alley as manager. He was noted for playing roles in Shakespearean tragedy.   C F-S

Mount Sandel, Co. Derry. An Early Mesolithic site, with hearths, pits and post-holes, on the estuary of the River Bann near Coleraine; an area of about 1,000 sq. m. was excavated by P. C. Woodman, 1973–7, revealing four hearths occupied in succession, associated with post-holes of a circular hut 6 m. (19 ft 6 in.) across, made of saplings and more lightly built on the S side. The hearths and rubbish-pits contained burnt remains, amongst them animal bones (including those of wild pig), hazelnut shells and flint tools; the pits yielded microliths, some tiny armatures of composite hunting weapons, some of insular type, some of chert; also bones of salmon, sea-bass, eel and flounder, and seeds of apple and water-lily. Bird remains included duck, pigeon, grouse, goshawk and capercailzie (wood-grouse). Core tranchet axes, flint picks, and two axeheads of polished type were also found. Radiocarbon sampling indicates an approximate date of 7000 BC.   M H
P. C. Woodman, 'A Mesolithic Camp in Ireland', *Scientific American*, 245, No. 2 (Aug. 1981), 92–100.

Moytirra (Mágh Tuireadh, Plain of the Pillars), Co. Sligo. Area on a ridge north of Lough Arrow, rich in megalithic remains and celebrated as the scene of two battles won by the Tuatha Dé Danann (*see* MYTHOLOGY). Remains include a WEDGE TOMB in Moytirra West which in 1884 yielded the inhumed burials of at least four adults and a child. With these were four Beakers related to the 'maritime' type, but with decorated zones uncharacteristically wide in relation to the plain zones between.   M H
W. G. Wood-Martin, 'On the Battle-ground and Ancient Monuments of Northern Moytirra', *JRSAI* 16 (1883–4), 442–70.

Muldoon, Paul (1951–   ). Poet; born in Co. Armagh, he has published three books, *New Weather* (1973), *Mules* (1977) and *Why Brownlee Left* (1980). He is a poet of humour and benign mischief, preferring irony to traditional heroism.   T McC

multiple cist cairn. A round cairn or adaptation of an existing burial mound, in which single burials of the Earlier BRONZE AGE are inserted in cists or pits, accompanied by Food Vessel pottery or deposited in Cinerary Urns. In some cases the burials are confined to one sector. *See* KNOCKAST, TARA, LONGSTONE.   M H

Murphy, Arthur (1727–1805). Journalist, actor, and lawyer; born in Co. Roscommon, he was educated at the English College at St Omer. He wrote many plays, including the comedies and farces *The Apprentice* (1756), *The Way to Keep Him* (1760), and *Three Weeks after Marriage* (1776); and the tragedies, *The Orphan of China* (1759) and *Zenobia* (1768).   I C R
Howard H. Dunbar, *The Dramatic Career of Arthur Murphy*, 1946; John P. Emery, *Arthur Murphy*, 1946.

Murphy, Richard (1927–   ). Poet; one of the best writers of the post-war generation, he is a master of the long descriptive poem, and an ambitious user of alliteration and half-rhyme. His publications include *Archaeology of Love* (1955), *Sailing to an Island* (1963), *The Battle of Aughrim* (1968), *High Island* (1974) and *Selected Poems* (1979). Originally a poet of isolated places, of the sea, sea birds and seals, Murphy later moved closer to homely themes, to poetry of friendship and nostalgia.   T McC

Murphy, Séamus (1907–74). Sculptor; born near Mallow, Co. Cork, he was a pupil of Daniel Corkery at the local National School. He studied modelling for a year at the Crawford School of Art, Cork (1921–2). From 1922 to 1930 he worked as an apprentice at J. A. O'Connor's stoneyard in Cork as a foliage carver. In 1931 he exhibited for the first time at the ROYAL HIBERNIAN ACADEMY and was awarded the Gibson Bequest, which enabled him to visit London and Paris (1932–3). On his return he worked again in O'Connor's stoneyard as a figure carver but in 1935 set up on his own. In Paris he executed *Prayer* and *Deirdre*, but his first commission was for the Clonmult Memorial, Midleton, Co. Cork, which was followed both by Irish commissions and others from San Francisco and St Paul, Minnesota. A fine example of his early style is the *Virgin of the Twilight* (1942). He

Murphy, Séamus. *The Virgin of the Twilight* (detail), 1942; carved from Kilkenny limestone, the over-life-size statue stands in Fitzgerald Park, Cork.

made many portrait busts of public figures, including Constance Markevicz and Jack Lynch. He saw himself very much in the tradition of Irish stone carving but he was not uninfluenced by his brief stay in Paris. In general he stood outside the modern movement in sculptural styles. He was a man of wide culture and his home in Cork was a centre for intellectual life. He was elected RHA in 1954.   JT
S. Murphy, *Stone Mad*, 1966.

Murphy, Suzanne (1946–   ). Singer; born in Limerick, she studied in Dublin with Veronica Dunne. She made her début as a soprano with the Irish National Opera 1976–80 and is currently with the English National Opera. She has sung also in Vienna and Milan.   A'GH

Murphy, Thomas (**Bernard**) (1936–   ). Playwright; born in Tuam, Co. Galway, he became Director of the ABBEY THEATRE and a symbolist playwright. His subjects include the terrors of the Irish who have emigrated (*Whistle in the Dark*, 1961), and those who have stayed at home (*A Crucial Week in the Life of a Grocer's Assistant*, 1978), in which dream sequences and stultifying real-life episodes illustrate the dilemma of a childlike 28-year-old trying to will himself to leave home.   BH

Murray, Ann (1948–   ). Singer, born in Dublin, she studied in Dublin and Manchester. She has appeared as a mezzo-soprano in opera at Aix-en-Provence, with the Paris Opéra, the New York City Opera and the Hamburg and Cologne State Operas. In 1981 she made her début at the Salzburg Festival and the Zurich Festivals. She has given many recitals, and records extensively.   AGH

music. Anglo-Norman settlers, who found little to praise in 12th-century Ireland, nonetheless expressed admiration for the skill of the hereditary musicians. Giraldus Cambrensis noted their 'rapid fingerwork', their 'unfailingly disciplined art' and their 'ornate rhythms and profusely intricate polyphony'. This standard was maintained throughout the Middle Ages, and the expertise of Irish harpers (*see* HARP) was recognized in Renaissance Italy. In Ireland the harper customarily provided accompaniment for the professional reciter who declaimed the work of the bard.

The old bardic system lingered on even after the demise of Gaelic society in the 17th century, and in the 18th century – outside the major cities – European music was hardly known. The blind harper CAROLAN (1660–1738) composed over three hundred melodies, widely dispersed and greatly loved. The Belfast Harp Festival in 1792 stimulated EDWARD BUNTING to transcribe the repertory of the aged participants and publish collections of traditional airs. Bunting's publications were the principal source of the airs adapted, at times cavalierly, by THOMAS MOORE for his *Irish Melodies*, sung and read throughout Europe in the 19th century, and they also inspired the later research and more extensive collections of PETRIE, JOYCE and others. These records enshrine the multifarious riches of the living tradition of Irish music.

In cosmopolitan 18th-century Dublin, music was cultivated at many levels, a notable feature being the concert seasons established for the benefit of the hospitals. Cousser (1660–1727), following his successes in Hamburg and London, came to Dublin in 1709, and was appointed Master of His Majesty's State Musick in Ireland in 1717, holding this title until his death. The Italian composer Francesco Geminiani (1687–1762) played and taught in Dublin from 1733 to 1740 and again from 1759 until his death at his house in Dame Street, which had a concert room attached. Thomas Arne, the leading English composer of his day, and his son Michael were other visitors held in high esteem; however, Handel's stay in Ireland was the most illustrious chapter in the city's chronicle, and the première of *Messiah*, on 13 April 1742, its acme. Following Handel's visit there was a great increase in musical activity in Dublin. In 1750 Pietro Castrucci (1679–1752), who had been the leader of Handel's orchestra in England, came to live in Dublin where he conducted concerts in the Rotunda.

Irish composers in the European tradition were few in number. Thomas Roseingrave (*c.* 1690–1766), assisted by the chapter of St Patrick's Cathedral (where his father was organist), was able to study in Italy. He became an intimate of Handel and Domenico Scarlatti

William Wallace, a noted composer of opera in the 19th century, whose *Maritana* was performed first in London and subsequently in Dublin and on the Continent.

and later resided in London and Dublin. He wrote operas and cantatas; a selection of his keyboard pieces, in the idiom of Scarlatti sonatas, appeared in many later anthologies.

Philip Cogan (1748–1833), born in Cork, was organist at both Dublin cathedrals, and for a while was Music Director to Emily, Duchess of Leinster. His private pupils included the Dublin-born tenor and composer Michael Kelly (1762–1826), who sang at the Vienna Court Opera for four years, and created the roles of Don Basilio and Don Curzio in Mozart's *Le nozze di Figaro* in 1787, and Thomas Moore. He published some sonatas in London and Edinburgh. Two piano concertos were the most adventurous works in his modest output. For his part, JOHN FIELD began his musical studies in his native Dublin, but left in 1793 at the age of eleven, and never returned.

After the 1800 Act of Union deprived the country of its Parliament and its artistic patrons, composers born in Ireland pursued careers abroad. In their time, WILLIAM WALLACE and MICHAEL BALFE were noted composers of opera: Balfe's *The Bohemian Girl* and Wallace's *Maritana* retained their popularity almost to the middle of this century. Their texts provide many allusions in the writings of JAMES JOYCE.

Sir Robert Stewart (1825–94), organist of St Patrick's Cathedral and Professor of Music at Trinity College, Dublin, wrote substantially for the Church. His Orchestral Fantasia on Irish Airs was performed at the Boston Peace Festival in 1872. The most notable musical figure of the 19th century to reside in his native city, he is commemorated by a statue on Leinster Lawn.

Sir Arthur Sullivan (1842–1900), who was born in England, was the son of an Irish bandmaster, he is principally known for his collaboration with W. S.

Gilbert in the series of Savoy Operas. His Irish Symphony in E minor (1864–6), a skilful and melodious work, has the distinction of pre-dating the symphonies of Dvořák and Tchaikovsky. This work was inspired by the landscape and character of Ireland, but does not quote folk-melodies.

Sir Charles Villiers Stanford (1852–1924), who was born in Dublin, became Professor of Music at Cambridge University and the Royal College of Music, London; he was renowned for his inspired teaching and ready wit. His pupils included Walford Davies, Vaughan Williams, Gustav Holst, Eugene Goossens and Arthur Bliss. A prolific composer of operas and orchestral, choral and chamber music, he wrote an Irish Symphony (1887) and Six Irish Rhapsodies, which incorporated familiar Irish melodies, treated ingeniously in a rather academic structure. He maintained his interest in Ireland, and a number of his songs have a decidedly Irish character. He published a collection of *Songs of Old Ireland* in 1882 and provided accompaniments to a new edition of Thomas Moore's *Irish Melodies*. Furthermore, he was the editor of the first printing of the Petrie Collection in 1902–5. He was knighted in 1902 and died in London; his ashes are interred in Westminster Abbey.

Victor Herbert (1859–1924) was born in Merrion Square, Dublin; he first sought fame in Germany, where he had studied, and subsequently in the USA. Principally an operetta composer, he also wrote an Irish Rhapsody. Sir HAMILTON HARTY's Irish Symphony, based on Irish folk-songs, is his most effective piece of orchestral music, while in his songs and symphonic poems the echo of idioms of traditional Irish singers can at times be heard.

The rising tide of nationalistic feeling in the last years of the 19th century inspired a remarkable new group of writers and artists. Music played a subservient but significant role. John F. Larchet (1884–1967), born in Dublin of a musical family, was the founder of a national school of Irish composers; he was associated with YEATS and LADY GREGORY at the ABBEY THEATRE for over thirty years. As Professor of Music at University College, Dublin (1921–58), he taught many of the composers now prominent in Ireland. He was a notable composer of songs, choral music and orchestral music wherein the elements of Irish folk-music were treated with a blend of modal and romantic harmonies. The influence of his taste and craftsmanship is clearly discernible in the works of Arthur Duff (1899–1956) and Eamonn Ó Gallchobhair (1906–), and persists in the music of T. C. Kelly (1917–) and Daniel McNulty (1920–). These composers have rarely attempted the larger forms, and their work is conservative in the best sense of the word.

A strong influence on cultural activities in Cork was wielded by the German-born ALOYS FLEISCHMANN, who was Professor of Music at the University there for forty-six years.

Irish composers have rarely studied with English masters, but Frederick May (1911–) is an exception, and the manner of his teacher Ralph Vaughan Williams is at times apparent in his music. May later

Cover design of selections from Michael Balfe's *The Bohemian Girl* (1843), arranged as a 'duet for two ladies voices'.

worked under Egon Wellesz in Vienna; his most personal and integrated work is the String Quartet (1936), which combines a searing lyrical intensity with a certain savage vigour. 'Songs from Prison' (1948), for baritone and orchestra, is somewhat more romantic, but is equally powerful and moving.

For his part, BRIAN BOYDELL has shown little interest in Irish traditional music. His work has remained consistently tonal and is influenced by Bartók and Hindemith. He has writen both for orchestra and for string quartet. A. J. POTTER, an exuberant and ebullient figure with a strong sense of the working professional, was a remarkably prolific composer, and GERARD VICTORY (himself a composer), who was appointed Director of Music for RTE in 1967, provided a hearing for every worthwhile piece by Irish composers.

The Irish composer most intimately concerned with Irish folk-music in the 20th century is SÉAN Ó RIÁDA. In 1961 he founded a group, Ceoltóirí Cualann, which has been a seminal force for all subsequent attempts at developing Irish traditional music in group form. While Ó Riáda is partially concerned with twelve-note technique, John Kinsella (1932–) has used it extensively since the early 1960s. His music is consistently serious in intent and purpose. As a devoted string quartet player himself, it is hardly surprising that his most personal revelation should occur in three Quartets which date respectively from 1960, 1968 and 1977. His 'Cello Concerto (1967) is a challenging piece on a large scale, as is his commemoration of Ó Riáda, 'A Selected Life' (1973), for choir and orchestra.

The Irish composer most concerned with avant-garde techniques is SEOIRSE BODLEY. The establishment of the Dublin Festival of 20th Century Music in 1969 has pointed the emergence of younger composers. John Buckley (1951–) was first noticed for a Brass Quintet

(1971). After a successful Wind Quintet (1976) he produced a major orchestral work, *Taller than Rome Spears* (1977). These Festivals have featured the work of three graduates of University College, Dublin, who have also studied abroad, utilize various avant-garde techniques and who receive regular European performances. Frank Corcoran (1944–), born in Co. Tipperary, was a pupil of Boris Blacher in Berlin and now resides in Stuttgart; his prolific output includes two Symphonies (1972 and 1978) and many pieces for mixed ensembles. Gerald Barry (1952–), born in Co. Clare, studied with Schat, Cerha and Stockhausen; he has also worked on music-theatre and film with Mauricio Kagel, who secured him commissions, notably at the Hamburg State Opera. A Concerto for Piano, Orchestra and Tape (1977) is representative of his enterprising talent. Raymond Deane (1953–), born in Co. Mayo, and also a Stockhausen pupil, is a more reflective musician with a distinctive style for piano writing, notable in the 25-minute *Orphica* and in his two Piano Sonatas.

In Northern Ireland, David Byers (1947–) has written some fine pieces for organ, much choral music and a group of works for unusual wind ensembles, of which *Pholypony* is the most intriguing. Philip Hammond (1951–) is, like Byers, a graduate of Queen's University, Belfast, sharing his interest in aleatoric methods. Hammond writes mainly for solo vocal and choral groupings and for instrumental ensembles.

performance. The Royal Dublin Society has since 1886 organized a series of recitals on Mondays from November to March each season, engaging eminent international ensembles and soloists, as well as Irish artists. Regular series of public concerts in Dublin were inaugurated in 1941 by Michael Bowles with the Radio Orchestra, which after 1945 was augmented (*see* RADIO). It became firmly established first under Jean Martinon and then under Hans Schmidt-Isserstedt, and standards were maintained under successive principal conductors (Milan Horvath, Tibor Paul and Albert Rosen) until 1981, when the Irish-born COLMAN PEARCE assumed the responsibility. In 1961 it became the Radio Telefis Eireann Orchestra. Its principal concerts in Dublin are repeated in Cork, Limerick and Galway. The Orchestra has toured in Britain and Europe, and has a sizable repertory of 20th-century music. RTE also maintains a Concert Orchestra for lighter entertainment, and a String Quartet based in Cork.

Since 1970 the New Irish Chamber Orchestra and the Ulster Orchestra have served other centres throughout the country. The NICO has toured Europe, the USA and China. In 1981 the Ulster Orchestra was expanded to 55 players under the direction of Bryden Thompson. The Irish Youth Orchestra was formed in 1970; under its conductor Hugh Maguire it has helped to stimulate the highest standards among young musicians.   AGH

musical instrument makers. Of the several skilled makers of harps, harpsichords and pianos, as well as organ-builders who lived and worked in Dublin in the

musical instrument makers. Semi-circular piano, marked 'Southwell Dublin fecit', 19th century. Ulster Museum.

18th century, the most famous was the German, Ferdinand Weber, whose workshop in Dublin flourished from 1739 until his death in 1784. The piano manufacture was continued by Weber's Irish apprentice, William Southwell, and his descendants. Weber's most important commission was the organ for Christ Church, Cork.   B de B

mythology. Irish mythology is for a number of reasons a somewhat complicated subject; while the material is relatively rich, it was transmitted by the Christian clergy of early Ireland who, though liberal in their attitudes, modified and transmuted it. For example, CORMAC MAC CUILENNÁIN, Bishop of Cashel (d. 908), tells us quite nonchalantly that Manannán mac Lir, the ancient sea-god associated with the Isle of Man especially, was a famous merchant and steersman who could predict the changes in the weather, 'whence the Irish and the British called him God of the Sea and said he was the Son of the Sea'. Quite apart from the fact that the Christian clergy edited much of it, the material is extremely rich and varied, ranging from the 'high' mythology of the ruling classes to localized cults and popular beliefs; some parts of the tradition go back to the common mythological gods and beliefs of the Celts generally others may be survivals of the lore of indigenous pre-Celtic peoples. And most of these materials were drawn upon by scholars and literary men to provide Ireland with a mythological pre-history, a kind of genealogical charter for all the dynasties and tribes of Ireland. The material then is rich: what it means is another matter.

The central mythological tale is *Cath Maige Tuired* ('The Battle of Mag Tuired'). The tale is as follows: Ireland had been inhabited by a number of peoples, including the Fir Bolg who ruled there, when the Túatha Dé Danann ('People of the Goddess Danu')

arrived in Ireland with four magic talismans – the stone of Fál, the sword of Nuadu, the spear of LUG and the cauldron of the DAGDA. They were skilled in druidic magic and came from the northern isles of the world, in Irish belief the home of magic. They challenged the Fir Bolg and demanded either battle or kingship, and they defeated the Fir Bolg in battle and won the sovereignty of Ireland. They in turn were challenged by a mysterious foe, the Fomuire. Nuadu, who was king of the Túatha Dé before their coming to Ireland, lost his hand in battle against the Fir Bolg and on that account he had to resign the kingship. In his place they chose Bres, son of the king of the Fomuire and daughter of Ériu, a woman of the Túatha Dé amongst whom Bres had been reared. Bres, however, lacked all the proper attributes of a king, especially royal generosity, and the lords of the Túatha Dé complained bitterly that 'their knives were not greased by him and no matter how often they visited him their breaths did not smell of ale'. Bres was deposed but he fled to his father's court and raised an army to do battle with the Túatha Dé. Dian Cécht, the God of Healing, fitted Nuadu with a silver hand – hence his name, Nuadu Airgetlám and the Túatha Dé prepared for the coming conflict. Lug, son of Cian of the Túatha Dé by Ethne, a woman of the Fomuire, arrives at the royal court of Nuadu, claiming that he is master of all the arts (*Samildánach*), and is admitted. Nuadu resigns the leadership to him and Lug prepares the Túatha Dé for the titanic battle with the Fomuire. All the craftsmen and sorcerers provide weapons and special powers – GOIBNIU, the smith, fashions spear-points that never miss and all touched by them 'will never taste life afterwards'; Dian Cécht, the leech, will cure every wounded man, the druids will bring showers of fire upon the Fomuire and the witches will enchant the trees and stones and turn them into an armed host. There was great slaughter on both sides, Lug slew his Fomorian grandfather, Balor of the Evil Eye, and Bres, the defeated king, is spared on condition that he will advise the Túatha Dé on agricultural practices and the Fomuire are banished from Ireland.

That, in outline, is the central mythological tale and it has been interpreted in different ways. T. F. O'Rahilly saw it as essentially the struggle between Balor and Lug. He saw Balor as another manifestation of the Irish single supreme deity (a sun-god), who appears in many different guises; the fundamental myth for O'Rahilly is the titanic struggle between the supreme lord of the Otherworld and the young hero-god (in the present case, Lug) who slays him with his own weapon, the thunderbolt. The French scholar Dumézil would argue that the tale fits into his tri-functional scheme of Indo-European mythologies and therefore the tale is an Indo-European and common Celtic inheritance. The first function has to do with the ruling of the universe, kingship, law and magic; the second has to do with force and especially the military force of the warrior-caste; the third has to do with agriculture, fertility and fecundity in plant and animal life. And these three functions correspond to three classes in society: the kings and druid-jurists, the warriors, and the agricultural producers. For him the

Túatha Dé make up the first two classes; they had the druids and sorcerers, all the arts and crafts, medicine and metalwork, but they lacked the third function. The story then tells of the conflict between the functions in which the third threatens to destroy the others until there is reconciliation and eventually a balance is struck between the two. More recently, the tale has been seen as a normative social paradigm which spells out, almost in parable fashion, how society should be organized. Men should not choose kings from the maternal side, as Bres was chosen. Kings should be generous, wise and responsible, unlike Bres, and those who are not so bring disaster upon society. Lug is the opposite in origins and behaviour to Bres; he has all the characteristics of the first two functions – he is royal and master of every craft – and in the end he spares Bres in return for agricultural prosperity and thus reconciles and mediates between the opposites.

The mythology of *Cath Maige Tuired* is 'high' mythology and has parallels in the mythology of other Indo-European peoples, but this in no way exhausts the richness of Irish mythology. Around the office of kingship there grew up many mythological beliefs. The most widely attested one is that of king and goddess. The kingdom is the feminine counterpart to the masculinity of the king. As the king grows old the sovereignty, imagined as a woman, becomes an old woman. The myth has given rise to a literary motif found frequently in Irish literature. For example, Lugaid Loígde was hunting with his brothers and a great snow fell upon them. They came upon a house with a great fire, food and drink in abundance, dishes of silver and beds of *findruine*, but with a hideous hag in the house. She offered them hospitality in return for sleeping with her. Only Lugaid Loígde accepted and after he had lain with her 'it appeared to him that the light of her countenance was like the sun rising in the month of May and the fragrance of her was like the smell of a flower garden. After this he cohabited with her and she said, "Good is thy journey for I am the sovereignty and you shall obtain the kingship of Ireland or one descended from thee shall." They afterwards took new viands and old drinks, and cups were distributed to them alone, and he cohabited with the sovereignty.'

A similar story is told of Niall mac Echach, ancestor of the Uí Néill. The royal inauguration was seen as a *banais rígi* ('wedding-feast of kingship') and was made up of two significant rituals: the bride offered her royal partner a drink and this was followed by sexual intercourse between king and sovereignty. The so-called Feast of Tara (*Feis Temro*) was such an inauguration rite and Medb (Maeve), goddess of Tara, whose name means 'she who makes men drunk', is imagined as the spouse of each king of Tara. The 'Hag of Beare' (*Caillech Bérre*) is one such territorial goddess in Munster, metamorphosed over the ages into a Christian nun. Under the just king, the land is prosperous and women and animals fecund, whilst under the sway of an evil king, the land grows barren and the goddess, in her turn, grows ugly, haggard and destitute, until she is restored to union with her rightful

mythology. The circular enclosure of Eamhain Macha (Navan Fort), Co. Armagh, seen from the air; this hillfort is an ancient royal site with mythological associations, the tree-ringed inner mound being a ritual structure. Cf. Tara.

spouse. These concepts have given rise to the idea of Ireland as a beautiful woman – an idea which lives on to this day – and to the romantic Arthurian tales of Percival and the 'Loathly Lady'.

The Old-Irish concept of the Otherworld can to a degree be recovered from the literature of early Ireland and it varies in mood and character. Sometimes, it is imagined as the land of the blessed (*Tír inna Beo*) or of the women (*Tír inna Ban*), the plain of pleasure (*Mag Mell*) where men and beautiful women live in unending happiness, where there is exquisite food and drink, beauty on all sides, and no sickness, sin, pain or death. This world is beyond human time, under the sea, under the ground, or in distant islands and may be reached through certain entrances in the natural world – through magic caves, beneath the Síd ('Fairy mound'), through being enveloped in a magic mist or by diving through the waters of a lake. However, it is not always seen in that way and there is a dark and sombre aspect to the concept of the Otherworld. SAMAIN is the feast of the dead. At this time, the natural order is suspended, the Síd is open and the spirits of the dead and the beings of the supernatural order intervene in the affairs of men. Beside this is the (perhaps more archaic) notion of Donn, Lord of the Otherworld, presiding over the never-ending feast of the dead.

The Otherworld was absorbed by early Christian scholars into their mythological pre-history of Ireland. The Túatha Dé were defeated and deprived of the sovereignty of Ireland by the sons of Míl, in mythological terms the real ancestors of the Irish. But the Túatha Dé forced the sons of Míl to compromise with them: the land was to be divided, so that all that was above ground belonged to the sons of Míl; all that was under the ground belonged to the Túatha Dé. And thus the Túatha Dé were said to have withdrawn underground to the Síd. Tírechán, writing towards the end of the 7th century, refers to them as *Dei Terreni*, and clerical writers are uncomfortable and ambiguous about them.

An early poem, 'Fiacc's Hymn', states:

> For Túaith hÉrenn baí temel
> Túatha adortais síde

('On the land of Ireland there was darkness; the peoples used to worship *síde*'.) Belief in the powers of the folk of the Síd certainly persisted and, in a remarkable instance, a monkish annalist writing in 1084 says that it was Oengus Óg, son of the Dagda, who revealed to Mac Gilla Lugáin, a frequenter of the Síd every Samain, the cause of the great plague which ravaged the population of Ireland in that year. For clerical writers and for the composers of literature and genealogy, the Túatha Dé were detached from the world of men generally, though they did intervene on occasion and these occasions are usually seen to be remote in past time. Sometimes suitably disguised, sometimes openly, as in the case of *Compert Mongán* (where Manannán mac Lir is the father of the hero Mongán), the gods of the Síd are the progenitors of human heroes and dynasties, and this continues – in a slightly modified way – the pagan tradition which saw the great royal lines as direct descendants of the gods. For the unlearned, the gods of the Síd remained gods or at least supernatural beings with vast powers to whom due deference had to be rendered and who were invoked, as the dairy-maids invoked Goibniu the artificer, at the appropriate points and crises of the agricultural year. At a humbler level than the literature of the learned, paganism and CHRISTIANITY could co-exist.

It is now difficult to reconstruct the Irish mythological pantheon, if ever there really was one. Many of the more important of the gods appear in *Cath Maige Tuired*: the Dagda, 'Good God', also called Eochaid Ollathair, 'The Great Father'; Nuadu Argatlám, the warrior-king; Goibniu, the smith-magician; Creidne, the worker in bronze and other metals; Luchta, the wright; Dian Cécht, the God of Healing; Ogma, the champion and also the God of Learning; Mac Ind Óc, 'The Divine Youth', also called Oengus; the Mórrígain, the Goddess of Battle – but tradition records many more besides. Amongst the most important is Brigid 'the exalted one', who is the Irish Minerva, patroness of the arts and crafts, of weaving, dyeing, healing and poetry. She and her two sisters (who really form a unity/trinity) are represented as daughters of the Dagda. Brigid is eponymous goddess of the Brigantes. Many of her characteristics have been transposed to her Christian equivalent, St Brigid of Kildare. Side by side with these well-known gods and goddesses were local gods, some of which survive as mere vestiges in the geographical nomenclature, as, for example, the god Moccos, a variant of whose cult remains in place-names like Torc and Cenn Tuirc. Others, such as Cernunnos, 'the horned god', are vaguely remembered in some of the qualities of the Ulster warrior, Conall Cearnach. Yet others, such as FINN, vestiges of whose cult are widespread in Celtic Europe, became the heroes of popular folk-tales and survived in the literature of the people almost until our own day.   DÓC

Nagle, Nano (Honoria; 1718–84). Foundress and pioneer in Roman Catholic education; born near Mallow, Co. Cork, she was educated in France and lived in Paris until returning to Ireland in 1746. About 1754 she started a school secretly in a two-room mud cabin in Cove Lane, Cork. Using an inheritance to fund her project and in defiance of the Penal Laws, by 1760 she had opened seven schools attended by several hundred pupils of both sexes. In 1771 she brought Ursuline nuns from France to asisst in her educational work and then founded an order devoted exclusively to the needs of the poor, the Presentation Sisters, who opened their first school at Cork in 1777. Their example inspired EDMUND IGNATIUS RICE, and their cultural influence through primary and secondary education has been considerable. The Presentation Sisters now have schools in Ireland, Britain, the USA, Australia, New Zealand and India. *See* EDUCATION.   B de B
Rt Rev. Dr Coppinger, *The Life of Miss Nano Nagle*, 1794; William Hutch, *Nano Nagle, her life, her labours and their fruits*, 1875; T. J. Walsh, *Nano Nagle and the Presentation Sisters*, 1959 (2nd ed. 1980).

Nash, John (1752–1835). Architect; born at Cardigan, Wales, this distinguished English architect accepted some Irish commissions and, being a master of theatrical effect, throve in the 'romantic' Irish landscape. His first Irish commission was Killymoon, Co. Tyrone (1802) – a small castle with a grim early-Gothic exterior. Lough Cutra, Co. Galway (1811) which is dramatically sited, is a compact version of Nash's East Cowes Castle on the Isle of Wight, and its construction was supervised by the brothers PAIN. Shanbally, Co. Tipperary (1812), was Nash's largest castle, while Rockingham (1810) was his largest Classical house. He added colonnades and pavilions to Caledon, Co. Tyrone (1812).   W G
Sir John Summerson, *The Life and Work of John Nash, Architect*, 1980.

National College of Art and Design. The present College is a direct descendant of the 18th-century drawing academy of the painter ROBERT WEST which was taken over by the DUBLIN SOCIETY in 1746 and, after several moves, eventually found a home in Kildare Street, Dublin, in 1815, where it remained until its central functions moved to Thomas Street in 1980. The Board of Trade took over the schools in 1849 and in 1854 they passed to the Department of Science and Art. When the State assumed complete ownership in 1877 the institution was renamed the Dublin Metropolitan School of Art. It was taken over by the Department of Agriculture and Technical Instruction in 1900 and in 1924 by the Department of Education.

The school was renamed the National College of Art in 1936 and became semi-autonomous by a statute of 1971 which set up the National College of Art and Design; subsequently the College was placed under the Higher Education Authority for funding purposes. The College awards its own diplomas; degrees are conferred by the National Council for Educational Awards.

The South Kensington system of art education was applied from 1854 until 1900, when a great surge of innovation took place: STAINED GLASS, enamelling, graphic design and other crafts were introduced, as well as WILLIAM ORPEN's Life Class. In later years still other subjects were added. The courses now leading to Diploma or Degree awards are: Fine Art, Visual Communications, FASHION and TEXTILES, Handcrafts, Industrial Design, Art Education, History of Art (with Fine Art or Design). JT

National Gallery of Ireland. The NGI opened in 1864 in Merrion Square, Dublin; the original building, designed by Francis Fowke, was enlarged and extended in 1968. It is one of the larger galleries in Europe, with a fine collection of works by Dutch masters and of the 17th-century French, Italian and Spanish schools, as well as a representative collection of Irish paintings. The principal benefactors have been Sir HUGH LANE, Sir Alfred Chester Beatty, the Countess of Milltown and GEORGE BERNARD SHAW, who bequeathed one-third of his estate to the Gallery. B de B

National Gallery of Ireland. Part of the façade, showing the portico added when the building was extended, 1899–1903; a new wing, to the right of the portico, was opened in 1968.

Nash, John. The battlemented Gothic castle, Lough Cutra, Co. Galway, designed in 1811, which has been restored in recent years.

National Library of Ireland. The Library was founded under an Act of 1877, establishing what had till then been the library of the Royal Dublin Society as a public institution governed by trustees. Its building in Kildare Street, by Sir Thomas Manly Deane (*see* DEANE AND WOODWARD) was begun in 1884 and opened in 1890. Its holdings of Irish material, both printed and in manuscript, are the most comprehensive in existence. MC

National Museum of Ireland. The Museum was founded under an Act of 1877, incorporating the antiquities collections of the Royal Irish Academy and the Natural History collections of the Royal Dublin Society (which latter were already housed in the building on Leinster Lawn built by the Society in 1857–9, and still devoted to the Natural History division). The Irish Antiquities and Art and Industry divisions are housed in the Kildare Street building which matches that of the NATIONAL LIBRARY. A smaller building recently acquired in Merrion Row is used for temporary exhibitions. MC

National Trust: Committee for Northern Ireland. The National Trust, founded in Great Britain in 1895, now covers England, Wales and Northern Ireland. Its Regional Office for Northern Ireland is at Rowallane, Saintfield, Co. Down.

Before 1921 the Trust had acquired only one Irish property (Kanturk Castle, Co. Cork), and this was subsequently handed over to the State. It was in 1937 that a group of local conservationists formed a Northern Ireland Committee to acquire White Park Bay, Co. Antrim. Since 1945 the work of the Trust in Northern Ireland has expanded enormously: it now has some 45 properties, including eight major country houses (CASTLECOOLE, Florencecourt, Castle Ward, Ardress House, Mount Stewart, Derrymore House, Springhill, The Argory), as well as many smaller buildings of importance. It also holds open spaces and substantial coastal stretches, and is actively concerned with nature conservation (Strangford Lough, Murlough Nature Reserve). Many of its properties are held inalienably under Act of Parliament: the Trust's function is primarily that of holding land, buildings and their contents for the benefit of the public (it publishes details of its properties and normal opening hours, members being admitted free of charge). The Trust does not normally engage in campaigning unless its own interests are directly affected, though it has been more active in this respect in Northern Ireland than in other regions. The Northern Ireland Committee enjoys a substantial degree of autonomy, but is in a position to draw upon the expertise and financial and other resources of the National Trust as a whole. The Trust had in 1982 about 7,500 members in Northern Ireland; it is a charitable body, established by its own special statutes and enjoying unusual privileges. It does not, however, receive any direct financial subvention from government sources towards its general purposes, which are principally financed from membership subscriptions, visitors' fees, gifts and legacies. CEBB

National Trust for Ireland. *See* TAISCE, AN.

Newgrange, Co. Meath. The site of a PASSAGE GRAVE at 61 m. (200 ft) above sea-level, in the Boyne cemetery between Dowth and Knowth; it has been known since 1699, when it was described by Edward Lhuyd. The tumulus is pear-shaped, measuring 78 × 85 m. (256 × 279 ft) in area and 11–13 m. (36–43 ft) in height, girdled with 97 oblong kerbstones, mainly decorated, of which three, including the entrance stone, were ornamented all over the outer face in an accomplished abstract style. Pollen preserved in samples of turves used in the construction of the tumulus provided evidence for the existence of a predominantly open landscape; seeds of wheat and barley were also found in the turves examined.

A slight incurve at the SE marks the entrance to a tomb 25 m. (82 ft) long with a chamber of cruciform plan, 6·50 m. (20 ft) above the floor; in this chamber are four stone basins, presumably for use in the burial ritual. Above the doorway is a rectangular roof-box, its lintel decorated with a lozenge pattern, through which the rising sun shines briefly onto the floor of the chamber on midwinter day.

Around the tomb, in a circle 16 m. (52 ft) from the kerb, there are twelve standing stones up to 2·50 m. (8 ft) high. Within the line of these, at the front of the tomb, O'Kelly discovered (in excavations begun in

Newgrange. View from the main chamber of the passage grave, *c.* 3200 BC, looking towards the entrance.

1962) a prolific early BRONZE AGE settlement with Beaker pottery. MH
M. J. O'Kelly, *Newgrange*, 1982.

Ni Chonaill, Eibhlin Dubh (*c.* 1748–1800). Poet; she is famous for her powerful poem 'Caoineadh Airt Ui Laoghaire' ('Lament for Art O'Leary'), written in her grief over the shooting of her husband. *See* POETRY. TMcC

Ni Chuilleanain, Eilean (1941–   ). Poet; a university teacher and co-editor of one of the best literary magazines, *Cyphers*, she is one of the best poets of recent years in Ireland. Her published work includes: *Acts and Monuments* (1972), *Site of Ambush* (1975), *Cork* (1977) and *The Rose Geranium* (1981). TMcC

Ni Dhomhnaill, Nuala (1952–   ). Gaelic poet. Her first collection, *An Dealg Droighin*, was published in 1981 shortly after her return to Co. Kerry after seven years residence in Turkey; it revealed her as a bright and most fascinating new talent in Irish-language poetry. TMcC

Nic Gearailt, Maire Aine (1946–   ). Poet; a native of the Corca Dhuibhne Gaeltacht. While working as a teacher in Dublin, she has published *Eiric Uachta* (1979), as well as essays and poems in Irish-language publications, *Comhair*, *Feasta* and *Innti*. TMcC

Nicholl, Andrew (1804–66). Painter; born in Belfast, he worked there and in Dublin and London, mostly painting watercolours. His early works were largely simple topographical views, but after a visit to Ceylon (Sri Lanka) in 1846 he developed a freer, more colourful manner and painted the exquisite flower pieces for which he is now remembered. AOC

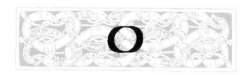

O'Brien, Dermod (1865–1945). Landscape, figure and genre painter; born in Co. Limerick, he was educated at Harrow and Trinity College, Cambridge. He visited Paris and Rome 1886–7, studied under Verlat in Antwerp, then transferred to Paris in 1891, to the Académie Julian, and afterwards to the Slade School in London. He shared a studio with Henry Tonks from 1899 and moved to Dublin in 1901. He was elected ARHA 1906, RHA 1907, and was PRHA from 1910 until his death. He was made an Honorary RA in 1912. C MacG

Lennox Robinson, *Palette and Plough*, 1948.

O'Brien, Edna (1930–). Writer; born at Tuamgraney, Co. Clare. Her first three novels, based on her own childhood in Co. Clare and early life in Dublin and London, achieved a *succès de scandale* in the 1960s, but were banned in Ireland. These early works (*The Country Girls*, 1960, *The Lonely Girl*, 1962, and *Girls in their Married Bliss*, 1964), were followed by novels of a more experimental nature, such as *A Pagan Place* (1970) and *Night* (1972). She transmutes her native Irishness, her more cosmopolitan experience and her womanhood to universality in such accomplished collections of short stories as *The Love Object* (1970) and *A Scandalous Woman* (1974), *Mrs Reinhardt and Other Stories* (1978) and the recently published *Returning: Tales* (1982). In her non-realist mode, the melancholy short novel *Johnny I hardly knew you* (1977) allusively explores the fragmented consciousness of a woman who has killed her young lover. She also writes non-fictional prose, such as *Mother Ireland* (1978), and plays, the latest being *Virginia* (1981). B H

G. Eckley, *Edna O'Brien*, 1974.

O'Brien, Flann. *See* O'NOLAN.

O'Brien, Kate (1897–1974). Writer; she was born and brought up in Limerick, which provides the setting for her first novel, *Without my Cloak* (1931). This won the James Tait Black and Hawthornden Prizes. A journalist and translator, she maintained a constant interest in Spanish literature and history, shown in *Farewell Spain* (1937) and *That Lady* (1946), about the fall of Philip II's mistress. Other novels include *Mary Lavelle* (1936), *The Land of Spices* (1941), and *As Music and Splendour* (1958). Her plays include *The Bridge* (1927) and *The Anteroom* (1936).

O'Brien, Kitty Wilmer (1910–82). Landscape painter; born at Quetta (now in Pakistan), she trained at the Royal Hibernian Academy Schools and in London. She worked in oils and in watercolour and was President of the Water Colour Society of Ireland and member of the RHA. She is best known for her watercolour and gouache paintings of Connemara and Dublin, and was a regular exhibitor in the many annual exhibitions in Ireland. C MacG

Ó Bruadair, Daibhí (*c.* 1625–1698). Gaelic poet; one of the best-known 17th-century poets, he was probably trained in a Munster BARDIC SCHOOL. Despite his prolific output and his masterful style, he was not successful in his effort to live the life of a professional poet in Co. Limerick. T McC

Ó Cadhain, Máirtín (1906–70). Writer; born at An Cnocán Glas, near Spiddal, Co. Galway, he became a National Teacher, university professor and writer of prose in Irish. His published works include: *Idir Shúgradh agus Dáiríre* ('Between Play and Seriousness'; short stories, 1939); *Cré na Cille* ('The Dust of the Cemetery'; a novel, 1949); and *An tSraith Dhá Tógáil* ('The Swath a-building'; short stories, 1970) and others. A A

O'Casey, Seán (1880–1964). Playwright; born in Dublin as John Casey, he was a labourer aged over forty when he had three tragi-comedies staged by the ABBEY THEATRE, each play taking Ireland's very recent history for its subject-matter and Dublin slums for its

O'Casey, Seán. A scene from *Shadow of a Gunman*, in a performance at the Abbey Theatre, April 1980.

setting. Although the success of *Juno and the Paycock* (1924), set in the Civil War, rescued the Abbey's finances, *The Plough and the Stars* (1926) caused riots because of its unheroic treatment of the Easter Rising, and its depiction of an Irish prostitute. O'Casey left Ireland, and thenceforward lived in exile; he died in Devon. He became estranged from the Abbey when *The Silver Tassie* (1928) was rejected because of its experimental second act, surrealistically representing World War I. Expressionism prevails in the plays of his exile, four propagandist 'prophetic' works reflecting his lifelong commitment to socialism and communism. *Red Roses for Me* (1942) deals with 'real' issues such as the Labour movement, nationalism and religious conflict, but its climactic scene is a symbolic dance of life. The satirical fantasies, all set in rural Ireland, include *Cock-a-Doodle-Dandy* (1949), in which a life-sized cockerel upholds the forces of life and joy against petty bureaucracy and narrow religious attitudes. O'Casey was also a gifted short-story writer and a waspish critic. His *Autobiographies* (1956–1963) are comic, acid and moving, showing – as all his work does – iconoclasm, compassion, and rage against poverty and oppression.   BH

David Krause, *Sean O'Casey, the Man and his Work*, 1960; ——, *Sean O'Casey and his World*, 1976; R. Ayling and M. J. Durkan, *Sean O'Casey, a Bibliography*, 1979; R. Ayling (ed.), *Sean O'Casey*, 1968; T. Kilroy (ed.), *Sean O'Casey*, 1975; E. O'Casey, *Sean*, London, 1971.

Ó Ceallachain, Diarmuid (1915–   ). Landscape painter; born in Cork, where he studied first at the Crawford Municipal School of Art, and later at the National College of Art, Dublin. He taught for many years in Cork at the Crawford Municipal School of Art. He has exhibited in all the major Irish national annual exhibitions, especially landscapes and portraits. Much of his work is in private collections, but some of his best and most characteristic work, such as *Dripsey Castle, Co. Cork*, may be seen in Cork at the Crawford Municipal Gallery.   C MacG

Ó Conaire, Pádraig (1883–1928). Writer; born in Galway, he was a writer of prose in Irish. His published works include: *Deoraíocht* ('Exile'; a novel, 1910); *Seacht mBua an Éirí Amach* ('The Seven Victories of the Rising'; short stories, 1918); and *An Crann Géagach* ('The Branched Tree'; short stories, 1919).   AA

O'Connor, Andrew (1874–1941). Sculptor; born in Massachusetts, he was the son of a sculptor from Scotland, who was his first teacher. He began his career in helping in the assembly of the Chicago World Exhibition, 1891–2; in 1894 he was working with Sargent in London. His first important commission was for the bronze doors of St Bartholomew's, New York. He settled in Paris in 1903, working for American commissions and exhibiting widely in Europe; in 1914 he returned to America and opened a studio at Paxton, Mass. During the 1920s he was living in Paris, and in the following decade he divided his time between there and Dublin. His vigorous model-ling style was largely derived from late 19th-century French sculpture, especially Rodin, but is rougher in handling. He identified with Ireland, despite his residence abroad, and left several examples of his work to the Hugh Lane Municipal Gallery of Modern Art, Dublin.   JT

Homan Potterton, *Andrew O'Connor*, exhibition catalogue, Trinity College, Dublin, 1974.

O'Connor, Frank (pseudonym of Michael O'Donovan; 1903–66). Writer; born in Cork, he became a Republican in the Civil War, and was imprisoned by the Free State Army. He began writing in the 1920s, and made fine English translations of Irish poetry. He became a director of the ABBEY THEATRE. Although he wrote two novels, his *forte* was the short story, as his first collection, *Guests of the Nation* (1931), shows; its title story is an example of O'Connor's vein of war story. Stories of childhood like 'First Confession' and 'My Oedipus Complex' illustrate an equally consistent strain of sympathetic humour. O'Connor's special field is the provincial middle class. His critical works include studies of the novel (*The Mirror in the Roadway*) and the short story (*The Lonely Voice*), and a history of Irish literature (*The Backward Look*, 1967).   BH

J. H. Matthews, *Frank O'Connor*, 1976; M. Sheehy (ed.), *Studies on Frank O'Connor*, 1969; M. Wohlgelernter, *Frank O'Connor: An Introduction*, 1977; F. O'Connor, *My Father's Son*, 1968.

O'Connor, James Arthur (c. 1792–1841). Painter; born in Dublin, he was self-taught as an artist. He first went to London with GEORGE PETRIE and FRANCIS DANBY in 1813, but returned to make a career as a fine topographical landscape painter of houses and parks. His views of Westport and Ballinrobe are famous. He went to live in London in 1822, though he returned for painting trips to Ireland. About this time he began painting his small, intense landscapes of wild scenery.

O'Connor, James. A characteristic landscape, *A Thunderstorm. The Wagon*, 1832. NGI.

XI **Osborne, Walter.** *Tea in the Garden*, 137 × 171 cm. (54 × 67½ in.), *c.* 1902. Hugh Lane Municipal Gallery of Modern Art, Dublin.

XII **O'Conor, Roderic.** *La Ferme de Lezaver*, 72 × 93 cm. (28½ × 36½ in.), 1894. NGI.

XIII **Orpen, Sir William.** *The Signing of the Peace in the Hall of Mirrors, Versailles, 28 June 1919*, one of the works specially painted by Orpen as Official Artist at the Paris Peace Conference; oil on canvas, 152 × 127 cm. (60 × 50 in.). Imperial War Museum, London.

On two occasions he visited Europe, including France, Holland and the Rhineland. As well as the obvious debt he owes to Dutch art, there is a marked affinity between his best works and those of Caspar David Friedrich.   A O C

O'Connor, Michael (*c.* 1801–1867). Stained-glass designer; born in Dublin, as a young heraldic artist he was apprenticed to Thomas Willement in London. After a period working in glass in Dublin, he returned to London where he settled in 1845, but continued to exhibit and receive commissions in Ireland. With his son Arthur he ran a highly successful, if commercial, firm in England.   N G B
Michael Wynne, 'Stained Glass in Ireland: principally Irish Stained Glass 1760–1963' (unpublished Ph.D. thesis, Trinity College, Dublin), 1975.

O'Conor, John (1947–   ). Pianist; born in Dublin, he studied in Dublin and Vienna, where in 1973 he won first prize in the Beethoven Competition and subsequently in 1975 the International Bösendorfer Competition. He has toured Japan on three occasions, and has played in Australia, USSR, the USA and throughout Europe. He is especially associated with the interpretation of keyboard works by Beethoven and JOHN FIELD.   A G H

O'Conor, Roderic (1860–1940). Landscape painter; born in Co. Roscommon, he studied at the Antwerp Academy in 1881 and, two years later, under Carolus Duran in Paris. He worked under the influence first of Alfred Sisley, and then of Signac and Seurat, but was subsequently much influenced by Van Gogh, and by the late 1880s by Gauguin (who asked him to go back with him to Tahiti, an invitation he refused, preferring to continue painting in Brittany; *see* pl. XII). He influenced several English artists, such as Clive Bell, Roger Fry, Matthew Smith and Duncan Grant, but had little direct contact with or influence upon Irish art in his own lifetime. O'Conor has been the subject of a television documentary made by RTE, and is well represented in public collections in Ireland, especially the Ulster Museum, Belfast, and the National Gallery and the Hugh Lane Municipal Gallery of Modern Art, Dublin.   C MacG

Ó Criomthain, Tomás (1856–1937). Writer; born on Great Blasket Island, Co. Kerry, he became a smallholder, fisherman and writer of prose in Irish. His main works are: *Allagar na hInise* ('Island Talk'; a diary, 1928); and *An tOileánach* ('The Islandman'; autobiography, 1929).   A A

O'Curry, Eugene (1796–1862). Calligrapher and translator; born in Co. Clare, he received no formal education, yet became one of the eminent scholars of his day in Ireland. After working for three years in the Ordnance Survey of Ireland, where he met JOHN O'DONOVAN. He worked as a cataloguer of Irish mss. in the Royal Irish Academy, Trinity College, Dublin, and the British Museum. A fine calligrapher, he made

beautiful facsimile copies of early mss. and he edited and translated important Irish texts. In 1854 he was appointed Professor of Irish History and Archaeology in the Catholic University of Ireland; three volumes of his lectures between 1857 and 1862 were published posthumously in 1873 as *The Manners and Customs of the Ancient Irish*.   B de B

Ó Dalaigh. The name of the greatest poetic family in Ireland whose activities stretch from Dalach, a pupil of St Colman in the 7th century, to PADRAIG J. DALY and AIDAN CARL MATHEWS (nephew of the scholar-President Cearbhall Ó Dalaigh) today. The most distinguished members of the family were: Muireadach Ó Dalaigh (*c.* 1180–*c.* 1250), the chief poet of the O'Donnells; Donnchadh Morr (*c.* 1175–1244), the brother of Muireadach, who was Ireland's greatest religious poet; Gofraidh Fionn Ó Dalaigh (*c.* 1320–*c.* 1385), who was a satirist; Aonghus Mac Doighre Ó Dalaigh (*c.* 1540–*c.* 1600), the chief poet of the O'Byrnes of Wicklow, an aristocratic and fervent war poet; Aonghus Ruadh Ó Dalaigh (*c.* 1550–1617), who was employed by the English to satirize different Irish families in order to foment trouble, but whose poisonous pen was abruptly silenced when he died by the sword in 1617. *See* POETRY.   T McC

O'Dea, James Augustine (Jimmy; 1899–1965). Comedian; born in Dublin, he became – from the early 1930s until his death – Ireland's most popular comedian, appearing in revues and pantomimes scripted by Harry O'Donovan. His characterization of 'Biddy Mulligan, pride of the Coombe' became famous on radio and on disc. During World War II he had a comedy programme on BBC radio, and in later years had his own TV series on RTE.   C F-S

Ó Direain, Mairtín (1910–   ). Poet; born on the Aran Islands, he is the best 20th-century Gaelic poet. One critic has stated that modernism in Gaelic poetry began with Ó Direain's *Cionnle Geala* (1943). In 1957 he published *Ó Morna agus Danta Eile*, which contained the best long poem in the language since BRIAN MERRIMAN's 'Cuirt an Mhean Oiche'. A volume of his collected poems, *Danta 1939–1979*, was published in 1980.   T McC

O'Donoghue, Gregory (1951–   ). Poet; born in Cork City. A collection of verse, *Kicking*, was published in 1975, and a large selection of recent work was published in *Exile* (Toronto) in 1978.   T McC

O'Donovan, John (1809–61). Antiquarian; born in Co. Kilkenny, he was outstanding as a scholar. He worked for three years in the Irish Record Office and then in the historical department of the Ordnance Survey of Ireland, when he visited every parish in the country, recording his copious observations on nomenclature and matters of antiquarian interest in letters which were edited long after his death by Rev. Michael O'Flanagan and published in fifty volumes between 1924 and 1932. O'Donovan's *A Grammar of the*

Irish Language was published in 1845; his greatest achievement was his translation of *The Annals of the Kingdom of Ireland by the Four Masters*, which appeared in a seven-volume edition, published in Dublin 1848–51 with a text in Irish type designed by GEORGE PETRIE. O'Donovan also contributed learned articles on history and topography to the *Dublin Penny Journal* and to the publications of the Irish Archaeological Society (of which he was a co-founder with EUGENE O'CURRY and JAMES TODD; his valuable *The Tribes and Customs of Hy Many*, from the 15th-century Book of Lecan, was published in 1843. Two other important works were published posthumously: his translation of *The Martyrology of Donegal*, edited by Bishop WILLIAM REEVES and Todd, 1864, and his text and translation of CORMAC MAC CUILLENÁIN's glossary, *Sanas Cormaic*, edited and annotated by WHITLEY STOKES.   B de B

O'Faolain, Seán (1900–). Writer; born John Whelan. Like FRANK O'CONNOR a native of Cork and a member of the IRA, he wrote stories, novels, a play, a travel book, translations of Irish poetry, criticism, autobiography and numerous biographies (of Constance Markievicz, Cardinal Newman, Daniel O'Connell, Hugh O'Neill and Wolfe Tone). His perceptive literary criticism included *The Short Story* (1948) and *The Vanishing Hero*, a study of the novelists of the 1920s (1956). *The Irish* (1947) surveys his countrymen from the Celts to the 20th century. A further contribution to Irish letters was his pioneering editorship of the liberal literary magazine *The Bell* from 1940 to 1946. The novelist Julia O'Faolain is his daughter.   B H
M. Harmon, *Sean O'Faolain; A Critical Introduction*, 1966; P. A. Doyle, *Sean O'Faolain*, 1968; M. Harmon (ed.), Sean O'Faolain Special Issue, *Irish Univ. Review*, vol. 6, Spring 1976.

O'Flaherty, Liam (1896–). Writer; born on the Aran island of Inishmore. He fought in the World War I in the Irish Guards, was wounded and discharged suffering from shellshock. He left the Catholic Church, became a Communist, fought in the Irish Civil War as a Republican, then started his literary career in England, encouraged by Edward Garnett; later he lived variously in Ireland, England, France and America. From his harsh experience he forged violent and often disturbing fiction. *Skerrett* (1932) depicts a schoolmaster's bitter struggle for moral and physical survival in an island community. *Famine* (1937) grimly details the destructive effects on peasant life of the potato famine in the 1840s. As well as fifteen novels and almost two hundred short stories, many about animals, he has written essays, biography, autobiography, and prose and poetry in Irish. Tension and death are subjects which pervade his fiction; his characters are monolithic, and their endurance is of heroic proportions.   B H
A. A. Kelly, *Liam O'Flaherty the Storyteller*, 1976; P. A. Doyle, *Liam O'Flaherty: An Annotated Bibliography*, 1972; P. F. Sheeran, *The Novels of Liam O'Flaherty*, 1976; J. N. Zneimer, *The Literary Vision of Liam O'Flaherty*, 1970.

Ogham. Secret writing based on a 20-letter alphabet derived from the Latin; each letter is signified by one or more lines or notches, up to a maximum of five. In its earliest form, it occurs on the upright edges of a standing stone, cut horizontally. The language of the inscriptions is Primitive Irish, the oldest form of Irish. The alphabet is:

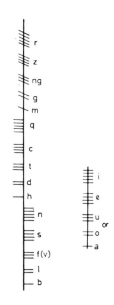

An inscription usually consists of personal names in a set formula: 'of x'; 'of x *maqi* [son of] y'; 'of x *avi* [grandson or descendant of] y'; 'of x *maqi y mucoi* [of the tribe of] z'. Over 300 Ogham stones are known in Ireland, 60% being in Cork and Kerry, the rest mainly in Munster and Leinster; smaller numbers are known in Wales, the Isle of Man and Scotland. The Irish stones date from *c.* 350–600, overlapping substantially with the period of early Christian sites. Claims to earlier use of Ogham from *c.* 200 have been advanced by a few scholars; *see* A. Ahlqvist, *Les Débuts de l'Étude du Langage en Irlande*, Amsterdam Studies in the Theory and History of Linguistic Science III, vol. 20.   MH

O'Grady, Desmond (1935–). Poet and teacher; one of the finest modern Munster poets. He has published numerous books, including *The Dark Edge of Europe* (1967) and *The Headgear of the Tribe* (1979).   T McC

O'Grady, Standish James (1846–1928). Writer; born at Castletown, Berehaven, Co. Cork, the son of a Protestant clergyman and small landowner, he grew up identifying himself with the Ascendancy, but as a young man he developed an enthusiasm for the early history of Ireland and its epic literature. His two-volume *History of Ireland* (1878–80), a free adaptation of those materials with emphasis upon the romantic and idealistic elements in them, so stirred the imagination

Ogham. One of the Dunloe stones, Coolmagort, Co. Kerry.

O'Grady, Standish. Portrait by John Butler Yeats, 1904.
NGI.

of the younger writers who were to constitute the Literary Revival that W. B. YEATS once declared, 'he started us all'. He also published vivid romances of Tudor Ireland. Though politically a Unionist, he felt his class had failed to live up to their responsibilities, and he attempted, futilely, in volumes of impassioned, Carlylean prose, to recall them to a sense of duty. He continued to contribute to the literary movement through his editorship of *All Ireland Review* (1900–7), but in the new century his vision seemed anachronistic and in his later years he became an increasingly isolated figure.　　　　　　　　　　　　　PLM
Phillip L. Marcus, *Standish O'Grady*, 1970.

Ó hAirtneide, Micheál (1941–　). Poet; born in Co. Limerick, he was for years (as Michael Hartnett) the most important English-language poet of Munster. Having published *Anatomy of a Cliché* (1967) and *A Farewell to English* (1975), he then decided to write in Irish only, his first book in the Gaelic *persona* being *Adnarca Broic* (1979).　　　　　　　　　TMcC

Ó Leochain, Seán (1943–　). Gaelic poet; educated at University College, Galway. He has published four collections of poetry, *Blath an Fheir* (1968), *An Dara Cloch* (1969), *Saol na bhFuioll* (1973) and *Idir Ord agus Inneoln* (1977).　　　　　　　　　　　　TMcC

O'Malley, Tony (1913–　). Landscape and figurative painter; born at Callan, Co. Kilkenny, he was largely self-taught and began to draw and paint whilst recovering from an illness. He painted landscapes in Kilkenny, Clare Island, Arklow, Enniscorthy and New Ross, and was also greatly influenced by the poetry of PADRAIC FALLON. After 1959 he divided his time between a home at St Ives in Cornwall and Callan. He signs his work 'Ó Maille'. He was given a major exhibition by the Arts Council of Ireland 1980/81 and was the subject of an RTE television documentary in 1982.　　　　　CMacG

O'Meara, Frank (1853–88). Landscape painter; born in Co. Carlow, he later lived in France and studied with Carolus Duran in Paris, and subsequently worked at Barbizon and Gretz. He is best known in Ireland for *Towards Evening and Winter*, now in the Hugh Lane Municipal Gallery of Modern Art, Dublin.　　　　　　　　　　　　　　CMacG

O'Murnaghan, Art (1872–1954). Artist and designer; a most imaginativve artist and one of the most versatile figures in modern Ireland, he joined the Dublin Gate Theatre at its inception (*see* THEATRES), and worked there as stage manager, actor and designer, as well as composing incidental music. In 1924 he resigned his pharmacy business on being engaged to produce *Leabhar na hAiseirghe* (*The Book of the Resurrection*). This illuminated memorial became his life's work, its extensive series of colourful and intricate Symbolist-cum-CELTIC REVIVAL designs on vellum occupying him for various periods until 1951. He evolved an original system of Celtic ornament, in

O'Murnaghan, Art. 'Eire page', designed in 1922 as part of a project for an illuminated book.

O'Neill, Daniel. *The First Born*, oil on canvas, 1949. Ulster Museum.

which the lines were taken direct from nature, and taught a course in it for a few years at the National College of Art. He also worked at landscape scenes in pastel and watercolour and a highly imaginative series of linocuts called 'Nature Rhythms', some of which he exhibited at the RHA. P L
P. Larmour, *Celtic Ornament* (1981).

O'Neill, Daniel (1920–74). Figurative painter; born in Belfast, he was largely self-taught and became a regular exhibitor at annual exhibitions in Dublin and elsewhere in Ireland. He lived for a period in London. His works can be found in public and private collections in Ireland, Great Britain and the USA. C MacG

O'Nolan, Brian (Flann O'Brien; Myles na Gopaleen; 1912–66). Writer; born at Strabane, Co. Tyrone, he became a civil servant. Using the pseudonym Flann O'Brien, he spun a fantastic web of fiction in his novels (four in English, one in Irish); and as Myles na Gopaleen he sustained a consistently funny column in the *Irish Times* for twenty-seven years. A skilled parodist, he mingled comedy and philosophy in rococo edifices set against intimately Irish backcloths, as in *The Dalkey Archive* (1964), whose cast includes St Augustine of Hippo (interviewed underwater); de Selby, a sinister inventor-cum-philosopher; Sergeant Fottrell, whose 'mollycule theory' involves the transmogrification of man to bicycle; Father Cobble, 'an Englishman but quite intelligent'; and James Joyce, discovered working as a barman in seaside Skerries, disowning all responsibility for *Ulysses* and wishing to become a Jesuit. B H
Ann Clissman, *Flann O'Brien: A Critical Introduction to his Writing*, 1975.

opera. In Ireland opera remained for many years an imported commodity. Arne's *Rosamond* was performed in Dublin in 1743 and Arne himself conducted Gay's *The Beggar's Opera* in Dublin, where travelling companies could be sure of enthusiastic audiences in the 18th century. Giuseppe Giordani, known as Giordanello (*c.* 1744–1798), conducted Italian operas in Dublin from 1774 until 1782, when his brother Tommaso (*c.* 1733–1806) settled there and conducted performances until his death. The tenor Michael Kelly (1762–1826) made his début in a Piccinni *opera buffa* at Dublin in 1779. In the 19th century the sumptuous Theatre Royal in Hawkins Street hosted visiting companies performing grand opera, comic opera and light opera until its destruction in 1882; one of its most brilliant first nights was the Drury Lane Company's performance of WILLIAM VINCENT WALLACE's *Maritana*.

The Carl Rosa Opera Co. (formed in 1874 and based in England), the Moody-Manners Company (1898–1916) and the O'Mara Company, formed in 1912 by the Irish tenor and impresario Joseph O'Mara (1866–1927) frequently performed in Dublin, Cork and Belfast, where the opulent Grand Opera House was built in 1895, and also included Irish provincial centres on their tours. These visits stimulated local societies in Waterford, Clonmel, Limerick, Kilrush and Galway, which until the mid-1960s presented one or two productions annually featuring cross-channel singers.

The Dublin Grand Opera Society was founded in 1941 by a group headed by Professor John F. Larchet (its President until 1967) and Colonel William T. O'Kelly (its Chairman until his death in 1979), with Colonel James Doyle as musical director. From modest beginnings it has expanded and flourished to become a powerful cultural influence.

In the immediate post-war years it welcomed companies from the Paris Opéra-Comique and from the Hamburg and Munich State Operas. A subvention from the Italian Government in the years 1953–65 enabled the Society to present many singers who were later to become famous at the highest international level; among them were Anna Moffo and Margherita Rinaldi, with Piero Capucilli, Luciano Pavarotti and Giuseppe di Stefano among the men. Anneliese Rothenberger and Joan Sutherland also appeared with the DGOS at crucial stages of their careers. Since 1947 the Society has had the collaboration of the RTE Symphony Orchestra. Among conductors can be numbered Desormière, Erede, Kempe, Mackerras and Patané. Napoleone Annovazzi has been the Society's principal conductor since 1961.

The Society's chorus and various management committees work voluntarily with the support of the Arts Council, 1,100 patron members and over 100 business guarantors. Its policy has been to present Irish singers of proven ability to team with distinguished visitors. Four or five Italian operas were presented over a three-week Spring season in Dublin, expanded since 1971 by a week in Cork, while in December – over two weeks – three productions are mounted to explore the French, German and Slavonic repertoire. To date 71 operas by 34 different composers (ranging from Gluck to Janáček) have been staged.

In Belfast the Northern Ireland Opera Trust (established in 1960) presents two operas each Spring and Autumn in the Opera House (beautifully restored in 1980), which has also recently welcomed the visiting Scottish Opera.

Dr Havelock Nelson founded the Studio Opera Group in 1950. It performs intimate operas throughout Northern Ireland and has occasionally visited Dublin and Drogheda. It has presented almost 100 different works, including many neglected one-act operas. The Group has been highly praised for its Mozart performances and for its initiative in staging many works by Benjamin Britten. It now averages four productions a year. Dr Nelson remains the Group's conductor.

The annual WEXFORD FESTIVAL, which attracts an international audience, has done much to stimulate interest in opera since 1951 and has a good record in discovering star singers.

The Irish National Opera (founded in 1965) tours smaller centres throughout Ireland. Its performances are given with piano accompaniment, but with imaginative sets and costumes. It nurtures emerging talent among Irish singers and provides them with invaluable experience. It has given 400 performances of eleven different operas. The INO was specially invited to give the première of *Twelfth Night* by James Wilson, an English composer resident in Ireland since 1947, at the Wexford Festival (1970), and to present Archie Potter's *The Wedding* at the ABBEY THEATRE in Dublin (1981).

The German composer Werner Egk (1901–) has written an opera, *Irische Legende*, produced at Salzburg in 1955, which is based on YEATS's *The Countess Cathleen*.   B de B/A G H

Ó Rathaille, Aogain (*c.* 1675–1729). Gaelic poet; born near Killarney, he seems to have had a knowledge of both English and Latin, as well as Irish. His genius spans the great divide of two sensibilities, that of the incomers of the Plantation and that of the native Gael, and the poems he wrote are full of great technical verve as well as reflecting the old pride of a ruined civilization.   T McC

Ó Riáda, Seán (1931–71). Composer; born in Cork, he became assistant director of music for Radio Telefis Eireann 1952, and subsequently studied in France and Italy before being appointed director of music at the ABBEY THEATRE.

His score for the historical film *Mise Eire* (*see* CINEMA) excited the enthusiastic admiration of the broader spectrum of the Irish people. Curiously, his involvement in folk-music is rarely noticeable in his best-known orchestral music. His major works bear the unusual title 'Nomos'. The first of these, sub-titled 'Hercules Dux Ferrariae' (1957), is for strings. It effectively and cleverly combines the modal theme with a limited use of twelve-note technique in an attractive set of variations. His most important work, 'Nomos' No. 20 (1963), has a text drawn from the Theban cycle of Sophocles. This is an hour-long dramatic work for baritone, choir and orchestra, which reflects on Fate, Life and Death and simultaneously attempts to gloss the history of Western musical evolution with its references to plainchant, organum and classical music.   A G H

Ó Riordain, Seán (1916–77). Gaelic poet; born at Ballyvourney, Co. Cork. The publication of his *Eireaball Spideoige* in 1952 introduced a peculiarly rich vocabulary and texture into Irish verse. *Linte Limbo* (1971), *Brosna* (1974, 1976) and *Tar Eis mo Bhais* (1978, 1979) carry the opposing powers of surging craft and personal melancholy. His thematic range is as broad as the technical gifts he displays, embracing religious and political themes, and both private and public elegies.   T McC

Ormond Manor House, Carrick-on-Suir, Co. Tipperary. This gabled Elizabethan Tudor house was built in the latter years of the 16th century by Thomas, 10th Earl of Ormond, after his return from the English Court. Apart from firing holes, the house had no fortification but was built adjacent to and

Ormond Manor House. The 16th-century mansion and (*left*) the adjacent, castle, now a ruin.

communicated with the earlier castle on the River Suir.

The great hall on the first floor of the house consists of an impressive long gallery decorated with stucco portraits of Elizabeth I and heraldic devices, which represent a rare example in Ireland of surviving 16th-century PLASTERWORK. There is a fine carved chimneypiece dated 1565 with armorial bearings and a Latin inscription. The building is now a National Monument. BdeB

Ormsby, Frank (1947–). Ulster poet; he is editor of the important magazine *The Honest Ulsterman*, and his first book, *A Store of Candles* (1977), was a Choice of the British Poetry Book Society. TMcC

O'Rourke, Miceál (1947–). Pianist; born in Dublin, he studied in Dublin and in Paris, where he has resided since 1971. He has toured twice in the USSR and in Poland. He has performed regularly in France and Belgium, is a frequent visitor to Ireland, and was enthusiastically received at his Boston début in 1979. He is noted as an interpreter of Chopin and Schumann. AGH

Orpen, Sir William Newenham Montague (1878–1931). Portrait, landscape and genre painter; born in Co. Dublin, he studied at the Metropolitan School of Art, Dublin, 1890–7, then at the Slade School, London. He was commissioned by Sir HUGH LANE to finish the series of portraits of well-known contemporary Irishmen, intended as the basis of the collection made for the foundation of the Dublin Municipal Gallery of Modern Art.

Orpen taught at the Metropolitan School of Art in Dublin 1902–14, and was arguably the most important influence on the rise of the native tradition in early 20th-century Irish painting. He was elected RHA 1908, RA 1921, and a member of New English Art Club 1900. He acted as an Official War Artist 1917–18,

and was Official Artist at the Paris Peace Conference in 1919 (*see* pl. XIII); he was knighted in 1918.

Orpen enjoyed considerable success as a fashionable portrait painter. He edited a general history of art (*The Outline of Art*, published 1923) and wrote two biographical works. After his death his reputation suffered a major decline, but some forty years later became subject to complete reappraisal. A major biography appeared in 1981, and a television documentary by RTE was devoted to his life and work. His works are to be found in all Irish public collections, as well as the Tate Gallery and the Imperial War Museum, London, and the Metropolitan Museum of Art, New York. CMacG

W. Orpen, *An Onlooker in France 1917–1919*, 1921; ——, *Stories of Old Ireland and Myself*, 1924; P. G. Konody and S. Dark, *William Orpen; Artist and Man*; 1932; Bruce Arnold, *William Orpen, Mirror to an Age*, 1981.

Osborne, Walter Frederick (1859–1903). Figurative, genre and landscape painter; born in Dublin, he was the son of William Osborne, an animal painter. He entered the Royal Hibernian Academy Schools in 1876, and later studied under Verlat in Antwerp and visited Brittany in 1882. He was elected ARHA 1883, RHA 1886, and a member of New English Art Club 1887. He exhibited at the Royal Academy. He painted many landscapes in the South of England. He became an assistant teacher to NATHANIEL HONE at the RHA Schools, but lived mostly from his portrait practice in Dublin. His landscape and subject pictures only came to be admired after his premature death from pneumonia. Works by Osborne were included in the major exhibition of Post-Impressionist painting held in 1979–80 at the Royal Academy, London, and the National Gallery of Art, Washington, D.C. He is also represented in the Tate Gallery, London; many of his best-known works are in the NGI and the Hugh Lane Municipal Gallery of Modern Art, Dublin. *See* pl. XI. CMacG

Jeanne Sheehy, *Walter Osborne*, 1974.

Ó Siadhail, Micheál. Poet; educated at Trinity College, Dublin, and the University of Oslo, he taught Irish for four years at TCD and subsequently at the Dublin Institute for Advanced Studies. He is the author of two collections of poetry, *An Bhliain Bhisigh* (1978) and *An Runga* (1980). TMcC

Ó Súilleabháin, Eoghan Rua (1748–84). Poet and wit; born in Co. Kerry, he was one of the most brilliant of the 18th-century Gaelic poets. Many of his poems are written in the AISLING genre; an outstanding example is 'Ceo Driochta' ('A Magic Mist'), full of his most characteristic music. TMcC

Ó Súilleabháin, Muiris (1904–50). Writer; born on Great Blasket Island, Co. Kerry. He became a member of the Garda Síochána (police force); as a writer of prose in Irish, his main work was *Fiche Blian ag Fás* ('Twenty Years A-Growing'; autobiography), 1933. AA

O'Sullivan, Seán. Portrait of Maude Gonne Mac Bride, charcoal, 1929. NGI.

O'Sullivan, Seán (1906–64). Portrait and landscape painter, designer and graphic artist; born in Dublin, he studied at the Metropolitan School of Art, Dublin, and worked in Paris (where he met JAMES JOYCE) in La Grande Chaumière and at Colarossi's. He was elected ARHA 1928, and RHA 1931. He is best known for his series of portraits, mainly drawings of contemporary figures, and also for his series of posthumous portraits of the leaders of the 1916 Rising. Examples of his work can be seen in the NMI and the NGI.   C MacG

Ó Tuairisc, Eoghan (1919–82). Poet, essayist, dramatist and critic; his best-known collections of poetry are *The Weekend of Dermot and Grace* (1964) and *Sidelines: a diary of poems* (1981), while his work in Irish has won many awards.   T McC

Ó Tuama, Seán (1926–). Poet and scholar; he is Professor of Modern Irish Literature at University College, Cork. He has written plays, as well as editing publications, including *The Gaelic League Idea* (1973) and *Poems of the Dispossessed* (1981). His collections of witty and intimate poems include *Faoilean ne Beatha* (1962) and *Saol fo Thoinn* (1978).   T McC

Owenson, Robert (*né* MacEóin; 1744–1812). Actor-manager; born in Co. Mayo, he was one of the very few native Irish-speakers on the stage. He was introduced to Garrick by OLIVER GOLDSMITH. He made his London début at Covent Garden in 1774, and became associated with Samuel Johnson's circle. He tried to initiate a National Theatre in Dublin, where only the work of Irish dramatists, actors and musicians would be presented, and took the Fishamble Street Theatre, but the venture failed for financial reasons.   C F-S

Pain, James (*c.* 1779–1877) and **George Richard** (*c.* 1793–1838). Architects; born in Isleworth, Middlesex, and London respectively, the sons of James Pain, a builder and surveyor, and grandsons of the architectural author William Pain. The brothers came to Ireland to supervise the building of Lough Cutra Castle for JOHN NASH. They divided their activities between Cork and Limerick – George Richard working in Cork and James in Limerick. Their first commission was Cork Gaol (1818), featuring a massive Doric portico influenced by George Dance. G. R. Pain rebuilt the North Chapel, Cork (1820), and St Patrick's, Cork (1836). Both brothers worked on the Court House, Cork (1835), while G. R. Pain designed 'Father Mathew's Church' (Holy Trinity, Cork; begun 1832). They built a series of Nash-style castles, including the huge Mitchelstown Castle, Co. Cork (1832), Dromoland, Co. Clare (1826), the picturesque Blackrock Castle, Co. Cork (*c.* 1830), Strancally, Co. Waterford (*c.* 1830), and Kinnity, Co. Offaly (1833). They designed numerous Church of Ireland churches in the ecclesiastical province of Cashel and several courthouses.   W G

painting. This general article is divided into two major sections, the first covering the period from the 17th century up to 1850, the second from 1850 to the present.

Painting from the 17th century to 1850
For a variety of reasons the history of Irish painting starts late in the 17th century. The most serious is the almost total lack of pictures dating from before 1660 – the result of the immensely destructive wars which plagued the country until the 1690s. Another is the preference shown in Ireland for TAPESTRY, which seems to have continued to be regarded as the normal decoration for great houses and castles later than in many countries. However, after the Restoration the situation changed rapidly: several professional painters settled in Dublin, attracted by the artistic tastes of the Viceroy, the Duke of Ormonde, and other major landowners who were rebuilding their properties. In 1670 the Guild of Cutlers, Painter-Steyners and Stationers was incorporated, though it never assumed an important role with artists, of whom James Gandy (1619–89), a minor follower of Van Dyck, came with Ormonde. Other resident portrait painters included the English-born and trained Thomas Pooley (1646–1723), and Gaspar Smitz (d. *c.* 1707), who was either Dutch or German. An important visitor was John Michael Wright, who was in Ireland in 1679 and painted a number of distinguished portraits. Smitz seems to have travelled to and from England quite considerably, and worked not only in portraiture but

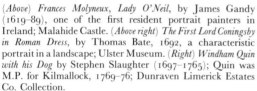

(*Above*) *Frances Molyneux, Lady O'Neil*, by James Gandy (1619–89), one of the first resident portrait painters in Ireland; Malahide Castle. (*Above right*) *The First Lord Coningsby in Roman Dress*, by Thomas Bate, 1692, a characteristic portrait in a landscape; Ulster Museum. (*Right*) *Windham Quin with his Dog* by Stephen Slaughter (1697–1765); Quin was M.P. for Kilmallock, 1769–76; Dunraven Limerick Estates Co. Collection.

as a teacher, restorer and still-life painter. During one of his English visits he almost certainly had as pupils in London, James Gandy's son, William, who worked in Ireland till the early 18th century, and GARRET MORPHEY, a native Irishman, and the finest resident painter in Ireland from the late 1680s to his death in 1716. He sometimes painted small whole-length portraits set in landscapes, which are stylistically close to the one known portrait by Thomas Bate, *The First Lord Coningsby in Roman Dress* (1692). Bate also worked as a landscape painter, executing a view of Dublin in the late 1690s.

The need for education resulted in early 18th-century artists going to England to study. Some then went on to Italy, staying there for several years. Unfortunately, this usually meant that such artists did not return to live in Ireland, as they found more work available in London than in Dublin. Irish patrons were, too, often more inclined to employ a foreign artist than a native-born painter, and many came from abroad during this period and achieved considerable success in Ireland. Stephen Slaughter (1697–1765), an Englishman, was one who made repeated visits,

painting somewhat naive portraits but with magnificently handled costume, which no doubt flattered his sitter's pride. CHARLES JERVAS was the only Irishman who, though based in London (where he became Principal Painter to the King in 1723), returned on long visits to Dublin. At his best he displays a fine, realist, style but frequently his work is lifeless, and it must have been a pleasure to Dubliners when JAMES LATHAM, home from the Continent, settled in the capital late in the 1720s and rapidly became the resident Establishment painter. His straightforward portraits, painted with a real feeling for colour and brushwork, produced few close followers other than Thomas Frye (1710–62), who made his career in England and did relatively few paintings, since he became the founder-manager of the Bow Porcelain Factory and an important mezzotint artist, scraping portraits and genre subjects of compelling and mysterious quality. Latham's friend, Philip Hussey (1713–83), was influenced by Slaughter in his pretty, early portraits. His later pictures include a charming group, *The Bateson Family*, and he may also have painted small-scale conversation pieces in the manner

(*Above*) A mezzotint portrait by Thomas Frye (1710–62), from a series published in London in 1760. (*Above right*) *The Bateson Family*, 1762, a notable group portrait by Philip Hussey (1713–83); Ulster Museum. (*Right*) *A Gentleman with a Gun and Dog* by Robert Hunter, the leading portraitist in Dublin from the 1750s to the 1780s; NGI.

of Arthur Devis. John Lewis (fl. 1740–69), a theatrical scene painter at the Smock Alley Playhouse, Dublin, was also active as a portraitist, one of his sitters being the actress PEG WOFFINGTON. Soon after Latham's death the young ROBERT HUNTER seems to have captured the market and for some thirty years he was the principal portrait painter in Dublin. His style changed, no doubt to suit his patrons, and one finds him painting fine whole-lengths in the manner of Francis Cotes, Rococo half-lengths and Devis-like small portraits, until he finally came under the influence of Reynolds.

The most important development of the 1720s and '30s was in landscape painting. Except for some topographical watercolours by mapmakers, and the superb drawings of Francis Place, done during his visit to Ireland in 1698/99, only a handful of 17th-century Irish landscapes survive. It was not until the Dutchman VAN DER HAGEN settled in Dublin, *c.* 1721, that landscape became an established mode in Ireland. His paintings, varying from topographical views of towns and houses, to views of romantic sites like Powerscourt Waterfall, were enormously influential on the landscape painters of his day, and for many years afterwards. Joseph Tudor (?1697–1759) relied closely on his style, while Anthony Chearnley (fl. 1740–85), a gentleman-amateur, combined an interest in landscape painting with antiquarian pursuits, drawing ruins, historical monuments and antiquities.

The problem of education came to a head in the 1730s when a group of gentlemen, including Samuel Madden and Thomas Prior, who were among the founders of the DUBLIN SOCIETY, decided that a school was vital not only to encourage the fine arts, but also design, in relation to the applied arts and manufactures. They began by sending pupils to a school recently opened by ROBERT WEST who was trained in France, as was his colleague James Mannin, either an Italian or a Frenchman. Between them they brought a knowledge of French art to Ireland. West's school was taken over by the Dublin Society in the 1740s and was at first divided into two departments or schools: Life under West, and Ornament and Landscape under Mannin. Pupils, who were usually in their teens, were taught drawing, using casts from the antique and engravings after the great masters. They normally stayed about two years and were either already apprentices, or were then apprenticed to a suitable master. Most Irish artists born after 1730 were pupils of the Schools, and the general excellence of art in Ireland in the second half of the century is a tribute to West and Mannin as teachers. Sometimes the Dublin Society arranged and paid for students to travel abroad; for instance they sent Matthew William Peters (1741–1814) to Italy. The schools do not seem to have taught oil painting, so that nearly all Irish 18th-century painters started their careers as excellent pastellists, including Peters and Martin Archer Shee

(*Above*) *An Actor between the Muses of Tragedy and Comedy* by Thomas Hickey, 1781. NGI.

(*Left*) *Self-portrait* by Robert Lucius West, dated 1816; West was a noted portraitist in the first quarter of the 19th century. NGI.

(1769–1850), whose careers were spent in England as portrait and subject-picture painters in oils; Shee became President of the Royal Academy in 1830. Many artists, however, had successful careers as pastellists. Of these ROBERT HEALY is famed for his charming grisaille portraits and HUGH DOUGLAS HAMILTON is best remembered for his small oval portrait heads. William Watson (d. 1765) drew larger portrait heads, but most Irish pastellists worked in the Healy/Hamilton manner. They included Francis Robert West (*c.* 1749–1809), the son of Robert West, and Charles Forrest (fl. 1771–80). Although the fashion for pastels died out in the third quarter of the century, their use continued into the 19th century.

Despite the flourishing conditions of the arts during the period of Grattan's Parliament (in the last two decades of the 18th century), the patronage for painters remained so limited that most of the best artists were forced to make their careers in London. Robert Hunter retained his position as the foremost portrait painter well into the 1780s and as late as 1792 he held an exhibition and sale of his paintings, a most unusual event at this time. He was succeeded by Hugh Douglas Hamilton, home from Rome in 1791, who, while abroad, had changed from pastel to oil painting and now excited much admiration for his whole-length portraits (often set in landscapes), especially after 1800 when exhibitions became regular annual events. William Cuming (1769–1852), Robert Lucius West (1774–1850), and Martin Cregan (1788–1870) were the best portraitists in the first quarter of the 19th century. Stephen Catterson Smith (1806–72), who was English by birth, spent most of his life in Dublin and was the main rival of these three.

Throughout the second half of the 18th century a number of foreign artists gave Hunter and Hamilton some competition, staying for three or four years and making quite a stir before they left. John Astley was in Dublin *c.* 1756–59 and Francis Wheatley 1779–83, when he recorded, in a series of large group portraits, the stirring events of the Volunteers (*see* pl. xv), and immortalized the high point of Anglo-Irish rule with his splendid *Grattan addressing the Irish House of Commons.* The American, Gilbert Stuart, was in Dublin 1787–93 and left behind many fine portraits, while George Chinnery, in the course of his visit 1795–1802, created a type of romantic portrait, new in Dublin, as well as painting many landscapes.

A very talented artist of Hunter's generation was NATHANIEL HONE the Elder who, sadly, while still young left for England, and established himself as a portrait painter in London. He worked against the taste of his own day in being more interested in Dutch painting than Italian, but the real damper on his career was his quarrel with Reynolds. A younger contemporary, Thomas Hickey (1741–1816), who attended the Dublin Society Schools, had an adventurous career working in London and Bath in the 1770s before setting sail for India where, apart from two brief visits home, he spent the rest of his life. His small whole-length portrait groups are his best work, especially those done when he was in India. Robert Fagan (1761–1816), who, although he was born in London (where his father, an expatriate Irishman, was a prosperous baker) and made his career in Italy, having an Irish father, considered himself Irish. He was an art dealer and archaeologist, and created some of the most original portraits of his period. But the greatest of the expatriate Irish painters was JAMES BARRY who, after a visit to Italy, made his career as a history painter in London. Barry was uncompromising, painting only the occasional portrait, but with great mastery. He went to London first in 1763 as the protégé of EDMUND BURKE, the author of *A Philosophical Enquiry into the Origin of our ideas of the Sublime and the Beautiful* (1757), which was in its day a major contribution to aesthetic theory; it was well known to Irish artists, and apart from its impact on Barry, Burke's views had a considerable importance for Irish landscape painting. GEORGE BARRET, who studied at the Dublin Society Schools, probably met Burke in Dublin; certainly he was much influenced by his love of nature in her 'terrible' moods and no doubt was urged by him to paint wild nature in her 'terrible' moods and not just well laid-out parks surrounding country houses. Barret became one of the earliest painters in Europe to treat landscape painting with emotive power and not from a purely topographical point of view. Robert Carver (fl. 1750–91), another Irish landscape painter, lived in London *c.* 1770, working as a theatrical scene painter; his landscapes are usually classical in composition but his 'Dublin Drop' for Drury Lane was famed for its exciting, realistic portrayal of Powerscourt Waterfall.

In the 1750s and '60s the landscape painters among the large colony of Irish artists in Rome included Robert Crone (*c.* 1718–79), James Forrester (*c.* 1730–76), Solomon Delane (d. 1812) and Hugh Primrose Dean (fl. 1758–84). Though little enough is known of their work now, these artists were considered by their contemporaries to be very fine painters and all but Dean were products of Mannin's teaching. This remarkable interest in Landscape, clearly fostered not only by the Dublin Society Schools, but by the patrons who were prepared to buy such work, meant that more landscape painters were able to make their careers in Ireland than portrait painters. The finest of these was THOMAS ROBERTS. He had, of course, attended the Dublin Society Schools but he had also been apprenticed to a most competent landscape painter, George Mullins (fl. 1763–75); unfortunately he died young, but he had worked with great energy for his aristocratic patrons, creating for them series of pictures not only of the parklands around their houses, but also of the scenery in the district. Roberts's style became very well known, as he exhibited these works with the Society of Artists, who were very active in Dublin during the 1760s and '70s, and thus the poetic atmosphere of his landscapes set the tone for many other painters. Roberts was also remarkable for conveying the distant vistas of Irish mountains and lakes, with their mysterious beauty. A contemporary of his, WILLIAM ASHFORD, began as an amateur, painting still-lifes, but perhaps inspired by Roberts' example, he started exhibiting landscapes in the 1770s and after Roberts' death in 1778 was far and away the most important landscape painter in Dublin. Ashford's serene and sunny pictures show an idyllic view of nature. He is said to have been a seascape painter of quality, though few of these are now known. By the early years of the 19th century THOMAS SAUTELLE

View of Dublin Bay with the Royal Charter School, by William Ashford, 1794. NGI.

ROBERTS (brother of Thomas Roberts) had developed his own romantic style, shaken off the influence of his elder brother, and was Ashford's only serious rival. Much of the work of all these landscape painters was done for the engravers (*see* ENGRAVING). The individual engravings of the first half of the century were superseded by books of views, the precursors of the illustrated travel books of the 19th century. Milton, who published his *Collection of Select Views from the different seats of the Nobility and Gentry in the Kingdom of Ireland* (1783–93) employed Roberts, Ashford and Wheatley, among other artists. This type of publication must have helped spread a knowledge of their work through a wide section of society. Thomas Sautelle Roberts issued aquatints from his own watercolours, and Jonathan Fisher (d. 1809) used his own paintings as the basis for sets of engraved views of Irish beauty sports, such as Carlingford Lough and Killarney, and even attempted a comprehensive set of 60 Irish views.

A landscape painter from Cork, NATHANIEL GROGAN, developed separately from these Dublin painters and concentrated more on the genre element in his paintings. Though Ashford and Wheatley were always interested in the figures in their landscapes, Grogan was alone in making them the focal point; it is not surprising, therefore, to find that, using Dutch art as his inspiration, he painted a number of fascinating scenes of Irish country life, including a Wake, an itinerant Preacher, figures drinking, a Fair, and a village schoolmaster. No other contemporary Irish artist can compete with Grogan as a genre painter, although a number of watercolourists worked on similar subjects. John Nixon (*c.* 1750–1818), drew a splendid *View of Cove*, 1794, which bustles with life; and George Grattan (1787–1819) during his short life attempted genre paintings both in oils and in watercolour, including the much admired *Blind Beggarwoman and Child* of 1807. Nixon was close to being a caricaturist, but watercolour and gouache were used throughout the century by a number of artists as a serious landscape medium. Thomas Walmsley (1763–1806) and Oben (James George O'Brien; fl. 1779–1819) were typical of the generation active around 1800. Perhaps the finest landscapes in gouache in the 18th century, however, remain Susannah Drury's *Views of the Giant's Causeway*, which won her a Dublin Society premium in 1740. Watercolour was also the medium of the antiquarian painters, and such architectural specialists as the two Maltons, Thomas and James. They were English but lived in Ireland for many years, mainly painting superb views of Dublin in watercolour and gouache.

After 1800 watercolour largely replaced pastels as the medium for small portrait studies. ADAM BUCK, from Cork, was the finest artist in this field but most of his career was spent in England and the Irish public were less well served by such artists as Robert Richard Scanlon (fl. 1826–64) and Felice Piccione (fl. 1830–42), an Italian who worked mainly in Belfast. Edward Hayes (1797–1864) continued the genre into the second half of the century. Adam Buck was the only watercolourist of note who worked both in that medium and in miniature, which has always been a specialized technique. In Ireland the earliest known exponents are Gaspar Smitz and Simon Digby, Bishop of Elphin (d. 1720), who, though an amateur, was famous for his miniatures. In the early 18th century several notable English miniaturists worked in Dublin, including Christian Friedrich Zincke, who worked in enamel and must have influenced Rupert Barber (fl. 1736–72), who practised in London and Bath, as well as Dublin. Zincke also influenced Nathaniel Hone, who was better known in his youth for his miniatures, both in enamel and on ivory. The great period for the art in Ireland was the second half of the century, when Gustavus Hamilton (*c.* 1739–1775), a Dublin Society trained artist, worked in Dublin and was succeeded by Horace Hone (1756–1825; son of Nathaniel), who worked there from 1782 until the Act of Union, when he returned to London. Although Hone was a very fine miniaturist, the greatest exponent of the art was Charles Robertson (1760–1821), who also worked in both England and Ireland. These painters worked in a style close to their English contemporaries and at their best they equal in quality Cosway and Smart. Other well-known Irish miniaturists were Sampson Twogood Roch (1759–1847) from Youghal, Co. Cork, and John Comerford (*c.* 1770–1832), who started as an oil painter but found miniatures more profitable; he worked in Kilkenny and Dublin.

Though very little decorative mural painting survives in Ireland today it was quite common in the 18th century, even being carried out in remote areas by artists who clearly had little formal training, such as J. Ryan (fl. *c.* 1780–96) who worked in Co. Galway. There are records of painted ceilings in Kilkenny Castle in the time of the first Duke of Ormonde, and other 17th-century work includes a set of horsemen (based on engravings after Diepenbecke) painted on coarse boards. Van der Hagen painted elaborate decorations in Curraghmore – these were destroyed later in the century – and Classical deities in grisaille (in imitation of sculpture) in another Co. Waterford house. Decoration of the latter variety fitted well into the elaborate PLASTERWORK of 18th-century Dublin houses, and Peter de Gree (d. 1789), a Dutch artist, had a successful practice in Ireland 1785–89. His imitation-stonework bas reliefs of putti and Classical figures survive in 52 St Stephen's Green, Dublin, and in several country houses. The sets of landscapes painted by such artists as Roberts and Mullins were probably used in much the same way, being inset into stucco decoration. But Barret went further when *c.* 1780 he painted, for William Locke at Norbury Park in England, a landscape room which gave the total illusion of being part of the view outside. In Ireland the Italian Gaspar Gabrielli was employed by Lord Cloncurry to create several landscape interiors at Lyons House, though none had the total illusion of Barret's work. A Dublin mansion decorated at the turn of the century, Aldborough House, had elaborate and, from descriptions, somewhat pretentious murals on the staircase; probably other Dublin houses had similar decorative schemes, but the only survivors are the Long Gallery in CASTLETOWN, Co. Kildare, with its Raphaelesque grotesques, and the ceiling at St Patrick's Hall in Dublin Castle painted by Vincent Waldré (1742–1814), with scenes from Irish history on either side of an allegory of George III with Liberty and Justice, which give the Hall a real feeling of grandeur.

The notion of artists exhibiting their work in an effort to establish and widen their reputations was slow to develop. Though private collections were probably always fairly easily accessible to the interested, the only way, until 1764, that the general public could see pictures was at auction sales, and at the exhibition of students' work held by the Dublin Society. In that year the Society of Artists in Ireland was founded in emulation of the London Society of the same name. Despite various internal arguments, annual exhibitions were held until 1780, when financial problems as well as dissension hit the Society and led to its collapse; it was not reformed until 1800 when exhibitions started again. The Dublin Society even built a fine Exhibition Hall in Hawkins Street which housed most of the shows until it was closed in 1819. The artists had, as usual, been fighting fierce battles and founding a great many rival institutions, but finally they reached agreement and the ROYAL HIBERNIAN ACADEMY was incorporated in 1823 with Ashford as its President; annual exhibitions were instituted in 1826.

The effect of the Act of Union on painting was immediate; it had an impact on patronage which took years for the arts to assimilate. The members of the old Irish Parliament were the educated, moneyed class who supported the arts. When they no longer needed to live in Dublin, Parliament having moved to London, their departure was a very serious blow to artists. Patronage was now in the hands of the professional classes, the doctors and lawyers, who (with much more limited means) not only bought less, but were more interested in establishing institutions, in spreading knowledge of the arts, and in research into the Celtic past. It took some time for the effects of the change to be felt, but the proliferation of art societies occurred at once. This led to many desirable results, including the foundation of the RHA; the holding of Old Master exhibitions, and the setting up of provincial societies leading to provincial art schools, notably in Belfast and Cork.

On the whole the new middle-class patrons wanted smaller pictures, liked watercolours, because they were cheaper, and needed townscapes or views of famous beauty spots as subjects for their landscapes. They also liked genre scenes, and a series of artistic families, the Sadlers, the Brocases and the Mulvanys, emerged to cater for their tastes. William Sadler II (c. 1782–1839) must have had a veritable factory to make repetitions of his most popular works, scenes like *The French Landing in Killala Bay* and *The Burning of Home's Emporium, Dublin.* Samuel Frederick Brocas (1792–1847) painted fine town views, often for engraving, while John George Mulvany (c. 1766–1838) preferred views of places like Kilmallock, famous for its medieval ruins. Other painters of the time who should be mentioned include Jeremiah Hodges Mulcahy (d. 1889), who painted landscapes, Richard Rothwell (1800–68), a romantic portrait and genre painter whose rich colouring was renowned; Nicholas Crowley (1819–57), whose genre paintings are lively and full of character; Joseph Haverty (1794–1854) was more sentimental and nationalist in his choice of subject, which included his famous *Limerick Piper*; John Henry Campbell (1757–1828) and his daughter Cecilia (1791–1857) both painted watercolours and oil landscapes, while Cecilia's husband, George Nairn (1799–1850), was a fine painter of horses. This genre was naturally always popular in Ireland and was largely in the hands of unknown painters or visiting English artists. Another specialization which became very popular in Ireland in the early 19th century was the painting of seascapes. The principal exponents were Richard Bridges Beechey (1808–95), Matthew Kendrick (c. 1797–1874), Edwin Hayes (1820–1904), and George Atkinson (1806–84).

The new patrons were true successors of the 18th-century antiquarians and were dedicated in their historical researches. Though mostly Protestant, they were all fascinated by the study of Celtic antiquity, not merely in its monuments but also its literature, its language and its life, which led them to explore such places as the Aran Islands, where they felt the ancient ways might survive. In art this corresponded with the romantic fascination felt in other European countries for medieval culture. Hence an artist like GEORGE PETRIE, who was an excellent watercolourist, but was more interested in research work than art, became an important figure among painters at the time, even briefly being President of the RHA. As a young man he had been a fellow-student and friend of JAMES ARTHUR O'CONNOR and FRANCIS DANBY who, like all the best artists of the post-Union generation, had to make their careers in England. While O'Connor retained links with Ireland, he lived in London painting small and often melancholy landscapes. Danby was a great success in London and in his later years in Paris. His was a more dramatic art, varying from large landscapes emphasizing the unimportance of man in the face of nature, to superb tranquil sunset seascapes.

The French Landing in Killala Bay, an abortive attempt in August 1798 to reinforce the United Irishmen, as depicted by William Sadler II; oil on panel. NGI.

An Emigrant Ship, Dublin Bay, Sunset, 1853, by Edwin Hayes, a painter who specialized in seascapes. NGI.

They were joined in London by DANIEL MACLISE from Cork, who became a major artist in England, painting great historical scenes including *The Death of Nelson* and *The Meeting of Wellington and Blücher at Waterloo* for the House of Commons in London. But he remained very much a nationalist Irishman, as can be gauged in the splendid *Marriage of Strongbow and Eva* (now in the National Gallery of Ireland) where the tragic end of Celtic civilization is stressed. The detailed handling of this subject owes much to Petrie's researches, though the artist who was most influenced by Petrie was another watercolourist, Frederick William Burton (1816–1900), who accompanied Petrie on several of his trips to the West and Aran. Burton's masterpiece, *The Meeting on the Turret Stairs*, is based on a Danish saga, but in its treatment it relies on Petrie's knowledge of early Irish as well as medieval costume and architecture. The importance of the use of watercolour is stressed by the fact that such subjects were now treated in what was originally considered an inferior medium. Michaelangelo Hayes (1820–77) also specialized in it, painting enormous pictures of battles,

(*Above*) *The Aran Fisherman's Drowned Child, c.* 1841, a dramatic social commentary by F. W. Burton; NGI. (*Above right*) A carefully executed watercolour by Michaelangelo Hayes (1820–77), *Sackville* (now O'Connell) *Street, Dublin*. (*Right*) A characteristic topographical study by Andrew Nicholl, *Clough-i-Stookman*, watercolour, *c.* 1828; Ulster Museum.

history and horses. However, the most original of the watercolourists was ANDREW NICHOLL from Belfast, who, apart from his topographical views, created numerous and enchanting pictures of wild flowers (*see* BOTANICAL ILLUSTRATION), usually painted in brilliant colour, through which a glimpse is caught of a country house or beauty spot. His work reveals a near-surrealist vision.   AOC

Painting from 1850 to the present
Although there was an increase in artists' societies of various types in 19th-century Ireland, the public was still not buying much in the way of native art, preferring, it seems, to import from abroad; the churches themselves were the leading offenders in this regard. The prevailing economic and political situation in Ireland between 1798 and 1850 was hardly conducive to the promotion of the fine arts at a general level. In the Dublin Exhibition of 1853, of the 1,023 pictures on show, only a handful were by Irish painters and almost 330 were Old Masters from various important collections, the balance being made up of modern English and Continental works.

With the decline in aristocratic patronage in the country, 'committee taste' got a firm hold on the public consciousness and so one finds in the 19th century the appearance of polite and learned societies for the advancement of the arts, and their dissemination and appreciation amongst all social classes. In the first half

of the century were founded: the ROYAL HIBERNIAN ACADEMY (1823); the Royal Irish Art Union (1839); the Cork Art Union (1841); and the National Art Union (1847). After 1850 there followed: the Dublin Art Union (1856); the Art Union of Ireland (1858); the Shilling Art Union (1860). The Society of Irish Artists and the Irish Institution led in turn to the creation of the NATIONAL GALLERY OF IRELAND which opened in 1864, and was incorporated by Act of Parliament in 1865. These developments, together with the establishment of a NATIONAL LIBRARY and the NATIONAL MUSEUM, testify to the general desire of the Irish for education and edification.

In another sense the rise and development of the provincial societies and schools of art assisted in the formation of a climate encouraging for the arts in 19th-century Ireland. In the north of the country the Belfast Association of Artists and the Fine Arts Society, founded in 1836 and 1843 respectively, led to the foundation of the Belfast School of Design which was to service the textile industry in that area. Derry had a School of Art by 1874. Further south, the Cork School of Design gave way in turn to the Crawford Science and Art Schools. The year 1852 saw the opening of schools of art in Limerick and the Waterford School of Practical Art & Design, followed by the Clonmel School of Art in 1854.

Despite all this activity, the position for the artist was not much improved, while a great deal of attention was being given to the training and development of the artisan and designer. The painter, unless he was producing either portraits or mainly topographical landscapes, had a thin enough time. It is therefore not surprising that many of the more active or ambitious artists sought fame and fortune in London, a wider area of patronage, and possible renown. The Act of Union, whatever its political consequences, had, in artists' terms, initiated a pattern of artistic haemorrhage which was to be a constant until the early years of the 20th century.

Amid the clamour aroused by the Famines, the dire social and economic aspects of Irish life and the political changes being wrought in Ireland, the painter continued to paint as if nothing had disturbed his social and artistic tranquillity, apparently barely affected by changes taking place all around. Even the most important painter of the period, NATHANIEL HONE, continued to paint in the manner which he had acquired abroad. FRANK O'MEARA passed most of his young life abroad, mainly in France, so that which might have been a crucial influence in terms of Irish art was largely lost to a wider audience. Of the younger generation, WALTER OSBORNE was perhaps more typical of the situation for the Irish painter. He had to paint in order to live, yet in his own lifetime he functioned principally as a portrait painter and a painter of genre pictures, in contrast with his subsequent reputation as the modern colourist/luminist painter. Osborne's great tonal works such as *Tea in the Garden* and *The People's Gardens, Dublin* were of little interest to polite Dublin society at the turn of the century.

Slightly younger than Osborne were WILLIAM J. LEECH and RODERIC O'CONOR and MARY SWANZY who, with the sculptor JOHN HUGHES, were to form part of the group of expatriate Irish artists seeking light and influences in continental Europe. There was no real political or philosophical cohesiveness in Irish art of the period, possibly because landscape, genre and portrait painting are practised essentially by individuals. With the possible and arguable exception of ORPEN and the Dublin School of Art, no real group evolved around a Master Painter in Ireland. The so-called Antwerp School was in reality only a group of Irish painters who in the last decade or so of the 19th century went to continental Europe, and some of whom visited and even studied in Antwerp, principally at Verlat's Academy. But so too, did many of them go to Paris to study at various academies and ateliers which were available to the young and not-so-young artists then flocking there.

The 19th-century Irish painter produced charming, affable, moral, decent and presumably appealing pictures for his audience. There was nothing that could shock the sensibilities of the public. Even when, in the middle of the century, the members of the Royal Hibernian Academy fought each other up and down the staircase of the Academy House in Abbey Street, it was more a question of personalities than of real differences of artistic theory. The schism which did result, however, was eventually healed and life settled down again in Academy House to remain largely

Le Petit déjeuner by Sarah Purser, a key figure in Irish art circles in the early years of the 20th century. NGI.

undisturbed until its destruction with all that it contained in the Rising of 1916.

A fundamental divide did occur in art in Ireland in the early years of the 20th century, when HUGH LANE, then a foppish young picture dealer of Irish origins, visited Dublin from London, and encountered the formidable personage of SARAH PURSER, the main character in the Irish art world of the period. It was she who introduced Lane to art in Ireland in 1901 at an exhibition of the works by Nathaniel Hone and JOHN BUTLER YEATS at 7 St Stephen's Green. He was so impressed by what he saw there that, although his own expertise lay in the field of Old Masters and Dutch art, he immediately bought a Hone and presented it to the Luxembourg Gallery, and he commissioned John Butler Yeats to paint a series of portraits of leading contemporary Irish figures of the literary, artistic and academic world. Eventually this project was to be taken over by William Orpen when Yeats, tiring of it, went to America. It was to be the beginning of the work which Lane undertook in the founding of a Modern Art Gallery for Dublin.

Even then, in 1907 Lane's intentions were very clear indeed. In the general introduction to a catalogue which he produced for the opening of his gallery (in which the Gaelic titles and the invitation card were translated by DOUGLAS HYDE and the catalogue entries made by the painter SARAH CECILIA HARRISON), Lane himself wrote '. . . I hope that this Gallery will always fulfil the object for which it is intended, and – by ceding to the National Gallery those pictures which, having stood the test of time, are no longer modern – make room for good examples of the movements of the day. ... Its influence must of necessity show itself in the next generation of artists, and of their critics. The opponents of the Gallery have been those who have not had the advantage of the study of these modern classics abroad, and who naturally cannot accept a standard so different from that which they have hitherto recognized.'

Irish art lovers were not slow to rise to the bait, and a tremendous campaign of misrepresentation and vilification took place both in the national press and socially. It was unfortunate for Lane that due to the shifting sands of Irish politics he had wandered into an area of great sensitivity, principally by treading on the toes of the newly prosperous Catholic professional class, who, already suspicious of new trends in art, were antagonistic towards Lane and aesthetes in general. Moreover, as the Trade Union movement showed itself sympathetic to Lane and his schemes to build a new art gallery, this roused the ire of the employer classes in Dublin who were locked in deadly combat with the Unions and Liberty Hall. The Unions for their part were naturally in favour of building an art gallery which would give employment to the massive pool of the unemployed, and they approved of the gallery which would subsequently be a focus for education at a wider level. Neither of these aims endeared themselves to the employer class, nor did it essentially recommend itself to the churchmen of the majority religion. Lane did eventually open his Municipal Gallery of Modern Art in 1908, but after protracted public rows about the building and financing of a new art gallery he removed some of the most important items of the loan collection to London, where, let it be said, they fared little better.

While Hugh Lane's initiative was highly significant in the development of trends in painting in Ireland in the 20th century, it could be argued that 1915 would be an appropriate date to take as an end to earlier fragmented phases. In that year SEÁN KEATING painted and exhibited his work *The Men of the West*. In this particular painting one can discern those attitudes which the new Ireland was to use as being emblematic of the revolutionary heroes in the War of Independence, and it would be easy to forget that when it was painted – in the year before the 1916 Rising – it had very different qualities to an audience whose very perception of the work is itself transformed by the traumatic events of 1916. Keating's painting meant that some kind of Irish identity had been forged between the Irish artist and the public.

Lane and, indeed, Irish art in the years that followed his initiative were unfortunate in that the course of both European and Irish history was at a crucial point of explosion. The confrontation between militant workers and the police as agents of the employers in Dublin in 1913, the conflict of World War I, the Howth gun-running, the 1916 Rising, the War of Independence, the Civil War and the land annuities controversy with Britain all produced a curious period

Abstract, an undated work by Mainie Jellett, one of the first Irish artists to be influenced by Cubism. NGI.

of stillness in Irish art practice which was prolonged by the advent of World War II.

It was in these circumstances that HARRY CLARKE's great window commissioned for the Labour building at the League of Nations centre in Geneva was declined, without thanks, by the Irish Government due to the epicene nature of the figurative work in the window. Yet the same Free State Government under W. T. Cosgrave could – at the prompting of Sarah Purser, who had founded the Friends of the National Collections – give Charlemont House in Parnell Square to the City of Dublin as a Modern Art Gallery in furtherance of the Irish claim to the disputed Lane Collection, then in London.

Many Irish artists did of course venture abroad to study, some to Holland, others to Spain and Italy. EVIE HONE and MAINIE JELLETT went to Paris to study under André Lhote and Albert Gleizes, bringing to Ireland on their return a modified form of Cubism. They were followed by a second wave of Lhote students, NORAH MCGUINNESS and JACK HANLON, who were to continue the Cubist tradition. During the years of World War II a group of mainly English painters – the White Stag Group – came to Ireland, and in 1943 the establishment of the Irish Exhibition of Living Art provided a plurality of exhibiting groups in Dublin.

To many it seemed that the Royal Hibernian Academy represented that group of painters who under the influence of the Literary Renaissance had looked to the Western Seaboard to establish some kind

XIV **painting.** *Landscape*, 175 × 116 cm. (69 × 45½ in.), by George Mullins, a work dating from the 1760s. Board of Works, Dublin.

XV **painting.** *The 2nd Lord Aldborough Reviewing the Volunteers in Belan Park* (detail) by Francis Wheatley, 1781, one of a series of large works commemorating the activities of the Volunteers. National Trust, Waddesdon Manor.

of Irish identity, seeking as its source the imagery of SYNGE, LADY GREGORY, Yeats and O'FLAHERTY, whereas the IELA was looking to avant-garde painting as seen through the French experience with modifications of Expressionism. Many of the same painters were, however, to be found in both groups, the reality being slightly different from the theory. All too often they were divided more by a clash of personalities than a difference of ideals, and the historical basis for much of what happened has little reference for the young painter of today. It was only in the early 1950s that the streams of activity became more mutually exclusive.

The other group exhibitions, for example, An t-Óireachtas, the Independent Artists, the Graphic Studio and the Project Arts Centre, as well as the activity of major picture dealers, also helped to change the face of Irish art by providing other outlets for younger artists, by exhibiting their works, and in a general way through exhibitions and information bringing many of their diverse accomplishments to the attention of a new public.

Deirdre McDonagh in the Brown Jacket Bookshop sold the works of Jack Yeats, then Victor Waddington became his agent, followed by Leo Smith in the Dawson Gallery, which with the Dublin Painters Group, the Water Colour Society, the Dublin Sketching Club and later on the Hendriks Gallery, gave a vitality and drive to Irish art in the 1950s and the early

Nude, oil on canvas, by Patrick Collins (b. 1910). Private Collection.

Garden Green by Norah McGuinness, 1962, in which Cubist influence is still to be seen. Hugh Lane Municipal Gallery of Modern Art, Dublin.

'60s. Given the size of the population and the consequently limited number of picture purchasers, the volume of this impetus is quite remarkable. In the 1950s the formation of an ARTS COUNCIL gave Irish art enormous momentum, and the Cultural Relations Committee of the Department of Foreign Affairs sent overseas some very good and representative exhibitions of work by Irish painters.

In the early 1960s the Scandinavian Report, *Design in Ireland*, gave the impetus for the foundation by William H. Walsh of the now famous KILKENNY DESIGN WORKSHOPS, which was the major effort to stimulate modern design practice in Irish industry and handcrafts, and in schools art history was introduced as a subject into the Leaving Certificate Examination in Secondary Education. The expansion of the National Gallery of Ireland under two Directors, Dr Thomas McGreevy and his immediate successor James White, led to an amazing upsurge in popular interest in painting in Ireland generally. McGreevy did not alas himself enjoy the full fruits of his long period as director: shortly after his retirement came the opening of the splendid new wing, and the income from the George Bernard Shaw Bequest enabled the NGI to compete with major European and American institutions in purchasing works of art.

The increasing number of newly prosperous in Ireland were now willing to spend money on art objects, and when MICHAEL SCOTT produced the first of

Escarpment, Glendalough, oil on canvas, by Patrick Hickey (b. 1927). Taylor Gallery, Dublin.

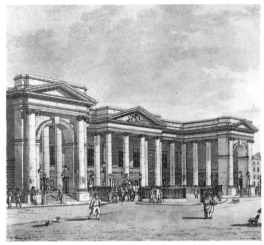

Parliament House. The colonnaded entrance court seen in an aquatint by James Malton, 1793 (detail).

the great international art exhibitions, ROSC, the Irish public if not quite prepared to accept modernism in all its forms, was certainly ready to go and look at it, and to participate in public debate about art and what they, the public, felt it was all about.

The thirty years between the end of World War II and the 1970s produced artists representing diverse and mainly conflicting groupings. The creation of Charles Haughey's scheme whereby artists resident in the State could be exempted from tax upon their artistic earnings, and the creation of AOSDÁNA (a scheme to honour creative and interpretive artists) follow upon the groundwork in those three decades by artists as divergent as: MAY GUINNESS, DIARMUID Ó CEALLACHAIN, HARRY KERNOFF, SOMHAIRLE MAC CANA, JACK B. YEATS, DANIEL O'NEILL, PAUL HENRY, GRACE HENRY, NORAH MCGUINNESS, MAURICE MACGONIGAL, BEATRICE GLENAVY, GEORGE CAMPBELL, NEVILLE JOHNSON, TONY O'MALLEY, NANO REID, JACK HANLON, PAT SCOTT, ANNE MADDEN, BRIAN BOURKE, MICHAEL FARRELL, LOUIS LE BROCQUY, ARTHUR ARMSTRONG, BRIAN FERRAN, BARRIE COOKE, PATRICK COLLINS, CECIL KING, ANNE YEATS, PAT HICKEY, PATRICK HENNESSY and ROBERT BALLAGH.

There remains in recent Irish art a continuum in tracing the line from the first political painting of Seán Keating in 1915 to the present-day work by Michael Farrell and Robert Ballagh, as well as the twin streams of activity in landscape painting and in the movement towards abstraction, the first represented by Paul Henry and Maurice MacGonigal and the latter by Norah MacGuiness and Cecil King.   C MacG
Anne Crookshank and The Knight of Glin, *The Painters of Ireland 1660–1920*, 1978; Bruce Arnold, *A Concise History of Irish Art*, 1969.

Pale, The. With reference to Ireland the term has been used loosely of the area of English influence in central-eastern counties. An identifiable Pale emerged by the mid-15th century, extending over parts of the counties of Dublin, Meath, Kildare and Louth, but its frontiers were subject to changes due to the periodic incursion of the Irish on its borders.   B de B

Parliament House, The (Dublin). Now the Bank of Ireland, this was the first building in the world designed and built to house a parliament. It was designed by Sir EDWARD LOVETT PEARCE in 1728 to fit between existing houses in the street line and included the colonnaded entrance court, the octagonal Commons chamber and the House of Lords; it was finished in 1739 after Pearce's death. JAMES GANDON added the Corinthian portico on the Westmoreland Street side in 1785 and Robert Parke added the Ionic portico, in Foster Place, in 1792. These porticos were linked to the original entrance by curved screen walls. After the Act of Union the Parliament House was sold to the Bank of Ireland, which employed FRANCIS JOHNSTON to dismantle the House of Commons, build the present cash office in place of the Court of Requests and rebuild screen walls so that they matched.   W G

passage grave. A type of Neolithic burial, of which some 250–300 examples are known in Ireland. In its classic form, it is a chamber approached by a passage under a round tumulus. In Ireland the chamber is often transeptal, the roof corbelled; the stones of walls, roof and kerb have carved designs. Simple forms with little or no passage are known, particularly in Antrim and Sligo. Irish tombs are often sited on hilltops and grouped in cemeteries. The finds with cremated burials are distinctive: Carrowkeel pottery, mushroom-head antler pins, hammer and other pendants and beads of semi-precious stones, and chalk and clay balls. No tools and weapons are found with burials. *See* CARROWMORE, DOWTH, KNOWTH, LOUGHCREW, NEWGRANGE, and STONE AGE.   M H

Patrick, Saint. The Romano-British Christian, whose name appears to have been Magonus Succatus Patricius, credited with the evangelization and conversion to CHRISTIANITY of the inhabitants of Ireland in the 5th century. The traditional date for the commencement of Patrick's mission – that given by the Irish annalists, 432 – is the year following that in which Pope Celestine I sent one Palladius to the Christians in Ireland as their first bishop. Two documents written by Patrick were transcribed into the BOOK OF ARMAGH. One is a brief autobiographical apology and testimony in Latin known as the *Confessio*; the other, also in Latin, known as the *Epistola* or *The Letter to Coroticus*, is a complaint to a chieftain who had abducted and enslaved some of Patrick's neophytes. In the *Confessio* Patrick named his place of origin but it has never been satisfactorily identified. In his youth he was abducted from his parents' villa and taken to Ireland where he remained for some years as a slave, returning there subsequently as a missionary. The earliest Patrician hagiographies to survive are the one by Tirechan, written *c.* 670, and the one by Muirchú, written about the close of the 7th century. Much of the corpus of Patrician legend, however, comes from the *Bethu Phátraic* (TRIPARTITE LIFE), an account compiled at the end of the 9th century, and from the 12th-century Latin life written by Jocelin of Furness.

The cave known as St Patrick's Purgatory, on an island in Lough Derg, was celebrated in Europe in the Middle Ages as the real entrance to Purgatory. It inspired a number of literary works including Marie de France's 2,000-word rhyming lay *L'Espurgatoire de Seint Patriz*, written *c.* 1190 and based on Henry of Saltrey's *Tractatus de Purgatorio S. Patricii*.

A revival of devotion to and interest in St Patrick accompanied the growth of Irish nationalism in the 18th century. JAMES BARRY painted his *St Patrick Baptizing the King of Cashel* in 1760–3. This subject and other miracles attributed to Patrick, especially the Banishment of the Snakes from Ireland, were popular in Irish religious art in the 19th century, when the saint himself was usually depicted as a venerable figure in contemporary episcopal vestments.   B de B

L. Bieler, *The Life and Legend of St Patrick*, 1949; B. de Breffny, *In The Steps of St Patrick*, 1982; R. P. C. Hanson, *Saint Patrick, His Origins and Career*, 1968.

Petrie, George. *Pilgrims at Clonmacnois*, watercolour; Petrie's interest in Ireland's past provided a stimulus for a number of contemporary artists. NGI.

Paulin, Tom (1949–). Poet; born in Leeds, England, but brought up in Belfast, he has published two carefully constructed collections, *A State of Justice* (1977) and *The Strange Museum* (1980).   T McC

Pearce, Colman (1938–). Conductor; born in Dublin, he has conducted the RTE Symphony Orchestra since 1966, and was appointed its Principal Conductor in January 1981. He has also appeared with orchestras in most European countries, in the USA and in Brazil. He has directed many important premières of Irish composers' works and of 20th-century music in general.   AGH

Pearce, Sir Edward Lovett (*c.* 1699–1733). Architect; he was a cousin of Sir John Vanbrugh, for whom he worked in London. He was probably the first architect to travel in Italy to see the buildings of antiquity at first hand, and while there he corresponded with the prominent architect Alessandro Galilei. His annotated copy of Palladio's *Quattro Libri* . . . survives, as do several of his drawings (in the Elton Hall collection). He is credited with the introduction of the Venetian and Diocletian window to Ireland. His surviving, authenticated works include: the obelisk and grotto at Stillorgan, Co. Dublin; the Palace at Cashel, Co. Tipperary (*c.* 1731); BELLAMONT FOREST, Co. Cavan (1729); Nos. 9 and 10 Henrietta Street, Dublin; CASTLETOWN, Co. Kildare (1722–32), which he supervised for Galilei; and the south side of the Upper Castle Yard and the PARLIAMENT HOUSE, begun in 1728, with its magnificent colonnaded entrance court and sumptuous House of Lords. He was appointed Surveyor-General (1730) for this last work, and was knighted in 1732. A number of other buildings have been attributed to him on stylistic grounds. He also sat as MP for Ratoath, Co. Meath. *See* pl. XVI.   WG

Maurice Craig, 'Sir Edward Lovett Pearce', *IGS Bulletin*, vol. xvii (1974), p. 10.

Peskett, William (1952–). Poet; by profession a science teacher in Ulster, he is a writer of unusual talent. He has employed the images of zoology with great effect in two collections, *The Nightowls Dissection* (1975) and *Survivors* (1980).   T McC

Petrie, George (1790–1866). Antiquary, topographical artist and musicologist; born in Dublin, he travelled extensively throughout Ireland, studying, sketching and describing ruins and collecting airs, the first printed edition of which eventually appeared 1902–5. In 1845 Petrie published *The Ecclesiastical Architecture of Ireland*, followed by his essay on *The Origin and Uses of the Round Towers of Ireland*, and edited *The Petrie Collection of the Ancient Music of Ireland* (1855). In 1857 he was elected PRHA. *See* also 'PETRIE CROWN'.   B de B

W. Stokes, *The Life and Labours in Art and Archaeology of George Petrie*, 1868.

'Petrie Crown'. A metal object of unknown provenance and unknown purpose. Formerly in the collection of GEORGE PETRIE and now in the National

'Petrie Crown'. The fragmentary Iron Age object, showing La Tène scroll decoration. NMI.

Museum of Ireland, it belongs to a small group of Iron Age objects decorated in a special manner. The design is in relief, produced by cutting away the background. The object consists of a decorated plate, pierced for attachment to a backing, which has been regularly cut away to create an openwork effect. Two concave roundels are attached to the plate and from the back of one of them, a hollow bronze horn extends. The horn and roundels bear elaborate, fine LA TÈNE scrollwork, some with suggestions of bird-headed endings and settings for enamel; one small stud survives. The object dates to about the 1st century AD.　　　MFR

Philosophic Society. The Society, which existed from 1683 to 1705, was founded in Dublin on the model of the Royal Society in London.　　　MC

photography. The earliest Irish photographer of whom records survive was Francis S. Beatty (1806–91) of Belfast. He used the daguerreotype process in 1839, shortly after its publication. The first portrait studio was opened in Dublin at the Rotunda by Doussin Dubreuil (active 1841–45), and this was soon followed by the establishment of a studio by Leon Gluckman (active 1843–67), who was the most important of these early practitioners. Beatty opened the first Belfast studio in 1842 and Cork's earliest studio was started by Edmund Harding (active c. 1843–65).

Photographs were included in exhibitions of the DUBLIN SOCIETY during the 1840s, but the first real photographic exhibition was that organized at the Dublin Exhibition of 1853. This showed works by local as well as foreign photographers.

The Dublin Photographic Society – renamed the Photographic Society of Ireland (P.S.I.) in 1858 – was founded in 1854; its founder-members included Sir

John J. Coghill (active 1853–65) and James Robinson (active 1853–70).

Notable individual photographers included John Shaw Smith (active 1850–60), who used the calotype process to record scenes in the Middle East in 1851, and William D. Hemphill (active 1857–65), whose scenes of Clonmel and its district photographed in stereo were published in a book in 1860.

Photography was also practised at many of Ireland's great houses including Clonbrock (Hon. Luke Dillon, active 1860–70), Lismore Castle (Francis Curry, 1814–96) and Birr Castle (the Countess of Rosse, active in the 1860s).

The International Exhibition held in Dublin in 1865 included an extensive photographic section containing works by many leading British as well as Irish practitioners. By that year views of Ireland were being produced by James Simonton (active 1855–70) and Frederick H. Mares (active 1860–80), while William Lawrence (1840–1932) began selling views in the early 1870s. In Belfast, Robert Welsh (active c. 1875–1900) produced an extensive series of views of the northern counties. During the 1880s and 1890s the most important Irish photographer was Alfred Werner (1859–1944), who used a giant camera to produce an almost life-size portrait of Maud Gonne in 1893.

The so-called 'Art Photographic' movement, active during the early years of the twentieth century, was responsible for the production of a great deal of banal and trite work. Photographs tended to be derivative of the sentimental painting of the period. These years were troubled ones in Ireland and provided exciting material for documentary photographers, the most outstanding of whom was Joseph Cashman (active 1910–30).

In 1921, a magazine, *The Camera*, was published in Dublin by William Harding (d. 1929); although originally intended to cater only for Ireland, it soon came to be recognized as one of the most enlightened organs on the subject. During the 1930s the influence of ideas from America and the Continent began to be apparent in the work of Irish photographers, among the most outstanding of whom at that time were Alex Day (active 1935–50) and F. R. McCormick (active 1930–42).

After World War II the number of Irish photographers increased greatly. Most work produced, however, was of low standard, the best practitioner being Richard Deegan (1909–73). From 1946 the Photographic Society began organizing biennial Irish Salons. These helped to keep local photographers in touch with international trends.

Until recently the only exhibitions in Ireland were those organized by the P.S.I. and the various clubs, but in 1978 came the opening in Dublin of the Gallery of Photography; this was responsible for generating a lot of fresh interest, culminating in the exhibition 'Out of the Shadows' (organized by the ARTS COUNCIL) in 1981, including works by over forty photographers, of whom Fergus Bourke, Rodney Tuach and Richard Haughton are probably the best known. In 1980, the Ulster Museum mounted an exhibition of

photography. A study by William D. Hemphill, *c.* 1862; Miss Osborne of Newton Anner, Co. Tipperary.

photography. *Child Study at Clonbrook House, c.* 1865, by the Hon. Luke Dillon.

photography. *Itinerant Caravan in Snow*, 1966, by Fergus Bourke.

photography by George Mott from his lavishly illustrated volume *The Land of Ireland* (1979), which has been published in English, American and German editions.

Photographic collections are housed in: National Library of Ireland; Photographic Society of Ireland; Public Record Office, Belfast; Ulster Museum; Ulster Folk Museum; and some county libraries hold collections relating to their areas. ECC

plasterwork. As an adjunct of architecture, decorative plasterwork, or stuccowork, is dependent on current architectural styles. When architecture flourished so did decorative plasterwork. However, there was one period, in the mid-18th century, when plasterwork developed into an art form independent of architecture.

Materials and technique: Decorative plasterwork was made of plaster of paris (hydrous calcium sulphate) mixed with water, the hardening being retarded by the addition of slaked lime. The plaster used as a base was keyed into oak or fir laths and reinforced with cattle hair, while raised work was reinforced with ash twigs, copper wire or nails. It was the lack of a suitable reinforcing agent which has caused so many bird's heads to fall off Irish plasterwork. Cornices and mouldings were run off with templates. Decoration such as modillion blocks, dentils and egg-and-dart were made in gelatine moulds, while foliage and figurative work etc. was worked by hand.

It seems likely that the art of decorative plasterwork was introduced with the trickle of Classical ideas which entered Ireland in the mid-16th century. The earliest recorded and finest surviving example of the period is in the ORMOND MANOR HOUSE, Carrick-on-Suir, Co. Tipperary (1565). The compartmented ceilings contain fretwork, coats-of-arms and initials. The wall friezes have panes with arabesques, portraits and allegorical figures. Native influences are seen at Bunratty, Co. Clare, where ceilings of *c.* 1620 are divided by ribs into panels which contain scroll and floral ornaments. Bunches of grapes and vine leaves were a favourite motif – they occur in a window

plasterwork. Ceiling in the Rococo style in Áras an Uachtaráin, with figures of putti, animals and birds in high relief; anonymous, 18th century.

plasterwork. An example of early 18th-century work in the House of Lords (now the Bank of Ireland): the La Touche ceiling, by an unidentified hand, based on Watteau's *Venus Wounded by Love.*

embrasure in the old Cashel cathedral – and were copied from carved stone ornament.

Little is known of 17th-century plasterwork, though the ceilings at Eyrecourt, Co. Galway (*c.* 1660), known from photographs, BEAULIEU, Co. Louth (*c.* 1670), and the Royal Hospital, KILMAINHAM (*c.* 1680), suggest that cornices were employed in conjunction with simple mouldings and raised beams with fretwork. This form may have been derived from ceiling construction where the heavy beams projected below the flat surface of the ceiling. Though Eyrecourt had palm leaves in the compartments and the Royal Hospital chapel ceiling is heavily encrusted with flowers, fruit and oak branches, figurative work was absent and most ceilings were plain. Early 18th-century examples include those at BELLAMONT FOREST, Co. Cavan, the House of Lords (now the Bank of Ireland; *see* PARLIAMENT HOUSE), 9 Henrietta Street, Dublin, and Howth Castle, Co. Dublin. (This form of compartmented plasterwork continued until the arrival of the FRANCINI brothers in the 1730s.)

The Francini brothers are credited with the introduction of figurative work into Ireland (*see* pl. XVII); they were contemporary with Artari and Bugatti in England. Though Italian, and using a style which ultimately derived from Italy, they were influenced by French Rococo and the designs of Jean Bérain (1637–1711). However, Cesare Ripa's *Iconologia* (1603) was a favourite source-book for the personification of Classical mythology. Watteau's *Venus Wounded by Love* was used as a model for the La Touche ceiling now in the Bank of Ireland. It belongs to a group of ceilings by an unknown hand, which include those at Mespil

House (now in the official residence of the President, Áras an Uachtaráin) and at Belvedere House, Co. Westmeath. The audacious Tracton House ceiling (*c.* 1746), now in Dublin Castle, is by another unknown hand. BARTHOLOMEW CRAMILLION was the last of the great figurative stuccodores to work in Ireland.

A distinctive Irish school of plasterwork developed in the 1750s, headed by ROBERT WEST. Figures are not a strong element of their work, which is typified by luxuriant foliage, putti and fruit and flowers, both in bunches and in baskets. The stuccodores excelled in musical trophies and stylized birds which are a cross between seagulls and pheasants. The strong sculptural element which typifies this period (at its height between 1755 and 1765) is often seen in the charming details befitting the owner or function of a particular building.

The earliest examples of Neo-Classical stuccowork are probably the ceilings in Dublin by Sir WILLIAM CHAMBERS, in Charlemont House (1762) and Leinster House (1767). The exact meeting point of Rococo and Neo-Classical can be seen in Powerscourt House, Dublin (1771), with Rococo work by James McCullagh and Adamesque work by MICHAEL STAPLETON in the same building. Richardson's *Book of Ceilings* (1776) and Columbani's *New Book of Ornament* (1775) were influential contemporary sources, while James Adam sent designs for Langford House, Dublin (demolished) and Headfort, Co. Meath; James Wyatt sent designs for Curraghmore, Co. Waterford, Westport, Co. Mayo, Leinster House, Dublin, and Mount Kennedy, Co. Wicklow. This period is particularly well documented through the accounts of the quantity accountant Bryan Bolger, who was active between the 1770s and the 1820s.

Provincial plasterers are less well documented than those working in Dublin. However, Patrick Osborne is an important figure who worked with masterful Rococo lightness. His work is found in the Mercy Hospital, Cork (1765–73), CASTLETOWN, Co. Kilkenny

plasterwork. Staircase ceiling in Powerscourt House, Dublin, 1771.

(for which his detailed accounts of 1774 have survived), the Chamber of Commerce at Waterford (*c.* 1780), and possibly Dunsandle, Co. Galway. Particularly charming Neo-Classical work is to be found in Co. Limerick at Glin Castle and Ash Hill Towers.

Early 19th-century stuccodores came increasingly under the control of architects, resulting in such work as at the Chapel Royal, Dublin Castle, by George Stapleton. As interiors became more severe, the role of the stuccodore diminished. However, the MORRISONS gave their stuccodores an opportunity to excel in virtuosity if not in invention. Christopher Moore worked on the dining room at CARTON, Co. Kildare, and Mr Popje at Kilruddery, Co. Wicklow. Further plasterwork executed under the Morrisons is to be seen at Ballyfin, Co. Laois, Fota, Co. Cork, and Baronscourt, Co. Tyrone.   WG
C. P. Curran, *Dublin Decorative Plasterwork of the 17th and 18th Centuries*, 1967.

Plunkett, James (pseudonym of James Plunkett Kelly; 1920–). Television producer and writer; born in Dublin, he was once an official in the Workers' Union of Ireland. He wrote his first play, *The Risen People*, about James Larkin and the 1913 Strike. His first novel, *Strumpet City* (1969), takes a panoramic view of Dublin, at the same time encompassing the Labour movement, Irish Socialism and the industrialization of Ireland. Its successor is *Farewell Companions* (1977).   BH

poetry. Although the evidence of such Irish epics as the TÁIN BÓ CUAILNGE ('The Cattle Raid of Cooley') shows that the Irish poetic imagination has a history going back over 2,000 years, Irish poetry was first committed to writing only in the 6th and 7th centuries. By the 8th century the clerical scholars (who had adapted the Latin alphabet to the IRISH LANGUAGE) had evolved many of the metrical systems that would survive for a thousand years. The earliest poems are brief *haiku*-like nature lyrics, spare in their descriptive beauty, written by monks whose perceptions of the world were brief afterthoughts that followed hours of divine contemplation, e.g.:

> Deep-red the bracken, its shape all gone
> The wild goose has raised his wonted cry.
>   (*trans. Kuno Meyer*).

However, the idea that monks initiated the composition of Irish poetry is a false one – they were preceded by a caste of professional poets, *fili* or *aes dana*.

The *file* was an aristocrat by nature and in outlook, who may have served an apprenticeship of up to twelve years and whose status in society was second only to that of the king. The power of the *file* lasted from pre-Christian times to the break-up of the old Gaelic order after the Battle of Kinsale (1601), and that power often focused within one family such as the Ó DALAIGHS or the Ó Cleirighs.

The period 1200–1600 was the golden era of the professional poets. Although society was continuously turbulent and war-torn, the *fili* remained miles from the nearest skirmish. They praised their warring chieftains, and reassured their masters with long genealogical verses. The poetry of this period strikes the modern reader as stuffy, boring and wantonly intricate; but that same poetry is one of the highest technical achievements in syllabic metre, or *dan direoch* ('perfect verse'). The *dan direoch* of the period – with its half-rhyme, end-rhyme, alliteration and consonance – would constitute a major achievement in any civilization.

The Ó Dalaigh family were the most prestigious and fruitful brood of professional-poet families. Muireadach Ó Dalaigh, poet of the O'Donnell's, had to flee to Scotland when he murdered O'Donnell's steward, but returned to the fold after composing a poem of apology. His most beautiful poem is a deeply personal work, 'M'anam do sgar riomsa a-raoir' ('My life left me last night'), a lament for his dead wife. Muireadach's brother Donnchadh Mor was considered by the Four Masters to be a religious poet of unsurpassable quality. His poem 'Truogh mo Thuras ar Loch Dearg' ('My Sorrowful Pilgrimage to Lough Derg') is one of repentance and real religious fervour. Before Donnchadh Mor died in 1244 his poems had become widely known and repeated. Yet another Ó Dalaigh, Aonghus Mac Doighre, was poet to the O'Byrnes of Wicklow. A number of his poems advanced a sense of nationhood and a perception of racial subjugation that were far in advance of the strictly familial and tribal perceptions of the time. The last great poet of the bardic period, the last to speak with the full authority of unsubjugated civilization, was Eochaidh Ó hEoghusa (O'Hussey), poet of the Maguires. In the winter of 1600, when he parted from his master Hugh Maguire,

O'Hussey wrote the ode that would resound through Gaelic civilization: a poem whose tone was perfectly conveyed in the translation by the 19th-century Mangan – 'Where is my Chief, my Master, this bleak night . . .?'

Although Kinsale (1601) is a watershed in the affairs of the Irish language, 'O'Husseys Ode' was by no means the final yelp of a defeated tongue. The underlying social system that supported an aristocratic caste of poets collapsed during the Elizabethan era, but Irish poetry remained a vibrant activity for two further centuries. Although its frontiers were narrowed, its life-chances pared away by English statutes, some of the finest Gaelic poets, such as Ó BRUADAIR, Ó RATHAILLE, BRIAN MERRIMAN and EIBHLIN DUBH NI CHONAILL, would emerge in the 17th and 18th centuries. One of the characteristics of the Gaelic poetry after the collapse of the Irish social order is the manner in which the sense of wounded pride persists, as if the later poets believed that all was *not* lost. The continuation of that sense of pride and the hope of redemption was best embodied in a new kind of poem – AISLING – which developed in the early 18th century. In this a vision-woman appeared to the entranced poet and promised the return of the Stuarts to Ireland.

The COURTS OF POETRY, those hot-beds of poetic pride and self-importance, survived in a less formal manner into the latter half of the 18th century. One particular Court of Poetry, that of Tadgh Ó Duinnin, bard of the MacCarthys, is recorded by Daniel Corkery in his *Hidden Ireland*. That particular 'Court' was later transferred from Ó Duinnin to Liam an Duna at Whitechurch, Co. Cork. In 1738 Seán Ó Murchu na Raithineach took over as chief poet, and he survived until 1762, having lived as a farmer and a semi-professional scholar-poet. There were many other such schools of poetry in Munster: in the Sliabh Luachra district near Killarney; in Croom, Co. Limerick, presided over by Seán Ó Tuama. At Ballymocoda a Court of Poetry was organized by Piaras Mac Gearailt. Seventeenth-century Ulster was also well-endowed with semi-professional poets. SEÁN DALL MAC CUARTA is probably the finest of the newer lyricists. His best-known poems, such as 'An Lonn Dubh Baite' ('The Drowned Blackbird') and 'Fáilte don Ean' ('Welcome to the Bird'), are written in a new form called *Tri Rainn agus Amhran* (literally, 'three verses and a song'); the first three verses are in loose syllabic metre, while the final verse was in popular song metre. Peader Ó Doirnin was another Ulster poet who had a superb knowledge of the complex poetics of the Bardic era but who chose to write with a more simple musical intention. His love-song 'Urchnoc Chein Mhic Cainte' ('The newly cultivated hill of Chein Mhic Chainte') is his most famous work, full of the music of words themselves –

A chiuinbhean tsuimh na gcuochann pearloch
Gluais lion fein ar ball beog

('O quiet sweet-natured woman of the pearly tresses,
Come away with me in a little while'.)

Cathal Buidha Mac Giolla Ghunna (1680–1756) was another Ulster poet. He had studied for the priesthood but abandoned his vocation and settled for the life of a wandering poet. His most famous composition, 'An Bonnan Bui' ('The Yellow Bittern'), has been universally translated and quoted by Irish poets as a final word on the need for heavy drinking – 'oir chan fhaigheann sibh traon i ndiadh bhur mbais' ('because you won't get a drop after you're dead').

Two great voices, those of Brian Merriman and Eibhlin Dubh Ni Chonaill, extend the world of Gaelic poetry as far as the 19th century. Merriman survived until 1803, Eibhlin Dubh (aunt of Daniel O'Connell, the Liberator) may have died in 1800. Merriman, an illegitimate child, was born near Ennistymon in Co. Clare. Although his compositions are few, he is famous for his great comic poem 'Cuirt an Mhean Oiche' ('The Midnight Court'). This 1,000 line *tour-de-force* describes an assembly of women presided over by Aoibheall, queen of the fairies. The poem is divided into five major sections; a prologue – which is a parody of the aisling form – three monologues and an epilogue. The poem uses bawdy descriptions of courtship, condemns agile priests for not marrying and marriage for its failure; finally, it praises all bastards in a riotous send-up of puritan Catholic values of the time. Eibhlin Dubh Ni Chonaill's fame rests also on her production of a single great poem – 'Caoineadh Airt Ui Laoghaire' ('Lament for Art O'Leary') – an elegy for her dead husband, officer of the Hungarian Hussars, who had returned to live on his family estate near Macroom, Co. Cork. Ó Laoghaire was shot dead by the bodyguard of the High Sheriff, Abraham Norris, with whom he had had a bitter dispute about a valuable horse. Eibhlin Dubh's poem is an elegy of exquisite proud beauty, one of the greatest poems in the Irish language –

Oir do shileas feinig
na marbh an saol tu
nuair cheannaios duit eide

('For I thought myself
that life could not kill you
when I bought your uniform')

The 19th century. In the early years of the century Irish was still used extensively and Gaelic poets continued to make their mark in a mild way – one thinks of Antoine Raifteiri (1784–1835), the folk poet of Co. Mayo, or of Amlaoibh Ó Súilleabháin (1780–1838), the poet, businessman and teacher of Callan, Co. Kilkenny – but it became increasingly difficult for a cultivated man to express himself in Gaelic only. Most of the material of high culture was now in the English language. While an Irish poet could turn a blind eye to the poems of Spenser or the Earl of Clancarty in the 17th century, he could not ignore the literary world of EDMUND BURKE and OLIVER GOLDSMITH in the 18th. The English language had thrust its way into the lives of the people so that a writer would be compelled to use English. Goldsmith and SWIFT are considered by many commentators to be the first mature literary voices of Ireland in English literature. Both were Englishmen by persuasion, outlook and tradition; their club-life is the club-life of London, their Irishness merely a local colour or quirk of character within the Englishness of their lives.

The 19th century produced little verse of high literary merit. The laureate of the early part of the century was undoubtedly THOMAS MOORE, who towers over second-rate Irish literature like a great weed. His 'melodies', sweet-sorrowful songs, were written to the music collected by PETRIE, Holden and BUNTING. Moore was a close friend of Byron and the first biographer of Lord Edward Fitzgerald: he shared with Byron a love of powerful openings such as

> The harp that once through Tara's halls
> The soul of music shed,
> Now hangs as mute on Tara's walls
> As if that soul were fled.

James Clarence Mangan (1803–49) is the first un-ambiguously indigenous Irish voice to surface in English poetry. His life was brief but fruitful: he produced 'versions' of Persian, Hindustani, Coptic and Irish poems that have an urgency wholly foreign to the anaemic ballads of the time, as in this example from 'Shapes and Signs':

> I see black dragons mount the sky,
> I see earth yawn beneath my feet –
> I feel within the asp, the worm
> That will not sleep and cannot die.

Many of Mangan's poems and translations appeared in print in the pages of the *Nation* newspaper, organ of the Young Ireland Movement, founded by THOMAS DAVIS.

Davis encouraged the translation and re-telling in verse of tales from Irish MYTHOLOGY. He had been preceded in this task by JAMES FERGUSON, who had published nineteen translations from the Irish in the *Dublin University Magazine*. Ferguson spent nearly thirty years trying to write a national epic based on a translation of 'Cath Muighe Rath' ('The Battle of Moyra'). He finished his task but failed ultimately in his ambition to unify political and cultural conscious-ness in one great work. Ferguson's work of translation is important, however, in that it paved the way for others to use Irish mythology as materials for poems in English. He succeeded in unearthing a cultural resource that would be employed in the Irish Literary Revival. One 19th-century achievement that was unknown to those literary men was the vast quantity of street-ballads and folk-songs that evolved within the slums and rural areas. The most famous balladeer of all was 'Zozimus', who would be recalled and invoked in the essays and poetry of W. B. Yeats.

The Irish Literary Revival. Criticism of the 19th century for its sentimentality ignores the fact that the century also produced W. B. YEATS, A.E., JAMES STEPHENS, LADY GREGORY and J. M. SYNGE – the backbone of the Irish Literary Revival. The movement of nationalism that was enshrined in the *Nation* and the habit of culture that was a heritage of Davis and Ferguson accelerated as the century progressed. After the bungling of the

Irish Party in the 1880s, the bulk of Irish hopes fell from the lap of Parnell into the arms of the Irish Post-Pre-Raphaelites. It took the shock of poetical failure to break up the more general idea of Irishness and focus it instead on specific acts of culture. 'Sgar an Solus' ('Spread the Light') was the motto of the Southwark Club which was formed into a larger literary com-mittee in January 1883. That literary club attracted the attention of one young poet whose work had begun to appear in the *Irish Fireside* and the *Dublin University Review*. The poet was W. B. Yeats, who was accom-panied to the early meetings by John Todhunter and Katherine Tynan.

Yeats was the greatest poet to come out of Ireland. One tends to see him as a giant consumer, taking energy from every source as his talent grew, from politics, Indian and Irish mythology, from friendship and love, from philosophy and the occult. His earliest poems, such as 'Anashuya and Vijaya' or 'The Indian to his Love', are full of the vague expressions of the English Pre-Raphaelites; but his discovery of Irish themes and his unrequited love for Maud Gonne tended to focus his talent and toughen his imagery. By the time he edited the Methuen *Book of Irish Verse* (1895) he would aim his talents at 'that educated and national public, which is our greatest need and perhaps our vainest hope'. Yeats was a committed writer, deeply concerned to heighten the value of his poetry. When he published *In the Seven Woods* (1904) he was concerned with the aims and processes of art, themes handled brilliantly in his first really excellent poem, 'Adam's Curse'.

Yeats became committed to many public activities; the formation of a National Theatre, the establishment of a Municipal Gallery in Dublin and to the endless attack on the philistine middle class of Ireland who felt no need for art. The Rising of 1916 had a profound effect on Yeats; one effect undoubtedly was the feeling of having been upstaged by inferior men. The poems that arose out of the event should be read as part of Yeats's therapy to retrain his *poetic* in the light of the new political situation. In 1917, the year he married George Hyde-Lees, Yeats published *The Wild Swans at Coole*. This book, with its great poems in praise of Lady Gregory's world – 'Her Praise' and 'In Memory of Major Robert Gregory', deepened the heroic strain in modern Irish poetry. It reasserted the frontier of wounded pride that one found earlier in the poems of Aogain Ó Rathaille and Eibhlin Dubh Ni Chonaill. Once he had found the heroic, Yeats used it with triumphant genius. His later books are full of the pride of race: *Michael Robartes and the Dancer* (1920) and *The Tower* (1928) assemble images of his family, characters from folklore and from his own prose-fiction, together with the last 1916 poetry. All of these images were woven into and tested by his philosophy of world birth and decay propounded in *A Vision* (1925).

Among Yeats's literary companions was A.E., whose first collection, *Homeward: Songs By The Way*, was published in 1894. A committed theosophist and philanthropist, A.E. would never allow his intellect to overcome his vision, so that his poetry remained fey and otherworldly. He was an indefatigable commentator on Irish affairs and a number of his essays, such as 'Thoughts for a Convention' and 'Idea of a Rural Community', still have great relevance to present-day Ireland. His 'Letters' also have profound consequences for Irishmen and place A.E. in the forefront of European literary peace-makers along with Romain Rolland and Hermann Hesse.

Poetry after Yeats. The generation that survived Yeats includes such fine poets as JOSEPH CAMPBELL, PADRAIC COLUM, F. R. HIGGINS, AUSTIN CLARKE and PATRICK KAVANAGH. Campbell and Colum will be remembered mainly for their simple lyrics that try to recapture the folk-poetry of an earlier era; one thinks of Campbell's 'The Old Woman' or 'The Dancer' and of Colum's 'A Drover' and 'A Poor Scholar of the Forties'. F. R. Higgins, a serious man and a more serious poet, will always be remembered for his beautiful poems 'The Boyne Walk' and 'Father and Son' –

> Only last week, walking the hushed fields
> of our most lovely Meath . . .

Austin Clarke was the most prolific poet of the post-Yeats era. His first book, *The Vengeance of Fionn* (1917), owed something to Yeats's *Wandering of Oisin*. His first *Collected Poems* appeared in 1936 after he had spent fifteen years in London, and in 1974 the Dolmen Press published a collected edition in three volumes. Between these years Clarke had founded the Dublin Verse Speaking Society with Robert Farren, had run the Lyric Theatre Company at the Abbey, published *Collected Plays* (1962), as well as autobiographical material and two volumes of poetry, *Flight to Africa* (1963) and *Old-fashioned Pilgrimage* (1967). As Clarke grew older, his satirical tooth grew sharp and long. He attacked institutions of State, the Catholic Church and the spiritual poverty of literary circles.

Patrick Kavanagh was another poet who wrote lyrics of exquisite and memorable beauty. Kavanagh had been a small farmer and his work is full of rural images, but his poems have none of the vagueness that one finds in the rustic lyrics of the 'Revival' period. His poems are urgent, they move with the speed of a really new poetic talent. Poems such as 'Spraying the Potatoes' and 'A Christmas Childhood' carry the hallmark of an Irish mysticism. In the late 1930s, Kavanagh moved to Dublin, a decision he often regretted. In the 1940s he published *A Great Hunger*, a long poem that studied the sexual and cultural deprivations of rural life, as well as the collection *A Soul for Sale*. The 1950s was Kavanagh's most traumatic period: he founded his own newspaper, *Kavanagh's Weekly*, became involved in a horrible libel case, and developed cancer of the lungs. He was an impatient man, short-tempered with those who were bumptious or over-serious. His *Collected Poems* were published in 1964, and he died three years later, leaving behind one of the most enduring collections of lyrics in Irish literature: poems like 'Shancoduff', 'Epic' and 'Canal Bank Walk'. Kavanagh's work does not travel well outside Ireland; his world view is deeply Catholic and rural, his piety is Irish. His work repays constant study,

as it reflects the only mystic voice to emerge from Irish Catholicism.

While Kavanagh and Clarke were the most powerful poetic presences in Dublin after Yeats, an Ulsterman, LOUIS MACNEICE, was the most distinguished expatriate poet. MacNeice had had an English education and he had come to prominence as a poet while linked with the left-wing writers of the 1930s. He was a philosopher and a classicist by training. These twin disciplines fostered his unique poetic voice of controlled emotions and melancholy. Irishness was a condition that constantly fascinated MacNeice. The lines in 'Dublin' perfectly demonstrate his relationship with the land that produced him:

> . . . she will not
> Have me alive or dead
> But yet she holds my mind.

His best book of the 1930s, *Autumn Journal* (1939), demonstrates both the range of his craft and the obsessions of a genteel Irishman.

In the early 1940s MacNeice returned from the USA, where he had been lecturing, to join the British war effort. At this time his intellectual capacity became more responsive and wide-ranging – he wrote the book *W. B. Yeats* (1941), and for the BBC the powerful radio play *The Dark Tower* (1946), as well as propaganda pamphlets like *Meet the U.S. Army* (1943). In the 1950s MacNeice's career lost its impetus: both *Ten Burnt Offerings* (1952) and *Autumn Sequel* (1954) were poorly received by critics. It has become a cliché to say that an artist finds new vigour in old age, but this is exactly what happened in MacNeice's case. In *Visitations* (1957), *Solstices* (1961) and the posthumous *The Burning Perch* (1963) he returns to classical preoccupations with death and decay, melancholy and despair.

After the mysticism of Kavanagh and the good grammar of MacNeice, we come to the high seriousness of THOMAS KINSELLA and JOHN MONTAGUE, the two distinctive voices to emerge from the late 1950s. Kinsella is the author of the most challenging poetry ever written in Ireland; his learning, his astonishing capacity to splinter the psyche within poems, have led him into the mainstream. In books like *Nightwalker and Other Poems* (1968) or *Notes from the Land of the Dead and Other Poems* (1972) he demonstrates a capacity to encompass and illuminate the darkest secrets of the human condition. John Montague, on the other hand, is a poet of the open territory, a poet of courtship and politics. From the expansive poems of *A Chosen Light* (1967) through the surreal *Tides* (1970) to the domestic worlds of *The Great Cloak* (1978) he uses the journeys of courtship, erotic love and childbearing as *loci* of larger statements. His single greatest work is a composite poem, both a tribal and intellectual analysis of the Ulster troubles, called *The Rough Field* (1972).

Three poets who preceded Montague and Kinsella chronologically but whose full importance did not emerge until the 1970s are THOMAS MACGREEVY, DENIS DEVLIN and BRIAN COFFEY. These three form an avant garde of international poetry within the Irish tradition, although Devlin is technically as conservative as Kavanagh. Coffey (b. 1905), the most intellectual and brilliant of that generation, published his *Selected Poems* as late as 1971, while his uncanny translations of Neruda appeared in 1973. MacGreevy was part of that group of Irish writers who lived in Paris in the 1920s and '30s. His *Poems* were published in 1934; individual works like 'De Civitate Hominum' and 'Nocturne of the Self-Evident Presence' he displays an ease of writing and a staccato rhythm that is more in tune with French achievements than with Irish poetry. Devlin published translations of St John Perse as well as his own work, the best of which is *Lough Derg and Other Poems* (1946).

Another poet whose career began in the early 1950s but whose burgeoning talent did not achieve full development until much later is RICHARD MURPHY, in *Sailing to an Island* (1963), and the *Battle of Aughrim* (1968). In his recent poetry he has moved away from his earlier seascapes; in poems like 'Tony White at Innisbofin 1959', 'Pier Bar' and 'Elixir' he has begun to explore the themes of power and nostalgia.

The late 1960s and early '70s saw the emergence of SEAMUS HEANEY, along with a group of accomplished poets from Ulster, notably MICHAEL LONGLEY, DEREK MAHON, PAUL MULDOON and James Simmons. Heaney's first two books, *Death of a Naturalist* (1966) and *Door into the Dark* (1969), invoke the special world of untroubled rural childhood, while *North* (1975) and *Field Work* (1979) focus on the more difficult themes of politics and love. Heaney is a poet of virtuosity, in particular when he uses the special imagery of bogland and farmland; his poems move with a language completely new and undiluted, as one feels, for example, when reading 'Exposure' or 'The Glanmore Sonnets'. Longley and Mahon are poets of grammar and erudition. Longley's books, particularly *Man Lying on a Wall* (1976) and *The Echo-Gate* (1980) combine severe ironic gesture with great learning in a successful effort to horrify the pleased reader. Mahon is a poet of unrelenting anguish who allows only the highest expressions of his art to live. Like Yeats, he is an indefatigable reviser; hence *Poems 1962–1978* is more than a collection of his previous work, it is reinterpreted eloquence.

Among the Irish-language poets who have been fruitful in contemporary Ireland are SEÁN Ó RIORDAIN, MÁIRTÍN Ó DIREAIN, MAIRE MAC AN TSAOI, and SEÁN Ó TUAMA. Seán Ó Riordain's work, particularly *Eireaball Spiedeoige* (1952) and *Tar Eis Mo Bhais* (1978), is sometimes pious in the manner of Kavanagh, while often intellectual and dense in the tradition of Denis Devlin or Kinsella. Mac An Tsaoi and Ó Tuama are both scholars for whom poetry is a professional area as well as a trait of character. Mac An Tsaoi is still a poet of deliberate simplicity, while Ó Tuama uses verse-drama as well as poetry to explore the attitudes and domestic pressures that precede human action and tragedy. A vibrant, even voracious, new generation of Irish-language poets has emerged in recent years; they include already established names like Thomas Mac Siomoin, CATHAL Ó SEARCAIGH, and MÍCHEAL Ó SIODHAIL, or the even newer NUALA NI DHOMHAILL and MÍCHEÁL Ó HAIRTNEIDE.

The success of such poetry publishers as Dolmen Press, Gallery Books and Raven Arts Press is symptomatic of the lively generation of younger poets now active in Ireland. In Ulster such new voices as FRANK ORMSBY and Medbh Mac Guckian have emerged, while in the Republic younger poets such as AIDAN CARL MATHEWS, THOMAS MACCARTHY or Dermot Bolger extend the range and develop muscle. New anthologies of verse like *Contemporary Irish Poetry* (1980) or *The Younger Irish Poets* (1982) have begun to demonstrate the range of activities on the contemporary scene.　　　　　　　　　　　　　　　　　　T McC

portal tomb. A simple rectilinear burial chamber of the Late Neolithic, having tall portals set inside the sidestones, and roofed by a capstone of great size. Often found at one end of a rectangular cairn, they occur mainly in Ulster, particularly mid-Ulster and Carlingford, and along both shores of the Irish Sea to Cornwall; about 150 examples are known in Ireland. *See* BALLYKEEL; STONE AGE.　　　　　　　　M H

Portumna Castle, Co. Galway. Built before 1618 for the 4th Earl of Clanricarde, but now only a shell, this was the most elegant and important strong-house of its day in Ireland; the house, with four projecting corner towers, consisted of three storeys over a basement, with four window bays between the towers. The ornate doorcase of the front door, with obelisks and strapwork, led to the Great Hall which extended the full width of the central four bays. The approach is through a series of axial gateways and courtyards.　　　　　　　B de B

Portumna Castle. The shell of the castle seen from across the courtyards.

Power, Tyrone. Lithograph by A. D'Orsay, 1839.

Pugh, Thomas and Richard. Clear glass goblet with engraved shamrock decoration, Dublin 1880.

Potter, A. J. (1918–80). Composer; born in Belfast, he studied under R. Vaughan Williams and settled in Dublin after World War II. His style is generally direct, at times sardonic and occasionally warmly romantic, cleverly concealing tone-rows and other academic devices in places. His *Piano Concerto da Chiesa* (1952) combines such disparate elements as a Chorale and an Irish slip jig. At his best, as in his *Sinfonia de Profundis* (1968) and his Second Symphony (in memory of President de Valéra), which received its posthumous première at Springfield, Mass., in December 1981, he communicates on equal terms with the musically sophisticated and the general listener. A television opera *Patrick*, screened in 1963, attracted wide notice and *The Wedding*, an amusing opera to his own libretto, was performed at the ABBEY THEATRE in June 1981. AGH

pottery. *See* CERAMICS.

Power, William Grattan Tyrone (1797–1841). Actor and playwright; born in Waterford, he started acting in Cardiff at the age of 14 and subsequently moved to London, after a time appearing almost exclusively in Irish parts. He starred in his own plays *Paddy Carey the Boy from Clogheen, The Irish Attorney, St Patrick's Eve*, etc. and in Mrs S. C. Hall's *The Groves of Blarney*. He visited America on prolonged tours on four occasions, and appeared regularly in Dublin until his death, by shipwreck, off Cape Cod. He was great-grandfather of the cinema actor Tyrone Power (1913–58) and the theatrical producer Sir TYRONE GUTHRIE. CF-S

Pugh, Thomas and **Richard.** Glass-makers. In the late 19th century the Pugh brothers produced high-quality engraved flint glass in Potter's Alley near Marlborough Place, Dublin. Their family had come from Stourbridge, Worcs., to the Cork Glass House (*see* GLASS) in the late 18th century. About 1855, Thomas and John Pugh joined with others in running a glass manufactory in Liffey Street, Dublin. In 1863 Thomas, his son Richard, and Thomas Leetch took over the lease of the old Potter's Alley Glasshouse and there continued production of clear and coloured glass (red, green, amber and purple) tableware, ornamental and chemical glassware, and lamps for railways and lighthouses. They employed master-engravers from Bohemia, Joseph Eisert and Franz Tieze, and they trained local men. Popular engraved decoration includes Bohemian deer and woodland scenes, fern decoration, and Celtic Revival motifs. Pieces were engraved also as souvenirs for national celebrations and for family occasions. MR

Pugin, Augustus Welby Northmore (1812–52). Architect; born in London, he was converted to Catholicism in 1835, the year which also marks the beginning of his career in architecture. Through his books, notably *The True Principles of Pointed or Christian Architecture* (1841), and his buildings Pugin did more than any other architect to foster the Gothic style in architecture. He believed that the form of a building should echo its function and that the building materials should reflect the character of the area in which they were used. Consequently his Irish churches are built of local stone, incorporate simple Irish motifs and have an air of austerity. He designed several churches in Co. Wexford, including Tagoat (1846) and the Cathedral at Enniscorthy (1843–50). His finest Irish work is the posthumously completed St Mary's Cathedral, Killarney (1842–55). W G

Phoebe Stanton, *Pugin*, 1971.

Purser, Sarah (1848–1943). Painter, designer and stained-glass artist; born in Co. Dublin, she trained at the Metropolitan School of Art, Dublin, in Paris at the Académie Julian, and in Italy. She returned to Dublin in 1878 and first exhibited at the Royal Hibernian Academy in that year. She was elected HRHA 1890, ARHA 1923 and RHA 1925. She was responsible for mounting the important joint exhibition of works by JOHN BUTLER YEATS and NATHANIEL HONE which was to result in HUGH LANE's patronage of those artists and his foundation of a modern art gallery in Dublin.

In 1903 she founded AN TÚR GLOINE, and in 1924 the Friends of the National Collections of Ireland to secure the safety of national treasures and to press for the return of the Lane pictures to Dublin. In 1930 she persuaded the head of the Irish Government, W. T. Cosgrave, to hand over Charlemont House in Dublin as the future home of the Lane Collection and the Modern Art Gallery. Examples of her own paintings are to be seen in all the national collections in Ireland. C MacG

Pye, Patrick (1929–). Painter and stained-glass designer; born in Winchester, he has lived in Dublin since 1932. He began painting with OISÍN KELLY at St Columba's College, Rathfarnham, and subsequently attended the National College of Art in Dublin. He was awarded the Mainie Jellett Scholarship for painting in Ireland. In 1955 he studied STAINED GLASS

at Dublin Art School, with Albert Troost in Holland, then with Patrick Pollen 1959–63. His first stained-glass commission was at LOUGHREA CATHEDRAL (1956); others include Glenstal Abbey, Co. Limerick (1957), Convoy, Co. Donegal (1968), and the Church of the Resurrection, Cave Hill Road, Belfast (1978). He is also noted for his many religious works and panel paintings in tempera. He is a founder-member of the Independent Artists Group and examples of his work are to be found in many public collections, including the Hugh Lane Municipal Gallery of Modern Art, Dublin. N G B/C MacG

Quin, James (1693–1766). Actor; born in Dublin, he was the illegitimate son of a barrister. He made his first appearance at Smock Alley in 1714. He moved to London, and became one of the leading actors of the era. Walpole, the prime minister, preferred his acting to that of Garrick. C F-S

Pye, Patrick. *The Mocking of Christ 3*, tempera on board. Private Collection.

Quin, James. The actor in the role of Falstaff; mezzotint by J. McArdell.

radio. Radio broadcasting may be said to have begun in Ireland in 1926 with a low-power 1-kw transmitter at McKee Barracks: the two earliest stations were known as Dublin 2RN and Cork 6CK; these became Radio Éireann under the jurisdiction of the Minister of Posts and Telegraphs. Radio Éireann's first coverage of a major event (for which a 60-kw transmitter was installed at Athlone) was of the Eucharist Congress in 1932. Early favourite programmes were Tommy O'Brien's opera requests, *Your Choice and Mine*, and the selections of disc-jockey Joe Linnane, both of which remained popular for decades, also radio plays and coverage of GAELIC ATHLETIC ASSOCIATION matches.

In 1970 the Government passed plans for Radio na Gaeltachta, beamed specifically to the Gaeltacht regions, with broadcasts in Irish. Studios in Kerry and Donegal are linked to the Gaeltacht studio in Connemara. This service devotes special attention to Irish music, stories and songs and also functions as a kind of archive, as it collects recordings of rapidly disappearing folk-arts like *Amhranaiocht ar an Sean-Nos* (singing in the old Irish traditional style) and the singing of highly ornamented and unaccompanied traditional songs.

Until the advent of TELEVISION programmes in the 1960s in Ireland, and especially in rural areas, the wireless set remained the primary source of home entertainment; radio broadcasting had, in consequence, a strong and widespread socio-cultural impact. The title Radio Telefís Éireann (RTE) was adopted in 1966 for the combined radio and television services. The second radio channel, opened in 1979, has freed the first channel for the more serious programmes. RTE has its own Symphony Orchestra and Concert Orchestra, its permanent choir, the RTE singers, and its Repertory Company with a permanent cast of actors and actresses, as well as a large library of historic recordings which include the voices of YEATS, SHAW and many other famous figures.　　　　EG

Rathcroghan (Crúachain), Co. Roscommon. An area 5 km. (3 miles) W of Tulsk, embracing at least 100 ancient monuments, including Early Iron Age burial mounds and RINGFORTS, on a set of NW/SE limestone ridges up to 150 m. (500 ft) above sea-level. Rathcroghan itself is a natural hillock, 63 m. (206 ft) across, scarped at the edges and with a small ring-barrow on top. Rathbeg, nearby to the W, is a small ring-barrow with three concentric banks, apparently faced with stone. Oweynagat (the Cats' Cave) is a limestone cave approached by a souterrain, two lintels of which have OGHAM inscriptions; it was reputedly the entrance to the Otherworld. The earliest monument of the complex is a COURT TOMB at Glenballythomas. Three stretches of roadway, the longest about 1 km. (1,100 yds), with sunken tracks bounded by low

parallel banks, run roughly E–W (cf. also the Banqueting Hall at TARA). In Irish MYTHOLOGY this is the seat of Ailill and Medb (Maeve), both celebrated in the TÁIN. At the SE edge of the complex is the inauguration-site of the O'Connor kings (*see* CARNFREE).　　　　MH

Rathgall, Co. Wicklow. A HILLFORT consisting of four concentric ramparts, covering 18 acres (7·28 hectares) on an E–W ridge at 135 m. (450 ft) above sea-level, E of Tullow; the central polygonal enclosure, 45 m. (150 ft) across, with a wall 1–8 m. (3–26 ft) thick, is medieval or later, while the other three ramparts are prehistoric. The site was excavated by B. Raftery in 1969–75 and 1978, revealing extensive evidence of Later Bronze Age, Early Iron Age and medieval occupation.

The bulk of evidence is Later Bronze Age, from the first half of the final millennium BC: a large circular post-built house, 15 m. (48 ft) in diameter, stood within an enclosing ditch 35 m. (115 ft) in diameter; a foundation burial(?) of an infant in this had gold ring-money as grave-goods. Outside this on the E side was a bronze-working centre which yielded some 4,000 fragments of clay moulds; to the S of this was a circular ditched burial enclosure, 16 m. (52 ft) in diameter, with three cremated burials, one in an upright coarse pot. Occupation debris included teeth of cattle and pigs. Other finds included *c*. 15,000 sherds of coarse pottery, 96 glass beads and ornaments of jet, amber and lignite, five gold ornaments, a chisel, tanged punch and socketed gouge, fragments of a spearhead, sword-blade and socketed axehead, the conical rivet of a cauldron, and 22 saddle-querns and a small number of grain-rubbers. *See* also EAMHAIN MACHA. Early Iron Age remains included an iron-smelting furnace; a medieval house, together with coins and potsherds, was also discovered.　　　　MH
B. Raftery, 'Rathgall and Irish Hillfort Problems', in D. Harding (ed.), *Hillforts*, 1976, pp. 339–57.

Reeves, Oswald (1870–1967). Artist and craftsman; born in England, he taught at the Metropolitan School of Art, Dublin, 1904–37. Under his direction Dublin enamels gained an international reputation. Emblematic and symbolical rather than pictorial, they were characterized by simplicity and subordination of detail. A bold modernism pervaded his later work, replacing the earlier faerie and symbolist modes. Works include tabernacle doors for the HONAN CHAPEL, Cork, and for Newry Cathedral; the triptychal war memorial, Grangegorman Church, Dublin; Mullingar Town Trophy; and the President's Trophy for the Irish Red Cross. He was Honorary Secretary to the Arts and Crafts Society of Ireland, and in 1909 organized the Guild of Irish Art Workers. *See* ARTS AND CRAFTS MOVEMENT.　　　　PL

Reeves, William (1815–92). Historian; born at Charleville, Co. Cork, he became Church of Ireland Bishop of Down, Connor and Dromore. He edited Adamnan's *Life of St Columba*, published in 1857, and was author of works on ecclesiastical history and co-editor (with J. H. TODD) of JOHN O'DONOVAN's translation

of the *Martyrology of Donegal*, 1864. He was President of the Royal Irish Academy in 1891. BdeB
Lady Ferguson, *Life of Reeves*, 1893.

Reid, Nano (1905–81). Landscape and figurative painter; born at Drogheda, Co. Louth, she studied at the Metropolitan School of Art under PATRICK TUOHY, LEO WHELAN, SEÁN KEATING and HARRY CLARKE. In 1927 she went to Paris to study at La Grande Chaumière, and then to the Central School of Art, London, and the Chelsea Polytechnic. She exhibited with the RHA, IELA, the Dublin Painters, and the Independent Artists. A retrospective exhibition of her work was held in 1974/75 in Dublin and Belfast. Examples of her work can be seen in the Hugh Lane Municipal Gallery of Modern Art, Dublin, the Crawford Municipal Gallery, Cork, and the Ulster Museum, Belfast. CMacG

Rice, Edmund Ignatius (1762–1844). Founder and educational pioneer; born near Callan, Co. Kilkenny, the son of a strong farmer, he pursued a successful business career in Waterford, but after the death of his young wife in 1789 he devoted himself increasingly to charitable works. Rice's spiritual mentors were St Ignatius Loyola and St Teresa of Ávila, and his mental world that of the Counter Reformation. The use of schools as a major instrument of proselytization of Irish Roman Catholics under the auspices of English evangelicalism made him aware of the need to provide alternative educational facilities for Catholics and so, inspired by NANO NAGLE and her Presentation Sisters, he opened a school at Waterford in 1803 (*see* CHRISTIAN BROTHERS). Shortly afterwards he formed a Congregation devoted to teaching, which received Papal approval in 1820 as the Institute of the Brothers of the Christian Schools of Ireland. Rice's latter years were clouded by a bitter controversy within the Congregation; he wished to extend its scope to include fee-paying schools which would provide an assured income with which to underwrite the maintenance of the free schools, but he was outnumbered by those who wished to restrict the work exclusively to the free education of the poor on the De La Salle method. The victory of those opposed to Rice's views led by the new Superior General, Brother Michael Paul Riordan, resulted in outrageous acts of insolence being perpetrated against the by then ailing founder of the Congregation. *See* EDUCATION. BB
J. D. Fitzpatrick, *Edmund Rice*, 1945; Desmond Rushe, *Edmund Rice, The Man and his Times*, 1981.

Richards, Shelah (1903–). Actress and director; after joining the ABBEY THEATRE in 1925 she created the parts of Nora in O'CASEY's *The Plough and the Stars*, Kate in ROBINSON's *The Big House*, Blanaid in JOHNSTON's *The Moon in the Yellow River*, etc. During World War II she presented independent seasons of new plays (which might not have passed the Irish censor) at the Olympia Theatre, Dublin. More recently she has directed plays for television. CF-S

(*Above*) **Reid, Nano.** *Tinkers at Slieve Breagh*, 1962. Collection An Chomhairle Ealaion, Dublin.

(*Right*) **Richards, Shelah.** Studio portrait of the leading actress.

Robinson, Lennox. Portrait by Dermod O'Brien, oil on canvas. NGI.

Roberts, John (1716–96). Architect, of Waterford; he is credited with the huge courtyard at Curraghmore, Co. Waterford (1740–52). He designed the Church of Ireland Cathedral, Waterford, in 1773, Waterford City Hall in 1782 and commenced the Catholic Cathedral in the same city in 1792. By his wife Mary Susanna Sautelle he was father of the artists THOMAS ROBERTS and THOMAS SAUTELLE ROBERTS.　　WG

Roberts, Thomas (1748–78). Painter; born at Waterford, he was a son of JOHN ROBERTS, architect. He studied at the DUBLIN SOCIETY Schools and also under George Mullins. Most of his career was spent in Dublin, where between 1766 and 1773 he exhibited 56 works at the Society of Artists. He visited London in 1775, working for Sir Watkin Williams Wynn and went for the sake of his health to Portugal in 1778, but died there. Most of his works comprise series of paintings done for Irish aristocratic patrons and they are, with their extraordinary poetic feeling for the atmospheric qualities of Ireland, the most evocative paintings of Irish scenery ever created, though many of his views are purely imaginary.　　AOC

Roberts, Thomas Sautelle (1760–1826). Painter; born at Waterford, he was the younger brother of THOMAS ROBERTS, and was training as an architect at the DUBLIN SOCIETY Schools when his brother died prematurely. He not only took his brother's name, Thomas, but changed his career to painting, probably completing his brother's unfinished works. After a spell in

England, where he painted in the Lake District, he returned to Ireland to become the foremost romantic landscape painter of the post-Union years, and a great influence on such artists as DANBY. His exciting free brushwork was very successful in depicting rocky river scenes and he could invoke the mysterious in his work. He was a notable watercolourist and much of his work was reproduced in aquatint. He was a founder-member of the ROYAL HIBERNIAN ACADEMY.　　AOC

Robinson, Esme Stuart Lennox (1886–1958). Theatre manager, playwright and director; born at Douglas, Co. Cork, he was the son of a Protestant clergyman. He devoted most of his career to serving the ABBEY THEATRE as manager, as director and producer of plays, and, from 1923 until his death, as a member of the Board of Directors. He also made an important contribution as a playwright, especially with his grim early plays *The Clancy Name* (perf. 1908), *The Cross Roads* (perf. 1909), and *Harvest* (perf. 1910). His later work was generally less powerful but showed greater variety; the better-known titles include *The Whiteheaded Boy* (perf. 1916), a popular comedy; *The Big House* (1926); and *Drama at Inish* (perf. 1933).　　PLM
Michael J. O'Neill, *Lennox Robinson*, 1964.

Robinson, Sir William (c. 1643–1712). Engineer and architect; nothing is known of his training, but he served as Surveyor-General in Ireland, where his most important work, the Royal Hospital, KILMAINHAM (1680–87), influenced the development of Classicism. He was also responsible for rebuilding at Kilkenny Castle in the 1680s and at Dublin Castle after the fire of 1684, as well as for repairs and additions to a number of forts, public buildings and churches, including St Mary's, Dublin, for which he designed at least the east window for the building of 1701.　　BdeB

Roche, Kevin (1922–). Architect; born in Dublin, where he trained and worked for MICHAEL SCOTT, before emigrating to the USA in 1948 to settle there. His most important achievements among over fifty major commissions are the TWA Terminal at Kennedy Airport, New York, and the Columbia Broadcasting System headquarters, New York. He was awarded the Pritziker Prize, 1982.　　BdeB

Rolleston, Thomas William Hazen (1857–1920). Poet, essayist and critic; born at Shinrone, Co. Offaly, he was with YEATS one of the earliest figures of the Irish Literary Revival. His *Treasury of Irish Poetry* was published in 1900.　　T McC

Rosc. The name Rosc, a medieval Irish word meaning 'poetry of vision', was chosen to express the ideals of the series of exhibitions held at four-yearly intervals in Dublin and elsewhere in Ireland since 1967. The first exhibition was conceived by the distinguished Irish architect MICHAEL SCOTT who was, from the inception of the series until his retirement in 1981, chairman of the executive committee.

XVI **Pearce, Sir Edward Lovett.** The ballroom in Dublin Castle, showing the sumptuous
decorative scheme designed by the architect; detail from an anonymous painting of a ball held in 1731.
Collection Col. N. G. Stopford Sackville.

Art experts from abroad were asked to select for the exhibition up to fifty practitioners in the visual arts representing current aspects. Associated exhibitions have been mounted to coincide with Rosc, exemplifying related and peripheral forms of the visual, decorative, and applied arts of Ireland or associated Celtic nations.   C MacG

Roscommon, Wentworth Dillon, 4th Earl of (?1633–1685). Poet; born in Ireland and educated in England and France, Lord Roscommon travelled widely in Europe before returning to England at the Restoration. A considerable landowner in Ireland, he was a member of the Irish parliament and a noted orator. A poet praised by Pope and Johnson, Roscommon is best remembered for his blank-verse translation of the *Ars Poetica* (1680) and his *Essay on Translated Verse* (1684).   I C R

Roscrea, Co. Tipperary. The Dublin–Limerick road separates the ROUND TOWER of St Cronan's Monastery from the mid-12th century Romanesque church, of which the west wall with *antae* and doorway with pointed gable survive. Close to the church are the fragments of a once-impressive 12th-century cross, and a much earlier carved pillar stands close to the modern Catholic church.   P H

round towers. These medieval towers are tall, slender stone structures, tapering inwards slightly towards the top, and capped by a conical roof; the tallest example at Kilmacduagh, Co. Galway, reaches a height of 34·28 m. (112 ft 6 in.), and normally the circumference varies between 14 m. and 17 m. (46–56 ft). The towers occur on monastic sites, and presumably originally stood close to churches. Devenish, Co. Fermanagh, is the only site where a second tower is known. In most examples, the usually round-headed doorway is placed between 1 m. and 4 m. (3–13 ft) above the ground; the tower on Scattery Island, Co. Clare, is the only example where the door is at ground-level. The raised level of the doorway has given rise to the suggestion that the entrance was placed well above ground-level for defensive purposes when the towers were used as places of refuge. It is possible that they were so used on occasions, but the occupants would then have been in danger of being burned alive if the towers were set on fire – which they sometimes were. At least in some instances, the towers would appear to have served as store-houses for books and monastic treasures, but their prime use is indicated by the old Irish word used to describe them – *cloigtheach*, meaning 'bell-house' or 'bell-tower'. The towers had a number of storeys within, each having a window; the top floor of the tower normally had four windows – one for each cardinal direction. None of the original floors survives, but some have been reconstructed (with interconnecting ladders), as at Monasterboice, Co. Louth. In almost all cases the doorway faces in an easterly direction.

The origin of the towers is hotly disputed. One of the most probable theories is that their shape originated in

round tower. The 12th-century tower at Timahoe, Co. Laois, showing the entrance above ground level.

the lands bordering the Mediterranean (where the much more recent Islamic minarets fulfil much the same function of calling the faithful to prayer), and that their form may have been transmitted to Ireland through the Carolingian Empire. Historical references to round towers span the period from 948 to 1238, and it was probably during this time-span that the majority were built, though some may conceivably be earlier. Some (e.g. Devenish, Co. Fermanagh, and Timahoe, Co. Laois) bear Romanesque decoration. Outside Ireland the only surviving free-standing round towers are one in the Isle of Man and two in Scotland, but their shape may be compared to those attached to continental European churches from the Carolingian period onwards. St Finghin's Church at Clonmacnois, Co. Offaly, incorporates a round tower within its structure, while rising from the stone roof of St Kevin's Church, Glendalough, Co. Wicklow, there is a miniature version of the upper part of a round tower.   P H
George Lennox Barrow, *The Round Towers of Ireland*, 1979.

Royal Dublin Society. *See* DUBLIN SOCIETY.

Royal Hibernian Academy of Arts. Founded by Royal Charter in 1823 with WILLIAM ASHFORD as President, the RHA held its first exhibition in Dublin

(*Opposite*) XVII **plasterwork.** The saloon at Carton, Co. Kildare, showing part of the Baroque ceiling decoration carried out by the Francini brothers in 1739; the overall theme is the 'Courtship of the Gods'.

in 1826, since when it has, with a few exceptions, held an annual exhibition. In the 1830s, for four successive years no work was sold from the exhibition, and the Academy was only saved by the foundation of the Royal Irish Art Union in 1839, which by buying original works, and commissioning engravings of others, helped the Academy to financial success. In 1916 its premises were destroyed by fire with all the records. The Academy has a President (PRHA), 23 full Members (RHA), 10 Associates (ARHA), and 10 Honorary Members (HRHA), all elected.   A O C

Royal Horticultural Society of Ireland. A group of gardeners from the Dublin area formed the Horticultural Society of Ireland which had its first formal meeting and its first show at Donnybrook in 1817.

A new constitution was adopted in 1830 and that year was regarded as the foundation date of the reformed society; the title Royal was granted in 1838 with the approval of Queen Victoria. After several moves the offices of the Society were transferred in 1974 to Thomas Prior House, Ballsbridge.   B de B

Royal Irish Academy. Founded in 1785 by the 1st Earl of Charlemont, the RIA is the premier learned insititution of Ireland. It is divided into two sections, one for the sciences and one for humane studies. Its *Dictionary of the Irish Language* is complete and its dictionary of modern Irish in progress. Its collection of antiquities formed the nucleus of the Irish antiquities division at the NATIONAL MUSEUM OF IRELAND, but it retains its priceless collection of Irish mss., forming part of its important library which is housed in the Academy House in Dawson Street.

The RIA publishes *Proceedings* for both sections, and administers excavation and other funds. The *New History of Ireland* is in progress under its auspices, and its *Atlas of Ireland* was published in 1979.   M C

Royal Irish Academy of Music. Situated in Westland Row, Dublin, the RIAM was founded in 1848 and reorganized in 1856; it is the senior institute in Ireland for the teaching of music in all its forms. An autonomous institution with 24 governors and a secretary, it is now partially funded by the Department of Education. Approximately 18,000 students at all levels are examined annually.   B de B

Royal Society of Antiquaries of Ireland. Originally founded in 1849 as the Kilkenny Archaeological Society; after two changes of name, it assumed its present title in 1890, having removed from Kilkenny to Dublin in 1868. Its present premises are at 63 Merrion Square, where its library is housed. Its *Journal* is published annually, usually in two parts.   M C

Russborough, Co. Wicklow. Commenced in 1741 by RICHARD CASTLE for Joseph Leeson, Earl of Milltown, the house has the longest façade (213 m.; 700 ft) of any in Ireland. The house was finished *c.* 1755 by FRANCIS BINDON. The lavishly decorated interior includes huge sculptural chimneypieces, extravagant use of mahogany, and Baroque plasterwork. Russborough (now open to the public) originally housed the famous Milltown Collection and now contains the important BEIT ART COLLECTION.   W G
Sir Alfred Beit, *Russborough* (Irish Heritage Series, no. 13).

Russell, George. *See* A.E.

Ryan, Richard (1946–   ). Dublin poet; he has published two excellent collections, *Ledges* (1970) and *Ravenswood* (1973).   T McC

Russborough. Overall view of the façade of the house and wings; the left-hand pavilion is obscured from view.

S

sacred trees. The cult of sacred trees and groves amongst the continental Celts is well attested. The *Nemeton* ('Sacred Place') of the Druids was often a sacred grove. Strabo tells us that the Celts of Galatia met at an assembly-place called Drunemeton ('Oak-Sanctuary'). The cult of sacred trees is very evident in Irish tradition. The five ancient sacred trees of Ireland – Bile Tortan, Eó Mugna, Eó Rossa, Cráeb Daithi and Bile Uisnig – are celebrated in early literature. Such trees grew on sacred inauguration-sites (*see* MYTHOLOGY), and the hewing down of the sacred tree of an enemy was a notable act of war and of symbolic conquest, such events being recorded in the annals as late as the 12th century. In a Christianized form, sacred trees were also associated with saints and with ecclesiastical sites and, of course, with holy wells. Belief in sacred trees, in one form or another, continued in Ireland down to recent times.   DÓC

St Macdara's Island, Co. Galway. Situated near Carna, the island has a small stone church measuring 4·57 × 3·42 m. (15 ft × 11 ft 3 in.) internally, with projecting *antae* rising to the top of the gable. The recently restored stone roof appears not to have been supported by an internal vault, and the imitations of shingles carved on the roof-stones suggest that the features of the church have been copied from an earlier wooden structure.   PH

St Molaise, Statue of. A large, hollow, two-piece, oak statue representing the 6th-century saint, Molaise of Devenish and Inishmurray, in priestly vestments. It is early medieval in date. A powerful sculpture, it is not at all marred by the somewhat exaggerated proportions of the head. The style is a native version of early Gothic. It was preserved until modern times in the Church of St Molaise in the monastery on the island of Inishmurray, Co. Sligo, and is now in the NMI. Because the scale of the statue was too great for the oratory, known as 'St Molaise's House', Catriona MacLeod, an authority on medieval wood-sculptures in Ireland, has suggested that the sculpture had been brought there for safe-keeping in relatively modern times from some larger, mainland foundation.   MFR

Samain. In Irish MYTHOLOGY Samain (November Eve) is the feast of the dead, when the boundaries between this world and the Otherworld were obliterated. Mongfhind, daughter of Fidach, died of poison, it is said, on November Eve and she was a witch; hence, according to a clerical writer's comment on popular belief, 'that is why Samain is called the "Feast of Mongfhind" by the rabble . . . wherefore women and the rabble address petitions to her at Samain'. On a more exalted literary level, contact with the Other-

St Macdara's Island. The small stone church as it appeared before restoration.

St Molaise, Statue of. The hollow oak statue, height 164·5 cm. (5 ft 4¾ in.). NMI.

world, for good or for evil, is made at Samain and on that night the Síd is open and its people are abroad in the world of men. Otherworld adventures and wooings begin at Samain. The vast corpus of belief and practice in regard to November Eve in folklore is the detritus of early Irish custom.   DÓC

Sayers, Peig (1873–1958). Storyteller and writer of prose in Irish; born at Vicarstown, Dunquin, Co. Kerry. Her main works are: *Peig* (autobiography; 1936); *Machnamh Seanmhná* (autobiographical; 1939) and *Scéalta ón mBlascaod* ('Stories from Blasket', folklore; 1938).   AA

Scott, Michael. The Ritz Cinema, Athlone, *c.* 1940 (from *The Irish Builder*).

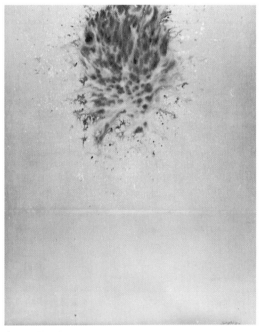

Scott, Patrick. *Yellow Device*, oil on canvas, 1962. Ulster Museum.

schools. *See* BARDIC SCHOOLS; HEDGE SCHOOLS; MONASTIC SCHOOLS; EDUCATION.

Scott, Michael (1905–   ). Architect; born at Drogheda, Co. Louth, he was educated in Dublin at Belvedere College, the Dublin School of Art and the Abbey Theatre School of Acting. He was in private practice from 1928 until he retired in 1977, but remained a consultant to the firm he established and which became Scott, Tallon, Walker in 1974 (senior partners: Robin Walker; Ronald Tallon; Niall Scott). Scott's work includes the Irish Pavilion for the New York World's Fair, 1939; Offices and Central Bus Terminal, Store Street, Dublin, 1953; Ballroom, Shelbourne Hotel, Dublin, 1956; Abbey Theatre, Dublin, completed 1965 (with Ronald Tallon). He became a Fellow of the Royal Institute of the Architects of Ireland in 1948, and was awarded that Institute's Triennial Gold Medal 1952–55; since that time he has received honorary doctorates and fellowships in Ireland, Great Britain and the USA and in 1975 was awarded the Royal Gold Medal of the Royal Institute of British Architects.   TÓB

Scott, Patrick (1921–   ). Abstract painter, and designer; born in Co. Cork, he studied architecture at University College, Dublin. He had a one-man show in Dublin in 1944. A member of the White Stag Group, he also exhibited with the Irish Exhibition of Living Art in 1946, and represented Ireland at the Venice Biennale in 1960, and received the Guggenheim International Award.

He designs tapestries for private and public buildings, many of these being made by V'soske Joyce Weavers, Co. Galway, and the French tapestry firm of Aubusson. He was represented in ROSC '80 in Dublin, and awarded a retrospective exhibition in 1981 at Trinity College, Dublin. His works are to be found in many public and private collections in Ireland, Great Britain and in the Museum of Modern Art, New York.   C MacG

Scott, William A. (1871–1921). Architect; as Professor of Architecture at University College, Dublin, from 1911 and a member of council of the Arts and Crafts Society of Ireland (*see* ARTS AND CRAFTS MOVEMENT), he was the most significant architect in Ireland in the early 20th century and an important designer of Celtic ornament. He was friendly with EDWARD MARTYN, W. B. YEATS and others in the IRISH REVIVAL, and occasionally collaborated with the sculptor Michael Shortall. In ecclesiastical and allied work he usually tended toward the revival of Irish forms, principally Romanesque, with a strong Byzantine element. In his work of a domestic nature he followed English 'arts and crafts' precepts, favouring vernacular forms, varied and local materials, and informal planning. A personal predilection for cubic massing and simple forms – a kind of proto-modernism – is evident in many of his other designs. Throughout, his work is characterized by a decided individuality and freshness. At once the most traditional and the most progressive of Irish architects – his Hostel at Lough Derg (1912) was a pioneer work in reinforced concrete – his example helped to pave the way for modern building design in Ireland (*see* ARCHITECTURE).

His works include churches at Spiddal, Co. Galway (1903–7), and Lough Derg, Co. Donegal (designed 1919; built 1926–31); Killyhevlin House, Co. Fermanagh (1903); Garden Village, Kilkenny (1906); Town Hall, Cavan (1909); and St Mary's College, Galway (1912). He also designed furnishings for LOUGHREA CATHEDRAL, Co. Galway (1903–8), the HONAN CHAPEL, Cork (1916), and Thoor Ballylee, Co. Galway (1917–19).   P L

Jeanne Sheehy, *The Rediscovery of Ireland's Past: The Celtic Revival, 1830–1930*, 1980; P. Larmour, *Celtic Ornament*, 1981.

Scully, Harry (fl. 1885–1930). Painter in watercolour and oils; born in Cork, he studied at the Cork School of Art, at Heatherly's Art School, London, and also on the Continent. He established a studio for teaching in Cork, and made frequent visits to Newlyn, Cornwall; he exhibited with the principal London galleries from 1887, also with the New Water Colour Society, the Royal Academy and the Royal Hibernian Academy. He was elected ARHA 1900, RHA 1906. He exhibited at the RHA for the last time in 1931, having gone to live in Orpington, Kent, during the Irish War of Independence.   C MacG

sculpture. There has been a sculptural tradition in Ireland which has continued – with some gaps– from the stone dolmens of the 3rd millennium BC to the land art of the present day. There are strong sculptural aspects to the burial mounds such as NEWGRANGE, *c.* 3200 BC, and the stone ring-forts of the Celtic settlers of the Iron Age, *c.* 500 BC–432 AD. Individual stone carvings of idols, and ritual objects like the TUROE STONE appear during this period.

Following the coming of CHRISTIANITY in the 5th century, from the 7th century onwards pillar stones with inscribed crosses were erected in monastic settlements; in many cases these stones appear to have had a sepulchral function. These slabs were probably influenced by British or Gaulish precedent, but they also echoed pre-Christian traditions in carrying OGHAM inscriptions. Simplified curved ornament was also usually added. As tokens of Christianity set in a monastery, the pillar stones look forward to the HIGH CROSS, a form probably derived from a processional cross made of wood and later translated into permanent stone form. In the early examples, the carved decoration is abstract, but by the 9th century it had developed to depict elaborate figured scriptural scenes.

There is a sculptural aspect to early Christian METALWORK, in which the pre-Christian abstract forms continued. In the Rinnagan Crucifixion plaque (8th century), we can see an attempt at figurative representation, but the real interest, as always, lies in the applied surface decoration which links it to jewellery, metalwork and ILLUMINATED MANUSCRIPTS. The VIKING invasions were crucial for introducing a new decorative

sculpture. The bronze Crucifixion Plaque from Clonmacnois, Co. Offaly. NMI.

treatment of interlacing and animals (which already existed in Irish art). These motifs blossomed in the 11th and 12th centuries and mingle with European Romanesque elements. Where figurative relief metalwork was attempted, as in the small Crucifixion Plaque from Clonmacnois, it was treated very schematically and symbolically, with little interest in three-dimensional effect.

During the 12th century the Romanesque style prevailed in Ireland. A late type of HIGH CROSS evolved, showing on one side Christ crucified in a long garment with a standing figure either beneath (as at Dysert O'Dea, Co. Clare) or, alternatively, on the other side (as at Roscrea). Where abstract interlaced ornament occurs, it is extremely shallow; the most detailed example of this is the shaft of the cross in the Market Square, Tuam, Co. Galway. Cut stone sarcophagi may have existed, although only one (in CORMAC'S CHAPEL, Cashel) is known: its elaborate interlacing is related to metalwork, e.g. the CROSS OF CONG. In Irish Romanesque churches (*see* ARCHITECTURE) there were no aisle column capitals comparable to the Continental examples. However, the doorways display a wealth of carving: stylized geometric decoration and animal and human heads – a form of decoration which has some parallels in French Romanesque. The carved tympanum of Cormac's Chapel (1134), shows a centaur fighting a monster and has some visual similarities to the hunting scenes on slabs and on the early high crosses.

In a certain sense, the outlines of the history of Irish sculpture can be traced through a study of tombs, from the megalithic period onwards, leading finally to the commemorative public statues of the modern period. This is particularly true of medieval or Gothic sculpture.

Following the Anglo-Norman invasion in 1169, and the consolidation of the colony in eastern Ireland,

The 12th-century high cross (with a figure of Christ and a second, standing, figure below), at Dysert O'Dea, Co. Clare.

Tomb-effigy of the Cantwell knight, Kilfane Church, Co. Kilkenny, c. 1320.

Norman bishops of Dublin were the first to have tombs made for themselves, following Continental and English precedent. Even abbots of Gaelic origin copied the Norman lead. Norman knights also followed this trend, e.g. the Cantwell knight at Kilfane Church, Co. Kilkenny. The stylistic precedent for both bishops and knights (as indeed for Irish Gothic architecture in general) was the art of the West of England. A number of English craftsmen came to Ireland in the early 13th century to work on Christ Church Cathedral, Dublin, where the carved aisle-capitals show the influence of West of England sculpture. The flowering of Anglo-Norman tomb sculpture – more noticeable in the late 13th and early 14th centuries – was cut short by the Black Death. The urbanized colonized easterly parts were most affected and there was consequently a decline in sculptural output and quality. At the same time, in the 14th century, there was a resurgence of the Gaelic Lords; and in the west a certain amount of sculpture was produced, associated with the new Franciscan friaries.

Apart from tombs, decorative capitals continued to offer scope for sculpture, e.g. at Ballintubber, Co. Mayo. Cloisters, too, offered opportunities, most notably at JERPOINT ABBEY, Co. Kilkenny, where the figures of gentlefolk and saints have been variously dated from 1400 to the early 16th century. Rich carved tracery can be found in many 15th-century abbeys, e.g. HOLY CROSS, Co. Tipperary. Decorative relief carving on walls and tombs is shallow and unlike the deeper carving of Flamboyant and Perpendicular Gothic abroad. Figure sculpture, where it occasionally appears, is very stilted, displaying little interest in the human form. Baptismal fonts sometimes have figure carving which is of mediocre quality. Similar shortcomings are evident in late-medieval carved wood statuary.

This general development of late-medieval sculpture is also found in figures in relief metalwork. The Domhnach Airgid Book shrine (an elaborate metal book-container) shows numerous figures in relief which still retain much of the hieratic stiffness of the Romanesque. The same could be said of the figure of Christ on the Processional Cross of 1479 from Ballylongford, Co. Kerry (now NMI). Bishop's croziers offered plenty of scope for both figurative and decorative metalwork: that of Cornelius O'Dea, Bishop of Limerick, has solidly modelled figurines of saints and excellent modelling of the decorated crochets and canopies.

A general revival of Irish medieval tomb sculpture took place in the mid-15th century. The Plunkett family in Co. Meath were leaders in this by commissioning tomb sculpture for their churches. The flat effigy was replaced by the tomb-chest which showed knights or bishops in relief effigy on top, with scenes of the Passion of Christ around the sides. The tomb-chest was an imitation of an idea long established in England and on the Continent. There is a marked contrast between the expertise of carving decorative elements and the lack of interest in the treatment of the human figure.

(*Above left*) Figure of St James the Less from a tomb panel by the workshop of Rory O'Tunney, at Jerpoint Abbey, Co. Kilkenny.

(*Above*) Kneeling figures of Sir Arthur Chichester and his wife in Carrickfergus church, Co. Antrim, erected *c.* 1614.

(*Left*) Detail of a misericord in St Mary's Cathedral, Limerick, *c.* 1480: a lion fighting with a wyvern.

In the West of Ireland in the late-medieval period, the wall-tomb was preferred to the tomb-chest. The tomb fronts were decorated with figures of saints, as at the Dominican Friary, Strade, Co. Mayo. There was a general decline in quality in the Gaelic regions in the early 16th century. The O'Tunney family was the leading sculptural workshop in Kilkenny and it was the first to identify its authorship by name. Their work was rather stylized, as was that of the Ormond School in Kilkenny. Neither can be compared to the naturalism or the late-medieval English or the Franco-Flemish schools. There was, however, one particularly note-worthy work – the tomb of Bishop Wellesley, *c.* 1539, now in Kildare Cathedral – a supreme achievement of Irish Gothic sculpture.

Also, apart from tombs, there is a certain amount of surviving Irish late-medieval religious woodcarving (to be seen in the NMI), which, with the exception of the misericords in St Mary's Cathedral, Limerick, is not of high quality.

The Gothic style continued throughout the 16th century and into the middle of the 17th – a period marked by wars and political disturbance. The Irish sculptural tradition was exhausted when the Italian Renaissance, through its Anglo-Flemish inter-pretation, appeared in Ireland in the 16th century.

It is evident that decorative patterns, rather than three-dimensional massing, was the main interest of ancient and medieval Irish sculptors. Consequently the man-centred aesthetics of the Italian Renaissance took a long time in dominating Irish art, quite apart from the unsympathetic conditions of patronage. Re-naissance influences came to Ireland as to England, simply as a modish decorative overlay, not a serious Classical form. With the establishment of new wealthy English settler landlords and the eclipse of the Church with the Reformation, sculpture is more often seen in great houses in coats-of-arms, PLASTERWORK and chimney-pieces. The best tomb sculpture follows the Jacobean pattern and was by English artists. The deceased is no longer shown supine but is often shown kneeling and surrounded by his wife and children.

The tomb of Sir Arthur Chichester, erected *c.* 1614 in Carrickfergus Church, Co. Antrim, and the monu-ment to the Earl of Cork in Youghal church, completed in 1620, exhibited a repertoire of the late Renaissance or Mannerist ornament: both the deceased are shown kneeling. In the Gaelic parts of Ireland more con-servative qualities in tomb sculpture persisted, e.g. the O'Conor Don memorial of 1624 in Sligo Abbey. The absence of political stability in the 16th and 17th centuries meant that, unlike England, there was little

Portrait of William Maple by Patrick Cunningham, 1753; height 76·2 cm. (30 in.). Royal Dublin Society.

development of unfortified country-house architecture with its attendant wood carving, stone statues and terraced gardens derived from Flemish-Renaissance prototypes.

Following the Restoration, the Baroque style is evident in the ornamental wood carving of the Huguenot James Tabary at the Royal Hospital, KILMAINHAM. In figurative work the style was introduced by William Kidwell, an Englishman, whose memorials show the deceased periwigged and reclining on an elbow. Kidwell also set a fashion in richly framed wall-tablets. The Rococo style in Irish plasterwork led by the FRANCINI brothers was continued by the native-born ROBERT WEST during the 1750s.

Reaction to the Baroque came with JOHN VAN NOST, of Anglo-Dutch extraction; he settled in Dublin c. 1749 and was paid by the DUBLIN SOCIETY to train a number of native-born sculptors, notably Patrick Cunningham and CHRISTOPHER HEWETSON, whose monument to Provost Baldwin, executed in Rome (1784) was the first Neo-Classical funerary monument in Ireland. There were study facilities for modellers at the Dublin Society's School during the second half of the 18th century, and the school had a formative influence on new talent in sculpture, as in the other plastic arts.

Neo-Classical architects like CHAMBERS (in the Marino Casino) and GANDON (in the Custom House) set

Life-size marble memorial to George Ogle, M.P. (d. 1814), by John Smyth, in St Patrick's Cathedral, Dublin.

Early Sorrow, life-size statue in plaster by Patrick MacDowell, 1847. Ulster Museum.

(*Above*) *Leenane: Connemara Trout* by Albert Power, 1944; green Connemara marble, height 48 cm (19 in.). NGI.

(*Right*) The bronze figure of Parnell by Augustus St Gaudens; detail from the Parnell Monument, unveiled in 1911.

the pace which the sculptors followed: Lord Charlemont brought Simon Vierpyl from Rome to carve the urns at the Casino. Vierpyl trained EDWARD SMYTH, whom Gandon employed on the Custom House and Four Courts. Smyth was a carver of vigorous outdoor sculpture and was succeeded as Head of the Sculpture School at the Dublin Society Schools by his son John – a more straightforward Neo-Classical sculptor who trained many of the emerging sculptors in Dublin in the early 19th century, notably JOHN HENRY FOLEY (who left Dublin in 1834 for a brilliant career in London). Patrick McDowell of Belfast also had a highly successful career in London. Other important sculptors of the early 19th century were Peter Turnerelli at Belfast, John E. Carew from Waterford and Thomas Kirk from Cork. JOHN HOGAN is somewhat different from the others in that, after his training in Cork, he settled in Rome (1824–49) where he created many funerary memorials, statues and busts for his native land; while Hogan remained devoted to the antique, Foley followed the newer tendencies (led by Chantrey in England) towards greater naturalism, abandoning allegory. In the later 19th century, Thomas Farrell, generally an undistinguished sculptor, was the leading practitioner in Dublin, his style containing elements of both Foley and Hogan. The Gothic Revival required a considerable amount of decorative stone carving – work which sustained several family stoneyards like those of the O'Sheas in Dublin and the Scannells in Cork. Commercial buildings in Dublin also required a good deal of ornamental carving, e.g. naturalistic foliation.

The influence of European modernism was felt belatedly in Ireland, as in England. Around 1900, the principal sculptor active and teaching at the Dublin Metropolitan School of Art was JOHN HUGHES. His figures of soldiers on the Victoria Memorial in Dublin, finished in 1903, show an awareness of the broken surfaces of Rodin's school. However, Hughes left Ireland for Italy and was replaced by OLIVER SHEPPARD as Head of Sculpture at the Metropolitan School; Sheppard was even more committed to plastic modelling, evident in some of his 'heroic' memorials. Albert Power, who also trained at the Metropolitan School, continued this idiom and made some fine monumental stone figures. Others, like the Irish-Americans A. St. Gaudens, Jerome Connor and ANDREW O'CONNOR, worked in a post-Rodinesque modelling tradition. The alternative stone-carving tradition continued in the work of SEAMUS MURPHY and Domhnall Ó Murchadha. There was little impact of the new materials and aesthetic of Continental 'modernist' sculpture. The Irish Exhibition of Living Art group of the 1940s was more significant for painting than for sculpture.

The post-war period has seen the wide-ranging if eclectic style of F. E. MCWILLIAM, a Belfast artist. OISIN KELLY has for the most part adhered to a quieter traditionalism, with a strong Irish character, working in wood very sensitively. Hilary Heron, Gerda Frommel and Ian Stuart have used stone and wood in more current tendencies. EDWARD DELANEY has rivalled Foley in the number of his public monuments in Dublin. John Behan, with his Dublin Art Foundry, has developed a centre for bronze casting for his own

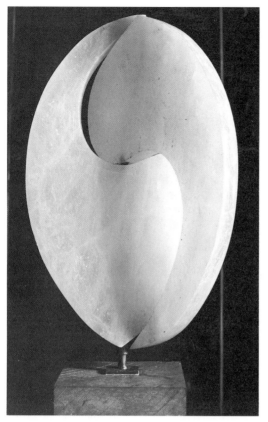

sculpture. *Alabaster Interlocking Shapes II* by Gerda Frommel, 1970; height 64 cm. (25 in.). The Bank of Ireland.

figurative work and that of others. Brian King has worked in minimal and land art, while Nigel Rolfe has led tendencies in performance art. Many, but far from all, of the main post-war international sculptural trends have been represented in Ireland.   JT

F. Henry, 'Irish Cistercian Monasteries and their carved Decoration', *Apollo*, October 1966; ——, *Irish Art in the Early Christian Period*, 1965; ——, *Irish High Crosses*, 1964; H. M. Roe, *Medieval Fonts of Meath*, Meath Arch. and Hist. Soc., 1968; J. Hunt, *Irish Medieval Figure Sculpture 1200–1600*, 2 vols., 1974; C. McLeod, 'Medieval Wooden Figure Sculpture in Ireland', *JRSAI* nos. 75 (1945) and 76 (1946); E. C. Rae, 'Irish Sepulchral Monuments of the later Middle Ages', *JRSAI*, no. 100 (1970); R. Stalley, *Architecture and Sculpture in Ireland 1150–1350*, 1971; H. Potterton, *Irish Church Monuments 1570–1850*, 1975; Rosc catalogues – *Irish Art in the 19th Century*, Cork 1971; *Irish Art 1900–1950*, Cork 1975; *Irish Art 1943–1973*, Cork 1980.

Semple, George (*c.* 1700–1781/2). Engineer and architect; born in Dublin, the son of a builder who had begun the family tradition of working as builders and architects. He built the spire of St Patrick's Cathedral in 1749 and commenced St Patrick's Hospital in the same year. He rebuilt Essex Bridge, Dublin, in 1753, the bridge at Graiguenamanagh, Co. Kilkenny (1760s), and is credited with others in the same county. He designed Headford, Co. Meath (1760).   WG

Shaw, George Bernard (1856–1950). Playwright; born in Dublin, he came from an Irish Protestant background and lived in Dublin until 1876. Then, as his fellow-countryman OSCAR WILDE was soon to do, he moved to London and involved himself in the English

(*Above*) sculpture. *Red Shift* (maquette in wood and plastic) by Brian King, 1969; height 38·1 cm. (15 in.). Ulster Museum.

(*Right*) Shaw, George Bernard. The eminent playwright in middle age at Rosslare.

literary scene. Unsuccessful as a novelist, he became one of the greatest modern playwrights and received the Nobel Prize for Literature in 1926. Although he was a perceptive observer of Ireland, he made it the central concern of only one of his major plays, *John Bull's Other Island* (1904). His comic genius, however, has frequently been treated as distinctively Irish. PLM

C. E. M. Joad, *Shaw*, 1949; Eric Bentley, *Bernard Shaw*, 1957; B. C. Rosset, *Shaw of Dublin: The Formative Years*, 1964; M. M. Morgan, *The Shavian Playground*, 1972.

Sheppard, Oliver (1865–1941). Sculptor; born at Cookstown, Co. Tyrone, where his father worked as a sculptor. The family settled in Dublin and he entered the Metropolitan School of Art. He was often a prizewinner in the National Art Competition run by the Dept. of Science and Art, South Kensington; in 1888 he won a Scholarship to the Central Art Training School there and studied under Edouard Lanteri. He probably spent a year in Paris. He taught first at Leicester, then Nottingham and then as assistant to Lanteri at South Kensington. In 1902 he became Instructor in modelling at the Dublin Metropolitan School of Art, and later Professor of Sculpture at the Royal Hibernian Academy, where he had exhibited regularly since 1887. His most famous work, *Cuchulainn*, was executed in 1911–12 but was subsequently selected as a memorial to the 1916 Rising for the GPO, Dublin. He made two fine memorials to the 1798 Rebellion for Co. Wexford and many busts. His style was heavily influenced by 'Belle Époque' sculpture – Rodinesque but with smoother surfaces. He was the chief sculptural influence in Ireland in the early years of the century. JT

Rosc catalogue, *Irish Art 1900–1950*, Cork 1975; J. Sheehy, *The Rediscovery of Ireland's Past*, 1980.

Sheridan, Frances (*née* Chamberlaine; 1724–66). Novelist and playwright; born in Dublin, she was secretly taught to read by her brother, against the wishes of their clergyman father. Author of the successful comedy, *The Discovery* (1763), she is best known for her sentimental novel, *Memoirs of Miss Sidney Bidulph* (1761), a sequel published in 1767, and a much-admired oriental tale, *The History of Nourjahad* (1767). She was the wife of THOMAS SHERIDAN and mother of RICHARD BRINSLEY SHERIDAN. ICR

Sheridan, Richard Brinsley (1751–1816). Playwright; born in Dublin, the son of the actor, THOMAS SHERIDAN and FRANCES SHERIDAN. He abandoned the law for the theatre, and the revised version of his first comedy, *The Rivals*, was a great success in 1775. His other major work, *The School for Scandal* (1777), was followed by the short rehearsal-play, *The Critic* (1779), and much later by a melodrama, *Pizarro* (1799), after Kotzebue. He entered the British House of Commons in 1780 and there pursued a notable career as a politician, renowned for his oratory. ICR

Madeleine Bingham, *Sheridan*, 1972; Lewis Gibbs, *Sheridan, his Life and his Theatre*, 1948.

Sheridan, Richard Brinsley. Portrait by J. Russell, 1788. National Portrait Gallery, London.

Sheridan, Thomas (1719–88). Actor-manager; born in Dublin, he was educated at Westminster School and Trinity College, Dublin. He ran the Smock Alley Theatre, 1743–58, and appeared in London at Drury Lane, Covent Garden, etc. He introduced important reforms which were emulated in British theatres, including the banishment of the audience from the stage and the payment of regular salaries to actors. He was the father of RICHARD BRINSLEY SHERIDAN. CF-S

shrines. Christian reliquaries, occurring in various shapes; some major examples are described below. *See also* DIMMA, BOOK OF.

shrines, house-shaped. This form of reliquary, common throughout Western Christianity, should perhaps be better described as 'tomb-shaped' or even 'church-shaped'. Usually made of wood covered with metal plates, the Irish examples surviving nearly complete are the Emly shrine (now in Boston), the Lough Erne shrines (NMI), the Breac Moedoc (NMI), and St Manchan's Shrine (described below). Most take the form of small oratories, such as the temple shown on the Temptation page of the BOOK OF KELLS. St Manchan's Shrine, however, is much larger than the others and consists of the gable part only. There are clear correspondences also with Early Christian composite stone tombs, such as that in Clones, Co. Monaghan. Wood-and-metal shrines may have attained great size, as the Irish finial fragments in the French National Museum of Antiquities at St Germain-en-Laye suggest. All surviving examples are equipped with tags for carrying straps, reflecting the practice of taking relics on circuit. The earliest Irish examples date from the 8th century. Closely similar shrines are known in

217

shrines. The Breac Moedoc, a well-preserved example of a house-shaped shrine with tags for carrying; the figures of saints in bronze are about 5 cm. (2 in.). in height. NMI.

Scotland (the Monymusk reliquary) and in Scandinavia (the 'Copenhagen' shrine) – the latter probably looted from Ireland by the VIKING invaders.

Shrine of the Cathach. This book shrine was made to preserve the 6th-century manuscript known as the CATHACH PSALTER, traditionally associated with St Colum Cille (Columba). The Cathach was one of the principal treasures of the O'Donnells and was enshrined, almost certainly at Kells, some time between *c.* 1062 and 1098. An inscription on it records that it was made at the behest of Cathbarr Ua Domnaill and Domnall Mac Robertaig, Abbot of Kells, by the craftsman Sitric Mac Meic Aeda (the Annals record the bringing of the relics of Colum Cille to Kells in 1090). Cathach is a nickname meaning 'battler' and the relic was traditionally carried round the O'Donnell army before battle to ensure victory. The shrine remained in the hereditary keepership of the O'Donnells, whose representative deposited it during the 19th century in the museum of the ROYAL IRISH ACADEMY, the contents of which passed, in 1891, to the NATIONAL MUSEUM OF IRELAND.

The shrine itself consists of a wooden box encased in metal plates; the sides and back bear their original ornaments including, on the short sides, two magnificent beast motifs in the Irish 'Ringerike' style executed in silver-and-niello inlay. Smaller original panels also survive with vegetal and other patterns originally sheeted in gold foil. The back is decorated in openwork of the general type familiar on shrines of this period. The front bears a 14th-century ecclesiastical figured scene. In the 18th century a silver case was made for the reliquary.

Shrine of St Lachtin's Arm. This arm-shaped reliquary 38·5 cm. (15¼ in.) in height, was made to enshrine the arm of St Lachtin of Freshford, Co. Kilkenny, patron of Donaghmore Church, Co. Cork. It is of bronze, inlaid with silver and niello and some gold (of which little remains), and contains a wooden core. The palm, nails

and back of the hand are inlaid with silver and decorated with scrolls and knotwork, both filigree and stamped. The arm is divided by four vertical bands carrying an inscription, and around the middle is an openwork collar in the Irish Urnes style. Thus the arm is organized into eight tall panels, some of which carry animal ornament and others interlacing. Two small horizontal bands at the base complete the decoration; the shrine is closed by a decorative cap. The inscription records, amongst others, the names Maelsechnaill Ua Cellachan, king of Munster, and Cormac son of Mac Carthaig, royal heir of Munster, suggesting that the object was made between 1118 and 1127.

The shrine was preserved at Donaghmore until the mid-18th century when it was acquired by Sir Andrew Fountaine of Narford Hall, Norfolk. At the Fountaine Sale it was purchased by the Government and deposited with the Royal Irish Academy in 1884; it is now in the NMI.

St Manchan's Shrine. This is the largest and most imposing shrine of its type in Ireland, 46·5 cm. (18 in.) in height. Standing on four legs, it is a gable- or roof-shaped reliquary of yew wood, decorated with panels of gilt-bronze interlaced animals in a style closely similar to that of the CROSS OF CONG; it therefore dates to the early 12th century. A large ornamental cross with bosses at the ends of the arms and in the centre decorates each main face. There are borders of red and yellow enamel at the sides and similar panels on the arms of the crosses. A series of relief figures was applied later in the 12th century. The shrine is equipped with four stout loops for carrying. Opened in the British Museum in 1935, it was found to contain a few crumbling bones, including part of a femur. It is preserved in the church at Boher, Co. Offaly.

Shrine of St Patrick's Bell. The *Annals of Ulster*, quoting the lost *Book of Cuanu*, record that the 'Clog and Edachta' ('Bell of the Will') was found in St Patrick's tomb in the year 552. St Colum Cille had it enshrined and given to the Church of Armagh. Whether this account is historical or not, an ancient bell was preserved at Armagh from early times. It is made of folded sheets of iron dipped in bronze and, in or about the year 1100, a new and sumptuous shrine was made for it at the behest of Domhnall O'Lochlann, King of Ireland, by the craftsman Cú Duilig Ó Inmainen and his sons, as the inscription on it records.

The bell is 19·4 cm. (7⅝ in.) high including the handle, and 13 × 10·1 cm. (5⅛ × 4 in.) wide at the base. The shrine, 25 cm. (10¼ in.) high, is bell-shaped (*see* pl. XIX) and has a sliding panel at the base, by means of which it can be opened and closed. The shrine is of bronze, decorated with panels of gold filigree, openwork panels with interlaced animals in a marvellously fluid version of the Irish Urnes style. The back is ornamented by a silver plate of pierced crosses. Two rock crystals (one clearly a botched replacement for missing ornaments) and eight glass studs are present, the glass probably being a later addition. The sides bear two projections holding rings for straps or chains.

Mentioned frequently in the *Annals*, the relic was in the hereditary custodianship of the O'Mulholland

shrines. The 'buckle' of the Moylough Belt Shrine, made of bronze with ornamental silver plates and an enamelled boss; probably 8th century. NMI.

silverwork. Two-handled cup with engraved coat-of-arms (of Archer?), by Thomas Williamson, Dublin, 1734–5. Victoria and Albert Museum, London.

family. The last representative died in 1858, bequeathing it to Adam MacClean of Belfast, from whose estate it was purchased by DR JAMES TODD. On Dr Todd's death it was acquired by the Royal Irish Academy, with whose collection it is now housed in the NMI.

Moylough Belt Shrine. Found in the course of turf digging in Co. Sligo in 1944, the shrine (now NMI) takes the form of an elaborate hinged metal belt. Inside it are fragments of leather, presumably the relic of a saint, whose name is not known. Made of tinned bronze, it is elaborately decorated with enamels, millefiori, stamped silver ornaments and cast animal patterns. The buckle is most elaborate in its design and clearly mimics large 6th/7th-century Germanic types. The dating of the object is somewhat controversial, but it is probably 8th century.   MFR

Síamsa Tíre. The National Folk Theatre Ltd, established 1968 by Pat Ahern as Síamsóirí na Ríochta. It was incorporated in Tralee in 1974, and rehoused in a restored older theatre in 1978. Irish folklore and folk-traditions are given a theatrical dimension through music, mime, song and dance. The company has toured in Britain, Europe and North America.   CF-S

silverwork. From *c.* 1500 silver was commonly worked in Ireland. The vast bulk of items made before *c.* 1650 that have survived are ecclesiastical, mostly chalices, many of which are datable from engraved inscriptions. The use of silver for domestic articles did not develop in Ireland to any great extent until after 1660. The manufacture of domestic silver continued to increase until it reached its height during the period 1750–1800, when there was a thriving manufacture not only in Dublin, but also in Cork and Limerick (see separate sub-entries below). After the Revocation of the Edict of Nantes in 1685 some Huguenot silver-smiths arrived in Ireland and brought a needed refinement to the styles of silver. During the latter part of the 17th century *chinoiserie* motifs, vertical flutes and gadrooned borders were the main features used in decoration. Irish domestic silver was at its most restrained from 1705 to 1740, being manufactured by craftsmen using heavy-gauge metal. It was a time of plain surfaces and elegant proportions, the decoration being mostly in the form of crests and coats-of-arms, the latter often in elaborately worked ornamental cartouches.

The emphasis on fine craftsmanship among the guilds led to the practice of apprenticeship as a means of training workmen in their trade, and the charter of 1637 ordered that an apprentice must serve seven years with a recognized master. The Goldsmiths Company was insistent on the necessity of this very full and careful training before any person could call himself a goldsmith or silversmith. This resulted in an exceptionally high standard of craftsmanship.

For the rich and well-to-do in the 18th century Ireland was a place of gaiety and high living. Entertaining was on a grand scale and the demand for table silver increased daily. Silver teapots came to Ireland *c.* 1702 and were in fashion until *c.* 1735, when they lost their popularity to china and porcelain pots and, apart from an occasional one made in Cork, do not appear to have been made between 1735 and 1770. The earliest ones were copied from the Chinese form, which had a globular body and were very small. The earliest Irish silver table-forks date from the late 17th century, long after they had come into use in continental Europe. The two-handled cup was an important part of any household, being used for communal drinking, at christenings, weddings and other celebrations. In one year Matthew West made nearly 500 such cups and had them hallmarked in Dublin. As well as every imaginable form of domestic plate, snuff boxes, nutmeg graters, shoe buckles, stocking buckles and sword handles suggest an age of stylish living. The aristocratic dish-ring is one of the more characteristic of Irish wares, being the forerunner of the insulated table-mat. Though invented in England *c.* 1704, the dish-ring was developed in Ireland from *c.* 1740, especially in the florid Rococo style which remained fashionable in Ireland until 1770.

Dish-ring with openwork design incorporating architectural motifs, Dublin, 1780; diameter 19·6 cm. (7¾ in.).

Parcel-gilt reproduction 'Tara Bracelet' by Waterhouse & Co., c. 1851, intended to complement the 'Royal Tara Brooches'. Ulster Museum.

This was a period of elaborate decoration, usually asymmetrical in form, known as chasing; it took two forms, flat chasing (which consisted of hammering the pattern on the surface with an iron tool shaped for the purpose), and repoussé work (which consisted of hammering the design on one surface, usually the inner, so that it appeared in relief on the other). This decoration developed into a peculiar Irish style which featured farmyard scenes with animals, shepherds and dairymaids, with churches and farm buildings, surrounded by large asymmetrical scrolls.

The Adam style of Neo-Classicism first made an appearance in Irish silver c. 1770 (although candlesticks had been made in this style from c. 1760) and lasted into the early 1880s. It was aimed at recapturing the simplicity and linear forms of Classical art based on the discoveries of Pompeii and Herculaneum. It was brought to England and developed by the Adam brothers. There is no special Irish version of this Classical influence. It is probably best remembered in Ireland for its beautiful bright-cut engraving, being a linear pattern cut into the surface with a sharp tool

called a graver to capture pools of shimmering light created by the movement of flickering candles. By the end of the century trade was again changing. This elegant period was being described as 'too much neatness and prettiness', although examples of bright-cut engraving occur well into the first half of the 19th century.

The 19th century opened with a disastrous period for design. The Act of Union had crushed any hope of cultural revival and the silversmiths in Ireland had to cope with competition from factory production in England which had brought the price of mass-produced silver wares within the reach of a growing middle-class market. Also, because of the abolition of tariffs, it was easier to import and assemble parts made in Birmingham than go to the high expense of making hand-wrought silver. Political pressures made it difficult for craftsmen to use the talents that had made Irish silver so important during the previous century. Many silversmiths closed shop and by 1850 not one was left in Cork or Limerick. A few managed to survive in Dublin, and carried on making silver with a heavy form of repoussé decoration similar to the Rococo period, but usually symmetrical in design and not as elegant in form. By 1840 a new interest was being shown in antiquarian studies and this had a most profound and striking effect in the making of silver and gold jewellery. In 1842 Waterhouse & Co. converted a copy of an antique fibula into a brooch and in 1849 the ROYAL IRISH ACADEMY gave permission to make copies of antique brooches in its collection. This was the start of a new revival in manufacturing of silver and gold objects, resulting in an extensive souvenir trade. This was further increased after the find of the 'TARA' BROOCH, which was sold to Waterhouse & Co. It became known as the Royal Tara brooch after Queen Victoria bought two copies. Many silversmiths followed Waterhouse's lead in this field and had displays at the Great Exhibition in London in 1851 and at the Dublin exhibitions of 1853 and 1856. Other Irish motifs, such as the shamrock, harp, Celtic cross and interlaced work, began to appear, and by the end of the century most silver carried one, if not all, of the above forms of decoration.

In 1894 the Arts and Crafts Society of Ireland (see ARTS AND CRAFTS MOVEMENT) was formed to foster artistic industries in Ireland and held its first exhibition in 1896. Several silversmiths, including Edmond Johnson, West & Sons, and Hopkins & Hopkins, exhibited copies of sugar bowls, cream jugs, Ardagh chalices (see ARDAGH HOARD) and METHERS, but nothing very original in design, as well as many copies of Irish brooches similar to ones exhibited in 1851 and 1852 by Waterhouse. Much the same could be said for the Arts and Crafts Society exhibition of 1899.

The silver and jewellery trades moved into the 20th century still copying old designs. The Roman Catholic Church began employing Irish craftsmen to manufacture ecclesiastical vessels for use both at home and by Irish Orders in the USA and elsewhere abroad; thus, like the Protestant Church in the 17th century, the Roman Catholic Church now became the main patron

(*Above*) Ornamented two-handled mether by Edmond Johnson, 1901; the design is derived from the ancient type of Irish drinking vessel, usually of wood or leather (cf. p. 152). Private Collection.

(*Right*) Rococo-style coffee pot by Daniel McCarthy, Cork, *c.* 1765. Ulster Museum.

to the silver and gold hollow-ware trade which continued until the 1960s following Vatican II, one of the results of which was a cutback in the use of elaborate altar-furnishings.

By 1926 the public were tiring of Celtic interlacing and round towers and shamrocks, as was evident in the designs for the new Irish Free State coinage of that year. This, however, did not apply to silverware, where this form of decoration continued and new schools of thought in design were almost non-existent. To try to counteract this the Company of Goldsmiths – for the first time since its foundation in 1637 – brought out a commemorative hallmark in the form of *An Claldheamh Solais* ('The Sword of Light'). This mark, which commemorated the 50th anniversary of the Rising of 1916, was stamped in addition to the existing hallmarks on all Irish-made articles of gold and silver (other than jewellery and watch-cases) during the year 1966; many pieces were commissioned and the silver trade showed an upward trend. A further mark in the form of the 8th-century gold gorget from Gleninsheen (NMI) was introduced in 1973 for one year to denote Ireland's entry into the European Economic Community. In 1980 the rise in the price of silver bullion resulted in an enormous cutback in the number of silver hollow-ware articles being manufactured. The jewellery trade continues with increasing competition not only from England but from Germany and Asian countries.

The greatest period for design in silver was the 18th century when items were hand-wrought and an apprenticeship scheme guaranteed a high standard of craftsmanship. The industrial revolution and factory-made wares in England, coupled with the Act of Union, dealt a hard blow to silversmiths of Ireland from which they have never fully recovered. A more detailed account of the history of the silversmiths of the three main centres – Cork, Dublin and Limerick – is given below.

D. Bennett, *Irish Georgian Silver*, 1972; K. Ticher, *Irish Silver in the Rococo Period*, 1972.

silversmiths of Cork. In addition to Dublin, the city of Cork had a thriving silver trade dated as far back as the 15th century. The goldsmiths were incorporated with several other guilds in 1656 and were given the title of 'The Master and Wardens and Company of the Society of Goldsmiths of the City of Cork'. During the 17th and early 18th centuries the Cork manufacturers used the emblems of a ship between two castles (or various derivative forms of these marks). These punches had more or less ceased to exist by the period of George I, and the use of the word 'sterling' (with various spellings and abbreviations) succeeded these marks. The word 'dollar' also occasionally appears on Cork silver, indicating that the piece was manufactured from Spanish dollars melted into ingots. There is no provision for any marks on Irish silver other than the harp crowned and the maker's mark (*see* Silversmiths of Dublin, below). All articles manufactured in Cork should have been sent to Dublin to be assayed and hallmarked. With the imposition of duty of 6*d.* per ounce under the 1729 Act and the institution, under the 1807 Act, of the compulsory stamp of the sovereign's head all plate manufactured in Ireland

Punch bowl with ribbed sides and scallop-shell decoration by Thomas Bolton, 1704. NMI.

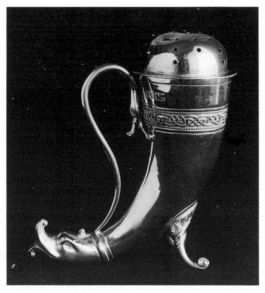

Sugar castor, by Edmond Johnson, probably one of a pair shown at the Arts and Crafts Society Exhibition, 1896, the design being based on the Charter Horn of the Cavanaghs. Private Collection.

should have been sent to Dublin for hallmarking when a return journey of 320 miles by coach or on horseback was anything but a practical proposition for a parcel of silver, with the prospect of a highwayman at every corner. The silver business was so lucrative in the 18th century that some of the best county families in the south of Ireland were glad to apprentice their younger sons to the leading silversmiths in Munster's capital. The trade thrived until the Act of Union at the start of the 19th century, which saw the abolition of most tariffs, a step which enabled silver to be imported fully

assembled into Ireland, hallmarked in Dublin and sold as being of Irish manufacture. By the mid-19th century there was not a single silversmith working in Cork.
silversmiths of Dublin. Silversmiths and goldsmiths appear to have been under the control of the guild system which entered Ireland in the wake of Anglo-Norman settlements in 1169. The charter of 1192 to the City of Dublin states that its citizens shall have 'all their reasonable guilds'. The earliest record of a named guild is a list of those admitted in 1226–7 to one known as the Dublin Guild Merchant; this list includes a goldsmith (a term applied also to silversmiths or anyone connected with the two trades). From the middle of the 14th century there are many wills which record bequests of domestic silver. Much of this was probably made in Ireland, but none survives.

To understand the workings of the goldsmiths' and silversmiths' trade it is requisite that we should turn back the pages of history to 1555, in which year the Guild of All Saints, whose charter – the date of which is unknown – had been accidentally burned, applied to the Common Council of the City of Dublin for recognition under the common seal of the city; this was granted in April 1557. This was not a new charter, merely a recognition that the original one was in existence before the fire and entitled the company to the same privileges as the other fraternities and guilds of the city. They were endowed with the rights which the original charter allowed, with one important exception. An insertion was included to the effect that the Mayor of Dublin, for the time being, should have oversight and correction of their orders as often as he should think expedient, which meant that the Common Council could interfere at any time in the affairs of the company. It also stated that none should be admitted to the fraternity except they be of 'English name and blode'. It also ordered that each craftsman was to stamp his wares with his mark, usually his initials, and then to submit the vessel to Goldsmiths Hall where it would be stamped with a lion, a harp and a castle. No pieces bearing these marks are extant.

This form of administration proved unsatisfactory and there appears to have been no proper control over the trade at this time. The year 1637 found its members petitioning the King, asking that they – the Guild of All Saints – might be incorporated by royal charter. Their petition was favourably received and on 22 December 1637 a charter was granted by Charles I. With the granting of this new charter the 'Wardens and Company of Goldsmiths of our said city of Dublin' (the title mentioned in the charter, being translated from abbreviated Latin) was put on a sound foundation and many of the orders set forth in that document remain applicable to the present day. It ruled that the punch of the artificer must be impressed on each piece of silver or gold. This was usually done before it was sent to Goldsmiths Hall for testing. The punch consisted of a metal die with the initials cut in reverse, and each craftsman had to register his punch or mark with the Master and Wardens, where it was recorded in the work book of the Company for reference and identification.

(Opposite) XVIII **stained glass.** Detail of a window by Sarah Purser in Loughrea Cathedral, showing St Brendan.

XIX Shrine of St Patrick's Bell. The bronze shrine, 25 cm. (10¼ in.) high, with intricate flowing decoration in the Irish Urnes style, *c.* 1100. NMI.

XX 'Tara' Brooch. The front of the 8th-century pseudo-penannular brooch, showing cast panels with filigree ornament and inset amber and glass; length 22·5 cm. (8⅞ in.). NMI.

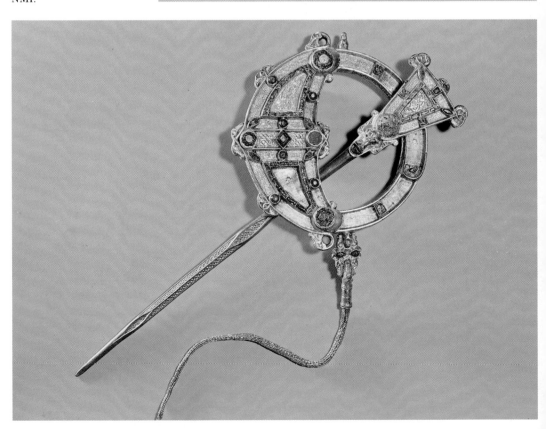

The charter prescribed the standard for gold and silver wares as being 22 carats for gold (pure gold is 24 carats), and 11 oz. 2 dwts of pure silver in every 12 Troy ounces of alloy. Pure silver, like pure gold, is too soft to fashion durable vessels, and the charter makes allowance for this by permitting a standard of fineness (which still applies today) equalling 925 parts of silver in every 1,000 parts of alloy. The metal for the remaining 75 parts per thousand in the alloy is not prescribed; it is usually copper. An assay office was established at Goldsmiths Hall and all gold and silver was tested there and, if found to be of the required standard, was stamped with a fineness mark in the form of a harp crowned. Any pieces of a lesser standard were required to be broken up.

The marks were introduced at the beginning of 1638, together with a date letter, not prescribed, denoting the year of manufacture in accordance with a practice adopted by the London Goldsmiths Company as early as 1478. In 1730 a fourth mark, the figure of Hibernia, was added to denote the payment of duty of 6d. an ounce. In 1784 came the introduction of two new standards for gold: 20 carats and 18 carats. The 20-carat standard is peculiar to Ireland, with a fineness mark in the form of a plume of three feathers; the numeral 20 also appears with the maker's mark on articles made of 20-carat gold. The 18-carat fineness mark is a unicorn's head; this became one of the most popular standards for gold jewellery. The numeral 18 also appears with the maker's mark on articles of 18-carat gold. In 1807 a further mark, the king's head, was introduced on gold and silver and the duty increased to 1/– per ounce. The king's head mark (the queen's at that time) was discontinued in 1890 when excise duties on silver and gold were abolished. An aditional fineness of 9 carats was introduced in 1854, with a fineness mark of a numeral 9 with the addition of the fineness expressed in parts per thousand, i.e. ·375. This is the lowest standard permitted. A further and final standard for gold was introduced in 1935 by Government Order for 14 carats, with a fineness mark of a numeral 14 and, in addition, the fineness expressed in parts per thousand, i.e. ·585. All the above-mentioned gold standards, i.e. 22, 20, 18, 14 and 9 carats, are still in use.

The Company of Goldsmiths carries out its functions of supervising the trade today in much the same way as it did in 1637. A board of 20 members is sworn in for life, and the offices of Master and two Wardens are rotated annually. The Assay Office, with a large staff headed by an assay master, daily tests all silver and gold, both manufactured and imported into the country, and applies the appropriate stamps. These hallmarks are so called because they are stamped at Goldsmiths Hall. The powers of the company, now in existence for nearly three and a half centuries, have been extended several times by Act of Parliament and by Government Order to meet changing conditions. Its original purpose – to protect the public from fraud when buying articles of gold and silver – still remains.
silversmiths of Limerick. The city of Limerick had a total of 15 corporations, consisting of smiths, carpenters, weavers, shoemakers, tailors, saddlers, masons, bakers, coopers, surgeon-barbers, butchers, tobacconists, tallow chandlers, hatters and brewers – the goldsmiths being part of the corporation of smiths. The earliest dated piece of Limerick silver is probably the Askeaton chalice, inscribed 'Ex do Simo Eaton Armr Per Askeaton Anno 1663'. The Eglish paten, however, has an inscription on the base with 1559 in Tudor lettering and also 'Ye Church of Eglish 1775'. The paten is in typical 16th-century style but it also bears the mark 'GM' (for George Moore, fl. 1748–84). The later inscription is poorly done and Moore may have had the paten in for repair and struck his mark on it.

During the 17th century the marks on Limerick silver consisted of the maker's mark, a castle gate and a star. It has been suggested that the latter marks derive from the middle of the century when Sir Geoffrey Galway added a fourth armorial tablet to the 15th-century tomb of Edmund Galway in St Mary's Cathedral. This fourth quartering, depicting Baal's Bridge, had been granted to John de Burgo of Galway in 1361 or 1364 for his spirited defence of that bridge. It shows the bridge with four arches guarded at each end by a castle, and the mark has two mullets above the bridge and one beneath it. It may be that the silversmiths adapted their mark from part of his arms, or it could be a variant on the arms of the city itself, a gateway between two towers. Many 17th-century pieces exist with these marks. Like those of Cork, the Limerick silversmiths seem to have adopted the sterling mark *c.* 1710, and for most of the 18th and 19th centuries their products bear the word 'sterling' and a maker's mark, often struck twice. One curious mark used by three Limerick silversmiths was a punch resembling the Crowned Harp punch used in Dublin (*see* above) but with the maker's initials replacing the strings of the harp. A fair quantity of silver was manufactured in Limerick from the mid-17th century up to *c.* 1820, by which time the Act of Union had dealt a hard blow to craftsmen generally in Ireland. Limerick was the third most important silver-manufacturing city in Ireland after Dublin and Cork. D B

D. Bennett/R. ffolliott, *The Irish Ancestor*, vol. x, no. 2 (1978).

Sinn Féin. As a doctrine of national self-reliance, Sinn Féin (meaning 'Ourselves alone') was formulated in 1905 by Arthur Griffith, patriotic journalist and subsequently first President of the Executive Council (Prime Minister) of the Irish Free State. The title was adopted in 1907 by the Sinn Féin League. From 1908 onwards, the movement, which brought together a number of small groups, was known simply as Sinn Féin. Its objectives were cultural, political and economic in nature. Reflecting the trends of the time, it stressed the individuality of the Irish nation in language and literature. Griffith saw in the restoration of an independent Irish parliament under the same Crown as Britain the answer to Ireland's political aspirations. Sinn Féin also advocated a high measure of economic self-sufficiency, but made little political headway before 1917, when in the wake of the Rising of

Skellig Michael. One of the cliff-top corbelled oratories overlooking the sea.

Smyth, Edward. Statue of Charles Lucas, 1722; marble, life size. City Hall, Dublin.

1916, it adopted a republican policy and strongly opposed the British plan to extend wartime conscription to Ireland. In 1921–2, the movement split on the issue of the Anglo-Irish Treaty and the Civil War (1922–4) followed. The republican wing continued to be called Sinn Féin under E. de Valéra's leadership, but, in 1926–7, he led a majority of the party into parliamentary politics under the name of Fianna Fáil. Since then, Sinn Féin has represented minority splinter groups of the republican movement.   KBN

Skellig Michael, Co. Kerry. The embodiment of the ascetic life-style of the early Irish monks, this island monastery – dedicated to the patron saint of high places – perches precariously on a platform 170 m. (560 ft) above the sea. It consists of the remains of six BEEHIVE HUTS and two corbelled oratories, as well as a small medieval church. Raided by the VIKINGS, the site was probably abandoned early in the 13th century.   PH

Smith, Sydney Bernard (1936–   ). Poet and wit; a specialist in satirical and humorous poetry. His recent publications are *Priorities* (1980), *Sensualities* (1981) and *Scurrilities* (1981).   T McC

Smyth, Edward (1749–1812). Sculptor; born in Co. Meath, he was trained in Dublin by Simon Vierpyl. His early work, the statue of Charles Lucas (in Dublin City Hall) designed in 1772, demonstrates his great talent in the tradition of late Baroque portraiture. He was employed as an artisan by Henry Darley, a building contractor, through whom he came into contact with GANDON in 1781. Gandon was impressed by him and gave him the commission to carve the ornamental stonework, riverine heads, Royal Arms, pediment figures and rooftop statues on the Custom House, where the surviving work is of excellent quality. He also carved statues and reliefs for Gandon's Four Courts (mostly destroyed by fire) and the King's Inns. Smyth also worked for the architect FRANCIS JOHNSTON at the Bank of Ireland, carving statues to Flaxman's designs after 1804, and at the Chapel Royal in Dublin Castle. He also carved some fine portrait busts. He became first head of the DUBLIN SOCIETY's School of Modelling in 1811. In general his work shows three-dimensional strength; however, his funerary memorials are disappointing. There is a certain late Baroque survival in Smyth's work and he was at his best in creating bold outdoor shapes; he was less at ease in the Neo-Classical idiom.   JT
W. Strickland, *Dictionary of Irish Artists* (1913); V. Barrow, 'Edward Smyth', *Dublin Historical Record*, xxxiii, no. 2, March 1980.

Smyth, John (fl. 1758–69). Architect. This Irish-born architect displayed great mastery of the Burlingtonian Palladian style. He designed St Thomas's church, Marlborough Street, Dublin (destroyed 1922) in 1758 and modelled it directly on Palladio's church of the Redentore in Venice. His other church, St Catherine's, Dublin (1769), has the finest 18th-century church façade in the city. He is credited with the building of the Provost's House, TRINITY COLLEGE, in 1759. WG

Solomons, Estella (1882–1968). Landscape and portrait painter and graphic artist; born in Dublin, she studied at the Royal Hibernian Academy schools under WALTER OSBORNE, at the Metropolitan School of Art in Dublin, and in London under WILLIAM ORPEN. She also studied at the Chelsea School of Art, and at Colarossi's in Paris. She was elected ARHA in 1925 and subsequently HRHA. She painted a series of portraits of leading contemporary literary, artistic and political figures, many of particular importance as she was a member of Cumann na mBan, assisted in the Rising of 1916, and was active thereafter in the Republican cause. She was married to the writer James Starkey (Seamus O'Sullivan). Her paintings and etchings are in many private and public collections in Ireland. CMacG
Hilary Pyle, *Portraits of Patriots*, 1966.

Somerville and Ross. Writers; Edith Œnone Somerville (1858–1949), born in Corfu of a Co. Cork family, and Violet Florence Martin (1862–1915), born in Co. Galway, were second cousins who met in 1886 and soon afterwards began writing fiction (as 'Somerville and Ross'). The collaboration is so perfect that it is almost impossible to distinguish individual contributions. They shared a Protestant Ascendancy background and supported the Union; at the same time they were well aware of the faults typical of their social class and much of their work chronicles the decline of the Big House. *The Real Charlotte* (1894) vividly depicts both Ascendancy society and the forces, internal and external, that were soon to bring about its virtual extinction. In a lighter vein, *Some Experiences of an Irish R. M.* (1899) was a great popular success. In these stories the authors exploit the comic potential of English, Anglo-Irish, and the native peasantry alike. After Martin's death in 1915, her cousin claimed to be still in regular communication with her, and books continued to appear as jointly authored. Nevertheless, the later work in general shows a falling off in quality, though *The Big House of Inver* (1925) offers a memorable picture of a once-proud tradition in its final stages of decay. PLM
Maurice Collis, *Somerville and Ross*, 1968; John Cronin, *Somerville and Ross*, 1972.

Souter, Camille (1929–). Painter; born in Northamptonshire and educated in Ireland, she was largely self-taught as a painter. She held her first 'one-man' show in 1956, and represented Ireland at the Paris Biennale in 1961. She received the Irish-American Cultural Institute Award in 1975; and won the Grand Prix International de l'Art Contemporain de Monte-Carlo, 1977. In 1980 she was awarded a major mid-term retrospective in the Douglas Hyde Gallery of Trinity College, Dublin. She is best known for her atmospheric, plastic, approach to landscape painting in Ireland, and is represented in all major Irish public collections. CMacG

Staigue Fort, Co. Kerry. A stone fort, 150 m. (500 ft) above sea-level, near the head of a small valley looking S near Castle Cove on the S side of Iveragh peninsula. The wall, which is 5 m. (16 ft 6 in.) thick at the base, 2 m. (6 ft 6 in.) at the top, and up to 5·50 m. (18 ft) high, encloses a circular area 27 m. (90 ft) across; ten flights of stairs running laterally in two tiers provide access to the top of the wall from the inner side. Access to the enclosure is by a lintelled doorway; there are two wall-chambers, at SW and NW. The wall is surrounded by a fosse 2·70 m. (9 ft) wide, with a low outer bank. The fort is probably in the Early Iron Age tradition. MH

stained glass. Although written evidence shows that long before the 18th century there were in Ireland windows glazed, sometimes with stained glass, none of the medieval glass excavated in recent years (e.g. at the Augustinian Abbey, Ballina, Co. Mayo, at HOLY CROSS ABBEY, Co. Tipperary, or at Kells Priory, Co. Kilkenny) or the few pieces still *in situ* have been proved to be of indigenous production; several examples have been shown to be of foreign manufacture. The dating and provenance of other random fragments available are as yet necessarily speculative. Fragments excavated in 1846 at St Canice's Cathedral, Kilkenny, may date back to the extensive glazing scheme carried out by Bishop Richard de Ledrede, *c.* 1354. If the Papal Nuncio's offer of £700 in 1645 had not been rejected, at least the reputedly magnificent east window might have escaped desecration only five years later, when Cromwell's troops 'broke down all the windows and carried away the glass'.

The small heraldic, narrative or genre panels, so popular in England in the 17th century after the Reformation and the destruction of the Lorraine glass-houses, were also imported into Ireland from Cromwell's departure onwards.

In the 18th century, three of the leading glass painters in England were Irish born or Dublin trained: THOMAS JERVAIS worked for distinguished patrons in Ireland and England; RICHARD HAND worked in Ireland for at least fifteen years before settling in England; and James Pearson (*c.* 1759–*c.* 1838), none of whose work has survived or been recorded in Ireland. Most windows in 18th-century England and Ireland were painted in enamelled colours on to rectangles of glass inserted into a lead or cast-iron grille and were based on cartoons or paintings by well-known Old Masters or contemporary painters. Showy, realistic but insipid ('washy' according to Horace Walpole), and devoid of religious feeling, they were neither real paintings nor stained glass.

Although the Gothic Revival and the inherent growing interest in the lost secrets of the chemical properties of medieval stained glass at times encouraged a more sensitive architectural approach, few of the many (over fifty) artists and studios working in Ireland in the 19th century reached a high standard; nevertheless, the craft thrived. At the beginning of the 19th century, the tradition of 'transparencies' painted on to glass continued for use on festive occasions, as well as for windows. In 1814 the glazing of Dublin Castle

stained glass. Memorial window to Lt Stephen H. Lewis of the Connaught Rangers (killed in action in 1915 at Gallipoli) in St Multose's, Kinsale, Co. Cork.

Chapel gave work to several established Dublin glaziers, notably Joshua Bradley of Hammond Lane. In the first half of the century, GEORGE M'ALLISTER provides a link between the two centuries, and ladies like Louisa Beaufort (at Collon, Co. Louth) and Louisa, Marchioness of Waterford, produced creditable designs. Well-known in England, where he established a thriving business, was the Dublin-born MICHAEL O'CONNOR. F. S. Barff's spirited Celtic Revival clerestory windows (1863) in St Patrick's Cathedral, Dublin, deviate from an increasingly eclectic sameness. Such was the Victorian demand for stained glass that respected firms like J. & D. Casey and Earley & Powell of Dublin and, before the end of the century, Watson & Co. of Youghal, Joshua Clarke of Dublin and Campbell Bros. and Ward & Partners of Belfast were faced with stiff competition not only from commercial English and Scottish firms but also the ubiquitous Mayers of Munich, with their assembly-line, mass-produced windows, who easily undercut small businesses obliged to import all their raw materials.

By the beginning of the 20th century EDWARD MARTYN, who blamed the 'speedy rise of cheap sham' on an uneducated public and clergy, felt that stained glass was the most degraded art in Ireland, but 'If we are determined to have bad work, it is better to have it bad Irish than bad foreign'. His campaign began with an invitation to the father of the English Arts and Crafts stained-glass revival, Christopher Whall (1849–1924) to make some windows for his family church at Ardrahan, Co. Galway, and to initiate stained-glass classes at the Metropolitan School of Art in Dublin. As Whall was already so committed in London, he sent a pupil, Alfred E. Child, and a glazier in his place.

By 1903, Martyn and SARAH PURSER the painter, had founded the Dublin workshop 'The Tower of Glass' (*see* TÚR GLOINE, AN). Child, MICHAEL HEALY and Sarah Purser made windows for LOUGHREA CATHEDRAL, An Túr's first major commission (*see* pl. XVIII). Catherine O'Brien, Beatrice Elvery (*see* GLENAVY, LADY), Ethel Rhind, WILHELMINA GEDDES and Hubert McGoldrick were also active shareholders, each working over differing periods and contributing to the high material and technical standards, imaginative originality and whimsical, often spiritual quality, which became hallmarks of the Irish stained-glass revival.

Unconnected with An Túr Gloine was HARRY CLARKE, trained in his father Joshua's business and by Child; among his intricately jewelled windows are eleven in the HONAN CHAPEL, Cork, and a number of minutely detailed miniature panels illustrating poems. The Clarke Studios trained or employed many of the next generation of craftsmen, e.g. Kathleen Quigley, William McBride (who founded the stained-glass Craftworkers Guild in 1919), Richard King, William Dowling and George Walsh. Although the many Arts and Crafts and Art Industries exhibitions (both in Ireland and elsewhere), journals such as *The Studio* and *The Irish Builder*, and commissions for memorial windows after World War I all helped to boost trade, imported work was a continual threat to the necessarily more expensive work of the Earley, Clarke and An Túr

Gloine Studios. By 1935, when EVIE HONE became a member of the latter studio, Irish stained glass was being sent all over the world and at its best was recognized as being of eminently high quality. Hone, trained in London and France as a painter, brought a loose painterly technique to the craft. Ireland's importance in the development of the modern movement at this period has been acknowledged by John Piper, who has written that the sympathetic influences of Geddes, Clarke and Hone were responsible for establishing positive constructive relations between stained glass and painting.

Although World War II adversely affected the art, Evie Hone acted as a bridge between the first generation of artist-craftsmen and women and the few younger individuals who now work in Ireland, most of whom drew inspiration from her: Patrick Pollen, who rented part of An Túr Gloine in 1953 on the strength of having seen her great window (1952) at Eton College, PATRICK PYE and Helen Moloney, who works in conjunction with the Derry architect Liam McCormick. Alan Tomlin, who inherited his father's Irish Stained Glass Studios in Dublin, and John Murphy, head of the Stained Glass Department at the National College of Art and Design, are among those descended from the Clarke Studios.

Unfortunately, by 1973 both the Earley and the Clarke Studios had closed down and the current revival of interest in the traditional, innovatory and secular aspects of the craft in Germany, America and England has so far largely bypassed Ireland.   N G B
Michael Wynne, 'Stained Glass in Ireland, principally Irish Stained Glass 1760–1963' (unpublished Ph.D. thesis, Trinity College, Dublin), 1975; Nicola Gordon Bowe, *Recent Irish Stained Glass*, 1982.

standing stone. A stone pillar, varying in height up to a maximum of 6 m. (20 ft), usually marking a burial of the Late Neolithic or Early Bronze Age, as at Carrownacaw, Co. Down; Punchestown, Co. Kildare; and LONGSTONE, Co. Tipperary. *See also* STONE ALIGNMENT; STONE CIRCLE.   M H

Stanyhurst, Richard (1547–1618). Historian; born in Dublin and educated at University College, Oxford. His 'Description of Ireland' and his historical account of Ireland during Henry VIII's reign appeared in Holinshed's *Chronicles* (1577). Following his notably unsuccessful translation into English of Virgil's *Aeneid*, I–IV (1582), he wrote only in Latin. His later works on Ireland include the pseudo-historical *De rebus in Hibernia gestis* (1584) and a life of ST PATRICK, *De Vita S. Patricii Hiberniae Apostoli* (1587). His work was attacked by both GEOFFREY KEATING and Sir JAMES WARE.   I C R

Stapleton, Michael (d. 1801). Stuccodore; his activity was first recorded when working on Powerscourt House, Dublin, in 1771. His Adamesque, Neo-Classical style had then already reached maturity and was strikingly different from Rococo work. He used repetitive patterns, produced by moulds, in low relief and emphasized by strong colours. He worked on the

Examination Hall in TRINITY COLLEGE in the 1780s, and later in the Chapel. His work is to be seen in Nos. 16 and 17 St Stephen's Green, Dublin (*c.* 1777); 34 and 35 North Great George's Street, Dublin (1783); Belvedere House, Great Denmark Street, Dublin (*c.* 1785); Mount Kennedy, Co. Wicklow (1780s); Lucan House, Co. Dublin (1790s); Dunsany Castle, Co. Meath; and Ardress, Co. Armagh. Laterly, as a builder, he was involved in the development of the Mountjoy Square area of Dublin.   W G

Stephens, James (1880/82–1950). Writer; born in Dublin, his childhood was a hard one, and he knew poverty and hunger. As a young man he became an ardent nationalist and supported Arthur Griffith's SINN FÉIN movement. The fantasies of LORD DUNSANY, the fiction of OSCAR WILDE, and the visionary poetry of William Blake were early influences upon his own writing, which blended realism, fantasy, philosophy, and whimsical comedy. His most important early work, the novel *The Crock of Gold* (1912), brought him popularity and critical acclaim. The Easter Rising of 1916 revived his interest in the Irish language and in the old Celtic literature, and led to a decade of intense literary activity. *Reincarnations* (1918) contained adaptations from the Irish of several poets. In *Irish Fairy Tales* (1920), *Deirdre* (1923), and *In the Land of Youth* (1924), he recreated traditional Irish stories, infusing them with his own idiosyncratic sensibility. His collections of poetry include *Insurrections* (1909), *Songs from the Clay* (1915) and *Kings and the Moon* (1938). In later years Stephens's vision darkened, partly as the result of his long study of Eastern thought; *Strict Joy* (1931) and *Kings and the Moon* (1938) exemplify this mood. A series of BBC broadcasts about literature represent a happier element in his later years.   P L M
Augustine Martin, *James Stephens, A Critical Study*, 1977; Hilary Pyle, *James Stephens*, 1965.

Sterne, Laurence (1713–68). Writer; born at Clonmel, Co. Tipperary, where his English father was an army officer, Sterne left Ireland at the age of ten and did not return. He became internationally famous as author of *Tristram Shandy* (1759–67) and *A Sentimental Journey* (1768). Attempts to claim him for Ireland have not been notably successful but JAMES JOYCE considered him 'my fellow-countrym[a]n'.   I C R

Stokes, Whitley (1830–1909). Philologist; born in Dublin, the son of Dr William Stokes, the friend and biographer of PETRIE. After practising law in England and a stint in the Indian Civil Service (where he served as President of the Indian Law Commission, 1879), Stokes devoted himself to Celtic studies and published numerous early Irish texts and glossaries. His *magnum opus*, the important *Thesaurus Palaeohibernicus* (co-edited by J. Strachan; 1901–10), made accessible the pre-11th century Irish glosses. His edited translation of *The Tripartite Life of Patrick* was published in 1887. Margaret Stokes (1832–1900), the antiquarian, who edited and published Lord Dunraven's *Notes on Irish Architecture*, 1875, was his sister.   B de B

Stone Age.

(*Left*) Saddle quern (for grinding cereals such as wheat or barley) from Newgrange, Co. Meath; such querns were in use in Ireland from *c.* 3500 BC. NMI.

(*Above left*) Decorated basin in one of the passages in the tumulus at Knowth, Co. Meath.

(*Above*) The dolmen at Proleek, Co. Louth, one of a number of such megalithic tombs surviving in Ireland.

Stone Age. The Mesolithic sites of MOUNT SANDEL and Lough Boora are the earliest sites inhabited by man in Ireland, being dated by radiocarbon to the millennium following 7000 BC. Both have yielded evidence of extensive fishing and fowling, of hunting wild pig and of gathering fruits. Both are sited on the water's edge, Mount Sandel on the estuary of the Bann some distance inland, and Lough Boora on a small peninsula on the edge of a lake in the tributary system of the Shannon. Mount Sandel had the remains of a circular post-built shelter 6 m. (20 ft) across. Both had implements of polished stone and narrow-blade micro-liths, the tiny pieces of chert and flint used to arm composite hunting weapons. This narrow-blade industry would be assigned to the Later Mesolithic in England and Wales.

A heavy blade industry consisting mainly of leaf-shaped 'Larnian' and 'Bann' flakes found in the Bann Valley north of Lough Neagh and in post-glacial raised beaches is assigned to a Later Mesolithic period. A series of successive sites on the Bann at Newferry, north of Lough Beg, having polished stone axeheads, fragments of bone points and bones of salmon and eel, are dated by radiocarbon to the period 5500–3500 BC and probably represent fishing stations on this fruitful river. A similar industry found in raised beaches of the maximum post-glacial marine transgression is thereby dated to the centuries before 3000 BC. Ox-bones found in these contexts at Glenarm, Rough Island, Ringneill Quay, Sutton and Dalkey Island are probably domesticated, thus indicating that the first agriculturists have arrived and that the Neolithic has begun.

The first farmers made clearances in the forest which covered a great part of the country in order to provide grazing for their cattle, sheep and goats and cultivation-patches for the cereals which they also imported. A combination of radiocarbon and pollen evidence tells of a significant tree-clearance, mainly of elm, before 3000 BC, followed in some cases by the appearance of the seeds or pollens of cereals. It may be that the simultaneous disappearance of elm over much of north and north-west Europe at this time is due to the introduction of elm disease by early farmers. Early field-systems fenced with stone walls and sealed under blanket bog at sites like BEHY in Co. Mayo document the nature of this clearance.

The cultural evidence from the earliest Neolithic is that plain shouldered pottery, kite-shaped arrowheads and Hollow Scrapers of flint and chert with polished axeheads of igneous rock mined at sites like TIEVEBULLIAGH form a Primary Neolithic assemblage which is found mainly in the northern half of the country. Rectangular post-built houses at Ballynagilly in Tyrone and BALLYGLASS in Co. Mayo are associated with this assemblage, as are 330 COURT TOMBS, apparently the earliest megalithic tombs in Ireland, found almost entirely north of a line from Clifden in Co. Galway to Dundalk in Co. Louth and with a pattern of siting which is both on the coastal plains and on the uplands, generally between 120 and 240 m. (400 and 800 ft). In Mayo their builders chose the well-drained eskers and avoided the drumlins of the eastern sector; rendzinas and grey-brown podzolics are favoured soils in Leitrim. About 40 excavated examples have yielded a record of cremated and inhumed burials with grave goods indistinguishable from the habitation assemblage.

Up to 300 PASSAGE GRAVES are grouped mainly in cemeteries centred on hilltops in the northern half of the country. Four large cemeteries, the Boyne Valley, LOUGHCREW, CARROWKEEL and Knocknarea-CARROWMORE, exhibit the finest architectural achievements of these great tomb-builders. The burial rite was multiple cremation, with which characteristic decorated hemispherical Carrowkeel bowls and a range of personal ornaments, pendants, beads and mushroom-head antler pins were deposited with enigmatic stone and chalk marbles; tools and weapons were never deposited. As in Atlantic Europe, a set of devices was carved on the tomb walls, sometimes combined in an ornamental scheme; this is found mainly in the inner reaches of passage and chamber and, in the Boyne Valley, also on the kerbstones surrounding the tumulus. The evidence suggests a dominant group who organized primary neolithic farmers into the work-force needed to bring the three Boyne Valley tombs and their tumuli, at NEWGRANGE, KNOWTH and DOWTH, to completion.

A Late Neolithic (LN) phase is marked by the appearance of a new group of pottery styles decorated with channelling or impressed cord and with a set of common motifs; these belong to three classes, Necked, Globular and Broad-rimmed, with a small remainder of exotic vessels. These are found with the established Primary Neolithic pottery and flint assemblage, occasionally with new Hollow-based arrowheads.

A new burial context, the inhumation of a single male in a stone cist under a round mound of layered construction, is found mainly in Leinster, as at LINKARDSTOWN; the new pottery is also found in PORTAL TOMBS and as secondary deposits in COURT TOMBS. New personal ornaments are disc-beads and barbell bone pins, copies of central European Uneticians types in metal and bone. Habitations are mainly in coastal and riverine situations; they include the defended hilltop enclosure of LYLES HILL. Small Spelt wheat is found with the range of cereals already introduced and saddle-querns are relatively common. Horse-bones, probably of animals used for draught, are also new.

This LN complex looks forward to more radical alterations in material culture, burial rite, siting and distribution in the Early Bronze Age (EBA) and looks east to Nordic and central Europe for its inspiration.
MH

stone alignment. A group of standing stones, arranged in one or more straight lines, often aligned NW/SE. Found with or near STONE CIRCLES in Cork/Kerry, where Castlenalact, 13 m. (43 ft) long, is the longest, and in mid-Ulster, where longer alignments are found.
MH

stone circle. A ring of standing stones, usually free-standing, sometimes contiguous, enclosing an open area, sometimes with a grave or burial-mound at the centre. They appear to have a ritual function and to

stone circle. The circle at Drombeg, Co. Cork, consisting of 17 stones, one of them recumbent.

date to Late Neolithic/Early Bronze Age times. Found in the Cork/Kerry area, e.g. at Drombeg, in mid-Ulster, e.g. at Beaghmore, and in groups near Cong, Co. Mayo, and LOUGH GUR.
MH

Stowe manuscript. The Stowe Missal and Gospel of St John (Royal Irish Academy, ms. D ii 3; 67 leaves, each measuring 145×114 mm.; $5\frac{3}{4} \times 4\frac{1}{2}$ in.) is an Irish minuscule with script angular rather than rounded, dating from c. 800. It contains extracts from St John's gospel and early liturgies of eucharist, baptism, and prayers for the sick. Perhaps written at the monastery of Tallaght and later used in Lorrha, Co. Tipperary, in the early 19th century it was in the Stowe House library of the Duke of Buckingham. A full-page portrait of St John shows the evangelist in traditional posture with eagle overhead, set in a framework of restrained knot-work interlace, with yellow and pink colouring. The initial letter of the gospel and capital P for the Peccavi prayer have lively and extraordinary ornamentation.
GOS

Strong, Eithne (1923–). Poet and short-story writer. She has published *Songs of Living* (1961), *Sarah, in Passing* (1974) and *Flesh – The Greatest Sin*, her most ambitious and successful work.
T McC

Strong, Rupert (1911–). Poet; born in London, he came to Dublin in the 1930s and trained as a psychoanalyst. A poet of wit, sex and memory, his publications include *Selected Poems* (1974) and *Come When You Can* (1981).
T McC

Stuart, Henry Francis Montgomery (1902–). Writer; born in Australia, he came to Ireland as a child. Although he represents today a major talent in the mainstream of international rather than specifically Irish literature, an Irish background frequently occurs in his novels of wartime and post-war Europe

and some of his work has an Irish setting (*Pigeon Irish*, 1932; *Redemption*, 1974). His *persona* is frequently that of the European 'Underground man', based on his own experiences. As a young poet, he married Maud Gonne's daughter Iseult (from whom he was later separated) and farmed in Co. Wicklow. Having been imprisoned for IRA activities in the 1920s, he spent the years 1940–5 in Germany where he had gone to lecture at the University of Berlin, and afterwards – in 1945 – was detained by the French occupation forces for alleged collaboration. After living in Paris (1949–51) and London, he returned to Ireland in 1958. The powerful autobiographical *Black List Section H* (1971) is distilled from this life, which also appears as fiction (*The Pillar of Cloud*, 1948). Other novels take the form of the parables (*Glory*, 1933). His fine late work, such as *Memorial* (1973), is an affirmation of the integrity with which he has pursued the artistic ideal. BH
H. Maxton *et al.*, *A Festschrift for Francis Stuart on his Seventieth Birthday*, 1972; J. H. Natterstad, *Francis Stuart*, 1974.

stucco. *See* PLASTERWORK.

Sullivan, Barry (1821–91). Actor; he began his career in Cork, after which he acted in Scotland and England. In 1858 he toured America in leading roles with enormous success. He played Benedick in *Much Ado About Nothing* to inaugurate the original Shakespeare Memorial Theatre, Stratford-on-Avon, in 1879. When he retired he claimed to have played Richard III 3,000 times. His statue, by Farrell, is in Glasnevin Cemetery, Dublin. CF-S

Swanzy, Mary (1882–1978). Landscape and genre painter; born in Dublin, she attended the Metropolitan School of Art, then studied in Paris under Delacluse and later in the studio of De La Gandara, at La Grande

Swanzy, Mary. *Landscape*, painted in a style suggesting Cubist influence deriving ultimately from Cézanne. NMI.

Chaumière and Colarossi's. She first exhibited at the Royal Hibernian Academy in 1905, and was elected HRHA in 1949. She lived mostly on the Continent and then in England. In 1968 she had a retrospective exhibition in Dublin and her work is represented in all public collections in Ireland. C MacG

Swift, Jonathan (1667–1745). Poet, pamphleteer, satirist and author; born in Dublin, he was educated at Kilkenny College and Trinity College, Dublin. Ordained into the Church of Ireland in 1695, he served briefly in Kilroot, near Belfast, before going to Moor Park, Surrey, to act as secretary to Sir William Temple. There he began his great satire, *A Tale of a Tub* (1704, 1710) and met Esther Johnson, the 'Stella' of his poems and the *Journal to Stella*. He returned to Ireland and the parish of Laracor near Dublin in 1700, but made several visits to London where he spent the years 1707–9 and 1710–13. He edited the journal *The Examiner* and wrote his enormously successful *The Conduct of the Allies* (1711) in support of Tory policy which condemned British military involvement in the War of the Spanish Succession. He became Dean of St Patrick's Cathedral, Dublin, in 1713. His leading Irish writings belong to the years 1720–9, and for his *Drapier's Letters* (1724), in which he argued against England's repressive economic policy towards Ireland, Swift was hailed as the 'Hibernian Patriot'. His subsequent disillusionment at Irish passivity is reflected in *A Modest Proposal* (1729) and in the invective of *The Legion Club* (1736). Always a considerable poet, Swift wrote much of his best work, including the *Verses on the Death of Dr. Swift* (1731), in the years 1728–36. His poetry carried more witty invective and insulted pride than the work of any Irish poet since Ó BRUADAIR. Although he was a gentleman-poet in the English high Augustan tradition, Vivian Mercier and JOHN MONTAGUE see him as a poet of the unbroken Irish tradition of comic bitterness. His most famous book, *Gulliver's Travels* (1726), confirms Swift as a supreme ironist and perhaps the greatest satirist in the language. ICR/T McC
Irvin Ehrenpreis, *Swift: The Man, His Works, and the Age*, 3 vols., 1962– ; A. L. Rowse, *Jonathan Swift, Major Prophet*, 1975; Brian Vickers (ed.), *The World of Jonathan Swift: Essays for the Tercentenary*, 1968.

Synge, John Millington (1871–1909). Playwright; born at Rathfarnham, Co. Dublin, he grew up in an atmosphere of intense evangelical Protestant piety. However, his orthodox faith did not outlast his adolescence, but manifested itself in metamorphosed form as a religious feeling for the natural world. After graduating from Trinity College, Dublin, in 1892, he was drawn to the Continent and spent the greater part of the next several years there, studying and writing. However, he had studied the Irish language and knew Celtic literature well; and his interest in the native tradition was greatly strengthened by exposure to the primitive life of the Aran Islands, which he visited for the first time in 1898. By 1902 he was writing plays for the nascent Irish theatre movement (*see* ABBEY

Synge, John Millington. Studio portrait of the playwright, taken before the onset of his serious illness in 1897.

THEATRE). Drama, as he had come to see it, required both 'joy' and 'reality'. The joyous element in his own meticulously crafted work arises largely from the 'poetic' prose of the plays, a heightened version, in English, of Irish peasant speech; it comes also from the vitality and energy he often found in the peasant character and valued so highly. But his corresponding commitment to reality led him to depict the weaknesses and vices of the people as well as their virtues, and this provoked hostile reactions from a considerable segment of the primarily nationalist audience. The dark but beautiful *Riders to the Sea* (publ. 1903, perf. 1904) was widely admired; but *The Shadow of the Glen* (1904), which dealt with a loveless marriage, became the subject of fierce controversy; and when *The Playboy of the Western World* (1907) showed Irish women competing for the love of an apparent parricide, there were riots in the theatre. His last play, *Deirdre of the Sorrows* (published posthumously in 1910), was written while he was dying of Hodgkins' disease; it uses an ancient legend as vehicle for a poignant dramatization of his own feelings about the ephemeral splendour of life and the imminence of death.

Synge also wrote poetry, and the Collected Poems (ed. Robin Skelton) appeared as the first volume of the four which make up his *Collected Works*, published 1961–8.　　　　　　　　　　　　　　　　PLM
David H. Greene and Edward M. Stephens, *J. M. Synge 1871–1909*, 1959; Declan Kiberd, *Synge and the Irish Language*, 1979.

Táin Bó Cualnge ('The Cattle Raid of Cooley'). Several recensions exist of this Old Irish epic, of which the one most likely to give any pleasure to the modern reader is the earliest one preserved, known as Recension I, which has been very well edited and translated by Cecile O'Rahilly. It has provided the base for KINSELLA's *The Táin*, an English paraphrase of the story, which it would be tempting to describe as the latest recension in the tradition. As a whole, the *Táin* is not very successful, since some of its parts do not seem to fit perfectly together and frequently contradict each other, but there are some splendid episodes. The most noteworthy are where the so-called boyhood deeds of the young Ulster hero Cú Chulainn are described, or in the vivid and precise picture of the army of Queen Mebd (Maeve) of Connacht setting out to take the Bull of Cooley from the Ulstermen. Sadly, what may be the most ancient and central part of the story still eludes modern scholarship, although some recent attempts give rise to the hope that the obscure passages, known as *rosc* or *retoiric*, may yet be elucidated properly.

The *Táin* has attracted a number of other stories into it and around it, so that the traditional saga-lists, found in the manuscripts, make a special group out of tales known as foretales or *remscéla* to the *Táin*. The most famous of these is probably *Longes mac nUislenn* ('The Exiles of the Sons of Uisliu'); the story, a familiar and popular theme, is of how the beautiful young Deirdre was betrothed to the old king, but fell in love with a fine young man and eloped with him, only to be killed by the king after some quite arresting episodes. The connection with the *Táin* is that some Ulstermen, including a son of King Conchobar of Ulster, take sides with Deirdre's beloved and subsequently turn against the Ulstermen on Maeve's side in the *Táin* itself. In others, the connection with the *Táin* is even less obvious, but one of them, *De chophur in da muccida* ('The Strife[?] of the two pig-keepers'), gives a mythological background to the struggle between the two bulls of Ulster and Connacht, something that may represent one of the original central motifs of the main story. Together, the *Táin* and the other stories belonging to the same arena are described as the Ulster cycle, which is perhaps the most important manifestation of early Irish prose literature.　　　　　　　　　　　　AA

Taisce, An (National Trust for Ireland, The). Founded in 1948, the National Trust is the most influential independent environmental body in Ireland. Under Irish planning law, Local Authorities are obliged to consult it on development in amenity areas. An Taisce's interests include the natural environment and the country's heritage of buildings, gardens, books and the arts. It is also concerned with the structure and characteristics of cities, towns and villages.

An Taisce has its national headquarters in Dublin, with a small professional staff; it also has many thousands of members, spread among associations around the country. It receives no Government grant and is wholly dependent on members' subscriptions, and on voluntary donations, to carry on its work.

The Council of An Taisce, which is elected annually, is its policy-making body. As well as the National Executive, there are a number of specialist committees devoted to: Planning; Trees; Education; Wildlife; Heritage Houses; and Gardens. An Taisce publishes its own *Journal*, which is an important reference on environmental matters. It also publishes from time to time reports on matters of concern, e.g. *Heritage at Risk* which dealt with the future of heritage houses, gardens and collections. This report influenced the Government in its legislation on taxation relating to heritage houses. An Taisce also owns a dozen properties around the country which are used for research or for public enjoyment.

Members of An Taisce have been invited by the Government to sit on State bodies, and it has representatives on the Water Pollution Advisory Council, Wildlife Advisory Council and two as Directors of An Foras Forbartha (the National Institute for Physical Planning). It is also represented on the Board of the Alfred Beit Foundation.

In the mid-1970s, An Taisce initiated the formation of two important related bodies: the Heritage Trust, which funds environmental projects, and the IRISH ARCHITECTURAL ARCHIVE.　　　　　CO'C

tapestry. Woven hangings of wool and silk, ornamented with vivid scenes of landscapes, interiors, men, animals, allegories, were favoured for use as wall-hangings in Irish castles from the late middle ages. In the 16th century, Piers, Earl of Ormond, with a view to introducing manufacturers to the town of Kilkenny, brought over from Flanders artificers in tapestry, diaper and carpets, but the manufacture did not extend beyond the supply of the castle and was soon discontinued. Tapestries which hung in the Manor House, Carrick-on-Suir, now stored at Kilkenny, including one depicting Samson and Delilah, may have come from that source but most tapestries in the country were imported.

In 1728, Robert Baillie, upholsterer and tapestry maker in Abbey Street, Dublin, commissioned WILLEM VAN DER HAGEN to 'take prospects' of six places to be depicted in six tapestries of Irish historical scenes for the House of Lords, Dublin.

About 1728 in Dublin, John van Beaver wove the tapestries 'The Defence of Derry' and 'The Battle of the Boyne' for the House of Lords (now the Bank of Ireland). In 1738, van Beaver worked and presented to the Weavers' Hall in Dublin a small tapestry portrait of George II (now in the USA); it bears the inscription:

> The workmanship of John Van Beaver
> Ye famous tapestry weaver.

In the present century tapestry work was encouraged again in the DUN EMER GUILD, where the piece

tapestry. Detail of 'The Battle of the Boyne' woven by John van Beaver for the House of Lords (now Bank of Ireland), Dublin, *c.* 1728.

entitled 'Smuainteac' ('Thoughtful'), now in the NMI, was woven in 1912–13 and the splendid dossal for the HONAN CHAPEL, Cork, *c.* 1917 to the design of Evelyn Gleeson and Katherine MacCormack.

The artist LOUIS LE BROCQUY has worked successfully in tapestry design; his large work 'Brendan the Navigator' (1963), measuring 4·25 × 5·50 m. (14 × 18 ft), woven at Aubusson in France by Tabard frères et soeur, hangs in the hall of the Carroll Group building, Grand Parade, Dublin.

Students are taught the technique at the NATIONAL COLLEGE OF ART AND DESIGN, Dublin; important commissions have been successfully executed by a number of graduates, including Evelyn Lindsay, Lillias Mitchell, Angela Forte, Sallie O'Sullivan, Leonora Fowler, Muriel Beckett and Alice Roden.　　　　　HLM

Tara, Co. Meath (Teamhair na Ríogh, High Place of the Kings). Sites, south of Navan, 150 m. (500 ft) above sea-level, on a ridge running N–S. There are several monuments, famous in MYTHOLOGY, dating from the STONE AGE and later. These were described *c.* AD 1000 by an antiquary who noted the names and positions of the visible monuments and wrote their mythical history in a tract of the *Dindshenchus*.

Two sites have been investigated. Ráth na Seanad ('Rath of the Synods'), excavated by S. P. Ó Ríordáin 1952–3, consists of a set of palisaded concentric banks surrounding a flat-topped mound covering burials by inhumation and cremation, and is dated to the early centuries AD by Roman pottery, glass and a lead seal; two gold torcs (now in the NMI) were found *c.* 1810 nearby. Dumha na nGiall ('Mound of the Hostages') is a PASSAGE GRAVE with a great quantity of cremated primary burials and a rich assemblage of typical finds, into which 50 individual burials of Early Bronze Age date were inserted, one of a youth with a necklace

Tara. Aerial view showing the principal earthworks within the large oval hillfort enclosure, measuring 290 × 245 m. (950 × 800 ft). Cf. mythology.

including segmented faience beads, *c.* 1400 BC (excavated 1955–60, by S. P. Ó Ríordáin and R. de Valéra).

Monuments also include, from N to S: Ráth Méadhbha, an EBA henge 200 m. (650 ft) across; Ráth Laoghaire and Ráth na Ríogh, EIA hillforts; the Forrádh and Teach Cormaic, conjoined EIA ringforts; Ráth Gráinne and the Claoinfherta (Sloping Trenches), three EIA burial mounds; and the famous Banqueting Hall (Teach Míodhchuarta), possibly a ceremonial roadway, aligned S towards the central group of monuments. There are two STANDING STONES: one of these, Lia Fáil (Stone of Destiny), alias Bod Feargusa (Penis of Fergus), now stands on the Forrádh ringfort, but early in the 19th century stood W of Dumha na nGiall.　　　　　　　　　　　　MH
S. P. Ó Ríordáin, *Tara, the Monuments on the Hill*, 1960.

'Tara' Brooch. Found in 1850 in material collapsed from a cliff at Bettystown, Co. Meath, this 8th-century pseudo-penannular BROOCH is now in the National Museum of Ireland. It has a diameter of 8·2 cm. (3¼ in.) and the length of the pin is 22·5 cm. (8⅞ in.). The name 'Tara' was attached to it by a dealer through whose hands it passed. The brooch – frequently said to be of bronze – is in fact made of cast silver-gilt; the broader parts of the ring, the hoop and the pin-head have, on the front, deep cast panels which carry elaborate filigree ornaments – animal designs, snakes, interlace and scrolls. Cast animal and bird heads, and their linked tails, form projecting loops and lunettes on the sides of the pin-head and ring. Amber and glass adorn the settings on the front (pl. xx), while the back is elaborately decorated with *kerbschnitt* animals, birds and scrollwork of Ultimate LA TÈNE type. Two silver panels on the pseudo-terminals have especially delicate patterns of that type – a wash of silver has been pierced to reveal the design in the underlying copper. A similar technique was used on a panel on the ring, where a film of gold has been cut through in the same manner. The pin-head is an elaborate construction attached to the ring by a loop of sophisticated design. The finely wrought pin is held in a socket in the pin-head which, on the front, appears as an elaborate animal mask. A chain of Trichonopoly work – knitted silver wire – is attached to the ring by means of a serpent's head grasping an elaborately decorated hinged tag which in turn pivots on a spindle grasped in the jaws of a further beast projecting from the side. The sophistication and variety of the ornaments make the 'Tara' brooch technically one of the three most accomplished pieces of 8th-century Irish metalwork. In the mid-19th century the brooch was copied and replicas sold (*see* SILVERWORK).　　　　　　　　　　　　MFR

Tate, Nahum (1652–1715). Playwright; born in Dublin, he was educated at Trinity College, Dublin. He had some success as a playwright and became Poet Laureate in 1692. His adaptation of *King Lear*, which omits the Fool and allows Cordelia to survive to marry Edgar, was played in the theatre until the mid-19th century. He wrote the libretto for Purcell's *Dido and Aeneas* and with Nicholas Brady published *A New Version of the Psalms* (1696).　　　　　ICR
H. F. Scott-Thomas, *The Life and Works of Nahum Tate*, 2 vols., 1932; Christopher Spencer, *Nahum Tate*, 1972.

Telescope, The Great. The telescope, which can be visited by the public in the demesne of Birr Castle, Co. Offaly, was completed and first used there by the 3rd Earl of Rosse in 1845; it remained the largest in the world for three-quarters of a century. The huge 1·90-m. (6-ft) speculum, which was cast in a peat-fired furnace at the bottom of the moat, and which is now on display in the Science Museum, London, enabled the Earl to see further into space than any man before.　　　　　　　　　　　　R

television. The Republic of Ireland's television broadcasting service put out its first public transmission on 31 December 1961. Mícheál Ó hEithir, the commentator on that occasion, subsequently became the country's best-known television presence. Regular transmissions began on 1 January 1962. An early popular programme, produced on a modest budget, was *School Around the Corner*, in which Paddy Crosbie visited nearly every school in the country, inviting bright pupils to do a turn or recount a funny story; the main rivals in popularity of this show were imported American cowboy, comedy and thriller features.

By the end of 1963 television was available throughout the 26 counties of the Republic, thanks to the four transmitters in Sligo, Clare, Carlow and Cork. Much later the six northern counties (which already had the BBC service) came into the reception radius through booster transmitters in Derry and Louth.

With the Broadcasting Authority (Amendment) Act in March 1966, the current title of Radio Telefis Éireann was adopted for both television and RADIO broadcasting. A second television channel, RTE 2, was launched on 2 November 1978. In 1981 half of the viewing hours of RTE's transmissions on its two channels were taken up by programmes imported from the USA, Britain, Canada and Australia; the American serial *Dallas* and the British serial *Coronation Street* ranked among the top ten most popular programmes. However, the role of Irish schools broadcasts, Telefís Scoile, has increased and helped other home-produced programmes to reach a level of 68 hours weekly in the winter and 46 in the summer; RTE 2 provided a further total of 39 viewing hours per week. Home-produced programmes in the top ratings were the national and international news bulletins (including the news read in Irish), sport and current affairs programmes, and Gay Byrne's *Late Late Show* on Saturday night, unfailingly iconoclastic in tone, which for two decades provoked widespread discussion. RTE was the first television station in the world to broadcast a daily *News for the Deaf*. Attempts to introduce high-quality theatre on the first channel were crowned by the production of JAMES PLUNKETT's *Strumpet City*, starring David Kelly, Frank Grimes and Donal McCann; it was also sold to a number of overseas networks.

Advertising time is allowed up to 10% of broadcasting time, with no more than $7\frac{1}{2}$ minutes in any given hour; strong restrictions apply to the advertising of alcoholic drinks and advertisements for cigarettes are forbidden. EG

textile manufacture. The history of textile manufacture is given here in accordance with the type of basic material used. See also separate entries on DYEING; CARPET-MAKING; EMBROIDERY; LACE; TAPESTRY; CROCHET; and KNITTING.

Wool. Of the many breeds of sheep in Ireland the best-known to hand-spinners are: the Mountain Blackface, the Galway and the Cheviot, all of which can thrive on rough grazing, the fleeces of the last two being particularly used for skirt and jacket materials; and the Suffolk Down, which need good pasture and provide fleeces for expert spinners suitable for stoles, scarves and cot blankets.

The earliest form of spinning was done with a wooden spindle shaft, usually about 30 cm. (12 in.) in length and a stone, bone or baked-clay whorl which acts as a weight to keep the spindle twirling and to put a twist in the prepared wool. A wooden spindle from a CRANNÓG at Ballinderry, Co. Offaly, *c.* 500–800, is among some early examples in the NMI. This simple method of spinning was replaced by the spinning-wheel, of which three types were used in Ireland: the Big Wheel, favoured in Connacht, at which the spinner stands turning the wheel with the right hand while drawing out the yarn with the left; a smaller type of wheel, favoured in Kerry, at which the spinner sits; and the Treadle or Flax Wheel, favoured in Donegal, which is propelled by foot. Efforts made by the Huguenot settler Louis Crommelin in 1685 to introduce the Picardy wheel were unsuccessful.

Two pieces of cloth sewn together and a tasselled horse-hair belt found at Armoy, Co. Antrim, used as a

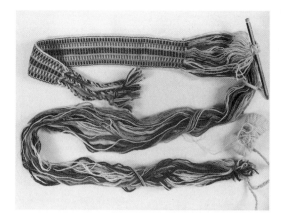

textile manufacture. An unfinished multi-coloured hand-braided crios (a woollen girdle) from the Aran Islands.

wrapping for a metal hoard and now in the NMI are dated to 900–600 BC. Shag cloth which has a curled surface is an ancient Irish textile; this was the material, dyed with madder, of the relic believed to be the cloak of St Brigid of Kildare in the 6th century. Heavy thick woollen material was used for medieval garments. Frieze, a type of coarse heavy woollen cloth, was manufactured widely; usually made in white and natural brown, this material was used for men's coats and capes (*see* COSTUME).

Repeated and serious obstacles placed in the way of the export of woollen fabrics from Ireland after the mid-17th century hampered the woollen trade; the once-flourishing woollen industry at Carrick-on-Suir and Clonmel, for example, failed at the end of the 18th century, and attempts in these towns to replace lost trade by the manufacture of flannel, ratteen and blankets proved unsuccessful after the Act of Union. The woollen trade was later boosted by Lady Aberdeen's foundation, the Irish Industries Association, 1886; by the efforts of the Congested Districts Board, 1891, whose projects to create employment included a woollen factory at Foxford, Co. Mayo, and quality-inspection of cloth at Ardara and Carrick, Co. Donegal; and more recently by the Royal Dublin Society (*see* DUBLIN SOCIETY), the Irish Society for Design and Craftwork, the Crafts Council of Ireland, and Bord Fáilte.

Martin Lally, a weaver living in a remote part of Ireland, described in 1954 how cloth was finished there. He used a hard warp and a soft weft to nap the cloth, with hand-carders, drops of honey and a cork pad to draw out the fibres into long curls.

High-quality tweed, of medium-to-heavy weight and in a variety of colours and weave, is still hand-made in Ireland (marl, fleck and mingled heather effects are popular); the weaving is done mainly in Co. Donegal, where it has been encouraged as a cottage industry.

Linen. Flax has a long history of use as a source of fibres: impressions of flax seeds occur on Late Bronze Age

textile manufacture. A Donegal hand-weaver working at the loom.

textile manufacture. Linen warping and weaving; engraving by William Hincks, *c.* 1790.

pottery. In the 7th century AD, an account of the church of the 5th/6th century of St Brigid's monastery at Kildare mentions linen hangings. It is known that by the 15th century yarn spun from flax in Ireland was exported to England and the Continent.

Damask linen, introduced in the 17th century by Huguenot refugees in Co. Armagh, brought Ireland fame; it is a mixed warp-faced, weft-faced fabric made chiefly of linen, and continued to be hand-woven in Ulster until the mid-1970s. A small quantity is still woven commercially on power looms. This is a jacquard weave, on reversible warp-faced satin pattern with weft-faced satin background. William III appointed Louis Crommelin as overseer of the Royal Linen Manufacture of Ireland. Linen manufacture was an important industry until its decline in the 19th century. In 1800, for example, there were twelve bleaching greens in Co. Cavan. In Co. Down, where the industry was of primary importance and Dromore was the most important market, cambric, fine linen, damask and drill were manufactured, as well as common household linens. In Co. Fermanagh in 1837 most families owned a spinning-wheel and reel and sold their homespun flax in the market towns. Linen was the staple manufacture of Co. Tyrone, where it was made and bleached for export, but by the 1830s two-thirds of that county's bleaching greens had fallen into disuse. However, following mechanization of the spinning and weaving of linen, Belfast became one of the greatest linen-producing centres of the world.

Silk. Silk imported from China and Japan forms the warp for Irish silk poplin, a silk-faced fabric with a fine worsted wool weft. A Dublin newspaper of 1704 advertised this textile as having equal proportions by weight of wool, 40 threads per inch, and silk, 280 to 420 threads per inch; this silk-and-wool mixture survived restrictions on woollen manufacture as the cloth could not be termed wool. Silk-poplin weaving is still carried on in Belfast.

During World War II, when silk was unobtainable in Ireland, efforts were made to start a silk farm by the Cistercian monks at Mount St Joseph Abbey, Roscrea, Co. Tipperary; they established that mulberry could be grown in Ireland, but on such a small scale that it was hardly an economic proposition. Nevertheless the monks persevered and with a couple of acres of mulberry bushes, could raise 30,000 silk worms in a season. Good looms and accessories were brought from Dublin and a noted silk weaver, Patrick Walsh, trained some of the monks in weaving. The undertaking lasted in all fifteen years, but eventually through lack of labour, had to be abandoned.

Cotton. The cotton trade was introduced in 1777 at Belfast. By 1800 about 27,000 persons were employed in and around the city in various branches of the industry; by 1810, 22,000 were employed in spinning, 25,000 in weaving and a further 5,000 in ancillary trades, but the boom was short-lived.   HLM

E. F. Sutton, *Weaving: The Irish Inheritance*, 1980; Lillias Mitchell, *Irish Spinning, Dyeing and Weaving*, 1978.

theatre. The Irish theatre is essentially a writers' theatre, and Irish playwrights have led the English-speaking theatre from the end of the 17th century until the present day. Though there have been fine Irish actors and actresses, and though fine theatre buildings have existed (and still exist), there has been no Irish equivalent of Roscius, Garrick, Siddons or Bernhardt, and no Irish theatre architecture to compare remotely with Epidaurus, the Globe, Drottningholm or, more recently, Minneapolis.

Following the Anglo-Norman invasion of 1169 miracle and morality plays were performed in Dublin and other centres of colonial administration. The Gaelic tradition was a bardic one, and, language difficulties apart, never came to terms with the theatrical form which presents a rehearsed fable in which actors portray recognizable characters before a large audience. Even since the IRISH LANGUAGE revival in the 20th century, few plays of real stature have been written and performed in Gaelic, despite State encouragement.

William Congreve (1670–1729), the master of the comedy of manners; portrait by Kneller. National Portrait Gallery, London.

George Farquhar (1678–1707), author of the Restoration comedies *The Recruiting Officer* and *The Beaux' Stratagem*; engraving by R. Clamp.

A moment from Act V, Scene 3, of Goldsmith's *She Stoops to Conquer* (first performed in 1773); engraving after Wheatley, 1791.

Religious plays in English were written and presented by John Bale in Kilkenny while he was Bishop of Ossory in the mid-16th century. English strolling players gave performances of secular plays during Elizabethan and Jacobean times, but it was not until 1637 that a purpose-built theatre (see next entry) was erected – at Werburgh Street, Dublin – during the Deputyship of the Earl of Strafford, but it only survived for four years. After the Restoration a theatre was opened at Smock Alley in Dublin, which though initially staffed by English players, eventually became an excellent training-ground for local talent. Many Irish actors and actresses during the 18th century found their way to England – among them Charles Doggett, ROBERT WILKS, JAMES QUIN, PEG WOFFINGTON, Kitty Clive, George-Anne Bellamy, Dorothea Jordan, SPRANGER BARRY, HENRY MOSSOP, THOMAS SHERIDAN, Richard Farren and John Moody. It was the writers, however, who really dominated the British theatre. Roger Boyle introduced Cornelian rhymed tragedy; WILLIAM CONGREVE excelled in the comedy of manners; and GEORGE FARQUHAR introduced a gentler, more rustic type of comedy to an over-sophisticated theatre. If Congreve's *The Way of the World* and Farquhar's *The Beaux' Stratagem* are the finest comedies of the late 17th/ early 18th centuries, OLIVER GOLDSMITH's *She Stoops to Conquer* and RICHARD BRINSLEY SHERIDAN's *The School for Scandal* occupy the same place in the later 18th century. Among the other Irish playwrights who kept the stages of Dublin and London busy during the 18th century were ARTHUR MURPHY (the leading exponent of sentimental comedy), Isaac Bickerstaffe, HUGH KELLY, Henry Jones, Andrew Cherry, and John O'Keefe (whose incomparable *Wild Oats* ran for two years in the Royal Shakespeare Company revival of the 1970s).

After the Act of Union of 1801 the Dublin, Belfast and Cork theatres largely became receiving-houses for London-based companies. The most celebrated 19th-century Irish actors were TYRONE POWER, BARRY SULLIVAN and DION BOUCICAULT – both Power and Boucicault were also playwrights, and enjoyed tremendous popularity in the USA; the latter's play *The Octoroon* is said to have been the first to treat the subject of Negro slavery seriously. OSCAR WILDE and GEORGE BERNARD SHAW continued the tradition of effervescent comedy. The ABBEY THEATRE introduced a new awareness of national identity; J. M. SYNGE, W. B. YEATS and SEÁN O'CASEY represent three strains of Abbey writing. SAMUEL BECKETT is the most important dramatist of the present time.   C F-S

W. S. Clark, *The Early Irish Stage*, 1955; Christopher Fitz-Simon. *The Irish Theatre*, 1983; Katherine Worth, *The Irish Drama of Europe from Yeats to Beckett*, 1978.

theatres. The façade of the Theatre Royal, Smock Alley, Dublin, founded 1662.

theatres. A brief history of theatre buildings in Ireland is given below, separated for convenience into sections on those in Dublin and those in the rest of the country.

Dublin theatres. The earliest purpose-built theatre in the British Isles outside London was the Werburgh Street Theatre, near Dublin Castle, opened in 1637 by John Ogilby, a Scot, and a member of the Lord Deputy's household. It closed after four years due to the Cromwellian interdict. The Theatre Royal in Smock Alley, known as the Smock Alley Playhouse, was the first theatre in the Restoration style to be built anywhere in the British Isles. It flourished from 1662 until 1787; many famous Irish and British actors performed there. The Aungier Street Theatre, designed by PEARCE in 1733, was run jointly with Smock Alley but closed in 1746 mainly due to competition from the Capel Street Theatre, which was also short-lived. A small theatre existed in Rainsford Street outside the city walls for a few years. The Crow Street Theatre was founded by SPRANGER BARRY and Henry Woodward in 1758 as a serious commercial rival to Smock Alley, which it outlived; it closed in 1821 due to serious financial difficulties when its patent was taken over by the London manager Henry Harris, who built the Theatre Royal in Hawkins St, which remained the leading Dublin playhouse until the end of the 19th century. (A smaller Theatre Royal flourished, confusingly, in Abbey St, 1837–9.) The building in Hawkins St was burned down in 1880 and replaced by the Leinster Hall, but this was again rebuilt as the Theatre Royal in 1897; in 1937 it was replaced by the magnificent art-deco Theatre Royal, subsequently demolished in the 1960s. The chief rival to the Hawkins St theatre from 1823 was the Adelphi in Brunswick St, redesigned as the Queen's in 1844; it was rebuilt in a unique neo-Celtic style in 1908, and demolished in

1965 after playing host to the ABBEY THEATRE company following the Abbey fire of 1951. Theatres which have disappeared were the Tivoli on Burgh Quay, the Capitol or La Scala in Prince's St, and the New Princess Theatre of Varieties in the Mechanics' Institute (which became the Abbey Theatre in 1904). The Assembly Rooms of the Rotunda Hospital were converted as the Gate Theatre by MÍCHEÁL MAC LÍAMMÓIR and HILTON EDWARDS in 1930, and also housed Longford Productions, the company formed by Edward and Christine Longford, from 1936 until 1960. The only large 19th-century theatres still in existence are the Gaiety in S. King St, and the Olympia (formerly the Empire Palace, and originally Dan Lowery's Music Hall). Dublin has had several studio or art theatres, including the Pike (fl. 1953–60), the Focus and the Project Arts Centre. The Eblana is situated in the central bus station, and the Oscar is a converted cinema in the suburb of Ballsbridge.

Provincial theatres. In Belfast the earliest-known theatre was 'The Vaults' (*c.* 1730). The 'new Theatre' was opened in Castle St, 1768; another, in Mill Gate, 1770; Ann St, 1778; off Rosemary St, 1784. Each closed with the opening of the next. In 1793 the Theatre Royal, Arthur Square, opened, and flourished until it became a cinema in the 1930s. In 1895 the Grand Opera House, designed by Matcham, was built in Great Victoria St; it became a cinema but was restored with the aid of Government funds in 1980. The late 19th-century Alhambra and Empire have been demolished, and the Royal Hippodrome, now a cinema, has lost its 19th-century façade.

The Ulster Group Theatre (fl. 1940–72) was the descendant of the Ulster Literary Theatre of the early 20th century and the Northern Drama League of the 1920s; it was formed by Harold Goldblatt and others,

theatres. The new Theatre Royal, Cork, at the time of its completion in 1867.

mainly to perform plays of Ulster interest. The Belfast Arts Theatre, founded by Hubert and Dorothy Wilmot in 1946, began as an avant garde company but with the move to larger premises its repertoire became more popular. In 1951 Mary O'Malley founded the Lyric Players Theatre as a tribute to the memory of w. b. yeats; in 1969 a new theatre was built in which a varied international repertoire is performed.

In Cork the earliest theatre was in N. Main St, opened in 1713 as a venue for the Smock Alley players from Dublin. The Theatre Royal in Dunscombe's Marsh was opened in 1736, possibly designed by pearce; it was superseded by the Theatre Royal in George's (Parnell) St in 1760. The Henry St and the Gentlemen's theatres both had short lives. The late 19th-century Palace is now a cinema. The Athenaeum on Lavitt's Quay, designed by Benson in 1866, subsequently named the Opera House, was burned down in 1955; in 1965 the new Opera House, by michael scott, was opened. The Group Theatre (fl. 1958–74) was an intimate venue for local and visiting companies under James N. Healy. The Southern Theatre Group (fl. 1959–71) used the Opera House as a touring base and specialized in the plays of john b. keane: it was re-formed as Theatre of the South Ltd. The Everyman Playhouse was opened in 1972 to house an existing amateur group and to receive visiting companies.

In Galway a theatre existed in 1739. Richard Martin built a new playhouse in Kirwin's Lane in 1783; it fell into disuse before 1800. A fine Town Hall, by richard morrison c. 1819, was the principal theatre until the Local Authority allowed its conversion to two cinemas. *Taibhdhearc na Gaillimhe*, the official Irish-language theatre, was founded by Liam Ó Bríain and others in Galway in 1928. In 1975 the Druid Theatre Company was formed to produce experimental as well as established plays in English.

In Limerick during the late 18th century plays were given in 'Peter's Cell' and in the Assembly House. The earliest purpose-built theatre, opened by Tottenham Heaphy in 1770, flourished until it was destroyed by fire in 1818. There was a theatre in George's St, 1810–c. 1822. In 1841 the new Theatre Royal was built by Joseph Fogerty in Lower Mallow St; it was accidentally burned down in 1922. A number of halls, including the Coliseum and the City, were used as theatres during the 20th century. In 1981 the Belltable Arts Centre, a reconstruction of the Coliseum, was opened.

In Waterford the earliest theatre was built in 1737 at the Abbey of the Black Friars. In 1784 a theatre was placed in the new City Hall, designed by john roberts: its interior was reconstructed in the mid-19th century, and survives as the oldest theatre in regular use in Ireland.

In Wexford the Theatre Royal in High St (replacing a short-lived theatre in Church Lane) was opened in 1830. During the 1940s it became a cinema. Since 1951 it has been the home of the wexford festival.

The Riverside Theatre, in the New University of Ulster at Coleraine, funded jointly by the University, the Local Authority and the arts council of northern ireland, and opened in 1976, is the best-equipped new theatre in Northern Ireland. cf-s
Christopher Fitz-Simon, *The Irish Theatre*, 1983.

Tievebulliagh, Co. Antrim. On this mountain near Cushendall, at an altitude of 300 m. (1,000 ft), W. J. Knowles discovered c. 1900 the first known igneous rock axe-factory. The site is marked by a thick deposit of *débitage*, flakes and rough-outs of the local porcellanite. The rough-outs travelled as far as Sligo, Limerick, Cork and Wicklow, into south-west Scotland and as far south in England as Kent; polishing appears to have been done not at the axe-factory but after dispersal. mh
W. J. Knowles, 'Stone Axe Factories near Cushendall', *JRSAI* 36 (1906), 383–94.

torc. Twisted plain gold, late Iron Age. NMI.

Todd, James Henthorn, D.D. (1805–69). Antiquary; born in Dublin, he was ordained in the Church of Ireland in 1832. He was editor of *The Christian Examiner*; co-founder with O'DONOVAN and O'CURRY of the Irish Archaeological Society, 1840; co-founder of St Columba's College; and Regius Professor of Hebrew and Librarian of Trinity College, Dublin, where he classified the Irish ms. collections. He was co-editor with WILLIAM REEVES of the *Martyrology of Donegal*, 1864, and his popular *St Patrick, Apostle of Ireland* was published in the same year. B de B

Todhunter, John (1839–1916). Poet, translator and teacher; born in Dublin, he was one of the earliest contributors to the Literary Revival in the late 19th century. He is best known for his *Irish Bardic Tales* (1896). T McC

Toland, John (1670–1722). Writer; born near Derry, and christened Junius Janus, Toland was reputedly the son of a Roman Catholic priest, but he converted to Protestantism at sixteen. He studied at the universities of Glasgow, Edinburgh, Leyden, and Oxford. The publication of his *Christianity not Mysterious* (1696), a work condemned by the Irish parliament to be burned by the common hangman, made him notorious as the leading deist of the age. In 1702, Toland acknowledged his indiscretion in publishing the book but his subsequent writings – which included many political works also – reveal him by turns as deist, freethinker, and proto-pantheist. I C R

torc. Strictly speaking, a torc is an ornament (ear-ring, neck- or arm-ring) produced by twisting bars or strips of gold. Originally used to produce bronze neck-rings in continental Europe, the technique was borrowed by insular craftsmen *c.* 1200 BC, and used to produce a variety of ornaments from bars of varied cross-section. Some torcs, such as the pair from the Rath of the Synods, TARA, are of large size and must have been conceived of as girdles. The tradition of torc-making is represented also in the IRON AGE by finds from Clonmacnois, Co. Offaly, and Somerset, Co. Galway. Controversy surrounds the debate on the sources of the gold used in many examples. M F R

tower house. This type of tall, usually square, defensible tower (varying in height from three to six storeys) was built in vast numbers in Ireland in the 15th and 16th centuries and less widely in the first half of the 17th as the staple house-fortification of the minor country landowners; such houses were especially numerous in counties Clare, Cork, Galway, Kilkenny, Limerick and Tipperary. The earliest datable examples from the early 15th century are in Co. Down. Most, if not all, would have stood within a walled enclosure, the bawn, which has seldom survived. Many tower houses were roofed with thatched straw; the owner's chamber was usually on the uppermost storey reached by a narrow stone stair. Good examples of the tower house may be seen at: Clara, Co. Kilkenny; Aughnanure, Co. Galway; Belvelly, Co. Cork; Roods-

town, Co. Louth; Rockfleet, Co. Mayo; Narrow Water, Co. Down; Rathmacknee, Co. Wexford; and Knockelly, Co. Tipperary, where the bawn is intact. Residential additions were made to a number of tower houses in the 17th and 18th centuries. B de B

town planning. The earliest planned towns in Ireland were built by English and Scottish colonists in the early 17th century. Contemporary theory linked urbanization with colonization and suggested that towns played an important role in administration and in the exploitation of the fruits of conquest. These towns were strategically sited, populated with Protestants and sometimes walled. Bandon, which was founded by Richard Boyle, is shown on a map of *c.* 1615 as having walls, a grid-iron plan, a market and sessions house. Derry is the best example, retaining its walls, gates and street plan. The smaller towns in Ulster, though not walled, had forts or bawns. After the Restoration many new manors were created and new towns built. Charleville, Co. Cork, was developed after the Earl of Orrery had built himself a house there. Likewise the Earl of Granard built Newtown Forbes, Co. Longford, and the Eyres laid out Eyrecourt, Co. Galway. The most important town of the period was Portarlington, Co. Laois, which was laid out by Sir George Rawdon in 1667.

Many existing towns were rebuilt or extended by their proprietors in the 18th century. Birr was extended by the Earls of Rosse in the mid-18th century with the laying out of a square dominated by a column. Stradbally, Co. Laois, was rebuilt in the 1740s with two rectangular squares and Castlewellan, Co. Down, with two polygonal squares. Maynooth, Co. Kildare, was rebuilt by the Duke of Leinster in the 1750s with a wide street which was an extension to the avenue to CARTON. Viscount de Vesci moved the town of Abbeyleix from a marshy site near his house to a dry site in 1776. Westport, Co. Mayo, was also moved to a new site, in the 1770s, where the streets were carefully related to the inclined site, thereby avoiding the more usual grid-iron pattern, and the local river was canalized down the mall. At Tullamore the Burys employed John Pentland and FRANCIS JOHNSTON to replan the town, while at Mitchelstown, Co. Cork, John Morrison built King Square in the 1780s and the PAIN brothers were involved in the development of the town in the 1820s. However, the majority of planned towns were based on a single street. Perhaps the most impressive of these is Cookstown, Co. Tyrone, which has a main street 40 m. (130 ft) wide and 2 km. ($1\frac{1}{4}$ miles) long.

The most important development in urban planning of the 18th century was the appointment, in 1757, of the Dublin Wide Street Commissioners. They realigned streets, laid out new streets and squares, standardized house heights and designed shop façades. Their achievements include Parliament, O'Connell, D'Olier and Westmoreland Streets. They supervised the development of Merrion Square, Upper and Lower Mount Street and Fitzwilliam Square; and their spirit prevailed in the layout of Mountjoy Square. Cork also had Commissioners, though their work was

town planning. Part of Merrion Square, Dublin, looking towards the neo-Greek St Stephen's church (1824); this, the second largest of the city's great squares, was laid out by John Ensor in 1726, under the supervision of the Dublin Wide Street Commissioners.

limited. In Limerick, Newtown Pery was laid out in a grid-iron plan which has been attributed to DAVIS DUCART.

Influenced by romantic landscape design, landlords began to create picturesque 'model' villages. In the 1820s Lady Belvedere added a semi-circular green to Tyrellspass, Co. Westmeath; slightly later Enniskerry, Co. Wicklow, was rebuilt in the Gothick style; at Adare, Co. Limerick, commenced in the 1830s, the houses were given heavy thatched roofs, wide eaves and rustic verandas, while at Ardagh, Co. Longford, the village – designed by J. Rawson Carroll in the 1860s – was Tudor in style. Talbot's Inch, Co. Kilkenny, designed in the Arts and Crafts style by W. A. SCOTT in 1904 for Lady Dysert, and Cushendun, Co. Antrim, by Clough Williams-Ellis, were the last model villages to be built. Because of fluctuating markets 18th-century industrial towns rarely survived. Prosperous, Co. Kildare, founded in 1780 as a cotton-spinning enterprise, failed within a few years. Lord Aldborough founded Stratford-on-Slaney, Co. Wicklow, in 1786 as an industrial settlement but it also failed, and the New Geneva project in Co. Waterford, for which JAMES GANDON drew up plans, never materialized. Some 19th-century industrial towns were more successful, however. Portlaw, Co. Waterford, built by the Malcolmsons, has a radial plan centred on the double entrance gates to the Malcolmson house and the mill. Sion Mills, Co. Tyrone, built by the Herdman family, is a dispersed settlement with the Herdman house lying between the village and the mill. The most

innovative was Bessbrook, Co. Armagh, established in 1846 by a Quaker mill-owner, John Richardson. There was no public house, police station or pawn shop in the town; instead there were churches, a community centre, savings bank and dispensary.

Land use and traffic management have been the main concern of 20th-century planners. The Abercrombie plan for Dublin (1922), though it was in the Beaux Arts tradition, was the first of this type. Manning Robertson, who assisted Abercrombie, prepared a Limerick City Plan in 1938 and a plan for Dublin in 1941. F. R. Hicks, influenced by the Garden Suburb Movement, laid out Mount Brown in the 1920s and Crumlin in the 1930s. The Bord-na-Mona villages, built since the 1950s, are the most attractive settlements in the garden-suburb idiom. The most striking recent development in town planning has been Shannon New Town (commenced 1960) by Frederick Rogerson. The design team for a similar new town, Craigavon, Co. Armagh (commenced 1965), was headed initially by Geoffrey Copcutt. In 1963 Arthur Swift and W. L. Waide designed a scheme for 12,000 people at Ballymun, Co. Dublin, but the tower-blocks have proved unsatisfactory and the experiment has not been repeated. The Myles Wright Plan for Dublin (1967) proposed Tallaght, Clondalkin and Blanchardstown as new towns, and these are now being built. As a direct result of the Local Government (Planning and Development) Act 1963, a School of Town Planning was established at University College, Dublin, and An Foras Forbartha (the National Institute of Physical Planning) was founded in 1964.   WG
R. A. Butlin (ed.), *The Development of the Irish Town*, 1977; P. Shaffrey, *The Irish Town*, 1975; A. McLoughlin, *Streets of Ireland*, 1981; D. Harkness and M. O'Dowd (eds.), *The Town in Ireland*, 1981.

Trevor, William (pseudonym of William Trevor Cox; 1928–   ). Writer; born in Mitchelstown, Co. Cork. Trevor, who has practised as a sculptor and as an advertising copywriter is, in his writing, a master of the telling and disturbing detail, in novels, short stories and plays for radio, television and stage. His preoccupations include old age (*The Old Boys*, 1964), the macabre (*The Children of Dynmouth*, 1976) and the volatility of human relationships (as in the collection *Angels at the Ritz*, 1975). In some of his finest work the pressures of Irish life afford opportunities for minute psychological analysis ('Attracta', 1978) or for a particular blend of pain and nostalgia ('The Ballroom of Romance', which appeared in a collection published in 1972 and was televised in 1982).   BH

Trinity College, Dublin. The College was founded in 1592 but its oldest surviving buildings are the 'rubrics' of *c.* 1700, with added Dutch gables of the 1890s. The library was begun in 1712 to designs of Col. THOMAS BURGH and still retains much of the original Classical joinery in the long room, though the ceiling was vaulted in 1860 by DEANE AND WOODWARD. Behind the 'rubrics' is RICHARD CASTLE's printing house of 1734, built in the form of a Doric temple. Castle also designed

Trinity College, Dublin. The long room of the (Old) Library, completed in the 1720s; engraving by James Malton, 1793.

Tuam Cathedral. The Romanesque chancel arch as incorporated by Sir Thomas Newenham Deane in the course of the 19th-century rebuilding.

the dining hall in the 1740s. The designer of the accomplished west front (1750s) has recently been established as the English architect Theodore Jacobsen. The Provost's House was started in 1759 and is a copy of General Wade's house in London by Lord Burlington, which in turn was based on Palladio. The façade is thought to be by JOHN SMYTH, while the interior, arguably the finest in Dublin, is attributed to Henry Keene. The PLASTERWORK is by Patrick and John Wall. The public theatre and chapel are from designs by Sir WILLIAM CHAMBERS, executed by Graham Myers and decorated by MICHAEL STAPLETON in the 1780s and 1790s. In the New Square is the Museum Building (1852–54) in the Venetian-Gothic style by Deane and Woodward. Both the Berkeley Library and the Arts Building (completed 1978) are by Ahrends, Burton and Koralek. *See* also EDUCATION. W G

K. C. Bailey, *A History of Trinity College Dublin 1892 to 1945*, 1947; R. B. McDowell and D. A. Webb, *Trinity College Dublin 1592 to 1952 – An Academic History*, 1982; E. McParland, 'Trinity College, Dublin', *Country Life*, clix (1976), pp. 1166, 1242, 1310; C. Maxwell, *A History of Trinity College Dublin 1591 to 1892*, 1946; J. W. Stubbs, *The History of the University of Dublin from its Foundation to the End of the 18th Century*, 1889; W. Urwick, *The Early History of Trinity College Dublin 1591 to 1660*, 1892.

Tripartite Life. The name given in English to the *Bethu Phátraic*, an account of the life and works of ST PATRICK written in Irish *c.* 895–901 and seemingly based on an earlier work now lost. It contains the foundation of much hallowed Patrician lore although most of its stories are undoubtedly apocryphal and frequently fantastic. B de B

W. Stokes (ed.), *The Tripartite Life of Patrick . . .*, 1887; K. Mulchrone (ed.), *Bethu Phátraic, The Tripartite Life of Patrick*, 1939.

Tuam, Co. Galway. St Mary's Cathedral, Tuam, incorporates part of the 12th-century fabric – a barrel-vaulted chancel with an unusually wide arch of six orders – dating from the period when the O'Conor High Kings of Ireland resided there. An early 14th-century choir with a richly carved east window was added to the chancel and served as the cathedral of one of the country's archbishoprics until the Reformation, and as the cathedral of the Church of Ireland diocese until the 19th century. Sir THOMAS DEANE's addition to the west of the chancel was completed in 1878 and now serves that purpose. In one corner of the cathedral is a fragment of a Romanesque cross; fragments of two others are mounted together in Tuam's Market Square. B de B

Tuohy, Patrick (1894–1930). Portrait, narrative and genre painter; born in Dublin, he was one of the first pupils at Patrick Pearse's school, St Enda's. In 1908 he studied under the sculptor William Pearse, who encouraged his interest in art, then entered the Metropolitan School of Art where he was a student of WILLIAM ORPEN. Tuohy taught in the Metropolitan School of Art from 1918, and first exhibited *A Mayo Peasant Boy* (painted in 1912) that same year. He was elected ARHA in 1926, and subsequently RHA. He spent long periods in Paris where he had painted portraits of JOYCE's family. Afterwards he lived in New York and died there. He is represented in the National Gallery of Ireland and the Hugh Lane Municipal Gallery of Modern Art, Dublin. C MacG

Túr Gloine, An (Tower of Glass, The). A purpose-built STAINED-GLASS workshop founded in 1903 at 24 Upper Pembroke Street, Dublin, by EDWARD MARTYN and SARAH PURSER. Co-operatively run, its principles were based on those of Christopher Whall (1849–1924) and the London firm of Lowndes & Drury (founded 1897): 'Each window should be in all its artistic parts

An Túr Gloine. Detail of the *St Simeon* window (1904) by Michael Healy in Loughrea Cathedral, showing the infant St John the Baptist.

Turoe Stone. The upper part of the stone, showing typical swirling La Tène decoration.

the work of an individual artist, the glass chosen and painted by the same mind and hand that made the design and drew the cartoon – in fact a bit of stained glass should be a work of free art (as in the mediaeval workshop days)'.

Except for Alfred Child (trained by Whall), the Studio's manager, his glazier Charles Williams and MICHAEL HEALY, who joined in 1903, the Studio's principal artists were graduates of Child's stained-glass classes (started in 1901) at the Dublin Art School: Beatrice Elvery (*see* GLENAVY), 1904–12; Catherine O'Brien (d. 1963), 1906–63; Ethel Rhind (d. 1952), 1908–39, who also worked effectively in *opus sectile*; WILHELMINA M. GEDDES, 1913–25; Hubert McGoldrick (1897–1967), 1920–45; and, later, EVIE HONE, 1935–44. The role of Sarah Purser, the principal shareholder, was largely administrative and supportive rather than artistic. Members of the studio made windows for LOUGHREA CATHEDRAL, An Túr Gloine's first major commission.

Regular exhibitors with the Arts and Crafts Society of Ireland (*see* ARTS AND CRAFTS MOVEMENT) from 1904 until 1925, all the members of An Túr belonged to the Guild of Irish Art Workers (founded 1909). In February 1925, the studio was registered as An Túr Gloine Stained Glass Works Ltd; in 1940, after Child's death, Catherine O'Brien became Secretary and Manager. In October 1944, after Sarah Purser's death, the company was dissolved; Miss O'Brien tok over the workshop premises until her death in 1963.

The Work Journals, Share Register and Minute Book of An Túr Gloine are deposited in the National Gallery of Ireland. N G B
Sarah Purser, *An Túr Gloine – 25th Anniversary Celebration*, 1928; James White and Michael Wynne, *Irish Stained Glass*, 1963; Peter Cormack, *Christopher Whall 1849–1924: Arts and Crafts Stained Glass Worker*, 1980.

Turoe Stone, Co. Galway. A decorated granite boulder of phallic appearance, 1·68 m. (5 ft 6 in.) high. now at Turoe House, 4 miles N of Loughrea, originally beside the nearby Rath of Feerwore. The upper 78 cm. (30 in.) of the stone is completely covered with LA TÈNE relief carving of outstanding quality, with thick-lobed spirals, triskeles and trumpet-curves; this is contained within a poor fret border. Similar La Tène decoration is found on stones at Castlestrange (Co. Roscommon), Killycluggin (Co. Cavan), Mullamast (Co. Kildare) and Derrykeighan (Co. Antrim). The Turoe Stone can be compared with similar decorated stones at Kermaria in Brittany and St Goar in the Rhineland. It is in the early IRON AGE tradition, and probably dates from the first century BC. M H
M. V. Duignan, 'The Turoe Stone, its Place in Insular La Tène Art', in P. M. Duval and C. F. C. Hawkes (eds.), *Celtic Art in Ancient Europe*, 1976, pp. 201–17.

Tynan, Katherine (1861–1931). Poet and novelist; born in Dublin, she was an intimate friend of W. B. YEATS. The characteristic features of her poetry are Catholic piety and the vagueness of the post-Pre-Raphaelite world. T McC

Ulster Architectural Heritage Society. The Society, whose offices are at 181a Stranmillis Road, Belfast, was formed in 1967 to promote the appreciation of good architecture of all periods (from the prehistoric era to the present); to encourage the preservation of buildings and groups of artistic merit or of historic importance; and to encourage public awareness and appreciation of the beauty, history and character of local neighbourhoods. While based in Belfast, its membership and interests extend throughout the nine counties of the Province. It is a campaigning body, which is consulted by public bodies, offers evidence at public enquiries and appeals, and frequently makes representations on planning, CONSERVATION and other issues. Its principal achievement was its successful campaign to secure legislation in Northern Ireland, similar to that in Great Britain, establishing a Historic Buildings Council, procedure for the statutory listing of buildings of note, and grant aid for the owners of such buildings. As a non-political, non-sectarian, non-profit-making organization and a recognized charity, the Society finances its activities mainly from the sales of its numerous and influential publications: of the two principal series, one comprises detailed surveys of towns, villages and districts on both sides of the border; the other consists of monographs on subjects connected directly or indirectly with Irish architectural history. The Society also arranges lectures, meetings and excursions, and maintains a close working relationship with other Irish conservation organizations, including regular exchange visits with members of the Dublin Civic Group. In 1982 the Society had about 1,300 members.　　　　　　　　　　　　CEBB

Ulster Museum (Belfast). Founded as the National Museum for Northern Ireland in 1962, the Ulster Museum is the greatly enlarged successor of the Belfast Municipal Museum and Art Gallery of 1892. The museum building by J. C. Wynne dates from the late 1920s, with an extension of 1971 by Francis Pym. It contains the important photographic collections of R. J. Welch, antiquities, the treasures salvaged from a Spanish Armada wreck, a costume collection, a fine art gallery and an especially strong section on industrial archaeology. Its offshoots are the Folk and Transport Museums at Cultra, Co. Down, and it is also connected with the notable Armagh County Museum.　　MC

Ulysses. Novel by JAMES JOYCE, begun 1914, published in 1922. Such technical features as the use of parallel myths and the various experiments with form, point-of-view and language place the novel within an international modernist tradition. However, Joyce, who once wrote that if he could 'get to the heart of Dublin' he could get to the heart of every city in the world, made the book also distinctively Irish. Working from memory, old newspapers, guidebooks (such as Thom's *Dublin Directory*), and details sent him by relatives, he meticulously reconstructed not only the physical appearance of the 'Hibernian metropolis' in 1904 but also the atmosphere, the personages of the day, and the major events with which they had been concerned (though he was perfectly willing on occasion to alter fact in the interest of plot, symbolism, and even motives such as hostility towards some of his real-life models). The major characters, though archetypalized, are at the literal level Irish; and even the Baroque complexity of style has been compared to masterpieces of indigenous art such as the BOOK OF KELLS.　　PLM
Richard Ellmann, *Ulysses on the Liffey*, 1972; C. H. Peake, *James Joyce: the Citizen and the Artist*, 1977.

universities. *See* EDUCATION.

Ussher, James (1581–1656). Antiquarian and scholar; born in Dublin, he was educated at Trinity College, Dublin, and ordained into the Anglican priesthood in 1601. Twice Vice-Chancellor of Trinity College, he was consecrated Bishop of Meath in 1621 and Archbishop of Armagh in 1625. He argued strongly for the separate identity of the Church of Ireland within the Anglican communion. Ussher left Ireland in 1640, never to return. He subsequently became Bishop of Carlisle and of Oxford. He wrote prolifically on ecclesiastical and biblical topics, researched early Irish history, and collected early Irish manuscripts, including the BOOK OF KELLS.　　ICR
C. R. Erlington, *The Life of James Ussher with an Account of his Writings*, 1848.

van der Hagen, Willem (d. 1745). Painter; coming from a Dutch family of painters, he worked in England before settling in Ireland *c.* 1721, where he became the country's first resident, professional, landscape painter. He also painted decorative murals (now all destroyed or removed) for houses in Co. Waterford, a ceiling in BEAULIEU, Co. Louth, as well as scenery for the Smock Alley Theatre, Dublin, decorations for Dublin Castle balls, and an altarpiece for St Michan's Church, Dublin (1721). His landscapes vary from topographical house views and architectural *capricci* to a painting of the Powerscourt waterfall, his last recorded work. He also made at least three views of Irish ports, Waterford (1736), Derry, and Carrickfergus, painted for a proposed, but never completed, series of tapestries to be woven in Dublin.　　AOC

Van Nost, John. Life-size bronze statue of George III, depicted as a Roman general, 1765. Mansion House, Dublin.

Van Nost, John (*c.* 1712–1780). Sculptor; born in London, where his father, a Dutchman, was a sculptor. The young Van Nost was apprenticed to Henry Scheemakers in London in 1726 and moved to Dublin *c.* 1749. There he was approved by the DUBLIN SOCIETY, for which he provided several busts. The Society's art schools, newly opened in 1746, sent promising young sculpture students to him. He introduced metropolitan standards of excellence to Dublin students like HEWETSON, Crawley, Cunningham and Foy. He had a very large and successful sculptural practice in Dublin. He made statues of George II, several works for the Rotunda pleasure gardens and Hospital, rooftop statues for Dublin Castle and numerous church memorials and busts. Van Nost's work was always of a good standard and was even outstanding in some instances. He followed the main direction of British sculpture of the day towards increasing Classical sobriety, avoiding the dramatic postures typical of the Baroque. His works complemented the Palladian style in Irish architecture.　　　　　　　　　　JT

W. Strickland, *Dictionary of Irish Artists*, 1913; H. Potterton, *Irish Church Monuments*, 1975.

Victory, Gerard (1921–). Composer; a civil servant, actor and producer before devoting himself to music, he was appointed Director of Music for Radio Telefís Éireann in 1967. His interest in serialism and avant-garde procedures dates from 1963. His music is eclectic, volatile in mood and manner; *Jonathan Swift – A Symphonic Portrait* (1970), written on a large scale, and first heard in 1972, is truly representative of his mature style; his *Four Tableaux for Large Orchestra* are rather more complicated. Dramatic and pictorial elements dominate two full-length operas, *Chatterton* and *Abelard and Heloise*. A continuous interest in providing 'entertainment' music is exemplified by his overtures *Cyrano de Bergerac* (1970) and *Olympic Festival* (1975).　　　　　　　　　　AGH

Vikings. The Scandinavian raiders who first came to Ireland in 795 but who later settled were mostly Norwegians. They were responsible for the foundation of Dublin in 841, and subsequently of other maritime towns such as Arklow, Wicklow, Wexford and Waterford, and probably also Cork and Limerick. By the end of the 10th century, a number of them had become Christians, and intermarried with the native Irish; these are referred to as Hiberno-Norse. A Viking cemetery at Islandbridge, Co. Dublin, yielded burials of some of the earliest-known Viking settlers. Recent excavations in the heart of Dublin (*see* WOOD QUAY) produced little material earlier than the 10th century, but revealed foundations of Viking houses of wood dating from the 10th to 12th centuries. Although Viking political power declined after the Battle of Clontarf (1014), it was only then that the Vikings – probably in Dublin – provided Irish art with a new range of animal ornament in the Scandinavian Ringerike and Urnes styles. These dominated the decoration of Irish works of art, particularly in the 12th century, as evidenced, for instance, by the CROSS OF CONG and St Manchan's Shrine (*see* SHRINES). Important instances of similar animal ornament are found embellishing Irish architecture, as on the doorway of CLONFERT CATHEDRAL, Co. Galway, and perhaps its finest testimony in stone is the 12th-century sarcophagus in CORMAC'S CHAPEL at Cashel.　　PH

P. G. Foote and D. M. Wilson, *The Viking Achievement*, 1970, Magnus Magnusson, *Vikings*, 1980.

Vikings. Silver coin of Sihtric III Silkbeard, *c.* 1015, from Dublin. British Museum.

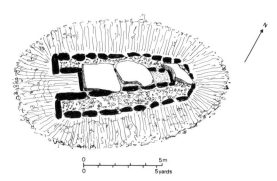

wedge tomb. Plan of a typical burial, showing the tapering outline of the tomb.

Wall, Mervyn Eugene Welply (1908–   ). Writer; born in Dublin, he spent his early life partly in Ireland and partly in Germany. He worked in the Civil Service, in Radio Éireann, and as Secretary of the Arts Council. His writing shows an unusual mixture of reality and fantasy, as in his play *Alarm among the Clerks* (1940). His inventive comic novels about a lay brother in Clonmacnois monastery, *The Unfortunate Fursey* (1946) and *The Return of Fursey* (1948), use medieval settings to satirize modern ireland.　　　BH

Wallace, William Vincent (1812–65). Composer; born at Waterford, he was a proficient organist and violinist at the age of fifteen and, although a Protestant, became organist at the R.C. Cathedral in Thurles, Co. Tipperary, at the age of eighteen and taught music there. He emigrated to Australia in 1835 and then travelled adventurously and extensively, performing in South America, the USA, Germany and Holland. His opera *Maritana* was produced in London at the Drury Lane Theatre in 1845 and in Ireland at the Theatre Royal, Dublin, in 1846, followed by performances in Vienna and other European capitals. His opera *Lurline*, first produced at Covent Garden in 1860, was a great success.

Wallace's sister Eliza, who made her début in his *Maritana* at Covent Garden in 1848, pursued a successful operatic career.　　　BdeB

Ware, Sir James (1594–1666). Historian; born in Dublin and educated at Trinity College, Dublin (which he later represented in the Irish Parliament), he devoted much of his life to research into early Irish history and literature, on which he began to publish in 1626. Among his many works are *De Scriptoribus Hiberniae* (1639), *De Hibernia et antiquitatibus ejus disquisitiones* (1654) and *De Praesulibus Hiberniae, Commentarius* (1665). Ware was the first to print Edmund Spenser's *View of the Present State of Ireland* (1633). An edition of Ware's works in English appeared in London in 1705.　　　ICR

Watters, Eugene. Poet and critic; *see* Ó TUAIRISC.

wedge tomb. A type of tomb, dating from the early BRONZE AGE, having a main burial chamber, frequently accompanied by an antechamber or portico distinguished from the chamber itself by a large closing-slab inside the flat façade. Such tombs face west and decrease in height and width from front to back. The cairn is economically built, revetted with outer walling only 50 cm. to 2 m. (1 ft 8 in. to 6 ft 6 in.) from the chamber walls. The roof, where present, is lintelled. Beaker and coarse pottery are frequently found with barbed-and-tanged arrowheads. *See* MOYTIRRA.　　　MH

West, Robert. Stucco decoration on the staircase of 86 St Stephen's Green, Dublin, 1765.

West, Robert (d. 1770). Painter; he trained in France and afterwards established a drawing school in Dublin which was taken over by the DUBLIN SOCIETY in the 1740s. The teaching of West and his assistant James Mannin was largely responsible for the high quality of the arts in Ireland from the 1750s onwards (*see* PAINTING).　　　AOC

West, Robert. Builder and stuccodore; he is first recorded as a plasterer in Dublin in 1752. He decorated the staircase of the Rotunda Hospital (1755) in a pedestrian manner, though his style developed quickly, as did his commissions. He decorated No. 4 Parnell Square and No. 9 Cavendish Row in 1756, followed in quick succession by No. 6 South Leinster Street and Mornington House. His finest work, strongly influenced by CRAMILLION, is in No. 20 Lower Dominick Street (*c.* 1755) – a house which he built for himself. Later work includes No. 56 St Stephen's Green (1760), with his brother, in the Chinese taste; and No. 86 St Stephen's Green (1765). Many houses, especially in the vicinity of Dublin, such as Newbridge, Malahide and Colganstown, have ceilings attributed to West. His work is notable for his command of composition and scale, his swirling foliage and squawking birds. These latter elements quickly became the hallmarks of a uniquely Irish school of PLASTERWORK.   W G

Wexford Festival. The birth of the Wexford Festival in 1951 was the result of a lecture given to Wexford Gramophone Society by Sir Compton Mackenzie who inspired in local physicians Tom Walsh, Des French and their friends the thought that staging opera in the little Theatre Royal was very much a possibility. Sir Compton became the Festival's first president.

The Festival has since developed and expanded with very considerable success, despite the constant problems of maintaining a high quality in opera and associated events and ensuring that the Theatre Royal remained an acceptable venue. There are the further difficulties of planning the programme more than 15 months ahead and sustaining the increasing pressure on an amateur council and the team of voluntary workers in a complex artistic enterprise based in a small town. However, Wexford, with 17,000 inhabitants, is of the right size, intimacy and layout to be dominated by the Festival, which takes place each year over twelve days in late October.

The operas chosen are in general rarely heard or of unusual nature. Surrounding the operas is a group of associated events such as recitals, choral concerts and important exhibitions in the field of the visual arts. The number of these exhibitions and the standard and variety of paintings, sculpture, silver, crafts, woodcarving and pottery have become an important festival feature. There are also fringe events, ranging from crab-fishing to films and flower shows.

The first opera to be mounted was an Irish one, BALFE's *Rose of Castile* in October 1951. It had a professional guest conductor and producer, three professional singers and an amateur chorus from the town. So began a festival which was to be driven forward by the enthusiasm of the town and Dr Tom Walsh, who continued as artistic director until 1966. The programme expanded in 1955 to include two operas, and developed further to three works from 1963. The orchestra is the RTE Symphony Orchestra and the Festival has concentrated always on top-class conductors, designers and producers and has helped to launch many young singers who went on to reach the peak of their profession, such as Geraint Evans, Janet Baker (in her first performance outside the chorus), Mirella Freni, Graziella Sciutti and Frederica von Stade.

Wexford Festival. A scene from the 1982 production of Haydn's *L'isola disabitata* (1779), a short work described by the composer as an 'Operette'.

Up to 1981 Wexford had produced 82 different operas, most of them sung in the original language. In the early days the trend was towards early 19th-century Italian opera, with some French and German works. More recently, and since 1970 in particular, the move has been towards a greater variety of composers, and a greater number of modern operas have been introduced into the repertoire. The pattern of three operas rotated through a 12-day programme is now well established and popular. The artistic policy of the Festival Council is to maintain a balanced programme, despite financial constraints, and it continues the successful formula of combining one more romantic or dramatic piece, one comedy and one which may be a novelty, a controversy or an experiment. The policy of producing operas rarely heard elsewhere and the consistently high standards of production draw critics and audiences from far and wide.   D E C P

Whelan, Leo (1892–1956). Portrait and genre painter; born in Dublin, he studied at the Metropolitan School of Art, Dublin, under WILLIAM ORPEN. His genre subjects and interiors are much prized and sought-after today by collectors, although during his lifetime he was best known for his portraits. He was elected ARHA 1920, RHA 1923.   C MacG

Wilde, Lady (*née* Jane Francesca Elgee; *c.* 1825–1896). Writer; born in Dublin. Inspired by the works and death of THOMAS DAVIS, she became a passionate supporter of the Young Ireland movement and translated and wrote poems and articles for *The Nation* in the 1840s under her pen-name 'Speranza'. Of greater merit were her works on Irish folklore published between 1884 and 1890. She was the wife of SIR WILLIAM WILDE and mother of OSCAR WILDE.   B de B

H. Wyndham, *Speranza*, 1951.

Wilde, Oscar Fingal O'Flahertie Wills (1854–1900). Playwright, poet, essayist and novelist, born in Dublin, his father was an expert on Irish antiquities and his mother had contributed patriotic poetry to the *Nation*. However, he preferred London, where he achieved fame before being imprisoned for two years for homosexual activities. Having turned his back on native subject-matter, he is connected to Irish tradition, if at all, by his sparkling wit. His most famous works include the novel *The Picture of Dorian Gray* (1890–1), the play *The Importance of Being Earnest* (perf. 1895), and *The Ballad of Reading Gaol* (1898).   P L M

Richard Ellmann (ed.), *Oscar Wilde: A Collection of Critical Essays*, 1969.

Wilde, Sir William Robert Wills (1815–76). Surgeon and antiquary; born near Castlerea, Co. Roscommon, he was the author of medical, topographical and Irish antiquarian works and compiler of an exemplary 3-volume catalogue of the antiquarian collection of the ROYAL IRISH ACADEMY, 1858–62; knighted in 1864, he was the father of OSCAR WILDE.   B de B

T. G. Wilson, *Victorian Doctor – The Life of Sir William Wilde*, 1942, reprinted 1974; T. de Vere White, *The Parents of Oscar Wilde*, 1967.

Wilks, Robert (*c.* 1665–1732). Actor; born at Rathfarnham, Co. Dublin, he trained under Ashbury at the Smock Alley Theatre, Dublin, before going to London, though returning to Dublin regularly. A lifelong friend of GEORGE FARQUHAR, who wrote several parts for him, he was highly regarded as Plume in *The Recruiting Officer* and Sir Harry Wildair in *The Constant Couple*.   C F-S

Willis, Richard Henry Albert (1853–1905). Painter and designer, born at Dingle, Co. Kerry, he was apprenticed as a boy to Arthur Hill, a Cork architect. He studied under JAMES BRENAN at the Cork School of Art and won a scholarship in the National Art Training School at South Kensington, London. Appointed headmaster of the Manchester School of Art in 1882, he resigned in 1892 to resume painting in London, where he exhibited at the Royal Academy. He succeeded his old teacher Brenan as head of the Metropolitan School of Art, Dublin in 1904. An Irish speaker himself, he was a strenuous supporter of the GAELIC LEAGUE and an enthusiast in the development of nationalism in Irish art education. He died at Ballinskelligs, Co. Kerry, where he often went to paint. His small landscapes and his enamels are much sought after by collectors and galleries alike.   C MacG

Woffington, Peg. The leading actress in the role of Mrs Ford in *The Merry Wives of Windsor*; mezzotint dated 1751. Theatre Museum, London.

Woffington, Margaret (Peg; *c.* 1714–1760). Actress; born in Dublin in very humble circumstances, she nevertheless excelled playing high-born ladies. Starting as a child performer, she appeared in Dublin at Aungier Street and Smock Alley (*see* THEATRES), where in 1740 she played the boy's part Sir Harry Wildair in FARQUHAR's *The Constant Couple*, the role which gained her initial success in London. She became the most celebrated actress in the British Isles, returning often to Smock Alley under SHERIDAN's management.   C F-S

Wood Quay (Dublin). The archaeological excavations on this 4-acre (1·8-hectare) site were among the largest of their kind ever undertaken in Europe. The excavations were carried out 1974–81 prior to the development of the site as a Civic Office complex by its owners, Dublin Corporation; they were directed by Patrick F. Wallace of the NMI and funded by the State. A succession of nine waterfronts was unearthed in the northern, riverward, part of the site; these ranged from palisaded earthen banks of the 10th-century VIKING age to a later stone wall and three wooden dockside revetments of the 13th-century Anglo-Norman period. Ten plots or properties of 10th-to early 12th-century date were excavated in the southern part of the site; in each of these plots were located the often intact foundation remains of up to a dozen houses built in succession of one another. Apart from the thousands of artefacts recovered (including several perfectly preserved organic remains, such as wood and textiles), the information on housing, urban environment, trade economy and town planning in Ireland's earliest town is of staggering proportions and will take years to exploit fully. PFW

woodwork. *See* FURNITURE.

Wyatt, James (1746–1813). Architect; although English, he dominated Irish country-house architecture for the last thirty years of the 18th century. His first Irish commission was Mount Kennedy, Co. Wicklow (1772), though work was not commenced till 1782, when it was executed by Thomas Cooley. Wyatt supplied designs for Abbeyleix, Co. Laois (1773–5), Gothic designs for Slane, Co. Meath (1775), and the dining room at Westport, Co. Mayo (1781). His visit to Ireland in 1785 was followed by work at Leinster House, Dublin (1785), and Curraghmore, Co. Waterford (*c.* 1787). His Irish career was crowned by the completion of the sublime house CASTLECOOLE, Co. Fermanagh (1790–8). WG

Wyatt, James. The dining room at Westport, Co. Mayo, designed by Wyatt in 1781; the stucco decoration is probably by Michael Stapleton.

Yeats, Anne (1919–). Painter and designer; born in Dublin, she is the daughter of WILLIAM BUTLER YEATS, and grand-daughter of JOHN BUTLER YEATS, the portrait painter. She studied at the Royal Hibernian Academy, Dublin, and became Designer, then Chief Designer, to the ABBEY THEATRE. She has exhibited in all the leading annual shows in Ireland, and also extensively on the Continent and in the USA. Examples of her work are to be found in the major public collections in Ireland. C MacG

Yeats, Jack B. (1871–1957). Painter, illustrator and writer; born in London, he was the son of the portrait painter, JOHN BUTLER YEATS, and was educated in Sligo. His family moved to Dublin 1880, and in 1887 to London where he studied at South Kensington School of Art, Chiswick Art School and Westminster School of Art. From 1891 he illustrated books, worked as a poster artist and wrote boys' stories. His first one-man exhibition was in London in 1897; he returned to Ireland in 1910. He exhibited at the Armory Show, New York, in 1913, and was elected ARHA 1916 and RHA 1917. He had a joint exhibition with William Nicholson at the National Gallery, London, 1942. Other major showings include the National Loan Exhibition in Dublin, 1945; a retrospective exhibition at Temple Newsam, Leeds, the Tate Gallery, London, and in Boston, Washington, San Francisco, Colorado, Toronto, Detroit and New York, 1951/52; and a Centenary Exhibition in Dublin, Belfast, and New York, 1971/72.

His most important works are to be found in many public galleries including the Hugh Lane Municipal Gallery of Modern Art, Dublin, the National Gallery of Ireland, the Yeats Museum, Sligo, the Tate Gallery, London, and in the Royal Collection. *See* also DUN EMER GUILD. C MacG

Thomas MacGreevy, *Jack B. Yeats; An Appreciation and Interpretation*, 1945; Hilary Pyle, *Jack B. Yeats: A Biography*, 1970.

Yeats, John Butler (1839–1922). Subject and portrait painter; born at Tullylish, Co. Down, he began his career as a barrister, working under Isaac Butt. When he was twenty-eight he took up painting, studied at Heatherley's Art School, London, and attended the Royal Academy Schools under Poynter from 1868. He was elected ARHA in 1887 (at which time he was a prominent figure in the Bedford Park Settlement, Chiswick) and RHA, 1892. He returned to Dublin in 1902, and between that date and 1907 he painted a great number of portraits of the important literary figures of the Irish Renaissance. Some of his best-known works, the series of portraits commissioned by Sir HUGH LANE, are in the Hugh Lane Municipal

Yeats, Jack B. *Self-portrait*, pencil drawing on paper, *c.* 1920. NGI.

Yeats, William Butler. Portrait by his father, John Butler Yeats. Hugh Lane Municipal Gallery of Modern Art, Dublin.

Gallery of Modern Art, Dublin, and others in the National Gallery of Ireland.

Yeats went to New York in 1907 intending to return but he never did, and died there. His sons JACK B. YEATS and W. B. YEATS remained in Ireland.   C MacG

William M. Murphy, *Prodigal Father: the Life of John Butler Yeats*, 1978.

Yeats, William Butler (1865–1939). Poet, dramatist, political figure; born in Dublin, he was Ireland's greatest poet and, as T. S. Eliot suggested, 'one of those few poets whose history is the history of our own time, who are a part of the consciousness of their age, which cannot be understood without them'. His background was Protestant; the distinguished family included his father JOHN BUTLER YEATS and his brother JACK YEATS, both brilliant painters. Although he was born in Dublin, it was the west of Ireland, especially Sligo (where his family had connections) and Galway, that most deeply impressed his imagination. His poetic career extends from the publication of *Mosada* (1886) and his first major collection, *The Wanderings of Oisin and Other Poems* (1889) to *Last Poems* (1939). Through long, conscious effort he effected a unity among his national, artistic and philosophical interest, so that his mature work fuses Irish and occult elements in verse of unrivalled lyric beauty and power.

He was also a major experimental dramatist. After playing a central role in the development of the Irish theatre movement and helping start the ABBEY THEATRE, he found inspiration in the Japanese Noh drama for esoteric dance-plays intended for a *coterie* audience. In all his literary work, creative tension is generated by the antinomies typical of his dualistic vision: youth and age, body and soul, the fallen world and ultimate reality, power and wisdom, life and art. The Nobel Prize in 1923 and his appointment as a Senator in the Irish Free State government (1922–28) brought recognition of his artistic and national achievements. Against the darkening background of the years leading up to World War II, he sought through his art to raise 'the heroic cry in the midst of despair' and to provide ideals that might shape the civilization of the future. Significant volumes of his work include the *Collected Poems* (1950), the *Collected Plays* (1952), *A Vision* (1937), and *Autobiographies* (1955). Yeats died in France, but his remains were brought to Ireland in 1948 and re-interred at Drumcliff, Co. Sligo, where, in accordance with his request, the following epitaph appears on his tomb:

> No marble, no conventional phrase;
> On limestone quarried near the spot
> By his command these words are cut:
> Cast a cold eye
> On life, on death
> Horseman, pass by!

PLM

Richard Ellmann, *Yeats: The Man and the Masks*, 1949; J. B. Hone, *Life of W. B. Yeats*, 1942; M. Mac Líammóir and Eavan Boland, *W. B. Yeats and his World*, 1971.

Appendix

List of museums, art galleries and libraries,
and houses, castles and gardens open to the public
(an asterisk indicates an individual entry in this
encyclopaedia)

MUSEUMS

Co. Antrim
*Ulster Museum, Botanic Gardens, Belfast

Co. Armagh
Armagh County Museum, The Mall, Armagh
Armagh Astronomy Centre, College Hill, Armagh
Regimental Museum, Sovereign's House, Armagh

Co. Carlow
Carlow County Museum, College Street, Carlow

Co. Cavan
Derragarra Folk Museum, Butlersbridge

Co. Clare
Bunratty Folk Park, Bunratty
Coosheen Folk Museum, Corbally, Kilkee
Craggaunowen Project, Quin

Co. Cork
Cork Public Museum, Fitzgerald Park, Cork
Cobh Museum, Scots Church, Cobh
Clock Tower Museum, Main Street, Youghal
Kinsale Regional Museum, Kinsale
West Cork Regional Museum, Clonakilty

Co. Donegal
Donegal Museum, Franciscan Friary, Rossnowlagh
Glencolumbkille Folk Museum, Glencolumbkille

Co. Down
Ulster Folk and Transport Museum, Cultra
   Manor

Co. Dublin
*National Museum of Ireland, Kildare Street,
   Dublin 2 (entrance to Natural History division
   is in Merrion Street)
National Maritime Museum, Haigh Terrace, Dun
   Laoghaire
Museum of Childhood, Palmerston Park, Dublin 6
Civic Museum, South William Street, Dublin 2
Museum of Broadcasting, 27 Lower Rathmines
   Road, Dublin 6
Aeronautical Museum, Dublin Airport

Kilmainham Jail Museum, Kilmainham, Dublin 8
Guinness Museum, James' Gate, James' Street,
   Dublin 8
James Joyce Museum, James Joyce Martello
   Tower, Sandycove

Co. Fermanagh
Enniskillen Museum, The Castle, Enniskillen

Co. Galway
Galway City Museum, The Spanish Arch, Galway
Aran Museum, Kilronan, Inishmore, Aran Islands
Museum Na nOilean, Inishmaan, Aran Islands

Co. Kerry
Muckross House, Killarney

Co. Kildare
Irish Horse Museum, The National Stud, Tully
Ecclesiastical Museum, St Patrick's College,
   Maynooth
Ballitore Museum, The Old Quaker Meeting
   House, Ballitore
Canal and Transport Museum, Old Grand Canal
   Hotel, Robertstown

Co. Kilkenny
Rothe House Museum, Parliament Street,
   Kilkenny

Co. Laios
Traction Engine Museum, The Green, Stradbally

Co. Limerick
Limerick Museum, John's Square, Limerick
The Hunt Collection, National Institute of Higher
   Education, Plassey, Castletroy
Aras De Valéra Museum, Bruree
Lough Gur Interpretive Centre, Lough Gur

Co. Louth
Transport Museum, Rathgory, Dunleer
Millmount Museum, Millmount, Drogheda

Co. Meath
Trim Museum, Trim

Co. Monaghan
Iniskeen Folk Museum, Iniskeen
County Museum, The Courthouse, Monaghan

Co. Offaly
Birr Castle Museum

Co. Sligo
County Museum, Stephen Street, Sligo

Co. Tipperary
County Museum, Parnell Street, Clonmel
Folk Museum, Toomevara

Co. Tyrone
Camp Hill Ulster-American Folk Park, Cappagh

Co. Waterford
Waterford Maritime Museum, The Quay,
    Waterford

Waterford Civic Museum, Reginald's Tower, The
    Quay, Waterford

Co. Westmeath
Athlone Castle Museum, The Castle, Athlone
Mullingar Museum, Market Square, Mullingar
Military Museum, St Columb's Barracks,
    Mullingar

Co. Wexford
Agricultural Museum, Johnstown Castle
Wexford Maritime Museum, The Quay, Wexford
County Museum, Castle Street, Enniscorthy

Co. Wicklow
Agricultural Museum, Glenealy
Arklow Maritime Museum, Old Technical School,
    St Mary's Road, Arklow
Castleruddery Transport Museum, Donard
Parnell Museum, Avondale House, Rathdrum

ART GALLERIES

Belfast
*Ulster Museum, Botanic Gardens, Belfast

Cork
Crawford Municipal Art Gallery, Emmet Place
Fota, Carrigtwohill

Dublin
*National Gallery of Ireland, Merrion Square
Hugh Lane Municipal Gallery of Modern Art,
    Parnell Square
National Portrait Collection, Malahide Castle
*Chester Beatty Gallery of Oriental Art,
    Shrewsbury Road

Kilkenny
Kilkenny Castle Art Gallery

Limerick
Municipal Art Gallery, Pery Square

Sligo
Sligo Art Gallery, Stephen Street

Waterford
Municipal Art Gallery, O'Connell Street

Co. Wicklow
*Beit Art Collection, Russborough, Blessington

LIBRARIES

*National Library, Kildare Street, Dublin 2
*Trinity College, Library, Dublin 2
*Royal Irish Academy Library, Dawson Street,
    Dublin 2
*National Gallery of Ireland, Art Reference
    Library, Merrion Square, Dublin 2
Dublin City Library, Pearse Street, Dublin 2
*Marsh's Library, St Patrick's Close, Dublin 8
King's Inn Library, Henrietta Street, Dublin 1
*Chester Beatty Library, Shrewsbury Road,
    Dublin 4
*Royal Dublin Society Library, Ballsbridge, Dublin 4
Representative Church Body Library, Braemor
    Park, Dublin 16
*Linenhall Library, Donegall Square, Belfast
Belfast Central Public Library, Royal Avenue,
    Belfast

Presbyterian Historical Society Library, Church
    House, Fisherwick Place, Belfast
The Diocesan Library, Cashel, Co. Tipperary
Cathedral Library, Armagh

In addition to the above important libraries there are
libraries in all the universities and most colleges. Most
counties have a County Library and some City
Libraries are well stocked. The library and papers of
the local historian, the Rev. William Carrigan, are in
the library of St Kieran's College, Kilkenny.

The Library of St Isidore's, the Irish Franciscan
College in Rome, contains much of Irish interest; some
of its contents were removed to Dún Mhuire, Seafield
Road, Killiney.

HOUSES AND CASTLES OPEN
TO THE PUBLIC

Co. Antrim
Carrickfergus Castle

Co. Armagh
Ardress House, Charlemont
Derrymore House, Bessbrook
The Argory, Charlemont

Co. Clare
Bunratty Castle
Knappogue Castle, Quin

Co. Cork
Blarney Castle
Bantry House
Dunkathel, Glanmire
Fota, Carrigtwohill
Riverstown House, Cork

Co. Derry
Hezlett House
Springhill, Moneymore

Co. Down
Castleward, Strangford
Mount Stewart, Newtownards

Co. Fermanagh
*Castlecoole, Enniskillen
Florencecourt, Enniskillen

Co. Galway
Thoor Ballylee, Gort
Dun Guaire Castle, Kinvara

Co. Kerry
Derrynane Abbey, Caherdaniel
Muckross House, Killarney

Co. Kildare
*Castletown House, Celbridge

Co. Kilkenny
Kilkenny Castle
Rothe House, Kilkenny
Edmund Rice's birthplace, Westcourt, Callan

Co. Limerick
Castlematrix, Rathkeale
Glin Castle, Glin (by arrangement only to groups
   of 10 or more)

Co. Mayo
Westport House

Co. Roscommon
Clonalis, Castlerea

Co. Sligo
Lissadell

Co. Tipperary
Cahir Castle
Damer House, Roscrea
*Ormond Manor House, Carrick-on-Suir

Co. Tyrone
Mellon farmhouse, Mountjoy
Wilson House, Strabane

Co. Westmeath
Tullynally Castle, Castlepollard

Co. Wicklow
Kilruddery, Bray (by arrangement only to groups
   of 10 or more)
Avondale, Rathdrum
*Russborough, Blessington

In addition to the above, some private house owners
will allow reasonable access to interested parties by
special arrangement. Among these are Birr Castle, Co.
Offaly, Dunsany Castle, Co. Meath, Slane Castle, Co.
Meath, Lismore Castle, Co. Waterford, *Castletown
(Cox), Piltown, Co. Kilkenny, Gurteen-le-Poer, Kil-
sheelan, Co. Tipperary, Abbeyleix, Co. Leix, Berming-
ham House, Tuam, Co. Galway. A number of other
houses now converted to commercial or institutional
use can usually be visited by prior arrangement, e.g.
Johnstown Castle, Co. Wexford, Ballyhaise, Co.
Cavan, Hazlewood, Co. Sligo, Ballyfin, Co. Laois,
Bellinter, Co. Meath, Gosford Castle, Co. Armagh,
Belfast Castle, and Bullock Castle, Dalkey, Co. Dublin.

Among the numerous houses or castles converted to
use as hotels or guest-houses are Dromoland Castle,
Co. Clare, Ashford Castle, Co. Galway, Cashel Palace,
Co. Tipperary, Kilkea Castle, Co. Kildare, Bargy
Castle, Co. Wexford, Longueville House, Mallow, Co.
Cork, and Assolas, Kanturk, Co. Cork.

GARDENS REGULARLY OPEN
TO THE PUBLIC

Co. Cork
Annesgrove, Castletownroche
Castle Gardens, Timoleague
Castlehaven House, Castletownsend
Creagh, Skibereen
Fota, Carrigtohill
Garinish Island (Ilnacullin), Glengariff

Co. Derry
Guy L. Wilson Daffodil Garden, New University
    of Ulster, Coleraine

Co. Down
Castlewellan
Mount Stewart, Greyabbey
Tollymore Forest Park
Rowallane, Saintfield

Co. Dublin
*National Botanic Gardens, Glasnevin
St Anne's, Clontarf
Howth Castle, Howth
Marley Grange
Fernhill, Sandyford.

Co. Fermanagh
Florencecourt

Co. Kerry
Derreen
Muckross House, Killarney

Co. Kildare
Japanese Gardens, Irish National Stud, Tully

Co. Laois
Abbeyleix

Co. Offaly
Birr Castle

Co. Waterford
Curraghmore, Portlaw
Lismore Castle

Co. Wexford
Johnstown Castle
John F. Kennedy Park

Co. Wicklow
Avondale
Mount Usher, Ashford
Powerscourt, Enniskerry

PRIVATE GARDENS OCCASIONALLY
OPEN TO THE PUBLIC

Co. Cork
Ashbourne House

Co. Donegal
Glenveagh
Carrablagh

Co. Down
Guincho

Co. Dublin
Beech Park, Clonsilla
Kilbogget, Killiney

Co. Kerry
Ardnagashel
Glenleam
Rossdohan

Co. Kildare
Kildangan, Monasterevan

Co. Limerick
Glenstal Abbey

Co. Sligo
Lissadell

Co. Tipperary
Ardsallagh, Fethard

Co. Waterford
Mount Congreve, Kilmeadon

Co. Wexford
Kilmokea House, Campile

Co. Wicklow
Kilruddery, Bray
Dargle Cottage, Enniskerry

Sources of illustrations

Individual illustrations are identified by page numbers, the position on the page being indicated where necessary by the following abbreviations: *a* = above; *al* = above left; *ar* = above right; *b* = below; *bl* = below left; *br* = below right; *c* = centre; *ca* = centre above; *cb* = centre below; *cl* = centre left; *l* = left; *r* = right.

Courtesy, Abbey Theatre, Dublin 42*r*, 73*l*, 100*l*, 101, 117;
Courtesy, Aer Rianta, Dublin 31*l*;
The Art Institute of Chicago 91;
The Bank of Ireland 216*a*;
Barber Institute of Fine Arts, Birmingham 49*a*;
Photo Bernand (Agence de Presse) 41*b*;
Photo Fergus Bourke 13*a*, 40*ar*, 193*ar*:
Peter Bridgewater 14, 17*b*;
Photo Studio Briggs 47*b*;
Courtesy, the Trustees of the British Museum, London 49*ca*, 81, 137, 179*l*, 246*r*;
Cambridge University Collection, copyright reserved 66*l*, 77*r*, 163;
Chandler Collection 193*bl*;
Photo Peter Chèze-Brown 94, 108*b*;
An Chomhairle Ealaíon, Dublin 68, 127*bl*, 149, 203*l*;
Commissioners of Public Works in Ireland 35*l*, 71*a*, 77*al*, 98, 118*a*, 124*r*, 127*ar*, 128*r*, 166, 173*a*, 209*a*, 212*a*, 212*b*, 226*a*, 230*al*, 230*r*, 231, 244*b*;
Photo *Connacht Tribune*, Galway 147*a*;
Courtauld Institute of Art, London 17*a*, 55, 105*b*, 114*l*, 246*l*;
Crawford Municipal Art Gallery, Cork 145*a*;
Department of the Environment, Belfast 24*r*, 28*br*;
Photo Hugh Doran 41*a*, 43*l*, 77*bl*, 208*l*,
E. Estyn Evans 247*a*;
Photo J. Fiennes 213*al*;
Photo Robin Glasscock 118*b*;
Courtesy, the Knight of Glin 93;
Green Studio, Dublin 72*b*, 84*l*;
The Hon. Desmond Guinness 104*a*, 113;
Photo Peter Harbison 16;
Hugh Lane Municipal Gallery of Modern Art, Dublin 71*b*, 87, 124*l*, 169*a*, 189*b*, 251*b*;
Imperial War Museum, London 170;
Courtesy, Irish Tourist Board 18*l*, 18*b*, 19*a*, 23*l*, 29*br*, 49*b*, 56*a*, 62, 65*r*, 69, 70*al*, 72*a*, 106, 121*r*, 147*bl*, 154, 165*a*, 167, 176, 194*l*, 194*r*, 195, 207, 215*r*, 216*br*, 219*l*, 226*b*, 234, 235, 247*b*;
John Ironside Photography, Wexford 248;
Susan Johnson 23*br*;

George Mott 15, 19*b*, 20, 21*l*, 21*ar*, 21*br*, 22, 23*ar*, 24*l*, 25, 27, 28*ar*, 29*ar*, 33*a*, 33*b*, 34*a*, 34*b*, 38, 58, 65*l*, 74, 77*cl*; 109*l*, 122*r*, 125, 127*al*, 131*r*, 143, 148*a*, 165*b*, 199, 200*b*, 213*bl*, 213*r*, 220*b*, 221*l*, 222*b*, 223, 228, 243*r*, 244*a*;
National Gallery of Ireland 13*b*, 26*b*, 40*l*, 63, 102, 105*a*, 110, 119, 121*l*, 123, 129*b*, 130*l*, 131*l*, 132*r*, 139, 150, 153, 157*a*, 157*b*, 168, 169*b*, 173*b*, 177, 179*br*, 180*l*, 180*r*, 181, 183*a*, 183*b*, 184*l*, 184*ar*, 185, 186, 187, 191, 204, 215*l*, 232, 251*a*;
Courtesy, the Trustees of the National Library of Ireland, Dublin 28*l*, 29*l*, 30*a*, 30*b*, 40*br*, 70*ar*, 112*r*, 136, 145*b*, 210*a*, 238*r*;
National Museum of Ireland, Dublin 48, 49*cb*, 50*bl*, 50*br*, 51, 60, 66*r*, 99*b*, 107*b*, 118*c*, 128*l*, 144, 151*l*, 152*a*, 152*b*, 174*a*, 192, 209*b*, 211, 218, 222*a*, 224*a*, 230*bl*, 236, 240*b*;
National Portrait Gallery, London 44, 103*a*, 134, 135, 178*br*, 217, 238*al*;
The National Trust (Waddesdon Manor) 188;
Courtesy, Maighread Ó Murchadha 159*a*;
Powerscreen Ltd, Carton 111;
Private Collections 36, 76, 97*l*, 100*r*, 178*l*, 189*a*, 201*l*;
Courtesy, Shelah Richards 203*r*;
Royal Dublin Society 214*a*, 237*r*;
Courtesy, William Ryan 206;
Photo Jeanne Sheehy 46*l*;
Courtesy, Mrs Silcock, Newtown, Co. Carlow 193*al*;
Photo Edwin Smith 57*a*, 95, 242, 250;
Photo Henk Snoek 32*a*, 32*c*;
Somerset Maugham Collection of Theatrical Paintings (on display in the National Theatre, London) 147*br*;
Stiftbibliothek St Gallen 114*r*;
Courtesy, Sotheby Parke Bernet & Co. 37, 220*a*;
Collection Col. L. G. Stopford Sackville 205;
Tate Gallery, London 109*r*;
Taylor Gallery, Dublin 190*l*;
Photo Howard Temple 237*l*;
Courtesy, Theatre Museum, London; (Harry R. Beard Collection) 200*a*, 201*r*, 240*a*, 249; (Enthoven Collection) 160, 161, 238*bl*;
The Board of Trinity College, Dublin 31*r*, 35*r*, 52, 53*r*, 57*b*, 79, 89, 99*a*, 103*b*, 120;
Ulster Museum, Belfast 75, 104*b*, 107*a*, 132*l*, 148*b*, 162, 174*b*, 178*ar*, 179*ar*, 184*br*, 210*b*, 214*br*, 216*bl*, 221*r*;
Victoria and Albert Museum, London 43*r*, 45, 56*b*, 59, 67, 73*r*, 84*r*, 92, 97*c*, 97*r*, 129*a*, 219*r*, 243*l*;
Courtesy, Wendy Walsh 46*r*.